D1489199

# JavaScript™
# by Example

## About Prentice Hall Professional Technical Reference

With origins reaching back to the industry's first computer science publishing program in the 1960s, and formally launched as its own imprint in 1986, Prentice Hall Professional Technical Reference (PH PTR) has developed into the leading provider of technical books in the world today. Our editors now publish over 200 books annually, authored by leaders in the fields of computing, engineering, and business.

Our roots are firmly planted in the soil that gave rise to the technical revolution. Our bookshelf contains many of the industry's computing and engineering classics: Kernighan and Ritchie's *C Programming Language*, Nemeth's *UNIX System Adminstration Handbook*, Horstmann's *Core Java*, and Johnson's *High-Speed Digital Design*.

PH PTR acknowledges its auspicious beginnings while it looks to the future for inspiration. We continue to evolve and break new ground in publishing by providing today's professionals with tomorrow's solutions.

PRENTICE
HALL
PTR

# JavaScript by Example

Ellie Quigley

PRENTICE HALL
PTR

PRENTICE HALL
Professional Technical Reference
Upper Saddle River, NJ 07458
www.phptr.com

**Library of Congress Cataloging-in-Publication Data**

Quigley, Ellie.
  JavaScript by example / Ellie Quigley.
    p. cm.
  ISBN 0-13-140162-9
    1. JavaScript (Computer program language) I. Title.

  QA76.73.J39Q54 2003
  005.13'3--dc21

                                                    2003050630


Production editor/compositor: *Vanessa Moore*
Cover design director: *Jerry Votta*
Cover designer: *Anthony Gemmellaro*
Manufacturing buyer: *Maura Zaldivar*
Editor-in-chief: *Mark Taub*
Editorial assistant: *Sarah Hand*
Marketing manager: *Curt Johnson*
Full-service production manager: *Anne R. Garcia*

**The publisher offers excellent discounts on this book when ordered in quantity for bulk
purchases or special sales. For more information, please contact:**
  **U.S. Corporate and Government Sales
  1-800-382-3419; corpsales@pearsontechgroup.com**

**For sales outside of the U.S., please contact:**
  **International Sales
  1-317-581-3793; international@pearsontechgroup.com**

Printed in the United States of America
1st Printing

ISBN   0-13-140162-9

Pearson Education Ltd.
Pearson Education Australia PTY, Limited
Pearson Education Singapore, Pte. Ltd.
Pearson Education North Asia Ltd.
Pearson Education Canada, Ltd.
Pearson Educación de Mexico, S.A. de C.V.
Pearson Education—Japan
Pearson Education Malaysia, Pte. Ltd.

# Contents

## A    JavaScript Web Resources    581

## B    HTML Documents: A Basic Introduction    583

# Preface

After years of teaching scripting languages, I recently decided it was time to try teaching JavaScript, and went on a search for the right book for my students. There were so many JavaScript books on the bookshelves, it was hard to know where to begin. I started buying one at a time, reading and sifting through them, always feeling that something was missing. Like Cinderella's shoe, I couldn't find the right fit. Either the book was too heavy on the technical side, but lacking in pictures and examples, or it was filled with slide shows, rollovers, and scrolling banners, but brief on the technical side. I wanted something that did both, a book that would demonstrate both the technical and the fun elements of JavaScript. I searched and searched, and found many excellent sources, but in the end, I couldn't find the perfect book for my class, so I decided to write my own.

With books and manuals piled high around my computer desk, I weeded through the best and the worst, gleaning out information and beginning to compile my new "By Example" book. I browsed through Internet tutorials and student guides, and studied Web pages, always looking for the best way to get the material across. I even delved into Adobe Photoshop and Macromedia Dreamweaver, while roaming from Maine to San Francisco with my digital camera, snapping pictures that would enhance my examples and add to the colorful side of JavaScript. And after much cutting and pasting, cropping and trimming, testing and trying, a new book has evolved—the one I was looking for. The shoe finally fits!

# Acknowledgments

Many thanks go to the folks at Prentice Hall: Mark L. Taub, editor-in-chief, and the most supportive person I know; Vanessa Moore, production editor, for being the very best in her business and for polishing a rough diamond into a gem. Thanks also to Dan Livingston and Tony Arguelles for technical proofing; Frank Peters for starting the idea; Steve Dobbins for setting the stage in San Francisco; my daughter, Jody Savage, for early proofing; and baby William and Christian for posing for pictures.

*Ellie Quigley*
*May, 2003*

# chapter

# 1

# Introduction to JavaScript

Click Here Now!

## 1.1   What JavaScript Is

JavaScript is a popular general-purpose scripting language used to put energy and pizzaz into otherwise dead Web pages by allowing a static page to interact with users and respond to events that occur on the page. JavaScript has been described as the glue that holds Web pages together.[1] It would be a hard task to find a commercial Web page, or almost any Web page, that does not contain some JavaScript code (see Figure 1.1).

JavaScript, originally called LiveScript, was developed by Brendan Eich at Netscape in 1995 and was shipped with Netscape Navigator 2.0 beta releases. JavaScript is a scripting language that gives life, hence LiveScript, to otherwise static HTML pages. It runs on most platforms and is hardware independent. JavaScript is built directly into the browser (although not restricted to browsers), Netscape and Microsoft Internet Explorer being the most common browsers. In syntax, JavaScript is similar to C, Perl, and Java; e.g., *if* statements and *while* and *for* loops, are almost identical. Like Perl, it is an object-oriented, interpreted language, not a compiled language.

Because JavaScript is associated with a browser, it is tightly integrated with HTML. While HTML is handled by its own networking library and graphics renderer, JavaScript programs are executed by a JavaScript interpreter normally built right into the browser. When the browser requests such a page, the server sends the full content of the document, including HTML and JavaScript statements, over the network to the client. When the page loads, HTML content is read and rendered line by line until a JavaScript opening tag is read, at which time the JavaScript interpreter takes over. When the closing JavaScript tag is reached, the HTML processing continues.

---

1. But the creator of JavaScript, Brendan Eich, says it's even more! In his article, "Innovators of the Net: Brendan Eich and JavaScript," he says, "Calling JavaScript 'the glue that holds web pages together' is short and easy to use, but doesn't do justice to what's going on. Glue sets and hardens, but JavaScript is more dynamic than glue. It can create a reaction and make things keep going, like a catalyst."

1

JavaScript handled by a browser is called client-side JavaScript. Although JavaScript is used mainly as a client-side scripting language, it can also be used in contexts other than a Web browser. Netscape created server-side JavaScript to be programmed as a CGI language, such as Perl or ASP, but this book will address JavaScript as it is most commonly used—running on the client side.

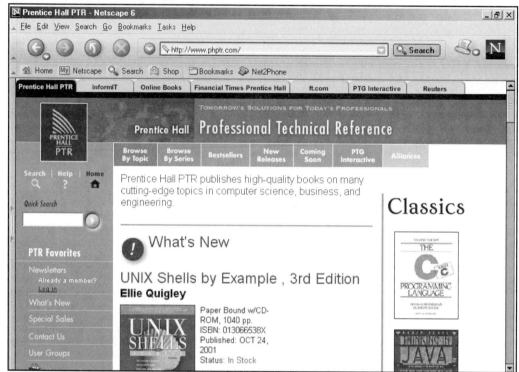

**Figure 1.1**   A dynamic Web page using JavaScript to give it life. For example, if the user rolls his mouse over any of the links or items in the navigation bars, those items will change color.

## 1.2   **What JavaScript Is Not**

JavaScript is not Java. Java was developed at Sun Microsystems. JavaScript was developed at Netscape. Java applications are independent of a Web page whereas JavaScript programs are embedded in a Web page and must be run in a browser window.[2] Java is a strongly typed language with strict guidelines while JavaScript is loosely typed and flexible. Java data types must be declared. JavaScript types such as variables, parameters, and function return types do not have to be declared. Java programs are compiled. JavaScript programs are interpreted by a JavaScript engine that lives in the browser.

---

2.  The JavaScript interpreter is normally embedded in a Web browser, but is not restricted to the browser. Servers and other applications can also use the JavaScript interpreter.

JavaScript is not HTML, but JavaScript code can be embedded in an HTML document and is contained within HTML tags. JavaScript has its own sytax rules and expects statements to be written in a certain way. JavaScript doesn't understand HTML, but it can contain HTML content within its statements. All of this will become clear as we proceed.

JavaScript is object based but not strictly object oriented because it does not support the traditional mechanism for inheritance and classes found in object-oriented programming languages, such as Java and C++. The terms private, protected, and public do not apply to JavaScript methods as with Java and C++.

JavaScript is not the only language that can be embedded in an application. VBScript, for example, developed by Microsoft, is similar to JavaScript, but is embedded in Microsoft's Internet Explorer.

# 1.3   What JavaScript Is Used For

JavaScript programs are used to detect and react to user-initiated events, such as a mouse going over a link or graphic. They can improve a Web site with navigational aids, scrolling messages and rollovers, dialog boxes, dynamic images, shopping carts, and so forth. JavaScript lets you control the appearance of the page as the document is being parsed. Without any network transmission, it lets you validate what the user has entered into a form before submitting the form to the server. It can test to see if the user has plug-ins and send them to another site to get the plug-ins if needed. It has string functions and supports regular expressions to check for valid e-mail addresses, social security numbers, credit card data, and the like. JavaScript serves as a programming language. Its core language describes such basic constructs as variables and data types, control loops, *if/else* statements, *switch* statements, functions, and objects.[3] It is used for arithmetic calculations, manipulates the date and time, and works with arrays, strings, and objects. JavaScript also reads and writes cookie values, and dynamically creates HTML based on the cookie value.

# 1.4   JavaScript and Events

HTML is static. It can be used to create buttons and boxes and fillout forms, but it cannot by itself react to user input. Normally, the browser bundles up the form information and sends it off to a server to be handled. But JavaScript is not static; it is dynamic. It can interact asynchronously with users on the client side. For example, when a user fills out a form; presses a button, link, or image; or moves his mouse over a link, JavaScript can respond to the event and interact dynamically with the user. For example, JavaScript can examine user input and validate it before sending it off to a server, or cause a new image to appear if a mouse moves over a link or presses a button. Events are discussed

---

3. The latest version of the core JavaScript language is JavaScript 1.5, supported by Netscape 6 and Microsoft Internet Explorer 5.5 and 6.

in detail in Chapter 12, "Handling Events," but you should be made aware of them right at the beginning because they are inherently part of what JavaScript does, and there will be examples throughout this text that make use of them.

The events are tied to HTML. In the following example, an HTML form is created with the *<form>* tag and its attributes. Along with the *type* and *value* attributes, the JavaScript *onClick* event handler is just another attribute of the HTML *<form>* tag. The type of input box is called a *"button"* and the value assigned to the button is *"Pinch me"*. When the user clicks on the button in the browser window, a JavaScript event, called *Click*, will be triggered. The *onClick* event handler is assigned a value which is the command that will be executed after the button has been clicked. In our example, it will result in an alert being sent to the user, displaying *"OUCH!!"*. See the output of Example 1.1 in Figures 1.2 and 1.3.

---

**EXAMPLE  1.1**

```
       <html>
       <head><title>Event</title></head>
       <body>
1          <form>
2             <input type ="button"
3                    value = "Pinch me"
4                    onClick="alert('OUCH!!')" >
5          </form>
       </body>
       </html>
```

---

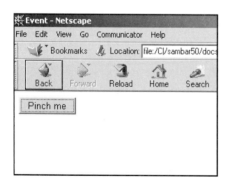

**Figure 1.2**  The *onClick* event is triggered when the button is pressed.

**Figure 1.3**   JavaScript handles the *onClick* event.

Some of the events that JavaScript can handle are listed in Table 1.1.

**Table 1.1**   JavaScript event handlers.

| Event Handler | What Caused It |
| --- | --- |
| onAbort | Image loading was interrupted. |
| onBlur | The user moved away from a form element. |
| onChange | The user changed a value in a form element. |
| onClick | The user clicked on a button-like form element. |
| onError | The program had an error when loading an image. |
| onFocus | The user activated a form element. |
| onLoad | The document finished loading. |
| onMouseOut | The mouse moved away from an object. |
| onMouseOver | The mouse moved over an object. |
| onSubmit | The user submitted a form. |
| onUnLoad | The user left the window or frame. |

## 1.5   What Versions? What Browsers?

When a user receives a page that includes JavaScript, the script is sent to the JavaScript interpreter, which executes the script. Since each browser has its own interpreter, there are often differences on how the code will be executed. And as the competing companies improve and modify their browsers, new inconsistencies may occur. There are not only different types of browsers to cause the incompatibilities but also different versions of the same browser.

### 1.5.1   Versions

JavaScript has a history. Invented by Netscape, the first version was JavaScript 1.0. It was new and buggy and has long since been replaced by much cleaner versions. Microsoft has a scripting language comparable to JavaScript called JScript. The Table 1.2 lists versions of both JavaScript and JScript.

**Table 1.2**   JavaScript and JScript.

| JavaScript or JScript Version | Browsers Supported |
|---|---|
| JavaScript 1.0 | Netscape Navigator 2.0, Internet Explorer 3.0 |
| JavaScript 1.1 | Netscape Navigator 3.0, Internet Explorer 4.0 |
| JavaScript 1.2 | Netscape Navigator 4.0–4.05, Internet Explorer 4.0 |
| JavaScript 1.3 | Netscape Navigator 4.06–4.7x, Internet Explorer 5.0 |
| JavaScript 1.5 | Netscape Navigator 6.0+, Mozilla (open source browser), Internet Explorer 5.5+ |
| JScript 1.0 | Internet Explorer 3 |
| JScript 2.0 | Internet Explorer 3 |
| JScript 3.0 | Internet Explorer 4 |
| JScript 4.0 | Internet Explorer 4 |
| JScript 5.0 | Internet Explorer 5 |
| JScript 5.5 | Internet Explorer 5 |

JavaScript is supported by Netscape 2, Explorer 3, Opera 3, and all newer versions of these browsers. In addition, HotJava 3 supports JavaScript, as do iCab for the Mac, WebTV, OmniWeb for OS X, QNX Voyager and Konqueror for the Linux KDE environment. NetBox for TV, AWeb and Voyager 3 for Amiga, and SEGA Dreamcast and ANT Fresco on RISC OS also support JavaScript.

### 1.5.2 Standardizing JavaScript (The EMCA Specification)

To guarantee that there is one standard version of JavaScript available to companies producing Web pages, ECMA (European Computer Manufacturers Association) is working with Netscape to provide an international standardization of JavaScript called ECMA-Script. ECMAScript is based on core JavaScript and behaves the same way in all applications that support the standard. The first version of the ECMA standard is documented in the ECMA-262 specification. After ironing out many of the inconsistencies between JavaScript and ECMA-262, JavaScript 1.3 is fully compatible with ECMA-262. The Netscape DevEdge or ECMA Web site has online documentation and PDF versions of the ECMA-262 specifications.

# 1.6 Where to Put JavaScript

Before learning JavaScript, you should be familiar with HTML and how to create an HTML document. This doesn't mean that you have to be an expert, but you should be familiar with the structure of HTML documents and how the tags are used to display various kinds of content on your browser. Once you have a static HTML document, then adding basic JavaScript statements is quite easy. (See Appendix B for an HTML tutorial.)

Client-side JavaScript programs are embedded in an HTML document between HTML head tags *<head>* and *</head>* or between the body tags *<body>* and *</body>*. Many developers prefer to put JavaScript code within the *<head>* tags, and at times, as you will see later, it is the best place to store function definitions and objects. If you want text displayed at a specific spot in the document, you may want to place the JavaScript code within the *<body>* tags (as shown in Example 1.2). Or you may have multiple scripts within a page, and place the JavaScript code within both the *<head>* and *<body>* tags. In either case, a JavaScript program starts with a *<script>* tag, and and ends with a *</script>* tag. And if the JavaScript code is going to be long and involved, or may be reused, it can be placed in an external file (ending in *.js*) and loaded into the page.

When a document is sent to the browser, it reads each line of HTML code from top to bottom, and processes and displays it. As JavaScript code is encountered, it is read and executed by the JavaScript interpreter until it is finished, and then the parsing and rendering of the HTML continues until the end of the document is reached.

**EXAMPLE** 1.2

```
1   <html>
2   <head><title>First JavaScript Sample</title></head>
3   <body bgcolor="yellow" text="blue">
4      <script language = "JavaScript"  type="text/javascript">
4         document.writeln("<h2>Welcome to the JavaScript
             World!</h1>");
5      </script>
6   <font size="+2">This is just plain old HTML stuff.</font>
7   </body>
8   </html>
```

## EXPLANATION

1    This is the starting tag for an HTML document.

2    This is the HTML *<head>* tag. The *<head>* tags contain all the elements that don't belong in the body of the document, such as the *<title>* tags, and JavaScript tags.

3    The *<body>* tag defines the background color and text color for the document.

4    This *<script>* tag is the starting HTML tag for the JavaScript language. JavaScript instructions are placed between this tag and the closing *</script>* tag. JavaScript understands JavaScript instructions, not HTML.

   The JavaScript *writeln* function is called for the document. The string enclosed in parentheses is passed to the JavaScript interpreter. If the JavaScript interpreter encounters HTML content, it sends that content to the HTML renderer and it is printed into the document on the browser. The normal HTML parsing and rendering resumes after the closing JavaScript tag is reached.

5    This is the ending JavaScript tag. The output is shown in Figure 1.4.

6    HTML tags and text continue in the body of the document.

7    The body of the document ends here.

8    This is the ending tag for the HTML document.

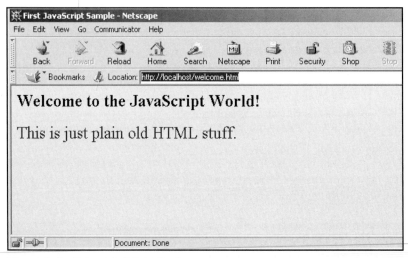

**Figure 1.4**   Example 1.2 output.

# 1.7 JavaScript and Old or Disabled Browsers

## 1.7.1 Hiding JavaScript from Old Browsers

There are many versions of browsers available to the public and 99 percent of the public uses Netscape or MSIE. So why worry? Well, just because a browser supports JavaScript, does not mean that everyone has JavaScript enabled. There are also some older text browsers that don't support JavaScript and with the advent of cell phones and Palm handhelds providing browser support but not JavaScript, there has to be some alternative way to address those Web browsers that do not have JavaScript. (See *http://www.internet.com/*.)

**HTML Comments.** If you put a script in a Web page, and the browser is old and doesn't know what a *<script>* tag is, the JavaScript code will be treated as regular HTML. So if you hide the JavaScript code within HTML comments, then the old browser will ignore it. If the browser has JavaScript enabled, then any HTML tags (including HTML comments) inserted between the *<script> </script>* tags will be ignored. See Examples 1.3 and 1.4.

---

**EXAMPLE 1.3**

```
      <html>
      <head><title>Old Browsers</title></head>
      <body><font color="0000F">
          <div align=center>
1         <script language="JavaScript"  type="text/javascript">
2             <!-- Hiding JavaScript from Older Browsers
3             document.write("<h2>Welcome to Maine!</h2>");
4             // Stop Hiding JavaScript from Older Browsers -->
5         </script>
          <img src="island.jpg" width=320 height=250 border=1>
          <br>Bailey's Island
      </body></html>
```

**EXPLANATION**

1  The JavaScript program starts here.

2  The *<!--* symbol is the start of an HTML comment and will continue until *-->* is reached. Any browser not supporting JavaScript will treat this whole block as a comment. JavaScript itself uses two slashes or C style syntax, */\* \*/*, and will ignore the HTML comment tags.

3  The *document.write* function displays this line in the page. Any HTML tags inserted in the quoted strings will be handled by the HTML renderer. JavaScript does not know how to interpret HTML by itself. If the browser supports JavaScript, the line *Welcome to Maine!* will appear just above the image. If the browser does not support JavaScript, this section of code is ignored. See the two examples of output shown in Figures 1.5 and 1.6.

**EXPLANATION** (CONTINUED)

4   This line starts with two slashes, the start of a JavaScript comment. This is done so that if JavaScript is interpreting this section, it won't see the HTML closing comment tag, -->. Why don't we want JavaScript to see the closing tag if it could see the opening tag? Because JavaScript would see the double dash as one of its special operators, and produce an error. Netscape's error:

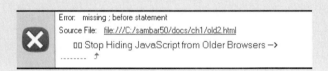

5   The JavaScript program ends here with its closing *</script>* tag.

**Figure 1.5**   Example 1.3 output in a JavaScript-disabled browser.

**Figure 1.6**   Example 1.3 output in a JavaScript-enabled browser.

## EXAMPLE 1.4

```
      <html><head><title>Enabled/Disabled Browsers</title>
      <script>
1     <!--> Sorry,
      <!--> you are not JavaScript enabled
2     <!-- hiding from non-JavaScript enabled browsers
          document.write("Testing to see if JavaScript is turned on.");
3     // done hiding -->
      </script>
      <head>
      <body></body>
      </html>
```

## EXPLANATION

1   The *<!-->* is like an empty HTML comment. JavaScript-enabled browsers will ig-
    nore these lines, just as they ignore the *<!-- hide...* line, because they begin with a
    comment marker. If the browser is disabled for JavaScript, this line and the next
    one start as empty HTML comments, causing the text that follows to be printed.

2   A non–JavaScript-enabled browser will see this as the start of another HTML com-
    ment, thus keeping the script section hidden.

**Netscape's *<noscript>* Tag.**   Netscape Navigator 3.0[4] provided a set of tags called
*<noscript></noscript>* that enable you to provide alternative information to browsers that
are either unable to read JavaScript or have disabled JavaScript. Today it's more likely
that JavaScript has been disabled for security reasons or to avoid cookies than it is to find
an old browser still in use. All JavaScript-enabled browsers recognize the *<noscript>* tag.
They will just ignore whatever is between *<noscript>* and *</noscript>*. Browsers that do
not support JavaScript do not know about the *<noscript>* tag. They will ignore the tags
but will display whatever is in between. See Example 1.5.

## EXAMPLE 1.5

```
      <html>
      <head>
      <title>Has JavaScript been turned off?</title>
      </head>
      <body>
1     <script language = "JavaScript" type="text/javascript">
2     <!--
          document.write( "<font color='green'><h2>" );
3         document.writeln("Your browser supports
          JavaScript!</h2></font>");
      // -->
```

---

4.  Warning: Netscape 2.0 always displays the contents of the *<noscript>* tag.

**EXAMPLE** 1.5 (CONTINUED)

```
        </script>
    4   <noscript>
            <font size="+1">
    5       Please turn JavaScript on if you want to see this page!<br>
            Netscape: <em>Edit/Preferences/Advanced/Scripts and
            Plugins</em><br>
            MSIE: <em>Tools/Internet Options/Security/Custom
            Level/Scripting</em></br>
    6   </noscript>
        </font>
        </body>
        </html>
```

**EXPLANATION**

1   The JavaScript program starts here with the opening *<script>* tag.

2   This is an HTML comment. This hides JavaScript from JavaScript-disabled browsers until the ending comment tag.

3   This line is displayed on the Web page only if JavaScript is enabled.

4   The *<noscript>* tag is read by browsers that support JavaScript. They will ignore everything between the *<noscript>* and *</noscript>* tags. Disabled browsers will not recognize the *<noscript>* tag and thus ignore them, displaying all text that follows.

5   JavaScript-disabled browsers will display the message shown in Figure 1.7. These instructions help the user enable JavaScript on Netscape 6+ and IE 5+ browsers. For directions on enabling/disabling JavaScript in all versions of Netscape and IE, see *http://www.lithosjigs.com/cart/enablejava.html*

6   The *</noscript>* tag ends here.

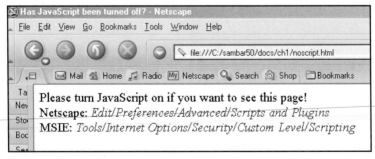

**Figure 1.7**   Output from Example 1.5.

# 1.8  **JavaScript from External Files**

When Web pages contain long scripts or functions that will be used by other documents, these scripts can be placed in external files. The external JavaScript files must end with a *.js* extension. The name of the external JavaScript file is assigned to the *src* attribute of the *<script>* tag in the HTML file. The name includes the full URL if the script is on another server, or just the script name if in the local directory. You can include more than one *.js* script in a file.

```
<script language="JavaScript" src="http://servername/javascriptfile.js">
</script>
```

**EXAMPLE** 1.6

```
        <html>
        <head><title>First JavaScript Sample</title>
1           <script language = "JavaScript" src="welcome.js">
2           </script>
        </head>
        </body>
3           <script language = "JavaScript">
4               document.write("<body bgcolor='yellow' text='blue'>");
                document.write("<font size='+3'>This is just plain old
                HTML stuff.
                </font>");
            </script>
        </body>
        </html>
```

**EXPLANATION**

1   The JavaScript *<script>* tag's *src* attribute is assigned the name of a file (name must end in *.js*) that contains JavaScript code. The file's name is *welcome.js* and it contains a JavaScript program of its own.

2   The JavaScript program ends here.

3   A new JavaScript program starts here.

4   The *document.write()* method displays output in the browser window.

## EXERCISES

1. What browser are you using? What version?

2. Where was JavaScript developed?

3. What is an example of a JavaScript event handler?

4. What is the difference between JavaScript and JScript?

5. Where do JavaScript tags go in an HTML page?

6. How do you set up JavaScript in an external file?

7. How do you hide JavaScript from older browsers?

8. What method sends output to the browser?

9. Write a JavaScript program that prints a welcome message. Check to see if Java-Script is enabled. Use comments to explain what you are doing.

# chapter
# 2

# Script Setup

## 2.1 The HTML Document and JavaScript

Unlike shell and Perl scripts, JavaScript scripts are not stand-alone programs. They are run in the context of an HTML document. When programming on the client side, the first step will be to create an HTML document in your favorite text editor, such as UNIX vi or emacs, or Windows Notepad[1] or WordPad. Since the file you create is an HTML document, its name must include either an *.html* or *.htm* extension. JavaScript programs are embedded within the HTML document between the *<script>* and *</script>* tags. **Please note that throughout the code examples in this book, any whitespace shown at the beginning of the lines is only for easier readability and you should not type it in your actual file.** The following example is an HTML file containing JavaScript code:

**The HTML file *hello.html.***

```
<html><head><title>Hello</title></head>
<body>
<script language="JavaScript">
    <!-- Hide script from old browsers.
    document.write("Hello, world!");
    // End the hiding here. -->
</script>
<p>So long, world.
</body>
</html>
```

---

1. If you are using Windows Notepad, be sure to turn off word wrap (under the Format menu) to avoid errors in your program.

## 2.1.1   Script Execution

Since a JavaScript program is embedded in an HTML document, you will execute it in your browser window. If using Netscape Navigator or Internet Explorer, follow these instructions:

1. Go to the File menu and open the file by browsing for the correct one.

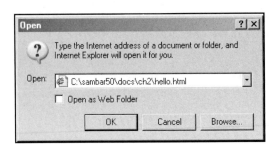

2. Click OK to open it. In this example, the file *hello.html* is displayed in the browser.

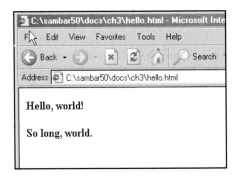

3. Or you can type the URL (complete address) in the navigation bar of your browser as shown here.

## 2.2 **Syntactical Details**

Rules, rules, rules. Just like English, French, or Chinese, all programming languages have their rules. Many of the rules are similar and many have individual quirks. But in order to do anything at all, you have to obey the rules, or your program simply won't work. If you have experience programming in other languages, you will find the JavaScript rules and syntax quite familiar, especially if you know Perl or languages derived from C. When you write JavaScript programs, you have to deal with HTML rules as well as JavaScript rules, since JavaScript does not stand alone.

### 2.2.1 **Case Sensitivity**

The HTML tags in a document are <u>not</u> case sensitive. If you type the *title* tag as *<title>*, *<Title>*, *<TItle>*, or any combination of upper or lowercase characters, the HTML renderer will not care. But JavaScript names, such as variables, keywords, objects, functions, and so on, <u>are</u> case sensitive. If, for example, you spell the Boolean value *true* with any uppercase letters (e.g., TrUE), JavaScript will not recognize it and will produce an error or simply ignore the JavaScript code. Although most names favor lowercase, some JavaScript names use a combination of upper and lowercase (e.g., *onClick*, *Math.floor*, *Date.getFullYear*).

### 2.2.2 **Free Form and Reserved Words**

JavaScript ignores whitespace (i.e., spaces, tabs, and newlines) if the whitespace appears between words. For example: A function name, such as *onMouseOver()*, *toLowerCase()*, or *onClick()*, cannot contain whitespace even though it consists of more than one word.

```
1. var name="Tom";          1 and 2 are equivalent statements
2. var     name   =
         "Tom";

3. onMouseOver()            3 and 4 are not the same
4. on  Mouse Over()
```

Whitespace is preserved when it is embedded within a string or regular expression. For example, the whitespace in the string, *"Hello        there"* will be preserved because it is enclosed within double quotes. Of course, you can't break up a word such as *switch*, *if*, *else*, *window*, *document*, and so on, because it would no longer be the same word. Because extra whitespace is ignored by the JavaScript interpreter, you are free to indent, break lines, and organize your program so that it is easier to read and debug.

There are a number of reserved words (also called keywords) in JavaScript. Being reserved means that keywords are special vocabulary for the JavaScript language and cannot be used by programmers as identifiers for variables, functions and labels, and the like. Words such as *if*, *for*, *while*, *return*, *null*, and *typeof* are examples of reserved words. Table 2.1 gives a list of reserved words.

**Table 2.1**   Reserved keywords.

| abstract  | boolean      | break  | byte       | case     | catch     |
|-----------|--------------|--------|------------|----------|-----------|
| char      | class        | const  | continue   | default  | delete    |
| do        | double       | else   | extends    | false    | final     |
| finally   | float        | for    | function   | goto     | if        |
| implements| import       | in     | instanceof | int      | interface |
| long      | native       | new    | null       | package  | private   |
| protected | public       | return | short      | static   | super     |
| switch    | synchronized | this   | throw      | throws   | transient |
| true      | try          | typeof | var        | void     | volatile  |
| while     | with         |        |            |          |           |

## 2.2.3   Statements and Semicolons

Just like sentences (which represent complete thoughts) in the English language, Java-Script statements are made up of expressions. The statements are executed top down, one statement at a time. If there are multiple statements on a line, the statements must be separated by semicolons. Although not a rule, it is good practice to terminate all statements with a semicolon to make it clear where the statement ends. Because JavaScript is free form, as long as statements are terminated with a semicolon, the lines can be broken, contain whitespace, etc. A statement results in some action unless the statement is a null statement, in which case, it does nothing.

The following two lines are both technically correct:

```
var name = "Ellie"      <- no semicolon, valid
var name = "Ellie";     <- better
```

The following line is incorrect:

```
var name = "Ellie"  document.write("Hi "+name);     <- wrong, two statements
```

It should be:

```
var name = "Ellie";  document.write("Hi " + name);   <- semicolon needed to
                                                         separate two statements
                                                         on the same line
```

If the statements are grouped in a block of curly braces, they act as a single statement.

```
if ( x > y) {  statement;  statement; }        <- Statements enclosed in curly
                                                  braces act as a single statement
```

### 2.2.4   Comments

A comment is text that describes what the program or a particular part of the program is trying to do and is ignored by the JavaScript interpreter. Comments are used to help you and other programmers understand, maintain, and debug scripts. JavaScript uses two types of comments: single-line comments and block comments.

Single line comments start with a double slash:

```
// This is a comment
```

For a block of comments, use the /* */ symbols:

```
/* This is a block of comments
   that continues for a number of lines
*/
```

### 2.2.5   The *<script>* Tag

JavaScript programs must start and end with the HTML *<script>* and *</script>* tags, respectively. Everything within these tags is considered JavaScript code, nothing else. The script tag can be placed anywhere within an HTML document. If you want the Java-Script code to be executed before the page is displayed, it is placed between the *<head>* and *</head>* tags. This, for example, is where function definitions are placed (see Chapter 7, "Functions"). If the script performs some action pertaining to the body of the document, then it is placed within the *<body>* and *</body>* tags. A document can have multiple *<script>* tags, each enclosing any number of JavaScript statements.

**FORMAT**

```
<script>
         JavaScript statements...
</script>
```

**EXAMPLE** 2.1

```
<script>
         document.write("Hello, world!<br>");
</script>
```

**Attributes.**   The *<script>* tag also has <u>attributes</u> to modify the behavior of the tag. The attributes are

- *language*
- *type*
- *src*

Any JavaScript-enabled browser can identify that the scripting language is JavaScript, if the *language* attribute is set to *JavaScript*[2] rather than, for example, *VBScript* or *JScript*. You normally set the language attribute as follows:

```
<script language="JavaScript">
```

Each time a new version of JavaScript is released, it contains new or modified features. Some browsers haven't caught up or do not support a newer version. Netscape Navigator 6.x, Internet Explorer 6, and Opera 5 all support JavaScript 1.5, but HotJava 3.0 doesn't. So to ensure that users of the various browser versions avoid problems when viewing pages that use JavaScript, the *language* attribute can be assigned a version number to specify what version of JavaScript is supported. If the browser doesn't recognize the version, the script will be totally ignored. You shouldn't have to worry about this if you are using the latest version of a particular browser, but just in case, here's how you specify a version number.

```
<script language="JavaScript1.5">
</script>
```

The *type* attribute is used to specify both the scripting language and the Internet content type.

```
<script language="JavaScript"
   type="text/javascript">
</script>
```

The *src* attribute is used when the JavaScript code is in an external file, the filename ending with a *.js* extension. The *src* attribute is assigned the name of the file, which can be prefixed with its location (e.g., a directory tree or URL).

```
<script language="JavaScript"
   type="text/javascript"
   src="sample.js">
</script>
```

```
<script language="JavaScript"
   type="text/javascript"
   src="directory/sample.js">
</script>
```

```
<script language="JavaScript"
   type="text/javascript"
   src="http://hostname/sample.js">
</script>
```

---

2. Although common to most scripts, the *language* attribute has been deprecated as of HTML 4.0 in favor of the *type* attribute.

# 2.3   **Generating HTML and Printing Output**

When you create a program in any language, the first thing you want to see is the output of the program displayed on a screen. In the case of JavaScript, you'll see your output in the browser window. Of course, browsers use HTML to format output. Although Java-Script doesn't understand HTML per se, it can generate HTML output with its built-in methods, *write()* and *writeln()*.

## 2.3.1   **Strings and String Concatenation**

A string is a character or set of characters enclosed in matching quotes. Since the methods used to display text take strings as their arguments, this is a good time to talk a little about strings. See Chapter 9, "JavaScript Core Objects," for a more complete discussion. All strings must be placed within a matched set of either single or double quotes; for example:

```
"this is a string" or 'this is a string'
```

Double quotes can hide single quotes; for example:

```
"I don't care"
```

And single quotes can hide double quotes; for example:

```
'He cried, "Ahoy!"'
```

Either way, the entire string is enclosed in a set of matching quotes.

Concatenation is caused when two strings are joined together. The plus (+) sign is used to concatenate strings; for example:

```
"hot" + "dog" or  "San Francisco" + "</br>"
```

For more information on strings, see Chapter 3, "The Building Blocks: Data Types, Literals, and Variables."

## 2.3.2   **The *write()* and *writeln()* Methods**

One of the most important features of client-side JavaScript is its ability to generate pages dynamically. Data, text, and HTML itself can be written to the browser on the fly. The *write()* method is a special kind of built-in JavaScript function used to output HTML to the document as it is being parsed. When generating output with *write()* and *writeln()*, put the text in the body of the document (rather than in the header) at the place where you want the text to appear when the page is loaded.

Method names are followed by a set of parentheses. They are used to hold the arguments. These are messages that will be sent to the methods, such as a string of text, the output of a function, or the results of a calculation. Without arguments, the *write()* and *writeln()* methods would have nothing to write.

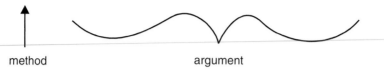

```
write("This is text that will be displayed by the browser");
```

method                                              argument

JavaScript defines the current document (i.e., the HTML file that contains the script) as a document object. (You will learn more about objects later.) For now, whenever you refer to the document object, the object name is appended with a dot and the name of the method that will manipulate the document object. In the following example the *write()* method must be prepended with the name of the document object and a period. The browser will display this text in the document's window. The syntax is

```
document.write("Hello to you");
```

The *writeln()* method is essentially just like the *write()* method, except when the text is inserted within HTML *<pre>* or *<xmp>* tags, in which case *writeln()* will insert a newline at the end of the string. The HTML *<pre>* tag is used to enclose preformatted text. It results in "what you see is what you get." All spaces and linebreaks are rendered literally, in a monopitch typeface. The *<xmp>* tag is an obsolete HTML tag that functions much like the *<pre>* tag.

## EXAMPLE 2.2

```
        <html>
        <head><title>Printing Output</title></head>
        <body bgcolor="yellow" text="blue">
        <b>Comparing the <em>document.write</em> and <em>document.writeln
                               </em> methods</b><br>
            <script language="JavaScript">
1           document.write("<h3>One, ");   // No newline
2           document.writeln("Two, ");
            document.writeln("Three, ");
3           document.write("Blast off....<br>");  // break tag
4           document.write("The browser you are using is " +
                           navigator.userAgent + "<br>");
5       </script>
6       <pre>
7       <script language="JavaScript">
8           document.writeln("With the <em>HTML &lt;pre&gt;
                               </em> tags, ");
            document.writeln("the <em>writeln</em> method produces a
                               newline.");
            document.writeln("Slam");
            document.writeln("Bang");
            document.writeln("Dunk!");
9       </script>
10      </pre>
        </body></html>
```

## EXPLANATION

1   The *document.write()* method does not produce a newline at the end of the string it displays. HTML tags are sent to the HTML renderer as the lines are parsed.

2   The *document.writeln()* method doesn't produce a newline either, unless it is in an HTML *<pre>* tag.

3   Again, the *document.write()* method does not produce a newline at the end of the string. The *<br>* tag is added to produce the line break.

4   The *document.write()* method does not produce a newline. The *<br>* tag takes care of that. *userAgent* is a special *navigator* property that tells you about your browser.

5   The first JavaScript program ends here.

6   The HTML *<pre>* tag starts a block of preformatted text; i.e., text that ignores formatting instructions and fonts.

7   This tag starts the JavaScript code.

8   When enclosed in a *<pre>* tag, the *writeln()* method will break each line it prints with a newline; otherwise, it behaves like the *write()* method (i.e., you will have to add a *<br>* tag to get a newline).

9   This tag marks the end of the JavaScript code.

10   This tag marks the end of preformatted text. The output is shown in Figure 2.1.

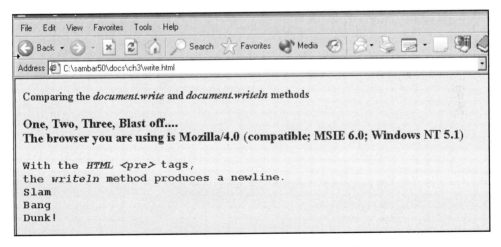

**Figure 2.1**   The output from Example 2.2 demonstrates the difference between the *document.write()* and *document.writeln()* methods.

## 2.4 About Debugging

Have you ever tried to draw a picture or do your resume for the first time without a mistake either in the layout, order, type, style, whatever? In any programming language, it's the same story. And JavaScript is no exception. It's especially tricky with JavaScript because you have to consider the HTML as well as the JavaScript code when your page doesn't turn out right. You might get errors on the console or get a totally blank page. Finding errors in a script can get quite frustrating without proper debugging tools. Before we go any further, this is a good time to get acquainted with some of the types of errors you might encounter.

### 2.4.1 Types of Errors

**Load or Compile Time.**    Load-time errors are the most common errors and are caught by JavaScript as the script is being loaded. These errors will prevent the script from running at all. Load-time errors are generally caused by mistakes in syntax, such as missing parentheses in a function or misspelling a keyword. You may have typed a string of text and forgotten to enclose the string in quotes, or you may have mismatched the quotes, starting with single quotes but ending with double quotes.

**Runtime.**    Runtime errors, as the name suggests, are those errors that occur when the JavaScript program actually starts running. An example of a runtime error would be if you asked the user for a number between 1 and 5 and he gave you a 7, or you put some code between the *<head></head>* tags and it should have been placed within the *<body></body>* tags, or you referenced a page that doesn't exist.

**Logical.**    Logical errors are harder to find because they imply that you didn't anticipate an event or that you inadvertently misused an operator, but your syntax was okay. For example, if you are checking to see if two expressions are equal, you should use the == equality operator, not the = assignment operator.

### 2.4.2 Debugging Tools

**The *javascript:* URL Protocol.**    For simple debugging or testing code, you can use the URL pseudoprotocol, *javascript:* followed by any valid JavaScript expression or expressions separated by semicolons. The result of the expression is returned as a string to your browser window, as shown in Example 2.3 and Figures 2.2 and 2.3.

**FORMAT**

```
javascript: expression
```

**EXAMPLE 2.3**

```
javascript: 5 + 4
```

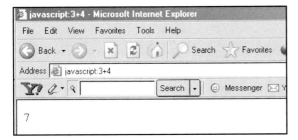

**Figure 2.2**   Internet Explorer and the *javascript:* protocol.

**Figure 2.3**   Netscape and the *javascript:* protocol.

**Netscape's JavaScript Console.**   Netscape 6 and 7 provide the JavaScript Console. You invoke it via the Tasks or Tools/Web Development menu, or by typing *java-script:* in the location bar of the browser. The JavaScript Console displays the lines containing the errors. Leave the console open and watch your errors build up. You can also type expressions to be evaluated.

**EXAMPLE   2.4**

```
      <html>
      <head>
      <title>First JavaScript Sample</title>

1     <script language = "JavaScript">
2        document.writeln("<h2>Welcome to the JavaScript World!</h1>);
3                             // Bug in line2:  Missing double quote!!
      </script>
      </head>
      <body bgcolor="yellow" text="blue">
      <font size="+2">This is just plain old HTML stuff.</font>
      </body>
      </html>
```

**EXPLANATION**

1   JavaScript code starts here.

2   In this line, the string starts with a double quote, but doesn't terminate with one. Since the quotes are not matched, JavaScript produces an error. If you go to the location window of the browser and type *javascript:* the console window will open with a list of program errors and little markers to show you where the potential error took place, as shown in Figures 2.4–2.8. You can leave the console window open and watch errors as they occur, using the clear button to start with a clean console window.

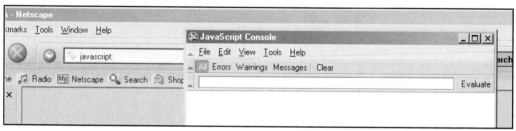

**Figure 2.4**   Type *javascript:* in the navigation bar and the console window will open.

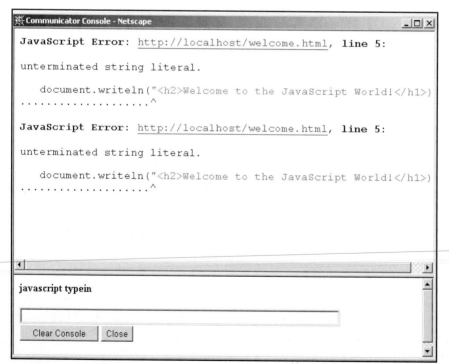

**Figure 2.5**   Netscape—The JavaScript Console indicates where errors are found.

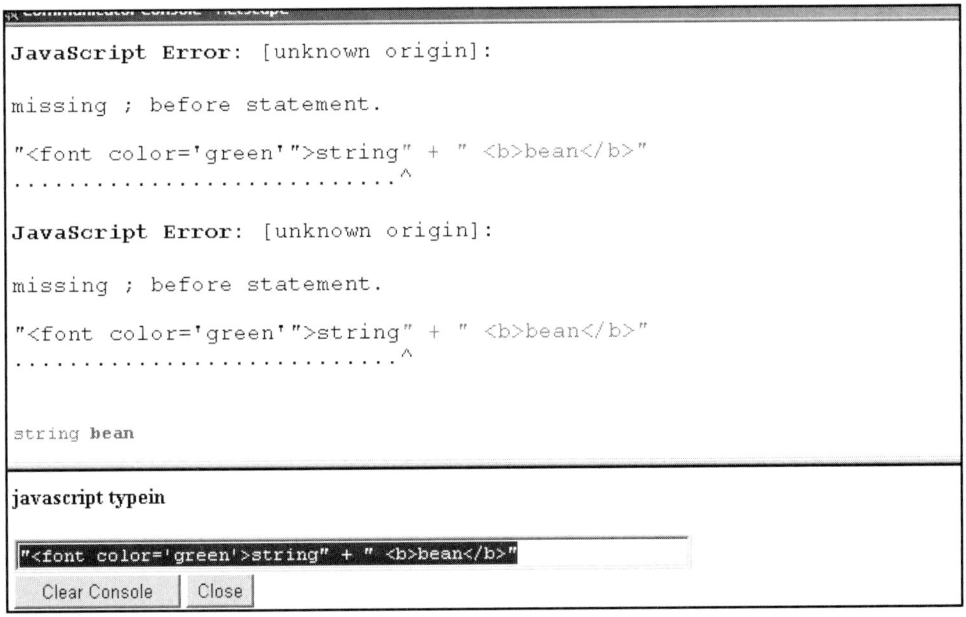

```
JavaScript Error: [unknown origin]:

missing ; before statement.

"<font color='green'">string" + " <b>bean</b>"
..........................^

JavaScript Error: [unknown origin]:

missing ; before statement.

"<font color='green'">string" + " <b>bean</b>"
..........................^


string bean
```

javascript typein

```
"<font color='green'>string" + " <b>bean</b>"
```

Clear Console   Close

**Figure 2.6**   Netscape—The JavaScript Console.

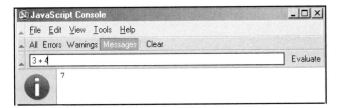

**Figure 2.7**   Netscape 7 console window.

**Figure 2.8**   Netscape and the *javascript:* protocol.

For JavaScript debuggers available for download for Netscape, go to *http://developer.netscape.com/software/tools/index.html*  or  *http://www.mozilla.org/projects/venkman/index.html* for the Netscape JavaScript debugger known as Venkman.

**Debugging in Explorer.**   Microsoft's Internet Explorer provides a debugging window as an advanced Internet option (see Figure 2.9). When an error occurs in your JavaScript program, a little triangle appears in the left-hand corner of the browser window. If you double-click the triangle, a debugging window opens explaining the error and the line number where it occurred (see Figure 2.10).

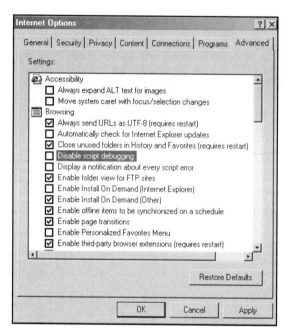

**Figure 2.9**   To enable debugging in IE, go to Tools > Internet Options > Advanced.

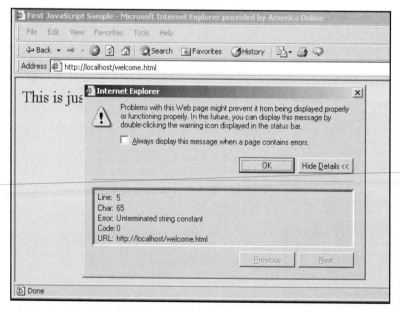

**Figure 2.10**
In Internet Explorer, look in left-hand bottom corner for a triangle.

Also see *http://msdn.microsoft.com/scripting/* to find the Microsoft Script Debugger (MSSD), a free debugging tool that works with IE 3.01 and above (see Figure 2.11). You can write and debug your scripts (called JScript by Microsoft) using this debugger.

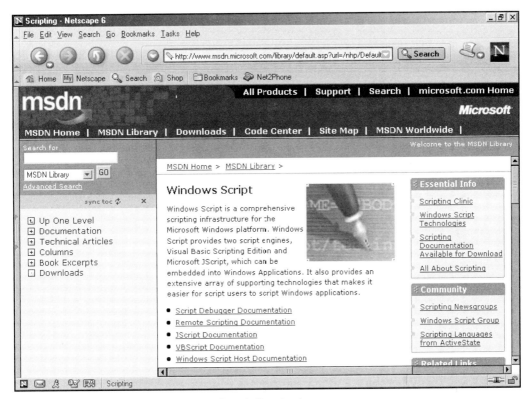

**Figure 2.11**   Web site for the Microsoft scripting tools.

## EXERCISES

1. What is a reserved word? Give an example.

2. Is JavaScript case sensitive?

3. What is the purpose of enclosing statements within curly braces?

4. What is the latest version of JavaScript? Where can you find this information?

5. What is the difference between the JavaScript *src* and *type* attributes?

6. How would you concatenate the following three strings with JavaScript?

   ```
   "trans"    "por"    "tation"
   ```

7. Write a script that demonstrates how concatenation works.

8. Create a JavaScript program that will print "Hello, world! Isn't life great?" in an Arial bold font, size 14, and make the background color of the screen light green.

9. Add two strings to the first JavaScript program—your first name and last name—concatenated and printed in a blue sans-serif font, size 12.

10. In the Location field of your browser, test the value of an expression using the *javascript:* protocol.

11. Find the errors in the following script:

    ```
    <html>
    <head>
       <title>Finding Errors</title>
    </head>
    <body bgcolor="yellow" text="blue">
    <script language="JavaScript"
       document.writeln("Two, ")
       document.writeln ("Three, ")
       document.write('Blast off....<br>");
    </script>
    </body>
    </html>
    ```

# 3

# The Building Blocks: Data Types, Literals, and Variables

## 3.1 Data Types

A program can do many things, including calculations, sorting names, preparing phone lists, displaying images, validating forms, ad infinitum. But in order to do anything, the program works with the data that is given to it. Data types specify what kind of data, such as numbers and characters, can be stored and manipulated within a program. JavaScript supports a number of fundamental data types. These types can be broken down into two categories, primitive data types and composite data types.

### 3.1.1 Primitive Data Types

Primitive data types are the simplest building blocks of a program. They are types that can be assigned a single literal value such as the number 5.7, or a string of characters such as *"hello"*. JavaScript supports three core or basic data types:

- numeric
- string
- Boolean

In addition to the three core data types, there are two other special types that consist of a single value:

- null
- undefined

**Numeric Literals.** JavaScript supports both integers and floating-point numbers. Integers are whole numbers and do not contain a decimal point; e.g., 123 and –6. Integers can be expressed in decimal (base 10), octal (base 8), and hexadecimal (base 16), and are either positive or negative values. See Example 3.1.

Floating-point numbers are fractional numbers such as 123.56 or –2.5. They must contain a decimal point or an exponent specifier, such as 1.3e–2. The letter "*e*" for exponent notation can be either uppercase or lowercase.

JavaScript numbers can be very large (e.g., $10^{308}$ or $10^{-308}$).

---

**EXAMPLE  3.1**

```
12345            integer
23.45            float
.234E-2          scientific notation
.234e+3          scientific notation
0x456fff         hexadecimal
0x456FFF         hexadecimal
0777             octal
```

---

**String Literals and Quoting.**    String literals are rows of characters enclosed in either double or single quotes.[1] The quotes must be matched. If the string starts with a single quote, it must end with a matching single quote, and likewise if it starts with a double quote, it must end with a double quote. Single quotes can hide double quotes, and double quotes can hide single quotes:

```
"This is a string"
'This is another string'
"This is also 'a string' "
'This is "a string"'
```

An empty set of quotes is called the null string. If a number is enclosed in quotes, it is considered a string; e.g., *"5"* is a string, whereas 5 is a number.

Strings are called constants or literals. The string value *"hello"* is called a string constant or literal. To change a string requires replacing it with another string.

Strings can contain escape sequences (a single character preceded with a backslash), as shown in Table 3.1. Escape sequences are a mechanism for quoting a single character.

**Table 3.1**    Escape sequences.

| Escape Sequence | What It Represents |
| --- | --- |
| \' | Single quotation mark |
| \" | Double quotation mark |
| \t | Tab |

---

1.  Any string without quotations marks surrounding it is considered the name of a variable.

**Table 3.1** Escape sequences. (continued)

| Escape Sequence | What It Represents |
|---|---|
| \n | Newline |
| \r | Return |
| \f | Form feed |
| \b | Backspace |
| \e | Escape |
| \\ | Backslash |
| **Special Escape Sequences** | |
| \XXX | The character with the Latin-1 encoding specified by up to three octal digits XXX between 0 and 377. \251 is the octal sequence for the copyright symbol. |
| \xXX | The character with the Latin-1 encoding specified by the two hexadecimal digits XX between 00 and FF. \xA9 is the hexadecimal sequence for the copyright symbol. |
| \uXXXX | The Unicode character specified by the four hexadecimal digits XXXX. \u00A9 is the Unicode sequence for the copyright symbol. |

## EXAMPLE 3.2

```
      <html>
      <head>
      <body>
1     <pre>
      <font size="+2">
2     <script language="JavaScript">
      <!-- Hide script from old browsers.
3         document.write("\t\tHello\nworld!\n");
4         document.writeln("\"Nice day, Mate.\"\n");
5         document.writeln('Smiley face:<font size="+3"> \u263a\n');
      //End hiding here. -->
      </script>
      </pre>
      </body>
      </html>
```

## EXPLANATION

1  The escape sequences will work only if in a *<pre>* tag or an alert dialog box.

2  The JavaScript program starts here.

3  The *write()* method sends to the browser a string containing two tabs (\t\t), *Hello*, a newline (\n), *world!*, and another newline (\n).

4  The *writeln()* method sends to the browser a string containing a double quote (\"), *Nice day, Mate.*, another double quote (\"), and a newline (\n). Since the *writeln()* method automatically creates a newline, the output will display two newlines: the default value and the \n in the string.

5  This string contains a backslash sequence that will be translated into Unicode. The Unicode hexidecimal character 233a is preceded by a \u. The output is a smiley face. See Figure 3.1.

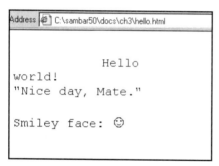

**Figure 3.1**  Escape sequences.

**Putting Strings Together.**    The process of joining strings together is called concatenation. The string concatenation operator is a plus sign (+). Its operands are two strings. If one string is a number and the other is a string, JavaScript will still concatenate them as strings. If both operands are numbers, the + will be the addition operator. The following examples output *"popcorn"* and *"Route 66"*, respectively.

```
document.write("pop" + "corn");
document.write("Route " +  66);
```

The expression *5 + 100* results in *105*, whereas *"5" + 100* results in *"5100"*.

**Boolean Literals.**    Boolean literals are logical values that have only one of two values, *true* or *false*. You can think of the values as yes or no, on or off, or 1 or 0. They are used to test whether a condition is true or false. When using numeric comparison and equality operators, the value *true* evaluates to 1 and *false* evaluates to 0. (Read about comparison operators in Chapter 5, "Operators.")

```
answer1 = true;
or
if (answer2 == false) { do something; }
```

**The *typeof* Operator.**   The *typeof* operator returns a string to identify the type of its operand (i.e., a variable, string, keyword, or object). You can use the *typeof* operator to check whether a variable has been defined because if there is no value associated with the variable, the *typeof* operator returns *undefined*.

## FORMAT

```
typeof operand
typeof (operand)
```

Example:
```
typeof(54.6)
typeof("yes")
```

## EXAMPLE 3.3

```
      <html>
      <head>
      <title>The typeof Operator</title>
      <script language="JavaScript">
1        document.write(typeof(55),"<br>");    // Number
2        document.write(typeof("hello there"),"<br>");   // String
3        document.write(typeof(true),"<br>");   // Boolean
      </script>
      </head>
      </html>
```

## EXPLANATION

1   The integer, 55, is a *number* type.

2   The text *"hello there"* is a *string* type.

3   The *true* or *false* keyword represent a *boolean* type. See Figure 3.2.

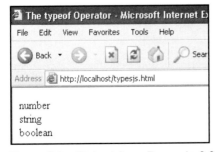

**Figure 3.2**   Output from Example 3.3.

**Null and Undefined.**   The difference between null and undefined is a little subtle. The *null* keyword represents "no value," meaning "nothing," not even an empty string or zero. It is a type of JavaScript object (see Chapter 8, "Objects"). It can be used to initialize a variable so that it does not produce errors or to clear the value of a variable, so that there is no longer any data associated with that variable, and the memory used by it is freed. When a variable is assigned *null*, it does not contain any valid data type.

A variable that has been declared, but given no initial value, contains the value *undefined* and will produce a runtime error if you try to use it. (If you declare the variable and assign *null* to it, *null* will act as a placeholder and you will <u>not</u> get an error.) The word *undefined* is not a keyword in JavaScript. If compared with the == equality operators, *null* and *undefined* are equal, but if compared with the identity operator, they are not identical (see Chapter 5, "Operators").

## EXAMPLE 3.4

```
        <html>
        <head>
        <title>The typeof Operator with Null and Undefined</title>
            <script language="JavaScript">
1               document.write("<em>null</em> is type   // null is an object
                    "+ typeof(null),"<br>");
2               document.write("<em>undefined</em> is type
                    "+ typeof(undefined),"<br>");
            </script>
        </head>
        </html>
```

## EXPLANATION

1   The *null* keyword is a type of object. It is a built-in JavaScript object that contains no value.

2   Undefined is returned when a variable has been given no initial value or when the *void* operator is used (see Table 5.17 on page 91). See output in Figure 3.3.

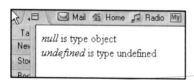

**Figure 3.3**  Output from Example 3.4.

## 3.1.2  Composite Data Types

We mentioned that there are two types of data: primitive and composite. This chapter focuses on the primitive types: numbers, strings, and Booleans—each storing a single value. Composite data types, also called complex types, consist of more than one component. Objects, arrays, and functions, covered later in this book, all contain a collection of components. Objects contain properties and methods; arrays contain a sequential list of elements; and functions contain a collection of statements. The composite types are discussed in later chapters.

## 3.2 Variables

Variables are fundamental to all programming languages. They are data items that represent a memory storage location in the computer. Variables are containers that hold data such as numbers and strings. Variables have a <u>name</u>, a <u>type</u>, and a <u>value</u>.

```
num = 5;              // name is "num", value is 5, type is numeric
friend = "Peter";   // name is "friend", value is "Peter", type is string
```

The values assigned to variables may change throughout the run of a program whereas constants, also called literals, remain fixed. (JavaScript 1.5 introduced constants and since they are so new, they are only recognized by Netscape 6.)

JavaScript variables can be assigned three types of data:

- numeric
- string
- Boolean

Computer programming languages like C++ and Java require that you specify the type of data you are going to store in a variable when you declare it. For example, if you are going to assign an integer to a variable, you would have to say something like:

```
int n = 5;
```

And if you were assigning a floating-point number:

```
float x = 44.5;
```

Languages that require that you specify a data type are called "strongly typed" languages. JavaScript, conversely, is a dynamically or loosely typed language, meaning that you do not have to specify the data type of a variable. In fact, doing so will produce an error. With JavaScript, you would simply say:

```
n = 5;
x = 44.5;
```

and JavaScript will figure out what type of data is being stored in $n$ and $x$.

### 3.2.1 Valid Names

Variable names consist of any number of letters (an underscore counts as a letter) and digits. The first letter must be a letter or an underscore. Since JavaScript keywords do <u>not</u> contain underscores, using an underscore in a variable name can ensure that you are not inadvertently using a reserved keyword. Variable names are case sensitive; e.g., *Name, name,* and *NAme* are all different variable names. Refer to Table 3.2.

**Table 3.2**  Valid and invalid variable names.

| Valid Variable Names | Invalid Variable Names |
| --- | --- |
| *name1* | *10names* |
| *price_tag* | *box.front* |
| *_abc* | *name#last* |
| *Abc_22* | *A-23* |
| *A23* | *5* |

## 3.2.2  Declaring and Initializing Variables

Variables must be declared before they can be used. To make sure that variables are declared first, you can declare them in the head of the HTML document. There are two ways to declare a variable: either explicitly preceded by the keyword *var,* or not. Although laziness may get the best of you, it is a better practice to always use the *var* keyword.

You can assign a value to the variable (or initialize a variable) when you declare it, but it is not mandatory, unless you omit the *var* keyword. If a variable is declared but not initialized, it is "undefined."

**FORMAT**

```
var variable_name = value;   // initialized
var variable_name;           // unitialized
variable_name;               // wrong
```

To declare a variable called *firstname,* you could say

```
var first_name="Ellie"
```

or

```
first_name ="Ellie";
```

or

```
var first_name;
```

You can declare multiple variables on the same line by separating each declaration with a comma. For example, you could say

```
var first_name, var middle_name, var last_name;
```

## EXAMPLE 3.5

```
        <html>
        <head>
        <title>Using the var Keyword</title>
            <script language="JavaScript">
1               var language="English";    // Variable is initialized
2               var name;    // OK, undefined variable
3               age;        //   Not OK!  var keyword missing   ERROR!
4               document.write("Name is "+ name);
            </script>
        </head>
        <body></body>
        </html>
```

## EXPLANATION

1   The variable called *language* is defined and initialized. The *var* keyword is not required here, but is recommended.

2   Because the variable called *name* is not initialized, the *var* keyword is required here.

3   The variable called *age* is not assigned an initial value. The *var* keyword is required. Without it, the program produces errors, shown in the output for Netscape and Explorer, in Figures 3.4 and 3.5, respectively.

4   This line will not be printed until the variable called *age* is defined properly. Just use the *var* keyword as good practice, even if it isn't always required!

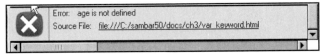

**Figure 3.4**  Netscape error (JavaScript Console).

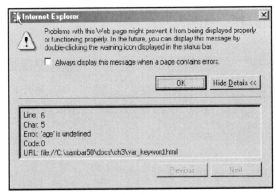

**Figure 3.5**  Internet Explorer error.

## 3.2.3 Dynamically or Loosely Typed Language

Remember, strongly typed languages like C++ and Java require that you specify the type of data you are going to store in a variable when you declare it, but JavaScript is loosely typed. It doesn't expect or allow you to specify the data type when declaring a variable. You can assign a string to a variable and later assign a numeric value. JavaScript doesn't care and at runtime, the JavaScript interpreter will convert the data to the correct type. Consider the following variable, initialized to the floating-point value of 5.5. In each successive statement, JavaScript will convert the type to the proper data type; see Table 3.3.

**Table 3.3**  How JavaScript converts datatypes.

| Variable Assignment | Conversion |
| --- | --- |
| var item = 5.5; | Assigned a float |
| item = 44; | Converted to integer |
| item = "Today was bummer"; | Converted to string |
| item = true; | Converted to Boolean |
| item = null; | Converted to the null value |

### EXAMPLE 3.6

```
    <html>
1      <head>
    <title>JavaScript Variables</title>
2   <script language="JavaScript">
3      var first_name="Christian";  // first_name is assigned a value
4      var last_name="Dobbins";     // last_name is assigned a value
5      var age = 8;
6      var ssn;       // Unassigned variable
7      var job_title=null;
    </script>
8   </head>
9   <body bgcolor="lightblue">
       <font="+1">
10     <script language="JavaScript">
11        document.write("<b>Name:</b> " + first_name + " "
              + last_name + "<br>");
12        document.write("<b>Age:</b> " + age + "<br>");
13        document.write("<b>Ssn:</b> " + ssn + "<br>");
14        document.write("<b>Job Title:</b> " + job_title + "<br>");
15        ssn="xxx-xx-xxxx";
16        document.write("<b>Now Ssn is:</b> " + ssn , "<br>");
       </script>
17   <body><p><img src="Christian.gif"></body>
    </html>
```

**EXAMPLE** 3.6 (CONTINUED)

Output:

```
11  Name: Christian Dobbins
12  Age: 8
13  Ssn: undefined
14  Job Title: null
16  Now Ssn is: xxx-xx-xxx
```

**EXPLANATION**

1 This JavaScript program is placed within the document head. Since the head of the document is processed before the body, this assures you that the variable definitions will be defined first.

2 This is where the first JavaScript program begins.

3 The string *"Christian"* is assigned to the variable called *first_name*.

4 The string *"Dobbins"* is assigned to the variable called *last_name*.

5 The number *8* is assigned to the variable called *age*.

6 The variable called *ssn* is not assigned any value at all. It is an uninitialized variable. The return value is *undefined*.

7 The value *null* is assigned to the variable called *job_title*. *Null* is used to set a variable to an initial value different from other valid types, but if used in an expression the value of *null* will be converted to the appropriate type.

8 The document head ends here.

9 The body of the document starts here.

10 A new JavaScript program starts here. All the variables declared in the head of the document are available here. Variables that are available throughout the entire document are called global variables.

11 The *document.write()* method concatenates the values of the strings with the + sign and sends them to the browser to display on the screen.

12 The value of the variable called *age* is displayed.

13 The variable called *ssn* was declared, but not initialized. It has no value, which JavaScript calls *undefined*.

14 The variable *job_title* was assigned *null*, a place-holder value. The *null* string is returned.

15 The variable *ssn* is assigned a string value. It is no longer *undefined*. Even though the variable was declared in the head of the document, as long as it was declared, it can be assigned a value anywhere else in the document.

16 The value of the variable *ssn* is displayed. Figure 3.6 shows the output in Internet Explorer.

**Figure 3.6**   Output from Example 3.6.

## 3.2.4   Scope of Variables

Scope describes where a variable is visible, or where it can be used, within the program. JavaScript variables are either of global or local scope. A global variable can be accessed from any JavaScript script on a page, as shown in Example 3.6. The variables we have created so far are global in scope.

It is often desirable to create variables that are private to a certain section of the program, thus avoiding naming conflicts and accidentally changing a value in some other part of the program. Private variables are called <u>local</u> variables. Local variables are created when a variable is declared within a function. Local variables must be declared with the keyword, *var*. They are accessible only from within the function from the time of declaration to the end of the enclosing block, and they take precedence over any global variable with the same name. (See Chapter 7, "Functions.")

## 3.2.5   Concatenation and Variables

To concatenate variables and strings together on the same line, the + sign is used. The + sign is an operator because it operates on the expression on either side of it (each called an operand). Sometimes the + sign is a string operator and sometimes it is a numeric operator when used for addition. Addition is performed when both of the operands are numbers. In expressions involving numeric and string values with the + operator, JavaScript converts numeric values to strings. For example, consider these statements:

```
var temp  = "The temperature is  " + 87;
 // returns "The temperature is 87"
```

```
var message =  25  + "  days till Christmas";
// returns "25 days till Christmas"
```

But, if both operands are numbers, then addition is performed:

```
var sum = 10 + 5;  // sum is 15
```

```
      <html>
      <head><title>Concatenation</title></head>
          <body>
              <script language="JavaScript">
1                 var x = 25;
2                 var y = 5 + "10 years";
3                 document.write( x + " cats" , "<br>");
4                 document.write( "almost " + 25 , "<br>");
5                 document.write( x + 4, "<br>");
6                 document.write( y, "<br>");
7                 document.write(x  +  5 + " dogs" , "<br>");
8                 document.write(" dogs"  + x + 5 , "<br>");

              </script>
          </body>
      </html>
```

Output:

```
3   25 cats
4   almost 25
5   29
6   510 years
7   30 dogs
8   dogs255
```

1   Variable *x* is assigned a number.

2   Variable *y* is assigned the string *510 years*. If the + operator is used, it could mean the concatenation of two strings or addition of two numbers. JavaScript looks at both of the operands. If one is a string and one is a number, <u>the number is converted to a string</u> and the two strings are joined together as one string, in this example, the resulting string is *510 years*. If one operand were *5* and the other *10*, addition would be performed, resulting in *15*.

3   A number is concatenated with a string. The number *25* is converted to a string and concatenated to *" cats"*, resulting in *25 cats*.

4   This time, a string is concatenated with a number, resulting in the string *almost 25*.

**EXPLANATION** (CONTINUED)

5   When the operands on either side of the + sign are numbers, addition is performed.

6   The value of *y*, a string, is displayed.

7   The + operators works from left to right. Since *x* and *y* are both numbers, addition is performed, *25 + 5. 30* is concatenated with the string *" dogs"*.

8   Since the + works from left to right, this time the first operand is a string being concatenated to a number, the number is converted to string *dogs25* and concatenated with string *5*.

## 3.3   Bugs to Watch For

Try to declare all your variables at the beginning of the program, even if you don't have values for them yet. This will help you find misspelled names faster. Watch that you use proper variable names. Don't used reserved words and words that are too long to remember or type easily. Remember that variable names are case sensitive. *MyName* is not the same as *myName*. Avoid giving two variables similar names, such as *MyName* and *myNames*. Avoid one-character differences in variable names, such as *Name1* and *Names1*. Even though you aren't always required to use the *var* keyword, do it anyway. It's safer. And, of course, be sure that the variables you use are spelled properly throughout the script.

When you use strings don't forget to enclose the strings in either double or single quotes. Quoting will get the best of programmers every time!

## EXERCISES

1. Create a script that uses the three primitive data types and prints output for each type. In the same script, print the following:

   ```
   She cried, "Aren't you going to help me?"
   ```

2. Go to *http://www.unicode.org/charts/PDF/U2600.pdf* and find a symbol. Use Java-Script to display one of the symbols in a larger font (+5).

3. Write a script that displays the number 234 as an integer, a floating-point number, an octal number, a hexadecimal number, and the number in scientific notation.

4. When is it necessary to use the *var* keyword?

5. Write a script that contains four variables in the head of the document: the first one contains your name, the second contains the value 0, the third one is declared but has no value, and the last contains an empty string. In the body of the document, write another script to display the type of each (use the *typeof* operator).

# chapter
# 4

# Dialog Boxes

## 4.1   Interacting with the User

Programs like to talk, ask questions, get answers, and respond. In the previous chapter, we saw how the *write()* and *writeln()* methods are used to send output to the browser. A method is how you do something, and JavaScript methods are the action words, the "doers" of the JavaScript language. They make things happen.

JavaScript uses dialog boxes to interact with the user. The dialog boxes are created with three methods:

- *alert()*
- *prompt()*
- *confirm()*

### 4.1.1   The *alert()* Method

We saw in the last chapter that the *write()* and *writeln()* were JavaScript methods used to send output to the Web page. Another way to send output to the browser is with the *alert()* method. The *alert()* method creates a little independent box—called a dialog box—which contains a small triangle with an exclamation point. A user-customized message is placed after the triangle, and beneath it, an OK button. When the dialog box pops up, all execution is stopped until the user presses the OK button in the pop-up box. The exact appearance of this dialog box may differ slightly on different browsers, but its functionality is the same.

The message for the alert dialog box is a string of text (or a valid expression) enclosed in double quotes, and sent as a single argument to the *alert()* method. HTML tags <u>are not rendered</u> within the message string but you can use the escape sequences, \n and \t.

## FORMAT

```
alert("String of plain text");
alert(expression);
```

Example:

```
alert("Phone number is incorrect");
alert(a + b);
```

## EXAMPLE 4.1

```
   <html>
   <head><title>Dialog Box</title></head>
   <body bgcolor="yellow" text="blue">
       <b>Testing the alert method</b><br>
1      <script language="JavaScript">
2          document.write("<font size='+2'>");
           document.write("It's a bird, ");
3          document.write("It's a plane, <br>");
4          alert("It's Superman!");
5      </script>
   </body>
   </html>
```

## EXPLANATION

1  The *<script>* tag starts the JavaScript program. The JavaScript engine starts executing code from here until the closing *</script>* tag. JavaScript does not understand HTML tags unless they are embedded in a string.

2  The *document.write()* method sends its output to the browser. The HTML *font* tag is embedded in the string and will be sent to the browser for rendering.

3  This is another *document.write()* method that outputs its text followed by a newline *<br>*.

4  The *alert()* method will produce a little dialog box, independent of the current document, and all processing will be stopped until the user presses the OK button. This little box can be moved around the screen with your mouse.

5  A closing *</script>* tag ends the JavaScript program. The output is shown in Figure 4.1.

**Figure 4.1**   Example 4.1 output using Netscape (left) and Internet Explorer (right).

---

**EXAMPLE   4.2**

```
      <html>
      <head>
      <title>Using JavaScript alert box</title>
1     <script language="JavaScript">
2         alert("Welcome to\nJavaScript Programming!");
3         var message1="Match your Quotes and ";
4         var message2="Beware of Little Bugs ";
5         alert(message1 + message2);
      </script>
      </head>
      </html>
```

**EXPLANATION**

1   The JavaScript program starts here with the *<script>* tag.

2   The *alert()* method contains a string of text. Buried in the string is a backslash sequence, *\n*. There are a number of these sequences available in JavaScript (see Table 3.1 on page 32). The *\n* causes a line break between the two strings. The reason for using the *\n* escape sequence is because HTML tags such *<br>* are not allowed in this dialog box. After the alert dialog box appears on the screen, the program will stop until the user presses the OK button.

3   The string *"Match your Quotes and "* is assigned to a variable called *message1*.

4   The string *"Beware of Little Bugs "* is assigned to the variable *message2*.

5   The *alert()* method not only accepts literal strings of text, but also variables as arguments. The + sign is used to concatenate the values of the two string together and create one string. That string will appear in the alert dialog box as shown in the output in Figure 4.2.

**Figure 4.2**   Output from Example 4.2.

## 4.1.2   The Prompt Box

Since JavaScript does not provide a simple method for accepting user input [as it does for sending output with *document.write()*], the prompt dialog box and HTML forms are used (forms are discussed in Chapter 11, "The Document Objects: Forms, Images, and Links"). The prompt dialog box pops up with a simple textfield box. After the user enters text into the prompt dialog box, its value is returned. The prompt dialog box takes two arguments: a string of text that is normally displayed as a question to the user, prompting him to do something, and another string of text which is the initial default setting for the box. If this argument is an empty string, nothing is displayed in the box. The prompt method always returns a value. If the user presses the OK button, all the text in the box is returned; otherwise *null* is returned.

**FORMAT**

```
prompt(message);
prompt(message, defaultText);
```

**Example:**

```
prompt("What is your name? ", "");
prompt("Where is your name? ", name);
```

## EXAMPLE 4.3

```
         <html>
         <head>
         <title>Using the JavaScript prompt box</title>
         </head>
         <body>
             <script language = "JavaScript">
1                var name=prompt("What is your name?", "");
2                document.write("<br>Welcome to my world! "
                     + name + ".</font><br>");
3                var age=prompt("Tell me your age.", "Age");
4                if ( age == null){     // If user presses the cancel button
5                    alert("Not sharing your age with me");
6                }
                 else{
7                    alert(age + " is young");
                 }
8                alert(prompt("Where do you live? ", ""));
             </script>
         </body>
         </html>
```

## EXPLANATION

1   The return value of the *prompt()* method is assigned to the variable called *name*. The *prompt()* method takes two arguments, one is the text that will prompt the user to respond. This text will appear above the prompt dialog box. The second argument provides default text that will appear at the far left, inside the box. If the second argument is an empty string, the prompt box will be empty.

2   After the user typed his response in the prompt textbox, the response was assigned to the variable *name*. The *document.write()* method displays that value on the screen.

3   The variable called *age* will be assigned whatever the user types into the prompt box. This time a second argument, *"Age"*, is sent to the *prompt()* method. When the prompt box appears on the screen, the word *Age* will appear inside the box where the user will type his response.

4   If the user presses the Cancel button, the value returned by the *prompt()* method is *null*. This *if* statement tests to see if the value of *age* is *null*.

5   If the return value was *null*, this line is printed in the alert dialog box.

6   This closing curly brace terminates the *if* block.

7   If the user did type something in the prompt dialog box, the return value was assigned to variable *age*, and is displayed by the alert dialog box.

8   The *prompt()* method is sent as an argument to the *alert()* method. After the user has pressed OK in the prompt box, the return value is sent to the *alert()* method, and then displayed on the screen. See Figures 4.3 through 4.7.

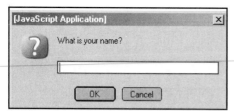

**Figure 4.3**   Prompt without a default argument.

**Figure 4.4**   Prompt with a default argument.

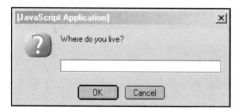

**Figure 4.5**   Prompt without a default.

**Figure 4.6**   User types in the prompt box.

**Figure 4.7**   The response is in an alert box.

### 4.1.3　The Confirm Box

The confirm dialog box is used to confirm a user's answer to a question. A question mark will appear in the box with an OK button and a Cancel button. If the user presses the OK button, *true* is returned; if he presses the Cancel button, *false* is returned. This method takes only one argument, the question you will ask the user.

**EXAMPLE 4.4**

```
        <html>
        <head>
        <title>Using the JavaScript confirm box</title>
        </head>
        <body>
            <script language = "JavaScript">
                document.clear   // Clears the page
1               if(confirm("Are you really OK?") == true){
2                   alert("Then we can proceed!");
                }
                else{
3                   alert("We'll try when you feel better? ");
                }
            </script>
        </body>
        </html>
```

**EXPLANATION**

1　The confirm dialog box takes only one argument, the question that you want to ask the user. It returns *true* if the user presses the OK button and *false* if he presses the Cancel button. He has to press either one in order to continue. If the return value is equal to *true*, then the *alert()* method on line 2 will be executed (see Figure 4.8).

2　The user pressed OK. The alert dialog box will display its message (see Figure 4.9).

3　If the user pressed Cancel, this alert dialog box will display its message (see Figure 4.9).

**Figure 4.8**　The confirm dialog box.

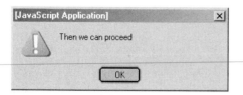 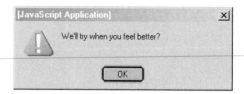

**Figure 4.9** After the user presses OK (left) or Cancel (right).

## EXERCISES

1. What is wrong with the following alert box?

```
alert("Hello<br>", "world!<br>");
```

Create a JavaScript program that produces the previous alert box. When the alert dialog box appears, what does the program do?

2. What is the return value of the prompt method if the user doesn't enter anything? Where is the return value stored?

3. Create a JavaScript program that prompts the user for a phone number and then asks him for confirmation.

# chapter

# 5

# Operators

## 5.1 About JavaScript Operators and Expressions

Data objects can be manipulated in a number of ways by the large number of operators provided by JavaScript. Operators are symbols, such as +, –, =, >, and <, that produce a result based on some rules. An operator manipulates data objects called operands; for example, 5 and 4 are operands in the expression 5 + 4. Operators and operands are found in expressions. An expression combines a group of values to make a new value, n = 5 + 4. And when you terminate an expression with a semicolon, you have a complete statement (e.g., n = 5 + 4;).

In the numeric <u>expression</u>, 5 + 4 – 2, three numbers are combined. The <u>operators</u> are the + and – signs. The <u>operands</u> for the + sign are 5 and 4. After that part of the expression is evaluated to 9, the expression becomes 9 – 2. After evaluating the complete expression, the result is 7. Since the plus and minus operators each manipulate two operands, they are called a binary operators. If there is only one operand, the operator is called a unary operator. If there are three operands, it is called a ternary operator. We'll see examples of these operators later in the chapter.

The operands can be either strings, numbers, Booleans, or a combination of these. We have already used some of the operators: the concatenation operator to join two strings together, the *typeof* operator to determine what data type is being used, and the assignment operator used to assign a value to a variable. Now let's look at a plethora of additional JavaScript operators and see how they manipulate their operands.

## 5.1.1   Assignment

An assignment statement evaluates the expression on the right-hand side of the equal sign and assigns the result to the variable on the left-hand side of the equal sign. The equal sign is the assignment operator.

```
var total = 5 + 4;
var friend = "Tony";
```

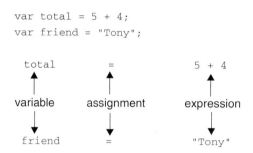

## 5.1.2   Precedence and Associativity

When an expression contains a number of operators and operands, such as $5 * 4 + 3 / -2.2$, and the order of evaluation is ambiguous, then JavaScript must determine what to do. This is where the precedence and associative rules come in. They tell JavaScript how to evaluate such an expression. Precedence refers to the way in which the operator binds to its operand, such as, should addition be done before division or should assignment come before multplication? The precedence of one operator over another determines what operation is done first. As shown in Table 5.1, the operators are organized as a hierarchy, the operators of highest precedence at the top, similar to a social system where those with the most power (or money) are at the top. In the rules of precedence, the multiplication operator is of higher precedence than the addition operator, technically meaning the operator of higher precedence binds more tightly to its operands. The assignment operators are low in precedence and thus bind loosely to their operand. In the expression $sum = 5 + 4$ the equal sign is of low precedence, so the expression $5 + 4$ is evaluated first and then the result is assigned to *sum*. Parentheses are of the highest precedence. An expression placed within parentheses is evaluated first; thus, in the expression $2 * (10 - 4)$, the expression within the parentheses is evaluated first and that result is multiplied by 2. When parentheses are nested, the expression contained within the innermost set of parentheses is evaluated first.

Associativity refers to the order in which an operator evaluates its operands: left to right in no specified order, or right to left. When all of the operators in an expression are of equal precedence, normally the association is left to right; in the expression $5 + 4 + 3$, the evaluation is from left to right. In Example 5.1, how is the expression evaluated? Is addition, multiplication, or division done first? And in what order, right to left or left to right?

In Table 5.1 the operators on the same line are of equal precedence. The rows are in order of highest to lowest precedence.

**Table 5.1**   Precedence and associativity.

| *Operator* | *Description* | *Associativity* |
| --- | --- | --- |
| () | Parentheses | Left to right |
| ++  − − | Auto increment, decrement | Right to left |
| ! | Logical NOT | Right to left |
| * / % | Multiply, divide, modulus | Left to right |
| + − | Add, subtract | Left to right |
| + | Concatenation | Left to right |
| <  <= | Less than, less than equal to | Left to right |
| >  >= | Greater than, greater than equal to | Left to right |
| = =  != | Equal to, not equal to | Left to right |
| = = =  !=  = | Identical to (same type), not identical to | Left to right |
| & | Bitwise AND | Left to right |
| \| | Bitwise OR | |
| ^ | Bitwise XOR | |
| ~ | Bitwise NOT | |
| << | Bitwise left shift | |
| >> | Bitwise right shift | |
| >>> | Bitwise zero-filled, right shift | |
| && | Logical AND | Left to right |
| \|\| | Logical OR | Left to right |
| ? : | Ternary, conditional | Right to left |
| = += − = *= /= %= <<= >>= | Assignment | Right to left |
| , | (comma) | |

## EXAMPLE 5.1

```
       <html><head><title>First JavaScript Sample</title>
    1  <script language = "JavaScript">
    2      var result = 5 + 4 * 12 / 4;
    3      document.write("<font size='+1'>result = " + result,"<br>");
    4  </script>
       </head>
       <body bgcolor="yellow" text="blue"></body>
       </html>
```

## EXPLANATION

1   This is the starting JavaScript tag.

2   The order of associativity is from left to right. Multiplication and division are of a higher precedence than addition and subtraction, and addition and subtraction are of higher precedence than assignment. To illustrate this, we'll use parentheses to group the operands as they are grouped by JavaScript. In fact, if you want to force precedence, use the parentheses around the expression to group the operands in the way you want them evaluated. The following two examples produce the same result:

```
var result = 5 + 4 * 12 / 4;
```

could be written

```
result = (5 + ( ( 4 * 12 ) / 4));
```

3   The expression is evaluated and the result is assigned to variable, *result*. The value of *result* is displayed on the browser.

4   This is the closing JavaScript tag.

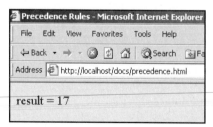

**Figure 5.1**   Output from Example 5.1.

**EXAMPLE 5.2**

```
      <html>
      <head>
      <title>Precedence and Associativity</title>
      </head>
      <body>
      <script language = "JavaScript">
1     var x = 5 + 4  * 12 / 4;
2     document.writeln( "<h3>The result is " + x + "<br>");
3     var x = ( 5 + 4 )  * ( 12 / 4 );
4     document.writeln("The result is " + x);
      </script>
      </body>
      </html>
```

**EXPLANATION**

1   The variable, called *x*, is assigned the result of the expression.

```
var x = 5 + 4 * 12 / 4;
```

results in

```
x = 5 + 48 / 4
```

results in

```
x = 5 + 12
```

results in

```
17
```

Since multiplication and division are higher on the precedence table than addition, those expressions will be evaluated first, associating from left to right.

2   The result of the previous evaluation, the value of *x*, is sent to the browser.

3   The expressions enclosed in parentheses are evaluated first and then multiplied.

```
var x = ( 5 + 4 )  * ( 12 / 4 );
```

results in

```
x = 9 * 3
```

results in

```
27
```

4   The result of the previous evaluation, the value of *x*, is sent to the browser. The output of the script is shown in Figure 5.2.

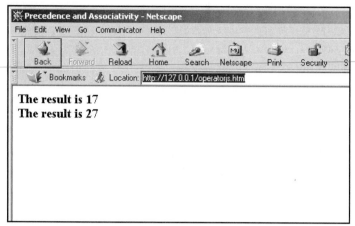

**Figure 5.2**  Output from Example 5.2.

## 5.2  Types of Operators

### 5.2.1 • Arithmetic Operators

Arithmetic operators take numerical values (either literals or variables) as their operands and return a single numerical value. The standard arithmetic operators are addition (+), subtraction (–), multiplication (*), and division (/). See Table 5.2.

**Table 5.2**  Arithmetic operators.

| *Operator/Operands* | *Function* |
| --- | --- |
| $x + y$ | Addition |
| $x - y$ | Subtraction |
| $x * y$ | Multiplication |
| $x / y$ | Division[a] |
| $x \% y$ | Modulus |

a.  The / operator returns a floating-point division in JavaScript, not a truncated division as it does in languages such as C or Java. For example, 1/2 returns 0.5 in JavaScript and 1/2 returns 0 in Java.

## EXAMPLE 5.3

```
        <html>
        <head><title>Arithmetic Operators</title></head>
        <body>
        <h2>Arithmetic operators</h2>
        <p>
1       <script language="JavaScript">
2           var num1 = 5;
            var num2 = 7;
3           var result = num1 + num2;
4           document.write("<h3>num1 + num2 = "+ result);
5           result = result + (10 / 2 + 5);
6           document.write("<h3>12 + (10 / 2 + 5) = " + result);
7       </script>
        </body>
        </html>
```

## EXPLANATION

1   This is the start of a JavaScript program.

2   Variables *num1* and *num2* are declared and assigned values 5 and 7, respectively.

3   The variable *result* is assigned the sum of *num1* and *num2*.

4   The results are displayed by the browser. Note that the + sign in this expression is used to concatenate two strings. When a string is concatenated to a number, Java-Script converts the number to a string. The value stored in the variable *result* is converted to a string and joined to the string on the left-hand side of the + sign.

5   The expression on the right-hand side of the = sign is evaluated and assigned to the variable, *result*, on the left-hand side of the = sign. (The parentheses are not needed, but used for clarity.) The browser output is shown in Figure 5.3.

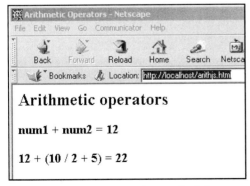

**Figure 5.3**   Ouput from Example 5.3.

## 5.2.2  Shortcut Assignment Operators

The shortcut assignment operators allow you to perform an arithmetic or string operation by combining an assignment operator with an arithmetic or string operator. For example, $x = x + 1$ can be written $x+=1$. See Table 5.3.

**Table 5.3**  Assignment operators.

| Operator | Example | Meaning |
|---|---|---|
| = | $var\ x = 5$; | Assign 5 to variable $x$. |
| += | $x\ += 3$; | Add 3 to $x$ and assign result to $x$. |
| −= | $x\ -= 2$; | Subtract 2 from $x$ and assign result to $x$. |
| *= | $x\ *= 4$; | Multiply $x$ by 4 and assign result to $x$. |
| /= | $x\ /= 2$; | Divide $x$ by 2 and assign result to $x$. |
| **= | $x\ **= 2$; | Square $x$ and assign result to $x$. |
| %= | $x\ \%= 2$; | Divide $x$ by 2 and assign remainder to $x$. |

---

**EXAMPLE 5.4**

```
    <html>
    <head>
    <title>Assignment and Shortcut Operators</title>
1   <script language = "JavaScript">
2      var num=10;
3      document.write("<font size='+1'>" + "<br>" +
           "num is assigned " + 10);
4      num += 2;
       document.write("<br>num += 2; num is " + num );
5      num -= 1;
       document.write("<br>num -= 1; num is " + num);
6      num *= 3;
       document.write("<br>num *= 3; num is " + num);
7      num %= 5;
       document.write("<br>num %= 5; num is " + num);
8   </script>
    </head>
    <body bgcolor="yellow" text="blue">
```

## EXPLANATION

1    JavaScript program starts here.

2    The variable *num* is assigned *10*.

3    Output is sent to the browser.

4    The shortcut assignment operator, +=, adds 2 to the variable *num*. This is equivalent to *num = num + 1;*.

5    The shortcut assignment operator, −=, subtracts 1 from the variable *num*. This is equivalent to *num = num - 1;*.

6    The shortcut assignment operator, *, multiplies the variable *num* by 3. This is equivalent to *num = num * 3;*.

7    The shortcut assignment modulus operator, %, yields the integer amount that remains after the scalar *num* is divided by 5. The operator is called the modulus operator or remainder operator. The expression *var%=5* is equivalent to *num = num % 5;*.

8    JavaScript ends here. The output is shown in Figure 5.4.

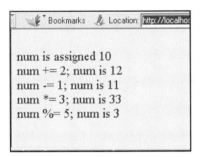

**Figure 5.4** Output from Example 5.4.

### 5.2.3   Autoincrement and Autodecrement Operators

To make programs easier to read, to simplify typing, and, at the machine level, to produce more efficient code, the autoincrement (++) and autodecrement (−−) operators are provided.

The autoincrement operator performs the simple task of incrementing the value of its operand by 1, and the autodecrement operator decrements the value of its operand by 1. The operator has two forms: the first form <u>prefixes</u> the variable with either ++ or −− (e.g., ++*x* or −−*x*); the second form <u>postfixes</u> (places the operator after) the variable name with either ++ or −− (e.g., *x*++ or *x*−−). For simple operations, such as *x*++ or *x*−−, ++*x* or −−*x*, the effect is the same; both ++*x* and *x*++ add one to the value of *x*, and both −−*x* and *x*−− subtract one from the value of *x*.

Now you have four ways to add 1 to the value of a variable:

- $x = x + 1$;
- $x += $ ;
- $x$++;
- ++$x$;

and four ways to subtract 1 from the value of a variable:

- $x = x - 1$;
- $x -= 1$;
- $x$--;
- --$x$;

Refer to Table 5.4. In "Loops" on page 101, you'll see these operators are commonly used to increment or decrement loop counters.

**Table 5.4**  Autoincrement and autodecrement operators.

| Operator | Function | What It Does | Example |
|---|---|---|---|
| ++$x$ | Pre-increment | Adds 1 to $x$ | $x = 3$; $x$++;   $x$ is now 4 |
| $x$++ | Post-increment | Adds 1 to $x$ | $x = 3$; ++$x$;   $x$ is now 4 |
| --$x$ | Pre-decrement | Subtracts 1 from $x$ | $x = 3$; $x$--;   $x$ is now 2 |
| $x$-- | Post-decrement | Subtracts 1 from $x$ | $x = 3$; --$x$;   $x$ is now 2 |

**Autoincrement and Autodecrement Operators and Assignment.**   The placement of the operators does make a difference in more complex expressions, especially when part of an assignment; for example, $y = x$++ is not the same as $y = $++$x$.

Start with:  $y = 0$ ; $x = 5$;

Pre-increment

$y = $++$x$;

Post-increment

$y = x$++;

**EXAMPLE  5.5**

```
        <html>
        <head><title>Auto-increment and Auto-decrement</title></head>
        <body>
            <script language = "JavaScript">
1               var x=5;
                var y=0;
2               y = ++x;        // add one to x first; then assign to y
                document.write("<h3>Pre-increment:<br>");
3               document.write("y is " +  y + "<br>");
                document.write("x is " + x + "<br>");
                document.write("----------------------<br>");
4               var x=5;
                var y=0;
5               y=x++;        // assign value in x to y; then add one to x

                document.write("<h3>Post-increment:<br>");
6               document.write("y is " + y + "<br>");
                document.write("x is " + x + "<br></h3>");
            </script>
        </body>
        </html>
```

**EXPLANATION**

1   The variables, *x* and *y*, are intialized to 5 and 0, respectively.

2   The pre-increment operator is applied to *x*. This means that *x* will be incremented <u>before</u> the assignment is made. The value of *x* was 5, now it is 6. The variable *y* is assigned 6. *x* is 6, *y* is 6.

3   The new values of *y* and *x* are displayed in the browser window.

4   The variables *x* and *y* are assigned values of 5 and 0, respectively.

5   This time the post-increment operator is applied to *x*. This means that *x* will be incremented <u>after</u> the assignment is made. The number 5 is assigned to the variable *y*, and then *x* is incremented by 1. So *x* is 5 and *y* is 6.

6   The new values of *y* and *x* are displayed in the browser window. See Figure 5.5.

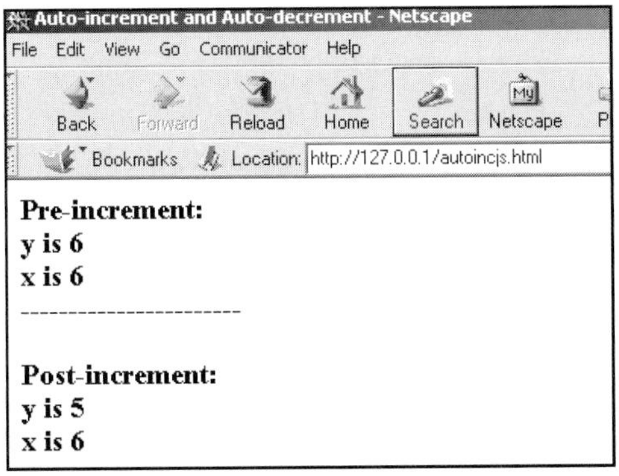

**Figure 5.5**
Output from Example 5.5.

## 5.2.4   Concatenation Operator

As shown in previous examples, the + sign is used for concatenation and addition. The concatenation operator, the + sign, is a string operator used to join together one or more strings. In fact, the concatenation operator is the only operator JavaScript provides to manipulate strings.

In the example, *"correct" + "tion" + "al"* , the result is *"correctional"*. If the operands are a mix of strings and numbers, JavaScript will convert the numbers to strings. For example, *"22" + 8* results in *"228"*, not *30*. If the operands are numbers, then the + sign is the addtion operator as in *5 + 4*. But suppose we say, *"22" * 1 + 4*. In this case, Java-Script sees the multiplication operator (*) and converts the string *"22"* to a number, resulting in *22 + 4* or *26*. Netscape Navigator provides the JavaScript console for testing these expressions or you can type *javascript:* in the URL, followed by the expression you want to test, as shown in Figures 5.6 and 5.7.

**Figure 5.6**   Evaluating expressions in the *javascript:* URL. The result of the test, *26*, is displayed in the browser window.

**Figure 5.7**   Concatenation of a string and a number.

The concatenation operator is summarized in Table 5.5. To explicitly convert strings to numbers, JavaScript provides built-in functions called *parseInt()* and *parseFloat()*, discussed in Sections 5.3.1 and 5.3.2, respectively.

**Table 5.5**  The concatenation operator.

| Operator | Example | Meaning |
|---|---|---|
| + | *"hot"* + *"dog"* | Concatenates (joins) two strings; creates *"hotdog"*. |
| | *"22"* + *8* | Converts number *8* to string *"8"*, then concatenates resulting in *"228"*. In statements involving other operators, JavaScript does not convert numeric values to strings. |
| += | *x =*"cow"*; x +=* *"boy"*; | Concatenates two strings and assigns the result to *x*; *x* becomes *"cowboy"*. |

## 5.2.5  Comparison Operators

When operands are compared, relational and equality operators are used. The operands can be numbers or strings. The result of the comparison is either *true* or *false*—a Boolean value. Strings are compared letter by letter (lexographically) using Unicode[1] values to represent the numeric value of each letter; thus, *"A"* is less than *"B"*, and when comparing *"Daniel"* with *"Dan"*, *"Daniel"* is greater than *"Dan"*. When comparing strings, JavaScript pads *"Dan"* with three spaces to make it the same length as *"Daniel"*. Refer to Table 5.6.

**Table 5.6**  Comparison operators.

| Operator/Operands | Function |
|---|---|
| $x == y$ | $x$ is equal to $y$ |
| $x != y$ | $x$ is not equal to $y$ |
| $x > y$ | $x$ is greater than $y$ |
| $x >= y$ | $x$ is greater than or equal to $y$ |
| $x < y$ | $x$ is less than $y$ |
| $x <= y$ | $x$ is less than or equal to $y$ |
| $x = = = y$ | $x$ is identical to $y$ in value and type |
| $x != = y$ | $x$ is not identical to $y$ |

---

1. Unicode is not supported in versions of JavaScript prior to 1.3. Unicode is compatible with ASCII characters. The first 128 Unicode characters correspond to the ASCII character set and have the same byte value.

**What Is Equal?**    In an ideal world, there would be equality between the sexes and among the races and religions, but in the real world equality is a debatable topic, often determined by governments. In JavaScript, operators determine the equality or inequality of their operands, based on more specific rules. When using the == or != equality operators, the operands may be of any given data type—numbers, strings, Booleans, objects, arrays, or a combination of these—and there are rules that govern whether they are equal. For example, two strings are equal when they have the same sequence of characters, same length, and same characters in corresponding positions. Two numbers are equal when they have the same numeric value. If a string is compared with a number, they are equal if the number has the same characters as the string; for example, *"500"* is equal to *500*. *NaN* (Not a Number) is not equal to anything, including *NaN*. Positive and negative zeros are equal. Two objects are equal if they refer to the same object. Two Boolean operands are equal if they are both *true* or both *false*. *Null* and *undefined* types are equal. To test any of the expressions shown in Table 5.7, use the JavaScript Console. Figure 5.8 shows an example using Netscape.

**Table 5.7**   Equality test with strings and numbers.

| Test | Are They Equal? |
|---|---|
| *"William" == "William"* | *true* |
| *"william" == "William"* | *false* |
| *5 == 5.0* | *true* |
| *"54" == 54* | *true* |
| *"5.4" == 5.4* | *true* |
| *NaN == NaN* | *false* |
| *null == null* | *true* |
| *−0 == +0* | *true* |
| *false == false* | *true* |
| *true == 1* | *true* |
| *null == undefined* | *true* |

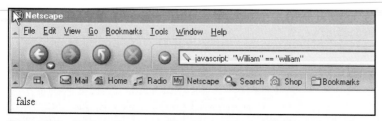

**Figure 5.8**   Testing the equality of two strings. Is *"William"* equal to *"william"*? Nope.

**What Is Identical?**   Men are equal; clones are identical. The === and !== equality operators test that its operands are not only of the same value, but also of the same data type. String *"54"* is equal to number *54*, but <u>not identical</u> because one is a string and the other is a number, even though their values are equal. See Table 5.8.

**Table 5.8**   Identity test with strings and numbers.

| *Test* | *Are They Equal?* |
| --- | --- |
| *"William" === "William"* | *true* |
| *"william" == "William"* | *false* |
| *5 == 5.0* | *true* |
| *"54" === 54* | *false* |
| *NaN == NaN* | *false* |
| *null == null* | *true* |
| *-0 == +0* | *true* |
| *false == false* | *true* |
| *true == 1* | *false* |
| *null == undefined* | *false* |

**Comparing Numbers.**   When the comparison operators are used to compare numbers, numeric values are compared; as in, is *50 > 45*? A Boolean value of either *true* or *false* is returned.

| | |
| --- | --- |
| *x > y* | *x* is greater than *y* |
| *x >= y* | *x* is greater than or equal to *y* |
| *x < y* | *x* is less than *y* |
| *x <= y* | *x* is less than or equal to *y* |

**EXAMPLE** 5.6

```
        <html>
        <head>
        <title>Comparing Numbers</title>
        </head><body>
1           <script language = "JavaScript">
2               var x = 5;
                var y = 4;
```

**EXAMPLE**  5.6 (CONTINUED)

```
3              var result = x > y;
4              document.writeln("<h3>The result is "+ result + ".<br>");
5              result = x < y;
6              document.writeln( "The result is " + result + ".<br>");
7          </script>
       </body>
       </html>
```

**EXPLANATION**

1   The JavaScript program starts here.

2   The variables x and y are assigned values to be compared later in the program.

3   If the value of x is greater than the value of y, a Boolean value of either *true* or *false* is returned and assigned to the variable *result*.

4   The Boolean result of the comparison is displayed by the browser. It is *true*; x is greater than y.

5   If x is less than y, *true* is assigned to the variable, *result*; otherwise it is assigned *false*.

6   The Boolean result of the comparison is displayed by the browser. It is *false*; x is not greater than y.

7   This tag marks the end of the JavaScript program. The output is shown in Figure 5.9.

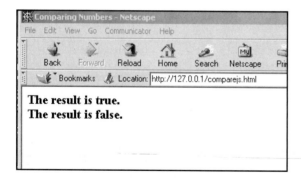

**Figure 5.9**   Output from Example 5.6.

**Comparing Strings.**   The difference between comparing strings and numbers is that numbers are compared numerically and strings are compared alphabetically, based on the ASCII character set. The strings are compared letter by letter, from left to right, and if they are exactly the same all the way to end, they are equal. Once a letter in one string differs from the corresponding letter in the second string, the comparison stops and each of the differing letters is evaluated. For example, if the string *"Dan"* is compared with *"dan"*, the comparison stops at the first letters *D* and *d*. *"Dan"* is smaller than *"dan"*, because the letter *D* has a lower ASCII value than the letter *d*. *D* has an ASCII decimal value of 68, and *d* has an ASCII value of 100.

To avoid the case-sensitivity issue when comparing strings, JavaScript provides the built-in string functions, *toUpperCase()* and *toLowerCase()*, discussed in "Free Form and Reserved Words" on page 17 and Table 9.10 on page 184.

| | |
|---|---|
| *"string1" > "string2"* | *"string1"* is greater than *"string2"* |
| *"string1" >= "string2"* | *"string1"* is greater than or equal to *"string2"* |
| *"string1" < "string2"* | *"string1"* is less than *"string2"* |
| *"string1" <= "string2"* | *"string1"* is less than or equal to *"string2"* |

## EXAMPLE 5.7

```
     <html>
     <head>
     <title>Comparing Strings</title>
     </head><body>
1        <script language = "JavaScript">
2            var fruit1 = "pear";
             var fruit2 = "peaR";

3            var result = fruit1 > fruit2;
4            document.writeln( "<h3>The result is "+ result + ".<br>");

5            result = fruit1 < fruit2;
6            document.writeln( "The result is " + result + ".<br>");

7            result = fruit1 === fruit2;
             // Are they identical; i.e., value and type are the same?
8            document.writeln( "The result is " + result + ".<br>");
         </script>
     </body>
     </html>
```

## EXPLANATION

1   This is the start of the JavaScript program.

2   The variables, *fruit1* and *fruit2*, are assigned to string values, differing by only one letter.

3   The string values are compared and a Boolean value of *true* or *false* will be returned and assigned to the variable, *result*. *"pear"* is greater than *"peaR"* because the *r* has an ASCII value of 114 and the *R* has an ASCII value of 82.

4   The result of the comparison in line 3 is *true* and the result is sent to the browser.

5   This time *"pear"* is compared to *"peaR"* with the less than operator. The result is *false*.

**EXPLANATION** (CONTINUED)

6    The result of the comparison in line 5 is *false* and the result is sent to the browser.

7    The identical equality operator is used. Since the strings are not identical, the result is false.

8    The result of the comparison in line 7 is false and the result is sent to the browser. The output of the script is shown in Figure 5.10.

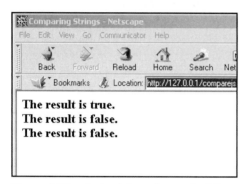

**Figure 5.10**   Output from Example 5.7.

## 5.2.6   Logical Operators

The logical operators allow you combine the relational operators into more powerful expressions for testing conditions and are most often used in *if* statements. They evaluate their operands from left to right, testing the Boolean value of each operand in turn: Does the operand evaluate to true or false? In the expression *if ( x > 5 && x < 10 )*, the *&&* is a logical operator. The expression simplified means, "if *x* is greater than 5 and *x* is also less than 10, then do something"; in the case of the logical AND (*&&*), if the first expression returns *true* and the second expression also returns *true*, then the whole expression is true. If instead of *&&* we used ||, the operator means OR and only one of the expressions must be true.

Sometimes the result of a test is not Boolean. When logical operators have numeric operands, such as 5 *&&* 6, the result of the entire expression is the value of the last evaluated expression. A numeric operand is true if it evaluates to any number that is not zero. *5*, *–2*, and *74* are all true. *0* is false. For example, when using the *&&* (AND) operator, both operands must be true for the whole expression to be true. The value returned from an expression such as 5 *&&* 6 is 6, the last value evaluated by the operator. 5 is not zero (true) and 6 is not zero (true), therefore, the expression is true. 5 *&&* 0, 0 *&&* 0 and 0 *&&* 5 all yield *0*, which is false. See Table 5.9.

The three logical operators are the logical AND, logical OR, and logical NOT. The symbol for AND is *&&*, the symbol for OR is ||, and the symbol for NOT is *!*.

**Table 5.9**   Logical operators and their functions.

| Operator/Operands | Function |
|---|---|
| *num1* && *num2* | True, if *num1* <u>and</u> *num2* are both true. Returns *num1* if evaluated to false; otherwise returns *num2*. If operands are Boolean values, returns true if <u>both</u> operands are true; otherwise returns false. |
| *num1* \|\| *num2* | True, if *num1* is true <u>or</u> if *num2* is true. |
| *! num1* | <u>Not</u> num1; true if *num1* is false; false if *num1* is true. |

**The && Operator (Logical AND).**   We all know the meaning of the English statement, "If you have the money <u>and</u> I have the time...." Whatever is supposed to happen is based on two conditions, and both conditions must be met. You must have the money <u>and</u> I must have the time. JavaScript uses the symbol && to represent the word AND. This operator is called the logical AND operator. If the expression on the left-hand side of the && evaluates to zero, null, or the empty string "",  the expression is false. If the expression on the left-hand side of the operator evaluates to true (non-zero), then the right-hand side is evaluated, and if that expression is also true, then the whole expression is true. If the left-hand side evaluates to true, and the right-hand side is false, the expression is false. If evaluated as Booleans, the same rules apply, except the returned value will be either Boolean *true* or *false*. See Table 5.10.

**Table 5.10**   Logical AND examples.

| Expression | What It Evaluates To |
|---|---|
| *true && false* | *false* |
| *true && true* | *true* |
| *"honest" && true* | *true* |
| *true && ""* | (empty string) |
| *true && "honest"* | *honest* |
| *5 && 0* | *0* |
| *5 && –6* | *–6* |
| *5 && false* | *false* |
| *null && 0* | *null* |
| *null && ""* | *null* |
| *null && false* | *null* |
| *"hello" && true && 50* | *50* |
| *"this" && "that"* | *that* |

## EXAMPLE 5.8

```
<html>
<head><title>Logical AND Operator</title>
</head>
<body bgcolor="lightblue">
<font="+1">
<script language="JavaScript">
    var answer = prompt("How old are you? ", "");
    if ( answer > 12 && answer < 20 ) {
        alert("Teenagers rock!");
    }
</script>
</body>
</html>
```

1
2

## EXPLANATION

1   The user is prompted for his age. The variable called *answer* is assigned the value he enters. (See Figure 5.11.)

2   If the value of *answer* is greater than 12 and also less than 20, the statement enclosed within the curly braces is executed: an alert box appears displaying *Teenagers rock!* (See Figure 5.12.) If the user enters any other value, nothing happens.

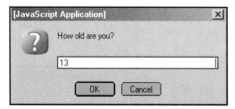

**Figure 5.11**   The user enters his age.

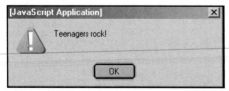

**Figure 5.12**   If the user enters his age and it is greater than 12 and less than 20, this alert box appears.

**The / / Operator (Logical OR).**　　In the English statement "If you have some cash <u>or</u> I have a credit card..." the word *or* is used in the condition. With the *or*, only one of the conditions must be met (hopefully that you have the cash!). JavaScript uses the || symbol to represent the logical OR. If the expression on the left-hand side of the || operator is evaluated as true (non-zero), the value of the expression is true, and no further checking is done. If the value on the left-hand side of the || operator is false, the value of the expression on the right-hand side of the operator is evaluated, and if true, the expression is true; that is, only one expression must be true. Once an expression returns true, the remaining expressions can be either true or false. It doesn't matter, as long as <u>one expression is true</u>. Refer to Table 5.11.

**Table 5.11**　　Logical OR examples.

| *Expression* | *What It Evaluates To* |
|---|---|
| *true || false* | *true* |
| *true || true* | *true* |
| *"honest" || true* | *honest* |
| *true && ""* | *true* |
| *true || "honest"* | *true* |
| *5 || 0* | *5* |
| *5 || –6* | *5* |
| *5 || false* | *5* |
| *null || 0* | *0* |
| *null || ""* | *(empty string)* |
| *null || false* | *false* |
| *"hello" || true || 50* | *hello* |
| *"this" || "that"* | *this* |

**EXAMPLE 5.9**

```
<html>
<head>
<title>Logical OR Operator</title>
</head>
<body bgcolor="lightblue">
<font="+1">
<script language="JavaScript">
```

**EXAMPLE   5.9 (CONTINUED)**

```
1       var answer = prompt("Where should we eat? ", "");
2       if ( answer == "McDonald's" || answer == "Taco Bell" ||
           answer == "Wendy's"){
3            alert("No fast food today, thanks.");
         }
   </script>
   </body>
   </html>
```

**EXPLANATION**

1   The user is prompted to choose a place to eat. The variable called *answer* is assigned the value he enters. (See Figure 5.13.)

2   If the value of *answer* is any one of *McDonald's* or *Taco Bell* or *Wendy's*, the statement enclosed within the curly braces, is executed: an alert box appears displaying *No fast food today, thanks*. (See Figure 5.14.) If he enters any other value, nothing happens.

**Figure 5.13**   The user enters a value.

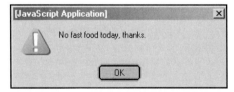

**Figure 5.14**   If the user enters any one of the values in line 2, this alert box appears.

**The *!* Operator (Logical NOT).**   In the English statement "That's *not* true!" the word *not* is used for negation: not true is false, and not false is true. JavaScript provides the NOT (*!*) operator for negation. The *!* operator is called a unary operator because it has only one operand; for example, *! true* or *! 5*. It returns *true* if the expression evaluates to false and returns *false* if the expression evaluates to true. See Table 5.12.

**Table 5.12**  Logical NOT examples.

| Expression | What It Evaluates To |
|---|---|
| ! "this" | false |
| ! 0 | true |
| !2 | false |
| ! false | true |
| ! null | true |
| ! undefined | true |

**EXAMPLE 5.10**

```
<html>
<head>
<title>Logical NOT Operator</title>
</head>
<body bgcolor="lightblue">
<font="+1">
<script language="JavaScript">
1       var answer = true;
2       alert("Was true. Now " + ! true);
</script>
</body>
</html>
```

**EXPLANATION**

1   The Boolean value *true* is assigned to the variable *answer*.

2   The expression sent to the alert dialog box, *! true*, negates the value *true*, (not true) making it *false*. (See Figure 5.15.)

**Figure 5.15**  The *!* operator caused *true* to become *false*.

In summary, the following example illustrates the logical operators and the values they return.

**EXAMPLE   5.11**

```
<html>
<head>
<title>Logical (Boolean) Operators</title>
</head>
<body>
<script language = "JavaScript">
1       var num1=50;
        var num2=100;
        var num3=0;
2       document.write("<h3>num1 && num2 is " + (num1 && num2) +
            ".<br>");
3       document.write("num1 || $num2 is " + (num1 || num2) +".<br>");
4       document.write("! num1 is " +   !num1   +".<br>");
5       document.write("!(num1 && num2) is " + !(num1 && num2) +
            ".<br>");
6       document.write("!(num1 && num3) is " + !(num1 && num3) +
            ".<br>");
</script>
</body>
</html>
```

**EXPLANATION**

1   Three variables, *num1*, *num2*, and *num3*, are initialized.

2   The *&&* operator expects both of its operands to be true, if the expression is to be true. A true value is any number that is not zero. In the expression, *50 && 100*, both operands are true. The value of the last true operand, *100*, is returned.

3   The *||* operator expects only one of its operands to be true if the whole expression is to be true. *50 || 100* is true because the first operand evaluates to a non-zero value. Because *50* is true and only one operand must be true, the evaluation stops here and *50* is returned.

4   The *!* (NOT) operator negates its operand. *! 50* means *! true*; that is, *false*.

5   Because the expression *num1 && num2* is enclosed in parentheses, it is evaluated first, resulting in *50 && 100*, *true*. Then the *!* (NOT) operator evaluates *! (true)*, resulting in Boolean *false*.

6   The expression, *num1 && num3*, enclosed in parentheses, is evaluated first. Since *num3* is *0*, the expression evaluates to false. *! (false)* is *true*. See Figure 5.16.

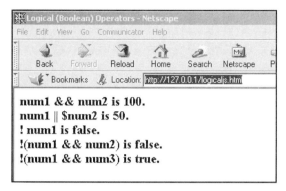

**Figure 5.16** Output from Example 5.11.

### 5.2.7 The Conditional Operator

The conditional operator is called a ternary operator because it requires three operands. It is often used as a shorthand method for *if/else* conditional statements. (See Chapter 6, "Under Certain Conditions.") Although we cover *if/else* in Chapter 6, the format below shows both the conditional operator and how it translates to an *if/else* statement.

**FORMAT**

```
conditional expression ? expression : expression
```

Examples:

```
x ? y : z     If x evaluates to true, the value of the expression
              becomes y, else the value of the expression becomes z

big = (x > y) ? x : y     If x is greater than y, x is assigned to
                          variable big, else y is assigned to
                          variable big
```

The same conditional operator as an *if/else* statement:

```
if (x > y) {
    big = x;
}
else{
    big = y;
}
```

## EXAMPLE 5.12

```
<html>
<head>
<title>Conditional Operator</title>
</head>
<body bgcolor="lightblue">
<font="+1">
<script language="JavaScript">
1    var age = prompt("How old are you? ", "");
2    var price = (age > 55 ) ? 0 : 7.50;
3    alert("You pay $" + price + 0);
</script>
</body>
</html>
```

## EXPLANATION

1   The user is prompted for input. The value he enters in the prompt box is assigned to the variable *age*. (See Figure 5.17.)

2   If the value of *age* is greater than 55, the value to the right of the *?* is assigned to the variable *price*; if not, the value after the *:* is assigned to the variable *price*.

3   The alert dialog box displays the value of the variable *price*. (See Figure 5.18.)

**Figure 5.17**   The user enters *12*. This value is assigned to variable *age* in the program.

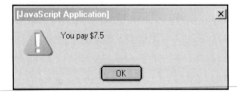

**Figure 5.18**   Since the age is not greater than *55*, the price is assigned *7.50*. (IE displays $7.50.)

## 5.2.8   Bitwise Operators

Bitwise operators treat their operands as a set of 32 bits (zeros and ones), rather than as decimal, hexadecimal, or octal numbers. For example, the decimal number nine has a binary representation of 1001. Bitwise operators perform their operations on such binary representations, but they return standard JavaScript numeric values. Refer to Table 5.13.

**Table 5.13** Bitwise operators.

| Operator | Function | Example | What It Does |
|---|---|---|---|
| & | Bitwise AND | $x$ & $y$ | Returns a $1$ in each bit position if both corresponding bits are $1$. |
| \| | Bitwise OR | $x \| y$ | Returns a $1$ in each bit position if one or both corresponding bits are $1$. |
| ^ | Bitwise XOR | $x$ ^ $y$ | Returns a $1$ in each bit position if one, but not both, of the corresponding bits are $1$. |
| – | Bitwise NOT | $-x$ | Inverts the bits of its operands. $1$ becomes $0$; $0$ becomes $1$. |
| << | Left shift | $x << y$ | Shifts $x$ in binary representation $y$ bits to left, shifting in zeros from the right. |
| >> | Right shift | $x >> y$ | Shifts $x$ in binary representation $y$ bits to right, discarding bits shifted off. |
| >>> | Zero-fill right shift | $x >>> b$ | Shifts $x$ in binary representation $y$ bits to the right, discarding bits shifted off, and shifting in zeros from the left. |

When using the bitwise operations &, |, ^, and –, each bit in the first operand is paired with the corresponding bit in the second operand: first bit to first bit, second bit to second bit, and so on. For example, the binary representation for 5 & 4 is 101 & 100.

```
    101        101        101
  & 100      | 100      ^ 100
  -----      -----      -----
    100        101        001
```

**Bitwise Shift Operators.**   The bitwise shift operators take two operands: the first is a quantity to be shifted, and the second specifies the number of bit positions by which the first operand is to be shifted. The direction of the shift operation is controlled by the operator used.

- << (left shift)
  This operator shifts the first operand the specified number of bits to the left. Excess bits shifted off to the left are discarded. Zero bits are shifted in from the right.

- >> (sign-propagating right shift)
  This operator shifts the first operand the specified number of bits to the right. Excess bits shifted off to the right are discarded. Copies of the leftmost bit are shifted in from the left.
- >>> (zero-fill right shift)
  This operator shifts the first operand the specified number of bits to the right. Excess bits shifted off to the right are discarded. Zero bits are shifted in from the left. For example, *19>>>2* yields 4, because 10011 shifted two bits to the right becomes 100, which is 4. For non-negative numbers, zero-fill right shift and sign-propagating right shift yield the same result.

Shift operators convert their operands to 32-bit integers and return a result of the same type as the left operator.

## EXAMPLE 5.13

```
        <html>
        <head>
        <title>Bitwise Operators</title>
        </head>
        <body bgcolor="lightblue">
        <font size="+1" face="arial">
        <h3> Testing Bitwise Operators</h3>
        <script language="JavaScript">
1           var result = 15 & 9;
            document.write("15 & 9  yields: " + result);
2           result = 15 | 9;
            document.write("<br> 15 | 9  yields: " + result);
3           result = 15 ^ 9;
            document.write("<br> 15 ^ 9  yields: " + result);
4           result = 9 << 2;
            document.write("<br> 9 << 2 yields: " + result);
5           result = 9 >> 2;
            document.write( "<br> 9 >> 2 yields: " + result);
6           result = -9 >> 2;
            document.write( "<br> -9 >> 2 yields: " + result);
7           result = 15 >>> 2;
            document.write( "<br> 15 >>> 2 yields: " + result);
        </script>
        </body>
        </html>
```

## EXPLANATION

1. The binary representation of 9 is 1001, and the binary representation of 15 is 1111. When the bitwise & (AND) operator is applied to *1111 & 1001*, the result is binary 1001 or decimal 9.

2. When the bitwise | (OR) operator is applied to *1111 | 1001*, the result is binary 1111 or decimal 15.

3. When the bitwise ^ (Exclusive OR) is applied to *1111 ^ 1001*, the result is binary 0110 or decimal 6.

4. 9<<2 yields 36, because 1001 shifted two bits to the left becomes 100100, which is decimal 36.

5. 9>>2 yields 2, because 1001 shifted two bits to the right becomes 10, which is decimal 2.

6. *–9 >> 2* yields –3, because the sign is preserved.

7. *15 >>> 2* yields 3, because 1111 shifted two bits to the right becomes 0011, which is decimal 3. For non-negative numbers, zero-fill right shift and sign-propagating right shift yield the same result.

```
Testing Bitwise Operators

15 & 9 yields: 9
15 | 9 yields: 15
15 ^ 9 yields: 6
9 << 2 yields: 36
9 >> 2 yields: 2
-9 >> 2 yields: -3
15 >>> 2 yields: 3
```

**Figure 5.19**  Output from Example 5.13.

# 5.3  Number, String, or Boolean? Datatype Conversion

As defined earlier, JavaScript is a loosely typed language, which really means that you don't have to be concerned about what kind of data is stored in a variable. You can assign a number to *x* on one line and on the next line assign a string to *x*, you can compare numbers and strings, strings and Booleans, and so on. JavaScript automatically converts values when it assigns values to a variable or evaluates an expression. If data types are mixed (i.e., a number is compared with a string, a Boolean is compared with a number, a string is compared with a Boolean), JavaScript must decide how to handle the expression. Most of the time, letting JavaScript handle the data works fine, but there are times when you want to force a conversion of one type to another. For example, if you prompt a user for input, the input is set as a string. But, suppose you want to perform calculations on the incoming data, making it necessary to convert the strings to numbers. When using the + operator you want to add two numbers that have been entered as strings, not concatenate them, so you will then need to convert the data from string to number.

JavaScript provides three methods to convert the primitive data types. They are:

- *String()*
- *Number()*
- *Boolean()*

### EXAMPLE 5.14

```
<html>
<head><title>The Conversion Methods</title></head>
<body>
<p>
<h3>Data Conversion</h3>
script language="JavaScript">
1      var num1 = prompt("Enter a number: ","");
       var num2 = prompt("Enter another number: ","");
2      var result = Number(num1) + Number(num2);
          // Convert strings to numbers
3      alert("Result is "+ result);
4      var myString=String(num1);
5      result=myString + 200;  // String + Number is String
6      alert("Result is "+ result);    // Concatenates 200 to the
                                        // result; displays 20200
7          alert("Boolean result is "+ Boolean(num2));  // Prints true
</script>
</body>
</html>
```

### EXPLANATION

1   The user is prompted to enter a number (see Figure 5.20). The variable *num1* is assigned the number. On the next line, *num2* is assigned another number entered by the user (see Figure 5.21).

2   The JavaScript *Number()* method converts strings to numbers. After the variables, *num1* and *num2* have been converted to numbers, the + sign will be used as an addition operator (rather than a concatenation operator), resulting in the sum of *num1* and *num2*. Unless converted to numbers, the string values *30 + 20* would be concatenated, resulting in *3020*.

3   The *alert()* box displays the sum of the two numbers entered by the user (see Figure 5.22).

EXPLANATION (CONTINUED)

4  The variable *num1* is converted to a string; its value is assigned to the variable, *result*.

5  The value of *myString, 20,* is concatenated to *200* and assigned to *result*. The result is *20200*.

6  The *alert()* box displays the result from line 5.

7  The value of *num2* is converted to Boolean, either *true* or *false*. Since the value of *num2* is not 0, *true* is displayed in the *alert()* dialog box.

**Figure 5.20**  The user is prompted to enter a number.

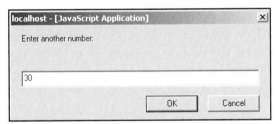

**Figure 5.21**  The user is prompted to enter another number.

**Figure 5.22**  The result is displayed.

## 5.3.1 The *parseInt()* Method

This method converts a string to a number. It starts parsing at the beginning of the string and returns all integers until it reaches a non-integer and then stops parsing. If the string doesn't begin with an integer, *NaN*[2] (not a number) is returned. For example,

---

2. NaN is not supported in JavaScript 1.0; instead of *NaN*, 0 is returned.

*parseInt("150cats")* becomes *150*, whereas *parseInt("cats")* becomes *NaN*. You can also use octal and hexadecimal numbers. In the two-argument format, the first argument to *parseInt()* is a string containing a number base (radix) ranging from 2 to 36. The default is base 10. In the statement, *parseInt("17", 8)*, the result is *15*. The first argument is the string to be parsed and the second argument, 8, is the number base of the number (here, octal 17). The value returned is decimal *15*. Refer to Tables 5.14 and 5.15.

**FORMAT**

```
parseInt(String, NumberBase);      Default base is 10
parseInt(String);
```

**Example:**

```
parseInt("111", 2);      7   (111 in base 2 is 7)
parseInt("45days");      45
```

**Table 5.14**  *parseInt(String).*

| String | Result |
|--------|--------|
| "hello" | NaN |
| "Route 66" | NaN |
| "6 dogs" | 6 |
| "6" | 6 |
| "-6" | –6 |
| "6.56" | 6 |
| "0Xa" | 10 |
| "011" | 9 |

**Table 5.15**  *parseInt(String, NumberBase).*

| String | Base | Result (decimal) |
|--------|------|------------------|
| "111" | 2 (binary) | 7 |
| "12" | 8 (octal) | 10 |
| "b" | 16 (hex) | 11 |

**EXAMPLE  5.15**

```
      <html>
      <head>
      <title>Using the parseInt() Function</title></head>
      <body><font face="arial size="+1">
      <b>
      <script language = "JavaScript">
1         var grade = prompt("What is your grade? ", "");
              // Grade entered as a string
2         grade=parseInt(grade);      // Grade converted to an integer
3         document.write("grade type is<em> " + typeof(grade));
4         grade+=10;
5         document.write("<em><br>After a 10 point bonus, your grade is "
                    + grade + "!<br>");
      </script>
      </body>
      </html>
```

**EXPLANATION**

1   The user is prompted to enter a grade. The string value entered in the prompt box is assigned to the variable *grade*. (See Figure 5.23.)

2   The *parseInt()* method will convert the grade to an integer value.

3   The *typeof()* operator returns the data type of the variable *grade*.

4   The value of *grade* is incremented by 10.

5   The new value of *grade* is sent to the browser. (See Figure 5.24.)

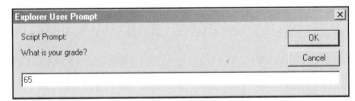

**Figure 5.23**   The user enters a grade.

**Grade type is *number*
After a 10 point bonus, your grade is 75!**

**Figure 5.24**   The new value of *grade* is displayed in the browser.

## 5.3.2   The *parseFloat()* Method

The *parseFloat()* method is just like the *parseInt()* method except that it returns a floating-point[3] number. A floating-point[3] number is a number that contains a fractional part, such as 3.0, –22.5, or .15. The decimal point is allowed in the string being parsed. If the string being parsed does not start with a number, *NaN* (not a number) is returned.

### FORMAT

```
parseFloat(String);
```

**Example:**

```
parseFloat("45.3 degrees");
```

**Table 5.16**   *parseFloat(String).*

| String | Result |
| --- | --- |
| "hello" | NaN |
| "Route 66.6" | NaN |
| "6.5 dogs" | 6.5 |
| "6" | 6 |
| "6.56" | 6.56 |

### EXAMPLE   5.16

```
      <html>
      <head>
      <title>Using the parseFloat() Function</title>
      <script language = "JavaScript">
1         var temp = prompt("What is your temperature? ", "");
2         temp=parseFloat(temp);
3         if(temp == 98.6){
4            alert("Your temp is normal");
          }
5         else{
             alert("You are sick!");
          }
      </script></head><body></body></html>
```

---

3.  The term "floating point" means that there are not a fixed number of digits before or after the decimal point; the decimal point floats.

## EXPLANATION

1    The user is prompted for input and the result is assigned as a string to the variable *temp*. (See Figure 5.25.)

2    The *parseFloat()* method converts the string into a floating-point number and assigns it to *temp*.

3    Although we haven't formally covered *if* statements, this example should be easy to follow. If the value of *temp* is equal to *98.6*, then the following block of statements will be executed.

4    If is the user entered 98.6, the alert box sends the message "*Your temp is normal*" to the browser.

5    If line 3 is not true, the block of statements following *else* is executed. An alert box will appear in the browser window saying, "*You are sick!*". (See Figure 5.26.)

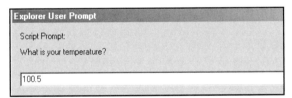

**Figure 5.25**   User enters a string. The *parseFloat()* method will convert it to a floating-point number.

**Figure 5.26**   Output from Example 5.16.

## 5.3.3 The *eval()* Method

The *eval()* method evaluates a string of JavaScript statements and evaluates the whole thing as a little program, returning the result of the execution.[4] If there is no result, *undefined* is returned.

---

4.  The *eval()* method takes a primitive string as its argument, not a *String* object. If a *String* object is used, it will be returned as is.

## FORMAT

```
eval(String);
```

**Example:**

```
eval("(5+4) / 3");
```

## EXAMPLE 5.17

```
      <html>
      <head>
      <title>The eval() Function</title>
      </head>
      <body bgcolor="lightblue">
      <font size="+1" face="arial">
      <script language="JavaScript">
1         var str="5 + 4";
2         var num1 = eval(str);
3         var num2 = eval(prompt("Give me a number ", ""));
4         alert(num1 + num2);
      </script>
      </body>
      </html>
```

## EXPLANATION

1   The string *"5 + 4"* is assigned to the variable *str*.

2   The *eval()* method evaluates the string expression *"5 + 4"* as a JavaScript instruction. The variable *num1* is assigned *9*, the sum of *5 + 4*.

3   The *eval()* method evaluates the string value that is entered into the prompt dialog box. (See Figure 5.27.) The *prompt()* method always returns a string value. If the value in the string is a number, *eval()* will convert the string to a number, return the number, and assign it to *num2*.

4   The *alert()* method displays the sum of *num1* and *num2* in the browser window. (See Figure 5.28.)

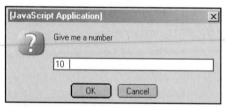

**Figure 5.27**   The *eval()* method converts the user input, a string, to a number.

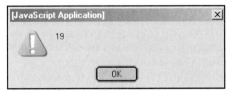

**Figure 5.28**   Output from Example 5.17.

# 5.4   **Special Operators**

In this chapter, we have covered the most commonly used JavaScript functions. Table 5.17 lists some of the other operators available to be discussed in later chapters when they are applicable.

**Table 5.17**   Other useful JavaScript operators.

| *Operator* | *What It Does* |
| --- | --- |
| , (comma) | Evaluates two expressions and returns the result of the second expression |
| *delete* | Deletes an object, an object's property, or an element at a specified index in an array |
| *function* | Defines an anonymous function |
| *in* (Netscape 6+, IE 5.5+) | Returns *true* if the property is a property of a specified object |
| *instanceof* (Netscape 6+, IE 5+) | Returns *true* if the object is of a given object type |
| *new* | Creates an instance of a user-defined object type or of one of the built-in object types |
| *this* | Keyword that you can use to refer to the current object |
| *void* | Specifies an expression to be evaluated without returning a value |

## EXERCISES

1. In the expression 6 + 4 / 2 % 2 what are the operands and in what order are they evaluated? Show operator preference by using parentheses.

2. How can JavaScript tell if the + is used for concatenation or addition? Write a short program to demonstrate.

3. a. If *x* is assigned the value of 5, what is *y* in the following two statements:
   ```
   y = --x;
   y = x--;
   ```
   b. Explain the output of the preceding two statements.

4. a. Are the following true or false:
   ```
   22 == "22"
   22 === "22"
   "2" > "100"
   ```
   b. Write a script to prove your answers to the preceding. In the same script, use the following two statements:
   ```
   document.write("3" + "4");
   document.write(3 + 4);
   ```
   c. Explain the output of the two preceding statements.

5. Example 5.8 prompts the user for his age. The user's response is assigned to the variable *answer* as a string value. Rewrite the program to assure that the age entered is a number before testing it. How do you do this?

6. Ask the user for a Fahrenheit temperature, and then convert it to Celsius. Use *parseFloat()*. To specify the precision of the number, see "The Number Object" on page 190 in Chapter 9. Formula for conversion: C = 5/9(F – 32).

7. The user is visiting Thailand. He has 65 U.S. dollars. Tell him how many baht that amounts to. There are approximately 42 baht to a U.S. dollar. Display an image of the Thai flag on the same page.

# chapter

# 6

# Under Certain Conditions

## 6.1  Control Structures, Blocks, and Compound Statements

If you were confronted with the above signpost, you'd have to decide which direction to take. People control their lives by making decisions, and so do programs. In fact, according to computer science books, a good language allows you to control the flow of your program in three ways. It lets you

- Execute a sequence of statements
- Branch to an alternative sequence of statements, based on a test
- Repeat a sequence of statements until some condition is met

Well, then JavaScript must be a good language. We've already used programs that execute a sequence of statements, one after another.

Now we will examine the branching and looping control structures that allow the flow of the program's control to change depending on some conditional expression.

The decision-making constructs (*if, if/else, if/else if, switch*) contain a control expression that determines whether a block of statements will be executed. The looping constructs (*while, for*) allow the program to execute a statement block repetitively until some condition is satisfied.

A compound statement or block consists of a group of statements surrounded by curly braces. The block is syntactically equivalent to a single statement and usually follows an *if, else, while,* or *for* construct.

## 6.2  Conditionals

Conditional constructs control the flow of a program. If a condition is true, the program will execute a block of statements and if the condition is false, flow will go to an alternate block of statements. Decision-making constructs (*if, else, switch*) contain a control expression that determines whether a block of expressions will be executed. If the condition after the *if* is met, the result is true, and the following block of statements is executed; otherwise the result is false and the block is not executed.

## FORMAT

```
if (condition){
    statements;
}
```

**Example:**

```
if ( age > 21 ){
    alert("Let's Party!");
}
```

The block of statements (or single statement) is enclosed in curly braces. Normally, statements are executed sequentially. If there is only one statement after the conditional expression, the curly braces are optional.

## 6.2.1   *if/else*

"You better pay attention now, or else . . . " Ever heard that kind of statement before? JavaScript statements can be handled the same way with the *if/else* branching construct. This construct allows for a two-way decision. The *if* evaluates the expression in parentheses, and if the expression evaluates to true, the block after the opening curly braces is executed; otherwise the block after the *else* is executed.

## FORMAT

```
if (condition){
    statements1;
}
else{
    statements2;
}
```

**Example:**

```
if ( x > y ){
    alert( "x is larger");
}
else{
    alert( "y is larger");
}
```

## EXAMPLE 6.1

```
        <html>
        <head>
        <title>Conditional Flow Control</title>
        </head>
        <body>
1       <script language=javascript>
            <!--  Hiding JavaScript from old browsers
            document.write("<h3>");
2           var age=prompt("How old are you? ","");
3           if( age >= 55 ){
4               document.write("You pay the senior fare! ");
5           }
6           else{
7               document.write("You pay the regular adult fare. ");
            }
            document.write("</h3>");
            //-->
8       </script>
        </body>
        </html>
```

## EXPLANATION

1   JavaScript program starts here.

2   The prompt dialog box will display the message *"How old are you?"*. Whatever the user types into the box will be stored in the variable *age*. (See Figure 6.1.)

3, 4   If the value of the variable *age* is greater than or equal to 55, line 4 is executed. (See Figure 6.2.)

5   This closing curly brace closes the block of statements following the *if* expression. Because there is only one statement in the block, the curly braces are not required.

6, 7   The *else* statement, line number 7, is executed if the expression in line 3 is false.

8   This tag marks the end of the JavaScript program.

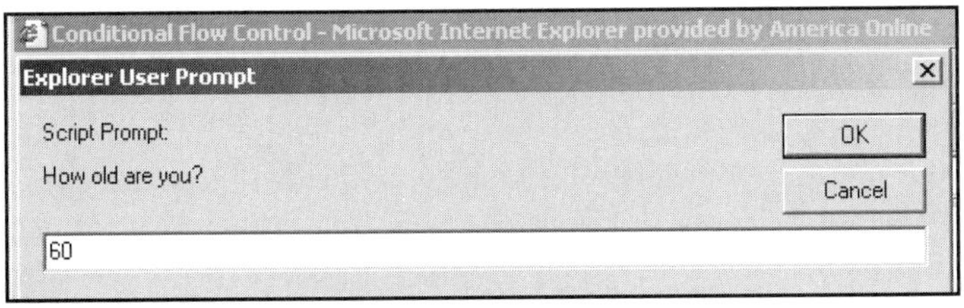

**Figure 6.1**   The user is prompted for input.

**Figure 6.2**   If the age was entered was greater than 55, this message is displayed.

### 6.2.2   *if/else if*

"If you've got $1, we can go to the Dollar Store; else if you've got $10, we could get a couple of movies; else if you've got $20 we could buy a CD . . . else forget it!" JavaScript provides yet another form of branching, the *if/else if* construct. This construct provides a multiway decision structure.

FORMAT

```
if (condition) {
    statements1;
}
else if (condition)  {
    statements2;
}
else if (condition)  {
    statements3;
}
else{
    statements4;
}
```

If the first conditional expression following the *if* keyword is true, the statement or block of statements following the expression are executed and control starts after the final *else* block. Otherwise, if the conditional expression following the *if* keyword is false, control branches to the first *else if* and the expression following it is evaluated. If that expression is true, the statement or block of statements following it are executed, and if false, the next *else if* is tested. All *else if*s are tested and if none of their expressions are true, control goes to the *else* statement. Although the *else* is not required, it normally serves as a default action if all previous conditions were false.

EXAMPLE 6.2

```
        <html>
        <head>
        <title>Conditional Flow Control</title>
        </head>
        <body>
1       <script language=javascript>
        <!--
        document.write("<H2>");
2       var age=eval( prompt("How old are you? ",""));
3       if( age > 0 && age <= 12 ){
4          document.write("You pay the child's fare. ");
        }
5       else if( age > 12 && age < 60 ){
6          document.write("You pay the regular adult fare. ");
        }
7       else {
           document.write("You pay the senior fare! ");
        }
           document.write("</H2>");
        //-->
8       </script></body></html>
```

**EXPLANATION**

1 JavaScript program starts here.

2 The prompt dialog box will display the message "*How old are you?*". Whatever the user types into the box will be converted to a number by the *eval()* method and then stored in the variable *age*.

3, 4 If the value of the variable *age* is greater than *0* and *age* is also less than or equal to *12*, then line 4 is executed.

5, 6 If the expression on line 3 is false, the JavaScript interpreter will test this line, and if the age is greater than 12 and also less than 60, the block of statements that follow will be executed. You can have as many *else ifs* as you like.

7 The *else* statement, line number 7, is executed if all of the previous expressions test false. This statement is called the default and is not required.

8 This tag marks the end of the JavaScript program.

## 6.2.3 *switch*

The *switch* statement is an alternative to *if/else if* conditional construct (commonly called a "case statement") and may make the program more readable when handling multiple options. It is supported in both Netscape Navigator and Internet Explorer.[1]

---

1. Added to JavaScript 1.2 and supported by Internet Explorer 4.0+ and Netscape 4+.

## FORMAT

```
switch (expression){
case label :
    statement(s);
    break;
case label :
    statement(s);
    break;
    ...
default : statement;
}
```

**Example:**

```
switch (color){
case "red":
    alert("Hot!");
    break;
case "blue":
    alert("Cold.");
    break;
default:
    alert("Not a good choice.");
    break;
}
```

The value of the *switch* expression is matched against the expressions, called labels, following the *case* keyword. The *case* labels are constants, either string or numeric. Each label is terminated with a colon. The default label is optional, but its action is taken if none of the other cases match the *switch* expression. After a match is found, the statements after the matched label are executed for that case. If none of the cases are matched, the control drops to the *default* case. The default is optional. If a *break* statement is omitted, all statements below the matched label are executed until either a *break* is reached or the entire *switch* block exits.

## EXAMPLE  6.3

```
<html>
<head>
<title>The Switch Statement</title>
</head>
<body>
<script language=javascript>
<!--
```

**EXAMPLE  6.3 (CONTINUED)**

```
1   var color=prompt("What is your color?","");
2   switch(color){
3      case "red":
           document.bgColor="color";
           document.write("Red is hot.");
4         break;
5      case "yellow":
           document.bgColor=color;
           document.write("Yellow is warm.");
6         break;
7      case "green":
           document.bgColor="lightgreen";
           document.write("Green is soothing.");
8         break;
9      case "blue":
           document.bgColor="#RRGGBB";
           document.write("Blue is cool.");
10        break;
11     default:
           document.bgColor="white";
           document.write("Not available today. We'll use white");
12        break;
13     }
       //-->
    </script>
    </body>
    </html>
```

**EXPLANATION**

1   The prompt dialog box will ask the user to type a color. After the user presses the OK button, the *switch* statement is entered. (See Figure 6.3.)

2   The *color* value of the *switch* expression is matched against the values of each of the *case* labels below.

3   The first *case* that is tested is *"red"*. If the user typed *red* as his choice, then the background color of the document's window will turn red and the message "*Red is hot.*" will be displayed in the document.

4   The *break* statement causes program control to continue after line 13. Without it, the program would continue executing statements into the next *case*, *"yellow"*, and continue doing so until a *break* is reached or the *switch* ends—and we don't want that.

## EXPLANATION, (CONTINUED)

5   The first case that is tested is *"red"*. If the user typed *yellow* as his choice, then the JavaScript interpreter will skip the *"red"* case and test the next one which is *"yellow"*. Since that value is matched successfully against the value of the *color* variable, the background color of the document's window will turn yellow and the message "*Yellow is warm.*" will be displayed in the document.

6   The *break* statement sends control of the program to line 13.

7   If *"red"* and *"yellow"* are not matched successfully against the value of the *color* variable, then *"green"* is tested, and if there is a match, then its block of statements is executed. (See Figure 6.4.)

8   The *break* statement sends control of the program to line 13.

9   If *"red"*, *"yellow"*, or *"green"* are not matched successfully against the value of the *color* variable, then *"blue"* is tested, and if there is a match, then its block of statements are executed. (The color is assigned the RGB hexidecimal value.)

10  The *break* statement sends control of the program to line 13.

11  The *default* statement block is executed if none of the above cases are matched.

12  This final *break* statement is not necessary, but is good practice in case you should decide to replace the *default* with an additional *case* label.

13  The final curly brace ends the *switch* statement.

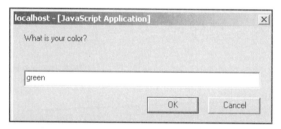

**Figure 6.3**   The user enters a color value.

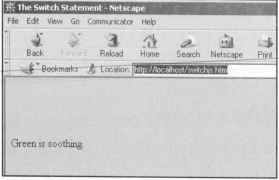

**Figure 6.4**   Output from Example 6.3. The *"green"* case was matched successfully.

# 6.3 Loops

Loops are used to execute a segment of code repeatedly until some condition is met. JavaScript's basic looping constructs are

- *while*
- *for*
- *do/while*

## 6.3.1 The *while* Loop

The *while* statement executes its statement block as long as the expression after the while evaluates to true; that is, non-null, non-zero, non-false. If the condition never changes and is true, the loop will iterate forever (infinite loop). If the condition is false control goes to the statement right after the closing curly brace of the loop's statement block.

The *break* and *continue* functions are used for loop control.

### FORMAT

```
while (condition) {
    statements;
    increment/decrement counter;
}
```

### EXAMPLE 6.4

```
    <html>
    <head>
    <title>Looping Constructs</title>
    </head>
    <body>
    <h2>While Loop</h2>
1   <script language="JavaScript">
        document.write("<font size='+2'>");
2       var i=0;    // Initialize loop counter
3       while ( i < 10 ){       // Test
4          document.writeln(i);
5          i++;    // Increment the counter
6       }       // End of loop block
7   </script>
    </body>
    </html>
```

1    The JavaScript program starts here.

2    The variable *i* is initialized to *0*.

3    The expression after the *while* is tested. If *i* is less than *10*, the block in curly braces is entered and its statements are executed. If the expression evaluates to false, (i.e., *i* is not less than *10*), the loop block exits and control goes to line 6.

4    The value of *i* is displayed in the browser window. (See Figure 6.5.)

5    The value of *i* is incremented by 1. If this value never changes, the loop will never end.

6    This curly brace marks the end of the *while* loop's block of statements.

7    The JavaScript program ends here.

**Figure 6.5**   Output from Example 6.4.

## 6.3.2  The *do/while* Loop

The *do/while* statement executes a block of statements repeatedly until a condition becomes false. Owing to its structure, this loop necessarily executes the statements in the body of the loop at least once before testing its expression, which is found at the bottom of the block. The *do/while* loop is supported in Netscape Navigator and Internet Explorer 4.0, JavaScript 1.2, and ECMAScript v3.

**FORMAT**

```
do
    { statements;}
while (condition);
```

EXAMPLE 6.5

```
            <html>
            <head>
            <title>Looping Constructs</title>
            </head>
            <body>
            <h2>Do While Loop</h2>
            <script language="JavaScript">
                document.write("<font size='+2'>");
1           var i=0;
2           do{
3               document.writeln(i);
4               i++;
5           } while ( i < 10 )
            </script>
            </body>
            </html>
```

**EXPLANATION**

1   The variable *i* is initialized to *0*.

2   The *do* block is entered. This block of statements will be executed before the *while* expression is tested. Even if the *while* expression proves to be false, this block will be executed the first time around.

3   The value of *i* is displayed in the browser window. (See Figure 6.6.)

4   The value of *i* is incremented by 1.

5   Now, the *while* expression is tested to see if it evaluates to true (i.e., is *i* less than *10*?). If so, control goes back to line 2 and the block is re-entered.

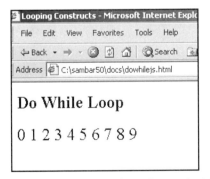

**Figure 6.6** Output from Example 6.5.

### 6.3.3   The *for* Loop

The *for* loop consists of the *for* keyword followed by three expressions separated by semicolons and enclosed within parentheses. Any or all of the expressions can be omitted, but the two semicolons cannot. The first expression is used to set the initial value of variables and is executed just once, the second expression is used to test whether the loop should continue or stop, and the third expression updates the loop variables; that is, it increments or decrements a counter, which will usually determine how many times the loop is repeated.

**FORMAT**

```
for(Expression1;Expression2;Expression3)
    {statement(s);}
for (initialize; test; increment/decrement)
    {statement(s);}
```

The above format is equivalent to the following *while* statement:

```
Expression1;
while( Expression2 )
    { Block; Expression3};
```

**EXAMPLE** 6.6

```
      <html>
      <head>
      <title>Looping Constructs</title>
      </head>
      <body>
      <h2>For Loop</h2>
      <script language="JavaScript">
         document.write("<font size='+2'>");
1        for( var i = 0; i < 10; i++ ){
2           document.writeln(i);
3        }
      </script>
      </body>
      </html>
```

**EXPLANATION**

1   The *for* loop is entered. The expression starts with step 1, the initialization of the variable *i* to *0*. This is the only time this step is executed. The second expression, step 2, tests to see if *i* is less than *10*, and if it is, the statements after the opening curly brace are executed. When all statements in the block have been executed and the closing curly brace is reached, control goes back into the *for* expression to the last expression of the three. *i* is now incremented by one and the expression in step 2 is retested. If true, the block of statements is entered and executed.

2   The value of *i* is displayed in the browser window. (See Figure 6.7.)

3   The closing curly brace marks the end of the *for* loop.

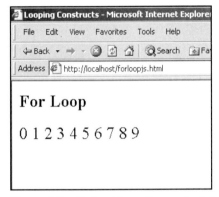

**Figure 6.7**   Output from Example 6.6.

### 6.3.4   The *for/in* Loop

The *for/in* loop is like the *for* loop, except it is used with JavaScript objects. Instead of iterating the statements based on a looping condition, it operates on the properties of an object. This loop is discussed in Chapter 9, "JavaScript Core Objects," and is only mentioned here in passing, because it falls into the category of looping constructs.

### 6.3.5   Loop Control with *break* and *continue*

The control statements, *break* and *continue*, are used to either break out of a loop early or return to the testing condition early; that is, before reaching the closing curly brace of the block following the looping construct.

**Table 6.1**  Control statements.

| Statement | What It Does |
|---|---|
| break | Exits the loop to the next statement after the closing curly brace of the loop's statement block. |
| continue | Sends loop control directly to the top of the loop and re-evaluates the loop condition. If the condition is true, enters the loop block. |

## EXAMPLE 6.7

```
    <html>
    <head>
    <title>Looping Constructs</title>
    </head>
    <body>
    <h2>While Loop</h2>
1   <script language="JavaScript">
        document.write("<font size='+2'>");
2       while(true) {
3           var grade=eval(prompt("What was your grade? ",""));
4           if (grade < 0 || grade > 100) {
                document.write("Illegal choice<br>");
5               continue;    // Go back to the top of the loop
            }
6           if(grade > 89 && grade < 101) {document.write("A<br>");}
7               else if (grade > 79 && grade < 90)
                        {document.write("B<br>");}
                else if (grade > 69 && grade < 80)
                        {document.write("C<br>");}
                else if (grade > 59 && grade < 70)
                        {document.write("D<br>");}
8               else {document.write("You Failed.<br>");}
9           answer=prompt("Do you want to enter another grade? ","");
10          if(answer != "yes"){
11              break;    // Break out of the loop to line 12
            }
12          document.write("So long.<br>");
    </script>
    </body>
    </html>
```

## EXPLANATION

1  The JavaScript program starts here.

2  The *while* loop is entered. The loop expression will always evaluate to true, causing the body of the loop to be entered.

3  The user is prompted for a grade, which is assigned to the variable *grade*.

4   If the variable *grade* is less than 0 or more than 100, "*Illegal choice*" is printed.

5   The *continue* statement sends control back to line 2 and the loop is re-entered, prompting the user again for his grade.

6   If a valid grade was entered, and it is greater than 89 and less than 101, the grade "*A*" is displayed.

7   Each *else/if* branch will be evaluated until one of them is true.

8   If none of the expressions are true, the *else* condition is reached and "*You Failed*" is displayed.

9   The user is prompted to see if he wants to enter another grade.

10, 11   If his answer is not *yes*, the *break* statement takes him out of the loop, to line 12.

## 6.3.6   Nested Loops and Labels

**Nested Loops.**   A loop within a loop is a nested loop. A common use for nested loops is to display data in rows and columns. One loop handles the rows and the other handles the columns. The outside loop is initialized and tested, the inside loop then iterates completely through all of its cycles, and the outside loop starts again where it left off. The inside loop moves faster than the outside loop. Loops can be nested as deeply as you wish, but there are times when it is necessary to terminate the loop owing to some condition.

**EXAMPLE   6.8**

```
        <html>
        <head>
        <title>Nested loops</title>
        </head>
        <body>
        <script language=javascript>
            <!--  Hiding JavaScript from old browsers
1           var str = "@";
2           for ( var row = 0; row < 6; row++){
3               for ( var col=0; col < row; col++){
                    document.write(str);
                }
4               document.write("<br>");
            }
            //-->
        </script>
        </body>
        </html>
```

## EXPLANATION

1   The variable *str* is assigned a string "@".

2   The outer *for* loop is entered. The variable *row* is initialized to 0. If the value of *row* is less than 6, the loop block (in curly braces) is entered (i.e., go to line 3).

3   The inner *for* loop is entered. The variable *col* is initialized to 0. If the value of *col* is less than the value of *row*, the loop block is entered and an @ is displayed in the browser. Next, the value of *col* will be incremented by 1, tested, and if still less than the value of *row*, the loop block is entered, and another @ displayed. When this loop has completed, a row of @ symbols will be displayed, and the statements in the outer loop will start up again.

4   When the inner loop has completed looping, this line is executed producing a break in the rows. (See Figure 6.8.)

**Figure 6.8**   Nested loops: rows and columns. Output from Example 6.8.

**Labels.**   Labels are identifiers followed by a colon and placed on a line by themselves. They can be named the same as any other legal identifier that is not a reserved word. They are used if you want to branch to some other part of the program. By themselves, labels do nothing. You name labels as you would name any other identifier. Labels are optional, but can be used to control the flow of a loop.  A label looks like this, for example:

```
Top:
```

Normally, if you use loop-control statements such as *break* and *continue*, the control is directed to the innermost loop. There are times when it might be necessary to switch control to some outer loop. This is where labels most often come into play. By prefixing a loop with a label, you can control the flow of the program with *break* and *continue* statements as shown in Example 6.9. Labeling a loop is like giving the loop its own name.

**EXAMPLE 6.9**

```
(A Demo Script)
1   outer:
        while(1){
        < Program continues here >
        }
2   middle:
        while(1){
3       if ( <expression is true> ) { break outer;}
        < Program continues here >
        }
4   inner:
        for (i=0; i<20; i++){
5       if ( <expression is true> ){ continue outer;}
        <Program continues here>
        }
6   document.write( "Out of all loops.<br>");
```

**EXPLANATION**

1   The label *outer:* is on a line by itself. It labels the *while* loop.

2   Here is another label called *middle:*. It will label the *while* loop below it.

3   If the expression is true, the *break* statement, with the label, causes control to go to line 6; it breaks out of the *outer:* loop.

4   This label applies to the *for* loop below it.

5   If the expression is true, the *continue* statement causes control to go back to line 1, the *outer:* loop.

## EXERCISES

1. Create a while loop that displays numbers as: 10 9 8 7 6 5 4 3 2 1.

2. Ask the user what the current hour is. If the hour is between 6 and 9 a.m., tell him, "Breakfast is served." If the hour is between 11 a.m. and 1 p.m., tell him, "Time for lunch." If the hour is between 5 and 8 p.m., tell him, "It's dinner time." For any other hours, tell him, "Sorry, you'll have to wait, or go get a snack."

3. Create a conversion table using the following formula:

   ```
   C = (F - 32) / 1.8;
   ```

   Start with a Fahrenheit temperature of 20 degrees and end with a temperature of 120 degrees; use an increment value of 5. The table will have two columns, one for Fahrenheit temperature values and one for those same temperatures converted to Celsius.

4. Ask the user for the name of the company that developed the JavaScript language. Alert him when he is wrong, and then keep asking him until he gets the correct answer. When he gets it right, confirm it.

5. Use a *switch* statement to evaluate the menu item selected to produce output similar to what you see below.

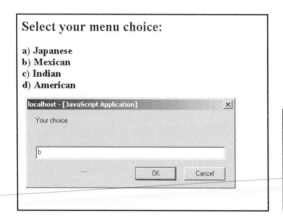

# chapter

# 7

# Functions

## 7.1 What Is a Function?

A pocket calculator performs certain functions. You push the buttons, send information to the calculator, it performs a calculation, and sends back the results. You don't care about what transpires inside the calculator, you just want the results. That's what a function does. Functions are self-contained units of a program designed to accomplish a specified task such as calculating mortgage payments, displaying random images, or checking for valid input. They can be used over and over again and thus save you from repetitive programming. They are also used to break up a program into smaller modules to keep it better organized and easier to maintain. JavaScript has a large number of its own built-in functions, and now you can create your own.

By definition, a function is a block of statements that not only performs some task, but also returns a value. A function is independent of your program and not executed until called. A function is often referred to as a "black box." It's like the pocket calculator: Information goes into the black box (or calculator) as input and the action or value returned from the box is its output. What goes on inside the box is transparent to the user. The programmer who writes the function is the only one who cares about those details. When you use *document.write()*, you send something like a string of text to the function, and it sends some text back to the browser. You don't care how it does its job, you just expect it to work. If you send bad input, you get back bad output or maybe nothing, hence the expression "Garbage in, garbage out."

Functions are like mini-scripts. They contain JavaScript statements that behave as a single command and can be called repeatedly throughout a program without rewriting the code.

The terms "function" and "method" are often used interchangeably. A method refers to a function that is used with JavaScript objects (covered in Chapter 8, "Objects"). A function, as used in this chapter, is a standalone block of statements, independent of the program until invoked by a caller.

### 7.1.1   Function Declaration and Invocation

Functions must be declared before they can be used. Normally functions are placed in the *<head>* tag of the HTML document to ensure that they are defined before used. Within the *<script>* tag itself, they can go anywhere. Function definitions can also be located in external JavaScript files (see "JavaScript from External Files" on page 13 of Chapter 1).

To define a function, the *function* keyword is followed by the name of the function, and a set of parentheses. The parentheses are used to hold parameters, values that are received by the function. The function's statements are enclosed in curly braces.

```
function bye() { document.write ("Bye, adios, adieu, au revoir..."); }
```

Once you define a function, you can use it. JavaScript functions are invoked by calling the function; for example, *bye()*. A function can be called directly from within the *<script>* tag, from a link, or called when an event is triggered, such as when the user presses a key. When called, the function's name is followed by a set of parentheses that may contain messages that will go to the function. These messages are called arguments.

To check whether the function has been defined or if it is truly a function, use the *typeof* operator; for example, *typeof(function_name)*.

## FORMAT

Function definition:

```
function function_name () {statement; statement;}
function function_name (parameter, parameter){statement; statement;}
```

Function call:

```
function_name();
function_name(argument1, argument2, ...)
```

## EXAMPLE 7.1

```
      <html>
      <head>
      <title>A Simple Function</title>
      <script language=JavaScript>
1         function welcome(){  // Function defined within <head> tags
2            var place="San Francisco";
3            alert("Welcome to "+ place + "!");
4         }
```

EXAMPLE 7.1 (CONTINUED)

```
5       welcome();     // Function call
</script>
</head>
<body bgcolor="lightblue">
<font face="arial" size-"+1">
<center>
<b>San Francisco</b><br>
6 <img src="sf.jpg" width=400 height=300 border=1>
</center>
</body>
</html>
```

**EXPLANATION**

1    Functions must be defined before they can be used. Therefore, functions are normally placed in a JavaScript program, between the HTML *<head></head>* tags. In this example, the function is defined, but it will not do anything until it is called from somewhere in the file.

     The *function* keyword is followed by the user-defined name of the function called *welcome* and a set of parentheses. The parentheses are used to hold parameters, information being received by the function. What the function actually does is defined in a set of statements enclosed within curly braces. The function statements are enclosed in a set of curly braces.

2, 3  This is the code that is run whenever the function is called. It is called the function definition. When this function is called, the string *San Francisco* will be assigned to the variable called *place* and the alert dialog box will display "*Welcome to San Francisco!*" in the browser window. (See Figure 7.1.)

4    This is the final closing curly brace that ends the function definition.

5    This is where the function is invoked or called. When the function *welcome()* is called, the statements within its definition will be executed.

6    Since the function is called in the head of the document, this image will not appear until the user presses the OK button in the alert dialog box. (See Figure 7.2.)

**Figure 7.1**  After the function *welcome()* is called, output is sent to the browser.

San Francisco

**Figure 7.2**   After the user presses the OK button in the alert box, this image loads.

**Passing Arguments.**   If a user wants to send values to a function, the values are enclosed in the parentheses right after the function name and sent as a comma-separated list of arguments when the function is called. The arguments are received by the function in a list of corresponding values called parameters. The names of the arguments are not necessarily the same names in the parameter list, but they correspond to the same values. These values can be assigned to local variables within the function. Local variables disappear when the function exits. JavaScript doesn't keep track of the number of arguments sent to the function to make sure they match up with the number of parameters specified in the function definition at the other end. If you send three arguments, and there are only two parameters defined within the function, the third argument is ignored. If you send three arguments, and there are four parameters waiting within the function, then the fourth parameter is *undefined*. It's similar to sending messages to an answering machine. If you send a message and the message machine is full, your message is ignored, and if you send a message and there's room for more messages, the message you sent is stored, and the unused space is still there, but not defined.

```
function_name(argument1, argument2, ...);    // function call (caller)




function_name(parameter1, parameter2...){    // function definition (receiver)
    result= parameter1 + parameter2;
   ...
}    // curly braces required
```

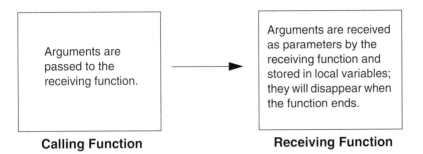

**Calling Function**                              **Receiving Function**

**Figure 7.3** In the analogy of the pocket calculator, you are the caller when you press the buttons, and the internal functions inside the calculator are the receiver.

## EXAMPLE 7.2

```
<html>
<head>
<title>Passing Arguments</title>
   <script language=JavaScript>
1      function greetings(pal){   // "Birdman!" is stored in pal
2      alert("Greetings to you, " + pal);
   }
   </script>
   </head>
   <body background="birdman.jpg">
3  <script language="JavaScript">
4      greetings("Birdman!");   // Passing an argument
   </script>
</body>
</html>
```

## EXPLANATION

1    The function, *greetings()*, has one parameter, called *pal*. This parameter holds a value that is sent to the function when it was called. The parameter name is any valid JavaScript variable name.

2    The alert method will display the string, *"Greetings to you, "* concatenated to the value stored in *pal*; in this example that value is *"Birdman!"*.

3    The JavaScript program is in the body of the document. It contains a function call that will invoke a function defined in the head of the document.

4    The function *greetings()* is called with one argument, *"Birdman!"*. This argument will be sent to the function, and assigned to the parameter, *pal*. If the function had been called in the head of the document as it was in Example 7.1, the background image would not appear until after the user pressed the OK button in the alert box (see Figure 7.4), but in this example, the image was loaded before the function was called.

**Figure 7.4**   Output from the *greetings()* function in Example 7.2.

**Calling a Function from a Link.**   A function can be called directly from a link, by using the JavaScript pseudoprotocol, *javascript:*, instead of a normal URL. The *javascript:* protocol and the function call are placed within quotes and assigned to the *href* attribute of the *<a>* tag. When the user clicks his mouse on the link, instead of the program going to the URL of another page, a JavaScript function will be called.

**EXAMPLE** 7.3

```
        <html>
        <head>
        <title>Functions</title>
1       <script language=javascript>
2           function greetings(){   // Function defined within <head> tags
                document.bgColor="lightblue";
3               alert("Greetings to you!");
            }
        </script>
        </head>
        <body><center>
4           <a href="javascript:greetings()"><big>Click here for
                Salutations</big>
            </a><br>
        </center>
        </body>
        </html>
```

1    The JavaScript program starts here in the head of the document. The function is defined within the head of the document to guarantee that it will be defined before being called.

2, 3   The function *greetings()* is defined. It is very simple. It causes the background color of the document to be a light blue color and causes an alert box to appear with a greeting message.

4    The *href* attribute of the link tag is assigned a string consisting of the *javascript:* pseudoprotocol, followed by the name of the function to be called. When the user clicks on this link, JavaScript calls the function, *greetings()*. (See Figure 7.5.)

**Figure 7.5**   After clicking on the link, the function is called, causing the alert dialog box to appear.

**Calling a Function from an Event.**   An event is triggered when a user performs some action, like clicking on a button or moving his mouse over a link. The function assigned to the event is called an event handler. When the event is triggered, the function is called. In the following example, when the user clicks on the Welcome button, the function is called.

```
     <html>
     <head<title>Functions and Events</title>
1    <script language=javascript>
2        function greetings(){  // Function definition
3            document.bgColor="pink";
             alert("Greetings and Salutations! ");
         }
     </script>
     </head>
```

EXAMPLE 7.4 (CONTINUED)

```
4      <body><center>
5        <form>
6          <input type="button"
7            value="Welcome button"
8            onClick="greetings();"
            >
         </form>
       </body>
       </html>
```

## EXPLANATION

1   The JavaScript program starts here. The function is defined in the head of the document.

2   The function *greetings()* is defined here.

3   The body of the function—what it does—is found here between the curly braces.

4   The body of the page starts here.

5   An HTML form starts here. It will be used to create a button input device.

6   The type of input device is a button.

7   The value that will be displayed in the button is *"Welcome button"*. (See Figure 7.6.)

8   When the user presses or clicks on the button, the *onClick* event will be triggered, causing the *greetings()* function to be called. The value assigned to the *onClick* event is a JavaScript function enclosed in quotation marks. (See Figure 7.7.)

**Figure 7.6**   When the button is pressed, the event is triggered.

**Figure 7.7**   A function is called after the event is triggered. The function "handles" the event.

**Calling a Function from JavaScript.**   In the first examples of this chapter, functions were defined in one JavaScript program and called from another. Although it is valid to define and call the function from the same JavaScript program, it is often desirable to define the function in the head of the document, to be sure it has been defined before it is called. Then you can call the function from a link, an event, or another JavaScript program. Since the document is defined within the *<body></body>* tags, the body is often the place from where you will call functions. The general rule of thumb is: If your script is designed to write data to the page, put the *<script></script>* tags within the *<body></body>* tags. Example 7.2 called a function from one JavaScript program within the body, but defined the function in another JavaScript program within the head.

**Scope of Variables in Functions.**   The scope of a variable describes where the variable is visible in the program; that is, where it can be used in the program. Variables declared outside of functions are global in scope, meaning they can be used or changed anywhere in the program. If a variable is declared within a function with the *var* keyword, then the variable is local in scope—the variable can be used only within the function where it is defined.

---

**EXAMPLE 7.5**

```
      <html>
      <head><title>Function Scope</title>
      <script language=javascript>
1         var name="William";
2         var hometown="Chico";
          function greetme(){
3             var name="Daniel";   // Local variable
              document.bgColor="lightblue";
4             document.write("<h2>In function, <em>name</em> is "
                              + name);
5             document.write(" and <em>hometown</em> is "+ hometown);
6         }
7         greetme();
8         document.write("<br>Out of function, <em>name</em> is "
                          + name);
9         document.write(" and <em>hometown</em> is " + hometown);
      </script>
      </head>
      </html>
```

**EXPLANATION**

1   The variable called *name* is global in scope. It is visible throughout the JavaScript program.

2   The variable called *hometown* is also global in scope and is visible throughout the program.

3  Any variables declared within a function with the *var* keyword are local to that function. In fact, you must use the *var* keyword when declaring local variables; otherwise, the variables will be global. The variable called *name* has been declared inside the function. This is a local variable and has nothing to do with the variable of the same name on line 1. This variable will go out of scope when the function ends on line 6, at which point the global variable will come back in scope.

4  The variable called *name* was defined inside this function and is local in scope. It will stick around until the function exits.

5  The global variable called *hometown* is visible here.

6  The closing curly brace marks the end of the function definition.

7  The function *greetme()* is called here.

8  The global variable called *name* has come back into scope.

9  The global variable called *hometown* is still in scope. (See Figure 7.8.)

In function, *name* is Daniel and *hometown* is Chico
Out of function, *name* is William and *hometown* is Chico

**Figure 7.8**   Output from Example 7.5.

## 7.1.2  Return Values

Functions may return values with a *return* statement. The *return* keyword is optional and can only exist within a function. When the *return* keyword is reached in a function, no further processing within the function occurs. A *return* can be used to send back the result of some task, such as a calculation, or to exit a function early if some condition occurs. If a function doesn't have a *return* statement, it returns the *undefined* value.

```
return;
return expression;
```

Example:

```
function sum (a, b) {
    var result= a + b;
    return result;
}
```

If the call to the function is made part of an expression, the returned value can be assigned to a variable. In the following example the *sum* function is called with two arguments, *5* and *10*. The *sum* function's return value will be assigned to the variable *total*.

```
var total=sum(5, 10);
```

---

**EXAMPLE** 7.6

```
      <html>
      <head>
      <title>Return Value</title>
      <script language=JavaScript>
1         function mileage(miles, gas){
2            return miles/gas;     // Return the result of the division
          }
      </script>
      </head>
      <body bgcolor="lightgreen"><font face="arial" size="+1">
      <center><img src="car-wave.gif"></center>
      <script language="JavaScript">
3         var distance=eval(prompt("How many miles did you
                           drive? ", ""));
          var amount=eval(prompt("How much gas did you use?", ""));
4         var rate = mileage(distance, amount);   // Return value
                                                  // assigned to rate
5         alert("Your mileage "+ rate  +" miles per gallon.\n");
      </script>
      </body>
      </html>
```

---

**EXPLANATION**

1   A function called *mileage()* is defined in this JavaScript program.

2   The *return* statement sends back to the caller of the function the result of the division. That returned value will be assigned to the variable, *rate*, on line 4.

3   The user is asked for input. The number of miles driven and the amount of gas used are assigned to the variables called *distance* and *amount*, respectively. (See Figure 7.9.)

4   The *mileage()* function is called, passing two arguments. Since the *mileage()* function is on the right-hand side of the assignment operator (the = sign), whatever is returned from the function will be assigned to the variable, called *rate*, on the left-hand side of the = sign.

5   The alert dialog box displays the value returned from the function: the number of miles used per gallon. (See Figure 7.10.)

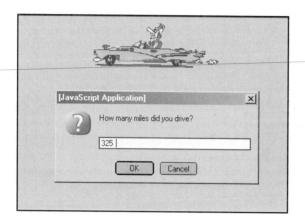

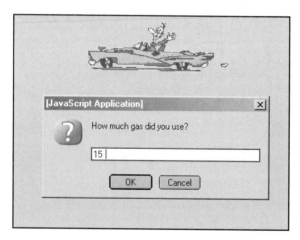

**Figure 7.9**    The user is asked for input.

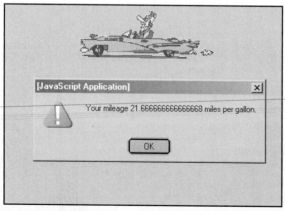

**Figure 7.10**    The number miles per gallon is returned by the *mileage()* function.

**Recursion.** Definition of recusion:

*recursion: See recursion.*

The above definition is a well-known joke in the computer world. JavaScript supports recursion. So what is it? A recursive function is a function that calls itself. It's a chain of function calls to the same function. The first time it calls itself is the first level of recursion, the second time is the second level, and so on. When a function calls itself, execution starts at the beginning of the function, and when the function ends, the program backs up to where it was when it called the function and starts executing from that point. Most importantly there must be a way to stop the recursion, or it will be infinite, and probably cause the program to crash.

## EXAMPLE 7.7

```
         <html>
         <head>
         <title>Recursion</title>
         <script language=JavaScript>
1            function upDown(num){
2                document.write("<b><font size='+1'>Level "
                              + num + "</b><br>");
3                if(num < 4){
4                    upDown(num + 1);    // Function calls itself
5                    document.write("<em>Level "+ num + "<em><br>");
                 }
             }
         </script>
         </head>
         <body bgcolor="lightblue">
         <h2>Recursion</h2>
         <script language="JavaScript">
6            upDown(1);
         </script>
         </body>
         </html>
```

## EXPLANATION

1   The first time this function is called it is passed the number 1.

2   The function prints out the level number, Level 1.

3   If the value of *num* is less than *4*, the function calls itself.

4   When the function calls itself, it adds 1 to the value of *num*. When the function calls itself it restarts execution at the top of the function, this time with the value of *num* equal to 2. Each time the function calls itself, it creates a new copy of *num* for that recursion level. The other copy is on hold until this one is finished. The function keeps calling itself and printing level numbers in bold text until the *if* statement fails; that is, until the value of *num* is not less than 4.

**EXPLANATION** (CONTINUED)

5   This line won't be executed until the recursion stops—when the value of *num* is
    *4*. When that happens, the current version of *upDown()* is finished, and we back
    off to the previous called function and start execution at line 5. This process con-
    tinues until all of the functions have completed execution.

6   This is the first call to the *upDown()* function. The argument is the number *1*. The
    output is shown in Figure 7.11.

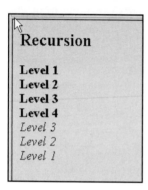

**Recursion**

**Level 1**
**Level 2**
**Level 3**
**Level 4**
*Level 3*
*Level 2*
*Level 1*

**Figure 7.11**   Output from Example 7.7.

### 7.1.3   Functions Are Objects

For a discussion on how functions behave as objects, see "Creating the Object with a
User-Defined Function" on page 133 in Chapter 8.

## 7.2   Debugging

When working with functions there are some simple syntax rules to watch for.

1. Did you use parentheses after the function name?
2. Did you use opening and closing curly braces to hold the function definition?
3. Did you define the function before you called it? Try using the *typeof* operator
   to see if a function has been defined.
4. Did you give the function a unique name?
5. When you called the function is your argument list separated by commas? If
   you don't have an argument list, did you forget to include the parentheses?
6. Do the number of arguments equal the number of parameters?
7. Is the function supposed to return a value? Did you remember to provide a variable or a place in the expression to hold the returned value?
8. Did you define and call the function from within a JavaScript program?

Figure 7.12 shows function errors displayed by the JavaScript Console in Netscape. These error messages make troubleshooting your scripts much easier.

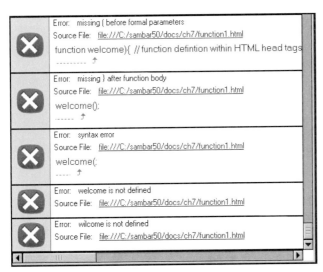

**Figure 7.12**   Function errors in the JavaScript Console (Netscape).

## EXERCISES

1. Copy the following file and execute it in your browser. What's wrong with it
   and why? Can you fix it?

```
<html><head><title>link</title>
<script language="JavaScript">
function addem(){
  var n = 2;
  var y = 3;
  document.write( n + y , "<br>");
}
</script>
</head>
<body bgcolor=red>
<a href="javascript:addem()">Click here</a>
<h2>Hello</h2>
</body>
</html>
```

2. Write a function that will calculate and return the amount that should be paid
   as a tip for a resturant bill. The tip will be 20 percent of the total bill.

3. Create a function called *changeColor()* that will be called when the user presses
   one of two buttons. The first button will contain the text "*Press here for a yellow
   background*". The second button will contain the text "*Press here for a light green
   background*". The function will take one parameter, a color. Its function is to
   change the background color of the current document.

4. What is recursion? What is the danger of using it?

5. Write a function that returns the total cost of any number of buckets of paint.
   Ask the user how many buckets he is going to buy and for the cost of one
   bucket. Ask him the color of the paint. Calculate and return what he owes.
   Change the color of the font to the color of the paint.

# chapter

# 8

# Objects

## 8.1 What Are Objects?

Objects are things we deal with every day. JavaScript deals with objects, as do most programming languages, and these languages are called object-oriented programming (OOP). Some people are apprehensive at the thought of tackling this kind of programming, and are perfectly happy to stick with top-down, procedural programs. But just as the everyday objects we use are not necessarily switchblades and chain saws, neither are programming objects. They are just a way of representing data. JavaScript is based on objects, so it's time to jump in.

When talking about JavaScript data types in Chapter 3, we discussed two types: primitive and composite. Objects are composite types. They provide a way to organize a collection of data into a single unit. Object-oriented languages, such as C++ and Java, bundle up data into a variable and call it an object. So does JavaScript.

When you learn about objects, they are usually compared to real-world things, like a cat, a book, or a triangle. Using the English language to describe an object, the object itself would be like a noun.

Nouns are described with adjectives. For the cat, it might be described as fat, furry, smart, or lazy. The book is old, with 400 pages, and contains poems. The triangle has three sides, three angles, and red lines. The adjectives that collectively describe these objects are called <u>properties</u> or attributes. The object is made up of a collection of these properties, or attributes.

In English, verbs are used to describe what the object can do or what can be done to it. The cat eats, sleeps, and meows. The book is read, its pages can be turned forward and backward, and it can be opened or closed by the reader. The triangle's sides and angles can be increased and decreased, it can be moved, and it can be colored. These verbs are called <u>methods</u> in object-oriented languages.

JavaScript supports several types of objects. They are as follows:

1. User-defined objects defined by the programmer
2. Core or built-in objects, such as Date, String, and Number (see Chapter 9)
3. Browser and Document objects (see Chapter 10)

## 8.1.1  Object Models and the Dot Syntax

An object model is a hierarchical tree-like structure used to describe all of the components of an object. When accessing an object in the tree, the object at the top of the tree is the root or parent of all parents. If there is an object below the parent it is called the child, and if the object is on the same level, it is a sibling. A child can also have children. A dot (.) is used to separate the objects when descending the tree; for example, a parent is separated from its child with a dot. In the following example, the *pet* object is subdivided into subordinate or child objects: a *cat* and a *dog*. The *cat* and the *dog* objects each have properties associated with them. In order to navigate down the tree to the cat's name, for example, you would stipulate *pet.cat.name,* and to get the dog's breed you would stipulate *pet.dog.breed.*

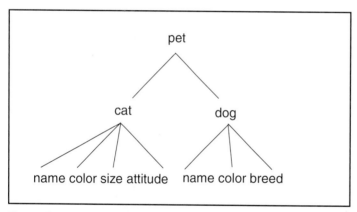

**Figure 8.1**    A hierarchical tree-like structure used to describe components of an object.

## 8.1.2  Creating an Object with a Constructor

JavaScript allows you to create an object in a number of ways, as discussed in detail in "User-Defined Objects" on page 131. One such way is with a constructor. A constructor is a special kind of method that creates an instance of an object. JavaScript comes with several built-in constructors. The *new* keyword precedes the name of the constructor that will be used to create the object.

```
var myNewObject = new Object(argument, argument, ...)
```

To create the *pet* object, for example, you could say:

```
var pet = new Object();
```

The *Object*() constructor, a special predefined constructor function, returns a reference to an object called *pet*, as shown in Example 8.1. The *pet* object has been instantiated and is ready to be assigned properties and methods.

```
<html>
<head><title>The Object() Constructor</title>
<script language = "javascript">
1       var pet = new Object();
2       alert(pet);
</script>
</head>
<body></body>
</html>
```

1   The *Object*() constructor creates and returns a reference to a *pet* object. It is an empty object; i.e., it has no properties.

2   The returned value from the *Object*() constructor is a reference to an object, as shown in the Figure 8.2.

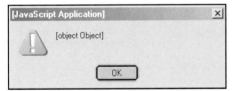

**Figure 8.2**   Output from Example 8.1.

The *pet* object could also be further subdivided as shown in Figure 8.1.

```
pet.cat = new Object();
pet.dog = new Object();
```

## 8.1.3   Properties of the Object

Properties describe the object and are connected to the object they describe with a dot. In Figure 8.1, the top object is the *pet* object. Although *cat* is an object in its own right, it is also considered a property of the *pet* object. In fact, any object subordinate to another object is also a property of that object. Both the *cat* and *dog* objects are properties of the *pet* object. The *cat* and the *dog* objects also have properties that describe them, such as *name*, *color*, *size*, and so forth.

To assign properties to the *cat* object, the syntax would be as follows:

```
pet.cat.name = "Sneaky";
pet.cat.color="yellow";
pet.cat.size="fat";
pet.cat.attitude = "stuck up";
```

## EXAMPLE 8.2

```
      <html>
      <head><title>The Object() Constructor</title>
      <script language = "javascript">
          var pet = new Object();
1         pet.cat = new Object();
2         pet.cat.name = "Sneaky";
          pet.cat.color = "yellow";
          pet.cat.size = "fat";
          pet.cat.attitude = "stuck up";
      </script>
      </head>
      <body></body>
      </html>
```

## EXPLANATION

1   New new object *cat* is created. It is subordinate to the *pet* object, so it is also a
    property of the *pet* object.

2   The *cat* object is assigned a *name* property with the value, *"Sneaky"*. It is also as-
    signed color, size, and attitude properties.

In JavaScript you might see the syntax

```
window.document.bgColor = "lightblue";
```

The *window* is the top object in the hierarchy, the parent of all parents; the *document*
is an object but, because it is subordinate to the *window*, it is also a property of the *window*
object. Although the background color, *bgColor*, is a property of the document object, by
itself it is not an object. (It is like an adjective because it describes the document.)

```
window
      document
            bgColor
```

## 8.1.4  Methods of the Object

Methods are special functions that object-oriented languages use to describe how the
object behaves or acts. The cat purrs and the dog barks. Methods, like verbs, are action
words that perform some operation on the object. For example, the *cat* object may have

a method called *sleep()* or *play()* and the dog object may have a method called *sit()* or *stay()*, and both of them could have a method called *eat()*.

The dot syntax is used to call the methods just as it was used to separate objects from their properties. The method, unlike the property, is followed by a set of parentheses.

```
pet.cat.play();
```

Methods, like functions, can take arguments, or messages that will be sent to the object:

```
pet.dog.fetch("ball");
```

A JavaScript example:

```
window.close();
window.document.write("Hello\n");
```

# 8.2  User-Defined Objects

All user-defined objects and built-in objects are descendants of an object called *Object*.

## 8.2.1  The *new* Operator

The *new* operator is used to create an instance of an object. To create an object, the *new* operator is followed by the constructor method. In the following example, the constructor methods are *Object()*, *Array()*, and *Date()*. These constructors are built-in JavaScript functions. A reference to the object is returned and assigned to a variable.

```
var car = new Object();
var friends = new Array("Tom", "Dick", "Harry");
var now= new Date("July 4, 2003");
```

## 8.2.2  The *Object()* Constructor

A constructor is a function (or method) that creates (constructs) and initializes an object. JavaScript provides a special constructor function called *Object()* to build the object. The return value of the *Object()* constructor is assigned to a variable. The variable contains a reference to the new object. The properties assigned to the object are <u>not</u> variables and are <u>not</u> defined with the *var* keyword. See Example 8.3.

## FORMAT

```
var myobj = new Object();
```

## EXAMPLE 8.3

```
       <html>
       <head><title>User-defined objects</title>
1          <script language = "javascript">
2              var toy = new Object();    // Create the object
3              toy.name = "Lego";         // Assign properties to the object
               toy.color = "red";
               toy.shape = "rectangle";
4          </script>
       </head>
       <body bgcolor="lightblue">
5          <script language = "javascript">
6              document.write("<b>The toy is  a " + toy.name + ".");
7              document.write("<br>It is a " + toy.color + " "
                              + toy.shape+ ".");
8          </script>
       </body>
       </html>
```

## EXPLANATION

1   JavaScript code starts here.

2   The *Object()* constructor is called with the *new* keyword to create an instance of an object called *toy*. A reference to the new object is assigned to the variable, *toy*.

3   The *toy* object's *name* property is assigned *"Lego"*. The properties describe the characteristics or attributes of the object. Properties are <u>not</u> variables. Do not use the *var* keyword.

4   This is the end of the JavaScript program.

5   A new JavaScript program starts here in the body of the page.

6   The global object called *toy* is available within the script. The value of the *toy* object's *name* property is displayed.

7   The values for the *color* and *shape* properties of the *toy* object are displayed.

8   This is the end of the JavaScript program. The output is shown in Figure 8.3.

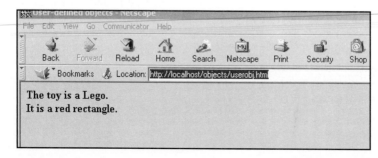

**Figure 8.3**  The *toy* object and its properties.

### 8.2.3  Creating the Object with a User-Defined Function

To create user-defined objects, you can create a function that specifies the object's name, properties, and methods. The function serves as a template or prototype of an object. When the function is called with the *new* keyword, it acts as a constructor and builds the new object, and then returns a reference to it.

The *this* keyword is used to refer to the object that has been passed to a function.

**EXAMPLE** 8.4

```
      <html>
      <head><title>User-defined objects</title></head>
      <script language = "javascript">

1         function book(title, author, publisher){
          // Defining properties
2             this.title = title;
3             this.author = author;
4             this.publisher = publisher;
5         }

      </script>
      <body bgcolor="lightblue"></body>
      <script language = "javascript">
6         var myBook = new book("JavaScript by Example",
                              "Ellie", "Prentice Hall");
7         document.writeln("<b>"  + myBook.title +
                          "<br>" + myBook.author +
                          "<br>" + myBook.publisher
              );
      </script>
      </body>
      </html>
```

**EXPLANATION**

1  This is a user-defined constructor function with three parameters.

2  The *this* keyword refers to the current object that is being created. The object is being assigned properties. The title of the book, *"JavaScript by Example"*, is being passed as the first parameter and assigned to the *title* property.

3  The author, *"Ellie"*, is assigned to the *author* property.

4  The publisher, *"Prentice Hall"*, is assigned to the *publisher* property.

5  This is the closing curly brace that terminates the function definition.

6  The variable, *myBook*, is assigned a reference to the newly created object.

7  The *title* property of the *myBook* object will be displayed. All of the properties of the *book* object are displayed in Figure 8.4.

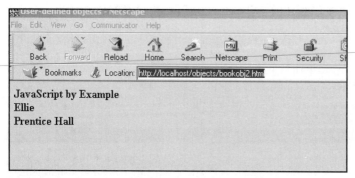

JavaScript by Example
Ellie
Prentice Hall

**Figure 8.4** Output from Example 8.4.

## 8.2.4 Defining Methods for an Object

The previous examples demonstrate how the constructor creates the object and assigns properties. But we need to complete the definition of an object by assigning methods to it. The methods are functions that let the object do something or let something be done to it. There is little difference between a function (see Chapter 7, "Functions") and a method, except that a function is a standalone unit of statements and a method is attached to an object and can be referenced by the *this* keyword.

**EXAMPLE 8.5**

```
    <html>
    <head><title>Simple Methods</title>
    <script language = "javascript">
1       function distance(r, t){  // Define the object
2           this.rate = r;         // Assign properties
            this.time = t;
        }
3       function calc_distance(){  // Define a function that will
                                   // be used as a method
4           return this.rate * this.time;
        }
    </script>
    </head>
    <body bgcolor="lightblue">
    <script language="javascript">
5       var speed=eval(prompt("What was your speed
                            (miles per hour)? ",""));
        var elapsed=eval(prompt("How long did the trip take?
                            (hours)?" ,""));
```

---

**EXAMPLE   8.5 (CONTINUED)**

```
6         var howfar=new distance(speed, elapsed);
                                      // Call the constructor
7         howfar.distance=calc_distance;  // Create a new property
8         var d = howfar.distance();      // Invoke method
9         alert("The distance is " + d + " miles.");
    </script>
    </body>
    </html>
```

**EXPLANATION**

1   This is the constructor function. It creates and returns a reference to an object called *distance*. It takes two parameters, *r* and *t*.

2   The object (referenced by the *this* keyword) is assigned properties.

3   The function *calc_distance()* will be used later as a method for the object.

4   The function returns the results of this calculation to the variable, *d*, on line 8.

5   The user is prompted for input in this statement and the next. (See Figure 8.5.) The string he enters is evaluated by the *eval()* method and assigned as a number to the variables *speed* and *elapsed*.

6   A new object called *howfar* is created with the *new* constructor. Two arguments are passed, the rate (in miles per hour) and the time (in hours).

7   A new property for the *howfar* object is created. It is assigned the name of the function, *calc_distance*, that will be used as a method. Note: only the name of the function is assigned without the parentheses. Putting them there would result in an error.

8   The method called *distance()* is invoked for the *howfar* object. The returned value is assigned to variable, *d*.

9   The alert box displays the distance traveled. (See Figure 8.6.)

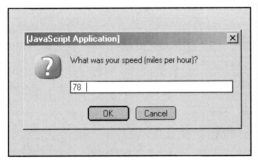
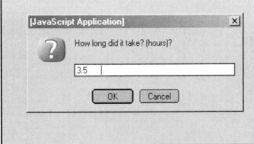

**Figure 8.5**   The user is prompted for input.

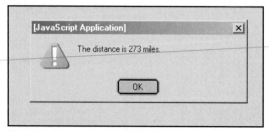

**Figure 8.6**   Final output displayed from Example 8.5.

**A Method Defined in a Constructor.**   Methods can automatically be assigned to an object in the constructor function so that the method can be applied to multiple instances of an object.

**EXAMPLE** 8.6

```
    <html>
    <head><title>User-defined objects</title>
    <script language ="javascript">
1   function book(title, author, publisher){    // Receiving
                                                 // parameters
2       this.pagenumber=0;        // Properties
        this.title = title;
        this.author = author;
        this.publisher = publisher;
3       this.uppage = pageForward;    // Assign function name to
                                      // a property
4       this.backpage = pageBackward;
    }
5   function pageForward(){    // Functions to be used as methods
        this.pagenumber++;
        return this.pagenumber;
    }
6   function pageBackward(){
        this.pagenumber--;
        return this.pagenumber;
    }
    </script>
    </head>
    <body bgcolor="lightblue">
    <script language = "javascript">
```

EXAMPLE   8.6 (CONTINUED)

```
7       var myBook = new book("JavaScript by Example", "Ellie",
                                "Prentice Hall" );   // Create new object
8       myBook.pagenumber=5;
9       document.write( "<b>"+ myBook.title +
                        "<br>" + myBook.author +
                        "<br>" + myBook.publisher +
                        "<br>Current page is " + myBook.pagenumber );
        document.write("<br>Page forward: " );
10      for(i=0;i<3;i++){
11          document.write("<br>" + myBook.uppage());
            // Move forward a page
        }
        document.write("<br>Page backward: ");
        for(;i>0; i--){
12          document.write("<br>" + myBook.backpage());
            // Move back a page
        }
</script>
</body>
</html>
```

## EXPLANATION

1   This is the constructor function that is used to build the object by assigning it properties and methods. The parameter list contains the values for the properties *title, author*, and *publisher*.

2   The *this* keyword refers to the *book* object. The *book* object is given a *pagenumber* property initalized to *0*.

3   A method is defined by assigning the function to a property of the *book* object. *this.uppage* is assigned the name of the function, *pageForward*, that will serve as the object's method. Note that only the <u>name of the method</u> is assigned to a property. There are no parentheses following the name. This is important. If you put parentheses here, you will receive an error message. When the method is called you use parentheses.

4   The property *this.downpage* is assigned the name of the function, *pageBackward*, that will serve as the object's method.

5   The function *pageForward()* is defined. Its purpose is to increase the page number of the book by one, and return the new page number.

6   The function *pageBackward()* is defined. Its purpose is to decrease the page number by one and return the new page number.

7   A new object called *myBook* is created. The *new* operator invokes the *book()* function with three arguments: the title of the book, the author, and the publisher.

8   The *pagenumber* property is set to *5*.

9   The properties of the object are displayed in the browser window.

10  The *for* loop is entered. It will loop three times.

11  The *uppage()* method is called for the *myBook* object. It will increase the page number by 1 and display the new value, each time through the for loop.

12  The *backpage()* method is called for the *myBook* object. It will decrease the page number by 1 and display the new value, each time through the loop. The output is shown in Figure 8.7.

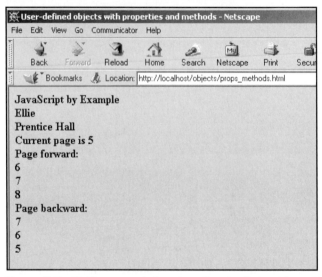

**Figure 8.7**   Calling user-defined methods. Output from Example 8.6.

**Properties Can Be Objects.**   In "Properties of the Object" on page 129 we said that any object subordinate to another object is also a property of that object; thus, if a parent object has objects below it in the hierarchy, those child objects are properties of their parent and separated from their parent with a dot. So how would you create subordinate objects? You create a subordinate object just as you create any other object—with a constructor method. The one thing you must remember is that if the object being created is already a property of another object, you cannot use the *var* keyword preceding its name. For example, *var pet.cat = new Object()* will produce an error because *cat* is a property of the *pet* object and properties are never variables. (See Figure 8.1.) Weird, huh?

**EXAMPLE** 8.7

```
<html>
<head><title>Properties Can be Objects</title>
    <script language = "javascript">
1       var pet = new Object();   // pet is an object
2       pet.cat = new Object();   // cat is a property of the pet
                                  // object. cat is also an object
3       pet.cat.name="Sylvester";  // cat is assigned properties
        pet.cat.color="black";
4       pet.dog = new Object();
        pet.dog.breed = "Shepherd";
        pet.dog.name = "Lassie";
    </script>
</head>
<body bgcolor="lightblue">
    <script language = "javascript">
5       document.write("<b>The cat's name is " +
                        pet.cat.name + ".");
6       document.write("<br>The dog's name is " +
                        pet.dog.name + ".");
    </script>
</body>
</html>
```

Output:

```
5   The cat's name is Sylvester.
6   The dog's name is Lassie.
```

**EXPLANATION**

1   A new *pet* object is created with the *Object()* constructor.

2   The *Object()* constructor creates a *cat* object below the *pet* in the object hierarchy; that is, a *cat* object subordinate to the *pet* object and also a property of it. You cannot precede *pet.cat* with the keyword *var* because properties are never considered variables.

3   The new object also has a property called *name* which is assigned a value, *Sylvester*.

4   The *Object()* constructor creates an *dog* object below the *pet* in the object hierarchy; that is, a *dog* object subordinate to the *pet* object and also a property of it.

5   The *name* property for the *cat* object is displayed.

6   The *name* property for the *dog* object is displayed.

## 8.2.5   Object Literals

When an object is created by assigning it a comma-separated list of properties enclosed in curly braces, it is called an object literal. Each property consists of the property name followed by a colon and the property value. An object literal can be embedded directly in JavaScript code.

### FORMAT

```
var object = { property1: value, property2: value };
```

Example:

```
var area = { length: 15, width: 5 };
```

### EXAMPLE   8.8

```
    <html>
    <head><title>Object Literals</title>
    </head>
    <body bgcolor="yellow">
        <script language = "javascript">
1           var car = {
2           make: "Honda",
            year: 2002,
            price: "30,000",
            owner: "Henry Lee",
3           };
4           var details=car.make + "<br>";
            details += car.year + "<br>";
            details += car.price + "<br>";
            details += car.owner + "<br>";
            document.write(details);
        </script>
    </body>
    </html>
```

### EXPLANATION

1   An object literal *car* is created and initialized.

2   The properties for the *car* object are assigned. Properties are separated from their corresponding values with a colon and each property/value pair is separated by a comma.

3   The object definition ends here.

4   The variable called *details* is assigned the properties of the *car* object for display. The output is shown in Figure 8.8.

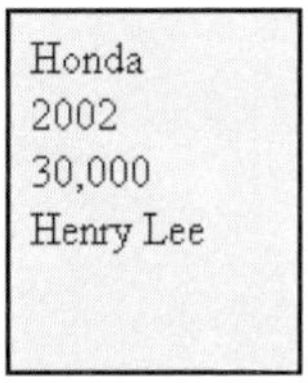

```
Honda
2002
30,000
Henry Lee
```

**Figure 8.8** Literal object properties. Output from Example 8.8.

## 8.3 Manipulating Objects

### 8.3.1 The *with* Keyword

The *with* keyword is used as a kind of shorthand for referencing an object's properties or methods.

The object specified as an argument to *with* becomes the default object for the duration of the block that follows. The properties and methods for the object can be used without naming the object. (If a method is used, don't forget to include the parentheses after the method name.)

---
**FORMAT**

```
with (object){
    < properties used without the object name and dot>
}
```

**Example:**

```
with(employee){
    document.write(name, ssn, address);
}
```

---
**EXAMPLE** 8.9

```
        <html>
        <head><title>The with Keyword</title>
        <script language = "javascript">
1       function book(title, author, publisher){
2           this.title = title;    // Properties
            this.author = author;
            this.publisher = publisher;
3           this.show = display;   // Define a method
        }
```

**EXAMPLE**  8.9 (CONTINUED)

```
4        function display(anybook){
5           with(this){    // The with keyword
6               var info = "The title is " + title;
                info += "\nThe author is " + author;
                info += "\nThe publisher is " + publisher;
7               alert(info);
            }
        }
    </script>
    </head>
    <body bgcolor="lightblue">
    <script language = "javascript">
8      var childbook = new book("A Child's Garden of Verses",
                                "Robert Lewis Stevenson",
                                "Little Brown");
9      var adultbook = new book("War and Peace",
                                "Leo Tolstoy",
                                "Penguin Books");
10     childbook.show(childbook);   // Call method for child's book
11     adultbook.show(adultbook);   // Call method for adult's book
    </script>
    </body>
    </html>
```

**EXPLANATION**

1  The *book* constructor function is defined with its properties.

2  The *book* object is described with three properties: *title*, *author*, and *publisher*.

3  The *book* object's property is assigned the name of a function. This property will serve as a method for the object.

4  A function called *display* is defined.

5  The *with* keyword will allow you to reference the properties of the object without using the name of the object or the *this* keyword. (See "The Math Object" on page 172 in Chapter 9.)

6  A variable called *info* is assigned the property values of a *book* object. The *with* keyword allows you to specify the property name without a reference to the object (and dot) preceding it.

7  The *alert* box displays the properties for a book object.

8  The constructor function is called and returns an instance of a new book object called *childbook*.

9  The constructor function is called and returns an instance of another book object called *adultbook*.

10  The *show()* method is called passing a reference to the *childbook* object.

11  The *show()* method is called passing a reference to the *adultbook* object.

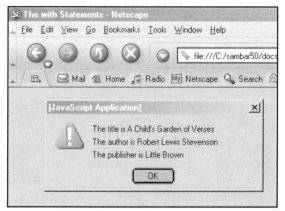

**Figure 8.9**  The *childbook* object and its properties.

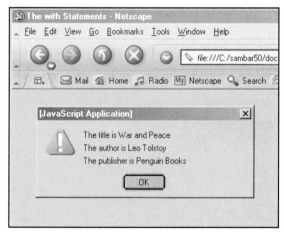

**Figure 8.10**  The *adultbook* object and its properties.

## 8.3.2  The *for/in* Loop

JavaScript provides the *for/in* loop, which can be used to iterate through a list of object properties or array elements. The *for/in* loop reads: for each property in an object (or for each element in an array) get the name of each property (element), in turn, and for each of the properties (elements), execute the statements in the block that follows.

The *for/in* loop is a convenient mechanism for looping through the properties of an object.

## FORMAT

```
for(var property_name in object){
    statements;
}
```

## EXAMPLE 8.10

```
    <html>
    <head><title>User-defined objects</title>
        <script language = "javascript">
1           function book(title, author, publisher){
2               this.title = title;
                this.author = author;
                this.publisher = publisher;
3               this.show=showProps;    // Define a method for the object
            }
4           function showProps(obj, name){
            // Function to show the object's properties
                var result = "";
5               for (var prop in obj){
6                   result += name + "." + prop + " = " +
                            obj[prop] + "<br>";
                }
7               return result;
            }
        </script>
    </head>
    <body bgcolor="lightblue">
        <script language="javascript">
8           myBook = new book("JavaScript by Example", "Ellie",
                            "Prentice Hall");
9           document.write("<br><b>" + myBook.show(myBook, "myBook"));
        </script>
    </body>
    </html>
```

## EXPLANATION

1   The function called *book* will define the properties and methods for a *book* object. The function is a template for the new object. An instance of a new *book* object will be created when this constructor is called.

2   This is the first property defined for the *book* object. The *this* keyword refers to the current object.

3   A function name called *showProps* is assigned to a property of the object, thus creating a method for the object.

4   The function called *showProps* is defined, tasked to display all the properties of the object.

5    The special *for/in* loop executes a set of statements for each property of the object.

6    The name and value of each property is concatenated and assigned to a variable called *result. obj[prop]* is used to key into each of the property values of the *book* object.

7    The value of the variable *result* is sent back to the caller. Each time through the loop, another property and value are displayed.

8    A *new book* object called *myBook* is created (instantiated).

9    The properties for the book object are shown in the browser window; see Figure 8.11. Notice how the method and its definition are displayed.

```
myBook.title = JavaScript by Example
myBook.author = Ellie
myBook.publisher = Prentice Hall
myBook.show = function showProps(obj, name) { var result = ""; for (i in obj) { result += name + "." + i + " = " + obj[i] + "
"; } return result; }
```

**Figure 8.11**  The *book* object's properties.

### 8.3.3  Extending Objects with Prototypes

Object-oriented languages support a feature called inheritance, where one object can inherit the properties of another. JavaScript implements inheritance with prototypes. As of Netscape Navigator 3.0, it is possible to add properties to objects after they have been created by using the *prototype* object.

JavaScript functions are automatically given an empty *prototype* object. If the function serves as the constructor for an object, then the *prototype* object can be used to implement inheritance. When the properties are assigned to a given object by a constructor function, the *prototype* object gets the same properties. Each time a new object of the same class is created, that object also inherits the *prototype* object and all the same properties. The good news is that even after an object has been created, it can be extended with new properties that will also become part of the *prototype*. Then any objects created after that will automatically inherit the new properties.

**What Is a Class?**    In object-oriented languages, the object's data describes the properties. The object, along with its properties and methods, is bundled up into a container called a <u>class</u>, and one class can inherit from another, and so on. Even though JavaScript doesn't have a class mechanism per se, it mimics the class concept with the constructor and its *prototype* object.

Each JavaScript class has a *prototype* object and one set of properties. Any objects created in the class will inherit the *prototype* properties. Let's say we define a constructor function called *Employee()* with a set of properties. The *prototype* object has all the same properties. The *Employee()* constructor function represents a class. The constructor is called and instantiates an object called *janitor*, and then the constructor is called again and instantiates another object called *manager*, and so on. Each instance of the *Employee()* class automatically inherits all the properties defined for the *Employee* through its *prototype*.

After an object has been created, new properties can be added with the *prototype* property. This is how JavaScript implements inheritance.

**EXAMPLE** 8.11

```
    <html>
    <head><title>User-defined objects and Inheritance</title>
    <script language = "javascript">
1       function Book(title, author, publisher){    // The Book class
            this.title = title;
            this.author = author;
            this.publisher = publisher;
            this.show=showProps;
        }
2       function showProps(obj,name){
            var result = "";
            for (var i in obj){
                result += name + "." + i + " = " + obj[i] + "<br>";
            }
            return result;
        }
    </script>
    </head>
    <body bgcolor="lightblue">
    <script language="javascript">
    // Add a new function
3       function lastEdition(){
            this.latest=prompt("Enter the latest edition for
                            "+this.title,"");
            return (this.latest);
        }
    // Add a new property with prototype
4   Book.prototype.edition=lastEdition;
5   var myBook=new Book("JavaScript by Example", "Ellie",
                        "Prentice Hall");
    // Define a new method
    document.write("<br><b>" + myBook.show(myBook,"myBook")+"<br>");
6   document.write("The latest edition is "+ myBook.edition()+"<br>");
    </script>
    </body>
    </html>
```

## EXPLANATION

1   The function called *Book* defines the properties and methods for a *Book* object. *Book* is a JavaScript class. Each object has a prototype whose properties it inherits. An instance of a new *Book* object will inherit all of these properties.

2   A function called *showProps* is defined. It uses the special *for* loop to iterate through all the properties of an object. It will be used to create a method for the *Book* object, called *show()*.

3   A function called *lastEdition()* is defined. It returns the latest edition of the book.

4   A new property is given to the *Book* object using the *prototype* property, followed by the property name, *edition*. This property is assigned the name of a function called *lastEdition*, thus creating a new method for the *Book* class.

5   A new *Book* object, called *myBook*, is created. It has inherited all of the original properties of the *Book* class, plus the new property defined by the *prototype* property, called *edition*.

6   The new method is called for the *myBook* object.

**Extending a JavaScript Object.**     Since all objects have the *prototype* object, it is possible to extend the properties of a JavaScript built-in object, just as we did for a user-defined object. (See Chapter 9, "JavaScript Core Objects.")

## EXAMPLE 8.12

```
    <html><head><title>Prototypes</title>
    <script language = "javascript">
    // Customize String Functions
1       function uc(){
2           var str=this.big();
3           return( str.toUpperCase());
        }
4       function lc(){
5           var str=this.small();
6           return( str.toLowerCase());
        }
7       String.prototype.bigUpper=uc;
8       String.prototype.smallLower=lc;

9       var string="This Is a Test STRING.";

10      string=string.bigUpper();
        document.write(string+"<br>");
11      document.write(string.bigUpper()+"<br>");
12      document.write(string.smallLower()+"<br>");
    </script>
    </head>
    <body bgcolor="lightblue"></body>
    </html>
```

## EXPLANATION

1   A function called *uc* is defined. It will manipulate a *String* object.

2   The *big()* method is an HTML method that will increase the font size (one size larger than the current font) for the *String* object.

3   The string will be returned with a larger font and all letters in uppercase.

4   A function called *lc* is defined. It will also manipulate the *String* object.

5   The *small()* method is an HTML method that will decrease the font size (one size smaller than the current font) for the *String* object.

6   The string will be returned with a smaller font and all letters in lowercase.

7   The function *uc* is assigned to the *String.prototype.bigUpper* property, creating a new method for the *String* object.

8   The function *lc* is assigned to the *String.prototype.smallLower* property, creating another new method for the *String* object.

9   This is the *String* object that will be manipulated by the new methods created by the *prototype* property.

10  When the *string.bigUpper()* method is called, the string is converted to uppercase with all letters in a bigger font.

11  The *string.bigUpper()* method is called again, creating a larger string all in capital letters.

12  When the *string.smallLower()* method is called, the string is converted to lower-case with all letters in a smaller font. See output in Figure 8.12.

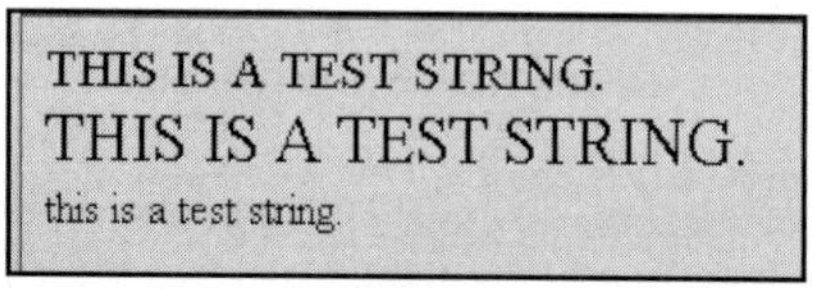

THIS IS A TEST STRING.
THIS IS A TEST STRING.
this is a test string.

**Figure 8.12**   Extending properties to a built-in class. Output from Example 8.12.

## EXERCISES

1. Create a *circle* object and a method that will calculate its circumference.

2. Write a function that will create a *clock* object.
   a. It will have three properties: *seconds*, *minutes*, and *hours*.
   b. Write two methods: *setTime()* to set the current time and *displayTime()* to display the time.
   c. The user will be prompted to select either a.m., p.m., or military time. The value he chooses will be passed as an argument to the *display()* method.
   d. The output will be either

      ```
      14:10:26 or 2:10:26
      ```

      depending on what argument was passed to the display() method.

# chapter
# 9

# JavaScript Core Objects

## 9.1　What Are Core Objects?

Like an apple, JavaScript has a core, and at its core are objects. Everything you do in JavaScript will be based on objects; you may create your own or use JavaScript's core objects, those objects built right into the language. JavaScript provides built-in objects that deal with date and time, math, strings, regular expressions, numbers, and other useful entities. The good news is that the core objects are consistent across different implementations and platforms and have been standardized by the ECMAScript 1.0 specification, allowing programs to be portable. Although each object has a set of properties and methods that further define it, this book does not detail every one, but highlights those that will be used most often. For a complete list of properties and objects, see the CD-ROM in the back of this book or go to *http://developer.netscape.com*.

## 9.2　Array Objects

An array is a collection of like values—called <u>elements</u>—such as an array of colors, an array of strings, or an array of images. Each element of the array is accessed with an index value enclosed in square brackets (see Figure 9.1). An index is also called a sub-script. There are two types of index values: a non-negative integer and a string. Arrays indexed by strings are called <u>associative arrays</u>.[1] In JavaScript, arrays are built-in objects with some added functionality.[2]

---

1. Creating a multidimensional array (i.e., an array with more than one index) is not officially supported by JavaScript, but can be simulated with some trickery.
2. Arrays were introduced in JavaScript 1.1.

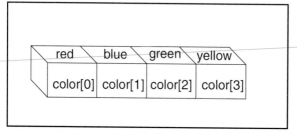

**Figure 9.1**   An *Array* object called *color.* Index values are in square brackets.

## 9.2.1   Declaring an Array

Like variables, arrays must be declared before they can be used. The *new* keyword is used to dynamically create the *Array* object. It calls the *Array* object's constructor, *Array()*, to create a new *Array* object. The size of the array can be passed as an argument to the constructor, but it is not necessary. Values can also be assigned to the array when it is constructed, but this is not required either. Let's examine some ways to create an array.

The following array is called *array_name* and its size is not specified.

```
var array_name = new Array();
```

In the next example, the size or length of the array is passed as an argument to the *Array()* constructor. The new array has 100 undefined elements.

```
var array_name = new Array(100);
```

And in the next example, the array is given a list of initial values of any data type:

```
var array_name = new Array("red", "green", "yellow", 1 ,2, 3);
```

Although you can specify the size of the array when declaring it, it is not required. JavaScript allocates memory as needed to allow the array to shrink and grow on demand. To populate the array, each element is assigned a value. Each element is indexed by either a number or string. If the array index is a number, it starts with 0. JavaScript doesn't care what you store in the array. Any combination of types, such as numbers, strings, Booleans, and so forth, are acceptable. Example 9.1 creates a new *Array* object called *book* and assigns strings to each of its elements.

**Using the *new* Constructor.**    To create an *Array* object, call the *Array()* constructor with the *new* keyword and pass information to the constructor if you know the size and/or what elements you want to assign to the array. Values can be added or deleted throughout the program; JavaScript provides a number of methods to manipulate the array (these are listed in "Array Methods" on page 158).

### EXAMPLE  9.1

```
<html>
<head><title>The Array Object</title>
<h2>An Array of Books</h2>
    <script language="JavaScript">
1       var book = new Array(6);    // Create an Array object
2       book[0] = "War and Peace";  // Assign values to its elements
        book[1] = "Huckleberry Finn";
        book[2] = "The Return of the Native";
        book[3] = "A Christmas Carol";
        book[4] = "The Yearling";
        book[5] = "Exodus";
    </script>
</head>
<body bgcolor="lightblue">
    <script language="JavaScript">
        document.write("<h3>");
3       for(var i in book){
4           document.write("book[" + i + "] "+ book[i]  + "<br>");
        }
    </script>
</body>
</html>
```

### EXPLANATION

1   The variable *book* is assigned a new *Array* object containing six elements.

2   The first element of the *book* array is assigned the string *"War and Peace"*. Array indices start at zero.

3   The special *for* loop is used to access each of the elements in the *book* array.

4   Each of the elements of the *book* array are displayed in the browser. (See Figure 9.2.)

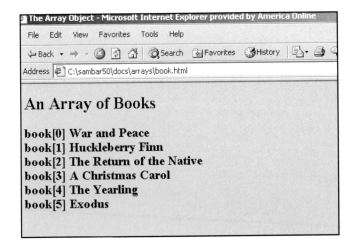

**Figure 9.2**
An array called *book* displays its elements. Output from Example 9.1.

**Populating an Array with a *for* Loop.** Populating an array is the process of assigning values to it. In Example 9.2, the *for* loop is used to fill an array. The initial value of the index starts at zero; the looping will continue as long as the value of the index is less than the final size of the array.

---

**EXAMPLE** 9.2

```
<html><head><title>The Array Object</title><body>
<body>
<h2>An Array of Numbers</h2>
<script language="JavaScript">
1      var years = new Array(10);
2      for(var i=0; i < years.length; i++ ){
3          years[i]=i + 2000;
4          document.write("years[" + i + "] = "+ years[i]
                            + "<br>");
       }
</script>
</body>
</html>
```

**EXPLANATION**

1  The *Array()* constructor is called to create a 10-element array called *years*.

2  The *for* loop starts with an initial value of *i* set to 0, which will be the value of the first index in the array. As long as the value of *i* is less than the length of the array, the body of the loop will be executed. Each time through the loop, *i* is incremented by 1.

3  The array is populated here. Each time through the loop, *years[i]* is assigned the value of *i + 2000*.

4  The value of the new array element is displayed for each iteration of the loop. (See Figure 9.3.)

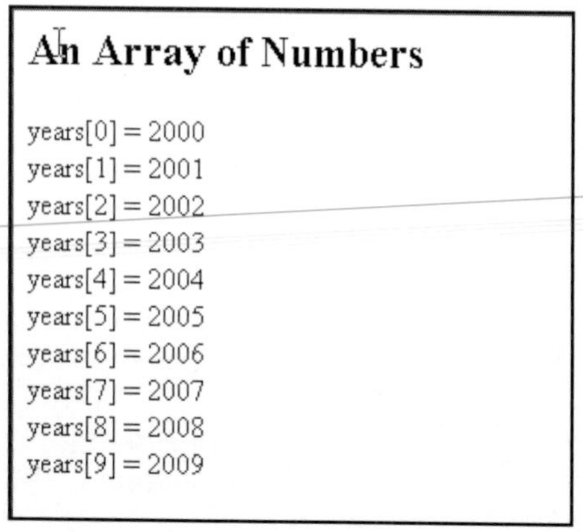

---

## An Array of Numbers

years[0] = 2000
years[1] = 2001
years[2] = 2002
years[3] = 2003
years[4] = 2004
years[5] = 2005
years[6] = 2006
years[7] = 2007
years[8] = 2008
years[9] = 2009

**Figure 9.3**
Output from Example 9.2.

**Creating and Populating an Array Simultaneously.**   When creating an array, you can populate (assign elements to) it at the same time by passing the value of the elements as arguments to the *Array()* constructor. Later on, you can add or delete elements as you wish. See Example 9.3.

**EXAMPLE** 9.3

```
     <html><head><title>The Array Object</title></head>
     <body>
     <h2>An Array of Colored Strings</h2>
     <script language="JavaScript">
1       var colors = new Array("red", "green", "blue", "purple");
2       for(var i in colors){
3           document.write("<font color='"+colors[i]+"'>");
4           document.write("colors[" + i + "] = "+ colors[i]
                            + "<br>");
         }
     </script>
     </body>
     </html>
```

**EXPLANATION**

1   A new array called *colors* is created and assigned five colors.

2   The special *for* loop iterates through each element of the colors array, using *i* as the index into the array.

3   The color of the font is assigned the value of the array element.

4   The value of each element of the colors array is displayed. The color of the font matches the value. (See Figure 9.4.)

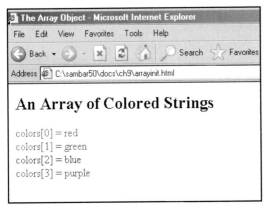

**Figure 9.4**   Each string is a different font color. Output from Example 9.3.

**Associative Arrays.**    An associative array is an array that uses a string as an index value, instead of a number. There is an association between the index and the value stored at that location. The index is often called a key and the value assigned to it, the value. Key/value pairs are a common way of storing and accessing data. In the following array called *states*, there is an association between the value of the index, the abbreviation for a state (e.g., *"CA"*), and the value stored there—the name of the state (e.g., *"California"*). The special *for* loop can be used to iterate through the elements of an associative array.

---

**EXAMPLE  9.4**

```
        <html><head><title>Associative Arrays</title></head>
        <body>
        <h2>An Array Indexed by Strings</h2>
1       <script language="JavaScript">
2           var states = new Array();
3           states["CA"] = "California";
            states["ME"] = "Maine";
            states["MT"] = "Montana";
4           for( var i in states ){
                document.write("The index is:<em> "+ i );
                document.write(".</em> The value is: <em>" + states[i]
                            + ".</em><br>");
            }
        </script>
        </body>
        </html>
```

---

**EXPLANATION**

1    The JavaScript program starts here.

2    The *Array()* constructor is called and returns a new *Array* object called *states*.

3    The index into the array element is a string of text, "CA".  The value assigned is *"California"*. Now there is an association between the index and the value.

4    The special *for* loop is used to iterate through the *Array* object. The variable, *i*, represents the index value of the array, and *states[i]* represents the value found there. It reads: For each index value in the array called *states*, get the value associated with it. (See Figure 9.5.)

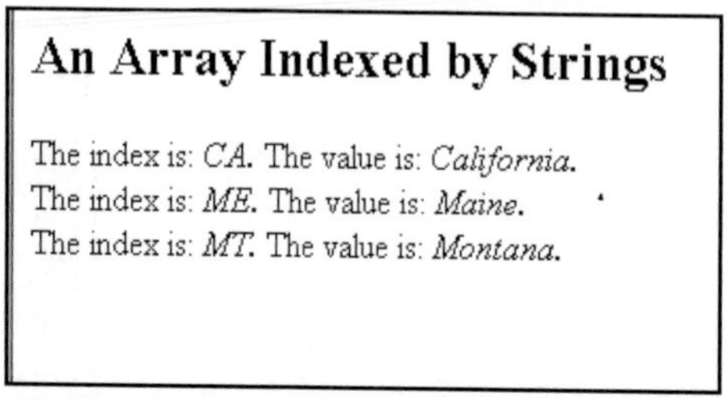

---

## An Array Indexed by Strings

The index is: *CA*. The value is: *California*.
The index is: *ME*. The value is: *Maine*.          •
The index is: *MT*. The value is: *Montana*.

**Figure 9.5**
An associative array.

# 9.3 Array Properties and Methods

Since an array is an object in JavaScript, it has properties to describe it and methods to manipulate it. The length of an array, for example, can be determined by the *length* property, and the array can be shortened by using the *pop()* method. For a complete list of array properties and methods, see Tables 9.1 and 9.2.

## 9.3.1 *Array* Object Properties

The *Array* object only has three properties. The most used is the *length* property which determines the number of elements in the array, that is, the size of the array.

**Table 9.1** *Array* object properties.

| Property | What It Does |
| --- | --- |
| *constructor* | References the object's constructor |
| *length* | Returns the number of elements in the array |
| *prototype* | Extends the definition of the array by adding properties and methods |

**EXAMPLE** 9.5

```
        <html>
        <head>
        <title>Array Properties</title>
        <h2>Array Properties</h2>
            <script language="JavaScript">
1               var book = new Array(6);      // Create an Array object
                book[0] = "War and Peace"; // Assign values to elements
                book[1] = "Huckleberry Finn";
                book[2] = "The Return of the Native";
                book[3] = "A Christmas Carol";
                book[4] = "The Yearling";
                book[5] = "Exodus";
            </script>
        </head>
        <body bgcolor="lightblue">
            <script language="JavaScript">
                document.write("<h3>");
```

**EXAMPLE  9.5 (CONTINUED)**

```
2            document.write("The book array has "   + book.length
                           + " elements<br>");
          </script>
        </body>
        </html>
```

```
(Output)
The book array has 6 elements.
```

**EXPLANATION**

1   A six-element *Array* object is declared.
2   The *length* property is used to get the length of the array. The length is 6.

## 9.3.2   Array Methods

Whether you have an array of colors, names, or numbers, there are many ways you might want to manipulate the array elements. For example, you might want to add a new name or color to the beginning or end of the array, remove a number from the end of the array, or sort out all the elements, reverse the array, and so on. JavaScript provides a whole set of methods for doing all of these things and more. See Table 9.2.

**Table 9.2**   Array methods.

| Method | What It Does |
| --- | --- |
| *concat()* | Concatenates elements from one array to another array |
| *join()* | Joins the elements of an array by a separator to form a string |
| *pop()* | Removes and returns the last element of an array |
| *push()* | Adds elements to the end of an array |
| *reverse()* | Reverses the order of the elements in an array |
| *shift()* | Removes and returns the first element of an array |
| *slice()* | Creates a new array from elements of an existing array |
| *sort()* | Sorts an array alphabetically, or numerically |
| *splice()* | Removes and/or replaces elements of an array |
| *toLocaleString()* | Returns a string representation of the array in local format |
| *toString()* | Returns a string representation of the array |
| *unshift()* | Adds elements to the beginning of an array |

**The *concat()* Method.**   The *concat()* method concatenates the elements passed as arguments onto an existing array (JavaScript 1.2), returning a new concatenated list.

## FORMAT

```
newArray=oldArray.concat(new elements);
```

Example:

```
names  = names.concat("green, "blue");
```

## EXAMPLE 9.6

```
        <html>
        <head><title>Array concat() methods</title>
        </head>
        <body>
        <script language="JavaScript">
1           var names1=new Array("Dan", "Liz", "Jody" );
2           var names2=new Array("Tom", "Suzanne");
            document.write("<b>First array: "+ names1 + "<br>");
            document.write("<b>Second array: "+ names2 + "<br>");
            document.write("<b>After the concatenation <br>");
3           names1 = names1.concat( names2);
            document.write(names1);
        </script>
        </body>
        </html>
```

## EXPLANATION

1   The first *Array* object, called *names1*, is created.

2   The second *Array* object, called *names2*,  is created.

3   After concatenating the *names2* array to *names1*, the result is returned to *names1*. The *concat()* method allows the elements of one array to be added to another.

```
First array: Dan,Liz,Jody
Second array: Tom,Suzanne
After the concatenation
Dan,Liz,Jody,Tom,Suzanne
```

**Figure 9.6**   The *concat()* method. Output from Example 9.6.

**The *pop()* Method.**    The *pop()* method deletes the last element of an array and returns the value popped off.

## FORMAT

```
var return_value=Arrayname.pop();
```

Example:

```
var popped = myArray.pop();
```

## EXAMPLE 9.7

```
     <html>
     <head><title>Array pop() method</title>
     </head>
     <body>
     <script language="JavaScript">
1        var names=new Array("Tom", "Dan", "Liz", "Jody");
2        document.write("<b>Original array: "+ names +"<br>");
3        var newstring=names.pop();   // Pop off last element of array
4        document.write("Element popped: "+ newstring);
5        document.write("<br>New array: "+ names + "</b>");
     </script>
     </body>
     </html>
```

## EXPLANATION

1   The *Array()* constructor creates a new array called *names* and intializes the array with four values: *"Tom"*, *"Dan"*, *"Liz"*, and *"Jody"*.

2   The contents of the array called *names* is displayed.

3   The last element of the array is removed. The value removed is returned and assigned to the variable called *newstring*.

4   The popped value is displayed.

5   The shortened array is displayed. (See Figure 9.7.)

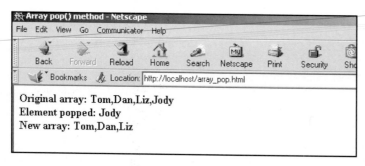

Original array: Tom,Dan,Liz,Jody
Element popped: Jody
New array: Tom,Dan,Liz

**Figure 9.7**
Output from Example 9.7.

**The *push()* Method.** The *push()* method adds new elements onto the end of an array, thereby increasing the length of the array. JavaScript allocates new memory as needed.

## FORMAT

```
Arrayname.push(new elements);   // Appended to the array
```

Example:

```
myArray.push("red", "green", "yellow");
```

## EXAMPLE 9.8

```
      <html>
      <head><title>Array push() method</title>
      </head>
      <body>
      <script language="JavaScript">
1         var names=new Array("Tom", "Dan", "Liz", "Jody");
2         document.write("<b>Original array: "+ names + "<br>");
3         names.push("Daniel","Christian");
4         document.write("New array: "+ names + "</b>");
      </script>
      </body>
      </html>
```

## EXPLANATION

1   An *Array* object called *names* is declared and intialized.
2   The contents of the array (i.e., all of its elements) are displayed.
3   The *push()* method appends two new elements, *"Daniel"* and *"Christian"*, to the end of the *names* array.
4   The array has grown. It is displayed in the browser window with its new elements. (See Figure 9.8.)

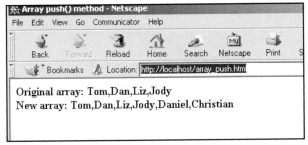

**Figure 9.8**  Output from Example 9.8.

**The *shift()* and *unshift()* Methods.**    The *shift()* method removes the first element of an array and returns the value shifted off; the *unshift()* method adds elements to the beginning of the array. These methods are just like *pop()* and *push()* except that they manipulate the beginning of the array instead of the end of it.

## FORMAT

```
var return_value=Arrayname.shift();
Arrayname.shift( new elements);    // Prepended to the array
```

Example:

```
var shifted_off = myArray.shift();
myArray.shift("blue","yellow");
```

## EXAMPLE 9.9

```
      <html>
      <head><title>Array shift() and unshift() methods</title>
      </head>
      <body>
      <script language="JavaScript">
1         var names=new Array("Dan", "Liz", "Jody" );
          document.write("<b>Original array: "+ names + "<br>");
2         names.shift();
          document.write("New array after the shift: " + names);
3         names.unshift("Nicky","Lucy");
          // Add new elements to the beginning of the array
          document.write("<br>New array after the unshift: " + names);
      </script>
      </body>
      </html>
```

## EXPLANATION

1   A new *Array* object called *names* is created.
2   The first element of the array is shifted off, shortening the array by 1.
3   The *unshift()* method will prepend to the beginning of the array, the names *"Nicky"* and *"Lucy"*, thereby making it longer by two elements. (See Figure 9.9.)

Original array: Dan,Liz,Jody
New array after the shift: Liz,Jody
New array after the unshift: Nicky,Lucy,Liz,Jody

**Figure 9.9**   The *shift()* and *unshift()* methods. Output from Example 9.9.

**The *slice()* Method.**   The *slice()* method copies elements of one array into a new array. The *slice()* method takes two arguments: the first number is the starting element in a range of elements that will be copied, and the second argument is the last element in the range, but this element is not included in what is copied. Remember that the index starts at zero, so that a beginning position of 2 is really element 3. The orginal array is unaffected unless you assign the result of the slice back to the original array.

---

**FORMAT**

```
var newArray = Arrayname.slice(first element, last element);
```

Example:

```
var ArraySlice = myArray.slice(2,6);   // ArraySlice contains elements
                                       // 2 through 5 of myArray.
```

---

**EXAMPLE  9.10**

```
        <html>
        <head><title>Array slice() method</title>
        </head>
        <body>
        <script language="JavaScript">
1           var names=new Array("Dan", "Liz", "Jody", "Christian",
                            "William");
            document.write("<b>Original array: "+ names + "<br>");
2           var sliceArray=names.slice(2, 4);
            document.write("New array after the slice: ");
3           document.write(sliceArray);
        </script>
        </body>
        </html>
```

---

**EXPLANATION**

1   This is the original array of names.

2   The *slice()* method will start at position 2, copy *Jody* into the new array, then *Christian*, and stop just before position 4, *William*. The original array is not affected by the slice.

3   The new array created by the *slice()* method is displayed. (See Figure 9.10.)

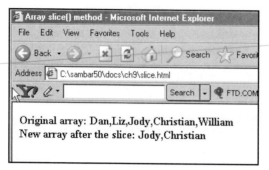

**Figure 9.10**   Using *slice()* to create a new array.

**The *splice()* Method.**   The *splice()* method [not to be confused with *slice()*] removes a specified number of elements from some starting position in an array and allows you to replace those items with new ones. (Don't confuse this method with the *slice()* method. Ropes, tapes, and films are spliced; bread, meat, and golf balls are sliced.)

**FORMAT**

```
Arrayname.splice( index position, number of elements to remove);
Arrayname.splice(index position, number of elements to remove,
                 replacement elements);
```

Example:

```
myArray.splice( 3, 2);
myArray.splice( 3, 2, "apples","oranges");
```

**EXAMPLE  9.11**

```
    <html>
    <head><title>Array splice() method</title>
    </head>
    <body>
       <script language="JavaScript">
       // splice(starting_pos, number_to_delete, new_values)
1          var names=new Array("Tom","Dan", "Liz", "Jody");
           document.write("<b>Original array: "+ names + "<br>");
2          names.splice(1, 2, "Peter","Paul","Mary");
3          document.write("New array: "+ names + "</b>");
       </script>
    </body>
    </html>
```

1    An *Array* object called *names* is declared and intialized.

2    The *splice()* method allows you to delete elements from an array and optionally replace the deleted elements with new values. The first arguments to the splice method od are *1, 2*. This means: start at element 1, and remove a length of 2 elements.  In this example, element 1 starts with *"Dan"* (element 0 is *"Tom"*). *"Liz"* is the second element. Both *"Dan"* and *"Liz"* are removed. The next three arguments, *"Peter"*, *"Paul"*, and *"Mary"*, are then inserted into the array, replacing *"Dan"* and *"Liz"*.

3    The new *names* array is displayed in the browser window. (See Figure 9.11.)

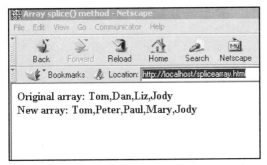

**Figure 9.11**    The *splice()* method. Output from Example 9.11.

## 9.4    The *Date* Object

JavaScript provides the *Date* object for manipulating date and time.[3] Like the *String* and *Array* objects, you can create as many instances as you like.

As we'll see, the *Date* object provides a number of methods for getting or setting specific information about the date and time. The date is based on the UNIX date starting at January 1, 1970 (in Greenwich Mean Time[4] [GMT]), and doesn't support dates before that time. Figure 9.12 gives you an idea of the difference between GMT and local time. Time is measured in milliseconds (one millisecond is one thousandth of a second). Since client-side JavaScript programs run on a browser, the *Date* object returns times and dates that are local to the browser, not the server. Of course, if the computer is not set to the correct time, then the *Date* object won't produce the expected results. Figure 9.13 shows a typical date and time control panel.

---

3.  For more information about the time and date, see *http://www.timeanddate.com/worldclock/*.

4.  Greenwich Mean Time (GMT) is now called Universal Coordinate Time (UTC). The current time in Greenwich, England is five hours + New York's present time, or eight hours + San Francisco's present time.

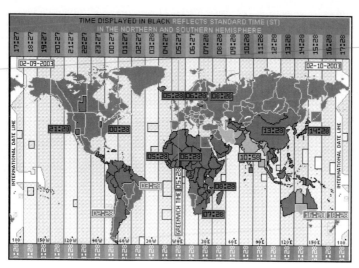

**Figure 9.12**   24-hour world time zones map with current time. Courtesy of
*http://www.worldtimezone.com/index24.html.*

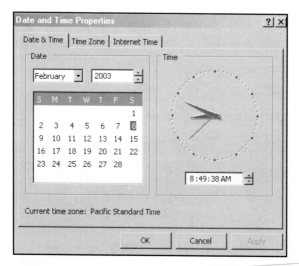

**Figure 9.13**   The computer's date and time settings.

If no arguments are passed to the *Date* object constructor, it returns the local date and
time (based on the accuracy of the clock on your client machine). There are five formats
that can be passed as arguments when creating a *Date* object. They are shown in Example 9.12.

**EXAMPLE 9.12**

```
var Date = new Date();    // The new constructor returns a Date object.
var Date = new Date("July 4, 2004, 6:25:22");
var Date = new Date("July 4, 2004");
var Date = new Date(2004, 7, 4, 6, 25, 22);
var Date = new Date(2004, 7, 4);
var Date = new Date(Milliseconds);
```

## 9.4.1 Using the *Date* Object Methods

The *Date* object comes with a large number of methods (see Table 9.3) and only a *prototype* property. For browser versions supporting *Date* methods, see *http://www.w3schools.com/js/js_datetime.asp*.

**Table 9.3** *Date* object methods.

| Method | What It Does |
| --- | --- |
| getDate | Returns the day of the month (1–31) |
| getDay | Returns the day of the week (0–6); 0 is Sunday, 1 is Monday, etc. |
| getFullYear | Returns the year with 4 digits* |
| getHours | Returns the hour (0–23) |
| getMilliseconds | Returns the millisecond* |
| getMinutes | Returns hours since midnight (0–23) |
| getMonth | Returns number of month (0–11); 0 is January, 1 is February, etc. |
| getSeconds | Returns the second (0–59) |
| getTime | Returns number of milliseconds since January 1, 1970 |
| getTimeZoneOffset | Returns the difference in minutes between current time on local computer and UTC (Universal Coordinated Time) |
| getUTCDate() | Returns the day of the month* |
| getUTDDay() | Returns the day of the week converted to universal time* |
| get UTCFullYear() | Returns the year in four digits converted to universal time* |
| getUTCHours() | Returns the hour converted to universal time* |
| getUTCMilliseconds() | Returns the millisecond converted to universal time* |
| parse() | Converts the passed-in string date to milliseconds since January 1, 1970 |

**Table 9.3**  *Date* object methods. (continued)

| Method | What It Does |
|---|---|
| *setDate(value)* | Sets day of the month (1–31) |
| *setFullYear()* | Sets the year as a four-digit number* |
| *setHours()* | Sets the hour within the day (0–23) |
| *setHours(hr,min,sec,msec)* | Sets hour in local or UTC time |
| *setMilliseconds* | Sets the millisecond* |
| *setMinutes(min,sec, msec)* | Sets minute in local time or UTC |
| *setMonth(month,date)* | Sets month in local time |
| *setSeconds()* | Sets the second |
| *setTime()* | Sets time from January 1, 1970, in milliseconds |
| *setUTCdate()* | Sets the day of the month in universal time |
| *setUTCFullYear()* | Sets the year as a four-digit number in universal time* |
| *setUTCHours()* | Sets the hour in universal time* |
| *setUTCMilliseconds()* | Sets the millisecond in universal time* |
| *setUTCMinutes()* | Sets the minute in universal time* |
| *setUTCMonth()* | Sets the month in universal time* |
| *setUTCSeconds()* | Sets the second in universal time* |
| *setYear()* | Sets the number of years since 1900 (00–99) |
| *toGMTString()* | Returns the date string in universal format |
| *toLocaleString* | Returns string representing date and time based on locale of computer as 10/09/99 12:43:22 |
| *toSource* | Returns the source of the *Date* object* |
| *toString* | Returns string representing date and time |
| *toUTCString* | Returns string representing date and time as 10/09/99 12:43:22 in universal time* |
| *UTC()* | Converts comma-delimited values to milliseconds* |
| *valueOf()* | Returns the equivalence of the *Date* object in milliseconds* |

* Starting with Netscape 4.0 and IE 4.0.

**EXAMPLE 9.13**

```
<html>
<head><title>Time and Date</title></head>
<body bgcolor="lightblue"><h2>Date and Time</h2>
<script language="JavaScript">
1       var now = new Date();      // Now is an instance of a Date object
        document.write("<font size='+1'>");
        document.write("<b>Local time:</b> " + now + "<br>");
2       var hours=now.getHours();
3       var minutes=now.getMinutes();
4       var seconds=now.getSeconds();
5       var year=now.getFullYear();
        document.write("The full year is " + year +"<br>");
        document.write("<b>The time is:</b> " +
            hours + ":" + minutes + ":" + seconds);
                document.write("</font>");
</script>
</body>
</html>
```

**EXPLANATION**

1   A new *Date* object called *now* is created. It contains a string: Thu Feb 6 20:02:02 PST 2003.

2   The variable called *hours* is assigned the return value of the *getHours()* method.

3   The variable called *minutes* is assigned the return value of the *getMinutes()* method.

4   The variable called *seconds* is assigned the return value of the *getSeconds()* method.

5   The variable called *year* is assigned the return value of the *getFullYear()* method, *2003*. The output is shown in Figure 9.14.

---

**Date and Time**

**Local time:** Thu Feb 06 2003 20:02:02 GMT-0800 (Pacific Standard Time)
**The time is:** 20:2:2

---

**Figure 9.14**   Output from Example 9.13.

## 9.4.2   Manipulating the Date and Time

JavaScript stores dates in milliseconds, so if you have more complicated calculations to perform, such as the number of days before a date, or between two dates, the information in Table 9.4 might be helpful in converting milliseconds to minutes, hours, days, and so forth.

**Table 9.4**   Basic units of time.

| Unit of Time | Milliseconds | |
|---|---|---|
| 1 second | 1000 | |
| 1 minute | second * 60 | (1000 * 60) |
| 1 hour | minute * 60 | (1000 * 60 * 60) |
| 1 day | hour * 24 | (1000 * 60 * 60 * 24 ) |
| 1 week | day * 7 | (1000 * 60 * 60 * 24 * 7 ) |

## EXAMPLE 9.14

```
   <html><head><title>Countdown 'till Christmas</title></head>
   <body bgColor="#00FF99">
   <font face="arial" size=5 color=red>
   <script language="JavaScript">
1      var today = new Date();
2      var fullyear = today.getFullYear();
3      var future = new Date("December 25, "+ fullyear);
4      var diff = future.getTime() - today.getTime();
       // Number of milliseconds
5      var days = Math.floor(diff / (1000 * 60 * 60 * 24 ));
       // Convert to days
6      var str="Only <u>" + days + "</u>  shopping days left
              \'til Christmas! ";
       document.write(str+"<br>");
   </script>
   </body>
   </html>
```

## EXPLANATION

1   A new *Date* object called *today* is created.

2   The *getFullYear()* method returns the year as 2003.

3   Another *Date* object called *future* is created.  It will contain the future date, Christmas, passed as its argument.

4   The difference between the future time and the present time is calculated and returned in milliseconds with the *getTime()* method.

5   The *Math* object is used to round down the result of converting milliseconds to days.

6   This string contains the number of days between the present date and Christmas. (See Figure 9.15.)

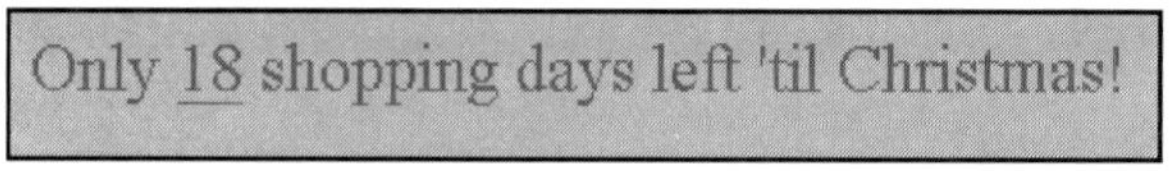

Only _18_ shopping days left 'til Christmas!

**Figure 9.15**   The number of days between two dates has been calculated.

### 9.4.3   Customizing the *Date* Object with the *prototype* Property

The *Date* object has a *prototype* property that allows you to extend the capabilities of the object. You can customize the time and the date by providing new methods and properties that will be inherited by all instances of this object. Since the *Date* object provides methods that return zero-based months, weeks, years, and other measures you may want to create a prototype method where *"January"* is month number 1 instead of 0, and the day is *"Monday"* instead of 1, etc.

**EXAMPLE   9.15**

```
        <html><head><title>The Prototype Property</title>
        <script language = "javascript">
        // Customize the Date
1       function weekDay(){
2           var now = this.getDay();
3           var names = new Array(7);
            names[0]="Sunday";
            names[1]="Monday";
            names[2]="Tuesday";
            names[3]="Wednesday";
            names[4]="Thursday";
            names[5]="Friday";
            names[6]="Saturday";
4           return(names[now]);
            }
5           Date.prototype.DayOfWeek=weekDay;
        </script>
        </head>
        <body bgcolor="pink">
        <font face="arial" size="+1">
        <center>
        <script language="JavaScript">
6           var today=new Date();
7           document.write("Today is " + today.DayOfWeek() + ".<br>");
        </script>
        </body></html>
```

**EXPLANATION**

1  The function called *weekday()* is defined.

2  The variable *now* is assigned a number representing the day of the week, where 0 is Sunday.

3  A new *Array* object called *names* is created. It will contain seven elements. Each element will be assigned the name of the weekday, e.g., *"Sunday"*.

4  The value in *now*, a number between 0 and 6, will be used as an index in the names array. If now is 6, then the value of *names[6]*, *"Saturday"*, will be returned.

5  A prototype method called *DayOfWeek* is assigned the name of the function that defines the method.

6  A new *Date* object is created with the *Date()* constructor method.

7  The new prototyped method is called, and returns the string value of today's date, *"Saturday"*. (See Figure 9.16.) The capabilities of the *Date* object have been extended to provide a method that will return the name of the weekday.

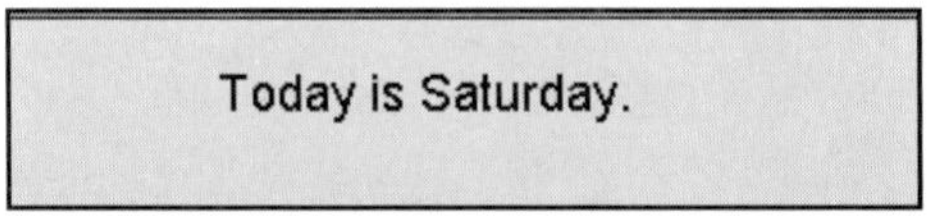

Today is Saturday.

**Figure 9.16**   The day is converted to a string.

## 9.5  The *Math* Object

The *Math* object allows you to work with more advanced arithmetic calculations, such as square root, trigonometric functions, logarithms, and random numbers, than are provided by the basic numeric operators. If you are doing simple calculations, you really won't need it.

Unlike other objects, you don't have to create an instance of the *Math* object with the *new* keyword. It is a built-in object and has a number of properties (see Table 9.5) and methods (see Table 9.6). The *Math* object always starts with an uppercase M.

**Table 9.5**   *Math* object properties.

| Property | Value | Description |
| --- | --- | --- |
| Math.E | 2.718281828459045091 | Euler's constant, the base of natural logarithms |
| Math.LN2 | 0.6931471805599452862 | Natural log of 2 |
| Math.LN10 | 2.302585092994045901 | Natural log of 10 |
| Math.LOG2E | 1.442695040888963387 | Log base-2 of E |

**Table 9.5**  *Math* object properties. (continued)

| Property | Value | Description |
|---|---|---|
| Math.Log10E | 0.4342944819032518167 | Log base-10 of E |
| Math.PI | 3.14592653589793116 | Pi, ratio of the circumference of a circle to its diameter |
| Math.SQRT1_2 | 0.7071067811865475727 | 1 divided by the quare root of 2 |
| Math.SQRT2 | 1.414213562373985145 | Square root of 2 |

**Table 9.6**  *Math* object methods.

| Method | Functionality |
|---|---|
| Math.abs(Number) | Returns the absolute (unsigned) value of *Number* |
| Math.acos(Number) | Arc cosine of *Number*, returns result in radians |
| Math.asin(Number) | Arc sine of *Number*, returns results in radians |
| Math.atan(Number) | Arctangent of *Number*, returns results in radians |
| Math.atan2(y,x) | Arctangent of *y/x*; returns arctangent of the quotient of its arguments |
| Math.ceil(Number) | Rounds *Number* up to the next closest integer |
| Math.cos(Number) | Returns the cosign of *Number* in radians |
| Math.exp(x)* | Euler's constant to some power (see footnote) |
| Math.floor(Number) | Rounds *Number* down to the next closest integer |
| Math.log(Number) | Returns the natural logarithm of *Number* (base E) |
| Math.max(Number1, Number2) | Returns larger value of *Number1* and *Number2* |
| Math.min(Number1, Number2) | Returns smaller value of *Number1* and *Number2* |
| Math.pow(x, y) | Returns the value of *x* to the power of $y(x^y)$, where *x* is the base and *y* is the exponent |
| Math.random() | Generates pseudorandom number between 0.0 and 1.0 |
| Math.round(Number) | Rounds *Number* to the closest integer |
| Math.sin(Number) | Arc sine of *Number* in radians |
| Math.sqrt(Number) | Square root of *Number* |
| Math.tan(Number) | Tangent of *Number* in radians |
| Math.toString(Number) | Converts *Number* to string |

* Returns the value of $E^x$ where E is Euler's constant and x is the argument passed to it. Euler's constant is approximately 2.7183.

**Square Root, Power of, and Pi.**　The *Math* object comes with a number of common mathematical constants (all uppercase), such as *PI* and natural log values, as well as methods to find the square root of a number, the power of a number, and so on. Example 9.16 demonstrates how to use some of these properties; the output is shown in Figure 9.17.

**EXAMPLE　9.16**

```
        <html>
        <head><title>The Math Object</title></head>
        <body>
        <h2>Math object Methods--sqrt(),pow()<br>
        Math object Property--PI</h2>
        <P>
        <script language="JavaScript">
1           var num=16;
            document.write("<h3>The square root of " +num+ " is ");
2           document.write(Math.sqrt(num),".<br>");
            document.write("PI is ");
3           document.write(Math.PI);
            document.write(".<br>"+num+" raised to the 3rd power is " );
4           document.write(Math.pow(num,3));
            document.write(".</h3></font>");
        </script>
        </body></html>
```

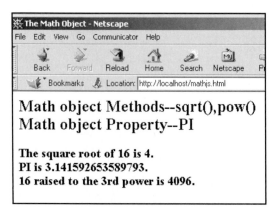

**Figure 9.17**　Output from Example 9.16.

## 9.5.1　Rounding Up and Rounding Down

There are three *Math* methods available for rounding numbers up or down. They are the *ceil()*, *floor()*, and *round()* methods (see Table 9.7 for examples). The differences between the methods might be confusing because all three methods truncate the numbers after the decimal point and return a whole number. If you recall, JavaScript also provides the *parseInt()* function, but this function truncates the number after the decimal point, without rounding either up or down.

**The *ceil()* Method.**   The *ceil()* method rounds a number <u>up</u> to the next largest whole number and then removes any numbers after the decimal point; thus, 5.02 becomes 6 because 6 is the next largest number, and –5.02 becomes –5 because –5 is larger than –6.

**The *floor()* Method.**   The *floor()* method rounds a number <u>down</u> to the next lowest whole number and then removes any numbers after the decimal point; thus, 5.02 now becomes 5, and –5.02 becomes –6.

**The *round()* Method.**   The *round()* method rounds <u>up</u> only if the decimal part of the number is .5 or greater. Otherwise, it rounds <u>down</u> to the nearest integer; thus, 5.5 is rounded up to 6, and 5.4 is rounded down to 5.

**Table 9.7**   Rounding up and down.

| Number | ceil() | floor() | round() |
|---|---|---|---|
| 2.55 | 3 | 2 | 3 |
| 2.30 | 3 | 2 | 2 |
| –2.5 | –2 | –3 | –2 |
| –2.3 | –2 | –3 | –2 |

**EXAMPLE** 9.17

```
      <html>
      <head><title>The Math Object</title></head>
      <body>
      <h2>Rounding Numbers</h2>
      <p>
      <h3>
      <script language="JavaScript">
1     var num=16.3;
      document.write("<I>The number being manipulated is: ", num,
                "</I><br><br>");
2     document.write("The <I>Math.floor</I> method rounds down: " +
                Math.floor(num) + "<br>");
3     document.write("The <I>Math.ceil</I> method rounds up: " +
                Math.ceil(num) +"<br>");
4     document.write("The <I>Math.round</I> method rounds to\
                the nearest integer: " + Math.round(num) + "<br>");
      </script>
      </h3>
      </body>
      </html>
```

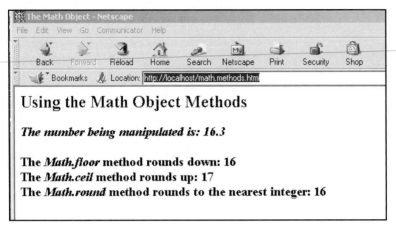

**Figure 9.18**  Output from Example 9.17.

## 9.5.2   Generating Random Numbers

Random numbers are frequently used in JavaScript programs to produce random images (such as banners streaming across a screen), random messages, or random numbers (such as for lotteries or card games). There are examples throughout this text where random numbers are used.

The *Math* object's *random()* method returns a random fractional number between 0 and 1 and is seeded with the computer's system time. (The seed is the starting number for the algorithm that produces the random number.) The *Math* object's *floor()* method truncates numbers after the decimal point and returns an integer.

---

**EXAMPLE  9.18**

```
        <html><head><title>Random Numbers</title>
        <font size="+1">
        <script language="JavaScript">
1       var n = 10;
2       for(i=0;  i < 10;i++){
        // Generate random numbers between 0 and 10
3           document.write(Math.floor(Math.random()* (n + 1)) +
                           "<br>");
        }
        </script>
        </head>
        <body></body>
        </html>
```

**EXPLANATION**

1   The variable *n* is assigned an initial value of *10*. This value will be the outside range of numbers randomly produced.

2   The *for* loop is entered and will cause the body of the block to be executed 10 times, thus producing 10 random numbers between 0 and 10.

3   The formula produces a random number between 0 and some number, *n*, using the *Math* object's *random* method. The output is shown in Figure 9.19.

```
0
8
5
10
8
7
5
4
1
6
```

**Figure 9.19**   Random numbers. Output from Example 9.18.

## 9.6   What Is a Wrapper Object?

The primitive man wraps himself up in an animal skin to keep warm or to protect his skin. A primitive data type can also have a wrapper. The wrapper is an object bearing the same name as the data type it represents. For each of the primitive data types (string, number, and Boolean), there is a *String* object, a *Number* object, and a *Boolean* object. These objects are called <u>wrappers</u> and provide properties and methods that can be defined for the object. For example, the *String* object has a number of methods that let you change the font color, size, and style of a string; and the *Number* object has methods that allow you to format a number to a specified number of significant digits. Whether you use the object or literal notation to create a string, number, or Boolean, JavaScript handles the internal conversion between the types. The real advantage to the wrapper object is its ability to apply and extend properties and methods to the object, which in turn, will affect the primitive.

## 9.6.1   The *String* Object

We have used strings throughout this book. They were sent as arguments to the *write()* and *writeln()* methods, they have been assigned to variables, they have been concatenated, and so on. As you may recall, a string is a sequence of characters enclosed in either double or single quotes. The *String* object (starting with JavaScript 1.1) is a core JavaScript object that allows you to treat strings as objects. The *String* object is also called a wrapper object because it wraps itself around a string primitive, allowing you to apply a number of properties and methods to it.

You can create a *String* object implicitly by assigning a quoted string of text to a variable, called a string primitive (see "Primitive Data Types" on page 31 of Chapter 3), or by explicitly creating a *String* object with the *new* keyword and the *String()* object constructor method. Either way, the properties and methods of the *String* object can be applied to the new string variable.

### FORMAT

```
var string_name = "string of text";
var string_name = new String("string of text");
```

Example:

```
var title="JavaScript by Example";
var title=new String("JavaScript by Example");
```

### EXAMPLE 9.19

```
    <html><head><title>The String Object</title></head>
    <body bgcolor=pink><font face="arial" size=+1>
    <h2>Primitive and String Objects</h2>
    <script language="JavaScript">
1       var first_string = "The winds of war are blowing.";
2       var next_string = new String("There is peace in the valley.");
3       document.write("The first string is of type<em> "+
                    typeof(first_string));
        document.write(".</em><br>The second string is of type<em> "+
4                   typeof(next_string) +".<br>");
    </script>
    </body>
    </html>
```

## EXPLANATION

1   This is the literal way to assign a string to a variable, and the most typical way. The string is called a string primitive. It is one of the basic building blocks of the language, along with numbers and Booleans. All of the properties and methods of the *String* object behave the same way whether you create a *String* literal or a *String* object as shown next. For all practical purposes, both methods of creating a string are the same, though this one is the easiest.

2   The *String()* constructor and the *new* keyword are used to create a *String* object. This is the explicit way of creating a string.

3   The *typeof* operator demonstrates that the first string, created the literal, implicit way, is a *String* data type.

4   The *typeof* operator demonstrates that this string, created with the *String()* constructor, is an object type. Either way, when properties and methods are applied to a string, it is treated as a *String* object. (See Figure 9.20.)

---

**Types of Strings**

The first string is of type *string*.
The second string is of type *object*.

---

**Figure 9.20**   Output from Example 9.19.

**The Properties of the *String* Object.**   The string properties (see Table 9.8) describe the attributes of the *String* object. The most common string property is the *length* property, which lets you know how many characters there are in a string. The *prototype* property allows you to add your own properties and methods to the *String* object, that is, you can customize a string.

**Table 9.8**   *String* object properties.

| Property | What It Does |
| --- | --- |
| *length* | Returns the length of the string in characters |
| *prototype* | Extends the definition of the string by adding properties and methods |

**EXAMPLE  9.20**

```
          <html><head><title>The String Object</title></head>
          <body bgColor="lightblue">
          <font face="arial" size=+1>
          <h3>Length of Strings</h3>
          <script language="JavaScript">
1             var first_string = "The winds of war are blowing.";
              var next_string = new String("There is peace in the valley.");
2             document.write("\""+first_string +"\" contains "+
                             first_string.length + " characters.");
3             document.write("<br>\""+ next_string+"\" contains "+
                             next_string.length+" characters.<br>");
              document.write("<font size=-1><em>...not to imply that war is
                             equal to peace...<br>");
          </script>
          </body>
          </html>
```

**EXPLANATION**

1  Two strings are created, one the literal way (a string primitive) and the other with the constructor method (a *String* object).

2  The *length* property is applied to the first string. When the property is applied to a literal string, it is temporarily converted to an object, and then after the operation, it is reverted back to a string primitive.

3  The *length* property is applied to the second string, a *String* object. (It is just a co-incidence that both strings are of the same length.) (See Figure 9.21.)

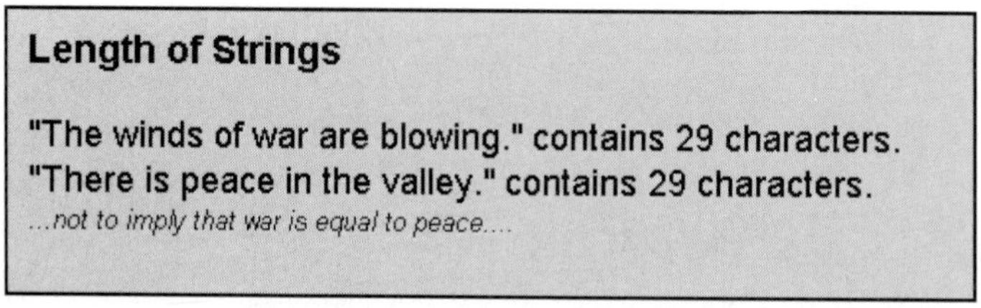

---

**Length of Strings**

"The winds of war are blowing." contains 29 characters.
"There is peace in the valley." contains 29 characters.
...not to imply that war is equal to peace....

**Figure 9.21**   Using the *String* object's *length* property. Output from Example 9.20.

**EXAMPLE** 9.21

```
<html><head><title>The Prototype Property</title>
<script language = "javascript">
// Customize String Functions
1       function ucLarge(){
            var str=this.bold().fontcolor("white").
               toUpperCase().fontsize("22");
            return( str);
        }
2       String.prototype.ucL=ucLarge;
</script>
</head>
<body bgcolor=black><center>
<script language="JavaScript">
3       var string="Watch Your Step!!";
4       document.write(string.ucL()+"<br>");
</script>
<img src="high_voltage.gif">
</body></html>
```

**EXPLANATION**

1   The *ucLarge()* function is defined. Its purpose is to generate and return an upper-case, bold, white font, with a point size of 22.

2   The *prototype* property allows you to customize an object by adding new properties and methods. The name of the customized method is *ucL*, which is the name of a new method that will be used by the *String* object. It is assigned the name (without parentheses) of the function *ucLarge()*, that performs the method's actions and returns a value.

3   A new string is created.

4   The prototyped method, *ucL()*, is applied to the *String* object, *str*. It will modify the string as shown in the output in Figure 9.22.

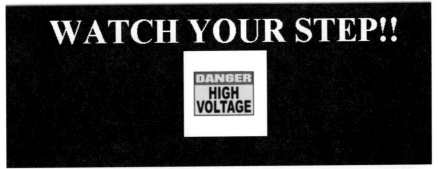

**Figure 9.22**   Using the *String* object's *prototype* property. Output from Example 9.21.

***String* Methods.**    There are two types of string methods: the string formatting meth-
ods that mimic the HTML tags they are named for, and the methods used to manipulate
a string such as finding a position in a string, replacing a string with another string, making a string uppercase or lowercase, and the like.

Table 9.9 lists methods that will affect the appearance of a *String* object by applying
HTML tags to the string, for example, to change its font size, font type, and color. Using
these methods is a convenient way to change the style of a string in a JavaScript program,
much easier than using quoted HTML opening and closing tags.

**Table 9.9**    *String* object (HTML) methods.

| Method | Formats as HTML |
|---|---|
| *String.anchor(Name)* | *<a name="Name">String</a>* |
| *String.big()* | *<big>String</big>* |
| *String.blink()* | *<blink>String</blink>* |
| *String.bold()* | *String* |
| *String.fixed()* | *<tt>String</tt>* |
| *String.fontcolor(color)* | *<font color="color">String</font>* <br> e.g., *<font color="blue">String</font>* |
| *String.fontsize(size)* | *<font size="size">String</font>* <br> e.g., *<font size="+2">String</font>* |
| *String.italics()* | *<i>String</i>* |
| *String.link(URL)* | *<a href="URL">String</a>* <br> e.g., *<a href="http://www.ellieq.com">String</a>* |
| *String.small()* | *<small>String</small>* |
| *String.strike()* | *<strike>String</strike>* (puts a line through the text) |
| *String.sub()* | *<sub>String</sub>* (creates a subscript) |
| *String.sup()* | *<sup>String</sup>* (creates a superscript) |

**EXAMPLE  9.22**

```
<html>
<head><title>String object</title>
</head>
<body bgcolor="yellow">
<font size="+1" face="arial">
<h2>Working with String Objects:</h2>
<script language="JavaScript">
1   var str1 = new String("Hello world!"); // Use a String constructor
2   var str2 = "It's a beautiful day today.";
    document.write(str1) + "<br>";
3   document.write(str1.fontcolor("blue")+"<br>");
4   document.write(str1.fontsize(8).fontcolor("red").
       bold()+"<br>");
5   document.write(str1.big()+ "<br>");
6   document.write("Good-bye, ".italics().bold().big() +
       str2 + "<br>");
</script>
</body></html>
```

**EXPLANATION**

1  A *String* object is created with the *String()* constructor.

2  A string primitive is created the literal way.

3  The *fontcolor()* method is used to change the color of the string to blue. This method emulates the HTML tag, *<font color="blue">*.

4  The *fontsize()*, *fontcolor()*, and *bold()* methods are used as properties of the string.

5, 6  The HTML method is concatenated to the string *"Good-bye, "* causing it to be displayed in italic, bold, big text. (See Figure 9.23.)

---

**Working with String Objects:**

Hello world!Hello world!

# Hello world!

Hello world!

*Good-bye,* It's a beautiful day today.

---

**Figure 9.23**  Properties of the *String* object are used to change its appearance and determine its size. Output from Example 9.22.

There are a number of methods (see Table 9.10) provided to manipulate a string.

**Table 9.10**  Methods for string manipulation.

| Method | What it Does |
|---|---|
| charAt(index) | Returns the character at a specified index position |
| charCodeAt(index) | Returns the Unicode encoding of the character at a specified index position |
| concat(string1, ..., stringn) | Concatenates string arguments to the string on which the method was invoked |
| fromCharCode(codes) | Creates a string from a comma-separated sequence of character codes |
| indexOf(substr, startpos) | Searches for first occurrence of substr starting at startpos and returns the startpos(index value) of substr |
| lastIndexOf(substr, startpos) | Searches for last occurrence of substr starting at startpos and returns the startpos (index value) of substr |
| replace(searchValue, replaceValue) | Replaces searchValue with replaceValue |
| search(regexp) | Searches for the regular expression and returns the index of where it was found |
| slice(startpos, endpos) | Returns string containing the part of the string from startpos to endpos |
| split(delimiter) | Splits a string into an array of words based on delimiter |
| substr(startpos, endpos) | Returns a subset of string starting at startpos up to, but not including, endpos |
| toLocaleLowerCase() | Returns a copy of the string converted to lowercase |
| toLocaleUpperCase() | Returns a copy of the string converted to uppercase |
| toLowerCase() | Converts all characters in a string to lowercase letters |
| toString() | Returns the same string as the source string |
| toUpperCase() | Converts all characters in a string to uppercase letters |
| valueOf | Returns the string value of the object |

**Methods That Find a Position in a String.**   A substring is a piece of an already existing string; thus *eat* is a substring of both *create* and *upbeat*, and *java* is a substring of *javascript*. When a user enters information, you want to see if a certain pattern of characters exist, such as the @ in an e-mail address or a zip code in an address. JavaScript provides a number of methods to assist you in finding substrings.

The *indexOf()* and the *lastIndexOf()* methods are used to find the first instance or the last instance of a substring within a larger string. They are both case sensitive. The first character in a string is at index value 0, just like array indices. If either of the methods finds the substring, it returns the position of the first letter in the substring. If either method can't find the pattern in the string, then a –1 is returned.

## EXAMPLE   9.23

```
        <html><head><title>Substrings</title>
        </head>
        <body bgcolor=lightgreen>
        <font face="arial" size="+1">
        Searching for an @ sign
        <script language="JavaScript">
1           var email_addr=prompt("What is your email address? ","");
2           while(email_addr.indexOf("@") == -1 ){
3               alert( "Invalid email address.");
                email_addr=prompt("What is your email address? ",""); }
            document.write("<br>OK.<br>");
        </script>
        </body></html>
```

## EXPLANATION

1   The user is prompted for his e-mail address and the input is assigned to a string called *email_addr*.

2   The loop expression uses the *indexOf()* String method to see if there is an @ symbol in the e-mail address. If there isn't, the *indexOf()* method returns –1 and the body of the loop is executed.

3   If the *indexOf()* method didn't find the @ substring, the alert box appears and the user is prompted again (see Figures 9.24 and 9.25). The loop terminates when the user enters an e-mail address containing an @ sign. Of course, this is just a simple test for validating an e-mail address; more elaborate methods of validation are discussed in Chapter 13, "Regular Expressions and Pattern Matching."

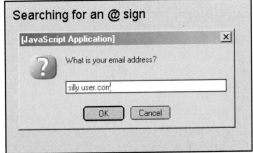

**Figure 9.24**   Using the *indexOf()* String method.

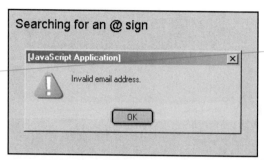

**Figure 9.25**  The user entered an e-mail address without the @ symbol.

**EXAMPLE** 9.24

```
<html>
<head><title>String Manipulation</title></head>
</head>
<body>
<h2>Working with String Manipulation Methods</h2>
<script language="JavaScript">
    function break_tag(){
        document.write("<br>");
    }
    document.write("<h3>");
1   var str1 = new String("The merry, merry month of June...");
    document.write("In the string:<em> "+ str1 );
2   document.write("</em> the first 'm' is at position " +
                    str1.indexOf("m"));
    break_tag();
3   document.write("The last 'm' is at position " +
                    str1.lastIndexOf("m"));
    break_tag();
4   document.write("<em>str1.substr(4,5)</em> returns<em> " +
                    str1.substr(4,5));
    break_tag();
    document.write(str1.toUpperCase());
    document.write("</h3>");
</script>
</body>
</html>
```

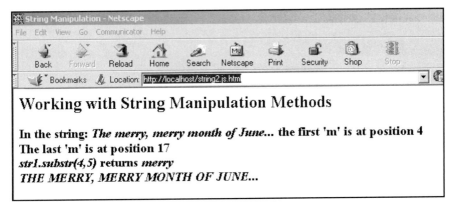

**Figure 9.26** Output from Example 9.24.

**Methods that Extract Substrings from a String.** You may have to do more than just find a substring within a string, you may need to extract that substring. For example, we found the @ in the e-mail address, now we may want to get just the user name or the server name or domain name. To do this, JavaScript provides methods such as *splice()*, *split()*, *charAt()*, *substr()*, and *substring()*.

**EXAMPLE 9.25**

```
      <html><head><title>Extracting Substrings</title>
      </head>
      <body bgcolor=lightgreen>
      <font face="arial" size="+1">
      Extracting substrings
      <font size="-1">
      <script language="JavaScript">
1         var straddr = "DanielSavage@dadserver.org";
          document.write("<br>His name is<em> " +
2             straddr.substr(0,6) + "</em>.<br>");
3         var namesarr = straddr.split("@" );
4         document.write( "The user name is<em> " + namesarr[0] +
                     "</em>.<br>");
5         document.write( "and the mail server is<em> " + namesarr[1] +
                     "</em>.<br>");
6         document.write( "The first character in the string is <em>" +
                     straddr.charAt(0)+ "</em>.<br>");
7         document.write( "and the last character in the string is <em>"
                     + straddr.charAt(straddr.length - 1)
                     + "</em>.<br>");
      </script>
      </body></html>
```

## EXPLANATION

1   A string is assigned an e-mail address.

2   The *substr()* starts at the first character at position 0, and yanks 6 characters from the starting position. The substring is *Daniel*.

3   The *split()* method creates an array, called *namesarr*, by splitting up a string into substrings based on some delimiter that marks where the string is split. This string is split using the @ sign as its delimiter.

4   The first element of the array, *namesarr[0]*, that is created by the *split()* method is *DanielSavage*, the user name portion of the e-mail address.

5   The second element of the array, *namesarr[1]*, that is created by the *split()* method is *dadserver.org*, the mail server and domain portion of the e-mail address.

6   The *charAt()* method returns the character found at a specified position within a string; in this example, position 0. Position 0 is the first character in the string, a letter *D*.

7   By giving the *charAt()* method the length of the string minus 1, the last character in the string is extracted, a letter g. (See Figure 9.27.)

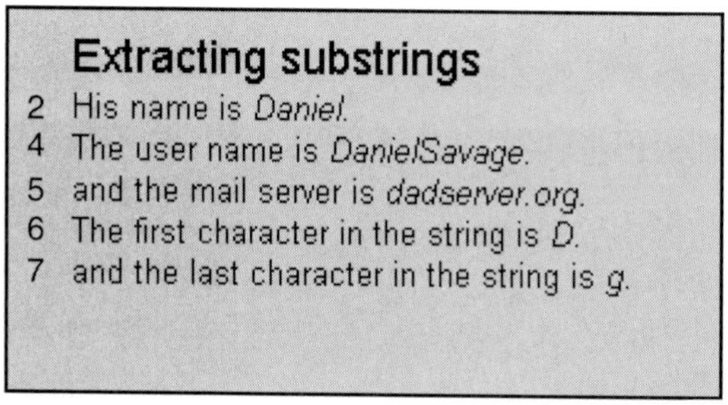

---

**Extracting substrings**

2   His name is *Daniel.*
4   The user name is *DanielSavage.*
5   and the mail server is *dadserver.org.*
6   The first character in the string is *D.*
7   and the last character in the string is *g.*

**Figure 9.27**   The *charAt()*, *split()*, and *substr()* methods. Output from Example 9.25.

**Search and Replace Methods.**   In word processing software you'll always find some mechanism to search for patterns in strings and to replace one string with another. JavaScript provides methods to do the same thing, using the *String* object. The *search()* method searches for a substring and returns the position where the substring is found first. The *match()* method searches a string for substrings and returns an array containing all the matches it found. The *replace()* method searches for a substring and replaces it with a new string. These methods are discussed again in Chapter 13, "Regular Expressions and Pattern Matching," in more detail.

EXAMPLE 9.26

```
      <html><head><title>Search and Replace</title>
      </head>
      <body bgcolor=lightgreen>
      <font face="arial" size="+1">
      Search and Replace Methods<br>
      <font size="-1">
      <script language="JavaScript">
1        var straddr = "DanielSavage@dadserver.org";
         document.write( "The original string is "+ straddr + "<br>");
         document.write( "The new string is "+
2        straddr.replace("Daniel","Jake")+"<br>");
3        var index=straddr.search("dad");
         document.write("The search() method found \"dad\" at
                        position "+ index +"<br>");
4        var mysubstr=straddr.substr(index,3);
         document.write("After replacing \"dad\" with \"POP\" <br>");
5        document.write(straddr.replace(mysubstr,"POP")+"<br>");
      </script>
      </body></html>
```

EXPLANATION

1    An e-mail address is assigned to the string variable *straddr*.

2    The *replace()* method takes two arguments, the search string and the replacement string. If the substring *Daniel* is found, it is replaced with *Jake*.

3    The *search()* method takes a subtring as its argument and returns the first position where a substring is found in a string. In this example the substring *dad* is searched for in the string *DanielSavage@dadserver.org* and is found at position 13.

4    The *substr()* method returns the substring found at position 13, 3 in the string, *DanielSavage@dadserver.org*: *dad*.

5    The substring *dad* is replaced with *POP* in the string. (See Figure 9.28.)

**Search and Replace Methods**
The original string is DanielSavage@dadserver.org
The new string is JakeSavage@dadserver.org
The search() method found "dad" at position 13
After replacing "dad" with "POP"
DanielSavage@POPserver.org

**Figure 9.28** The *search()* and *replace() String* methods. Output from Example 9.26.

## 9.6.2  The *Number* Object

Now that we've travelled this far in JavaScript, have you wondered how to format a floating-point number when you display it, as you can with the *printf* function in C or Perl? Well, the *Number* object, like the *String* object, gives you properties and methods to handle and customize numeric data. The *Number* object is a wrapper for the primitive numeric values (see Chapter 2, "Script Setup"), which means you can use a primitive number type or an object number type and JavaScript manages the conversion back and forth as necessary. The *Number* object was introduced in JavaScript 1.1.

The *Number()* constructor takes a numeric value as its argument. If used as a function, without the *new* operator, the argument is converted to a primitive numeric value, and that number is returned; if it fails, *NaN* is returned. The *Number* object has a number of properties and methods, as listed in Tables 9.11 and 9.12.

**FORMAT**

```
var number = new Number(numeric value);
var number = Number(numeric value);
```

Example:

```
var n = new Number(65.7);
```

**Table 9.11**  The *Number* object's properties.

| Property | What It Describes |
|---|---|
| MAX_VALUE | The largest representable number, 1.7976931348623157e+308 |
| MIN_VALUE | The smallest representable number, 5e–324 |
| NaN | Not-a-number value |
| NEGATIVE_INFINITY | Negative infinite value; returned on overflow |
| POSITIVE_INFINITY | Infinite value; returned on overflow |
| prototype | Used to customize the *Number* object by adding new properties and methods |

**Table 9.12**  The *Number* object's methods.

| Method | What It Does |
|---|---|
| *toString()* | Converts a number to a string using a specified base (radix) |
| *toLocaleString()* | Converts a number to a string using local number conventions |
| *toFixed()*[a] | Converts a number to a string with a specified number of places after the decimal point |
| *toExponential()* | Converts a number to a string using exponential notation and a specified number of places after the decimal point |
| *toPrecision()* | Converts a number to a string in either exponential or fixed notation containing the specified number of places after the decimal point |

a.  These methods are part of the ECMA 3.0, IE5.5+, Netscape 6.0+.

**Using Number Constants and Different Bases.**  The constants *MAX_VALUE*, *MIN_VALUE*, *NEGATIVE_INFINITY*, *POSITIVE_INFINITY*, and *NaN*, are properties of the *Number()* function, but are not used with instances of the *Number* object; thus, *var huge = Number.MAX_VALUE* is valid, but *huge.MAX_VALUE* is not. *NaN* is a special value that is returned when some mathematical operation results in a value that is not a number.

The methods provided to the *Number* object manipulate instances of number objects. For example, to convert numbers to strings representing different bases, the *toString()* method manipulates a number, either primitive or object. See Example 9.27.

**EXAMPLE**  9.27

```
<html>
<head><title>Number Contants</title>
</head>
<body bgcolor=orange><font color="black" size="+1">
<h2>
Constants
</h2>
<script language="JavaScript">
1    var largest = Number.MAX_VALUE;
2    var smallest = Number.MIN_VALUE;
3    var num1 = 20;    // A primitive numeric value
4    var num2 = new Number(13);    // Creating a Number object
     document.write("<b>The largest number is " + largest+ "<br>");
     document.write("The smallest number is "+ smallest + "<br>");
```

**EXAMPLE   9.27 (CONTINUED)**

```
5        document.write("The number as a string (base 2): "+
                  num1.toString(2));
6        document.write("<br>The number as a string (base 8): "+
                  num2.toString(8));
7        document.write("<br>The square root of -25 is: "+
                  Math.sqrt(-25) + "<br>");
      </script>
      </body>
      </html>
```

**EXPLANATION**

1    The constant *MAX_VALUE* is a property of the *Number()* function. This constant cannot be used with an instance of a *Number* object.

2    The constant *MIN_VALUE* is a property of the *Number()* function.

3    A number is assigned to the variable called *num1*.

4    A new *Number* object is created with the *Number()* constructor and assigned to *num2*.

5    The number is converted to a string represented in binary, base 2.

6    The number is converted to a string represented in octal, base 8.

7    The square root of a negative number is illegal. JavaScript returns *NaN*, not a number, when this calculation is attempted. (See Figure 9.29.)

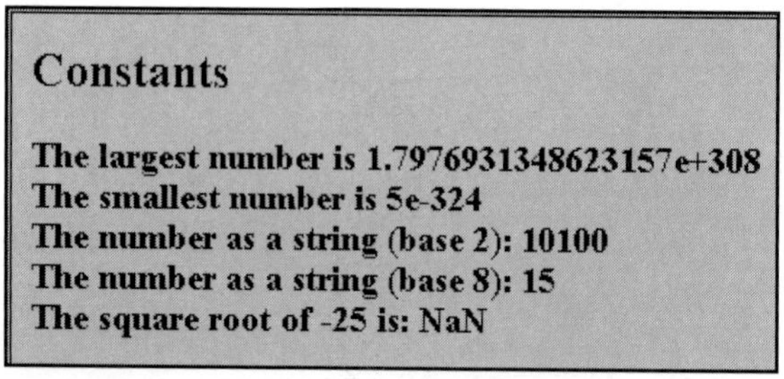

---

**Constants**

The largest number is 1.7976931348623157e+308
The smallest number is 5e-324
The number as a string (base 2): 10100
The number as a string (base 8): 15
The square root of -25 is: NaN

---

**Figure 9.29**    Constants, number conversion, and *NaN*. Output from Example 9.27.

**Formatting Numbers.**    To convert floating-point numbers to a string with a specified number of significant digits, JavaScript provides the *toFixed()* and *toExponential()* methods.

EXAMPLE   9.28

```
        <html>
        <head><title>Number Object</title>
        </head>
        <body bgcolor=orange><font color="black" size="+1">
        <h2>
        Formatting Numbers
        </h2>
        <script language="JavaScript">
1           var n = new Number(22.425456);
2           document.write("<b>The unformatted number is " + n + "<br>");
3           document.write("The formatted number is "+ n.toFixed(2) +
                         "<br>");
4           document.write("The formatted number is "+ n.toFixed(3) +
                         "<br>");
        </script>
        </body>
        </html>
```

**EXPLANATION**

1    A new *Number* object is created and assigned to the variable *n*.

2    The value of the number is displayed as a large floating-point number, 22.425456.

3    The *Number* object's *toFixed()* method gets an argument of 2. This fixes the decimal point two places to the right of the decimal point and rounds up if necessary. The new value is 22.43.

4    This time the *toFixed()* method will format the number with three numbers to the right of the decimal point. (See Figure 9.30.)

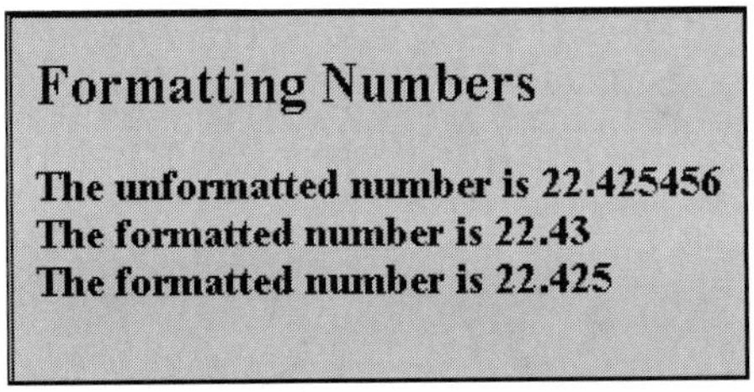

**Formatting Numbers**

The unformatted number is 22.425456
The formatted number is 22.43
The formatted number is 22.425

**Figure 9.30**   Using the *toFixed()* *Number* method. Output from Example 9.28.

### 9.6.3   The *Boolean* Object

The *Boolean* object was included in JavaScript 1.1. It is used to convert a non-Boolean value to a Boolean value, either *true* or *false*. There is one property, the *prototype* property, and one method, the *toString()* method, which converts a Boolean value to a string; thus, *true* is converted to *"true"* and *false* is converted to *"false"*.

## FORMAT

```
var object = new Boolean(value);
```

Example:

```
var b1 = new Boolean(5);
var b2 = new Boolean(null);
```

## EXAMPLE 9.29

```
        <html><head><title>Boolean Object</title>
        </head>
        <body bgcolor=aqua>
        <font face="arial" size="+1"><b>
        The Boolean Object<br>
        <font size="-1">
        <script language="JavaScript">
1           var bool1= new Boolean( 0);
            var bool2 = new Boolean(1);
            var bool3 = new Boolean("");
            var bool4 = new Boolean(null);
            var bool5 = new Boolean(NaN);
2       document.write("The value 0 is boolean "+ bool1 +"<br>");
        document.write("The value 1 is boolean "+ bool2 +"<br>");
        document.write("The value of the empty string is boolean "+
                    bool3+ "<br>");
        document.write("The value of null is boolean "+ bool4+ "<br>");
        document.write("The value of NaN is boolean "+ bool5 +"<br>");
        </script>
        </body></html>
```

## EXPLANATION

1   The argument passed to the *Boolean* object constructor is the initial value of the object, either *true* or *false*. If the initial value is *0*, the empty string *""*, *NaN*, or *null*, the result is *false*; otherwise, the result is *true*.

2   The *Boolean* object's values are displayed as either *true* or *false*. (See Figure 9.31.)

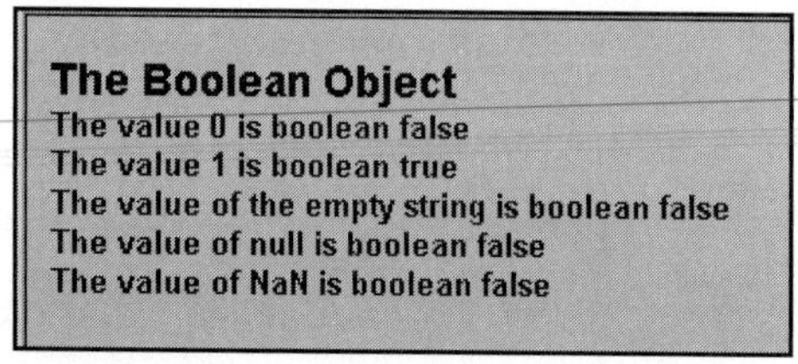

---

**The Boolean Object**
The value 0 is boolean false
The value 1 is boolean true
The value of the empty string is boolean false
The value of null is boolean false
The value of NaN is boolean false

**Figure 9.31**   *True* or *False*? Output from Example 9.29.

### 9.6.4  The *Function* Object

The *Function* object (added in JavaScript 1.1) lets you define a function as an object dynamically. It allows a string to be defined at runtime and then compiled as a function. You can use the *Function()* constructor to create a variable that contains the function. Since the function has no name, it is often called an anonymous function and its arguments are passed as comma-separated strings. The last argument is the body of statements that will be executed when the function is called. If the *Function()* constructor does not require arguments, then the body of statements, treated as a string, will be passed to the *Function()* constructor to define what the function is to do. Since functions are objects, they also have properties (see Table 9.13) and methods (see Table 9.14).

Function objects are evaluated each time they are used, causing them to be slower in execution than normal JavaScript functions.

**Table 9.13**   Properties of the *Function* object.

| Property | What It Does |
|----------|--------------|
| *length* | Returns the number of arguments that are expected to be passed (read only) |
| *prototype* | Allows the object to be customized by adding new properties and methods |

**Table 9.14**   Methods of the *Function* object.

| Property | What It Does |
|----------|--------------|
| *apply()** | Allows you to apply a method from one function to another |
| *call()* | Allows you to call a method from another object |

\* Supported on versions Netscape 4.06+ and Internet Explorer 5.5+.

**FORMAT**

```
var nameOfFunction = new Function (arguments, statements_as_string: }
```

**Example Function Definition:**

```
var addemUp = new Function ( "a", "b", "return a + b;" );
```

**Example Function Call:**

```
document.write(addemUp (10, 5));
```

**EXAMPLE** 9.30

```
        <html><head><title>Function Object</title>
        </head>
        <body bgcolor=lightgreen>
        <font face="arial" size="+1">
        <center>
        Anonymous Functions and the Function Constructor<p>
        <script language="JavaScript">
1           var sum = new Function("a","b", "return a + b; ");
2           window.onload =  new Function ( "document.bgColor='yellow';");
3           document.write( "The sum is " + sum(5,10)+ "<br>");
            document.write( "The background color is yellow<br>");
        </script>
        </body></html>
```

**EXPLANATION**

1   A variable called *sum* is a *Function* object, created by the *Function()* constructor. It has two arguments, *"a"* and *"b"*. The function statements are the last string in the list. These statements will be executed when the function is called.

2   This *Function()* constructor only has one argument, the statement that will be executed when the function is called. Since the function is assigned to the *onload* event method for the *window* object, it will act as an event handler and cause the background color to be yellow when the document has finished loading.

3   The *sum* function is called with two arguments. (See Figure 9.32.)

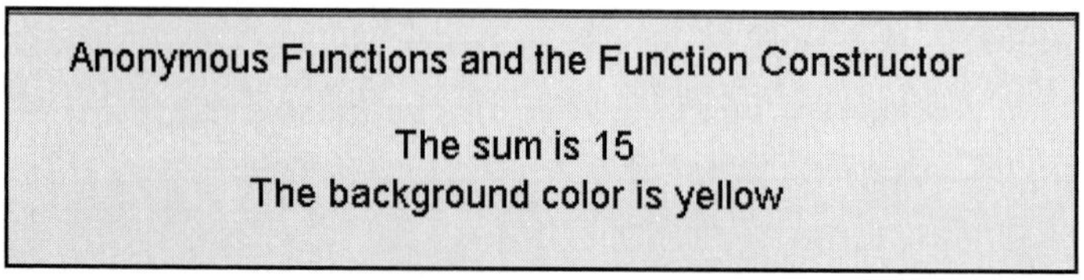

---

**Anonymous Functions and the Function Constructor**

**The sum is 15**
**The background color is yellow**

---

**Figure 9.32**   Output from Example 9.30.

### 9.6.5 The *with* Keyword Revisited

In Chapter 8, we used the *with* keyword with user-defined objects to make it easier to manipulate the object properties. Recall that any time you reference the object within the block following the keyword, you can use properties and methods without the object name. This saves a lot of typing and reduces the chances of spelling errors, especially when the properties have long names. The *String* object is used in the following example to demonstrate how *with* is used.

**EXAMPLE 9.31**

```
<html><head><title>The with Keyword</title>
</head>
<body>
<h2>Using the <em>with</em> keyword</h2>
<p>
<h3>
<script language="JavaScript">
    var yourname=prompt("What is your name? ","");
    // Create a string object
    with(yourname){
        document.write("Welcome " + yourname + " to our planet!!<br>");
        document.write("Your name is " + length + " characters in
                       length.<br>");
        document.write("Your name in uppercase: " + toUpperCase() +
                       ".<br>");
        document.write("Your name in lowercase:  " + toLowerCase() +
                       ".<br>");
    }
</script>
</h3>
</body></html>
```

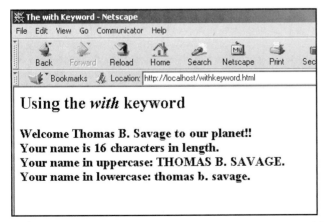

**Figure 9.33** Using the *with* keyword to reference an object.

## EXERCISES

1. Create an array of five animals. Use a *for* loop to display the values stored there. Now add two more animals to the end of the array and sort the array. (Use Java-Script's built-in array methods.) Display the sorted array.

2. Create an associative array called *colors*. Each element of the array is a string representing the color, e.g., *red* or *blue*. Use the *for/in* loop to view each element of the array with a color of the font the same color as the value of the array element being displayed.

3. Create a function that will return the current month by its full name. Use the *Date* object to get the current month. Months are returned as 0 for January, 1 for February, 2 for March, etc. Output should resemble:

   ```
   The current month is January.
   ```

   Hint: You can create an array, starting at index 0, and assign a month value to it; e.g., *month[0]="January"* or use a *switch* statement, e.g., *case 0: return "January"*.

4. An invoice is due and payable in 90 days. Write a function that will display that date.

5. How many days until your birthday? Write a function to calculate it.

6. To calculate the balance on a loan, the following formula is used:

   $$PV = PMT * ( 1 - (1 + IR )^{-NP}) / IR$$

   *PV* is the present value of the loan; *PMT* is the regular monthly payment of the loan; *IR* is the loan's interest rate; *NP* is the number of payments remaining. Write a JavaScript statement to represent this formula.

7. Using the formula to calculate the loan balance from the last exercise, write a function that will calculate the principle balance left on a loan where the monthly payments are $600, the annual interest rate is 5.5%, and there are 9 years remaining on the loan. Use the *toFixed() Number* method to format the output.

8. Apply the *ceil()*, *floor()*, and *round()* methods to the number 125.5567 and display the results.

9. Create an array of 10 fortune cookies that will be randomly displayed each time the user reloads the page.

10. Create a string prototype that can be used to create an italic, Verdana font, point size 26.

11. Calculate the circumferance of a circle using the *Math* object.

12. Write a JavaScript program that uses the *Array* and *Math* objects. Create an array of 5 sayings, for example: *"A stitch in time saves 9"*, or *"Too many cooks spoil the broth"*. Each time the Web page is visited, print a random saying.

13. a. Use the *Date* object to print today's date in this format:

    ```
    Today is Friday, June 16, 2003.
    ```

    b. Calculate and display the number of days until your next birthday.
    c. Create a prototype for the *Date* object that will print the months starting at 1 instead of 0.

14. a. Create a *String* object containing *"Jose lived in San Jose for many years."*
    b. Find the index for the second *Jose*.
    c. Get the substring *ear* from *years*.
    d. Display the string in a blue, italic font, point size 12, all uppercase.

# chapter
# 10

# The Browser Objects: Navigator, Windows, and Frames

## 10.1 JavaScript and the Browser Object Model

JavaScript programs are associated with a browser window and the document displayed in the window. The window is a browser object and the document is an HTML object. In the browser object model, sometimes called BOM, the window is at the top of the tree, and below it are objects: *window, navigator, frames[], document, history, location,* and *screen.* See Figure 10.1.

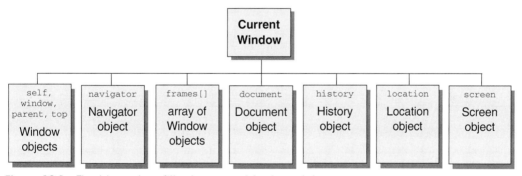

**Figure 10.1**  The hierarchy of the browser object model.

If you are writing a JavaScript program that needs to manipulate the window, then you would use the *window* object and properties and methods associated with it. For example, the *status* property of the *window* object is used when you want to display text in the status bar, and the window's *alert* method allows you to send a message to a dialog box.

The document object model refers to the HTML document and all the elements and attributes associated with it. Since your Web page is so closely linked to HTML (or XML), JavaScript uses the document object model, also called DOM, to access the HTML elements and attributes within a page. The document is the root of this model.

Each HTML element is assigned to an object: there are image objects, form objects, link objects, and so on (see Figure 10.2). (See Chapter 11, "The Document Objects," for more on document objects and the document object model.)

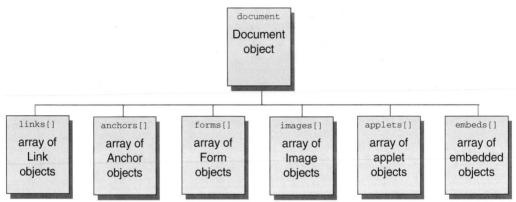

**Figure 10.2**   The hierarchy of the document object model.

By combining the browser and document object models, JavaScript allows you to manipulate all of the elements in a page as objects, from the window down the hierarchy, as shown in Figure 10.3.

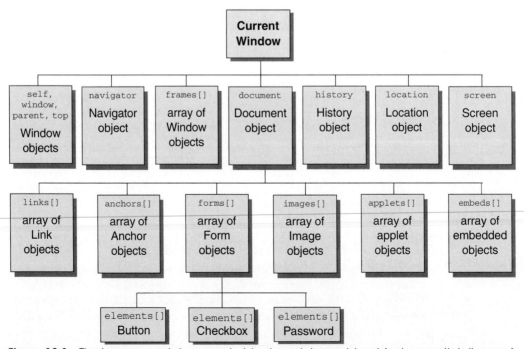

**Figure 10.3**   The browser and document object models combined (only a partial diagram).

### 10.1.1 Working with the *navigator* Object

The *navigator* object contains properties and methods that describe the browser. Netscape Navigator and Internet Explorer support the *navigator* object, but some browsers do not.

The *navigator* object can be used for platform-specific checking to determine the version of the browser being used, whether Java is enabled, what plug-ins are available, and so on.

Table 10.1 lists the properties that describe the *navigator* object.

**Table 10.1** Properties of the *navigator* object.

| *Property* | *What It Describes* |
|---|---|
| *appCodeName* | Code name for the browser |
| *appName* | Name of the browser |
| *appVersion* | Version of the browser |
| *mimeTypes* | An array of MIME types supported by the browser |
| *platform* | The operating system where the browser resides |
| *userAgent* | HTTP user-agent header sent from the browser to the server |

**EXAMPLE 10.1**

```
        <html>
        <head><title>Navigator Object</title></head>
        <body>
1       <script language="JavaScript">
            document.write("<font size=+1><b>\
            The properties of the \"navigator\" object are:</b><br>");
2           for(var property in navigator){
3               document.write(property + "<br>");
            }
        </script>
        </body>
        </html>
```

**EXPLANATION**

1  The JavaScript program starts here.

2  The special *for* loop assigns, in turn, each property of the *navigator* object to the variable called *property*.

3  Each property of the *navigator* object is displayed in the browser window. See Figures 10.4 and 10.5.

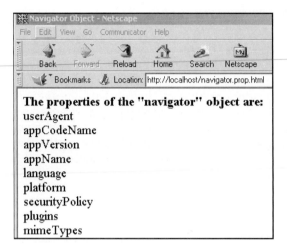

**Figure 10.4**    In Netscape Navigator, the browser window displaying the properties of the *navigator* object. Output from Example 10.1.

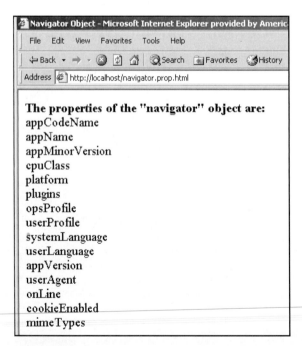

**Figure 10.5**    In Internet Explorer, the browser window displaying the properties of the *navigator* object. Output from Example 10.1.

**What Is Your Browser's Name? Version Number?** Browsers support different features, properties, and methods; for example, Internet Explorer may display a page in a slightly different form than Netscape Navigator, one version of Netscape might support a feature not supported by an older version, a version of IE might not support a feature supported by Netscape, and so on. Then if you take into consideration all the other browsers and their unique features, it can be tricky to please all of the browsers all of the time or even some of the browsers all of the time. Browser detection allows you to check for specific browser names, versions, whether cookies are enabled, what types of plug-ins are loaded, and so on. The *navigator* object contains a number of properties that allow you to detect information about the user's browser so you can customize your Web page in a way that is transparent to the user.

**What Is a Browser Sniffer?** A browser sniffer is a program that makes browser detection easy. Many Web sites provide free browser sniffers that determine the types of different browsers. If you want to know more about your browser, go to *http://www.perlscriptsjavascripts.com/js/browser_sniffer.html*.

**EXAMPLE 10.2**

```
    <html><head>
    <title>The Navigator Object</title></head>
    <body>
    <h2>About The Browser</h2>
    <script language="JavaScript">
1       var BrowserName= navigator.appName;
2       var BrowserVersion = navigator.appVersion;
3       var BrowserAgent= navigator.userAgent;
        var platform=navigator.platform;
        document.write("<font size='+1'>");
4       document.write("<b>The Browser's name  is:</b> " +
                    BrowserName + "<br>");
5       document.write("<b>The Browser version is:</b> " +
                    BrowserVersion + "<br>");
6       document.write("<b>The Browser's \"user agent\" is:</b> " +
                    BrowserAgent + "<br>");
7       document.write("<b>The Browser's platform is:</b> " +
                    platform + "<br>");
        document.write("</font>");
    </script>
    </body>
    </html>
```

### EXPLANATION

1   The value of the *navigator* object's *appName* property is assigned to variable *BrowserName*. The value is the name of the browser.

2   The value of the *navigator* object's *appVersion* property is assigned to variable *BrowserVersion*. The value is the current version of the browser.

3   The value of the *navigator* object's *userAgent* property is assigned to variable *BrowserAgent*. The value is sent from the browser to the server in the HTTP header as the user agent.

4   The common name of the browser, *Netscape* or *Microsoft Internet Explorer*, is displayed.

5   The version number of the browser is displayed.

6   User-agent strings, as shown in this *navigator* property,  are one of many environmental variables used to identify a program to HTTP or mail and news servers, for usage tracking and other purposes (*HTTP_USER_AGENT*). User agents can be browsers, spiders, robots, crawlers ,and the like. For a database of user agents, see *http://www.icehousedesigns.com/useragents/*. For a complete descripton of each part of the user-agent string see *http://www.mozilla.org/build/user-agent-strings.html*.

7   The operating system is in the navigator's *platform* property. The Windows operating system is the platform on which this browser is currently running. See Figures 10.6 and 10.7 for the complete output.

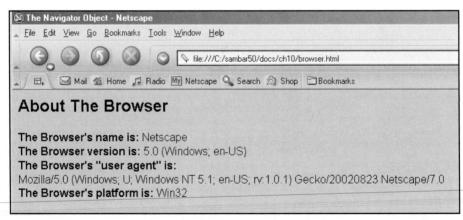

**Figure 10.6**   The output from Example 10.2 shown in Netscape Navigator.

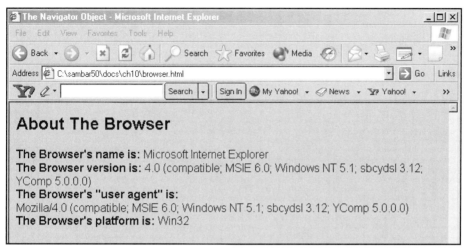

**Figure 10.7**   The output from Example 10.2 shown in Internet Explorer.

**Detecting Plug-Ins.**   Plug-ins are special software programs that can be downloaded to add the ability to listen to audio, watch videos and movie clips, display animation, and create special image viewing files. Some examples of plug-ins are Macromedia Shockwave or Flash player, Adobe Acrobat Reader, and RealNetworks RealPlayer. Plug-ins can be platform dependent and their MIME types may vary as well. If you are using Netscape, go to the Help menu and select About Plug-ins to get more information about the plug-ins supported on your client.

The *plugins[]* array of the *navigator* object (starting with Navigator 3) contains a complete list of installed plug-ins and can be numerically indexed to see all plug-ins installed for this browser, specifically Netscape. Each element of the *plugins[]* array represents a *plugin* object. The properties of the *plugin* object are shown in Table 10.2. When you use the HTML *<embed>* tag in a document, you are creating a *plugin* object. Each instance of the *<embed>* tag creates another object. See "The embeds Object" on page 346 in Chapter 11, and the discussion on page 210 of the *<object>* tag for embedding objects.

**Table 10.2**   Properties of the *plugin* object.

| Property | What It Describes |
|---|---|
| *description* | A description of the plug-in |
| *filename* | The disk filename of the plug-in |
| *length* | The number of elements in the *plugins[]* array's *mimeType* object; e.g., *navigator.plugins["Shockwave"].length* |
| *name* | The name of the plug-in |

**EXAMPLE** 10.3

```
        <html><head><title>Plugin Detection</title></head>
        <script language="JavaScript">
1           function pluginDetector(type) {
2               if (navigator.plugins[type]){
                    return true;
                }
                else{
                    return false;
                }
            }
        <body bgcolor="magenta">
        <font face="verdana">
        <script language="JavaScript">
3           var plugin = prompt("What plugin do you want to check
                                for?","");
4           if (pluginDetector(plugin)){      // Does the browser
                                               // support plug-ins?
                alert("You have the plugin "+ plugin);
            }
            else{
                alert("Don't have the plugin");
            }
        </script>
        </body></html>
```

**EXPLANATION**

1   A JavaScript function, called *pluginDetector()*, is defined. It takes one parameter, the name for a type of plug-in.

2   If the plug-in is installed, the function will return true; otherwise false.

3   The user is asked to input the name of a plug-in he would like to check for. See Figure 10.8.

4   If the *pluginDectector()* function returns true, the alert message will report that the user's browser supports the named plug-in. See Figure 10.9.

**Figure 10.8**
Checking for a Netscape
plug-in called Shockwave Flash.

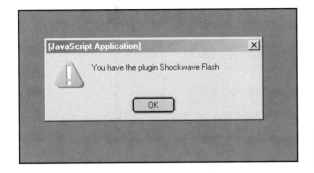

**Figure 10.9**
The plug-in is installed.

## EXAMPLE 10.4

```
        <html><head><title>Plugin Detection</title>
        </head><body bgcolor="lightgreen">
        <font face="arial" size="+1">
        <h2>Installed Plugins (Netscape)</h2>
        <script language="JavaScript">
1       for ( var i = 0;i < navigator.plugins.length; i++){
2       document.write ("<br>"+navigator.plugins[i].name+"<br>");
3           if(navigator.plugins[i].description){
                document.write ("<font size='-1'>"+
4               navigator.plugins[i].description+
                "<font size='+1'<br>");
            }
        }
        </script>
        </body></html>
```

## EXPLANATION

1   The *plugins[]* array consists of a list of plug-ins that have been installed in this browser. The *for* loop is used to go through the array, one by one, listing each plug-in. The *length* property specifies the number of elements in the *plugins[]* array. If using IE for Windows, then you will need to use the HTML *<object>* tag and identify a class ID.
    (See *http://msdn.microsoft.com/library/default.asp?url=/workshop/components/activex/activex_ovw_entry.asp* for a tutorial on ActiveX.)

2   The *name* property specifies the actual name of the plug-in.

3   The *description* property gives more detail about what the plug-in does. If it is not null, the block is entered.

4   A description of the plug-in is displayed, as shown in Figure 10.10.

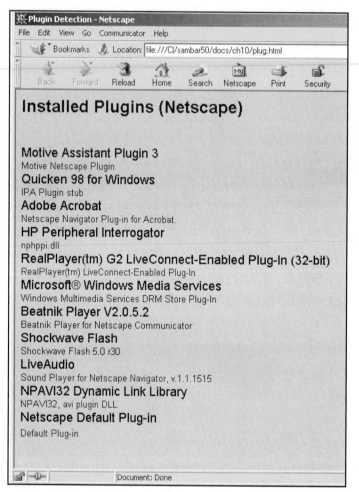

**Figure 10.10**   Netscape plug-ins.

**What Is ActiveX?**    Athough IE 4 defines the *plugins[]* array, it is always empty because Internet Explorer for Windows versions 5.5 SP2 and 6.0 no longer support Netscape-style plug-ins. Instead of plug-ins, Microsoft has something called ActiveX controls.

IE for Windows uses ActiveX controls instead of Netscape plug-ins or Java applets. ActiveX controls are used as a means to embed objects or components into a Web page. Online spreadsheets, word processors, patches, and timers are examples of such components. The plug-ins we describe here are ActiveX controls and can be downloaded from vendor sites on the Internet. You can add ActiveX controls to your Web pages by using the standard HTML *<object>* tag. The *<object>* tag takes a set of parameters that specify which data the control should use and define its appearance and behavior.

**EXAMPLE  10.5**

```
              <html><head>A Sample of ActiveX Control
              <title>ActiveX Example</title></head>
              <body>
      1       <object id="realaudio1" width=0 height=0
      2       classid="clsid:CFCDAA03-8BE4-11CF-B84B-0020AFBBCCFA">
      3       <param name="_ExtentX" value="0">
              <param name="_ExtentY" value="0">
              <param name="AUTOSTART" value="0">
              <param name="NOLABELS" value="0">
      4       </object>
              </body>
```

**EXPLANATION**

1   The ActiveX control is found in the *<body>* of the HTML document. It starts with the *<object>* tag to represent the ActiveX control. The ID contains information about the type of control; in this example, the ID is *RealAudio1*.

2   Then *classid* is assigned *clsid*, which gives the location of the control: in CFCDAA03-8BE4-11CF-B84B-0020AFBBCCFA.

3   The parameters are used to control the appearance and functionality of the control.

4   The ActiveX control is closed with the *</object>* tag.
    (See *http://msdn.microsoft.com/library/default.asp?url=/workshop/ components/activex/activex_ovw_entry.asp* for a tutorial on ActiveX.)

**What Are MIME Types?**   MIME stands for Multi-purpose Internet mail extensions.[1] It is a standard format for sending mail messages across the Internet. Now it is used to exchange all kinds of file types across the Internet, such as audio, video, and image files. All browsers have a list of MIME types. JavaScript 1.1 implemented the *mimeType* object (see Table 10.3). These objects are predefined JavaScript objects that allow you to access the *mimeTypes[]* array, a property of both the *navigator* object and the *plugin* object. (Note: The *mimeTypes[]* array will not produce output in IE.)

   *audio/x-pn-realaudio-plugin* is an example of a MIME type for RealPlayer G2 LiveConnect-Enabled Plug-In.

---

1. Available with NN3+ and IE5+ on the Mac, but not on Windows IE.

**Table 10.3**  Properties of the *mimeType* object.

| Property | What It Describes |
|---|---|
| *description* | A description of the MIME type |
| *enabledPlugin* | A reference to the *plugin* object for this MIME type |
| *suffixes* | A string of filename extensions allowed for this MIME type; e.g., jpeg, jpg, jpe, jfif, pjpeg, pjp object; e.g., *navigator.plugins["Shockwave"].length* |
| *type* | The name of the MIME type; e.g., *image/jpeg* |

---

**EXAMPLE 10.6**

```
<html>
<head><title>Mime Detection</title>
</head><body bgcolor="lightgreen">
<font face="arial">
<h2><u>Mime Types (Netscape)</u></h2>
<b>
<script language="JavaScript">
    for ( var i=0;i < navigator.mimeTypes.length;  i++){
1       if(navigator.mimeTypes[i].enabledPlugin != null){
            document.write ("<br></em><font size='+2'>"+
2           navigator.mimeTypes[i].type+"<br>");
            document.write("<font size='+1'>
            Enabled Plugin Name: <em>"+
3           navigator.mimeTypes[i].enabledPlugin.name+"<br>");
            document.write("</em>Description: "+ "<em>"+
4           navigator.mimeTypes[i].description+
            "<br></em>Suffixes: "+ "<em>"+
5           navigator.mimeTypes[i].suffixes+"<br>");
            }
    }
</script>
</body></html>
```

**EXPLANATION**

1   If the MIME type for a plug-in is not null, the information about it is printed.

2   This is the MIME type of the plug-in, such as *application/x-mplayer2* or *application/x-shockwave-flash.*

3   This is the enabled plug-in referred to by this MIME type.

4   The MIME type is described; such as Acrobat(*.pdf) or Network Interface Plugin (*.nip).

5   The suffixes are the filename extensions that this MIME type supports, such as .rpm, .wav, .pdf, and so on. Partial output is shown in Figure 10.11.

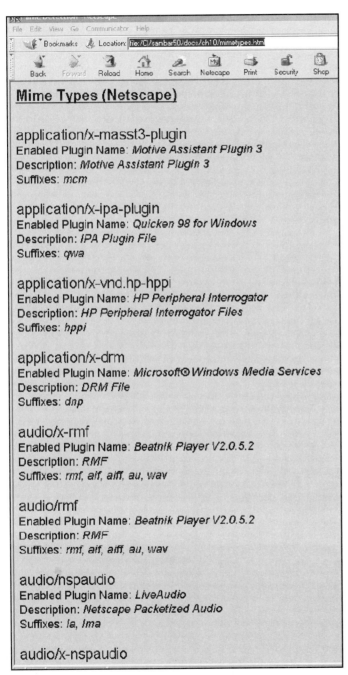

**Figure 10.11** MIME types. Output from Example 10.6 (partial list).

## 10.1.2   Working with the *window* Object

The *window* object is where all the action happens in a browser. It's at the top of the Java-Script hierarchy, and is automatically defined for each window that you open, as represented in Figure 10.12. When you start up your browser, you may stay in the current window until you exit the browser, or you may have any number of windows open at the same time. Within each window you browse the Internet, read e-mail, search for cheap airline tickets, and buy a new book. Each new page you bring up is a document within the current window. The window is often partitioned into independent display areas, called frames, which are windows within windows. (Frames are discussed in "Working with Frames" on page 231.)

**Figure 10.12**   Any number of windows, each with assorted objects.

The *window* object comes with a number of properties and methods. Since it is the basis of all objects, the name of the *window* object can be excluded when applying methods to it; for example, it is not necessary to specify *window.alert("Watch out!")* or *window.document.write("OK")*. You simply use *alert("Watch out!")* or *document.write("OK")*.

When a user clicks on a button or rolls the mouse over a link, an event occurs which often effects the behavior of a window. Such user-intiated events are discussed in Chapter 12, " Handling Events."

**The *window* Object's Properties and Methods.**   The *window* object has a number of properties, which are also objects in their own right. Table 10.4 lists those properties and how they describe the attributes of the window.

**Table 10.4**   Properties of the *window* object.

| *Property* | *What It Describes* |
|---|---|
| *closed* | True if the window is closed |
| *defaultStatus* | The default status message displayed in the status bar at the bottom of the window |
| *document* | The document object that is currently displayed in the window |
| *frames* | An array of frame objects within the window |
| *history* | The *history* object containing the URLs last loaded into the window |
| *length* | The number of frames within the window |
| *location* | The URL of the current window |
| *name* | The name of the window |
| *offscreenBuffering* | Used to draw new window content and then copy it over existing content when complete; Controls screen updates |
| *opener* | The window that opened the current window |
| *parent* | Indicates a window that contains another window (used with frames) |
| *screen* | Displays information about the screen, e.g., height, width (in pixels)[a] |
| *self* | Refers to the current window |
| *status* | Specifies a temporary message in the status bar, resulting user interaction |
| *top* | The topmost window containing a particular window (used with frames) |
| *window* | Identifies the current window being referenced |

a.   A new property of the window object, version 4 and above of Netscape and Internet Explorer.

The *window* object also has a number of methods that define its behavior, such as how to open, close, scroll, and clear a window. They are listed in Table 10.5.

**Table 10.5**  Methods of the *window* object.

| Method | What It Does |
|---|---|
| *alert(text)* | Creates a triangular dialog box with a message in it |
| *blur()* | Removes focus from the window |
| *clearInterval(interval)* | Clears a previously set interval timer |
| *clearTimeOut(timer)* | Clears a previously set timeout |
| *close()* | Closes a window |
| *confirm()* | Creates a dialog box for user confirmation |
| *focus()* | Gives the focus to a window |
| *open(url, name, [options])* | Opens a new window and returns a new *window* object |
| *prompt(text, defaultInput)* | Creates a dialog prompt box to ask for user input |
| *scroll(x, y)* | Scrolls to a pixel position in a window |
| *setInterval(expression, milliseconds)* | After a specified interval, evaluates an expression (see Examples 10.10 and 10.12) |
| *setInterval(function, milliseconds, [arguments])* | After a specified interval, evaluates a function (see Examples 10.10 and 10.12) |
| *setTimeout(expression, milliseconds)* | After a timeout period has elapsed, evaluates an expression (see Examples 10.10, 10.11, and 10.13) |
| *setTimeout(function, milliseconds, [arguments])* | After a timeout period has elapsed, evaluates a function (see Examples 10.10, 10.11, and 10.13) |

**Opening and Closing Windows.**   You can open a new browser window by going to the *File* menu and selecting *New → Window* (Netscape and IE), or you can open a new window from a JavaScript program with the window's *open* method.

## FORMAT

```
var window_object = window.open("url", windowname, [options]);
```

Example:

```
var winObj= window.open("http://localhost/windows/winter.jpg",
    "winter","width=1150,height=350,resizable=yes,scrollbars=yes,
    location=yes");
```

## EXAMPLE 10.7

```
    <html>
    <head><title>Opening a New Window</title>
    <script language="JavaScript">
1       function newWindow(){
2           var winObj=open("winter.jpg", "winter");
        }
    </script>
    </head>
    <body bgColor="lightblue">
        <h2>Winter Scene from the Old Country</h2>
        <h3>Click here to see through my winter window<br>
3       <a href="javascript:newWindow()">Winter Scene</a></h3>
    </body>
    </html>
```

## EXPLANATION

1   The JavaScript function *newWindow* is defined.

2   The *open* method is called and returns a *window* object that is assigned to the variable, *winObj*. The first agument to the *open* method is the URL of the new window; in this case the document is an image file called *winter.jpg* located in the current directory. The name to be associated with this window is *winter*.

3   When the user clicks on the line *Winter Scene*, the JavaScript user-defined function, *newWindow*, is called (see Figure 10.13). This function is responsible for opening the new window. Instead of a URL, the HTML *<a href>* tag is assigned name of a JavaScript function. The *javascript:* label allows the function to be called when the user clicks on the link. Without the *javascript:* label, the browser will try to find a URL address called *newWindow()*, and fail.

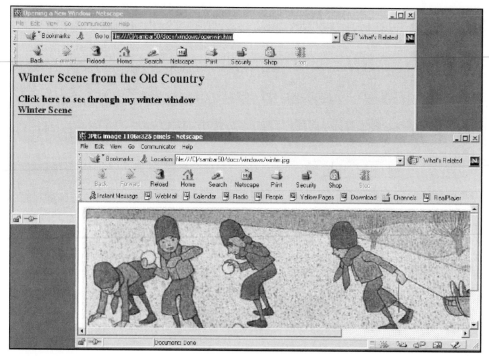

**Figure 10.13**   A new window showing a winter scene is opened.

The *window* object's *open()* method has a number of options that allow you to further customize the new window. They are listed in Table 10.6.

**Table 10.6**   The *open()* method and its options.

| Option | Values | Gives the Window |
|---|---|---|
| *directories()* | yes/no *or* 1/0 | Directory buttons |
| *height* | integer value | Height in pixels |
| *location()* | yes/no *or* 1/0 | A location box |
| *menubar()* | yes/no *or* 1/0 | A menu bar |
| *resizable* | yes/no *or* 1/0 | The ability to be resized |
| *scrollbars* | yes/no *or* 1/0 | Scrollbars along the side |
| *status()* | yes/no *or* 1/0 | A status bar |
| *toolbar()* | yes/no *or* 1/0 | A toolbar |
| *width* | integer value | Width in pixels |

**EXAMPLE   10.8**

```
      <html>
      <head><title>Opening a New Window with Parameters
          and Closing It</title>
      <script language="JavaScript">
1         function newWindow(){
2             winObj=window.open("http://localhost/windows/winter.jpg",
                  "winter","width=1150,height=350,resizable=yes,
                  scrollbars=yes,location=yes");
3             winObj.focus();
4             //winObj.blur();
          }
5         function closeWindow(){
6             winObj.close();
          }
      </script>
      </head>
      <body bgColor="lightblue">
      <h2>Winter Scene from the Old Country</h2>
      <h3>Click the link to see my winter window<br>
7         <a href="javascript:newWindow()">Winter Scene</a>
      <p>When you are ready to close the window, click here<br>
8         <a href="javascript:closeWindow()">Close the window</a></h3>
      </body></html>
```

**EXPLANATION**

1   The function *newWindow()* is defined.

2   The *open()* method is passed the URL of the jpeg image file that will be displayed in the new window called *winter*. The width and height of the new window are 1150 and 350 pixels, respectively. The window is resizeable and has scrollbars. A location box appears in the top of the new window. The name of the *window* object created by the open method is *winObj*. It is important that you use no spaces or linebreaks between the commas in the list of parameters.

3   The *focus()* method brings the new window into focus: it appears in front of the parent window or any other windows.

4   The *blur()* method (commented out) would push the window behind any other windows that are open.

5   The user-defined function, *closeWindow()*, is defined.

6   The reference to the *window* object, *winObj*, will call the *close()* method to close the new window that was opened.

7   The *newWindow* function is called when the user clicks on the link <u>Winter Scene</u>. The label, *javascript:*, prevents the link from trying to activate a URL, and instead goes to the JavaScript program and calls the function *closeWindow()*. See Figure 10.14.

8   When the user clicks on this link, the new window will be closed. The original or parent window will remain in the browser. If the name of the new *window* object is not provided, the *close()* method will try to close the parent window.

**Figure 10.14** Opening a new resizeable window with a scrollbar and size dimensions in pixels. Output from Example 10.8.

**Moving and Resizing a Window.** JavaScript provides several methods with which to resize and move a *window* object. The window can be moved or resized absolutely, or relative to its current position or size. The numbers, given as arguments, are the pixel coordinates. They are listed in Table 10.7.

**Table 10.7** Move and resize methods.

| Method | Example | What It Does |
|---|---|---|
| *moveBy* | *moveBy(20,20)* | Moves the window relatively by 20 pixels |
| *moveTo* | *moveTo(0,0)* | Moves to the top, left-hand corner of the screen |
| *resizeBy* | *resizeBy(15,10)* | Resizes the window relatively by 15 × 10 pixels |
| *resizeTo* | *resizeTo(450,350)* | Resizes the window absolutely to 450 × 350 pixels |

## EXAMPLE 10.9

```
<html>
<head><title>Move a New Window</title>
<script language="JavaScript">
    function directions(){
1       winObj=window.open("myplace.html","myplace",
            "width=200,height=300,resizable=no");
2       winObj.moveTo(0, 0); // Move window to top left-hand corner
3       winObj.focus();
4       parent.window.moveTo(215, 0);  // Move the parent window
5       parent.window.resizeTo(400,400);   // Resize browser window

    }
    function closeWindow(){
        winObj.close();

    }
</script>
</head>
<body bgColor="lightblue">
<h2>We've moved!</h2>
For directions to our new place,
<br>
click the button
6   <form >
        <input type="button"
            value="Simple Directions"
7           onClick="directions();">
    <p>When you are ready to close the window, click here<br>
    <a href="javascript:closeWindow()">Close the window</a></h3>
</body>
</html>
```

## EXPLANATION

1   A new *window* object is created. If the resizeable option is turned off, the user will not be able to maximize the window. A maximized window cannot be moved with the *moveTo()* method.

2   The *moveTo()* method determines the position where the window will be moved. The arguments 0,0 represent the *x,y* coordinates (column,row) in pixels.

3   The new window will be put into focus, meaning it will be at the top of the window hierarchy, in front of all the other windows.

4   The parent window is the original window we started in. It is moved to coordinates 215 × 0 pixels.

5   The parent (original) window is resized to 400 × 400 pixels.

6   This is the start of a simple HTML form. It creates a simple input device called a button on the screen.

7   This is the *onClick* event. When the user presses the button, the event is triggered and the handler, a function called *directions()*, will be called. The new window is moved to the top left-hand corner and put into focus. See Figure 10.15.

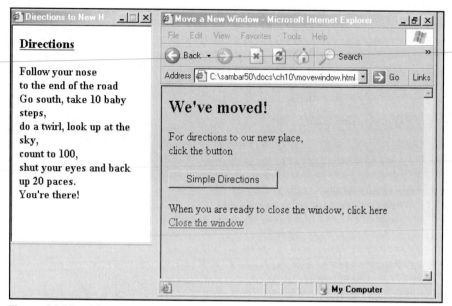

**Figure 10.15** After moving, focusing, and resizing both the new window and the parent window. Output from Example 10.9.

**Creating Timed Events.** The *window* object provides a method that acts like an alarm clock so that you can time when you want certain things to happen in your program. The *setTimeout()* method evaluates an expression after a specified amount of time. The *setTimeout()* method has two arguments: a quoted expression, and the time in milliseconds to delay execution of the expression. (A minute contains 60,000 milliseconds, so 30 seconds would be 30,000 milliseconds.) Since JavaScript sees time in terms of milliseconds, Table 10.8 gives you a little conversion table to help determine the time in milliseconds.

**Table 10.8** Basic units of time.

| Unit of Time | Milliseconds | |
|---|---|---|
| 1 second | 1000 | |
| 1 minute | second * 60 | (1000 * 60) |
| 1 hour | minute * 60 | (1000 * 60 * 60) |
| 1 day | hour * 24 | (1000 * 60 * 60 * 24) |
| 1 week | day * 7 | (1000 * 60 * 60 * 24 * 7) |

If a function contains a *setTimeout()* method that in short intervals keeps invoking the function, the result can give the effect of continuous motion such a scrolling panorama or message, or even animation.[2] Often, timers are used to scroll messages in the title or status bars repeatedly. You must decide what is tasteful on your Web page and what is annoying, but that aside, we use *setTimeout()* and *clearTimeout()* methods for scheduling something to happen in the future.

As of JavaScript 1.2, the *setInterval()* and *clearInterval()* methods were introduced for automatically rescheduling the execution of code at defined intervals.

The *setTimeout()* method is a window method. It takes two parameters:

1. The statements to execute, enclosed in quotes
2. The time in milliseconds to wait before the statements are executed

## FORMAT

```
var timeout = setTimeout("expression", delaytime);
var timeout= setInterval("expression", intervaltime);
```

Example:

```
var timeout = setTimeout("timer()", 15000);   // In 15 seconds call the
                                               // function "timer()"
var timerId = setInterval("scroller()", 500);  // In .05 seconds call
                                               // "scroller()"
```

To clear the timed event use the *clearTimeout()* or *clearInterval()* methods:

```
clearTimeout(timeout);
clearInterval(timerID);
```

## EXAMPLE 10.10

```
    <head><title>The setTimeout method</title>
    <script language="JavaScript">
1       function changeStatusBar(){
2           window.status = "See me now before I disappear!";
3           timeout =setTimeout("window.status=''", 6000);
            // alert(timeout);  This value differs in Netscape and IE
        }
    </script>
    <body>
    <center>
    <font face=arial size=3 color=blue>
    The timeout is set for 6 seconds.
    <br>
4   <img src="alarm.jpg" border=2>
    <p>
    Watch the status bar
    <br>
```

---

2. For an example of a timer to create animation, see Chapter 15, "Dynamic HTML: Style Sheets, the DOM, and JavaScript."

EXAMPLE 10.10 (CONTINUED)

```
5    <form>
        <input type="button"
        value="click here"
6       onClick="changeStatusBar();">
     </form>
     </center>
     </body>
     </html>
```

EXPLANATION

1    A JavaScript function, called *changeStatusBar()*, is defined. Its purpose is to print a message in the status bar of the window for six seconds.

2    A string value is assigned to the status property of the window. The string "*See me now before I disappear!*" will appear in the status bar at the bottom of the window.

3    The *setTimeout()* method is a window method. After six seconds, the status bar will be set to an empty string.

4    This is an image of a clock that displays on the screen, just for decoration.

5    An HTML form starts here. The user will see a button, with the text "*click here,*" on the button.

6    When he presses the button, the *onClick* event is triggered, causing the event handler, *changeStatusBar()*, to be invoked. See Figure 10.16.

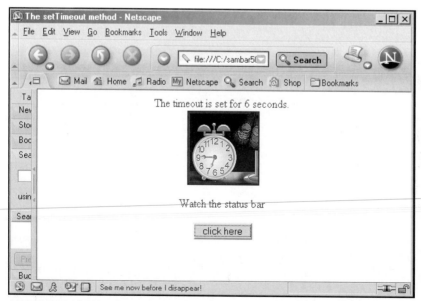

**Figure 10.16**   Click the button and watch the status bar. Output from Example 10.10.

EXAMPLE 10.11

```
        <html>
        <!-- This script is a modification of a free script found at
           the JavaScript source.
           Author: Asif Nasir (Asifnasir@yahoo.com)
         -->
        <head>
        <script language="JavaScript">
1           var today = new Date();
2           var future = new Date("December 25, 2003");
3           var diff = future.getTime() - today.getTime();
                            // Number of milliseconds
4           var days =Math.floor(diff / (1000 * 60 * 60 * 24 ));
                            // Convert to days
5           var str=
               "Only " + days + "  shopping days left until Christmas!";
6           function scroller(){
7              str = str.substring(1, str.length) + str.substring(0,1);
8              document.title=str;
9              window.status=str;
10             setTimeout("scroller()", 300);   // Set the timer
            }
        </script>
        </head>
        <body onLoad = "scroller()">
        <b>
        <font color=green size=4>
        Get Dizzy. Watch the title bar and the status bar!!
        <br>
11      <image src="christmasscene.bmp">
        </body>
        </html>
```

## EXPLANATION

1   The *Date()* constructor creates an instance of a new Date object, called *today*.

2   Another Date object is created with the date "*December 25, 2003*" assigned to the variable, called *future*. It would probably be a good idea to make the year a variable, so that we are not always looking at 2003. Try the *getFullYear()* method to get the current year in four digits.

3   The difference in milliseconds between the future time and the current time is assigned to the variable called *diff*.

4   The milliseconds of time are converted into days, and the result is rounded down by the Math object's *floor()* method.

5   The string variable, "*Only (number of days goes here) shopping days left until Christmas!*", is assigned to *str*.

6   A function called *scroller()* is defined.

**EXPLANATION** (CONTINUED)

7   This looks kind of tricky, but here's what's happening. The *substr()* method extracts everything between the first character and the rest of the string *substr(1, str.length)*, resulting in "*nly 19 shopping days left until Christmas!*". Next, another *subtsr(0,1)* method extracts the first character from the string, the "*O*". The "*O*" is added onto the end of the new string, resulting in "*nly 19 shopping days left until Christmas!O*" and after .03 seconds the *scroll()* function will be called again. Then the string will become "*ly 19 shopping days left until Christmas!On*", and then "*19 shopping days left until Christmas!Onl*" and so on. Since the *substr()* method is being called so rapidly, the effect is a scrolling banner.

8   The new string, *str*, created by the two *substr()* methods will appear in the document's title bar. Every time the function is called (i.e., every .03 seconds), the new string will appear, giving a scrolling effect.

9   The new string will also appear in the status bar of the window.

10  The timer is set here. The first argument is the name of the function that will be called, and the second argument is how often it will be called, in this case, once every 300 milliseconds or .03 seconds (300/1000). The display is shown in Figure 10.17.

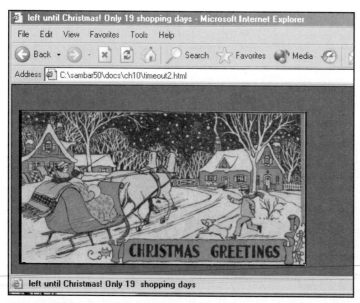

**Figure 10.17**   The string "*Only 19 shopping days left until Christmas!*" scrolls continuously in the title bar and in the status bar. How annoying!

**EXAMPLE 10.12**

```
        <html><head><title><Timeout></title>
        <script language="JavaScript">
1       var today = new Date();
2       var future = new Date("December 25, 2003");
3       var diff = future.getTime() - today.getTime();
                        // Number of milliseconds
        var days =Math.floor(diff / (1000 * 60 * 60 * 24 ));
                        // Convert to days
        var str=
            "Only " + days + "  shopping days left until Christmas! ";
4       function startup(){
5          setInterval("scroller()",500);
        }
6       function scroller(){
            str = str.substring(1, str.length) + str.substring(0,1);
            document.title=str;
            window.status=str;
        }
        </script>
        </head>
7       <body onLoad = "startup()" bgColor=red>
        <b><font color=green size=4>
        Get Dizzy. Watch the title bar and the status bar!!
        <br>
        <image src="christmasscene.bmp">
        </body>
        </html>
```

**EXPLANATION**

1   The *Date()* constructor creates an instance of a new Date object, called *today.*

2   Another Date object is created with the date *"December 25, 2003"* assigned to the variable, called *future.* It would probably be a good idea to make the year a variable, so that we are not always looking at 2003. Try the *getFullYear()* method to get the current year in four digits.

3   The difference in milliseconds between the future time and the current time is assigned to the variable called *diff.* The milliseconds of time are converted into days, and the result is rounded down by the Math object's *floor()* method.

4   A function called *startup()* is defined. It contains the timer method, *setInterval().*

5   The *setInterval()* method is executed and calls *scroller()* at intervals of 500 milliseconds, and will continue to do so until the window is exited or the *clearInterval()* method is called. In Example 10.11 we used *setTimeout()* instead of *setInterval().*

6   The *scroller()* function is being called every .05 seconds to send a string to the title bar and status bar of the window. It is explained in detail in Example 10.11. See Figure 10.17 for output.

7   When the document has finished loading, the *onLoad* event is triggered. It will call the *startup()* function and change the background color to red.

**Scrolling.**   Scrolling allows you to move to a particular place in text or an image. If you open up another window, you may want to scroll to a particular place in the window based on the user's selection from a menu in the main window, or you may want to use scrolling to produce an animated effect. For example, if you have a large image that can't be seen in the new window, you can set up scrolling so that you start at the left-hand side of the image and slowly move to the right-hand side and back again, giving a panoramic effect. Scrolling may have different behavior on different browsers.[3]

The *scrollTo()* method takes two arguments, the horizontal and vertical coordinates in pixels to represent the window position, where 0,0 would scroll to the left-hand top corner of the window, and position 0,350 would scroll down 350 pixels from the starting position, and 350,0 would scroll to the right 350 pixels from the starting position, and so on.

## FORMAT

```
window_object.scrollTo(horizontal_pixel_position,vertical_pixel_position);
```

Example:

```
parent.window.scrollTo(0,350);
```

## EXAMPLE  10.13

```
      <html>
      <head><title>Scrolling through Autumn</title>
      <script language="JavaScript">
1        winObj=window.open("fallscene.gif","mysscene",
         "width=350,height=292,resizable=no");  // Create the new window
                                                 // with an image.
2        winObj.moveTo(0, 0);
3        winObj.focus();
4        var pixelpos=0;
5        var ImgWidth=1096;
6        var pixelstep = 2;
7        var timeout;
8        function startScroll(){
```

---

3. Example 10.13 works fine on the Netscape browser, but does not work on Internet Explorer because the image is scaled to fit the window no matter what size it is. For this example to work in IE, go to Tools → Internet Options → Advanced → Multimedia, then uncheck the "Enable Automatic Image Resizing" option.

**EXAMPLE   10.13 (CONTINUED)**

```
9           if (pixelpos <= (ImgWidth - 350)){
                    // Check that scrolling is still within the
                // boundaries of the window.
10            pixelpos += pixelstep;
11            winObj.scrollTo(pixelpos,0);    // Go to that position in
                                              // the new window
12            timeout=setTimeout("startScroll()",20);
           }
       }

13     function scrollAgain(){
           pixelpos = 0;  // Reset the horizontal pixel position to 0
14         startScroll();    // Start scrolling again
       }
       function stopHere(){
15         clearTimeout(timeout);  // Stop the clock to stop scrolling
       }
       function closeWindow(){
16         winObj.close();
       }
    </script>
    </head>
    <body bgColor="lightgreen">
    <font face="arial" size=4 >
    <b><br><center>
    A Window into an Autumn Day
    <form>
17     <input type="button"
           value="Start scrolling"
           onClick="startScroll();">
       <input type="button"
           value="Stop scrolling"
           onClick="stopHere();">
       <input type="button"
           value="Start over"
           onClick="scrollAgain();">
    </form>
    <font size=-1>
    <p>When you are ready to close the window, click here<br>
18  <a href="javascript:closeWindow()">Close the window</a></h3>
    </body>
    </html>
```

## EXPLANATION

1   A new *window* object is created. It will contain a .gif image of a fall scene.

2   The new *window* object is moved up to the top left-hand corner of the browser (coodinates 0,0).

3   The *focus()* method puts the window on top of all other opened windows.

4   The initial pixel position that will be used for scrolling is set to 0.

5   The variable *ImgWidth* is assigned *1096*, which will be used to represent the size of the image in pixels.

6   Each time the image moves to the right, it will be moved 2 pixels in intervals of .02 seconds.

7   A variable called *timeout* is declared. It will hold the value returned from the *setTimeout()* method.

8   A function called *startScroll()* is defined. It will start the image scrolling from the left of the screen to the right. If the scrolling is stopped before it reaches the end, this function will start scrolling where it left off.

9   If the value of the variable *pixelpos* is less than the width of the window, keep going.

10  Add one to the pixel postition.

11  Scroll horizontally to the new pixel position in the window. Moves over one pixel to the right.

12  Set the *timeout* to 20 milliseconds: scroll the image to the right, 50 times per minute.

13  A function called *scrollAgain()* is defined.

14  Scrolling starts again.

15  Stops the scrolling by clearing or turning off the timer.

16  This function closes the window.

17  Three buttons will be displayed. A function to start, stop, or restart the scrolling will be called depending on which button the user presses.

18  If the user clicks on this link, the window with the image will be closed. See Figures 10.18 and 10.19.

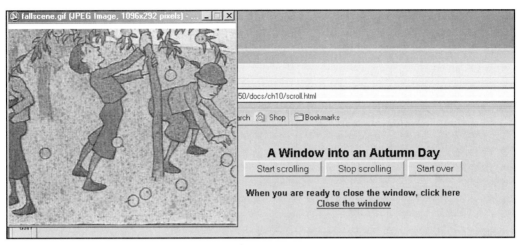

**Figure 10.18**   The new window on the left has a scene that will scroll by slowly; it can be stopped, and then restarted.

**Figure 10.19**   This is the scene that will be scrolling by in the small window above.

### 10.1.3   Working with Frames

When you look out the window from the room where you might be at the moment, it may be one big pane of glass like a picture window, or the window may be divided up into panes of squares or rectangles, as shown in Figure 10.20.

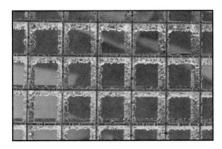

**Figure 10.20**
Windows can have many frames.

The browser is a virtual window that can be divided up into frames—independent windows, like panes, within the main window, where each frame is used to display different information. Frames were invented by Netscape.[4] Web designers have debated the merit of using frames because they are often misused and have some distinct disadvantages discussed later in this chapter.

The file that defines the layout of the frames is called the parent window, and each of the frames it describes is called a child (see Figure 10.21). Although you can't see the parent window, it will show up in the browser's source for the page.

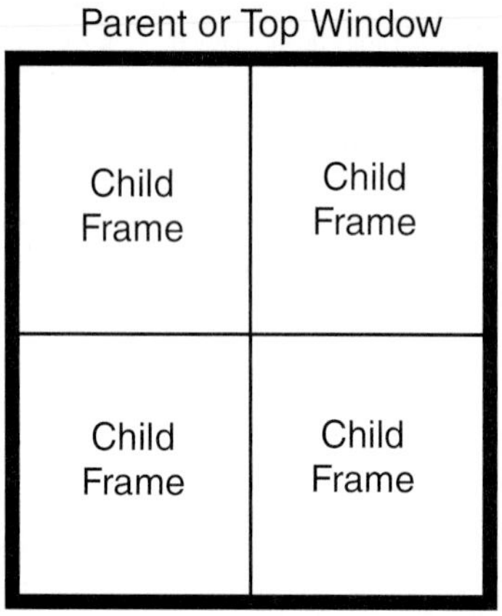

Parent or Top Window

| Child Frame | Child Frame |
|---|---|
| Child Frame | Child Frame |

**Figure 10.21**   The parent window is divided into child frames.

To build frames in a Web page, you use the HTML *<frameset>* tags instead of the *<body>* tags (see Table 10.9). At least three files are needed to create frames. The first file defines the layout of the frames (or subwindows) by defining the size and position of the frames. The *rows* and *cols* attributes of each frameset specify how much room the frame will need within the window. These values use exact pixels as a default, although you can also use percentages to represent a section of the window, or an asterisk * to allocate leftover space. (These size values will be shown in Examples 10.14 and 10.15.)

**Creating HTML Frames.**   In Example 10.14 the window is divided into two frames: a left-hand frame that takes up 25 percent (in columns) of the window and a right-hand frame that takes up 75 percent (in columns) of the rest of the window. Since files are required to accomplish this, the main file defines the frameset, the second file contains the HTML code for the left-hand frame, and the third file contains the HTML code for the right-hand frame.

---

4. Netscape versions below 2.0 do not support frames.

**Table 10.9**    HTML frame tags.

| Tag | Attribute | What It Does |
|-----|-----------|--------------|
| *<FRAMESET>* | | Defines a collection of frames or other framesets |
| | *BORDER* | Sets frame border thickness (in pixels) between all the frames |
| | *FRAMEBORDER* | Draws 3D separators between frames in a frameset. A value of *1* or *yes* turns frame borders on; a value of *0* or *no* turns them off |
| | *ROWS* | Defines the number and size of rows in a frameset |
| | *COLS* | Defines the number and size of columns in a frameset |
| *<FRAME>* | | Defines attributes of specific frames |
| | *NAME* | Used by JavaScript to reference the frame by name |
| | *SRC* | The URL or location of the frame |

## EXAMPLE 10.14

```
      <html>
      <head><title>Frame Me!</title></head>
      <!-- Creating the framesets for two files -->
      <!-- This file is named: framesets.html -->
1     <frameset cols="25%,75%">
2        <frame src="leftframe.html" >
3        <frame src="rightframe.html" >
4     </frameset>
      </html>
----------------------------------------------------------------
      <html>
      <head><title>Left Frame</title></head>
      <!--This file is named: leftframe.html -->
5     <body bgColor="yellow">
      <h2>
6     Just to show you that this is the left frame
      </h2>
      </body>
      </html>
----------------------------------------------------------------
      <html>
      <head><title>Right Frame</title></head>
7     <!--This file is named: rightframe.html -->
8     <body bgColor="lightgreen">
      <h2>
      Just to show you that this is the right frame
      </h2>
      </body>
      </html>
```

## EXPLANATION

1  This is the parent file that defines how the window will be divided into frames. The first frame will take up 25 percent of the page in columns and the second frame will take up the rest of the page, 75 percent.

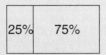

2  The frame *src* attribute is assigned the URL of the first HTML file, *leftframe.html*, that will be displayed in the window.

3  The frame *src* attribute is assigned the URL of the second HTML, *rightframe.html*, that will be displayed in the window.

4  The frameset definition ends with the *</frameset>* tag.

5  The background color of the left-hand frame will be yellow.

6  This text appears in the left frame.

7  This section represents the right-hand frame.

8  The background color of this frame is light green. See Figure 10.22.

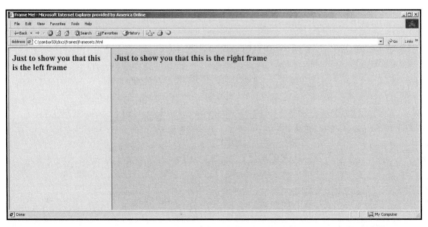

**Figure 10.22**  Two vertically positioned frames. Output from Example 10.14.

The next example shows a window partitioned into three horizontal frames.

EXAMPLE  10.15

```
      <html>
      <head><title>Frame Me!</title></head>
      <!-- This file simply defines the frames; it points to other
           HTML files (not shown) that comprise the HTML
           content  -->
1     <frameset rows="130,*,*" frameborder="yes"
          border="1" framespacing="0">
2         <frame src="topframe.html" >
3         <frame src="main.html" scrolling="no">
          <!--main.html is the middle frame -->
          <frame src="bottomframe.html" >
4     </frameset>
      </html>
```

**EXPLANATION**

1  This time the frameset will be divided up into three sections by rows. The first frame will be a horizontal frame consisting of 130 pixels in a row. Based on the amount of space taken up by the first frame, the remaining frames will be allocated whatever space is left in the window. There are three frames that will be placed horizontally on the page.

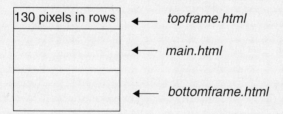

2  This is the URL to the first frame, *topframe.html*, which will be at the top of the window.

3  This is the URL to the second frame, *main.html*, which will be in the middle of the window.

4  This is the URL to the third frame, *bottomframe.html*, which will be at the bottom of the window.

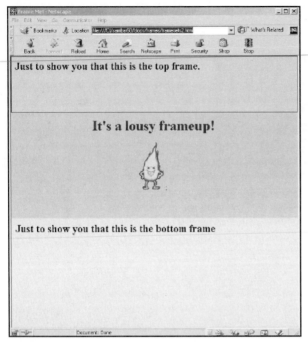

**Figure 10.23** Three horizontal frames created in Example 10.15.

**The *frame* Object.**   HTML frames in JavaScript are represented as an array of frame objects. The *frames[]* array is a property of the *window* object and is referenced with the window's parent property. Each element of the array represents a frame in the order in which it appears in the document; thus, *window.parent.frames[0]* would reference the first frame defined in a frameset (see Figure 10.24). If you name the frame, then you can reference the frame element by its name. If the frame is named *leftframe*, it can be referenced as *window.parent.leftframe*.

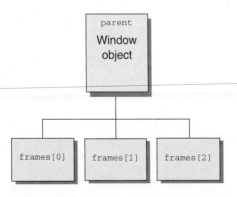

**Figure 10.24** The JavaScript hierarchy.

Since frames are just little windows, they share many of the same properties and methods of the *window* object. See Table 10.10 for a list of properties and Table 10.11 for a list of methods.

**Table 10.10** Properties of the *frame* object.

| Property | What It Describes |
| --- | --- |
| *document* | The document currently loaded in the frame |
| *frames* | An array of frames |
| *length* | The number of elements in the frames array; i.e., the number of frames |
| *name* | The name of the frame assigned to the HTML name attribute |
| *parent* | The main window from which the child frames are defined |
| *self* | The current frame |
| *top* | The window that started the script |
| *window* | The current window or frame |

**Table 10.11** Methods of the *frame* object.

| Method | What It Does |
| --- | --- |
| *blur()* | Removes focus from the frame |
| *clearInterval()* | Clears a timed interval |
| *clearTimeout()* | Clears a timeout |
| *focus()* | Puts focus into the frame |
| *print()* | Invokes a print dialog box |
| *setInterval()* | Sets a timed interval |
| *setTimeout()* | Sets a timeout |
| *unwatch()* | Unsets the watchpoint |
| *watch()* | Sets a watchpoint on a frame property; if a property changes, calls a function |

**Creating Menus and Navigation Bars.**    Since frames can be used to divide a page, it is common to use one of the frames as a menu of items and the other as the main page where a page is loaded depending on the user's selection. If one frame contains a selection of links, then it can serve as a navigation bar. When the user clicks on a link, the page at that URL will be loaded into the main frame.

In Example 10.16 the frames are defined for two frames. Example 10.17 displays the content of the two frame files. The left-hand frame will represent a menu of links. The background color in the right-hand frame will change when the user clicks on a link in the left-hand frame.

---

**EXAMPLE**  10.16

```
      <html>
      <head><title>Frame Me!</title></head>
      <!--Creating the framesets for two frames -->
      <!--This HTML file is named: framedef.html -->

1     <frameset cols="25%,75%">
2         <frame src="leftmenu.html"  name=lframe>
3         <frame src="rightcolor.html" name=rframe>
4     </frameset>
      </html>
```

**EXPLANATION**

1   The HTML *<frameset>* tag replaces the *<body>* tag when working with frames. The size is determined by the *ROWS* and *COLS* attributes of the *<frameset>* tag. In this example, the first frame will occupy 25 percent of the window, and the second frame will occupy 75 percent of the window (in columns). The default is to set *ROWS* and *COLS* in pixels. (*ROWS* and *COLS* are not case sensitive.)

2   The first frame, named *lframe* occupies 25 percent of the left-hand side of the window. Its content is in an *src* file called *leftmenu.html*.

3   This frame, called *rframe*, occupies 75 percent of the right-hand side of the window. Its content is in an *src* file called *rightcolor.html*.

4   The HTML *</frameset>* tag ends the definition of the frames.

EXAMPLE   10.17

```
        <html>
        <head><title>Left Frame</title>
        <!--This HTML file is named: leftmenu.html -->
1       <script language="JavaScript">
2           function setBgColor(color){
3               parent.frames[1].document.bgColor=color;
                // Or use the frame's name: parent.rframe.document.bgColor
            }
        </script>
        </head>
        <body bgColor="white">
        <h3>
        Pick a color:
        <br>
4       <a href="javascript:setBgColor('red')">red</a>
        <br>
        <a href="javascript:setBgColor('yellow')">yellow</a>
        <br>
        <a href="javascript:setBgColor('green')">green</a>
        <br>
        <a href="javascript:setBgColor('blue')">blue</a>
        </h3>
        </body>
        </html>
        ----------------------------------------------------------------
        <html>
        <head><title>Right Frame</title></head>
        <body>
        <h2>
        This is the frame where colors are changing.<br>
        In your javascript function, this is frame[1].
        </h2>
        </body>
        </html>
```

## EXPLANATION

1   A JavaScript program starts here.

2   A function called *setBgColor()* is defined. It takes one parameter, a reference to a color being passed by the user.

3   Going down the document tree, start with the parent window, to the second frame, *frames[1]* (remember array subscripts start at 0), to the frame's document, and then the document's property, *bgColor*. Assign a color.. This assignment will cause the background color in the right-hand frame to change.

4   When the user clicks on any of the following links, the JavaScript function *setBg-Color()* will be called, with the color sent as an argument to the function. The *javascript:* pseudo URL prevents the link from going to a real URL. The display is shown in Figure 10.25.

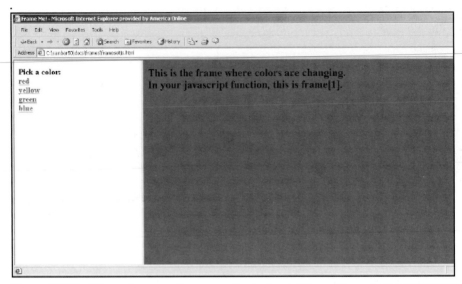

**Figure 10.25**   When the user clicks on a link in the left-hand frame, the background color in the right-hand frame changes. Ouput from Example 10.17.

**Using the *top* Property to Keep the Main Window out of a Frame.**   If you create a Web page, it should load into the user's main browser window, not in one of the frames. You can use the location method to force your page to load in the main window by putting the JavaScript code shown in Example 10.18 into the *<head>* portion of the page. Every window and frame has a *top* property, a reference to the topmost *window* object currently loaded in the browser. (See "The location Object" on page 244.)

**EXAMPLE 10.18**

```
     <html><head><title>Forcing the Frame</title>
1    <script language = "JavaScript">
2        if (window != top) {     // True if window is not the top
                                   // window in the hierarchy
3            top.location.href = location.href;
                                   // Put this window on top
         }
     </script>
4    <body bgcolor="lightblue">
     <h1>
     The important page that we're talking about
     <h2>
     </body>
     </html>
```

## EXPLANATION

1   The script begins here.

2   If the current window is not at the top of the window hierarchy in the browser, the statement in the block is evaluated. The *top* property references the highest object in the window hierarchy.

3   If the current window isn't at the top of the window hierarchy (if it's not the main window), this assignment forces the page, *location.href*, into the main window, *top.location.href*.

4   This is the body of the fictitious page that will be loaded into the main window of whoever views it.

**Collapsing Toolbars and Menu Bars.**   You don't always necessarily want to look at the toolbar or menu bar. It can be in the way of what you're viewing in the main page. Example 10.19 collapses the frame in order to bring the main frame to the foreground so that it will be viewed in the entire window.

## EXAMPLE   10.19

```
<html>
<head>
<title>Untitled Document</title>
<meta http-equiv="Content-Type"
    content="text/html; charset=iso-8859-1">
</head>
<frameset cols="117,450" rows="*">
    <frame src="toctoolbar.html" name="menu">
    <frame src="tocmain.html" name="main">
</frameset>
<noframes><body bgcolor="#FFFFFF">
</body></noframes>
</html>
------------------------------------------------------------
(The Startup Main Page)
<html>
<head>
<title>Untitled Document</title>
<meta http-equiv="Content-Type" content="text/html;
    charset=iso-8859-1">
</head>
<body bgcolor=yellow>
<h1>This is the main page</h1>
<body bgcolor="#FFFFFF">
</body>
</html>
------------------------------------------------------------
```

**EXAMPLE   10.19** (CONTINUED)

```
(The Menu Bar Page)
<html>
<head>
<title>Menu Bar</title>
<meta http-equiv="Content-Type" content="text/html;
    charset=iso-8859-1">
<script language="javascript">
    var myUrl;
1   function openSite(url){
2       parent.main.location = url;
3       myUrl=url;
    }
4   function collapse(){
        if ( ! myUrl){
5           parent.location = "tocmain.html";}
        else{
6           parent.location=myUrl;      // Force this page into the
                                        // parent location
        }
    }
</script>
</head>
<body bgcolor="#FFFFFF">
7  <p><a href="javascript:openSite('tocmain.html')">Home</a><p>
   <p><a href="javascript:openSite('http://ellieq.com');">
      Page 1</a></p>
   <p><a href="javascript:openSite('http://prenticehall.com');">
      Page 2</a></p>
   <p><a href="javascript:openSite('http://google.com');">
      Page 3</a></p>
8  <p><a href="javascript:collapse();">Hide Menu</a><p>
</body>
</html>
```

**EXPLANATION**

1   A function called *openSite* is defined. It takes one parameter, the URL of the Web site.

2   The parent is the main window where the frames are defined. *main.location* is the frame on the right-hand side of the toolbar. It was named *main* when the framesets were defined. The main frame is assigned the URL of one of the Web sites after the user clicks on a link in the menu bar.

3   The global variable *url* gets the URL of the current Web site shown in the right frame.

4   The function called *collapse()* is defined. Its function is to make the right frame fit into the whole window, hiding the menu bar.

5   If the user hasn't selected any page prior to selecting Hide Menu, the main frame will take up the whole window. The *location* property of the *window* object refers to the location of the parent window, the main window from where the frames were created.

6  The *location* property of the parent window is assigned the URL of the window currently being viewed in the right-hand frame. This forces the right frame to take up the entire window. The menu bar is no longer displayed.

7  This list of links makes up the menu bar and is in the left-hand frame.

8  When the user clicks this link, the *collapse()* function is called, and the menu disappears causing the right frame to take up the entire window.

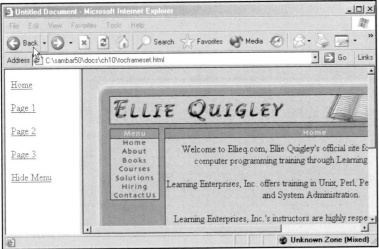

**Figure 10.26**  Two frames, a menu, and the main frame.  The user clicked on Page 1.

**Figure 10.27**  The user clicked *Hide Menu*. The larger frame has expanded to fill the entire page. Backpaging will take you back to the menu.

## 10.1.4  The *location* Object

The *location* object is a property of the *window* object and is used to access the URL of the document currently loaded in the window. In previous examples, we have seen *location* as a *window* property, but because it is really also an object itself, it also has properties used to describe the different parts of a URL. (See Table 10.12.)

If you are writing a page containing frames, the entire page may not be picked up by a search engine, such as Yahoo! or Google. Anyone linking to your page via the search engine will only get part of the page, not the complete frameset. Also, when a page is divided into frames, the visitor cannot bookmark the page if the browser is not in the top frameset. The location object can be used to make sure the topmost window is the one currently loaded in the browser. (See "Using the top Property to Keep the Main Window out of a Frame" on page 240.)

### FORMAT

```
javascript: window.location.href = "URL";
javascript: window.location.replace("URL");
```

**Example:**

```
javascript: window.location.href = "http://www.legos.com/";
javascript: window.location.replace("http://www.legos.com/");
```

**Table 10.12**  Properties of the *location* object.

| Property | What It Describes in the URL |
|---|---|
| *hash* | If it exists, the anchor part |
| *host* | The hostname:port |
| *hostname* | The hostname |
| *href* | The entire URL |
| *pathname* | The pathname |
| *port* | The port number |
| *protocol* | The protocol and colon |
| *search* | The query string |

**Table 10.13**  Methods of the *location* object.

| Method | What It Does |
|--------|--------------|
| *reload()* | Reloads the current URL |
| *replace()* | Replaces the current page with a new one |
| *unwatch()* | Removes a watch point on the location property |
| *watch()* | Sets a watch point on the *location* property; i.e., calls a function if the property changes |

Two methods of interest are *replace()* and *reload()*. The *replace()* method is used to change the location of the current page; that is, to point to another page. It is similar to the *href* property, but where *href* puts the new page at the top of the history list, the *replace()* method removes the current page from the history list and replaces it with the new page. The *reload()* method behaves like the browser's Reload button. It causes the window's current document to be reloaded.

**Loading a New Page into a Frame with the *location* Object.**  In Example 10.20, the *location* object changes the location of the current page. By selecting a Web site, the user is taken to that site, which is displayed in the bottom frame of a frameset.

**EXAMPLE  10.20**

```
(The file defining the framesets)
<html><title>Changing Location</title>
<html>
<head><title>Frames</title></head>
<frameset rows="130,*" frameborder="yes" border="8"
        framespacing="0">
    <frame src="location.html" scrolling="no">
    <frame src="emptyframe.html" >
</frameset>
</html>
----------------------------------------------------------------
(The empty file which will be the bottom frame)
<html>
<head><title>Empty Frame</title>
</head>
<body>
</body>
</html>
----------------------------------------------------------------
```

**EXAMPLE  10.20 (CONTINUED)**

```
<html><head><title>Changing Location</title>
</head>
<script language="JavaScript">
1      function loadPage(urlAddress){
2          parent.frames[1].location.href = urlAddress;
       }
</script>
</head>
<body bgcolor="F8C473">
<font size="+1" face=arial,helvetica>
Pick your bookstore and we'll take you there!
3   <form>
       <input type="button"
          value="Amazon"
4         onClick="loadPage('http://amazon.com');">
       <input type="button"
          value="Borders"
          onClick="loadPage('http://borders.com');">
       <input type="button"
          value="Prentice Hall"
          onClick="loadPage('http://prenhall.com');">
</form>
</body>
```

**EXPLANATION**

1  When the function *loadPage()* is called, it gets the URL address of the bookstore as its only parameter and assigns the address to the *location* object.

2  There are two frames in this document. The first frame contains the buttons with the names of bookstores to pick from—Amazon, Borders, and Prentice Hall. The second frame is empty until the user makes a selection. This statement assigns the URL of the chosen bookstore to the *location* object by traversing the JavaScript hierarchy, starting at the parent window, to the bottom frame, *frames[1]* and to the *href* property of the *location* object. By doing this, the browser will find the home page of the bookstore, and display it in the bottom frame.

3  The HTML form starts here. It is a form that displays three graphical buttons. When the user presses on one of the buttons, a function called *loadPage()* will be invoked and the bottom frame will display its Web page.

4  The JavaScript *onClick* event is triggered when the user clicks on the button. The function called *loadPage()* will be called with the URL of the bookstore. The display is shown in Figure 10.28.

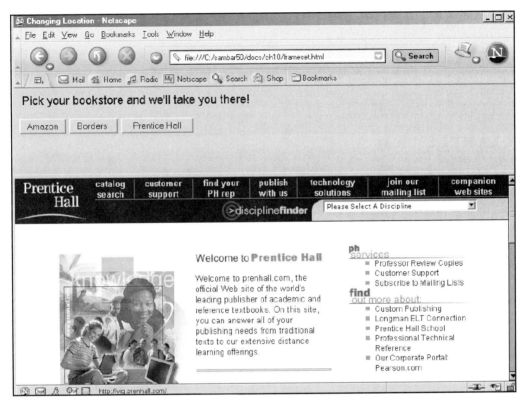

**Figure 10.28**   Two frames: The top frame puts the location of the bookstore in the bottom frame.

### 10.1.5   The *history* Object

The *history* object is a property of the *window* object. It keeps track of the pages (in a stack) that the user has visited. The *history* object is most commonly used in JavaScript to move back or forward on a page, similar to the back button and forward button supported by your browser. The *history* object can reference only those pages that have been visited; that is, those pages on its stack. It has a *length* property and three methods called *go()*, *back()* and *forward()*.[5]

---

5.  Not predictable on Netscape 6.

## FORMAT

Examples:

```
history.go(-3)    // Go back three pages
history.go(2)     // Go forward three pages
back()            // Same as history.go(-1)
forward()         // Same as history.go(1)
```

## EXAMPLE 10.21

```
    <html><head>
    <title>The History Object</title>
    </head>
    <script language="JavaScript">
        function loadPage(urlAddress){
1           parent.frames[1].location.href = urlAddress;
        }
    </script>
    </head>
    <body>
        <font size="+1" face=arial,helvetica>
        <form name="form1">
        <input type="button"
            value="Amazon"
            onClick="loadPage('http://amazon.com');">
        <input type="button"
            value="Borders"
            onClick="loadPage('http://borders.com');">
        <input type="button"
            value="Barnes&Noble"
            onClick="loadPage('http://barnesandnoble.com');">
        </form>
        <form name="form2">
2       <input type="button"
            value="go back"
3           onClick="javascript: history.go(-1);">
4       <input type="button"
            value="go forward"
5           onClick="javascript: history.go(1);">
        </form>
    </body>
    </html>
```

## EXPLANATION

1   When the user presses the back or forward buttons, he will be moved back and forth to pages opened in the bottom frame of the page. This line loads the page. The other two files that set up the frames are shown in Example 10.20.

2   This input button will be used if the user wants to go back to the previous page.

3   The *history.go(-1)* method will send you back to the previous page you have visited. If nothing happens, you haven't been anywhere yet.

4   This input button will be used if the user wants to move to the next page.

5   If you move forward and nothing happens, it's because you don't have anything on the history stack yet; you haven't gone anywhere. But once you load a new page, then go back, you will be able to move foward. The *history.go(1)* method will then move you forward one page. Output is shown in Figures 10.29 and 10.30.

**Figure 10.29**   The user can go back to the previous page or move forward to the next page in the history stack. Output from Example 10.21.

**Figure 10.30**   The user presses the "go back" button to go to the previous page he visited. Output from Example 10.21.

## 10.1.6 The *screen* Object

The *screen* object is a property of the *window* object and is automatically created when a user loads a Web page. It gives you access to the various properties of the user's screen such as its height, width, color depth, and so on. These are listed in Table 10.14. This can be helpful when designing pages that will require specific dimensions. For example, if the user's available screen width is less that 650 pixels (640×480), you may want to load a smaller image, whereas if it is over 1000 pixels (1024×768), a larger image can be loaded. There are no event handlers for this object.

**Table 10.14** Properties of the *screen* object.

| Property | What It Describes |
| --- | --- |
| availHeight | The pixel height of the screen, minus toolbars, etc. |
| availLeft | The *x* coordinate of the first pixel, minus toolbars, etc. |
| availTop | The *y* coordinate of the first pixel, minus toolbars, etc. |
| availWidth | The pixel width of the screen, minus toolbars, etc. |
| colorDepth | The maximum amount of colors that the screen can display |
| height | The pixel height of the screen |
| pixelDepth | The number of bits per pixel of the screen |
| width | The pixel width of the screen |

**EXAMPLE 10.22**

```
        <html><head><title>Screen Properties</title>
        </head>
        <body bgcolor="orange" > <font face=verdana>
        <script language="JavaScript">
        document.write("<b>The Screen</b><br>");
        document.write("<table border=2>");
        document.write("<tr><th>Screen Property</th><th>Value</th>");
    1   document.write("<tr><td>Height</th><th>",screen.height,"
                </td></tr>");
        document.write("<tr><td>Available Height</th><th>",
    2       screen.availHeight,"</td></tr>");
        document.write("<tr><td>Width</th><th>",screen.width,"
                </td></tr>");
        document.write("<tr><td>Available Width</th><th>",
```

EXAMPLE  10.22 (CONTINUED)

```
3        screen.availWidth,"</td></tr>");
    document.write("<tr><td>Color Depth</th><th>",
4        screen.colorDepth,"</td></tr>");
    document.write("</table>");
    </script>
    </body>
    </html>
```

## EXPLANATION

1  The *height* property of the *screen* object contains the height of the screen in pixels.

2  The available height is the height minus any toolbars or other objects attached to the window.

3  The *width* property of the *screen* object contains the width of the screen in pixels.

4  The *colorDepth* refers to the maximum number of colors that the screen can display in bit format. The display is shown in Figure 10.31.

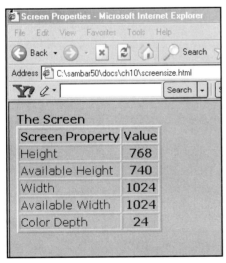

**Figure 10.31**  Tables showing properties of the *screen* object in Internet Explorer (left) and Netscape (right).

## EXERCISES

1. In a new window, print all the properties of the *navigator* object.

2. Write a script that will display the name of your browser, the version, and the operating system you are using. (Use the *parseInt()* function to print just the version number.)

3. Does your browser support Shockwave Flash? Write a JavaScript program to show whether the plug-in is installed.

4. Create two links, one to open a new window and one to close it. The new window will display this message in a big font: *The eye is the window to your soul.* The new window will be positioned in the left-hand corner of your screen, will be resizable, have a scrollbar, and it will have the focus.

5. Create an HTML document that contains four frames (i.e., four panes in a window, as in Figure 10.21). Each frame will display a different image. In another window, use JavaScript to display the number of frames in the original window and the name of the original window.

6. Create a program that produces a page containing frames. The first frame will span across the top of the page and contain a centered heading entitled, *A Virtual Zoo.* A second frame will be used as a navigation bar at the left-hand side of the screen. It will contain links to five animals. When the user presses a link, an image of that animal will appear in a frame of its own to the right side of the navigation bar.

7. In an alert dialog box, display the pixel height, width, and color depth of your screen. Each value will be separated by a newline.

8. Create a program that will create a digital clock in the status bar. Use the *setInterval()* method to update the status bar once every minute with the current time.

# chapter

# 11

# The Document Objects:

## 11.1 The Document Object Model

In Chapter 10 we addressed the browser object model. The properties and methods of different browsers vary since there is no standard for defining what a browser does. The document object model (DOM), on the other hand, deals specifically with a document, and there are now standards that dictate how the objects in an HTML (or XML) page should be represented. The DOM is a hierarchical tree-like structure,consisting of a collection of objects, all relating to the document. According to the World Wide Web Consortium (WC3), a DOM is a platform- and language-independent object model that "allows programs and scripts to dynamically access and update the content, structure, and style of documents."[1] It mimics the structure of the document it models. When working with JavaScript, the DOM mimics the HTML document. Each element of an HTML document, such as an image, form, link, or button, can be represented as a JavaScript object, and each object contains properties and methods to describe and manipulate these objects. (See *http://www.w3.org/TR/REC-DOM-Level-1/level-one-html.html* for more on HTML-specific DOMs.)

The W3C abstract states: "The Document Object Model provides a standard set of objects for representing HTML and XML documents, a standard model of how these objects can be combined, and a standard interface for accessing and manipulating them. Vendors can support the DOM as an interface to their proprietary data structures and APIs, and content authors can write to the standard DOM interfaces rather than product-specific APIs, thus increasing interoperability on the Web."[2]

The W3C defines DOM Level 1 to create an industry standard for all browsers, fully supported by Netscape 6 and Internet Explorer 5 and 6. The standard consists of two parts: the first defines how to navigate and manipulate the HTML and XML structure for the core objects, properties, and methods; the second defines a set of objects strictly

---

1. World Wide Web Consortium (W3C), *http://www.w3.org/DOM/*.
2. World Wide Web Consortium (W3C), *http://www.w3.org/TR/1998/REC-DOM-Level-1-19981001/*.

related to HTML. In addition to DOM Level 1, there are two other levels, still in progress. What all that boils down to is that the DOM specifies a standard set of objects that will work with HTML and XML documents no matter what browser, no matter what scripting language.

Example 11.1 shows an HTML document and how it is represented structurally.

---

**EXAMPLE  11.1**

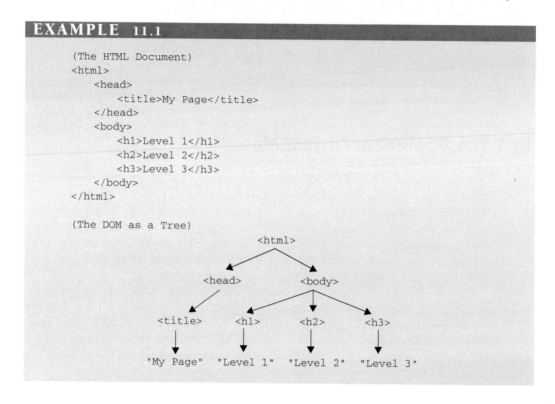

```
(The HTML Document)
<html>
    <head>
        <title>My Page</title>
    </head>
    <body>
        <h1>Level 1</h1>
        <h2>Level 2</h2>
        <h3>Level 3</h3>
    </body>
</html>


(The DOM as a Tree)
```

---

The DOM hierarchy—a tree structure, similar to a family tree—consists of parents and children called <u>nodes</u> (no, not nerds, but nodes). Each leaf in the tree is called a node. The topmost node, the *<html>* tag, is the root node. The *<head>* and *<body>* tags are child nodes of the *<html>* parent node. If the nodes are at the same level, they are called siblings, like a real family. Nodes may have a parent and a number of child nodes. The DOM provides a set of objects, with properties and methods, that allow access to this tree structure within a JavaScript program. With the advent of dynamic HTML, the DOM has control over every element of a Web page, and specifies base objects such as *Node*, *NodeList*, and *NamedNodeMap*, and high-level objects to represent all elements of the document. We'll see more on dynamic HTML and the DOM in Chapter 15, "Dynamic HTML: Style Sheets, the DOM, and JavaScript." For now we will use the DOM to navigate through the document object and its children, and see how to manipulate these objects with their many  properties and methods.

## 11.1.1 The JavaScript Hierarchy

Since the JavaScript document objects are arranged in a DOM hierarchy, each node in the tree can be referenced using the dot syntax. In JavaScript, the *window* object is at the top of the tree, the ultimate parent because everything takes place within the window. The window is called the *top*, *self*, or *parent* object. It has child nodes. They are listed below:

1. The *navigator* object
2. The *frames* object
3. The *history* object
4. The *location* object
5. The *document* object
6. The *screen* object
7. The *event* object

We discussed the window as part of the browser object model in the last chapter. The DOM is concerned only with those nodes that make up the document object. Documents contain text, images, forms, links, etc. The most commonly used object is the <u>*document object*</u>. Subordinate to the *document* object are another set of objects, its children:

1. The *anchors* object
2. The *images* object
3. The *forms* object
4. The *links* object
5. The *applets* object
6. The *embeds* object

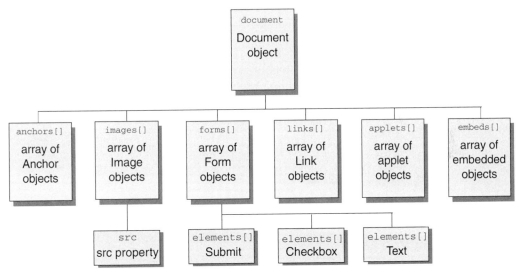

**Figure 11.1** The document model.

**Revisiting the Dot Syntax.** To refer to an object, you start with the *window* object (*parent*), followed by a dot, then the next object in the hierarchy, then another dot, and so on until you reach the desired object; for example, *window.location* or *window.docu-ment.forms[0]*. When referencing a child of the *window* object it is not necessary to include the *window*, because JavaScript knows that the window is at the top of the tree. Instead of saying *window.document.bgColor*, you can simply say *document.bgColor*.

## 11.1.2 The Document Itself

The *document* object is a property of the *window* object, and if the window is partitioned into frames (subwindows), each frame is a property of the *window* object.

Every window (or frame) contains a *document* object that corresponds to the HTML document shown in the window. This object corresponds mainly to the body of the document—that is, what is inserted between the *<body></body>* tags—although it can also be found in a limited way within the *<head></head>* tags. JavaScript programs manipulate this object to bring life to otherwise dead, static pages. Since the *document* object is below the *window* object, the *document* object can be represented as a property of the *window* by saying *window.document*. The *forms* object is an array of objects below the *document* object, so the *forms* object is a property of the *document* object and is represented as *window.document.forms[]*.

As stated before, because the *window* object is at the top of the hierarchy, any objects just below it, such as the *document* or *location* objects, are *window* properties and the word *window* is not required; thus, specifying *window.document.bgColor* is the same as *document.bgColor.*

The syntax for describing the background color (*bgcolor*) property for a document object is shown in the following example:

```
document.bgColor = "yellow";
```

**Document Properties.**   The *document* object is defined when the HTML *<body>* tag is encountered on the page and stays in existence until the page is unloaded, and the *<body>* tag has a number of attributes that define the appearance of the page. The *document* object has properties that correspond to the HTML *<body>* tag attributes, as shown in Tables 11.1 and 11.2. The properties of the *document* object are shown in the output of Example 11.2. (See Chapter 12, "Handling Events," for events that are associated with the *<body>* tag.)

**Table 11.1**   HTML *<body>* tag attributes.

| Attribute | What It Specifies |
|---|---|
| alink | Color of an active link; i.e., while the mouse is on the link |
| background | URL of a background image |
| bgcolor | Background color of the page |
| fgcolor | Text or foreground color |
| link | Color of an unvisited link |
| vlink | Color of a visited link |

**Table 11.2**  Some *document* object properties.

| Property | What It Describes |
|---|---|
| *anchors[]* | An array of *anchors* objects |
| *applets[]* | An array of *applets* objects, relating to Java applets |
| *bgColor, fgColor* | Determines the background color and text color, related to the HTML *<body>* tag |
| *cookie* | Allows reading and writing HTTP cookies (see Chapter 14, "Cookies") |
| *domain* | A security property for Web servers in the same domain |
| *forms[]* | An array of *forms* objects, related to the HTML *<form>* tag |
| *images[]* | An array of *images* objects, related to the HTML *<img>* tag |
| *lastModified* | A string with the date when the page was last modified |
| *linkColor, alinkColor, vlinkColor* | Determines the color of unvisited links, active links, and visited links, respectively; related to link attributes of the HTML *<body>* tag |
| *links[]* | An array of *links* objects, related to the HTML *<a href>* tags |
| *location* | The URL of the document (deprecated) |
| *referrer* | URL of the document that linked the browser to this document |
| *title* | The title of the current document, related to the text between the *<title></title>* tags found in the head of the document |
| *URL* | A string containing the URL of the document |

**EXAMPLE  11.2**

```
        <html><head><title>Looping through Object Properties</title></head>
        <body>
        <script language="JavaScript">
1           var props=new Array();
2           for ( var property in window.document){
3               props.push(property);
            }
4           for(i=0;i<props.length; i++){
5               document.write( props[i] + " ");
                if( i>0 && i%3 == 0 ){
                    document.write("<br>");
                }
            }
        </script>
        </body></html>
```

## EXPLANATION

1   A new array object called *props* is created with the *Array()* constructor.

2   The *for/in* loop allows you to enumerate (list one by one) the properties of an object, in this case the *document* object. The body of the *for/in* loop is executed once for each property of the *document* object. If a property has been flagged as read-only, it will not be listed.

3   Each time through the loop, a new property of the *document* object is pushed onto the *props* array.

4   This *for* loop iterates through the *props* array to list the properties that were assigned to it.

5   Each property of the *document* object is displayed in groups of three. The output differs somewhat on different browsers.

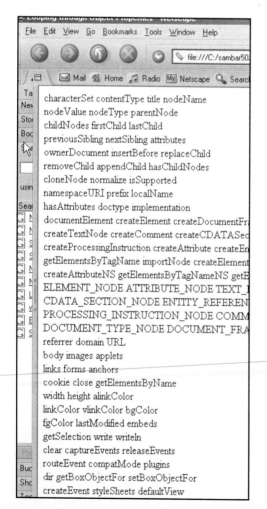

**Figure 11.2**
Using the *for/in* loop to display the properties of the *document* object.

**Using the *document* Object Properties in JavaScript.** The following example demonstrates how the properties that describe the document are used in a JavaScript program. The *write()* method displays a description of each of these properties as they pertain to the current document. The background color is silver, the text is forest green, the unvisited link is blue, and the visited link is purple.

## EXAMPLE 11.3

```
      <html><head><title>Document Object Properties</title></head>
      <body bgColor="silver" text="forestgreen" link="blue"
                     vlink="purple">
      <font face="arial" size="+2">
      <script language="JavaScript">
          var beg_tag="<em>"; end_tag="</em><br>";
          document.write("The location of the document"+ beg_tag +
1             document.location + end_tag);
          document.write("The document's title: "+ beg_tag+
2             document.title + end_tag);
          document.write("The background color: "+ beg_tag+
3             document.bgColor + end_tag);
          document.write("The link color is: "+ beg_tag+
4             document.linkColor + end_tag);
          document.write("The text color is: "+ beg_tag+
5             document.fgColor + end_tag);
          document.write("The document was last modified: "+ beg_tag +
6             document.lastModified + end_tag);
      </script>
7     <a href="thanks.stm">Thanks!</a>
      </body></html>
```

## EXPLANATION

1 This property contains the location of the document; i.e., the full path name to the document.

2 This property contains the title of the document, shown in the title bar at the top of the window.

3 This property describes the hexidecimal color of the document's background, in this example, silver.

4 This property describes the hexidecimal color of links, blue in this example.

5 This property describes the hexidecimal color of the text, forest green in this example.

6 This displays the date and time when the document was last modified.

7 The link will change color from blue to purple once it has been visited. Complete output is shown in Figure 11.3.

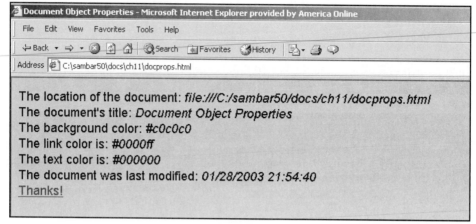

**Figure 11.3**  Document properties. Output from Example 11.3.

**The *document* Object Methods.**   The *document* object has methods to tell the object how to behave or what to do. Table 11.3 lists these methods. We have used the *write()* and *writeln()* methods throughout this text to send output to the screen dynamically, as shown below:

```
document.writeln("<h2>Welcome to the JavaScript World!</h1>");
```

Methods, like properties, use the dot syntax to define the object they are manipulating; for instance, *document.clear()* or *window.open()*. (The parentheses differentiate a method from a property.)

**Table 11.3**  Methods of the *document* object.

| Method | What It Does |
|---|---|
| *clear()* | Clears the current document window |
| *close()* | Closes the document window for writing |
| *focus()* | Brings the document into focus |
| *open()* | Begins a new document, erasing the old one |
| *write()* | Writes and appends text into the current document |
| *writeln()* | Same as *write()*, but appends a newline if in a *<pre>* tag |

When you open a new document, the current document will be replaced with a new document and all of its content overwritten. Example 11.4 opens a new document in an existing frame. The original text in the document is overwritten. After the document is opened, it must be closed.

EXAMPLE 11.4

```
<html>
<head><title>Frame Me!</title></head>

<!-- Creating the framesets for two files -->
<!-- This HTML file is named: framedef.html -->

<frameset cols="25%,75%">
<frame src="leftframe.html" name=lframe>
<frame src="rightframe.html" name=rframe>
</frameset>
</html>
-----------------------------------------------------------------
<html>
<head><title>Right Frame</title></head>

<!-- This file is named: rightframe.html -->

<body bgColor="lightgreen">
<h2>
Just to show you that this is the right frame
</h2>
</body>
</html>
-----------------------------------------------------------------
<html>
<!-- This file is named: leftframe.html -->
<head><title>Left Frame</title></head>
<body bgColor="yellow"><font face="verdana">
<h2>
left frame writes to right frame
</h2>
<script language="JavaScript">
    // Methods of the document object
1       parent.frames[1].document.open();
2       parent.frames[1].document.write("<body bgcolor='black'>",
            "<font color='white'>",
            "<h1>Hey brother, let me write all over you!</h2>");
3       parent.frames[1].document.close();
</script>
</body>
</html>
```

**EXPLANATION**

1   From the left frame, *parent.frames[0]*, the right frame is referenced as *parent.frames[1]*. A new document is opened in the right-hand frame with the *open()* method. Whatever was in that frame is erased by the new document. The *open()* method is optional because when the *write()* method is called, JavaScript will automatically open a new document and send the output there. There are times when this might happen, and you didn't want to overwrite everything. Since the document is parsed top to bottom, if the browser has finished parsing, then any attempts to write to the document will cause the whole thing to be overwritten. This might happen if you call a function as a result of some event being triggered.

2   The *write()* method sends content to the right-hand frame, including the background color, the color of the font, and a string of text. Take note that the *write()* [and *writeln()*] methods take a comma-separated list of arguments. In previous examples, we used the + (the concatenation operator) to join the strings together, but here, commas are used to separate the strings. The *write()* method displays its arguments in the order they are given.

3   The document in the right-hand frame is officially closed. Whereas the *open()* method was optional, the *close()* method is required. When using Internet Explorer, the content of the frame remained unchanged after closing the frame, but with Netscape, the old document reappeared. See Figures 11.4 and 11.5.

**Figure 11.4**   Left frame opened a new document in right frame, replacing what was there.

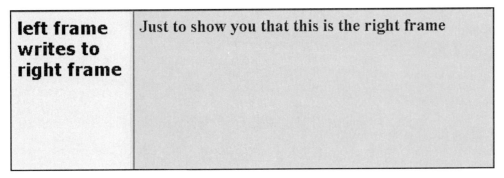

**Figure 11.5** After the document in the right-hand frame is closed, the original document reappears (Netscape 7).

# 11.2 Introduction to Forms

At the heart of the Web is the form. It is used to pass information from the browser to the server. Anytime you go online and order a book, trade at an auction, fill out a survey, or send an e-mail using a Web browser, you are working with a form.

An HTML form offers you a number of ways to accept input, such as radio buttons, checkboxes, pop-up menus, and text boxes; these are called virtual input devices. Once the form has been filled out by a user, it normally is sent to a server where the input is processed by a server-side program, such as a CGI, ASP, or PHP application.

## 11.2.1   HTML Review of Forms

All forms are in HTML documents. They begin with a *<form>* tag and its attributes, followed by the input fields where the user enters form information, and end with a *</form>* tag.

```
<form action="URL to server program" method="post">
The body of the form goes here, including input devices for filling out
the form (see Table 11.4 for a complete example).
</form>
```

The *action* attribute is assigned the URL of the server program that will be executed when the data is submitted by pressing the submit button.

A *method* attribute may be assigned to the *<form>* tag. The *method* attribute indicates how the form will be processed. The *get* method is the default (and does not need to be specified) and the *post* method is the most commonly used alternative. The *get* method is preferable for operations that will not affect the state of the server; that is, simple document retrieval, database lookups, and the like. The *post* method is preferred for handling operations that may change the state of the server, such as adding or deleting records from a database. (See Appendix C for a complete discussion.)

The browser gets input from the user by displaying fields that can be edited. The fields are created by the HTML *<INPUT TYPE=key/value>* tag. These fields appear as checkboxes, text boxes, radio buttons, and other forms. The data that is entered into the form is sent to the server in an encoded string format in a name/value pair scheme. The value represents the actual input data. Before the server-side program is called, Java-Script can be used to validate the data that was entered into the form by using event handlers.

If the form is not going to be sent to the server for processing, then the *action, target,* and *method* attributes are not necessary.

A summary of the steps in producing a form follows:

1. START: Start the form with the HTML *<form>* tag.
2. ACTION: The *action* attribute of the *<form>* tag is the URL of the server-side (CGI) script that will process the data input from the form. For a complete discussion of CGI, see Appendix C.
3. METHOD: Provide a method on how to process the data input. The default is the *get* method.
4. CREATE: Create the form with buttons, boxes, and whatever looks attractive using HTML tags and fields.
5. SUBMIT: Create a submit button so that the form can be processed. This will launch the CGI script listed in the *action* attribute.
6. END: End the form with the *</form>* tag.

## 11.2.2   Input Types for Forms

Table 11.4 shows the various form input types.

**Table 11.4**   HTML form input types.

| Input Type | Attribute | Description |
|---|---|---|
| *button* | *name* | Creates a generic button for user input. It has no default action. |
| *text* | *name, size, maxlength* | Creates a text box for user input. *size* specifies the size of the text box. *maxlength* specifies the maximum number of characters allowed. |
| *textarea* | *name, size, rows,cols* | Creates a text area that can take input spanning multiple lines. *rows* and *cols* specify the size of the box. |
| *password* | *name, value* | Like text box but input is hidden. Asterisks appear in the box to replace characters typed. |
| *checkbox* | *name, value* | Displays a square box that can be checked. Creates name/value pairs from user input. Multiple boxes can be checked. |

**Table 11.4** HTML form input types. (continued)

| Input Type | Attribute | Description |
|---|---|---|
| radio | name, value | Like checkboxes, except only one button (or circle) can be checked. |
| select | name, option, size, multiple | Provides pop-up menus and scrollable lists. Only one can be selected. Attribute *multiple* creates a visibly scrollable list. A *size* of 1 creates a pop-up menu with only one visible box. |
| file | name | Specifies files to be uploaded to the server. MIME type must be *multipart/form-data*. |
| hidden | name, value | Provides name/value pair without displaying an object on the screen. |
| submit | name, value | When pressed, executes the form; launches *cgi*. |
| image | src, value, align | Same as submit button, but displays an image instead of text. The image is in a file found at *src*. |
| reset | name, value | Resets the form to its original position; clears all input fields. |

First let's see how input gets into the form by looking at a simple document (see Figure 11.6) and the HTML code used to produce it (see Example 11.5). The user will be able to click on a button or enter data in the text box. The input in this example won't be processed when the submit button is pressed. Nothing will be displayed by the browser.

**EXAMPLE 11.5**

```
        <html><head><title>An HTML Form</title></head>
        <body><b>
1       <form action="/cgi-bin/bookstuff/form1.cgi" method="post"><p>
        <fieldset><legend><font size="+1"> All About You</legend>
        <p><font size="-1" color="blue">
        Type your name here:
2       <input type="text" name="namestring" size="50">
        <p>
        Talk about yourself here:<br>
3       <textarea name="comments" align="left" rows="5" cols="50">I was
            born...
        </textarea>
        <p>
        Choose your food:<b>
```

**EXAMPLE   11.5 (CONTINUED)**

```
4   <input type="radio" name="choice" value="burger">Hamburger
    <input type="radio" name="choice" value="fish">Fish
    <input type="radio" name="choice" value="steak">Steak
    <input type="radio" name="choice" value="yogurt">Yogurt
    <p>
    <b>Choose a work place:</b><br>
5   <input type="checkbox" name="place" value="LA">Los Angeles
    <br>
    <input type="checkbox" name="place" value="SJ">San Jose
    <br>
    <input type="checkbox" name="place" value="SF" checked>
        San Francisco
    <p>
    <b>Choose a vacation spot:</b><br>
6   <select multiple name="location">
        <option selected value="hawaii"> Hawaii
        <option value="bali">Bali
        <option value="maine">Maine
        <option value="paris">Paris
    </select>
    <p></fieldset>
7   <input type="submit" value="Submit">
8   <input type="reset" value="Clear">
9   </form>
    </body>
    </html>
```

**EXPLANATION**

1   This is the beginning of a *<form>* tag that specifies where the browser will send the input data and the method that will be used to process it. The default method is the *get* method. When the data is submitted, a server-side program, usually a CGI script, will be executed by the server. The CGI script is located under the server's root directory in the *cgi-bin* directory, the directory where CGI scripts are normally stored. In this example, the CGI script is stored in a directory called *bookstuff* below the *cgi-bin* directory.

2   The input type is a text box that will hold up to 50 characters. When the user types text into the text box, that text will be stored in the user-defined *name* value, *namestring*. For example, if the user types *Stefan Lundstrom*, the browser will assign to the query string, *namestring=Stefan Lundstrom*. If assigned a *value* attribute, the text field can display a default text string that appears in the text box when it is first displayed by the browser.

3   The user is asked for input. The text area is similar to the text field, but will allow input that scans multiple lines. The *<textarea>* tag will produce a rectangle named "comments" with dimensions in rows and columns (5 rows × 50 columns) and an optional default value (*I was born...*).

**EXPLANATION** (CONTINUED)

4    The user is asked to pick from a series of menu items. The first input type is a list of radio buttons. Only one button can be selected at a time. The input type has two attributes: a *type* and a *name*. The value of the *name* attribute *"choice"*, for example, will be assigned *"burger"* if the user clicks on the *Hamburger* option. *choice=burger* is passed onto the CGI program. And if the user selects *Fish, choice=fish* will be assigned to the query string. These key/value pairs are used to build a query string to pass onto the CGI program after the submit button is pressed.

5    The input type this time is in the form of checkboxes. More than one checkbox may be selected. The optional default box is already checked. When the user selects one of the checkboxes, the value of the *name* attribute will be assigned one of the values from the *value* attribute; *place=LA* if *Los Angeles* is checked.

6    The user is asked for input. The *<select>* tag is used to produce a pop-up menu (also called a drop-down list) or a scrollable list. The *name* option is required. It is used to define the name for the set of options. For a pop-up menu, the *size* attribute is not necessary; it defaults to 1. The pop-up menu initially displays one option and expands to a menu when that option is clicked. Only one selection can be made from the menu. If a *size* attribute is given, that many items will be displayed. If the *multiple* attribute is given (as *<select multiple name="whatever">*), the menu appears as a scrollable list, displaying all of the options.

7    If the user clicks the submit button, the CGI script listed in the form's *action* attribute will be launched.

8    If the reset button (*"Clear"*) is pressed, all input boxes are reset to their defaults.

9    This tag ends the form. The output is shown in Figure 11.6.

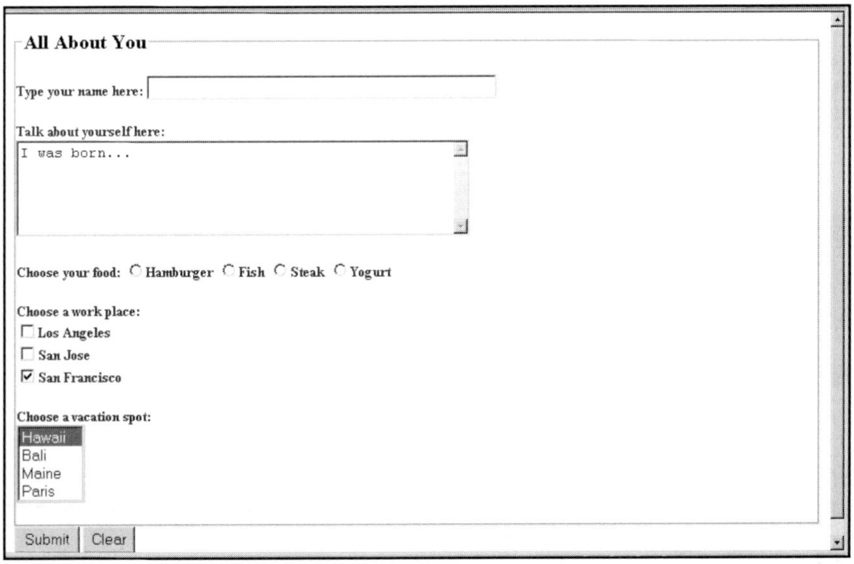

**Figure 11.6**    A simple HTML form. Output from Example 11.5.

## 11.2.3   JavaScript and the *forms* Object

In the previous example, the HTML form had nothing to do with JavaScript. After a form has been filled out, the information is normally sent from the browser to a server in a URL encoded format. The server then calls a CGI program to handle the information. So where does JavaScript come into all of this? Well, before sending the form off to the server, JavaScript can check to see if the form was filled out properly. If we like, every input field can be validated by JavaScript. It can check for empty fields. It can check for a valid credit card number, e-mail address, zip code, and so on. In addition, rather than having the user submit the form, submission can be controlled by JavaScript with its own *submit()* method. And by naming the forms, JavaScript can handle multiple forms and input types, respond to user-initiated events, and call functions to handle the data that was submitted.

As shown in the HTML Example 11.5 a document may have a number of HTML forms and input types such as simple text boxes, radio buttons, checkboxes, and so on. JavaScript provides objects that parallel HTML tags; for example, the JavaScript *forms* object parallels the HTML *<form>* tag and the JavaScript *elements* object parallels the input devices such as radio buttons or checkboxes.

In this section we will focus on the structure of the JavaScript *forms* object and how to use it in terms of the DOM. In Chapter 12, "Handling Events," you will learn how to catch the form before it is sent to the server. In Chapter 13, "Regular Expressions and Pattern Matching," you will learn how to check all the input fields of a form before processing it, using the magic of regular expressions and pattern matching.

**The *forms[]* Array.**   Since the document contains forms, the *forms* object is also a property of the *document* object. Every time you create a form in a given document, the browser creates a unique form object and assigns it as an element of an array, called the *forms[]* array. The index value of the array, starting at 0, corresponds to the order in which the form occurs in the document; the first form is assigned to *forms[0]*, and each successive form would get the next index value. When accessing a form from JavaScript, the first form to appear in the page would be referred to as *document.forms[0]* and the next form *document.forms[1]*, and so on. See Figure 11.7.

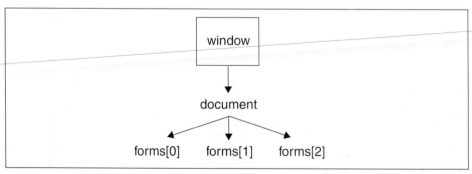

**Figure 11.7**   How the *forms()* array is created.

If you name the form (*name* is an attribute of the HTML *<form>* tag), you can use that name to represent the JavaScript *forms* object. Rather than saying *document.forms[0]* or *document.forms[1]*, you can reference the form by its name. For example, if the first HTML form is named *myform1*, the corresponding JavaScript object, *document.forms[0]*, can now be referenced as *document.myform1*.

**The *elements[]* Array.**     HTML forms contain input types like buttons and text boxes, also called fields. Similarly, the JavaScript *forms* object consists of a property called *elements*. This is a JavaScript array that parallels all of the HTML fields within the form. Each of the input types in the *elements[]* array is also an object in its own right. See Figure 11.8.

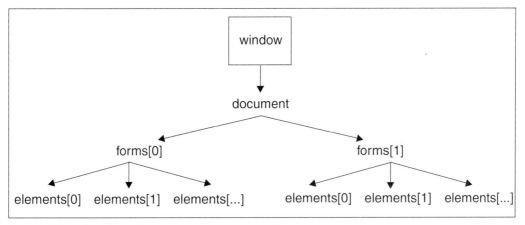

**Figure 11.8**   How the *elements[]* array is created.

When going down the DOM hierarchy, *document.forms[0].elements[0]* refers to the first field in a form. The *elements* objects also contains properties, such as the *name*, *type*, and *value* of the field. For example, *document.forms[0].elements[0].name* references the name of the field and *document.forms[0].elements[0].type* references the type of the field, such as *submit, reset, button, text, radio*, or *checkbox*.

If you name the field or input types, those names can be used to reference the corresponding JavaScript object. For example, *document.myform1.yourname.value* is easier to read and type than *document.forms[0].elements[0].value*, although they reference the same field value.

The following example contains two forms, each containing input types. The name of the first form is *form1* and the name of the second form is *form2*. Each form is an element of the *forms[]* array.

**EXAMPLE 11.6**

(Two Forms)

```
<form name="form1">
    <input type="text"
        name="yourname">: Type your name here<br>
    <input type="button"
        name="button1"
        value="Push Button">
</form>

<form name="form2">
    <input type="radio"
        name="veggie1"
        value="bean">Beans
    <input type="radio"
        name="veggie2"
        value="carrot">Carrots
</form>
```

(Object Hierarchy)

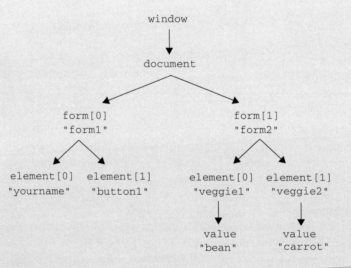

| HTML | JavaScript Object | JavaScript Named Object |
|------|-------------------|-------------------------|
| `<form name="form1">` | `document.forms[0]` | `document.form1` |
| `<input type="text"`<br>`    name="yourname"` | `document.forms[0].elements[0]` | `document.form1.yourname` |
| `<input type="button">`<br>`    name="button1">` | `document.forms[0].elements[1]` | `document.form1.button1` |
| `<form name="form2">` | `document.forms[1]` | `document.form2` |
| `<input type="radio">`<br>`    name="veggie1">` | `document.forms[1].elements[0]` | `document.form2.veggie1` |

**Properties and Methods.** The *forms* object is a property and child of the *document* object. Each form is an element of the *forms[]* array and each form has properties that correspond to the HTML attributes of the form as well as properties that describe the form. As discussed previously, these properties may be objects in their own right; for example, the *button* property of the form is also an object with its own properties. Some of the properties of the *forms* object are listed in Table 11.5 and methods are listed in Table 11.6. Properties of the *elements* object are listed in Table 11.7.

**Table 11.5** Properties of the *forms* object.

| *Property* | *What It Describes* |
| --- | --- |
| *action* | The URL to the server (where the form is sent) |
| *button* | An object representing a generic button |
| *checkbox* | An object representing a checkbox field |
| *elements* | An array containing an element for each form field (radio button, checkbox, button, etc.) defined within a form |
| *encoding* | MIME type (*application/x-www-urlencoded* or *multipart/form-data*) |
| *FileUpload* | An object representing a file-upload form field |
| *hidden* | An object representing a hidden field in a form |
| *length* | The number of fields defined within the form |
| *method* | *get* or *post* (how the form is sent to the server) |
| *name* | The name of the form |
| *password* | An object representing a password field |
| *radio* | An object representing a radio button field |
| *reset* | An object representing a reset button |
| *select* | An object representing a selection list |
| *submit* | An object representing a submit button |
| *target* | References the HTML target tag attribute, the name of the frame where the user's reponse to the submitted form will be displayed |
| *text* | An object representing a text field |
| *textarea* | An object representing a text area field |

**Table 11.6** Methods of the *forms* object.

| Method | What It Does |
|---|---|
| *reset()* | Resets the form fields to their default values (see page 290) |
| *submit()* | Submits a form |

**Table 11.7** Properties of the *elements* object.

| Property | What It Describes |
|---|---|
| *form* | The name of the form object where the element was defined (read-only) |
| *name* | The name of the input device as specified in the HTML *name* attribute (read-only) |
| *type* | The type of input device, such as radio, checkbox, password, etc. (read-only) |
| *value* | The text that is associated with the input device, such as the text entered into the text area or text box, the text that appears in a button, etc. (read/write) |

## 11.2.4 Naming Forms and Buttons

**How JavaScript References a Form by Name.** The *<form>* tag has a *name* attribute that allows you to give your form a name. It is somewhat easier and more readable to reference a form by its name than by using the array syntax, such as *forms[0]* and *forms[1]*.

In the following example, two HTML forms are created: one contains a text box, and the other a button. Each of the forms is given a name with the *name* attribute. In the JavaScript program, the two forms are accessed by walking down the JavaScript tree hierarchy, starting at the top of the tree, separating each of the nodes with a dot.

## EXAMPLE   11.7

```
       <html>
       <head><title>Naming Forms object</title></head>
       <body>
1      <form name="form1">
          Enter your name:
2         <input type="text"
             name="namefield"
             value="Name: ">
3      </form>

4      <form name="form2">
5         <input type="button" value="Press here">
6      </form>
       <font size="+1">
7      <script language="JavaScript">
          // How do we reference the form in JavaScript?
          // Go down the document tree: window/document/form.property
          // The window object can be left off, since it is at the top
8         document.write( "The first form is named: "+
                     window.document.form1.name);
9         document.write( "The second form is named: "+
                     document.form2.name);
       </script>
       </body></html>
```

## EXPLANATION

1   This is the first HTML form, named *form1*.

2   The input type for this form is a rectangular text field with a default value *"Name: "*.

3   This tag ends the form.

4   This is the second form, named *form2*.

5   The input type for this form is a button with the value *"Press here"*, which will appear as text in the button.

6   This tag ends the second form.

7   The JavaScript program starts here.

8   To display the name of the first form, descend the JavaScript tree, starting at the *window*, to the *document*, to the form named *form1*, to its *name* property.

9   To display the name of the second form, descend the JavaScript tree as in line 8. This time we left out the *window* object, which is fine because Javascript knows that the *window* is always at the top of the tree. See Figure 11.9.

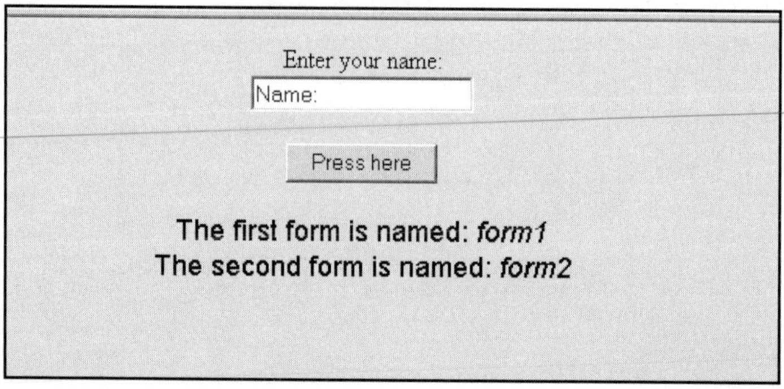

Enter your name:

Name:

Press here

**The first form is named: *form1***
**The second form is named: *form2***

**Figure 11.9**   Name those forms!

The elements and properties of the HTML *<form>* tag are shown in Table 11.8.

**Table 11.8**   *<form>* tag elements and properties.

| Object | Property | Purpose |
| --- | --- | --- |
| button | name, type, value | A general purpose GUI button |
| checkbox | checked, defaultChecked, name, type, value | A set of (or one) clickable boxes allowing multiple selections |
| FileUpLoad | name, type, value | A field allowing a file to be submitted as part of a form |
| hidden | name, type, value | A field where the content is not shown in the form |
| password | defaultValue, name, value | A field for entering a password, masking the real characters typed |
| radio | checked, defaultChecked, name, type, value | A set of (or one) clickable boxes allowing only one selection |
| reset | name, type, value | A button that clears and resets the form fields |
| select | length, name, options, selectedIndex, type, value | A pop-up or scrolling list of items from which to choose |
| submit | name, type, value, | A button used for submitting form data |
| text | defaultValue, name, type, value | A rectangular field allowing one line of input |
| textarea | defaultValue, name, type, value | A rectangular box allowing multiple lines of input value |

**How JavaScript References the Form Elements by Name.**   Each form object is an element of the *forms[]* array and each form contains input types such as buttons, text boxes, checkboxes, and so on. Each of the input types is also stored in an array called *elements[]* in the order the input device in found in the document. In the following example, there is one form, called *myform*. It contains two elements, button input types, named *button1* and *button2*, respectively.

---

**EXAMPLE 11.8**

```
        <html><head><title>Naming Buttons</title>
        </head>
        <body bgcolor="cyan"><font face="arial">
        <b>Naming buttons<br>
        <font size="+1">
1       <form name="myform">
2          <input type="button" name="button1" value="red"></input>
3          <input type="button" name="button2" value="blue"></input>
4       </form>
        <script language="JavaScript">
            document.write("<b><br>Form name is: </b><em>"
5          +document.myform.name);
            document.write("</em><b><br>Name of first button is:</b><em> "
6          +document.myform.button1.name);
            document.write("</em><b><br>Value of button1 field:</b><em> "
7          +document.myform.button1.value);
            document.write("</em><b><br>Name of second button is:</b><em> "
           +document.myform.button2.name);
            document.write("</em><b><br>Value of button2 field:</b><em> "
           +document.myform.button2.value);
        </script>
        </body>
        </html>
```

**EXPLANATION**

1   The HTML form starts here. It is named *myform*. JavaScript can now reference the form by its name.

2   The input type is a button named *button1* and assigned a value of *red*. JavaScript can now reference the button by its name.

3   The input type is a button named *button2* and assigned a value of *blue*.

4   The form ends here.

5   Within the JavaScript program the form is referenced by its name. It is a property of the *document* object. Without naming the form, it would be referenced as *document.forms[0].name*.

6   The name assigned to the first button is displayed. See Figure 11.10. Without naming the form or the button, it would be referenced as *document.forms[0].elements[0].value*. Easy to misspell words here. The first time I wrote this program, I spelled *myform.name* as *myform1.name*; the output was *form[0] is null or not an object*. See Figure 11.11.

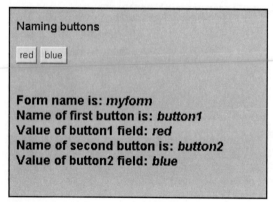

**Figure 11.10**   Name that button!

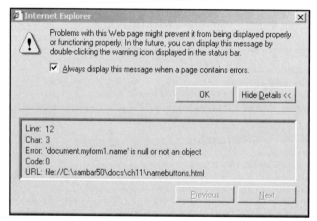

**Figure 11.11**   What went wrong? Watch your spelling! We tried to reference a form by the wrong name!

In the following example, the document contains two named forms, *myForm1* and *myForm2*. Each of the forms contain input types: the first form contains a text box and the second form contains three buttons. A JavaScript program gets access to the forms and properties by using their names to reference them.

**EXAMPLE 11.9**

```html
        <html><head><title>Form and Element Properties</title>
        </head>
        <body>
1       <form name="myForm1">
            Enter something:
2           <input name="enter"
                type="text"
                value="hello">
        </form>
3       <form name="myForm2">
        Button test<br>
4           <input type="button" name="button1" value="red"></input>
            <input type="button" name="button2" value="blue"></input>
            <input type="button" name="button3" value="green"></input>
        </form>
        <script language="JavaScript">
            document.write("<b><br>Form name is: </b><em>"
5           +document.myForm1.name);
            document.write("</em><b><br>Number of button fields:</b><em> "
6           +document.myForm2.length);
            document.write("</em><b><br>Value of the text field:</b><em> "
7           +document.myForm1.enter.value);
            document.write("</em><b><br>Value of button1 field:</b><em> "
8           +document.myForm2.button1.value);
            document.write("</em><br><br><b>The name of the first form,
            <em>document.forms[0].name,</em> is: </b>"
9           +document.forms[0].name);
            document.write("<br><b>The name of the second form, <em>
            document.forms[1].name,</em> is: </b>"
            +document.forms[1].name);
            document.write("<p><b>Accessing the \"elements[]\" <em>name,
            type, </em>and</em><em> value</em> properties: </b>");
10          for(var i = 0; i < document.myForm2.length; i++){
11              document.write("<br>name: " +
                document.myForm2.elements[i].name +"<br>");
12              document.write("value: "
                +document.forms[1].elements[i].value+"<br>");
                document.write("type: "
                +document.forms[1].elements[i].type
                +"<br>");
            }
        </script>
        </body>
        </html>
```

**EXPLANATION**

1  The HTML form is named *myForm1*, accessible in JavaScript as *document.forms[0]* or *document.myForm1*.

2  The HTML input type is a text field, named *enter* and accessible in JavaScript as *document.MyForm1.elements[0]* or *document.myForm1.enter*.

3  Another HTML form, called *myForm2* is started.

4  The HTML input type for the second form is a set of simple button devices, each one named *button1*, *button2*, and *button3*, respectively.

5  The *name* property for the first form is used by JavaScript to display the form name.

6  The *length* property for the second form is used by JavaScript to display the number of fields defined within the form. There are three buttons, so the length is 3.

7  The value in the text field called *enter* is displayed (whatever the user typed into the text box).

8  The *value* property of the first button, *red*, is the text you see inside the first button.

9  The *name* property of the first form, *myForm1*, is displayed.

10  The *for* loop is entered to iterate through each of the field elements in the second form.

11  The *name* property of the second form, *myForm2*, is displayed.

12  The value and type property for the three elements of the second form are displayed, one at a time. Instead of using names to represent each of the field elements, they are accessed with their element array names. See Figure 11.12.

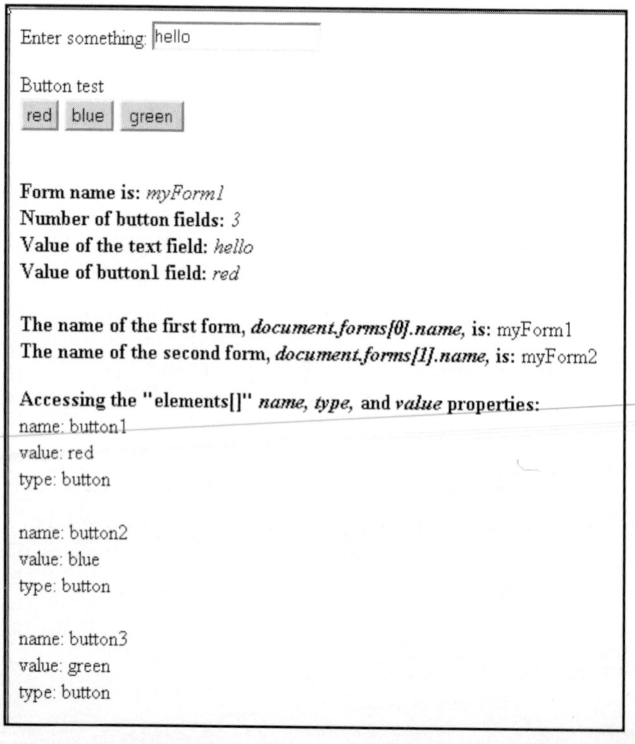

---

Enter something: hello

Button test
red  blue  green

**Form name is:** *myForm1*
**Number of button fields:** *3*
**Value of the text field:** *hello*
**Value of button1 field:** *red*

**The name of the first form,** *document.forms[0].name,* **is:** myForm1
**The name of the second form,** *document.forms[1].name,* **is:** myForm2

**Accessing the "elements[]"** *name, type,* **and** *value* **properties:**
name: button1
value: red
type: button

name: button2
value: blue
type: button

name: button3
value: green
type: button

**Figure 11.12**
Naming forms and their elements.

## 11.2.5   Submitting Fillout Forms

**Submitting an HTML Form <u>Without</u> JavaScript.**   When the user clicks on a submit button, the form is normally sent right off to the server for further processing by another application such as a CGI script. Before the server gets the form, its content is gathered by the browser, encoded, and then sent to the URL address supplied in the *action* attribute of the form. (In the previous examples, the *action* attribute was not used because there was no reason to process the sample forms.) The application on the server side is started up to decode and process the form information. From there, an acknowledgement may be sent back to the user, an e-mail delivered, the processed information sent to a database, or whatever else we define. Now let's look at an example of an HTML form and how it is submitted to a server application.

### EXAMPLE 11.10

```
    <html><head><title>An HTML Form</title></head>
    <body><b>
1   <form action="/cgi-bin/bookstuff/form1.cgi" method="post"><p>
    <fieldset><legend><font size="+1"> All About You</legend>
    <p>
2   Type your name here:
    <input type="text" name="namestring" size="50">
    <p>
3   <b>Choose a work place:</b><br>
    <input type="checkbox" name="place" value="LA">Los Angeles<br>
    <input type="checkbox" name="place" value="SJ">San Jose<br>
    <input type="checkbox" name="place" value="SF" checked>San
            Francisco<p>
    <b>Choose a vacation spot:</b><br>
4   <select multiple name="location">
        <option selected value="hawaii"> Hawaii
        <option value="bali">Bali
        <option value="maine">Maine
        <option value="paris">Paris
    </select>
    <p></fieldset>
5   <input type="submit" value="Submit">
6   <input type="reset" value="Clear">
7   </form>
    </body>
    </html>
```

### EXPLANATION

1   The form starts here. The *action* attribute contains the URL of the server program that will get the form. The method being used (how the form will be sent) is the *post* method. This is the most common method used with forms.

2   The user is asked to type something into a text field box.

3   The user is asked to check a box for his place of work.

## EXPLANATION (CONTINUED)

4 The user is asked to select a vacation spot from a select menu, or drop-down list.

5 When the user clicks the submit button, the form is sent to the URL (server program) assigned to the *action* attribute of the *<form>* tag.

6 If the user presses the Clear button, all fields will be reset to their defaults.

7 This tag marks the end of the form. See Figure 11.13.

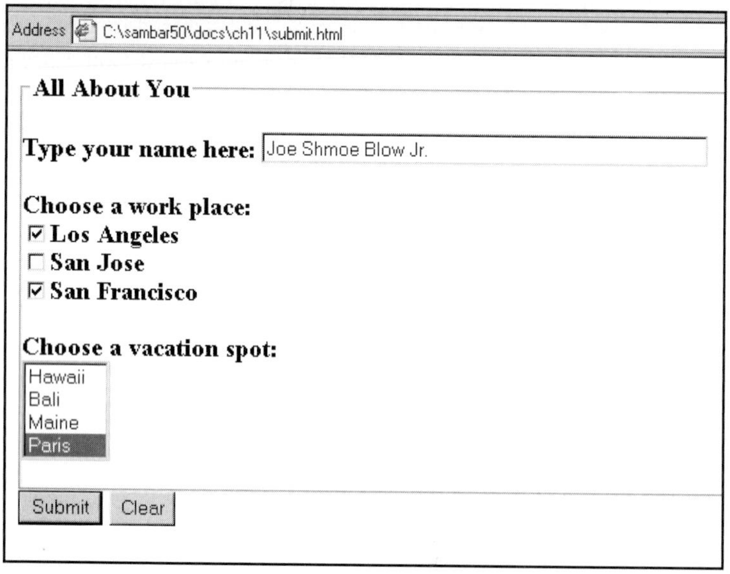


**Figure 11.13** A filled-out HTML form awaiting submission to the server.

**Submitting a Form with an Image.** The image input type gives you another way to submit a form. You can replace the standard submit button with a graphical image. The *src* attribute must be included to specify the location (URL) of the image. As with other image tags, the *alt* attribute (HTML 4.0) should be used to give replacement text for browsers that cannot load the image. Many browsers rely on either the *name* or *value* attribute as alternate text, so if there is any doubt, all three attributes for the same purpose should be used.

## EXAMPLE 11.11

```
     <html><head><title>An Image Input Type</title>
     <body bgcolor="magenta"> <font size="+1">
     <center>
     Enter your name:
     <br>
1    <form action="example.cgi" method="post">
2       <input type="text" size=50 >
        <p>
```

EXAMPLE 11.11 (CONTINUED)

```
3          <input type="image" src="submit.gif" alt="submit">
           <br>
4          <input type="reset">
5       </form>
        </center>
        </body>
        </html>
```

**EXPLANATION**

1   The HTML form starts here.

2   The input type is text. The user enters his name here.

3   The input type is a graphical submit button. When the user clicks on the image, the form will be submitted and sent to the CGI program assigned to the form's *action* attribute. The *src* attribute is assigned the URL of the *submit.gif* image. If the image can't be loaded, the *alt* attribute will cause the word "submit" to appear where the image should go.

4   When the user presses the Reset button, the text box will be cleared.

5   The HTML form ends here.

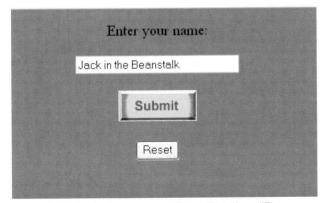

**Figure 11.14**   An image as a Submit button (IE).

**Submitting a Form <u>with</u> JavaScript (Event Handlers).**   A discussion of forms would be incomplete without mentioning how JavaScript implements form events (See Chapter 12, "Handling Events," for a complete discussion.) Events are triggered by a user when he initiates some action, like pressing a key, clicking his mouse on a button, or moving his mouse over a link. When such an action occurs, the browser detects it, and depending on what event is triggered, something will be done in response. A function may be called, a form can be validated—something happens. See Figure 11.15.

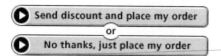

**Figure 11.15**   The user initiates an action, and an event is triggered.

With a form, an event handler allows you to control whether the form is submitted or cleared. For example, after the user has filled out the form, normally it is sent right off to a CGI, PHP, or ASP program on the server side to be processed. But if a JavaScript event handler is set up, then when the user presses the submit button, the handler can check the input data, and based on what comes in, determine whether to go ahead with the submission of the form data or reject it. That way, the user doesn't have to wait for the form to go to the server, have it validated there, and then sent back for mistakes that he could have corrected right away. (See "Form Validation with Regular Expressions" on page 446 in Chapter 13 for a complete discussion.) Likewise, before clearing all the values typed into the form, an event handler can confirm with the user that this is really what he wants to do, before resetting all the input devices to their default values.

With forms there are two event handlers that allow you to catch the form before it goes to the server. They are the *onClick* event handler and the *onSubmit* event handler. The *onReset* event can be used to clear the form's input devices or to stop them from being cleared.

**The *onClick* Event Handler.**   One way to either accept or reject the submission is to use the *onClick* event handler. The *onClick* event handler is an attribute of the HTML *submit* or *button* input type. When the user presses the button, the event is triggered, and if the handler function returns *true*, the form will be submitted; otherwise, it will be rejected.

**EXAMPLE  11.12**

```
      <html><head><title>onClick Event Handler and Forms</title>
      <script language="JavaScript">
1        function readySubmit(){
            if(confirm("Are you ready to submit your form? ")){
               return true;
            }
            else{
               return false;
            }
         }
      </script>
      </head>
      <body>
2     <form action="/cgi-bin/testform.cgi"
         method="post">
      Enter your user id:
```

EXAMPLE   11.12 (CONTINUED)

```
3     <input type="text"
          name="textbox"
          value="">
      <br>
      Type your password:
      <input type="password"
          name="secret">
      <p>
4     <input type="submit"
          onClick="readySubmit();">
      </body></html>
```

EXPLANATION

1   The JavaScript function called *readySubmit()* is defined. It will display a confirm
    dialog box. If the user clicks the OK button, a *true* value will be returned and the
    form will be submitted. If the user clicks the Cancel button, *false* will be returned,
    and the form will be stopped.

2   The form starts here. When submitted, it will go to the server-side CGI program.
    The URL of the CGI program is assigned to the *action* attribute of the HTML
    *<form>* tag.

3   The input types for this form are a text field and a password field.

4   When the user clicks the submit button, the *onClick* event handler is triggered. It
    will handle the event by invoking the JavaScript function called *readySubmit()*.

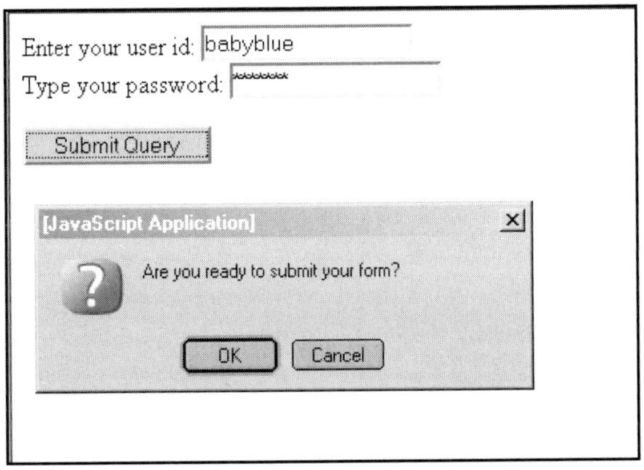

**Figure 11.16**   Submitting a form and the *onClick* event.

**The *onSubmit* Event Handler.**   Another important form event handler, called *onSubmit*, will also be triggered when the user presses the submit button or the Enter key, just
before the form is submitted. The *onSubmit* event handler is added as an attribute of the
*<form>* tag, (and only the *<form>* tag), to control what happens when the user presses the
submit button. When a function is assigned to the *onSubmit* event handler, if the value

returned by the function is *true*, the form will be submitted to the server, but if it returns *false*, the form will be stopped and the user will be given a chance to re-enter data in the form. The following example produces the same output as the previous one, but notice the placement of the handler. Instead of being associated with a button, it is associated with the form and set as an attribute of the *<form>* tag.

---

**EXAMPLE   11.13**

```
        <html>
        <head><title>onSubmit Event Handler and Forms</title>
        <script language="JavaScript">
1           function readySubmit(){
                if(confirm("Are you ready to submit your form? ")){
                    return true;}
                else{
                    return false;}
            }
        </script>
        </head>
        <body>
        <form action="/cgi-bin/testform.cgi"
            method="post"
2           onSubmit="return(readySubmit());" >
        Enter your user id:
        <input type="text"
            name="textbox"
            value="">
        <br>
        Type your password:
        <input type="password"
            name="secret">
        <p>
3       <input type="submit" >
        </body>
        </html>
```

---

**EXPLANATION**

1   The JavaScript function called *readySubmit()* is defined. It will display a confirm dialog box. If the user clicks the OK button, a *true* value will be returned and the form will be submitted. If the user clicks the Cancel button, *false* will be returned, and the form will be stopped.

2   The *onSubmit* event is an attribute of the HTML *<form>* tag. It will catch the form just before it is sent off to the server. When the user presses the submit button, the event handler *readySubmit()* will be invoked. If the event handler is called by the *onSubmit* attribute of the *<form>* tag, an explicit *return* must be used.

3   The input type is a submit button. When the user presses this button, the Java-Script *onSubmit* event is triggered. (See line 2.)

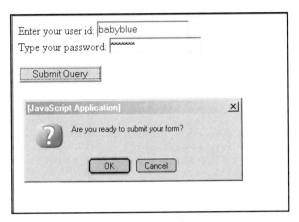

**Figure 11.17**  Submitting a form and the *onSubmit* event.

**The *onReset* Event Handler.**    The HTML reset button allows the user to clear the form fields and set them back to their default values. JavaScript will let you set up an *onReset* event handler to either accept or reject this action. This event handler can be used to make sure that clearing an entire form is really what you want to do before it's too late, especially if you've done a lot of typing and don't want to re-enter all that data.

## EXAMPLE 11.14

```
       <html>
       <head><title>The onReset Event</title>
       <script language="JavaScript">
1          function resetAll(){
2              if(confirm("Do you want to reset the form to its default
                          values? ")){
3                  return true;
               }
               else{
4                  return false;
               }
           }
       </script>
       </head>
       <body>
5      <form action="/cgi-bin/testform.cgi"
           method="post"
6          onReset="return resetAll();" >
       Enter your user id:
7      <input type="text"
           name="textbox"
           value="">
       <br>
```

**EXAMPLE  11.14 (CONTINUED)**

```
      Type your password:
8     <input type="password"
          name="secret">
      <p>
      <input type="submit"
          onClick="readySubmit();">
9     <input type="reset"
          value="Reset Form">
      </body>
      </html>
```

**EXPLANATION**

1   The function called *resetAll()* is defined. It is invoked when the *onReset* event is triggered.

2   If the user presses OK when he sees this confirm dialog box, a *true* value will be returned by this function, allowing the reset to clear all the input fields and set them back to their original values.

3   The value *true* is returned

4   If a value of *false* is returned by this function, the reset action will be dismissed.

5   The form starts here.

6   When the user presses the reset button the *onReset* event handler is triggered, causing the JavaScript function called *resetAll()* to be invoked.

7, 8   The input types for this form are a text field and a password field.

9   The reset button is used to reset the form fields back to their original values. When this button is pressed, the *onReset* event will be triggered. See Figure 11.18.

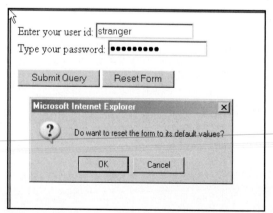

**Figure 11.18**    The user pressed the Reset Form button. The dialog box confirms the choice before the input boxes are reset to their default values.

**The *this* Keyword.**   The *this* keyword is especially helpful when dealing with forms. The *this* keyword refers to the current object. For forms containing multiple items, such as checkboxes, radio buttons, and text boxes, it is easier to refer to the item with the *this* keyword than by using its full name when calling a function.

When using an event handler, the *this* keyword always refers to the object that triggered the event. If the event is triggered from within the *<form>* tag, *this* refers to the current form, but if it is triggered by an element within the form, such as an input device, then it references that element. Each element has a *form* property that references the form in which it was created. In the following segment of an HTML document, note that when the *onClick* event handler is triggered within the first *button* input type, the *form* property is used to reference the form itself, whereas in the second button, the *this* keyword refers to the current button.

## FORMAT

```
<form>                                      <-- The JavaScript form object
<input type="button"                        <-- This a JavaScript element
   value="Print Form Stuff"
   onClick="display_formval(this.form);" >  <-- this keyword references the
                                                form object by using the
                                                element's form property

<input type="button"
   value="Print Button Stuff"
   onClick="display_buttonval(this);" >     <-- this keyword references the
                                                current object, the button

</form>
```

## EXAMPLE  11.15

```
        <html>
        <head><title>An HTML form and the "this" keyword and
            Event Handler</title>
        <script language="JavaScript">
1           function checkForm(yourinfo){
2               if(yourinfo.namestring.value == ""){   // Check for an
                                                        // empty string
                    alert("Please type in your name");
                    return(false);
                }
                else{
                    return(true);
                }
            }
        </script>
        </head>
        <body><b>
```

**EXAMPLE  11.15 (CONTINUED)**

```
          <form name="info" action="/cgi-bin/bookstuff/form1.cgi"
             method="post"
   3         onSubmit="return checkForm(this)"><p>
          <font size="+1"><p>
          Type your name here:
   4      <input type="text" name="namestring" size="50">
          <p>
   5      <input type="submit" value="Submit">
          <input type="reset" value="Clear">
          </form>
          </body>
          </html>
```

**EXPLANATION**

1    The function called *checkForm()* is passed an argument called *yourinfo*, which contains a reference to the form created on line 3.

2    When following the document object model hierarchy, *yourinfo* refers to *document.forms[0]* or *document.info.yourinfo.namestring.value* refers to the text field called *namestring* and the input value assigned to it after the user has entered something in the text box.

3    The *onSubmit* handler sends one argument, *this*, to the function *checkForm()*. The keyword *this* is a shorthand name for the current object; in this example the current object is a form, *document.forms[0]*.

4    The HTML input type is a text field called *namestring* that will display up to 50 characters.

5    The HTML input type is a submit button. When the user presses this button, the *onSubmit* handler in line 3 is triggered. If the return value from the function *check_Form* is *true*, the form will be submitted to the server, located at the URL shown in the *action* attribute of the form named *info*.

**Using the *button* Input Type Rather than *submit*.**    As shown in the previous examples, before the browser sends data to the server, an *onSubmit* or *onClick* event handler is triggered when the user presses the submit button or the Enter key. But what if you don't want the form to go off to the server? Then you will have to reject the submission or the browser will reset all the field values to their defaults.

If the form is *not* going to submit data to a server, the *button* input type can be used instead of the *submit* button. The *button* object has no default behavior and is used as a triggering device so that when the user presses the button, it causes something to happen. The *onClick* event handler is commonly used with buttons and is set as an attribute of the *button* input type. The *onClick* event handler is triggered when the user clicks the button associated with it.

EXAMPLE 11.16

```
           <html>
           <head><title>button input type</title>
           <script language="JavaScript">
1              function greetme(){
                   alert("Why did you click me like that? ");
               }
           </script>
           </head>
           <body>
2          <form name="form1">
           <!-- event handler for a button is an attribute for its
               input type -->
3          <input type="button"
               value="Click me!"
4              onClick="greetme()">
           </form></body>
           </html>
```

EXPLANATION

1   This function called *greetme()* is called when the user clicks on the button device.

2   A form called *form1* is started.

3   The input type is a simple graphical *button* containing the text *Click me!*

4   When the user presses the button, the *onClick* event handler is triggered and the function called *greetme()* is called. It will send an alert dialog box to the screen, as shown in Figure 11.19.

**Figure 11.19**  Forms and buttons.

**The *submit()* and *reset()* Methods.** In addition to event handlers, JavaScript provides two methods for the *forms* object, the *submit()* and the *reset()* methods. These methods emulate the event handlers of the same name: the *submit()* method submits the form just as though the user had pressed the submit button, and the *reset()* method resets the form elements to their defaults just as if he had typed the reset button. Neither of these methods trigger the *onSubmit* or *onReset* event handlers. (Note that the methods must be spelled with lowercase letters.)

**EXAMPLE 11.17**

```
      <html><head><title>An HTML Form</title></head>
      <body>
      <b>
1     <form name=myForm
          action="http://localhost/cgi-bin/environ.pl"
          method="post">
      <p>
      <fieldset><legend><font size="+1"> All About You</legend>
      <p><font size=3 color="blue">
      Type your name here:
2     <input type="text"
          name="namestring"
          size="50">
      <p>
      Talk about yourself here:<br>
3     <textarea name="comments"
          align="left"
          rows="5" cols="50">I was born...
      </textarea>
      <p>
      <b>Choose a work place:</b><br>
4     <input type="checkbox"
          name="place"
          value="LA">Los Angeles
      <br>
      <input type="checkbox"
          name="place"
          value="SJ">San Jose
      <br>
      <input type="checkbox"
          name="place"
          value="SF"
          checked>San Francisco
      <p></fieldset>
      </form>
      <p>
```

EXAMPLE 11.17 (CONTINUED)

```
5   <a href="#" onClick="javascript: myForm.submit();">
    Click here to submit this form</a>
    <p>
6   <a href="#" onClick="javascript: myForm.reset();">
    Click here to reset this form</a>
    </body>
    </html>
```

EXPLANATION

1   The form called *myForm* starts here. When the form is submitted, it will go to the address assigned to the *action* attribute, and the method—how the form is sent—is the *post* method.

2   The text field input type will accept a line of text from the user.

3   The text area box will accept up to 5 rows of text from the user.

4   The user can select any of the checkboxes. The default, *San Francisco*, is checked.

5   The link has been deactivated with the #. When the user presses the link, the *onClick* event will be triggered and cause the JavaScript *submit()* method to be invoked. The form data will be sent to the URL assigned to the *action* attribute of the form. The URL is a CGI program residing on the local server. Note that there is no need for the submit button here.

6   The link has been deactivated with the #. When the user presses the link, the *onClick* event will be triggered and cause the JavaScript *reset()* method to be invoked. The input boxes will all be cleared and set back to their default values.

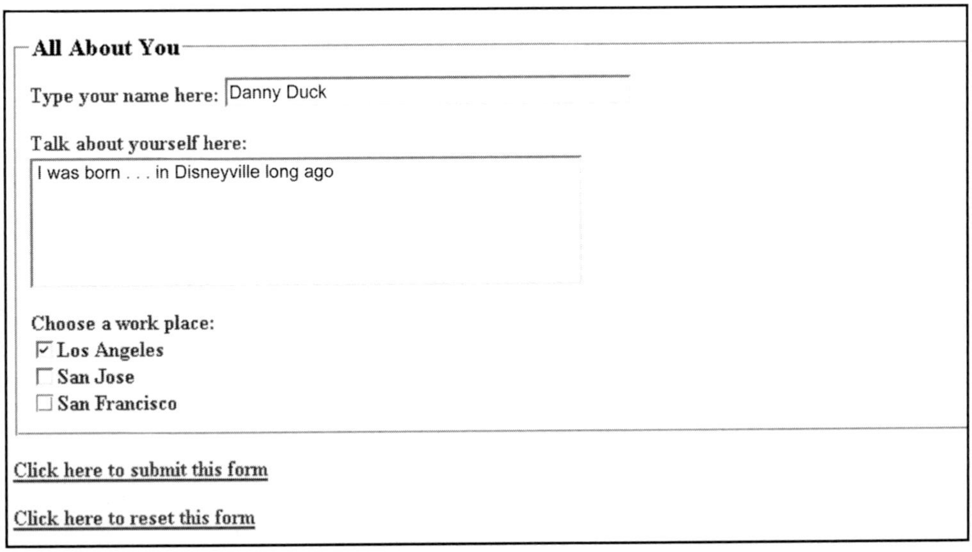

---

**All About You**

Type your name here: Danny Duck

Talk about yourself here:

I was born . . . in Disneyville long ago

Choose a work place:
☑ Los Angeles
☐ San Jose
☐ San Francisco

Click here to submit this form

Click here to reset this form

**Figure 11.20**  When the user clicks one of the links, either the *submit()* or the *reset()* method will be invoked.

**Displaying A Form's Content in a Pop-Up Window.**   After filling out a form, you may want to display the form content for confirmation before submitting it to a server. This can be done by creating another window, called a pop-up, and outputting the form data dynamically into that window. Example 11.18 uses JavaScript to open a new window to display the gathered form data from another file.

**EXAMPLE   11.18**

```
      <html><head><title>Display Form Input</title>
      <script language="JavaScript">
1     function showForm(myform) {
2         NewWin=window.open('','','width=300,height=200');
3         name_input="<b>Your name: " + myform.user_name.value
              + "</b><br>";
4         NewWin.document.write(name_input);
          phone_input="<b>Your phone: " + myform.user_phone.value
              + "</b><br>";
5         NewWin.document.write(phone_input);
      }
6     function close_window(){
          NewWin.window.close();
      }
      </script>
      </head><hr>
      <body><h3> Display form data in a little window</h2><p>
7     <form name="formtest" >
8         Please enter your name: <br>
          <input type="text" size="50" name="user_name">
          <p>
          Please enter your phone: <br>
          <input type="text" size="30" name="user_phone">
          <p>
9         <input type="button"
              value="show form data"
              onClick="showForm(this.form)";>
      </form>
      <font size="+1">
10    <a href="javascript:void(0)" onClick="close_window()">
      Click here to close little window</a>
      </font>
      </body>
      </html>
```

## EXPLANATION

1   A JavaScript function called *showForm()* is defined. Its only parameter is a reference to the name of the form; in this example, *myform*.

2   A new *window* object is created with the window's *open()* method.

3   The variable called *name_input* is assigned a string that will contain HTML tags and the value that was assigned to the form's text field.

4   The document of the new window will display the string value assigned to the variable *name_input* in line 3.

5   The document of the new window will display the string value assigned to *phone_input*.

6   This function will close the new window.

7   The HTML form called *formtest* starts here.

8   The input type for this form consists of two text fields that will be used to obtain the name and the phone of the user.

9   When the *button* input device is clicked, the *onClick* handler will be invoked. This is when you will see the new little window appear on the screen with all the form data.

10  The JavaScript *void(0)* operator has the effect of deactivating the link so that it will not try to go to some URL when clicked (like the # in Example 11.17). Instead, event handler *close_window()* will be invoked and the little window that was opened to display the form data, will be closed. See Figure 11.21.

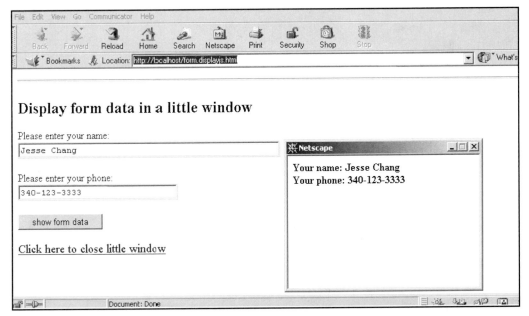

**Figure 11.21**   Form data is displayed in another window, called a pop-up window.

## 11.2.6   Programming Input Devices

With JavaScript, you can alter the contents of the form's input devices dynamically. Since each input device is an object, each has properties and methods, and can be manipulated like any other JavaScript object (i.e., it can be assigned to, changed, deleted, etc.). You can program checkboxes, assign values to text areas and text boxes, change the value in fields, add choices to drop-down menus, verify password entries, and do all of this on the fly. The following section shows you how to program input devices.

**The *text* Object.**    The *text* object parallels the HTML text field *<input type="text">* and also has name and value fields. To reference a text field from JavaScript, go down the document tree, starting at the *document*, then to the *form*, and then the *text* element. To get a value in the text field, for example, you would use the following syntax:

```
document.form1.textbox1.value,
```

where *form1* is the name of the form and *textbox1* is the name of the text field. Shown in Figure 11.22 is the JavaScript object hierarchy for the *text* object. Table 11.9 lists its properties and Table 11.10 lists its methods.

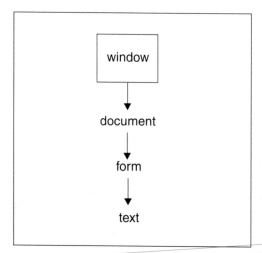

**Figure 11.22**   The *text* object within the JavaScript hierarchy.

**Table 11.9**  Properties of the *text* object.

| Property | What It Describes |
|---|---|
| *defaultValue* | The value assigned to the *value* attribute, and the default value the user sees in the text box when it first appears |
| *form* | The name of the form where the text box is defined |
| *name* | The name used to reference the text box |
| *type* | The type of the input device; i.e., *text* |
| *value* | The value attribute that will be assigned whatever the user types in the text box |

**Table 11.10**  Methods of the *text* object.

| Method | What It Describes |
|---|---|
| *blur()* | Removes focus from the object |
| *focus()* | Puts focus on the object |
| *handleEvent()* | Invokes the handler for a specified event (JavaScript 1.2) |
| *select()* | Selects or highlights text in the box |
| *unwatch()* | Turns off the watch for a particular property |
| *watch()* | Watches, and when a property is changed, calls a function |

**EXAMPLE 11.19**

```
      <html>
      <head><title>Text Boxes</title></head>
      <body bgcolor="pink">
1        <form name="form1">
         Enter your name:<br>
2            <input type="text"
                name="namefield"
                size=30 value="Name: "
3                onFocus="document.form1.namefield.select()">
4                // onFocus="this.select()">
         </form>
      <font face=arial size="+1">
      <script language="JavaScript">
      // How do we reference the form in JavaScript?
      // Go down the document tree: document.form[].element.property
```

**EXAMPLE   11.19 (CONTINUED)**

```
5   document.write( "The type of the input device is:<em> "+
        document.form1.namefield.type);
    document.write( "<br></em>The textbox is named:<em> "+
        document.form1.namefield.name);
    document.write( "<br></em>The value in the text field is:<em> "+
        document.form1.namefield.value);
    document.write( "<br></em>The size of the text field is:<em> "+
        document.form1.namefield.size);
    </script>
    </body><html>
```

**EXPLANATION**

1   The form starts here in the body of the document.

2   The input type is a text box, named *namefield* with a default value *"Name: "*.

3   When the mouse cursor is clicked in this box, the *onFocus* event is triggered and the *select()* method causes the value in the text box to be highlighted.

4   Instead of using the long, drawn-out, DOM hierarchy, the *this* makes it easier to reference this input type.

5   The properties for the text box, named *namefield*, are accessed using the DOM hierarchy. The output is shown in Figure 11.23.

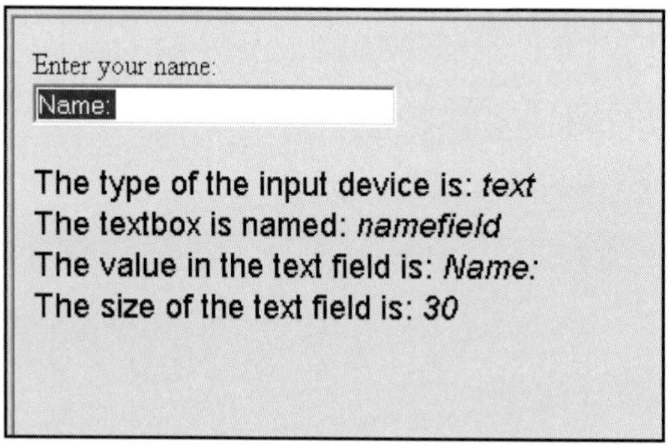

Enter your name:
| Name: |

**The type of the input device is:** *text*
**The textbox is named:** *namefield*
**The value in the text field is:** *Name:*
**The size of the text field is:** *30*

**Figure 11.23**   The text box and its properties.

EXAMPLE 11.20

```
1    <html>
     <head><title>Assigning Value on the Fly to a Text
         Field</title></head>
     <body bgcolor="aquamarine">
     <font face=arial size="+1">
1    <form name="form1">
     Enter your name
2        <input type="text"
3            name="yourname"
             size=60>
             <p>
             Click in the box
4        <input type="text"
5            name="message"
             size=60
6            onClick="this.value='Greetings and Salutations, '+
                         document.form1.yourname.value+ '!';">
             <p>
7        <input type="reset">
     </form>
     </body>
```

EXPLANATION

1 An HTML form called *form1* is started.

2 The input type for this form is a text box that will hold up to 60 characters.

3 The name of the text box is *yourname*.

4 The second input type is also a text box.

5 The name of this text box is *message*.

6 The *onClick* event handler is triggered when the user clicks inside this text box. It concatenates the message "*Greetings and Salutations*" to whatever was typed in the first box, and assigns that value to this text box, called *message*.

7 To clear all the boxes, the user can click on the Reset button. See Figures 11.24 and 11.25.

**Enter your name** Elvis

**Click in the box**

Reset

**Figure 11.24** The user enters his name in the first text field.

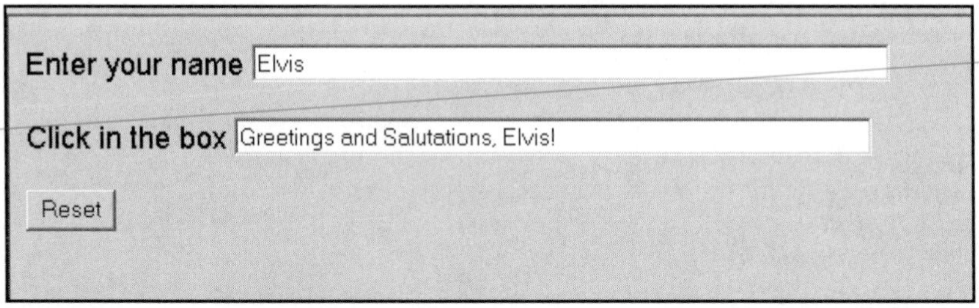

Enter your name
Elvis
Click in the box
Greetings and Salutations, Elvis!
Reset

**Figure 11.25** When the user clicks in the second text box, a message appears.

**The *password* Object.** The *password* object is much like the *text* object except that the input does not appear as text, but as asterisks or bullets, depending on the browser. The idea is to prevent a snoopy onlooker from seeing what is being typed in the box, but this is hardly a safe or secure type of password. If you look at the source of the HTML document, anywhere the actual password is spelled out, it appears in plain text for the viewer of the source.

The *password* object parallels the HTML password field *<input type="password">* and also has name and value fields. To reference a text field from JavaScript, you go down the document tree, starting at the *document*, the *form*, and then the *text* element. To get a value in the text field, for example, you would use *document.form1.passwd.value*, where *form1* is the name of the form and *passwd* is the name of the password field. Figure 11.26 shows the JavaScript object hierarchy for the *password* object. Tables 11.11 and 11.12 show properties and methods of the *password* object.

window
document
form
password

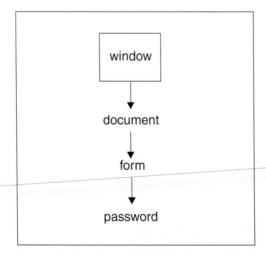

**Figure 11.26** The *password* object within the JavaScript hierarchy.

**Table 11.11** Properties of the *password* object.

| Property | What It Describes |
|---|---|
| *defaultValue* | The value assigned to the *value* attribute, and the default value the user sees in the password box when it first appears |
| *form* | The name of the form where the password box is defined |
| *name* | The name used to reference the password box |
| *type* | The type of the input device (i.e., *password*) |
| *value* | The value attribute that will be assigned whatever the user types in the password box |

**Table 11.12** Methods of the *password* object.

| Method | What It Describes |
|---|---|
| *blur()* | Removes focus from the password box |
| *focus()* | Puts focus on the password box |
| *handleEvent()* | Invokes the handler for a specified event (JavaScript 1.2) |
| *select()* | Selects or highlights text in the box |
| *unwatch()* | Turns off the watch for a particular property |
| *watch()* | Watches, and when a property is changed, calls a function |

**EXAMPLE 11.21**

```
     <html>
     <head><title>Password Boxes</title>
     <script language="Javascript">
1        function verify(pw){
2           if ( pw.value == "letmein" ){
               alert("The chamber door will open now!");
            }
3           else{
               alert("Sorry, you cannot enter. Please leave.");
            }
         }
     </script>
     </head>
     <body bgcolor="#330033"><font color="FFCCFF">
     <center>
     <h2> Welcome To The Secret Chamber<h2>
     <img src="wizard.jpg"><br>
     To enter, a password is required:<br>
```

**EXAMPLE** 11.21 (CONTINUED)

```
4   <form name="form1">
5   <input type="password"
        name="passwfield"
        size="30"
6       onBlur="return verify(this)">
    </form>
7   <input type=button value="Knock to verify">
    <font face=arial size="+1">
    </body>
```

**EXPLANATION**

1     The function called *verify()* is defined with one parameter, a reference to a *password* object.

2     If the value of the password box is equal to the string *letmein*, the user is told he can enter.

3     If the user didn't type in the correct password, he will be sent a message in an alert box.

4     The HTML form named *form1* starts here.

5     The input type is a password box. When the user types something into the box, a series of dots appears.

6     The *onBlur* event handler function, called *verify()*, is invoked when the user leaves the box and clicks his cursor anywhere else on the page. The purpose of the handler is to check that the user typed in a correct password.

7     When the user clicks on the button, the *onBlur* event handler is triggered. See Figures 11.27 and 11.28.

**Figure 11.27**   The *password* object.

**Figure 11.28**   The user enters a password that isn't correct and receives the alert message.

**The *textarea* Object.**   If you don't have enough room to say it all in a text field, then you can use the text area box for multiple lines of input. The *textarea* object parallels the HTML *<textarea>* tag. The number of characters in a line is specified with the *cols* attribute of the *<textarea>* tag, and the number of rows in the box are specified by the *rows* attribute. If the *wrap* attribute is defined, when the user reaches the end of a line, a newline will be inserted and the input will start on the next line; otherwise a scrollbar will appear. The *textarea* object, like the *text* object, has a number of properties and methods that make it possible to access and change the text area from within a JavaScript program. These are shown in Tables 11.13 and 11.14.

To reference a text area box from JavaScript, you go down the document tree, starting at the *document*, then to the *form*, and then the *textarea* element. To get a value in the text area box, for example, you would use *document.form1.textarea1.value*, where *form1* is the name of the form, and *textarea1* is the name of the text area. Figure 11.29 shows the JavaScript object hierarchy for the *textarea* object.

**Table 11.13**  Properties of the *textarea* object.

| Property | What It Describes |
|---|---|
| *defaultValue* | The value assigned to the *value* attribute, and the default value the user sees in the text area when it first appears |
| *form* | The name of the form where the text area is defined |
| *name* | The name used to reference the text area |
| *type* | The type of the input device; i.e., *textarea* |
| *value* | The value attribute that will be assigned whatever the user types in the text area |

**Table 11.14**  Methods of the *textarea* object.

| Method | What It Describes |
|---|---|
| *blur()* | Removes focus from the text area box |
| *focus()* | Puts focus on the text area box |
| *handleEvent()* | Invokes the handler for a specified event (JavaScript 1.2) |
| *select()* | Selects or highlights text in the text area box |
| *unwatch()* | Turns off the watch for a particular property |
| *watch()* | Watches, and when a property is changed, calls a function |

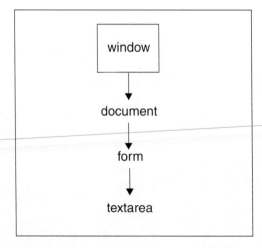

**Figure 11.29**  How the *textarea* object is created within the JavaScript hierarchy.

**EXAMPLE 11.22**

```
        <html>
        <head><title>Text Area Boxes</title></head>
        <font face=verdana>
        <body bgcolor="lightgreen">
        <form name="form1"><b>
            Finish the story
        <br><b>
1       <textarea name="story" rows=8 cols=60 >
            Once upon a time, there were three little ...
        </textarea>
        </form>
        <script language="JavaScript">
            document.write( "The type of the input device is:<em> "+
2               document.form1.story.type);
            document.write( "<br></em>The text area is named:<em> "+
3               document.form1.story.name);
            document.write( "<br></em>The number of rows in the text area
4               is:<em> "+ document.form1.story.rows);
            document.write( "<br></em>The value in the text area is:<em> "+
5               document.form1.story.value);
            document.write( "<br></em>The number of cols in the text area
6               is:<em>"+ document.form1.story.cols);
        </script>
        </body>
        </html>
```

**EXPLANATION**

1   An HTML text area is defined. Its name is *story* and it consists of 8 rows and 60 columns. The text, "*Once upon a time, there were three little...*" appears in the text area.

2   The name of the text area is *story*. It is a *textarea* object. Its type is *textarea*.

3   The value of the *name* property is displayed.

4   The *rows* property of the text area contains the number of rows that were assigned in the *rows* attribute of the text area.

5   This is the value of the text that appears inside the box.

6   The *cols* property of the text area contains the number of columns that were assigned in the *cols* attribute of the text area. The output is shown in Figure 11.30.

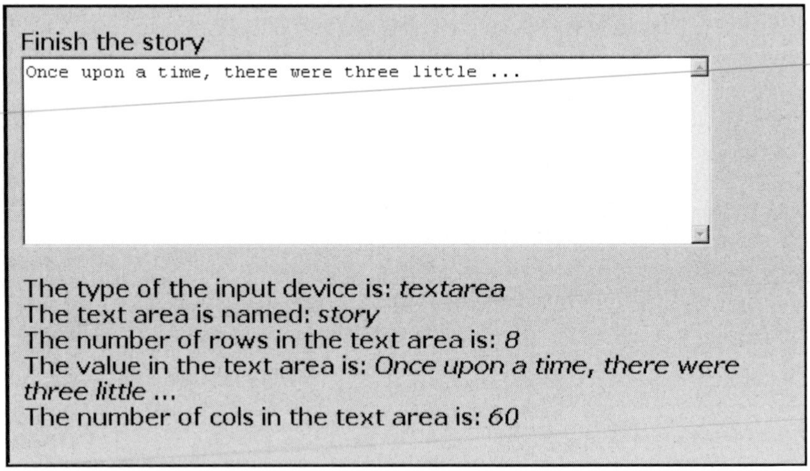

Finish the story

```
Once upon a time, there were three little ...
```

The type of the input device is: *textarea*
The text area is named: *story*
The number of rows in the text area is: *8*
The value in the text area is: *Once upon a time, there were three little ...*
The number of cols in the text area is: *60*

**Figure 11.30**   The *textarea* object.

**Selection Lists  (Drop-Down Menus).**     The HTML *<select>* tag defines a field for display as a drop-down or a scrolling box. A select list consists of menu items called options. JavaScript supports a *select* object. The *select* object can be named but the options cannot. However, the *select* object has an *options* property that is an array of all the option items, so that if you have to get access to one of the options, you can use the options array. The *selectedIndex* property contains a number that represents the index number of the option that has been selected. If, for example, the first option in the menu is selected, then the value of the *selectedIndex* property is 0 (since array elements start at 0). To get a value in the selection list, you could use, for example, *document.form1.select1.options[0].value*, where *form1* is the name of the form, *select1* is the name of the *select* object, and *options[0]* is the first option in the list. Tables 11.15 and 11.16 list the properties and methods of the *select* object. Figure 11.31 shows the JavaScript object hierarchy for the *select* object.

**Table 11.15**   Properties of the *select* object.

| *Property* | *What It Describes* |
|---|---|
| *form* | The name of the form where the select is defined |
| *length* | The number of items in the select list; same as *options.length* |
| *name* | The name used to reference the select menu |
| *options[]* | An array of option objects describing each of the selection options. Can modify select options (Javascript 1.1). The options object has properties: *index length, text, selected, value* |

**Table 11.15**  Properties of the *select* object. (continued)

| Property | What It Describes |
|---|---|
| *selectedIndex* | The integer index value of a selected option, −1 if no option is selected. This value can be modified. If set to an index value, that option is *selected*, and all others *deselected* |
| *type* | Two possible values for the select object; if *multiple* is on, the value is *select-one* and if not, *select-multiple* |

**Table 11.16**  Methods of the *select* object.

| Method | What It Does |
|---|---|
| *blur()* | Removes focus from the select box |
| *focus()* | Puts focus in the select box |
| *handleEvent()* | Invokes the handler for a specified event (JavaScript 1.2) |
| *unwatch()* | Turns off the watch for a particular property |
| *watch()* | Watches, and when a property is changed, calls a function |

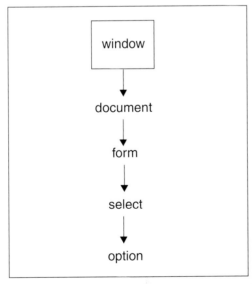

**Figure 11.31**  How the *select* object is created within the JavaScript hierarchy.

**EXAMPLE** 11.23

```
      <html>
      <head><title>Drop Down Menus</title></head>
      <body bgcolor=lightgreen>
      <font face=arial >
      <b>Select a Course
1     <form name="form1">
2        <select name="menu1" size="4" >
3            <option name="choice1" value="Perl1">Intro to Perl</option>
             <option name="choice2" value="Perl2">Advanced Perl</option>
             <option name="choice3" value="Unix1">Intro to Unix</option>
             <option name="choice4" value="Shell1">Shell
                Programming</option>
4        </select><p>
      </form>
5     <script language="JavaScript">
         document.write("The name of the selection list is ",
6            document.form1.menu1.name);
         document.write("<br>The number of items in the selection list
7            is ", document.form1.menu1.length);
         document.write("<br>The item currently selected is option["+
8            document.form1.menu1.selectedIndex + "]");
         document.write("<br>The text in the first selection is "+
9            document.form1.menu1.options[0].text);
         document.write("<br>The text in the second selection is "+
             document.form1.menu1.options[1].text);
      </script>
      </body>
      </html>
```

**EXPLANATION**

1   The HTML form named *form1* starts here. The *name* and *value* attributes are not really necessary here because this form is not being sent to a server.

2   The *select* tag starts a drop-down list named *menu1*; it has four options.

3   The options that will appear in the menu are listed.

4   This ends the select list.

5   The JavaScript program starts here. It displays the properties of the *select* object.

6   The name of the *select* object is displayed.

7   The number of options in the select list is displayed.

8   The index value of the option selected by the user is displayed. If no option has been selected, the value of *selectedIndex* is −1. If one has been selected, the index value of the option is displayed. The options are in an array where the index starts at 0. The first option is at index 0, the second option is index 1, and so on.

9   The actual text shown in the list for the first option is displayed, followed by the text in the second selection. The output is shown in Figures 11.32 and 11.33.

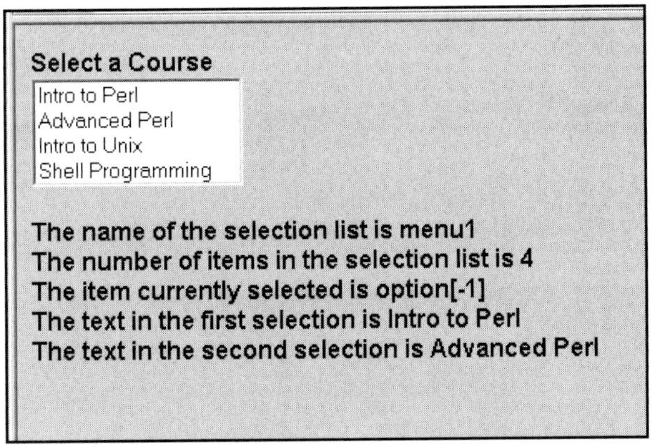

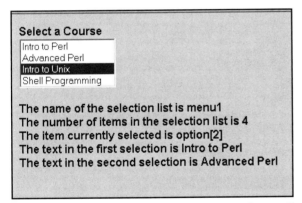

**Figure 11.32** A selection list's properties before anything has been selected.

**Figure 11.33** A selection list's properties after an item has been selected.

---

**EXAMPLE 11.24**

```
    <html>
    <head><title>Drop-Down Menus</title>
    <script language="JavaScript">
1       function schedule(f){
2           if(f.menu1.selectedIndex == 0){
            // Could also say: document.form1.menu1.selectedIndex
3           f.text1.value="PL100, Feb 3-7, 9am to 5pm, Room 2133,
                Dr. Baloney "
            // Could also say: document.form1.text1.value
            }
```

**EXAMPLE  11.24** (CONTINUED)

```
            if(f.menu1.selectedIndex == 1){
            f.text1.value="PL200 Feb 10-13 9am to 5pm, Room 209B,
                Ms. Eclectic";
            }
            if(f.menu1.selectedIndex == 2){
            f.text1.value="UX101 Mar 2-6 9am to 5pm, Room 209,
                Mr. Nerdly";
            }
            if(f.menu1.selectedIndex == 3){
            f.text1.value="SH201 Apr 10-13 9am to 5pm, Room 209B,
                Miss Bashing";
            }
        }
    </script>
    <body bgcolor=lightgreen>
    <font face=arial >
    <b>
4   <form name="form1">
    Select a Course<br>
5       <select name="menu1" size="4" onChange="schedule(this.form)">
6           <option name="choice1" value="Perl1">Intro to Perl</option>
            <option name="choice2" value="Perl2">Advanced Perl</option>
            <option name="choice3" value="Unix1">Intro to Unix</option>
            <option name="choice4" value="Shell1">Shell
                Programming</option>
        </select><p>
7   <input type="text" name="text1" size=60 />
    </form>
    </body></html>
```

**EXPLANATION**

1   A function called *schedule()* is defined. The parameter, *f*, represents the *form* object; i.e., *document.form1*.

2   If the first item in the select menu is checked, the *selectedIndex* value is 0. The number represents the index into the *options[]* array, where *options[0]* is the first option.

3   If the first option was selected in the menu, then the value of the text box, called *textbox1*, is assigned a string describing the "*Intro to Perl*" course. This assignment updates the text box field dynamically.

4   The form, named *form1*, starts here.

5   The select menu called *menu1* will contain a list of four options. The *onChange* event will be triggered for this event as soon as something is entered in one of the options.

6   An option list for the select input device is created. This will produce a menu with choices.

7   An input text box device, named *text1*, is created. The output is shown in Figures 11.34 and 11.35.

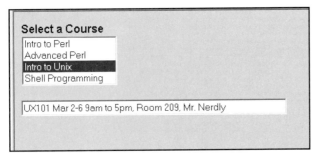

**Figure 11.34** After the user selected the third option in the menu, the text box is updated dynamically.

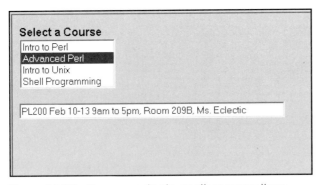

**Figure 11.35** The user selects another menu item.

*Multiple Selects*
If you use the *multiple* attribute of a select list, more than one option can be selected. To select more than one item, hold down the Control key while clicking on an item. If more than one item is chosen, the *selectedIndex* value will indicate only the first one that was selected. To test whether more than one option has been selected, you can use the *selected* property of the *options* object. This property will result in *true* if an option has been selected; *false* otherwise. See Example 11.25.

```
<html>
<head><title>Drop Down Menus</title>
<script language="JavaScript">
1      function showme(form){
2          var choices="";
```

**EXAMPLE** 11.25 (CONTINUED)

```
3              for (i=0;i< form.vacation.options.length;i++){
4                 if( form.vacation.options[i].selected == true){
5                    choices += form.vacation.options[i].text+"\n";
                  }
               }
6              alert(choices);
            }
   </script>
   <body bgcolor=lightgreen>
   <font face=arial >
   <b>
7  <form name="form1" onSubmit="showme(this);">
   Where do you want to go? <br>
8  <select name="vacation" size=4 multiple>
       <option>Maui
       <option>Jamaica
       <option>Bali
       <option>Virgin Islands
   </select>
   <p>
   <input type="submit">
   <input type="reset">
   </form>
   </body>
   </html>
```

**EXPLANATION**

1   The function called *showme()* is defined. It is passed one parameter, a reference to a *form* object.

2   The variable called *choices* is declared and assigned an empty string.

3   The *for* loop is entered. The initial value, *i*, is set to 0. As long as the value of *i* is less than the length of the options array, the body of the loop will be entered; thus, as long as we haven't looped through all the options in the menu, the loop will be entered.

4   If the option from the menu was selected, the *selected* property will evaluate to *true*.

5   If an option was selected, the variable, called *choices*, will be assigned the text value of the option; perhaps *Maui* or *Bali* will be assigned to *choices*. Each time through the *for* loop, if an option is selected, it will be appended to the variable, resulting in a string that contains all of the selected options.

6   The alert dialog box will display the string value containing all the options that were selected.

7   The HTML form called *form1* starts here.

8   The HTML select menu called *vacation* starts here. It will contain four menu options, and allow multiple selections. See Figure 11.36.

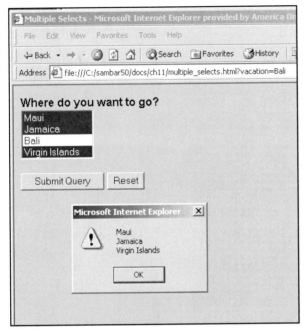

**Figure 11.36**  *Multiple selections were made by the avid traveller.*

**Radio Buttons.**  Like the buttons on an old-fashioned radio, you can only push one button when using HTML radio buttons. When a radio button is checked, it is selected, and when another button is checked, the previously checked one is deselected. In short, only one button at a time can be checked. This type of button is useful if you want a user to be able to select only one of a list of items.

**Figure 11.37**  *Play that tune! HTML radio buttons are similar to buttons on an old-fashioned radio: only one can be pressed at a time.*

Radio buttons are created with the HTML *<input type="radio">* and are represented in JavaScript as a *radio* object with specific properties and methods used to manipulate the object. Each button is a property of the *radio* object and assigned to an array of elements in the order they are placed in the form. The *checked* property of the *radio* object specifies whether a button was checked. It returns Boolean *true* if the button was selected, and *false* if not.

To reach a value in the radio list, for example, you would use: *document.form1.radio1*, where *form1* is the name of the form, and *radio1* is the name of the *radio* object.

Figure 11.38 shows the JavaScript object hierarchy for the *radio* object. Tables 11.17 and 11.18 list the properties and methods of the *radio* object.

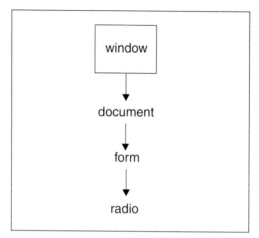

**Figure 11.38**   How the *radio* object is created within the JavaScript hierarchy.

**Table 11.17**   Properties of the *radio* object.

| Property | What It Describes |
| --- | --- |
| *checked* | Is true if the radio button was selected, false if not |
| *defaultChecked* | Refers to the checked attribute of the radio input tag—what the user sees as a default checked box when the buttons first appear |
| *form* | The name of the form where the radio buttons are defined |
| *name* | The name used to reference the radio input tag |
| *type* | Refers to the type attribute of the radio input tag |
| *value* | Refers to the value attribute of the radio input tag |

**Table 11.18**   Methods of the *radio* object.

| Method | What It Does |
| --- | --- |
| *blur()* | Removes focus from the select box |
| *click()* | Simulates a mouse being clicked on the button |
| *focus()* | Puts focus in the select box |

**Table 11.18** Methods of the *radio* object. (continued)

| Method | What It Does |
| --- | --- |
| *handleEvent*() | Invokes the handler for a specified event (JavaScript 1.2) |
| *unwatch*() | Turns off the watch for a particular property |
| *watch*() | Watches, and when a property is changed, calls a function |

**EXAMPLE  11.26**

```
     <html>
     <head><title>Radio Buttons</title>
     <script name="JavaScript">
1        function changeBg(f){
2            for (var i = 0; i < f.color.length;i++){
3              if(f.color[i].checked){
4                  document.bgColor= f.color[i].value;
                  }
              }
            }
     </script>
     </head>
     <body bgcolor="#CCFFFF">
     <font face="arial"><b>
5    <form name="formradio">
     Pick a background color:<p>
6    <input type=radio
         name="color"
         value="#0099CC">dark cyan<br>
     <input type=radio
         name="color"
         value="#339966">teal<br>
     <input type=radio
         name="color"
         value="#F33CC">magenta<br>
     <input type=radio
         name="color"
         value="#FFFF66">light yellow<br>
     <input type=radio
         name="color"
         value="#FF9933">light orange<br>
     <p>
     <input type=button
7        value="Click for Color" onClick="changeBg(this.form);">
     <input type=reset>
     </form>
     </body>
     </html>
```

## EXPLANATION

1  A function called *changeBg()* is defined. It will take one parameter, a reference to the form where the radio buttons are defined. The parameter *f* could also be written using the DOM hierarchy: *document.form[0]* or *document.formradio* (the form's name).

2  The *for* loop is entered. The variable, *i*, will be used to index through each of the elements of the *radio* object. The name *color* is a reference to each object in the forms *elements[]* array. The *length* property specifies how many radio buttons were created in the form. When all of the buttons have been tested, the loop will exit.

3  If a radio button was checked, the *checked* property will return *true*.

4  If checked, the color of the background will be changed by assigning the value of the radio button's *value* attribute to the *bgColor* property of the document.

5  The form is defined. It is named *formradio*.

6  The input type is a radio button, named *color*. Only one button can be selected. The value is a hexidecimal color code.

7  When the user clicks this button, the *onClick* event handler is triggered and the handler function *changeBg()* is called, using the *this* keyword and the *form* object as its argument.

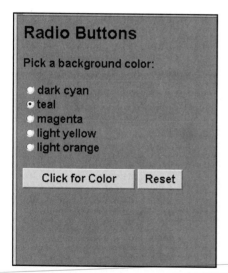

**Figure 11.39**   Using radio buttons; only one can be checked.

**Checkboxes.**   Although radio buttons can only be checked once, a user can check as many checkboxes as he wants. When a checkbox is clicked, it is on, and when it is not, it is off.

Checkboxes are created with the HTML *<input type="checkbox">* and are represented in JavaScript as a *checkbox* object with specific properties and methods used to manipulate the object. Each checkbox is a property of the *checkbox* object and assigned to an array of elements in the order they are placed in the form. The *checked* property of the *checkbox* object specifies whether a box was checked. It returns true if checked, and false if not.

To reach a value in the checkbox list, you could use, for example, *document.form1.check1*, where *form1* is the name of the form, and *check1* is the name of the *checkbox* object. Figure 11.40 shows the JavaScript object hierarchy for the *checkbox* object. Tables 11.19 and 11.20 list the properties and methods of the *checkbox* object.

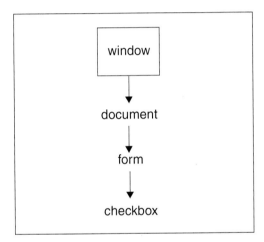

**Figure 11.40**   How the *checkbox* object is created within the JavaScript hierarchy.

**Table 11.19**   Properties of the *checkbox* object.

| Property | What It Describes |
|---|---|
| *checked* | Returns true if the checkbox is checked |
| *defaultChecked* | Returns true if the *<input>* tag includes the *checked* attribute, a default box that is initially checked; otherwise, returns false |
| *form* | The name of the form where the checkbox is defined |
| *name* | A string that names the checkbox |
| *type* | The type of input device; i.e., *checkbox* |
| *value* | The text assigned to the value attribute |

**Table 11.20**  Methods of the *checkbox* object.

| Method | What It Does |
|---|---|
| *blur()* | Removes focus from the checkbox |
| *click()* | Simulates a mouse being clicked in the checkbox |
| *focus()* | Puts focus in the checkbox |
| *handleEvent()* | Invokes the handler for a specified event (JavaScript 1.2) |
| *unwatch()* | Turns off the watch for a particular property |
| *watch()* | Watches, and when a property is changed, calls a function |

**EXAMPLE  11.27**

```
        <html>
        <head><title>Checkboxes</title>
        <script name="JavaScript">
1          function check(f){
              var str="";
2              for (var i = 0; i < f.topping.length;i++){
3                  if(f.topping[i].checked){
4                      str += f.topping[i].value + "\n"; // Create a string
                                                         // of items checked
                                                         // by the user
                  }
              }
5              f.order.value=str;        // Put str value into the text area
          }
6          function OK(){
              var result= confirm("Are you sure you are ready to
                  order?  ");
              if(result == true){
7                  document.formchbox.submit();
              }
              else { return false;}
          }
        </script>
        </head>
        <body bgColor="#CCFF33">
        <font face="verdana"><b>
        <table border="4"><tr><td><b>Checkboxes</b></td></tr></table>
8       <form name="formchbox"
            method="post"
            action="/sambar50/cgi-bin/chb.pl" >
            Pick your pizza toppings:<p>
```

**EXAMPLE 11.27 (CONTINUED)**

```
 9   <input type="checkbox"
         name="topping"
         value="tomatoes">Tomatoes<br>
     <input type="checkbox"
         name="topping"
         value="salami">Salami<br>
     <input type=checkbox
         name="topping"
         value="pineapple">Pineapple<br>
     <input type=checkbox
         name="topping"
         value="Canadian bacon">Canadian bacon<br>
     <input type=checkbox
         name="topping"
         value="anchovies">Anchovies<br>
     <input type=checkbox
         name="topping"
         value="extra cheese">Extra cheese<br>
     <p><font size="-1">
     Pizza Toppings
     <br>
10   <textarea name="order" rows=6 cols=35
11       onFocus="javascript:check(this.form);">
         Click here to check your order!!
     </textarea>
     <p>
     Press the pizza man to order!
     <br>
12   <input type=image src="Pizza_chef.gif"
         onClick="javascript:return OK();">
     <br>
     <input type=reset value="Clear the form">
     </form>
     </body>
     </html>
```

**EXPLANATION**

1   A JavaScript function called *check()* is defined. It takes one parameter, a reference to a form. Instead of *f*, the form could also be referenced as *document.forms[0]* or *document.formchbox*.

2   A *for* loop is entered to go through each of the checkboxes in the form. The name of the checkbox object is *topping*. The *length* property refers to how many checkboxes were defined. After all of the checkboxes have been inspected, the loop exits.

3   If the checkbox element, called *topping[i]*, is checked, the *check* property has a value *true*; otherwise *false*.

4   A string called *str* is assigned the value stored in the checkbox, and for each box that is checked, its value will be appended to the string.

**EXPLANATION** (CONTINUED)

5   After all of the checkboxes have been tested, their values will be found in the *str* variable. These values are assigned to the text area box, called *order.*

6   A function, called *OK()*, is defined. Its purpose is to confirm that the user is ready to submit his order.

7   If he clicks OK in the confirmation box, the checkbox's *submit()* method is invoked. Otherwise, nothing happens.

8   The HTML form called *formchbox* is defined.

9   The input type is a checkbox, named *topping*. Each of the checkbox choices are created for this form.

10  An HTML text area, named *order*, is defined. It consists of 6 rows and 35 columns.

11  When the text area gets focus, (that is, when the user clicks his mouse anywhere in the text area box), the hander *check()* is invoked. A reference to this form is passed as an argument.

12  This is an image input type used instead of a submit button. When the user clicks on the image of the pizza man, the *OK()* handler will be invoked.

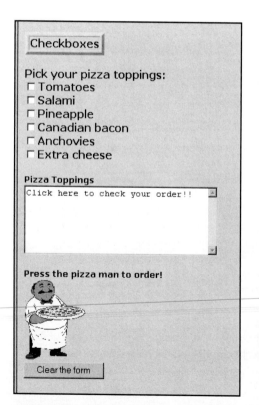
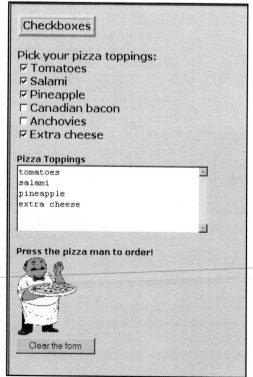

**Figure 11.41**   The initial form with empty checkboxes (left) and after the user has clicked on some of the checkboxes (right).

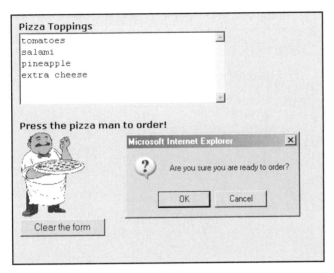

**Figure 11.42** When the user clicks on the pizza man, a confirmation box appears.

### 11.2.7 Simple Form Validation

Have you ever filled out a form to buy something, clicked the submit button, waited, waited, and then received a big red message saying that the card number you entered was invalid? And then after all that waiting, you had to retype the entire form because all of the fields were reset? By letting JavaScript do some preliminary checking of the form input for obvious mistakes and erroneous information, you can save the user a lot of time and aggravation. Then, after the preliminary checking is done, the form is ready to go off to a server program, such as Perl or PHP, where it can be further validated and processed. This section will show you a little about validating forms: doing preliminary checking to see if a password is the correct length, making sure a field isn't empty, checking for unwanted characters, and more. Chapter 13, "Regular Expressions and Pattern Matching," shows you how to validate e-mail addresses, credit cards, zip codes, names, phone numbers, social security numbers, and the like by using regular expressions, a powerful pattern matching tool provided by JavaScript.

**Checking for Empty Fields.** Forms often have mandatory fields that must be filled out before the form can be submitted. The following example checks for empty fields.

## EXAMPLE 11.28

```
                <html><head><title>An HTML Form and the onSubmit Event
                    Handler</title>
                <script language="JavaScript">
1               function checkForm(yourinfo){
2                   if(yourinfo.namestring.value == "" ||
                    yourinfo.namestring.value == null){
                                    // Check for an empty string or null value
3                   alert("Please type in your name");
4                   return(false);
                    }
                    else{
5                       return(true);
                    }
                }
                </script>
                </head>
                <body>
                <b>
6               <form name="info" action="/cgi-bin/bookstuff/form1.cgi"
                    method="post"
7                  onSubmit="return checkForm(document.info)"><p>
                <font size="+1"><p>
                Type your name here:
8               <input type="text" name="namestring" size="50">
                <p>
9               <input type="submit" value="Submit">
                <input type="reset" value="Clear">
                </form>
                </body>
                </html>
```

## EXPLANATION

1   The function called *checkForm()* has one argument, *yourinfo*, which is a reference to the form defined on line 6.

2   If the user didn't enter anything into the text box, the value of the input type will be null. The expression *if(yourinfo.namestring.value == "")* checks for an empty field.

3   The user didn't enter anything into the text box, an alert dialog box will appear on the screen, and after he presses OK, he will have a chance to fill out the form again.

4   If *false* is returned from this function, the form will not be submitted to the server.

5   If *true* is returned from this function, the form will be submitted to the server.

**EXPLANATION** (CONTINUED)

6    The HTML form starts here. The form, *document.forms[0]*, is named *info*. The *action* attribute contains the URL of the program that will process the form, a CGI script on the server. The *method* attribute defines the HTTP method that determines how the data will be sent to the server.

7    The *onSubmit* event is an attribute of the HTML *<form>* tag. It is triggered when the user presses the submit button. The event handler is a function called *check-Form()*. Its parameter is the name of the form, *document.info* (also could use its array name: *document.forms[0]* ). (See the *this* keyword in the next example.) The *return* keyword is required when using the *onSubmit* event handler. One of two values will be returned: either *true* or *false*.

8    The input type for this form is a text field box. Its name is *namestring* and it can hold a string of up to 50 characters.

9    The input type is the submit button. When the user presses this button, the *on-Submit* event handler on line 7 is activated. See Figure 11.43.

**Figure 11.43**   Using the *onSubmit* event handler to stop a form if the user didn't enter anything in the field.

**Checking for Alphabetic Characters.**   If checking input fields for alphabetic characters, such as a user name, the following example will go through a loop evaluating each character in a string to guarantee it is an alphabetic. See Chapter 13, "Regular Expressions and Pattern Matching," for more on this type of validation.

**EXAMPLE 11.29**

```
       <html><head><title>Verifying a Name</title>
       <script language="JavaScript">
1          function validate(form){
2              if(alpha(form.first) == false){
                   alert ("First name is invalid");
                   return false;
               }
3              if(alpha(form.last) == false){
                    alert("Last name is invalid");
                    return false;
               }
                 return true;
           }
4          function alpha(textField ){
5              if( textField.value.length != 0){
6                  for (var i = 0; i < textField.value.length;i++){
7                      var ch= textField.value.charAt(i);
                       // alert(ch);  # Using alert to see what characters
                                      // are coming in
8                      if((ch < "A" || ch > "Z") && (ch< "a" || ch >"z")){
                           return false;
                       }
                   }
               }
               else {
9                  return true;
               }
           }
       </script>
       </head>
       <body bgcolor="lightgreen">
       <font face=verdana>
       <b>
10     <form name="alphachk" onSubmit="return validate(this);">
       Enter your first name:
       <br>
11     <input name="first"
           type="text"
           size=60>
       <p>
       Enter your last name:
       <br>
12     <input name="last"
           type="text"
           size=60>
       <p>
13     <input type=submit value="Check it out">
       <input type=reset>
       </form>
       </body>
       </html>
```

# EXPLANATION

1 A JavaScript function called *validate()* is defined. It takes one parameter, a reference to a *form* object.

2 The *if* expression invokes a function, called *alpha()*, and passes the text object to it. The first name is validated by the *alpha()* function. If *false* is returned, the block is entered and the user is alerted that he did not enter a valid first name. If this function returns *false* to the *onSubmit* handler that invoked it, on line 10, the form will not be submitted.

3 As in line 2, the *alpha()* function is being called, only this time to verify the last name of the user.

4 The function called *alpha()* is defined. All the validation work is done here. This function will validate that the user entered something in the text box, and that what he entered is alphabetic characters, and only alphabetic characters, either uppercase or lowercase.

5 If the length of characters entered in the text field is not equal to 0, then the block is entered.

6 The *for* loop is used to check each character, one at a time, that was entered in the text field.

7 The *charAt()* string method returns a character at a specified position in the string. Each time through the loop, a new character is assigned to the variable, *ch*.

8 This is the test for alphabetic characters. Since each character is represented internally as an ASCII number, ( "A" is ASCII 65, "B" ASCII 66, etc.), any character outside the range "A" to "Z" and "a" to "z" is not an alphabetic character.

9 If *true* is returned by the *alpha()* function, the form will be submitted.

10 The name of the form is *alphachk*. The *onSubmit* event is triggered when the user presses the submit button on line 13.

11 The input type is a text field, called *first*. This is where the user will enter his first name.

12 The input type is a text field, called *last*. This is where the user will enter his last name.

13 The input type is a submit button. When the user presses this button, the *onSubmit* event is triggered, and if the form was valid, it will be submitted to the server. (In this example, it isn't going anywhere, because the *action* attribute of the form wasn't specified.) See Figure 11.44.

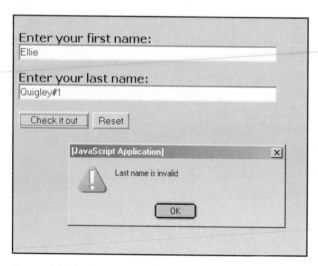

**Figure 11.44**   The user enters a valid first name and an invalid last name.

**Checking E-Mail Addresses.**   You are frequently asked to include your e-mail address when filling out a form. There are some requirements for a valid e-mail address such as *TommyTucker@somewhere.com*. One requirement is that there is an @ symbol after the user name, and that there is at least one dot (.) in the address. The following example is a preliminary check for the existence of both of those characters, but it is far from a complete check. See Chapter 13, "Regular Expressions and Pattern Matching," for a much more robust version of e-mail validation using regular expressions.

**EXAMPLE 11.30**

```
        <html><head><title>Checking Email</title>
        <script language="JavaScript">
1           function email(form){    // Validate the address
2               if(form.address.value.indexOf("@") != -1 &&
                    form.address.value.indexOf(".") != -1){
                alert("OK address!");
3               return true;
                }
                else {
                alert("Invalid address");
4               return false;
                }
            }
        </script>
        </head>
        <body bgcolor="lightgreen">
        <font face=verdana>
        <b>
        <center>
```

EXAMPLE  11.30 (CONTINUED)

```
5    <form name="mailchk"
         action="/cgi-bin/ml.pl"
         method="post"
         onSubmit="return email(this);">
     Enter your email address:
     <p>
6    <input name="address"
         type="text"
         size=60>
     <p>
7    <input type=submit value="Check it out">
     <input type=reset>
     </form>
     </center>
     </body>
     </html>
```

**EXPLANATION**

1   A JavaScript function called *email()* is defined. It takes one parameter, a reference to a form.

2   If the string method, *indexOf*, does not return a –1, then the @ character and a dot (.) were found in the value entered by the user in the text box, and an alert message will let the user know his e-mail address is okay. This is where the validation takes place.

3   If *true* is returned, the form will be submitted.

4   If *false* is returned, the form is stopped, and will not be submitted.

5   The HTML form, called *mailchk*, starts here. The *onSubmit* event will be triggered when the user presses the submit button on line 7.

6   The form's input type is a text box named *address* that will hold up to 60 characters.

7   When the user presses the submit button, the *onSubmit* handler on line 5 is triggered. It invokes the handler function, called *email*, and passes a reference to the form as an argument. See Figures 11.45 and 11.46.

Enter your email address:
john@baloney.edu
Check it out
Reset
[JavaScript Application]
OK address!
OK

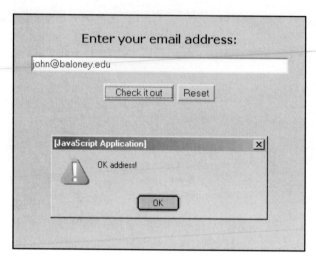

**Figure 11.45** The user enters a valid e-mail address.

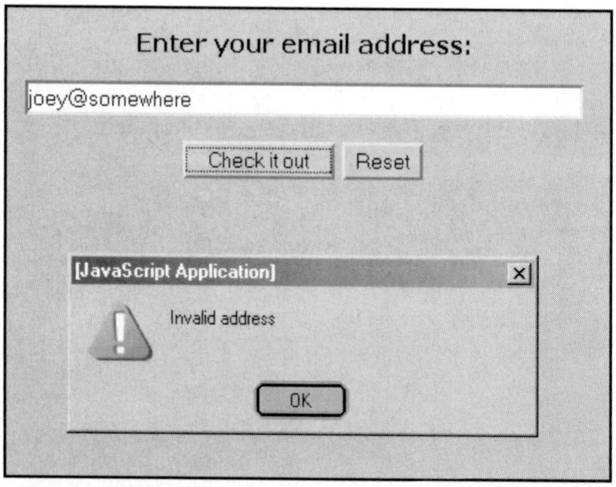

Enter your email address:
joey@somewhere
Check it out
Reset
[JavaScript Application]
Invalid address
OK

**Figure 11.46** The user enters an invalid e-mail address. A dot is missing in the address.

**Checking Password Fields.** There are a number of checks made on password entries. Does it have the right number of characters? Does it contain one numeric character? Is it case sensitive? The following example is a simple validation routine to check for alphanumeric characters and that the number of characters in the password field is not less than six.

**EXAMPLE** 11.31

```
     <html><head><title>Verifying a Password</title>
     <script language="JavaScript">
1        function valid(form){
2            if( form.pass.value.length == 0 ){
                 alert("Please enter a password");
                 return false;
             }
3            if( form.pass.value.length < 6 ){
                 alert("Password must be at least 6 characters");
                 return false;
             }
             for (var i = 0; i < form.pass.value.length;i++){
                 var ch= form.pass.value.charAt(i);
4                if((ch < "A" || ch > "Z") && (ch< "a" || ch >"z")
                     && (ch < "0" || ch > "9")){
                     alert("Password contains illegal characters");
                     return false;
                 }
             }
5            alert("OK Password");
             return true;
         }
     </script>
     </head>
     <body bgcolor="red">
     <font face=verdana>
     <b><center>
6    <form name="passchk" onSubmit="return valid(this);">
         Enter your password:
     <br>
7    <input name="pass"
         type="password"
         size=33>
     <p>
     <input type=submit value="Submit Password">
     <input type=reset>
     </form>
     </center>
     </body>
     </html>
```

## EXPLANATION

1   A JavaScript function called *valid()* is defined. It takes one parameter, a reference to a form.

2   If the password entered by the user has a length of 0 characters, an alert message is sent.

3   If the password entered by the user has a length of less than 6 characters, an alert message is sent.

4   If the value of the password entered by the user contains any character that is not an alphabetic character and not a number, an alert message is sent.

5   If the password was at least 6 characters and contained only alphanumeric characters (letters and numbers), then the validation test was passed, and the user is alerted. A value of *true* is returned to the *onSubmit* handler, allowing the form to be submitted.

6   The HTML form called *passchk* is started here. Its *onSubmit* handler is triggered when the user presses the submit button.

7   The input type is a password box, called *pass*. This is where the user will enter his password. See Figure 11.47.

**Figure 11.47**   The user enters a password of less than 6 characters (left) or enters a password that contains illegal characters (right).

# 11.3 Introduction to Images

A picture is worth a thousand words. Whether it's a slide show, banner, movie, or photo album, the Web contains a huge collection of images. Any time you buy something online, there is usually an image associated with the item, maybe a small image, and then a bigger image if you want more detail. Whatever it is, a book, a house, a pair of shoes, or a toy, we like to see it before we put it in our virtual shopping cart and pay the money.

Images can be links, clickable image maps, banners, marquees, billboards, or rollovers—you name it. With HTML, the images you load are static, and just sit on the page. They cannot be changed without loading a brand-new page, and loading a lot of images takes time. JavaScript brings a new dimension to working with images. Instead of viewing a static image on the page, now you can create rollovers, slide shows, cycling banners, and more. You can create dynamic images that can be changed on the fly, adding animation and drama to your Web page. Before getting into the fun of images, we will look at how JavaScript views the image. In Chapter 12, "Handling Events," and Chapter 15, "Dynamic HTML: Style Sheets, the DOM, and JavaScript," you utilize what you learn here to see the full potential of image creation with JavaScript.

## 11.3.1   HTML Review of Images

Before using images with JavaScript, the following section reviews the basics of using images in a static Web page.

**Table 11.21**   HTML image tags.

| Tag | Attributes | Description |
| --- | --- | --- |
| IMG | | Starting tag for loading an image. |
| | ALIGN | Floats the image either to the left or right side of the page, or aligns the image with text in directions, *texttop, top, middle, absmiddle, bottom,* or *absbottom.* |
| | ALT | Alternative text in case the image doesn't appear. |
| | BORDER | The width in pixels of an image border. |
| | HEIGHT | Height of the image in pixels. |
| | HSPACE | Adds space, in pixels, to both the right and left sides of the image. |
| | SRC | Contains the URL, location of the image relative to the document root of the Web page. |
| | VSPACE | Adds space, in pixels, to both the top and bottom of the image. |
| | WIDTH | Width of the image in pixels. |
| MAP | | Starting tag for an image map. Image maps link areas of an image with a set of URLs. Clicking on an area of the map sends the user to that page. |
| | ID | The name of the image map. |
| | NAME | Also the name of the image map. |

**Table 11.21**   HTML image tags. (continued)

| Tag | Attributes | Description |
|---|---|---|
| AREA | | Defines the clickable areas of the image map. |
| | ALT | Describes what happens when the user clicks. |
| | COORDS | Determines the shape of a rectangle, circle, or polygon in x,y pixel coordinates. |
| | HREF | The address of the page that will appear when the user clicks in a particular area. |
| | SHAPE | Assigned a *type*, where *type* represents the shape of the area. |

**Using an Image in an HTML Web Page.**   The following example is an HTML file linked to an image. In this example, we review the way inline images are created in a document.

**EXAMPLE**   11.32

```
<html>
<head><title>HTML Images</title></head>
<body bgcolor="lightblue">
<h2>  This Is Baby William</h2>
1  <img src="baby.jpg" alt="baby" border=2 align="left" hspace="10"
2      width="220" height="250">
3  <pre>
Father calls me William,
    sister calls me Will,
Mother calls me Willie,
   but the fellers call me Bill!
Mighty glad I ain't a girl--
    ruther be a boy,
Without them sashes, curls, an' things
    that's worn by Fauntleroy!
Love to chawnk green apples
    an' go swimmin' in the lake--
Hate to take the castor-ile
    they give for belly-ache!
Most all the time, the whole year round,
    there ain't no flies on me,
But jest 'fore Christmas
    I'm as good as I kin be!
</pre></body>
</html>
```

Eugene Field, *Jest 'Fore Christmas*, in *Childcraft*, Vol. 2, (Chicago: Field Enterprises, Inc., 1949).

## EXPLANATION

1 The image *src* attribute defines where the image is located. This image, *baby.jpg*, is located where the HTML file called *image.html* is found, normally under the document root of your browser. If the image can't be loaded, the *alt* attribute specifies text that will appear in its place. The image will be aligned at the left-hand side of the page and will have a thin black border around it. There will be 10 pixels of space on both the left- and right-hand sides of the image. This keeps the text from jamming up too close to the picture.

2 The *width* and *height* attributes of the *img* tag allow you to specify the size of your image in pixels. If you right-click on an image (Windows), a pop-up window will appear where you can select Properties to obtain info about your image.

3 This is a *<pre>* tag that is followed by all the text that appears at the right-hand side of the image. See Figure 11.48.

**Figure 11.48** Using images in an HTML page. Output from Example 11.32.

## 11.3.2 JavaScript and the *image* Object

The *image* object is a property of the *document* object and gives you access to the images that have been loaded into a document. It corresponds to the HTML *<img>* tag. As each HTML form is a JavaScript element of the *forms[]* array, each image is assigned to the *images[]* array[3] in the order in which the image appears within the document. The first

3. Implemented starting in JavaScript 1.1.

image would be represented as *document.image[0]*, the next as *document.image[1]*, and so on. As with forms, images can also be named. The properties for the *image* object correspond to the HTML attributes of the <img> tag, such as *width, height, border, vspace,* and *hspace,* are shown in Table 11.22.[4] As of Netscape 6 and Internet Explorer 4, it is possible to assign values to these properties to dynamically change the size, shape, and border of the image. There are no common methods for the *image* object.

JavaScript also provides the *image* object with event handlers that are triggered when the image is loaded, a mouse crosses the image, or the image is replaced when the user clicks on a link. The event handlers are discussed in Chapter 12, "Handling Events."

For preloading offscreen images, JavaScript provides an image constructor. The constructor is used if you have large images that will take time to download or images that are being replaced dynamically within the page. The images are preloaded into memory (but not displayed) and available from the cache when the user requests them, thus making the response time much faster.

**Table 11.22**  *image* object properties.

| Property | HTML <IMG> Attribute | Description |
|---|---|---|
| *border* | *border* | An integer value determining the width of an image border in pixels |
| *complete* | | A Boolean value returning true if Navigator has finished downloading the image |
| *height* | *height* | An integer representing the height of the image in pixels |
| *hspace* | *hspace* | An integer representing the horizontal space (pixels) around the image |
| *lowsrc* | *lowsrc* | Specifies an optional image to display for a low-resolution device |
| *name* | *name* | A string containing the name of the image |
| *prototype* | | Used to add user-specified properties to an *image* object |
| *src* | *src* | A string containing the path and name of the image |
| *vspace* | *vspace* | An integer representing the vertical space (pixels) around the image |
| *width* | *width* | An integer representing the width of the image in pixels |

---

4.  These properties are common to both Netscape and Internet Explorer. IE, however, supports many more than those listed here.

**Replacing Images Dynamically with the *src* Property.**   By changing the *src* property of an image, it is possible to dynamically replace one image with another. You can create an array of images with the *Array()* constructor, and dynamically assign any one of these images to the *src* property of the JavaScript *images[]* array.

**EXAMPLE** 11.33

```
     <html>
     <head><title>HTML Images</title>
     <script language="JavaScript">
1        var myImages=new Array("baby1.jpg", "baby2.jpg", "baby3.jpg",
                               "baby4.jpg");
2        index_val=0;
3        function next_image(){
4            index_val++;
5            if (index_val < myImages.length){
6                document.images["display"].src = myImages[index_val];
                 // could say document.display.src or
                 // document.images[0].src
             }
7            else{
                 index_val=0;
                 document.images["display"].src = myImages[index_val];
             }
         }
8        function previous_image(){
             index_val--;
9            if (index_val >= 0){
                 document.images["display"].src = myImages[index_val];
             }
10           else{
                 index_val=myImages.length - 1;
                 document.images["display"].src = myImages[index_val];
             }
         }
     </script>
     </head>
     <body bgcolor="cornflowerblue">
     <h2>  Baby Gallery</h2>
11   <img name="display" src="baby.jpg" width="220" height="250" >
     <br>
12   <a href="javascript:next_image()">
     Go to next baby<br>
     </a>
13   <a href="javascript:previous_image()">
     Go to previous baby<br>
     </a>
     </body>
     </html>
```

## EXPLANATION

1   The array *myImages* consisting of four images is created by the *Array()* constructor.

2   The index value for the array is assigned to a variable called *index_val*.

3   A function called *next_image()* is defined. When called, the function will cause the next image in the array to be displayed.

4   By increasing the value of the index, the next image in the array will be accessed.

5   As long as the end of the array hasn't been reached, the block will be entered and the new image displayed.

6   The name of the image, *display*, is used as an index into the *images[]* array to reference the default image by name. By assigning a new image (from the *myImages* array) to the images *src* property, the current image will be replaced by the new image.

7   If the end of the array has been reached, the statements within the *else* block will be executed, resetting the array index back to the beginning, index 0.

8   A function called *previous_image()* is defined. When called, it will go backward in the array and cause the previous image to be displayed.

9   If the index value is still ≥0, we are still within the boundaries of the array.

10  If by subtracting one from the index value, we have ended up with a value of –1, we are out of the bounds of the array, and will set the index value back to the size of the array, its length –1.

11  This is the initial image displayed on the screen before the user initiates an action.

12  When this link is clicked, the JavaScript function called *next_image()* is invoked.

13  When this link is clicked, the JavaScript function called *previous_image()* is invoked. See Figure 11.49.

**Figure 11.49**   Output from Example 11.33.

EXAMPLE   11.34

```
      <html>
      <head><title>HTML Replacing Images</title></head>
      <body bgcolor="cornflowerblue">
      <h2>  This Is Baby William</h2>
  1   <img name="display" src="baby.jpg" width="220" height="250" >
      <script language="JavaScript">
  2       var myImages=new Array("baby1.jpg", "baby2.jpg", "baby3.jpg");
  3       var n = prompt("Pick a number between 1 and 3","");
  4       n--;
  5       document.images["display"].src = myImages[n];
                 // document.images[0].src = myImages[n]
      </script></body>
      </html>
```

## EXPLANATION

1   An HTML inline image called *display* is created. Its source is a file called *baby.jpg* with the width and height defined in pixels.

2   An array object called *myImages* is created with the *Array()* constructor. The elements of the array are three *.jpg* files.

3   The user is prompted to pick and number between 1 and 3, which will determine which image will be displayed. The user input is assigned to variable *n*.

4   Array indices start at 0. The user entered a number between 1 and 3, and since *n* will be used as an index into the array, it must be decremented to produce an index number ranging from 0 to 2.

5   The images array can be indexed by number or name. In this example, *display* is the name given to the default image shown on the screen, *baby.jpg*. By changing the *src* property, the default image will be replaced by any one of the images listed in the *myImages* array.  See Figure 11.50.

**Figure 11.50**   Output from Example 11.34 (left) after the user picks a number (right).

**Preloading Images and the *Image()* Constructor.**   If you assign a new image to the *src* property of an *image* object, there may be some lag in the time it takes to download the image from the server. And if you have a slow connection, this can be a real turnoff, to the point that you don't even bother to wait for the image to load. To solve this problem, the *Image()* constructor allows you to preload an offline image; this puts the image in the browser's cache before it is used. This technique of caching the image makes the response time much faster, especially when you have large images, animation, rollovers, and the like. The *Image()* constructor can also define the size (height and width, in pixels) of the cached image. For seamless transition when replacing one image with another, both images should be of the same size. To use the *Image()* constructor, see below.

## FORMAT

```
var newImage = new Image();
var newImage = new Image(height, width)
newImage.src = "image.gif";
```

Example:

```
var myImage = new Image(200,300);
myImage.src = "baby.gif";
```

**A Simple Rollover with a Mouse Event.**   We talked about event handlers with the *form* object and now we will demonstate the use of an event handler with the *image* object. For a complete discussion, see Chapter 12, "Handling Events." The objective of the next example is to change the image when the mouse rolls over a link, and to change it back when the mouse moves away from the link. There are two images involved: the image that initially appears on the page and the image that replaces it when the mouse rolls over the link associated with it. Both of the images are preloaded with the *Image()* constructor. The JavaScript *onMouseOver* event handler is triggered when the user's mouse moves onto the link, and the *onMouseOut* event is triggered when the mouse moves away from the link.

## EXAMPLE 11.35

```
        <html>
        <head><title>Preloading Images</title></head>
        <h2>  This Is Baby William</h2>
        <script language="JavaScript">
1           if(document.images){
2               var baby1=new Image();        // Preload an image
3               baby1.src="baby1image.jpg";
            }
            if (document.images){
4               var baby2=new Image();        // Preload an image
```

---

**EXAMPLE 11.35 (CONTINUED)**

```
5              baby2.src="baby2image.jpg";
        }
    </script>
    <body bgcolor="cornflowerblue">
6   <a href="#" onMouseOver="document.willy.src=baby2.src;"
7                onMouseOut="document.willy.src=baby1.src;">
8   <img name="willy"
        src="baby1image.jpg"
        align="left"
        alt="baby"  border=2  hspace="10"
        width="220" height="250">
    </body>
    </html>
```

**EXPLANATION**

1    Dynamic images are not available on browsers older than Navigator 3 and IE 4. The *if* statement checks for the existance of the *image* object. If the *image* object is unavailable, this block will not be executed.

2    The *Image()* constructor creates and preloads a new *image* object called *baby1*.

3    The *src* property is assigned the name of the external image file called *baby1image.jpg*.

4    The *Image()* constructor creates and preloads a new image object called *baby2*.

5    The *src* property is assigned the name of the external image file called *baby2image.jpg*.

6    The # (hash mark) disables the link so that the browser does not try to go to a URL when clicked. The link is an image. The *onMouseOver* event handler is triggered when the user's mouse moves onto the link, and the *onMouseOut* event handler is triggered when the user's mouse moves away from the link (image). When the mouse moves over the image, the baby image changes from the first image to the second one. When the mouse is moved away from the image, the original image is displayed. Going down the JavaScript hierarchy, we start with the *document*, then to *willy* (*images[0]* or *images["willy"]*), then to the *src* property that is assigned the *image* object. One image is replaced with another.

7    When the mouse is moved away from the link, the intial image *baby1image.jpg* will reappear on the screen.

8    The initial external image called *baby1image.jpg* is named *willy* and is aligned on the left-hand side of the screen. The output is shown in Figure 11.51.

  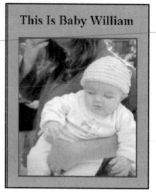

**Figure 11.51**  Before the mouse rolls over the image (left), as the mouse hovers over the image (middle), and when the mouse moves away from the image (right).

**Randomly Displaying Images and the *onClick* Event.**  By using the *Math* object's *random()* method, it is sometimes fun to randomly generate pictures from a list of images. Example 11.36 demonstrates how to change the *src* attribute of an *image* object by using a random number as the index of an elment in an image array. All of the images are preloaded by using the *Image()* constructor, greatly improving on the time it takes to load the images.

---

**EXAMPLE  11.36**

```
     <html>
     <head><title>Preloading Images</title></head>
     <script language="JavaScript">
1        ImageHome=new Array(3);
2        for(var i=0; i<3; i++){
             ImageHome[i]=new Image();
         }
3        ImageHome[0].src="baby1.jpg";
         ImageHome[1].src="baby2.jpg";
         ImageHome[2].src="baby3.jpg";
4        function myRandom(){
5            var n=ImageHome.length - 1;
6            var randnum=Math.floor(Math.random() * (n + 1));
7            document.images["display"].src = ImageHome[randnum].src;
         }
     </script>
     </head>
```

EXAMPLE   11.36 (CONTINUED)

```
<body bgcolor="cornflowerblue"><center>
<h2>  This Is Baby William</h2>
8   <img name="display"
        src="baby.jpg"
        border=5
        width="200" height="250" >
    <p>
    <form>
9   <input type="button"
        value="Click Here for Baby Picture"
10      onClick="myRandom()"
        >
    </form>
    </center>
    </body>
    </html>
```

**EXPLANATION**

1   The *Array*() constructor creates an *array* object to consist of three elements. This array will be used to hold three images.

2   The *Image*() constructor will preload and cache three images and assign them to the array created in line 1.

3   The *src* property of the first element of the *image* array is assigned an image called *baby1.jpg*. Each array element is assigned a different image.

4   The function called *myRandom*() is defined. It produces a random number that will be used as the index into the image array, causing a random picture to be displayed on the screen.

5   The variable called *n* is assigned the value of the length of the image array minus 1.

6   The variable called *randnum* is assigned a random whole number between 1 and 3, the value returned from the *Math* object's random method.

7   Instead of using a number to access the image array, a string is used. The string is the name given to the HTML image defined on line 8. This is the image that initially appears in the browser window. In the JavaScript tree, this image is represented as *document.images[0].src* or *document.display.src* or *document.images["display"].src*. Either way, this image will be replaced with the value of the image in the array *ImageHome[randnum].src*.

8   The inline image, called *baby.jpg* is displayed on the screen when the program starts. It is named *display*.

9   This form input type creates a button on the screen.

10  When the user clicks the button, the *onClick* event is fired up, and the event is handled by calling  *myRandom*(), which displays a random image. See Figure 11.52.

**Figure 11.52**   Each time the user clicks the button, a random picture is displayed.

# 11.4 Introduction to Links

Links are fundamental to the Web. They get you where you want to go, and often take you so far away that you forgot where you were when you started. In fact, Web crawlers are programs that use links to move all over the Internet. HTML hypertext links are usually created by assigning a Web address or a filename to the HTML *<a href>* tag, for example:

```
<a href = "URL address ">Go Home </a>
```

## 11.4.1  JavaScript URLs

With JavaScript, you can also assign a function to the *<a href>* tag that will be launched when the user clicks his mouse on the link. For example,

```
<a href="javascript: function_name(arguments);">  Do Something </a>
```

or, to use an event handler with a link (see Chapter 12, "Handling Events"):

```
<a href=javascript: onClick="return handler(arguments)" >
```

## 11.4.2 The *links* Object

The *links* object is a property of the *document* object and gives you access to the hypertext links that have been loaded into a document. It corresponds to the HTML *<a href>* tag. As each HTML form is a JavaScript element of the *forms[]* array, and each image is assigned to the *images[]* array, so each link is assigned to the *links[]* array in the order in which the link appears within the document. The first link would be represented as *document.links[0]*. The properties for the *links* object are shown in Table 11.23.[5] There are no methods common to both Netscape Navigator and Internet Explorer for the *links* object.

A *links* object contains a URL, similar to the window's *location* object, and shares the same properties. See "The location Object" on page 244. There are nine events that can be triggered by a link: *onClick, onDblClick, onKeyDown, onKeyPress, onKeyUp, onMouseDown, onMouseUp, onMouseOver,* and *onMouseOut.* (For details, see Chapter 12, "Handling Events.")

**Table 11.23**  Properties of the *links* object.

| Property | What It Describes |
|---|---|
| *hash* | Anchor part of the URL (if any) |
| *host* | The hostname:port part of the URL |
| *hostname* | The hostname (machine) part of the URL |
| *href* | The entire URL |
| *pathname* | The pathname part of the URL |
| *port* | The port part of the URL |
| *protocol* | The protocol part of the URL, including the colon following |
| *search* | The query string part of the URL |
| *target* | The HTML target attribute of the link |

---

5. These properties are common to both Netscape and Internet Explorer. IE, however, supports many more than are listed here.

EXAMPLE 11.37

```
      <html><title>Using Links </title>
      </head>
      <h2>Links and their Properties</h2>
      <body>
1     <a href="http://search.yahoo.com/bin/search?p=javascript">
      Search for JavaScript Stuff</a>
      <p>
2     <a href="http://google.com" >Go to Google</a>
      <p>
      Click here for Yahoo <br>
3     <a href="http://www.yahoo.com">
      <img src="yahoo.bmp">
      </a>
      <script language = "JavaScript">
4        document.write("<br><b>This document contains "
            +document.links.length + " links.<br></b>");
5         for (i = 0; i< document.links.length; i++){
             document.write("<u>document.links["+i+"]:</u><br>");
             document.write("<b>hostname:</b> "
                +document.links[i].hostname +"<br>");
6            document.write("<b>href: </b>"
                +document.links[i].href +"<br>");
7            document.write("<b>pathname:</b>"
                +document.links[i].pathname +"<br>");
8            document.write("<b>port:</b> "
                +document.links[i].port +"<br>");
9            document.write("<b>query:</b> "
                +document.links[i].search +"<br>");
10           document.write("<b>protocol:</b> "
                +document.links[i].protocol +"<br><br>");
          }
      </script>
      </body>
      </html>
```

**EXPLANATION**

1   This link goes to the Yahoo! search engine and searches for the word "javascript."
2   This link goes to the Google search engine.
3   This link goes to the Yahoo! search engine.
4   The size of the *links[]* array is determined by the *length* property. It displays the number of links in the document.
5–10  The *for* loop is used to iterate through the links array and display some of its properties. The output is shown in Figure 11.53.

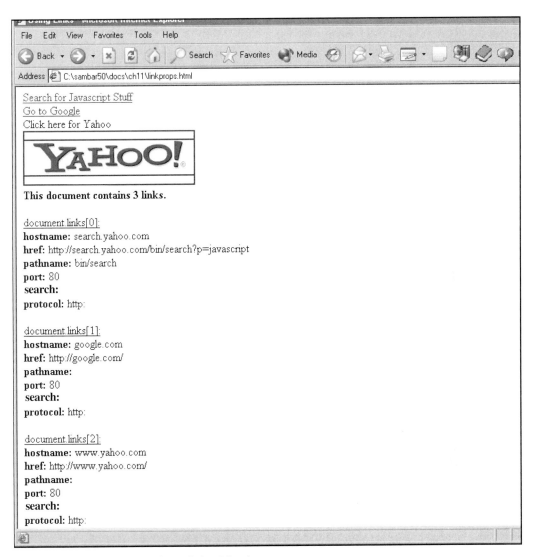

**Figure 11.53** Properties of the *links* object.

**EXAMPLE   11.38**

```
        <html><title>Using Links </title>
        <head>
   1    <map name="my_image_map">
   2    <area shape="rect" href="union4.jpg" coords="157,117,287,203">
        <area shape="rect" href="union1.jpg" coords="10,12,134,96">
        <area shape="rect" href="union2.jpg" coords="171,12,286,91">
        <area shape="rect" href="union3.jpg" coords="5,118,132,201">
        <area shape="default" href="christmas.jpg">
   3    </map>
        </head>
        <body>
        <h2>Christmas on Union Square</h2>
   4    <img src="union1.jpg"   width=300 height=240
   5    usemap="#my_image_map">
        <script language="JavaScript">
            var lstr = "<ul>";
   6        for ( var i = 0; i < document.links.length; i++ ){
                lstr += "<li><a href=" + document.links[i].href;
                lstr += ">link[" + i + "] </a>\n";
            }
   7        lstr += "</ul>";
   8        document.open();
   9        document.write(lstr);
  10        document.close();
        </script>
        </body>
        </html>
```

**EXPLANATION**

1   This is the start of an image map.

2   This is an image map[a] that creates rectangular "hotspots" on the default Christ-mas image displayed on the page. By pressing one of the hotspots, a link to a Christmas image is activated and displayed in the browser. (All of the scenes were taken at Union Square in San Francisco just before dusk.)

3   The HTML image map tag ends here.

4   This is the default image that appears on the screen.

5   A string called *lstr* is created by iterating through the *links[]* array.

6   For each HTML hyperlink created in the document, there is a corresponding ele-ment in the JavaScript *links[]* array. The string *lstr* will contain HTML links for each of the images created in the image map part of the document. This string will be created and dynamically displayed in a new document.

7   The last HTML tag, to end the bullet list, is closed, and concatenated to the *lstr* string.

8   The document's *open()* method opens a new HTML document.

9   The string *lstr* is displayed in the new document. It contains the bulleted list of links.

10   The document that was opened, is closed. The output is shown in Figure 11.54.

a.   The image map was created by Macromedia's Dreamweaver.

**Figure 11.54**   By pressing in any corner of the image or by clicking on a link, a new image will be displayed.

### 11.4.3   The *anchor* Object

An anchor is a place in an HTML document that can be reached with a link. Anchors allow you to access specific parts of a Web page. JavaScript 1.1 introduced the *anchor* object, which represents an HTML *<a>* element. The *anchors* object is a property of the *document* object and gives you access to the links that have been loaded into a document. As each HTML hypertext link is a JavaScript element of the *links[]* array, and each image is assigned to the *images[]* array, so each anchor is assigned to the *links[]* array in the order in which the anchor appears within the document. The first anchor would be represented as *document.anchors[0]*. The only standard property defined for the *anchor* object is the *name* property. Any other properties found with this object are browser specific and not supported by the W3C DOM standard. There are no methods common to both Netscape Navigator and Internet Explorer for the *anchor* object.

## 11.4.4  The *embeds* Object

The *embeds* object (Navigator 3.0), like the *forms* and *image* objects, creates an array representing each embedded object in a page, such as a movie, spreadsheet, or audio clip, in the order the object is found in the page. The first embedded object is assigned to *embeds[0]*, the second to *embeds[1]*, and so on. You can also index the *embeds[]* array by string; just use the name of the embedded object in quotes.

   In the following example, when the page is loaded, the embedded sound clip will automatically start playing, and will be stopped if the user presses the link, "Stop that noise!". The assumption is that you are using Netscape Navigator with the LiveAudio plug-in installed. Not all audio plug-ins support *.wav* files. It is more likely that you have a newer version of Netscape or are using IE or Opera, in which case you are probably using RealPlayer by RealNetworks or Microsoft's Windows Media Player. The example is just a demonstration of how the *embeds* object is used in JavaScript.

---

**EXAMPLE** 11.39

```
     <html><head>
     <script language="JavaScript">
1        function playme(){
2            if (document.embeds){
3                if(navigator.appName == "Netscape")
                 //document.embeds[0].play();
4                document.classical.play();
             }
             else{
5                document.embeds[0].run();
             }
         }
6        function stopSound(){
             document.classical.stop();
         }
     </script>
     </head>
7        <body onLoad="playme();" bgcolor="green" link="white">
     <center>
     <font face="arial" size=+1 color="white">
     <h2>Beethoven's 5th Symphony Playing...</h2>
```

## EXAMPLE   11.39 (CONTINUED)

```
8    <embed src="Beeth5th.wav"
        name="classical"
        hidden=true   <!-- hide Live Audio's control panel -->
        loop=false
        volume=100
        autostart=true>
9    <a href="javascript:stopSound()">Stop that noise!</a>
     <br>
     <img src="noteserver.jpg" border="2" width=500 height=200>
     </body></html>
```

## EXPLANATION

1   The JavaScript function called *playme()* is defined. It will be used to start the music file.

2   If there is an *embeds[]* array in the document, enter the *if* block.

3   If the browser is Netscape Navigator, start the music with LiveAudio's *play()* method. Communicator doesn't come with LiveAudio; you may user RealPlayer instead. The methods will differ for *play()* and *stop()*.

4   The *play()* method starts the music.

5   On other browsers, the *run()* method will start the music. You may try *DoRun()* and *DoStop()* for Real Player.

6   A function called *stopSound()* is defined.

7   Once the document has finished loading, the function *playme()* will be invoked.

8   The source attribute of the *<embed>* tag is assigned the name of the audio clip, *Beeth5th.wav*, which will be started automatically.

9   When the user clicks on this link, the *stopSound()* function is invoked.

**Figure 11.55**   Plays the embedded *.wav* file until it is finished or the user presses the link.

**Figure 11.56**   The *stop()* method isn't supported in IE. The music plays until the clip finishes.

## EXERCISES

1. What's a BOM? What's a DOM?

2. Create an HTML document that contains two forms. One form consists of a text field, the other a text area. Name the forms and the input devices. Use Java-Script to print out the names and values in the forms.

3. Add a button to the last example. If the user clicks it, display the form content in another window.

4. Create two text fields. In one text field, the user will enter his birth month and day. Write a JavaScript program that will print the number of days until his birthday in the second text field.

5. Write a JavaScript function that will finish the story in Example 11.22.

6. Write a multiple choice quiz. It has five questions and the user can only select one answer. After he selects an answer, alert him if he is wrong, and show him the correct answer in a separate text box field.

7. Change Example 11.36 so that a confirmation box will appear, asking the user to confirm his vacation choices. The vacation choices will be listed in a pop-up window.

8. Create a JavaScript program called *slideshow.html* that will produce a slide show. It will contain an array of four images. Preload the images. A timer will be set so that a new image replaces another image every 10 seconds. If the user presses a button labeled Start, the timer starts the image replacement and if he presses a button labeled Stop, the timer stops it.

9. Create a form that uses a text input type. Ask the user to type his name in uppercase letters. The submit button will be an image. Validate that the form is not empty and that the user typed his name in only uppercase letters. Send the form to a CGI program if it is valid.

# chapter

# 12

# Handling Events

## 12.1 Introduction to Event Handlers

We have been talking about events since Chapter 1, "Introduction to JavaScript," because events are inherently part of almost all Web pages and they make the pages interactive and dynamic. JavaScript events are asynchronous, meaning that they can happen at any time. They are actions that are initiated by a user visiting a Web page; for example, if the user submits a form or moves the mouse over a link or an image, he may trigger an event.[1] When an event occurs, JavaScript can execute code in response to the user's action. As shown in previous examples, if the user presses the submit button, Java-Script may check to see if a form was filled out properly; or if the mouse moves over a link, JavaScript may replace one image with a new one. JavaScript's response to one of these user-initiated events is called <u>event handling</u>. If the user presses a button, for example, JavaScript may handle the event by calling a function that will perform some designated task, such as to open a new window or bring a window into focus or submit a fillout form.

JavaScript event handlers are not enclosed between *<script></script>* tags. Event handlers are attributes of HTML tags (specified in the HTML 4 specification). If the event is associated with a form tag, then it will be an attribute of the *<form>* tag, and if associated with a link, it will be an attribute of the *<a href>* tag, and so on. The string that is assigned to the event handler is the command that will be executed when the event is triggered by the user. The command is a JavaScript built-in function or user-defined function. The function will be called when the event is triggered.

Whereas a property or method may be associated with a single object, events are usually associated with a collection of objects. The *onClick* event handler, for example, may be associated with a form's input tag, but it could also be associated with a link tag, or an image map area, or a simple button.

---

1. An event is initiated by a user. The event itself may be blur, click, change, or the like. The event handler is the event preceded with "*on*". For example, *onBlur* and *onClick* are attributes of an HTML tag, and are used to handle the event for which they are named.

(Note the spelling convention used for the event handlers. The first word, *on*, is all lowercase, and the first letter of each subsequent word is capitalized. Unless the event is being used as a method in a JavaScript program (see "Event Handlers as JavaScript Methods" on page 356), it is not case sensitive. Using *onClick* or *onclick* are both fine.)

Consider the following example:

```
<form><input type="button"
             value="Wake me"
             onClick="wakeupCall()">
</form>
```

The HTML *<form>* tag contains an input tag with three attributes: *type*, *value*, and *onClick*. The input type is a *"button"*; it has a value of *"Wake me"*, and a JavaScript event handler called *onClick*. The *onClick* event handler is assigned a function called *"wakeupCall()"*. When the user clicks the button labeled *Wake me!*, the *onClick* event handler is triggered, and the *wakeupCall()* function will be executed, as demonstrated in Example 12.1 and shown in Figure 12.1.

## EXAMPLE 12.1

```
        <html>
        <head><title>Wake up call</title>
1       <script language="javascript">
2          function wakeupCall(){      // Function is defined here
3              setTimeout('alert("Time to get up!")',5000);
           }
4       </script>
5       </head>
        <body bgcolor="lightblue">
6       <form>
7          <input type="button"
8              value="Wake me"
9              onClick="wakeupCall()">
        </form></body></html>
```

## EXPLANATION

1   The start of the JavaScript program.

2   The *wakeupCall()* function is defined in the JavaScript program, between the *<script></script>* tags. When the user clicks the form button, the function assigned to the event handler is called; that is, *wakeupCall()* is called. The function itself is defined in a JavaScript program, even though it is called from outside the program.

3   The timer is set for 5,000 milliseconds. The alert dialog box will pop up on the screen five seconds after the user clicks the button.

4   End of the JavaScript program.

5   End of the HTML *<head>* tag.

6   This is the start of an HTML *<form>* tag.

**EXPLANATION** (CONTINUED)

7    The type of form uses a *"button"* input type.

8    The value is shown in the button as the text, *"Wake me"*.

9    The *onClick* event is assigned the name of a function. When the user presses the button, the *onClick* event handler, *wakeupCall()*, will be called.

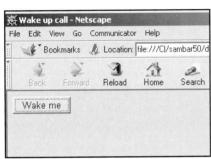 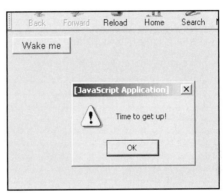

**Figure 12.1**   Before clicking the button (left); after clicking and waiting five seconds (right).

A list of JavaScript event handlers and their uses is given in Table 12.1.

**Table 12.1**   JavaScript events and what they do.

| Event Handler | What It Affects | When It Happens |
|---|---|---|
| *onAbort* | Images | When image loading has been interrupted. |
| *onBlur* | Windows, frames, all form objects | When focus moves out of this object except *hidden*; e.g., when the cursor leaves a text box. |
| *onChange* | Input, select, and text areas | When a user changes the value of an element and it loses the input focus. Used for form validation. |
| *onClick* | Links, buttons, form objects, image map areas | When a user clicks on an object. Return false to cancel default action. |
| *onDblClick* | Links, buttons, form objects | When a user double-clicks on an object. |
| *onDragDrop* | Windows | When a user drops an object, such as a file, onto the browser window. |
| *onError* | Script | When an error in the script occurs; e.g., a syntax error. |
| *onFocus* | Windows, frames, all form objects | When a mouse is clicked or moved in a window or frame and it gets focus; except *hidden*. |

**Table 12.1**   *JavaScript events and what they do. (continued)*

| Event Handler | What It Affects | When It Happens |
|---|---|---|
| onKeyDown | Documents, images, links, forms | When a key is pressed. |
| onKeyPress | Documents, images, links, forms | When a key is pressed and released. |
| onKeyUp | Documents, images, links, forms | When a key is released. |
| onLoad | Body, framesets, images | After the document or image is loaded. |
| onMouseOut | Links (and images within links) | When the mouse moves away from a link. |
| onMouseOver | Links (and images within links) | When the mouse moves over a link. Return true to prevent link from showing in the status bar. |
| onMove | Windows | When the browser window is moved. |
| onReset | Forms reset button | When the forms reset button is clicked. Return false to stop reset. |
| onResize | Windows | When the browser window changes size. |
| onSelect | Form elements | When a form element is selected. |
| onSubmit | Forms | When you want to send a form to the server. Return false to stop submission to the server. |
| onUnload | Body, framesets | After the document or frameset is closed or reset. |

## 12.1.1   Creating the Event Handler

There are two parts to setting up an event handler:

1. The event handler is assigned as an attribute of an HTML tag such as a document, form, or link. If you want the event to affect a document, then it would become an attribute of the *<body>* tag; if you want the event to affect a button, then it would become an attribute of the form's *<input>* tag, and if you want the event to affect a link, then it would become an attribute of the *<a href>* tag. For example, if the event is to be activated when a document has finished loading, the *onLoad* event handler is used, and if the event happens when the user clicks on an input device, such as a button, the *onClick* event handler is fired up.

```
<body onLoad="alert('Welcome to my Web site')"; >
<form>
<input type="button"
   value="Tickle me "
   onClick="alert('Hee hee ho hee')";
</form></body>
```

2. The next step is to assign a value to the event handler. The value may be a built-in method such as *alert()* or *confirm()*, a user-defined function, or a string of JavaScript statements. Although the event handler is an attribute of an HTML tag, if a user-defined function is assigned to the event handler, then that function must be defined either in a JavaScript program or as direct script statements (separated by semicolons).

And be careful with quotes! The handling function must be enclosed within either double or single quotes. If you have double quotes within the function, surround the whole thing in single quotes, and if you have single quotes within the function, either escape the single quote with a backslash, or surround the whole thing in double quotes.

```
built-in method    -->     onClick="window.open('myhome.html', 'newWin')"


user-defined function -->  onUnLoad="timeOver();"


group of statements -->    onChange="if (!checkVal(this.value, 1, 10)){
                                this.focus();  this.select();}"
```

## EXAMPLE 12.2

```
      <html>
      <head><title>An event</title></head>
1     <body bgcolor="magenta" onUnload="alert('So long, stranger!')";>
      <center>
2     <form>
3     <input type="button"
4        value="Click here to be alerted"
5        onClick='alert("Watch out! An asteroid is approaching
                        earth!")'>
6     </form>
      </center>
      </body>
      </html>
```

## EXPLANATION

1  The *<body>* tag contains the *onUnload* event handler. When the user browses to another page or exits the page, the *alert()* method will be triggered. Normally you would use this event for a quick cleanup or exit function, such as closing a window or clearing a page. Starting some time-consuming process at this point would be annoying to the user, since he is trying to leave this page without silly delays. The only purpose for this example, is to demonstrate when the event happens.

2  The form starts here with the *<form>* tag.

3  The input type for this form is *"button"*.

**EXPLANATION** (CONTINUED)

4    The value on the button is *"Click here to be alerted"*.

5    The *onClick* event is an attribute of the HTML form's input tag. When the user clicks the mouse on the button (the *onClick* event), the *alert()* method is called. See Figure 12.2.

6    The HTML form tag ends here. The output is shown in Figure 12.2.

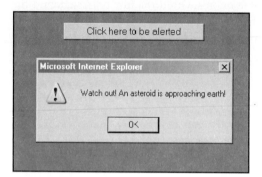

**Figure 12.2**    When the user presses the button, the *onClick* event is activated (left); when the page is refreshed or exits, the *onUnload* event is activated (right).

## 12.2  Event Handlers as JavaScript Methods

An event handler is an attribute of an HTML tag. Since HTML elements are also treated as objects in a JavaScript program, there are a number of event methods that can be used to simulate events (see Table 12.2). When an event method is applied to an object, the object to which it refers behaves as though the event has happened; e.g., the *click()* method behaves like the *onClick* event, the *blur()* method behaves like the *onBlur* event, and so on.[2] The event method is applied to the object with the dot syntax, as are all other methods; e.g., in a JavaScript program you might see something like the following:

```
document.test.button1.click(), window.focus()
```

**Table 12.2**    Event methods.

| Event Method | Event Handler It Simulates | Effect |
| --- | --- | --- |
| *blur()* | *onBlur* | Removes focus from windows, frames, form fields |
| *click()* | *onClick* | Simulates a mouse click in form fields |

2.  Event methods behave as though the event has happened but in themselves do not trigger an event handler. For example, the *click()* method does not trigger the *onClick* event handler.

**Table 12.2**   Event methods. (continued)

| Event Method | Event Handler It Simulates | Effect |
| --- | --- | --- |
| *focus()* | *onFocus* | Puts focus in a window, frame, form field |
| *reset()* | *onReset* | Clears the form fields |
| *select()* | *onSelect* | Selects or highlights text in a form field |
| *submit()* | *onSubmit* | Submits a form |

---

## EXAMPLE   12.3

```
    <html>
    <head><title>Simulation Methods</title></head>
    <body bgcolor="yellow">
1   <form name="myform"
2       action="http://localhost/cgi-bin/doit.pl"
        method="post">
    Enter your name:<br>
        <input type="text"
            name="namefield"
            size="30"
            value="Name: "
3           onFocus="this.select()">
    <p>
    Enter your address:<br>
4       <input type="text"
            name="addressfield"
            size="30"
            value="Address: "
5           onFocus="this.select()">
    <p>
    </form>
6   <a href="#" onClick="javascript: document.myform.submit();">
    Click here to submit your form</a>
    <p>
7   <a href="#" onClick="javascript:document.myform.reset();">
    Click here to reset your form</a>
    </body>
    </html>
```

## EXPLANATION

1   A form named *myform* is started.

2   This is the URL where the form will be processed after it is submitted.

3   The *onFocus* event handler is assigned an event method called *select()*. For *this* textbox, when the mouse cursor is clicked in the box, the *onFocus* event is triggered and the event is handled by highlighting or selecting the text in the box.

**EXPLANATION** (CONTINUED)

4  Another text box is defined to hold the user's address.

5  When the cursor is moved into this field, the text box gets focus and the *select()* method is called to highlight this box, as in line 3.

6  A deactivated link is assigned an *onClick* event handler. When the user clicks on the link, the JavaScript code is executed. The pseudo *javascript:* protocol is followed by a reference to the form and a *submit()* method, which causes the form to be submitted when the user clicks on the link.

7  A deactivated link is assigned an *onClick* event handler. When the user clicks on the link, the JavaScript code is executed. The pseudo *javascript:* protocol is followed by a reference to the form and a *reset()* method, which clears the form fields. See Figure 12.3.

**Figure 12.3**  The focus is in the first box and the field is selected (highlighted).

## 12.2.1  Return Values

Sometimes the event handler's return value is necessary if a certain action is to proceed. The browser's default actions can be suppressed by returning a false value, or a form's submission can be completed by sending back a true value. For example, if the *onSubmit* handler gets a true value back from a function or method, then a form may be submitted to the server, and if not, the form will be stopped. In Chapter 11, "The Document Objects: Forms, Images, and Links," we saw that when validating a form, return values are used. The following example illustrates these return values.

**EXAMPLE   12.4**

```
        <html><head><title>An HTML Form and the onSubmit Event
           Handler</title>
        <script language="JavaScript">
1           function checkForm(yourinfo){
2               if(yourinfo.namestring.value == "" ||
                    yourinfo.namestring.value == null){
                    // Check for an empty string or null value
3               alert("Please type in your name");
4               return(false);
                }
                else{
5               return(true);
                }
            }
        </script>
        </head>
        <body>
        <b>
6       <form name="info" action="/cgi-bin/bookstuff/form1.cgi"
           method="post"
7           onSubmit="return checkForm(document.info)"><p>
        <font size="+1"><p>
        Type your name here:
8       <input type="text" name="namestring" size="50">
        <p>
9       <input type="submit" value="Submit">
        <input type="reset" value="Clear">
        </form>
        </body>
        </html>
```

1   The function called *checkForm()* has one argument, *yourinfo*, which is a reference to the form defined on line 6.

2   If the user didn't enter anything into the text box, the value of the input type will be null. The expression *if(yourinfo.namestring.value == "")* checks for an empty field.

3   The user didn't enter anything into the text box. An alert dialog box will appear on the screen, and after he presses OK, he will have a chance to fill out the form again.

4   If *false* is returned from this function, the form will not be submitted to the server.

5   If *true* is returned from this function, the form will be submitted to the server.

6   The HTML form starts here. The form, *document.forms[0]*, is named *"info"*. The *action* attribute contains the URL of the program that will process the form, a CGI script on the server. The *method* attribute defines the HTTP method that determines how the data will be sent to the server.

7   The *onSubmit* event handler is an attribute of the HTML *<form>* tag and is triggered when the user presses the submit button. The event handler is a function called *checkForm()*. Its parameter is the name of the form, *document.info* (also could use its array name: *document.forms[0]*). The *return* keyword is required when using the *onSubmit* event handler. One of two values will be returned: either *true* or *false*.

8   The input type for this form is a text field box. Its name is *"namestring"* and it can hold a string of up to 50 characters.

9   The input type is the submit button. When the user presses this button, the *onSubmit* event handler on line 7 is activated. See Figure 12.4.

**Figure 12.4**   Using the *onSubmit* event and return values. If the return value is *true* the form is submitted; otherwise, it is stopped.

# 12.3 Handling a Window or Frame Event

A window is the main Web page, unless it is divided up into frames. There are a number of events that will affect windows and frames; these are described in Table 12.3. The following examples illustrate some of the events that affect windows and frames.

**Table 12.3**   Window and frame events.

| Event Handler | When It Is Triggered |
|---|---|
| onBlur | When the mouse moves away from the window or frame and it loses focus |
| onFocus | When the mouse is clicked or moved in a window or frame and it gets focus |
| onLoad | When a document or image has finished loading |
| onMove | When a window is moved[a] |
| onUnLoad | When a page is exited or reset |

a.   The *onMove* event handler in Netscape Navigator 4.0 is enabled only for the *window* object.

### 12.3.1   The *onLoad* and *onUnLoad* Events

The *onLoad* event handler is invoked when a document, its frameset, or images have completely finished loading. This includes the point at which all functions have been defined and scripts have been executed, and all forms are available. This event can be helpful in synchronizing the loading of a set of frames, particularly when there may be large images that need to be loaded or all of the frame data hasn't arrived from the server.

The *onUnLoad* event handler is invoked when the page is exited or reset.

**EXAMPLE   12.5**

```
     <html><head><title>Mouse Events</title>
1    <script language="JavaScript">
2       var sec=0;
3       function now(){
             var newdate= new Date();
             var hour=newdate.getHours();
             var minutes=newdate.getMinutes();
             var seconds=newdate.getSeconds();
             var timestr=hour+":"+minutes+":"+seconds;
4            window.setInterval("trackTime()", 1000);
5            alert("Your document has finished loading\n"+
                 "The time: "+timestr);
         }
6       function trackTime(){
7            sec++;
         }
8       function howLong(){
             alert("You have been browsing here for "+ sec+" seconds");
         }
     </script>
     </head>
9    <body background="blue hills.jpg" onLoad="now();"
```

## EXAMPLE   12.5 (CONTINUED)

```
10      onUnLoad="howLong();">
    <font face="arial,helvetica" size=5>
    When you leave or reload this page, <br>an alert dialog box
    will appear.
    </body>
    </html>
```

## EXPLANATION

1   The JavaScript program starts here.

2   A global variable called *sec* is declared.

3   The user-defined function *now()* contains several of the *Date* object's methods to calculate the time. This function is used to keep track of how long the user browses from the time the page is loaded until it is exited.

4   The *window* object's *setInterval()* method is set to call the function *trackTime()* every 1,000 milliseconds (one second) starting when the document is loaded until it is unloaded.

5   The alert dialog box pops up when the page finishes loading.

6   This is a user-defined function that keeps track of the number of seconds that have elapsed since the page was loaded.

7   The variable called *sec* is increased by one each time *trackTime()* is called.

8   This function is called when the page is exited or reloaded. It is the event that is triggered by the *onUnLoad* handler on line 10.

9   When the document has finished loading, the *onLoad* event handler is triggered. The *onLoad* event handler is an attribute of the *<body>* tag. The event handler is assigned a function called *now()* that sets up a timer that will go off every second while the page is opened. After a second passes another function called *trackTime()* will keep updating a variable that stores the number of seconds that have elapsed. The background attribute of the HTML *<body>* tag is set to an image of blue hills.

10  The *onUnLoad* event handler is triggered when the user either leaves or reloads the page. See Figure 12.5.

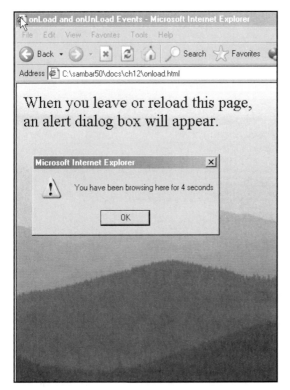

**Figure 12.5**
If you exit, or press the reload button,
this alert box appears.

### 12.3.2   The *onload()* and *ununload()* Methods

The *onload()* method, *window.onload()*, simulates the *onLoad* event handler. The *ununload()* method, *window.ununload()*, simulates the behavior of the *onUnload* event handler. All JavaScript event methods must be in lowercase, such as *onload()* or *ununload()*. The event handlers themselves, used as HTML attributes, are not case sensitive, so *ONUNLOAD*, *onUnLoad*, and *onunload* are all acceptable.

### 12.3.3   The *onFocus* and *onBlur* Event Handlers

When an object has the focus, it is waiting for the user to do something, such as press a button, click on a link, start or stop an animation. If you are moving between frames, the frame where the mouse is pointing has the focus, and when the cursor moves out of the frame, it loses focus or is "blurred." The *onFocus* event handler allows you to initiate a window or frame type function when the mouse is moved into a window, and the *onBlur* event handler is triggered when you leave a window or frame. When a window has focus, it becomes the top window in a stack of windows. The following example changes the background color of the left frame to pink when it goes into focus and to yellow when it goes out of focus. The status bar at the bottom of the window reflects what frame has the focus.

**EXAMPLE  12.6**

```
    <html>
    <head><title>Frame Me!</title></head>
1   <frameset cols="25%,75%">
2       <frame src="leftfocus.html" name="left">
3       <frame src="rightfocus.html" name="right" >
    </frameset>
    </html>
---------------------------------------------------------------------
    <!-- The right frame file -->
    <html>
4   <head><title>Right Frame</title></head>
5       <body bgColor="lightblue">
    <font face="arial" size=4> right frame<br>
    </body>
    </html>
---------------------------------------------------------------------
    <html>
    <head><title>Left Frame</title>
6   <script language="JavaScript">
7       function focus_on_me(){
            document.bgColor="pink";    // Current doc is the left frame
8           window.status="focus leftframe";
        }
9       function defocus_me(){
            parent.left.document.bgColor="yellow";   // Another way to
                                                     // reference
10          window.status="focus rightframe";    // See the status bar
        }
    </script>
    </head>
11      <body onFocus="focus_on_me()"        // Event handlers
12          onBlur="defocus_me()"
            bgColor="lightgreen">
            <image src="signs.jpg">
        </body>
    </html>
```

**EXPLANATION**

1   In this example, there are three files involved with frames. This is the HTML file that defines the frameset. It consists of a main window divided into two frames, a left frame consisting of 25 percent of the window, and right frame consisting of 75 percent of the window.

2   The left-hand frame's source code is in a file called *leftfocus.html*.

3   The right-hand frame's source code is in a file called *rightfocus.html*.

4   This HTML document is the content for the right-hand frame.

5   The background color of the right-hand frame is *lightblue*.

6   This is the start of the JavaScript program found in the file called *leftfocus.html*.

**EXPLANATION** (CONTINUED)

7   This user-defined function, called *focus_on_me()*, is called when the *onFocus* event handler is triggered; that is, when the user's cursor has focus in that window. It assigns a pink background color to the left-hand frame by going down the JavaScript hierarchy: *parent.left.document.bgcolor*.

8   The status bar in the window is assigned the string *"focus leftframe"*. Look in the status bar.

9   This user-defined function, called *defocus_me*, is called when the *onBlur* event handler is triggered; that is, when the user's cursor loses focus in that window. It assigns a yellow background color to the right-hand frame by going down the JavaScript hierarchy: *parent.right.document.bgcolor*.

10  The status bar in the window is assigned the string *"focus rightframe"*. Look in the status bar.

11  An *onFocus* event handler is assigned to the *<body>* tag for the file called *leftfocus.html*. As soon as focus goes into this window (frame), the handler's function called *focus_on_me()* is called.

12  An *onBlur* event handler is assigned to the *<body>* tag for *leftfocus.html*. When focus leaves this frame (i.e., the user clicks his mouse in another window), the function called *defocus_me()* is called. The output is shown in Figure 12.6.

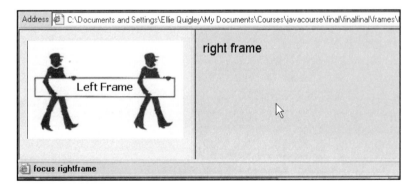

**Figure 12.6**   When focus is on the left frame, it turns pink. When focus leaves the left frame, it turns yellow. Notice the mouse pointer is in the right frame. That's where the focus is. Check the status bar.

## 12.3.4   The *focus()* and *blur()* Methods

The *focus()* and *blur()* methods behave exactly the same as their like-named events. These methods are applied to an object, such as a window or form object, and are called from the JavaScript program. When the *focus()* method is applied to an object, it will cause that object to be in focus and when the *blur()* method is applied to an object, it will lose its input focus.

**EXAMPLE** 12.7

```
         <html>
         <head><title>The focus and blur methods</title>
         <script language="JavaScript">
1            function newWindow(){
2                winObj=window.open("summertime.jpg",
                 "summer","width=650,height=200,resizable=yes,
                 scrollbars=yes,location=yes");
3                winObj.moveTo(0,0);   // Move to left-hand corner of screen
4                winObj.focus();       // New window gets the focus
                 //windObj.blur();
             }
5            function closeWindow(){
6                winObj.close();       // Close the new window
             }
         </script>
         </head>
         <body bgColor="lightgreen">
         <h2>Summer Scene from the Old Country</h2>
         <form>
             <input type=button
                 value="Open Window"
7                onClick="javascript:newWindow();">
             <input type=button
                 value="Close Window"
8                onClick="javascript:closeWindow();">
         </form>
         </body>
         </html>
```

**EXPLANATION**

1   A user-defined function, called *newWindow()*, will create a new *window* object with the *window* object's *open()* method, specified with a number of options to further define the window.

2   The new *window* object is an image called *summertime.jpg*.

3   The new window is moved to the left-hand corner of the screen, pixel position (0,0).

4   The new window gets focus. It will be on top of all the other windows.

5   This user-defined function is responsible for closing the new window.

6   The *close()* method of the *window* object causes the new window to be closed.

7   When the user clicks this button, the *onClick* event handler is triggered, and a new window will be opened.

8   When the user clicks this button, the *onClick* event handler is triggered, and the new window will be closed. The output is shown in Figures 12.7 and 12.8.

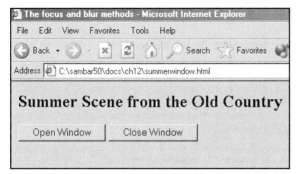

**Figure 12.7**   The parent window.

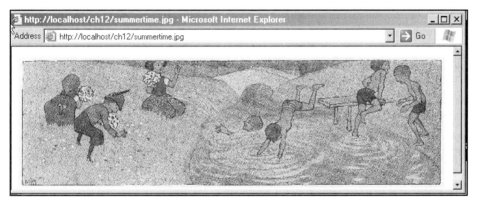

**Figure 12.8**   The new window is in focus and will appear on top of its parent window.

# 12.4 Handling Mouse Events

In many previous examples, we've seen uses of the *onClick* event handler to initiate an action when a user clicks his mouse in a button or on a link. There are a number of other events that can be fired up because of some action of the mouse. When the user moves the mouse pointer over a link, image, or other object, the *onMouseOver* event handler is triggered, and when he moves the mouse pointer away from an object, the *onMouseOut* event is triggered. Table 12.4 lists events that are triggered when mouse movement is detected.

**Table 12.4**  Mouse events.

| Event Handler | When It Is Triggered |
| --- | --- |
| onClick | When the mouse is clicked on a link and on form objects like button, submit |
| onDblClick | When the mouse is double-clicked on a link, document, form object, image |
| onMouseDown (NN6+) | When the mouse is pressed on a link, document |
| onMouseMove (NN6+) | When the mouse touches the link, form object |
| onMouseOut | When a mouse is moved out of a link, image map |
| onMouseOver | When a mouse is moved over a link, image map |
| onMouseUp | When the mouse is released from a link, document |

## 12.4.1   How to Use Mouse Events

The *onMouseOver* and *onMouseOut* event handlers occur when the user's mouse pointer is moved over or out of an object. The *onMouseMove* event occurs when the mouse just touches the object. In the following example, every time the user touches the button labeled *onMouseMove* with his mouse, a function called *counter()* is invoked to keep track of the number of mouse moves that have taken place. That number is displayed in an alert dialog box, as shown in Figure 12.9. If the user double-clicks his mouse anywhere on the page, the a message will appear, and if OK is clicked, the window will be closed.

**EXAMPLE  12.8**

```
    <html><head><title>Mouse Events</title>
1   <script language="JavaScript">
2      var counter=0;
3      function alertme(){
          alert("I'm outta hea!");
4          window.close();
       }
5      function track_Moves(){
6          counter++;
          if(counter==1){
             alert(counter + " mouse moves so far!");
          }
          else{
             alert(counter + " mouse moves so far!");
          }
       }
    </script>
    </head>
```

## EXAMPLE 12.8 (CONTINUED)

```
7    <body bgColor="CCFF00" onDblClick="alertme()";>
     <p><font face="arial" size=3>
        Double click anywhere on this page to get out!
     <p>
        When the mouse moves over the link, an event is triggered.
8    <a href="#" onMouseOver="alert('Event: onMouseOver');">onMouseOver
     </a><p>
     When the mouse moves away from a link, an event is triggered.
9    <a href="#" onMouseOut="alert('Event: onMouseOut');">onMouseOut
     </a><p>
     When the mouse moves in or out of the button, a function<br>
     is called that keeps track of how many times the mouse touched
     the button.
10   <form>
          <input type="button"
              value="onMouseMove"
11            onMouseMove="track_Moves();">
     </form>
     </body>
     </html>
```

## EXPLANATION

1  A JavaScript program starts here.

2  A global variable called *counter* is initialized.

3  If the user double-clicks his mouse anywhere on the page, an alert dialog box will appear; if he OKs it, the window will be closed.

4  The *window's close* method causes the current window to be closed.

5  This function is called when the *onMouseOver* event handler is triggered. This event happens when the user touches his mouse on an object, in this case, a button object.

6  The counter is incremented by one every time the user touches the button.

7  The *onDblClick* event handler is an attribute of the HTML *<body>* tag. When the user double-clicks his mouse, the *alertme()* function will be called, and the window closed.

8  The *onMouseOver* event handler is an attribute of the *<a href>* link tag. It is triggered anytime the user moves his mouse over the link. (The link has been deactivated by using the # sign.) When this event occurs, the *alert* method is called.

9  The *onMouseOut* event handler is an attribute of the *<a href>* link tag. Any time the user moves his mouse away from this link, the event is triggered, and the *alert* method is called.

10  The form starts here. The input type is a button.

11  When the user's mouse touches the button, the *onMouseMove* event handler is triggered, and the *track_Moves()* function is called. This function will simply increment a counter by one, each time it is called, and then alert the user.

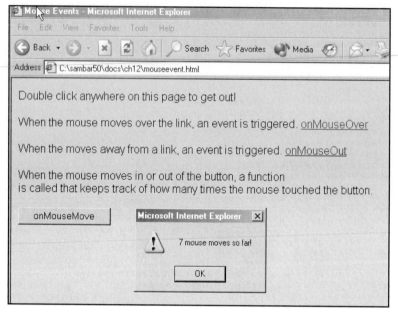

**Figure 12.9**  •  Links and mouse events.

## 12.4.2   Mouse Events and Images—Rollovers

The *onMouseOver* and *onMouseOut* event handlers are commonly used to create a roll-over, an image that is replaced with a different image every time the mouse moves over a link or image. (See "A Simple Rollover with a Mouse Event" on page 336 in Chapter 11.) In the following example, if the user touches the first link, the picture of the first mouse will be replaced with a new picture, giving the illusion that the mouse's eyes are moving.

---

**EXAMPLE**   12.9

```
      <html><title>Mouse Events</title>
      </head>
      <body bgColor="orange">
    1 <a href="#" onMouseOver="document.mouse.src='mouse.gif'">
         onMouseOver </a><p>
    2 <a href="#" onMouseOut="document.mouse.src='mouse2.gif';">
         onMouseOut</a><p>
    3 <img src="mousestart.gif" width=300 height=150 name="mouse">
      </body>
      </html>
```

## EXPLANATION

1. The *onMouseOver* event handler is assigned to a deactivated link (# causes the link to be inactive). When the mouse rolls onto the link, the event is triggered, and a new image, called *mouse.gif* will replace the original image, *mousestart.gif*.

2. The *onMouseOut* event handler is assigned to another deactivated link, this time with another image of the mouse. When the mouse rolls away from the link, the event is triggered, and a new image, called *mouse2.gif* will replace the last image, *mouse.gif*. By rolling the mouse back and forth, the mouse's eyes seem to move. The words "*hi*" and "*bye*" also keep changing.

3. This is the original image that is displayed before the links are touched. See Figure 12.10.

**Figure 12.10** Original display (left), as the mouse moves over the link (middle), and as the mouse moves away from the link (right).

### 12.4.3 Creating a Slide Show

By using a timer with an event, you can do all sorts of fun things with images. You can create scrolling banners, rotating billboards, button rollovers, and more. The following example is a simple slide show. Four images are preloaded and each image is assigned to an array element. When the user moves his mouse onto one of the pictures, a new picture will replace the previous one every two seconds, and when he moves his mouse away from the image, the show stops. Any time the mouse moves over the image, the show starts again.

**EXAMPLE  12.10**

```
        <html>
        <head><title>The Four Seasons</title>
        <script language="JavaScript">
1           var season = new Array();
2           var indx = 0;
3           var timeDelay=2000;
4           if(document.images){
5               season[0]=new Image();
6               season[0].src="winter.jpg";
                season[1]=new Image();
                season[1].src="summer.jpg";
                season[2]=new Image();
                season[2].src="fall.jpg";
                season[3]=new Image();
                season[3].src="spring.jpg";
            }
7           function changeSeason(){
8               var size= season.length - 1;
                if( indx < size ) {
                    indx++;
                }
                else {
                    indx = 0;
                }
9           document.times.src= season[indx].src;
10          timeout=setTimeout('changeSeason()', timeDelay);
            }
11          function stopShow(){
12              clearTimeout(timeout);
            }
        </script>
        </head>
        <body bgcolor="cornflowerblue"><center><font face="arial">
        <h2>The 4 Seasons</h2><b>
        To see slide show, put your mouse on the image.<br>
        Move your mouse away from the image, to stop it.
13      <a href="javascript:void(null);"
            onMouseOver="return changeSeason();"
            onMouseOut="return stopShow()">
14      <img name="times" src="winter.jpg" align="left"
        border=8  hspace="10" width="700" height="200">
        </a>
        <br>
        </body>
        </html>
```

## EXPLANATION

1   A new *Array* object, called *season* is declared. It will be used to store an array of images.

2   A global variable called *indx* is declared and initialized to 0.

3   The value 2000 is assigned to another global variable, called *timeDelay*.

4   If this browser has an image object, then an array of objects is created with the *Image()* constructor.

5   Using the *Image()* constructor preloads and caches the images. Each new image object is assigned to an element of the *season* array.

6   The first element of the *season* array gets a *new Image* object. The *src* property (the location and name of the image) is *winter.jpg*, located in the present working directory.

7   A user-defined function called *changeSeason()* is defined. It is called when the *on-MouseOver* event handler is triggered by the user moving his mouse onto the image. Its purpose is to replace one image with another image in the *season* array, every 2 seconds, for as long as the user's mouse is on the image. (It might be nice to add a little Vivaldi audio clip here to enhance the show!)

8   The size of the array is its length − 1 since array indices start at 0. As long as the array size isn't surpassed, the index value will keep being incremented by 1.

9   This is where image replacement happens. The name of the original image is *times* (line 14) and it is referenced by JavaScript using the DOM hierarchy: *docment.times.src* is assigned a new image from the *season* array, *season[indx].src*. The new image will be displayed.

10  The *window* object's *setTimeout()* method will be set to call the *changeSeason()* function every 2,000 milliseconds (2 seconds). Every 2 seconds a new image is displayed as long as the user keeps his mouse on an image.

11  The user-defined function called *stopShow()* is defined. It is called when the *on-MouseOut* event is triggered by the mouse moving away from the image. It turns off the timer, stopping the slide show.

12  The *setTimeout()* method is cleared.

13  The link has two mouse event handlers, *onMouseOver* and *onMouseOut*. The pseudo URL, *javascript:void(null)*, deactivates the link and ensures that if there is a return value from the event, it will be nullified. Since neither of the events return anything, it would be enough to just use the protocol as *javascript:*. The display is shown in Figures 12.11 and 12.12.

**Figure 12.11**   Watch the seasons change every 2 seconds.

**Figure 12.12**   Spring image (top), summer image (middle), and fall image (bottom) are all part of the slide show created in Example 12.10.

## 12.5 Handling Link Events

In many of the previous examples, links have been used to trigger events. When the user clicked or moved his mouse over a link, a link event was triggered. One link event, *onClick*, gets sent whenever someone clicks on a link. As we saw with mouse events, *onMouseOver* and *onMouseOut* also cause a link event to occur.

**Table 12.5** Link events.

| Event Handler | When It Is Triggered |
|---|---|
| *onClick* | When the mouse is clicked on a link |
| *onMouseOut* | When a mouse is moved out of a link |
| *onMouseOver* | When a mouse is moved over a link |

### 12.5.1 JavaScript URLs

We have seen JavaScript code in a *javascript:* URL throughout this text. In the example using mouse events, the event handler was assigned to a link and the link was deactivated with the *javascript:* protocol followed by a hash mark:

```
<a href="#" onClick='alert("This hotlink is out of service!");
   return false;'>Click here</a>
```

or by using the *void* operator to guarantee that any return value from the function will be discarded:

```
<a href="javascript:void(0);" onMouseOver="return changeSeason();"
```

In either case, the link was not supposed to take the user to another location, but instead to handle an event or call a function. (Make sure that any function calls in the URL have been defined.) Another note: if the "#" causes the browser to jump to the top of the page when the link is clicked, you can add a return *false* statement inside the *onClick* handler to keep the browser from checking the content of the *href*.

The following simple example uses the *onClick* event handler with a deactivated link and the return statement; the display is shown in Figure 12.13.

**EXAMPLE 12.11**

```
<html><head><title>Deactivate the hotlink</title></head>
<body>
<center>
<a href="#" onClick='alert("This hotlink is out of service!");
   return false;'>Click here</a>
</center>
</body>
</html>
```

**Figure 12.13**  The user clicked on a deactivated link.

# 12.6 Handling a Form Event

As discussed in Chapter 11, "The Document Objects: Forms, Images, and Links," the *document* object has a *forms* property. It contains an array of all the forms that have been defined in the document. Each element of the array is a *form* object and the number in the index of the array represents the order in which the form appeared on the page. The first form would be *document.forms[0]*. Each form contains elements, also represented as an array. The elements represent the input types of the form, such as a checkbox, radio button, or text field. By naming each of the forms and its respective elements, it is much easier to work with them in JavaScript. (See Chapter 11 for a complete discussion of the *forms[]* array.) There are a number of events associated with the form's elements. Many of them were also covered in Chapter 11. They are listed in Table 12.6.

**Table 12.6**  Event handlers for the form's elements.

| Object | Event Handler |
| --- | --- |
| *button* | *onClick, onBlur, onFocus* |
| *checkbox* | *onClick, onBlur, onFocus* |
| *FileUpLoad* | *onClick, onBlur, onFocus* |
| *hidden* | *none* |
| *password* | *onBlur, onFocus, onSelect* |
| *radio* | *onClick, onBlur, onFocus* |
| *reset* | *onReset* |
| *select* | *onFocus, onBlur, onChange* |
| *submit* | *onSubmit* |
| *text* | *onClick, onBlur, onFocus, onChange* |
| *textarea* | *onClick, onBlur, onFocus, onChange* |

### 12.6.1 Buttons

One of the most common GUI form elements is the button. The button object has no default action and is normally used to trigger an event such as the *OnClick* event. HTML 4 allows you to create a *<button>* tag without the *<input>* tag.[3] There are several buttons associated with a form; the buttons are called:

- *submit*
- *reset*
- *button*

If an event is an attribute of a form tag, then the event occurs when the user presses one of the buttons associated with the form object.

### 12.6.2 *this* for Forms and *this* for Buttons

The *this* keyword refers to the current document and is especially helpful when dealing with forms. In forms that contain multiple items, such as checkboxes, radio buttons, and text boxes, it is easier to refer to the item with the *this* keyword, than by using its full name when calling a function or an event handler. (Examples of the *this* keyword are shown in Chapter 11.)

In a form, *this* could be the form itself or one of the input devices. With an event handler, the *this* keyword by itself references the current object, such as an input device, whereas *this.form* references the form object where the input device was created.

---

**EXAMPLE 12.12**

```
       <html><head><title>The this keyword</title>
       <script language="JavaScript">
1          function display_formval(myform){
               alert("text box value is: " + myform.namestring.value );
           }
2          function display_buttonval(mybutton){
               alert("button value is: " + mybutton.value);
           }
       </script>
       </head>
       <body><b>
       <hr>
3      <form name="simple_form">
           <p>
           Type your name here:
           <input type="text" name="namestring" size="50">
           <p>
```

---

3. The *<button> </button>* tags give greater flexibility to the appearance of the button by allowing HTML content to be displayed instead of plain text that is assigned to the value attribute of a button created using the *<input type="button">*.

**EXAMPLE   12.12 (CONTINUED)**

```
4        <input type="button"
             value="Print Form Stuff"
5            onClick="display_formval(this.form);" >
         <input type="button"
             value="Print Button Stuff"
6            onClick="display_buttonval(this);" >
         <input type="reset" value="Clear">
     </form>
     </body></html>
```

**EXPLANATION**

1    The function called *display_formval()* is defined. Its only parameter is a reference to a form started on line 3. The purpose of this function is to display the text that the user typed in a text box, called *"namestring"*. The function is called when the *onClick* event handler is triggered on line 5.

2    The function called *display_buttonval()* is defined. Its only parameter is a button input type, defined on line 4. It displays the value in the button.

3    This is the start of a form named *simple*.

4    The input type is a button in the form named *simple*.

5    The *onClick* event handler is triggered when the user presses this button. The argument sent to the *display_formval()* function, *this.form*, is a reference to the form object. Without the *form* property, the *this* keyword would refer to the current object, the button. See line 6. Rather than using the full JavaScript hierarchy to reference a form, the *this* keyword simplifies the process.

6    The *onClick* event is triggered when the user presses this button. Since the handler is assigned to the button, the *this* keyword is a reference to the button object. The display is shown in Figure 12.14.

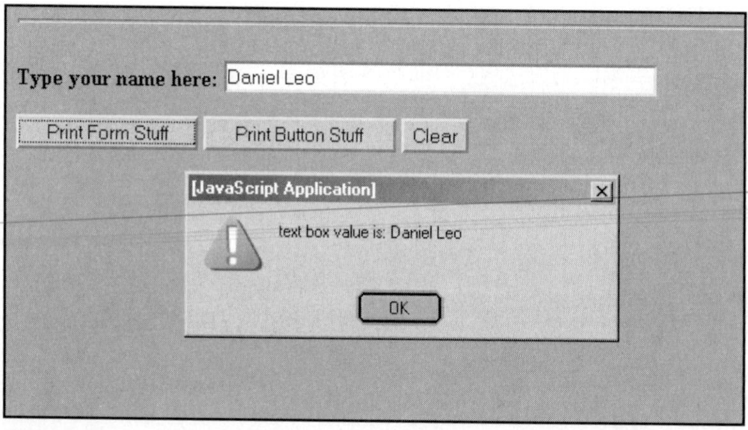

**Figure 12.14**   The user clicked on the Print Form Stuff button.

### 12.6.3 Forms and the *onClick* Event Handler

The *onClick* event handler is used most often in forms. The click event occurs when a button in a form, such as a radio or checkbox, is pressed. It also happens when an option is selected in a Select menu. In Chapter 11, we used many examples of the *onClick* event handlers. Here are a few more.

---

**EXAMPLE** 12.13

```
    <html>
    <head>
    <title>Event Handling and Forms</title>
    <script language=javascript>
1       function greetme(message){
            alert(message);
        }
    </script>
    </head>
    <body bgcolor=white>
    <h2>
    Greetings Message
    </h2>
    <hr>
2   <form>
3      <input type="button" value="Morning"
4         onClick="greetme('Good morning. This is your wakeup
          call!')">
       <input type="button" value="Noon"
          onClick="greetme('Let\'s do lunch.')">
       <input type="button" value="Night"
          onClick="greetme('Have a pleasant evening.\nSweet
          dreams...')">
    </form>
    </body>
    </html>
```

---

**EXPLANATION**

1    A simple function called *greetme()* is defined. It will be called each time the user presses one of three buttons and send an alert message to the screen.

2    The HTML form starts here.

3    The input type for this form is three buttons, respectively labeled, *"Morning"*, *"Noon"*, and *"Night"*. See Figure 12.15.

4    When the user presses a button, the *onClick* event is fired up, and the *greetme()* function is called with a string. See Figure 12.16. Watch the quotes in the string. Because the outside quotes are double quotes, the inner quotes are single. And if the outer set of quotes had been single quotes, the inner set would be double. It's very easy to ruin a program just because the quoting is off, as you well know by now if you've gone this far in the book.

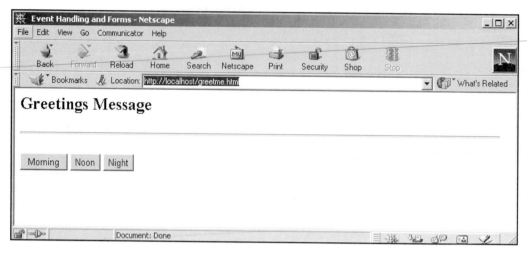

**Figure 12.15**   Three buttons waiting for a user to click one of them.

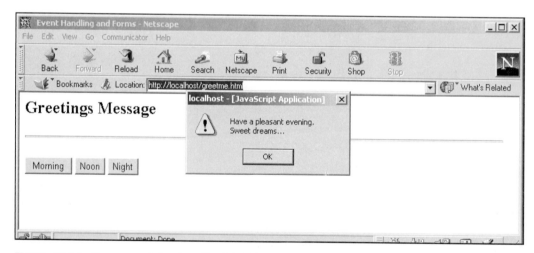

**Figure 12.16**   The user clicked on the Night button.

## 12.6.4   Event Handlers and Event Methods Working Together

You'll find that many JavaScript programs use a combination of event handlers and event methods, especially when working with forms. The following example uses event handlers and event methods. It creates a random number between 1 and 10, and asks the user to guess what the number is. As soon as the document is loaded, the *onLoad* event handler is triggered, and when the user presses the button, the *onClick* handler is fired up. The *focus()* method is used to put focus in the text box where the user will enter his guess.

EXAMPLE   12.14

```
       <html>
       <head><title>Event Handling</title>
       <script language="JavaScript">
       var tries=0;
1          function randomize(){
               // Random number is set when the document has loaded
               var now=new Date();
               num=(now.getSeconds())%10;    // Very cool!
               num++;
           }
2          function guessit(form){
           // Function is called each time the user clicks the button
               if (form.tfield.value == num){
                   alert("Correct!!");
3                  form.tfield.focus();
                   n=0;
                   randomize();
               }
               else{
                   tries++;
4                  alert(tries + " Wrong. Try again.");
                   form.tfield.value="";   // Clear the text box
                   form.tfield.focus();    // Put the cursor in the text box
               }
           }
       // End hiding from old browsers -->
       </script>
       </head>
       <body bgcolor="lightgreen"
5          onLoad="randomize()">   <!--Call function when page is loaded-->
       <center>
       <b>Pick a number between 1 and 10</b>
       <form name="myform">
6          <input type="textbox" size=4
               name="tfield">
               <p>
7          <input type="button"
               name="button1"
8              value="Check my  guess"
               onClick="guessit(this.form)">
       </form>
       </body>
       </html>
```

This script was modified from one written by Andree Growney available at *http://www.htmlgoodies.com/primers/jsp/hgjsp_.html.*

## EXPLANATION

1    A function called *randomize()* is defined. It will create a random number by dividing the number of seconds by 10 and returning the remainder (modulus); for example, 59/10 would return the number 9. Then, by adding 1 to that, we get 10.

2    The function called *guessit* will take one argument, a reference to the form. Its purpose is to see if the number entered by the user, *form.tfield.value*, matches the value of the random number calcuated in the *randomize()* function.

3    The *focus()* method puts the cursor in the text field.

4    If the user guessed wrong, the alert dialog box appears and tells him so, the text field is cleared, and focus is put there.

5    Once the document has loaded, the *onLoad* event handler is triggered, causing the function *randomize()* to be called. This sets the initial random number for the program.

6    The form's input type is a text box. This is where the user will enter his guess.

7    This input type is a button.

8    When the user clicks on this button, the *onClick* event handler is triggered, causing the *guessit()* function to be called with *this* form as an argument. The display is shown in Figures 12.17 and 12.18.

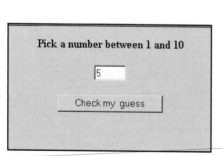

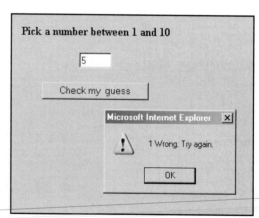

**Figure 12.17**   The user makes a guess (left), but is told he guessed wrong (right).

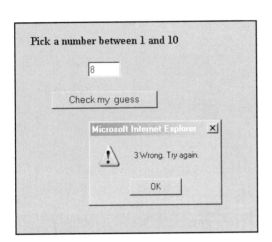
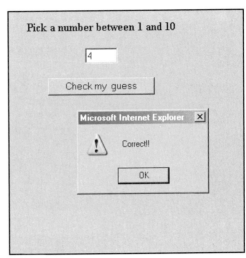

**Figure 12.18**  After three wrong guesses (left), the user finally got it (right).

## 12.6.5  Forms and the *onFocus* and *onBlur* Event Handlers

The *onFocus* event handler is triggered when a form element has focus: the cursor is sitting in the box, waiting for key input or in the case of a button, for the Enter key to be pressed. The *onBlur* event is triggered when the form element loses focus: when the cursor is moved away from the input device.

**EXAMPLE  12.15**

```
     <html>
     <head><title>Using the onFocus Event Handler</title>
     <script language="JavaScript">
1        function handler(message){
2            window.status = message;     // Watch the status bar
         }
     </script>
     </head>
     <body bgcolor="magenta"><b>The onFocus Event Handler
     <i>(When you click in one of the boxes, focus goes to the status
        bar)</i>
3    <form name="form1">
         <p>Type your name:
4        <input type="text"
             name="namestring"
             size="50"
5            onFocus="handler('Don\'t forget to enter your name')">
         <p>Talk about yourself here:<br>
```

## EXAMPLE 12.15 (CONTINUED)

```
6        <textarea name="comments"
             align="left"
7            onFocus="handler('Did you add comments?')"
             rows="5" cols="50">I was born...
         </textarea><p>
         <input type="button"
             value="submit">
         <input type="reset"
             value="clear">
     </form>
     </body>
     </html>
```

## EXPLANATION

1    A user-defined function called *handler()* is defined. It takes a string as its only parameter.

2    The string message, *"Don't forget to enter your name"* (or *"Did you add comments?"*) is passed to the function and assigned to the window's status bar.

3    The HTML form starts here.

4    The first input type is a text box.

5    The text box contains the attribute for the *onFocus* event handler. When this box has focus, the event will be fired up and call the *handler()* function.

6    A text area is defined to hold user comments.

7    The text area contains the attribute for the *onFocus* event handler. When this box has focus, the event will be fired up and call the *handler()* function. See Figure 12.19.

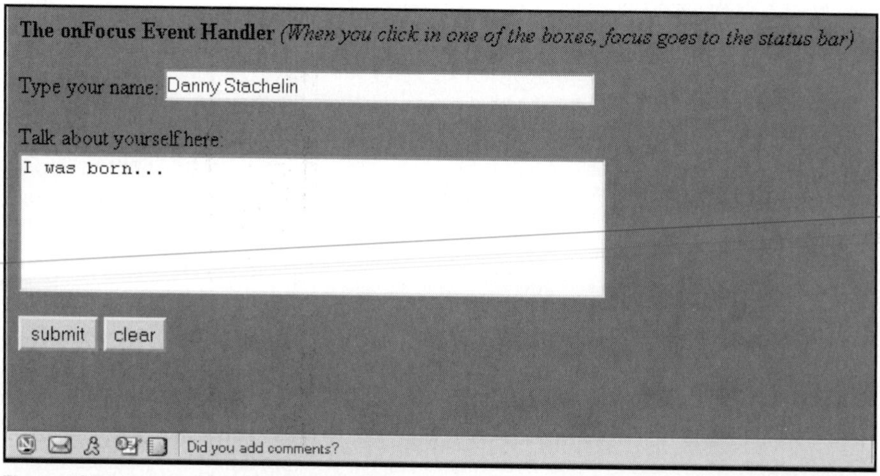

**Figure 12.19** Look at the status bar.

### 12.6.6 Forms and the *onChange* Event Handler

The *onChange* event handler is triggered after the user modifies the value or contents of an HTML input, select, or text area element in a form, and then releases the mouse. This is another event handler that can be useful in checking or validating user input.

---

**EXAMPLE 12.16**

```
        <html>
        <head><title>onChange Event Handler</title>
        </head>
        <body>
1       <form>
            Please enter your grade:
2       <input type="text" onChange="
            grade=parseInt(this.value);   //Convert to integer
3           if(grade < 0 || grade > 100){
                alert('Please enter a grade between 0 and 100');
            }
4           else{
                confirm('Is '+ grade + ' correct?');
            }
5       " >
6       </form>
        </body>
        </html>
```

**EXPLANATION**

1   The HTML form starts here.

2   The input type is a text field. The *onChange* event is triggered when something changes in the text field box, such as a user entering input.

   Instead of assigning a function to the handle the event, the JavaScript statements are enclosed in double quotes and will be parsed and executed when the event is triggered. It might be less error prone to write a function than to try to keep this whole section of code together in quotes.

3   If the input assigned to grade is less than 0 or greater than 100, it is out of the legal range, causing an alert box to appear.

4   If the input was within the limits, then the else block is executed. A confirm box will appear to verify that this is what the user meant to type.

5   This quote marks the end of the JavaScript statements, and the > marks the end of the input type tag.

6   The HTML form ends here. The actions of the handler are shown in Figures 12.20 through 12.22.

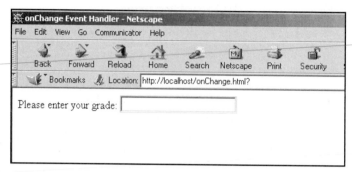

**Figure 12.20**   The user enters no value at all: there is no change.

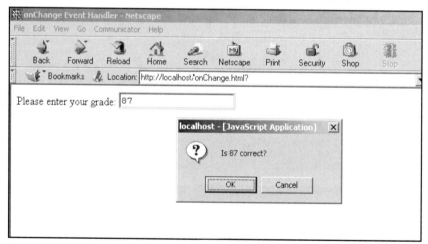

**Figure 12.21**   The user enters a value. A change has taken place. The *onChange* handler is invoked.

**Figure 12.22**   User enters a value. The *onChange* handler is invoked. The value entered was out of range, causing the alert box to appear.

## 12.6.7 Forms and the *onSubmit* Event Handler

The *onSubmit* event handler was discussed in detail in Chapter 11, but it is included again in this chapter since it is such an important form event. You will see this event again in Chapter 13, "Regular Expressions and Pattern Matching." If you recall, the *onSubmit* event is an attribute of the HTML *<form>* tag and is triggered when the user presses the submit button after filling out a form. This event allows the programmer to validate the form before sending it off to the server. If the return value from the event handler is true, the form will be submitted; if false it won't be submitted. The following examples demonstrate two different validation programs using an *onSubmit* event handler.

**EXAMPLE 12.17**

```
        <html><head><title>The onSubmit Event Handler</title></head>
        <body font="arial" size=3>
        <script language="JavaScript">
1       function popUp(){
2           newWin=window.open('','NewWin','toolbar=no,
                status=no,width=500,height=200');
3           newWin.document.write("<h3>Form data</h3>");
            newWin.document.write("<b>Your name is:</b> " +
                document.form1.namestring.value);
            newWin.document.write("<br><b>Your address is: </b>" +
                document.form1.address.value);
        }
        </script>
        <b> <hr>
4       <form name="form1" onSubmit="popUp();">
        <p>
        Type your name:
5       <input type="text"
            name="namestring"
            size="50">
        <p>
        Type in your address:
        <input type="text"
            name="address"
            size="80">
        <p>
6       <input type="submit" value="Submit form">
        <input type="reset" value="Clear">
        </form></body>
        </html>
```

## EXPLANATION

1   A function called *popUp()* is defined. It will cause a pop-up window to appear with data that was entered into a form.

2   This is where the new *window* object is created and assigned properties.

3   The *write()* method will send its output to the new window.

4   The HTML form starts here. When the submit button is pressed, the *onSubmit* event handler will be triggered and call the *popUp()* function, causing a new pop-up window to appear containing the information that the user typed into the form. At this point the program could ask the user if the data is valid and continue to process the information by sending it to a server. Since the *action* attribute for the HTML form hasn't been defined, nothing will happen.

5   The input types for the form are defined here as two text boxes, one for the user's name and one for his address.

6   The submit button is created here. When the user submits the form, the *onSubmit* handler on line 4 will be triggered. The action is shown in Figures 12.23 and 12.24.

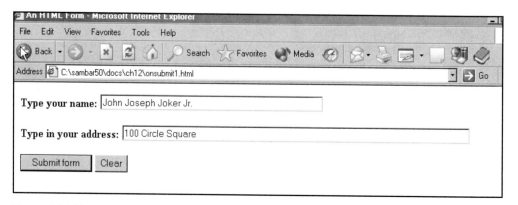

**Figure 12.23**   The fillout form.

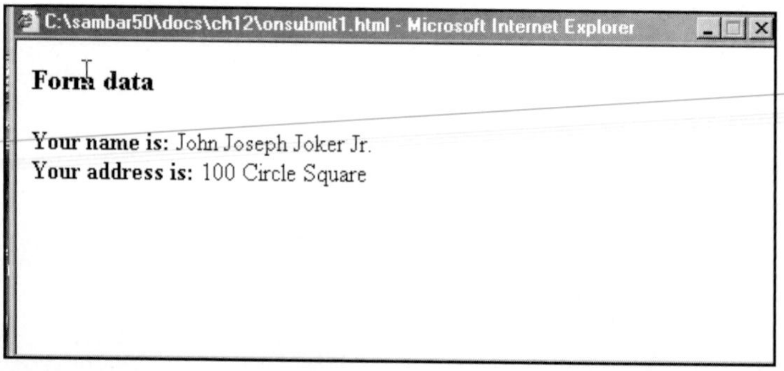

**Figure 12.24**   Pop-up window with form data after submit.

**EXAMPLE   12.18**

```
<html><title>Check it Out!</title>
<head>
<script language="JavaScript">
// Script modified from original found at
// http://javascript.internet.com
1       function okForm(form){
            if (form.accept.checked == true){
                return true;}
            else{
                alert("Please check the box!");
                form.accept.focus();
                return false;}
        }
</script>
</head>
<body bgcolor="silver">
<font face="arial,helvetica" size=2>
<b>Thank you for your order. Check the box to continue.</b>
2    <form action="/cgi-bin/checkout.pl"
        method="post"
3       onSubmit="return okForm(this)">
<input type="checkbox"
        name="accept"
        value="0"  >
4    <input type="submit"
        value="Go to checkout" >
        <input type="button"
        value="Go to Home Page"
5       onClick="window.location.replace('http://localhost');" >
</form>
</body>
</html>
```

**EXPLANATION**

1   A function called *okForm()* is defined. The function is called by the *onSubmit* event handler. Its purpose is to ensure that a checkbox has been checked. If it has, the return value is *true*, and the form will be submitted. If not, the user will be reminded to check the box, *false* will be returned, and the form will not be submitted. See Figure 12.25.

2   The *action* attribute is the URL of the server where the form data will be sent for processing, once it has been submitted.

3   The *onSubmit* event handler is triggered when the user presses the submit button for this form.

4   When this submit button is pressed, the *onSubmit* handler on line 3 is triggered.

5   When the user presses this button, the *onClick* handler will be fired up, and cause the current window to be replaced with another window, the home page for the site.

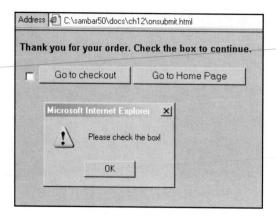

**Figure 12.25**   The user didn't check the box.

# 12.7 Handling Key Events: *onKeyPress*, *onKeyDown*, and *onKeyUp*

As of JavaScript 1.2, keyboard actions, not just mouse actions, can be detected in Java-Script programs. This is useful, for example, in certain types of game programs where keyboard entry must be detected to determine the next action. The *onKeyPress*, *onKey-Down*, and *onKeyUp* event handlers are triggered when the user presses a key and releases it. The *onKeyPress* event is a combination of two actions: after you press down on the key, the event happens just at the point you release it. The other two key events happen as soon as you press a key down (*onKeyDown*) and then when you release it (*onKeyUp*). The *onKeyDown* and *onKeyPress* events keep firing continuously as long as the user keeps a key depressed, whereas the *onKeyUp* event fires once when the user releases the key. Some browsers may differ in the way they handle key events.

**EXAMPLE 12.19**

```
      <html><head><title>Key Events</title></head>
1     <body bgcolor="yellow" onKeyPress="
2        if(navigator.appName=='Netscape')
3           alert('The key pressed:'+ event.which +
4              'ASCII'+ String.fromCharCode(event.which))
         else
5           alert('The key pressed:'+ event.keyCode +
                 'ASCII'+ String.fromCharCode(event.keyCode));">
      <font face = "verdana">
      <b>Press any key on your keyboard and see what happens!</b>
      </body>
      </html>
```

## EXPLANATION

1 The body tag is assigned an *onKeyPress* event handler. If the user presses a key anywhere in the body of the document, the event is triggered, causing an alert method to appear and display the value of the key.

2 First we check to see if the browser being used is Netscape. Netscape and IE use different properties to describe the numeric value of the key being pressed.

3 The *which* property of the event object describes the numeric ASCII value for the key that was pressed. (See more of the event object on page 394.)

4 The *String* method *fromCharCode()* converts the ASCII value of the key to the character value that is shown on the key; e.g., ASCII 65 is character "A".

5 If the browser isn't Netscape, the alternative for this example is Internet Explorer. IE uses the *keyCode* property to represent the numeric value of the key being pressed. The *fromCharCode() String* method converts the number to a character. The output is displayed for both browsers in Figures 12.26 and 12.27.

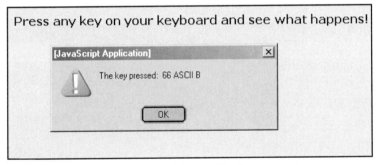

**Figure 12.26** Netscape 7 and the *onKeyPress* event.

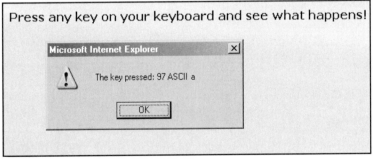

**Figure 12.27** Internet Explorer and the *onKeyPress* event.

**EXAMPLE  12.20**

```
        <html>
        <head><title>Key Events</title>
        </head>
        <body bgcolor="white"><font face="arial">
        <center><img src="key.gif"></center>
        <center><b><h2>Events</h2>
        <h3>
        <br>A <font color="blue">blue </font>bouncing arrow will appear
        when you press a key down<br>and a <font color="red">red</font>
        jumping arrow appears when you release the key<br></b>
    1   <form>
            Type something in the box:
    2       <input type="text" size=10
    3       onKeyDown="document.Arrow.src='images/down_arrow.gif'"
    4       onKeyUp="document.Arrow.src='images/up_arrow.gif'">
            <input type=reset value="reset">
        </form>
    5   <img src="images/up_arrow.gif" name="Arrow">
        </body></html>
```

**EXPLANATION**

1   The HTML form starts here.

2   The input type is a text box field that will hold 10 characters.

3   The *onKeyDown* event occurs when a user presses one of the keys on his keyboard. This event is assigned an image of a blue, bouncing down arrow that will appear as soon as the key is pressed and disappear when the key is released.

4   The *onKeyUp* event occurs when a user releases a key. This event is assigned an image of a red, bouncing up arrow that is always bouncing when the keys are not being used, since it is set as the default image on line 5.

5   This is the default image named *Arrow*; it will be displayed when the document loads. See Figure 12.28.

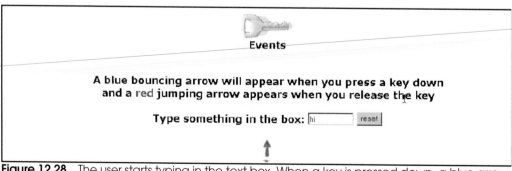

**Figure 12.28**   The user starts typing in the text box. When a key is pressed down, a blue arrow starts bouncing down. When the key is released, the red arrow starts bouncing upwards

# 12.8 Handling Error Events

## 12.8.1  The *onError* Event

The error event fires when a JavaScript error has occurred (window) or when an image cannot be found (image elements).

---

**EXAMPLE** 12.21

```
<html><head><title>Wake up call</title>
<script language="javascript">
    function wakeupCall(){      // Function is defined here
        timeout=setTimeout('alert("Time to get up!")',2000);
    }
 </script>
</head>
<body bgcolor="white">
<form>
<center>
<p>
1  <image src="Image/java_steam.gif"
2      onError="alert('Image is having trouble loading!')">
<p>
<input type="button"
    value="Wake me"
    onClick="wakeupCall()">
</form>
<center>
</body>
</html>
```

---

**EXPLANATION**

1  The *<image>* tag identifies the *src* of a *.gif* image to be loaded from a subdirectory called *Image*.

2  The *onError* event handler is triggered when an error occurs while loading the image. See Figure 12.29.

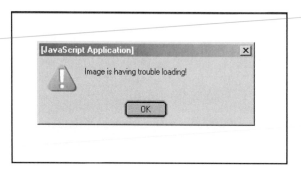
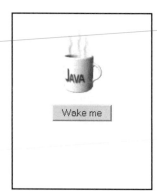

**Figure 12.29**   The *onError* Event handler was triggered because the image *src* was wrong (left), and after the image loads (right).

## 12.9 The *event* Object

*Event* objects are sent to an event handler with each event that occurs within a document. The object provides information about the event, described by its many properties, but is implemented differently in Netscape Navigator and in IE. Table 12.7 provides a list of the properties for Netscape Navigator and Internet Explorer.

**Table 12.7**   Properties of the *event* object.

| Property | What It Describes |
|---|---|
| *altKey, ctrlKey, shiftKey* | Set to true or false to test if Alt, Shift, or Control keys were pressed when the event occurred (IE) |
| *button* | The mouse button that was pressed (IE) |
| *cancelBubble* | Set to true or false to cancel or enable event bubbling |
| *clientX* and *clientY* | The cursor's horizontal and vertical position in pixels, relative to the Web page in which the event occurred (IE) |
| *data* | Array of URLs for dragged and dropped (NN) |
| *fromElement* and *toElement* | The HTML element being moved to or from (IE) |
| *height* and *width* | Height and width of the window (NN) |
| *keyCode* | The Unicode key code associated with a keypress event (IE) |
| *layerX* and *layerY* | Horizontal and vertical cursor position within a layer (NN) |
| *modifiers* | The bitmask representing modifier keys such as Alt, Shift, Meta, etc. (NN) |

**Table 12.7**  Properties of the *event* object. (continued)

| Property | What It Describes |
|----------|------------------|
| *offsetX* and *offsetY* | The cursor's horizontal and vertical position in pixels, relative to the container in which the event occurred (IE) |
| *pageX* and *pageY* | Horizontal and vertical cursor position within a Web page (NN) |
| *reason* | Used to indicate the status of a data transfer for data source objects (IE) |
| *returnValue* | The return value of the event handler, either *true* or *false* (IE) |
| *screenX* and *screenY* | Horizontal and vertical cursor position within a screen (NN) |
| *srcElement* | Same as *target* for IE |
| *srcFilter* | Specifies the filter object that caused an *onfilterchange* event (IE only) |
| *target* | Object for captured events (NN) |
| *type* | The type of event that occurred (NN) |
| *which* | A numeric value for the mouse button that was pressed or the ASCII value of a pressed key (NN) |
| *x* and *y* | The cursor's horizonal and vertical position in pixels, relative to the document in which the event occurred (IE) |

**EXAMPLE  12.22**

```
    <html><head><title>Event Properties</title>
    </head>
    <body bgcolor="yellow"
    <font face = "verdana">
    <!--Internet Explorer has src.Element property-->
    <!--Netscape has target property-->
1   <form name="form1"
2     onSubmit="alert(event.type + ' ' + event.srcElement);">
3     <input type=button
          name="mybutton"
          value="Click here"
4         onClick="alert(event.type + ' ' +event.target);">
      <input type=submit>
    </form>
    </body>
    </html>
```

## EXPLANATION

1   The HTML form starts here.

2   When the user presses the submit button for this form, the *onSubmit* event is fired up. It will cause an alert message to appear displaying two event properties: the *type* of the event and the *srcElement* (Internet Explorer) property of the object to which the event was sent. See the left of Figure 12.30.

3   The input type for this form is a button with the value "*Click here*" appearing in the button.

4   When the *onClick* event is triggered, an alert message will appear displaying two event properties: the *type* of the event and the *target* (Netscape) property or object to which the event was sent. See the right of Figure 12.30.

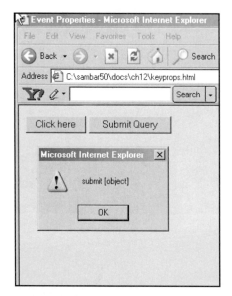
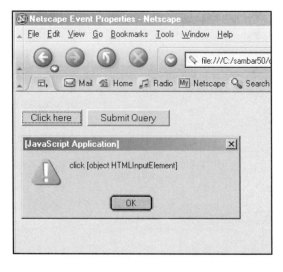

**Figure 12.30**   Displaying the event object's property in Internet Explorer (left), and Netscape (right).

## EXERCISES

1. Create three buttons, labeled *Shoot movies*, *Shoot guns*, and *Shoot basketballs*. When the user presses any button, use the *onClick* event handler to call a function that will send a message based on which button was pressed.

2. Rewrite Example 12.19 to create a JavaScript function that will test for the browser type and handle the event.

3. Create a form that contains a two text fields to receive the user's name and address, respectively. When the user leaves each text field, use the *onBlur* event handler to check if the user entered anything in the respective field. If he didn't, send him an alert telling him so, and use the *focus()* method to return focus back to the text field he just left.

4. Create a form that will contain a text box. When the user enters text, all the letters will be converted to lowercase as soon as he clicks anywhere else in the form. (Use the *onChange* event handler.)

# 13

# Regular Expressions and Pattern Matching

## 13.1 What Is a Regular Expression?

A user is asked to fill out an HTML form and provide his name, address, and birth date. Before sending the form off to a server for further processing, a JavaScript program checks the form to make sure the user actually entered something, and that the information is in the requested format. We saw in the last chapter some basic ways that Java-Script can check form information, but now with the addition of regular expressions, form validation can be much more sophisticated and precise. Before getting into form validation, we will delve into regular expressions and how they work. If you are savvy with Perl regular expressions (or the UNIX utilities, *grep, sed,* and *awk*), you may move rapidly through this section, since JavaScript regular expressions, for the most part, are identical to those found in Perl.

A regular expression is really just a sequence or pattern of characters that is matched against a string of text when performing searches and replacements. A simple regular expression consists of a character or set of characters that matches itself. The regular expression is normally delimited by forward slashes; for example, */abc/*.

Like Perl, JavaScript[1] provides a large variety of regular expression metacharacters to control the way a pattern is found. The metacharacters are used to control the search pattern; you can look for strings containing only digits, only alphas, a digit at the beginning of the line followed by any number of alphas, a line ending with a digit, and so on. When searching for a pattern of characters, the possibilities of fine-tuning your search are endless.

Again, JavaScript regular expressions are used primarily to verify data input on the client side. When a user fills out a form and presses the submit button, the form is sent to a server, and then to a CGI script for further processing. Although forms can be validated by a CGI program, it is more efficient to take care of the validation before sending

---

1. JavaScript 1.2, NES 3.0 JavaScript 1.3 added *toSource()* method. JavaScript 1.5, NES 6.0 added *m* flag, non-greedy modifier, non-capturing parentheses, lookahead assertions. ECMA 262, Edition 3.

the script to the server. This is an important function of JavaScript. The user fills out the form and JavaScript checks to see if all the boxes have been filled out correctly, and if not, the user is told to re-enter the data before the form is submitted to the server. Checking the form on the client side allows for instant feedback, and less travelling back and forth between the browser and server. It may be that the CGI program does its own validation anyway, but if JavaScript has already done the job, it will still save time and inconvenience for the user. With the power provided by regular expressions, the ability to check for any type of input, such as e-mail addresses, passwords, social security numbers, and birthdates is greatly simplified.

The first part of this chapter delves into the construction of regular expressions and how to use regular expression metacharacters. The second part of the chapter applies this information to validating form input.

## 13.2 Creating a Regular Expression

A regular expression is a pattern of characters. JavaScript regular expressions are objects. When you create a regular expression, you test the regular expression against a string. For example, the regular expression /green/ might be matched against the string *"The green grass grows"*. If *green* is contained in the string, then there is a successful match.

Building a regular expression is like building a string. If you recall, you can create a *String* object the literal way or you can use the *String()* constructor method. To build a regular expression object, you can assign a literal regular expression to a variable, or you can use the *RegExp* constructor to create and return a regular expression object.

### 13.2.1   The Literal Way

To create a regular expression object with the literal notation, you assign the regular expression to a variable. The regular expression is a pattern of characters enclosed in forward slashes. After the closing forward slash, options may be provided to modify the search pattern. The options are *i*, *g*, and *m*. See Table 13.1.

**Table 13.1**   Options used for modifying search patterns.

| Option | Purpose |
| --- | --- |
| *i* | Used to ignore case |
| *g* | Used to match for all occurrences of the pattern in the string |
| *m* | Used to match over multiple lines |

**FORMAT**

```
var variable_name = /regular expression/options;
```

Example:

```
var myreg = /love/;
var reobj = /san jose/ig;
```

If you are not going to change the regular expression, say, if it is hard-coded right into your script, then this literal notation is faster, since the regular expression is evaluated at runtime.

## 13.2.2   The Constructor Method

The constructor method, called *RegExp()*, creates a *RegExp* object. The *RegExp()* constructor takes one or two arguments. The first argument is the regular expression; it is a string representing the regular expression, for example, *"green"* represents the literal regular expression */green/*. The second optional argument is called a <u>flag</u> such as *i* for case insensitivity or *g* for global. The constructor method is used when the regular expression is being provided from some other place, such as from user input, and may change throughout the run of the program. This method is handled at runtime.

**FORMAT**

```
var variable_name = new RegExp("regular expression", "options");
```

Example:

```
var myreg = new RegExp("love");
var reobj = new RegExp("san jose", "ig");
```

**Testing the Expression.**   The *RegExp* object has two methods that can be used to test for a match in a string, the *test()* method and the *exec()* method, which are quite similar. The *test()* method searches for a regular expression in a string and returns *true* if it matched and *false* if it didn't. The *exec()* method also searches for a regular expression in a string. If the *exec()* method succeeds, it returns an array of information including the search string, and the parts of the string that matched. If it fails, it returns *null*. This is similar to the *match()* method of the *String* object.  Table 13.2 summarizes the methods of the *RegExp* object.

**Table 13.2**  Methods of the *RegExp* object.

| Method | What It Does |
| --- | --- |
| exec | Executes a search for a match in a string and returns an array |
| test | Tests for a match in a string and returns either *true* or *false* |

**The *test()* Method.**    The *RegExp* object's *test()* method is used to see if a string contains the pattern represented in the regular expression. It returns a *true* or *false* Boolean value. After the search, the *lastIndex* property of the *RegExp* object contains the position in the string where the <u>next</u> search would start. (A string starts at character position 0.) If a global search is done, then the *lastIndex* property contains the starting position after the last pattern was matched. (See Example 13.4 to see how the *lastIndex* property is used.)

Steps to test for a match:

1. Assign a regular expression to a variable.
2. Use the regular expression *test()* method to see if there is a match. If there is a match, the *test()* method returns *true*; otherwise, returns *false*. There are also four string methods that can be used with regular expressions. (See "String Methods Using Regular Expressions" on page 408.)

## FORMAT

```
var string="String to be tested goes here";
var regex = /regular expression/;        // Literal way
var regex=new RegExp("regular expression");     // Constructor way
regex.test(string);    // Returns either true or false
```

or

```
/regular expression/.test("string");
```

Example:

```
var myString="She wants attention now!";
var regex = /ten/     // Literal way
var regex=new RegExp("ten");     // Constructor way
regex.test(myString);    // Looking for "ten" in  myString
```

or

```
/ten/.test("She wants attention now!");
```

**EXAMPLE  13.1**

```
        <html>
        <head>
        <title>Regular Expression Objects the Literal Way</title>
        <script language = "JavaScript">
1           var myString="My gloves are worn for wear.";
2           var regex = /love/;      // Create a regular expression object
3           if (regex.test(myString)){
4               alert("Found pattern!");
            }
            else{
5               alert("No match.");
            }
        </script>
        </head><body></body>
        </html>
```

**EXPLANATION**

1   *"My gloves are worn for wear."* is assigned to a variable called *myString*.

2   The regular expression */love/* is assigned to the variable called *regex*. This is the literal way of creating a regular expression object.

3   The *test()* method for the regular expression object tests to see if *myString* contains the pattern, *love*. If *love* is found within *gloves*, the *test()* method will return *true*.

4   The alert dialog box will display *Found pattern!* if the *test()* method returned *true*.

5   If the pattern */love/* is not found in the *myString*, the *test()* method returns *false*, and the alert dialog box will display its message, *No match.*

**EXAMPLE  13.2**

```
        <head>
        <title>Regular Expression Objects with the Constructor</title>
        <script language = "JavaScript">
1           var myString="My gloves are worn for wear.";
2           var regex = new RegExp("love");      // Creating a regular
                                                 // expression object
3           if ( regex.test(myString)){
4               alert("Found pattern love!");
            }
            else{
5               alert("No match.");
            }
        </script>
        </head><body></body>
        </html>
```

## EXPLANATION

1    The variable called *myString* is assigned *"My gloves are worn for wear."*

2    The *RegExp()* constructor creates a new regular expression object, called *regex*. This is the constructor way of creating a regular expression object. It is assigned the string *"love"*, the regular expression.

3    The *test()* method for the regular expression object tests to see if *myString* contains the pattern, *love*. If it finds *love* within *gloves*, it will return *true*.

4, 5   The alert dialog box will display *Found pattern!* if the *test()* method returned *true*, or *No match.* if it returns *false*. See Figure 13.1.

**Figure 13.1**    *"My gloves are worn for wear."* contains the pattern *love*.

**The *exec()* Method.**    The *exec()* method executes a search to find a match for a specified pattern in a string. If it doesn't find a match, *exec()* returns null; otherwise it returns an array containing the string that matched the regular expression.

## FORMAT

```
array = regular_expression.exec(string);
```

Example:

```
list = /ring/.exec("Don't string me along, just bring me the goods.");
```

```
        <html>
        <head>
        <title>The exec() method</title>
        <script language = "JavaScript">
1           var myString="My lovely gloves are worn for wear, Love.";
2           var regex = /love/i;      // Create a regular expression object
3           var array=regex.exec(myString);
4           if (regex.exec(myString)){
                alert("Matched! " + array);
            }
            else{
                alert("No match.");
            }
        </script>
        <body></body>
        </html>
```

**EXPLANATION**

1   The string *"My gloves are worn for wear."* is assigned to *myString*.

2   The regular expression */love/* is assigned to the variable *regex*.

3   The *exec()* method returns an array of values that were found.

4   If the *exec()* method doesn't return *null*, then there was a match. See Figure 13.2.

**Figure 13.2**  The array returned by *exec()* contains *love*.

## 13.2.3  Properties of the *RegExp* Object

There are two types of properties that can be applied to a *RegExp* object. The first type is called a <u>class property</u> (see Table 13.3) and applies to the *RegExp* object as a whole, not a simple instance of a regular expression object. For example, the *input* property contains the last string that was matched, and is applied directly to the *RegExp* object as *RegExp.input*. The other type of property is called an <u>instance property</u> and is applied to an instance of the object (see Table 13.4); for example, *mypattern.lastIndex* refers to the position within the string where the next search will start for this instance of the regular expression object, called *mypattern*.

**Table 13.3**   Class properties of the *RegExp* object.

| Property | What It Describes |
| --- | --- |
| *input* | Represents the input string being matched |
| *lastMatch* | Represents the last matched characters |
| *lastParen* | Represents the last parenthesized substring pattern match |
| *leftContext* | Represents the substring preceding the most recent pattern match |
| *RegExp.$\** | Boolean value that specifies whether strings should be searched over multiple lines; same as the multiline property |
| *RegExp.$&* | Represents the last matched characters |
| *RegExp.$_* | Represents the string input that is being matched |
| *RegExp.$'* | Represents the substring preceding the most recent pattern match (see the *leftContext* property) |
| *RegExp.$'* | Represents the substring following the most recent pattern match (see the *rightContext*property) |
| *RegExp.$+* | Represents the last parenthesized substring pattern match (see the *lastParen* property) |
| *RegExp.$1,$2,$3...* | Used to capture substrings of matches |
| *rightContext* | Represents the substring following the most recent pattern match |

**Table 13.4**   Instance properties of the *RegExp* object.

| Property | What It Describes |
| --- | --- |
| *global* | Boolean to specify if the g option was used to check the expression against all possible matches in the string |
| *ignoreCase* | Boolean to specify if the i option was used to ignore case during a string search |
| *lastIndex* | If the g option was used, specifies the character position immediately following the last match found by *exec()* or *test()* |
| *multiline* | Boolean to test if the m option was used to search across multiple lines |
| *source* | The text of the regular expression |

**EXAMPLE   13.4**

```
        <html>
        <head><title>The test() method</title>
        </head>
        <body bgcolor=silver>
        <font face="arial" size="+1">
        <script language = "JavaScript">
1           var myString="I love my new gloves!";
2           var regex = /love/g;     // Create a regular expression object
3           var booleanResult = regex.test(myString);
            if ( booleanResult != false  ){
4               document.write("Tested regular expression <em>"+
                    regex.source + ".</em> The result is <em>"
                    + booleanResult + "</em>");
                document.write(".<br>Starts searching again at position " +
5                   regex.lastIndex + " in string<em> \"" +
6                   RegExp.input + "\"<br>");
                document.write("The last matched characters were: "+
7                   RegExp.lastMatch+"<br>");
                document.write("The substring preceding the last match is:
8                   "+ RegExp.leftContext+"<br>");
                document.write("The substring following the last match is:
9                   "+ RegExp.rightContext+"<br>");
            }
            else{ alert("No match!"); }
        </script></body>
        </html>
```

**EXPLANATION**

1   The string object to be tested is created.

2   A regular expression object, called *regex*, is created.

3   The *test()* method returns *true* or *false* if the regular expression is matched in the string.

4   The *source* property is applied to *regex*, an instance of a *RegExp* object. It contains the text of the regular expression, */love/*.

5   The *lastIndex* property is applied to an instance of a *RegExp* object. It represents the character position right after the last matched string.

6   The *input* class property represents the input string on which the pattern matching (regular expression) is performed.

7   *lastMatch* is a class property that represents the characters that were last matched.

8   *leftContext* is a class property that represents the left-most substring pattern that precedes the last pattern that was matched; here, whatever string comes before */love/*.

9   *rightContext* is a class property that represents the right-most substring pattern that follows the last pattern that was matched; here, whatever string comes after */love/*. Output is shown in Figure 13.3.

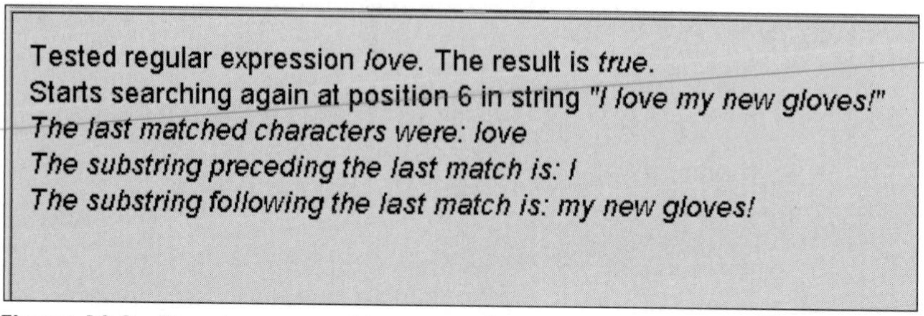

Tested regular expression *love*. The result is *true*.
Starts searching again at position 6 in string *"I love my new gloves!"*
*The last matched characters were: love*
*The substring preceding the last match is: I*
*The substring following the last match is: my new gloves!*

**Figure 13.3**   Regular expression properties.

## 13.2.4   String Methods Using Regular Expressions

In addition to the *RegExp* object's *test()* and *exec()* methods, the *String* object provides four methods that also work with regular expressions.

**Table 13.5**   *String* object regular expression methods.

| Method | What It Does |
| --- | --- |
| *match(regex)* | Returns substring in *regex* or *null* |
| *replace(regex, replacement)* | Substitutes *regex* with replacement string |
| *search(regex)* | Finds the starting position of *regex* in string |
| *split(regex)* | Removes *regex* from string for each occurrence |

**The *match()* Method.**   The *match()* method, like the *exec()* method, is used to search for a pattern of characters in a string and returns an array where each element of the array contains each matched pattern that was found. If no match is found, returns *null*. With the g flag, *match()* searches globally through the string for all matching substrings.

**FORMAT**

```
array = String.match(regular_expression);
```

Example:

```
matchList = "Too much, too soon".match(/too/ig);
```

**EXAMPLE** 13.5

```
         <html>
         <head>
         <title>The match() Method</title>
         </head><body>
         <font size="+1"><font face="arial, helvetica">
         <script language = "JavaScript">
1            var matchArray = new Array();
2            var string="I love the smell of clover."
3            var regex = /love/g;
4            matchArray=string.match(regex);
5            document.write("Found "+ matchArray.length +" matches.<br>");
         </script>
         </body>
         </html>
```

**EXPLANATION**

1   A new array object is created.

2   The variable called *string* is assigned *"I love the smell of clover."*

3   The regular expression called *regex* is assigned the search pattern *love*. The g modifier performs a global search: multiple occurrences of the pattern will be returned.

4   The *match()* method is applied to the string. The regular expression is passed as an argument. Each time the pattern */love/* is found in the string it will be assigned as a new element of the array called *matchArray*. If the g modifier is removed, only the first occurrence of the match will be returned, and only one element will be assigned to the array *matchArray*.

5   The length of the array, *matchArray*, tells us how many times the *match()* method found the pattern */love/*.  See Figure 13.4.

```
Found 2 matches.
```

**Figure 13.4**   The pattern *love* was found twice in the string.

**The *search()* Method.**   The *search()* method is used to search for a pattern of characters within a string, and returns the index position of where the pattern was found in the string. The index starts at zero. If the pattern is not found, –1 is returned. For basic searches, the *String* object's *indexOf()* method works fine, but if you want more complex pattern matches, the *search()* method is used, allowing you to use regular expression metacharacters to further control the expression. (See "Getting Control—The Metacharacters" on page 414.)

```
var index_value = String.search(regular_expression);
```

Example:

```
var position = "A needle in a haystack".search(/needle/);
```

**EXAMPLE  13.6**

```
    <html>
    <head>
    <title>The search() Method</title>
    </head><body bgcolor="yellow">
    <font size="+1">
    <font face="arial, helvetica">
    <script language = "JavaScript">
1       var myString="I love the smell of clover."
2       var regex = /love/;
3       var index=myString.search(regex);
        document.write("Found the pattern "+ regex+ " at position "
                     +index+"<br>");
    </script>
    </body>
    </html>
```

**EXPLANATION**

1   The variable called *myString* is assigned the string, *"I love the smell of clover."*

2   The variable called *regex* is assigned the regular expression /love/. With the search() method, using the g modifier is irrelevant. The index position of the pattern where it is first found in the string, is returned.

3   The *String* object's *search()* method returns the index position, starting at zero, where the regular expression, *regex*, is found. See Figure 13.5.

---

> Found the pattern /love/ at position 2

**Figure 13.5**  The *search()* method found the pattern starting at character position 2, where 0 is the beginning character.

**The *replace()* Method.**   The *replace()* method is used to search for a string and replace the string with another string. The *i* modifier is used to turn off case sensitivity and the *g* modifier makes the replacement global; that is, all occurrences of the found pattern are replaced with the new string. The *replace()* method is also used with the grouping metacharacters. (See "Grouping or Clustering" on page 442.)

```
string = oldstring.replace(regular_expression, replacement_value);
```

Example:

```
var str1 = "I am feeling blue".replace(/blue/, "upbeat");
   ( str1 is assigned: "I am feeling upbeat.")
```

**EXAMPLE  13.7**

```
        <html>
        <head>
        <title>The replace() Method</title>
        </head>
        <body bgcolor="yellow">
        <font size="+1">
        <font face="arial, helvetica">
        <script language = "JavaScript">
1          var myString="Tommy has a stomach ache."
2          var regex = /tom/i;   // Turn off case sensitivity
3          var newString=myString.replace(regex, "Mom");
           document.write(newString +"<br>");
        </script>
        </body>
        </html>
```

**EXPLANATION**

1   The variable called *myString* is assigned the string *"Tommy has a stomach ache."* Note that the pattern *Tom* or *tom* is found in the string twice.

2   The variable called *regex* is assigned the regular expression */tom/i*. The *i* modifier turns off the case sensitivity. Any combination of uppercase and lowercase letters in the pattern *tom* will be searched for within the string.

3   The *String* object's *replace()* method will search for the pattern, *regex*, in the string and if it finds the pattern will replace it with *Mom*. If the g modifier were used, all occurrences of the pattern would be replaced with *Mom*. For example, */tom/ig* would result in *"Mommy has a sMomach ache."*

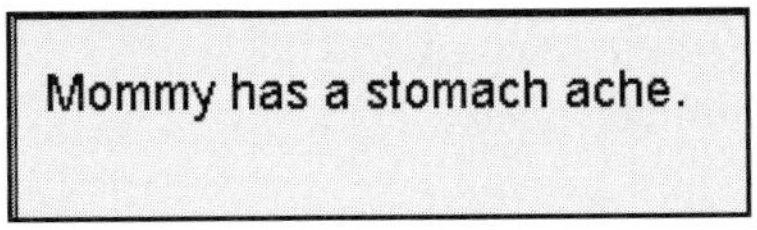

Mommy has a stomach ache.

**Figure 13.6**   The first occurrence of *Tom*, uppercase or lowercase, is replaced with *Mom*.

**The *split()* Method.**     The *String* object's *split()* method splits a single text string into
an array of substrings. In a real-world scenario, it would be like putting little crayon
marks at intervals on a piece of string and then cutting the string everywhere a mark
appeared, thus ending up with a bunch of little strings. In the JavaScript world, the
crayon mark is called a <u>delimiter</u>, which is a character or pattern of characters that marks
where the string is to be split up. When using the *String* object's *split()* method, if the
words in a string are separated by commas, then the comma would be the delimiter and
if the words are separated by colons, then the colon is the delimiter. The delimiter can
contain more complex combinations of characters if regular expression metacharacters
are used.

## FORMAT

```
array = String.split( /delimiter/ );
```

Example:

**splitArray = "red#green#yellow#blue".split(/#/);**
     *(splitArray is an array of colors. splitArray[0] is "red")*

## EXAMPLE  13.8

```
    <html>
    <head><title>The split() Method</title></head>
    <body>
    <font size="+1">
    <font face="arial, helvetica">
    <script language = "JavaScript">
1       var splitArray = new Array();
2       var string="apples:pears:peaches:plums:oranges";
3       var regex = /:/;
4       splitArray=string.split(regex);   // Split the string by colons
5       for(i=0; i < splitArray.length; i++){
            document.write(splitArray[i] + "<br>");
        }
    </script>
    </body>
    </html>
```

## EXPLANATION

1   A new array object is created.

2   The variable called *string* is assigned a colon-delimited string of text.

3   The variable called *regex* is assigned the regular expression /:/.

4   The *String* object's *split()* method splits the string using colons as the string delim-
    iter (marks the separation between words), and creates an array called *splitArray*.

5   Each of the array elements is displayed in the page. See Figure 13.7.

**Figure 13.7**   The string is split on colons.

```
        <html>
        <head>
        <title>The split() Method</title>
        </head>
        <font size="+1">
        <font face="arial, helvetica">
        <script language = "JavaScript">
1           var splitArray = new Array();
2           var myString="apples        pears,peaches:plums,oranges";
3           var regex = /[\t:,]/;   // Delimeter is a tab, colon, or comma
4           splitArray=myString.split(regex);
            for(i=0; i < splitArray.length; i++){
5               document.write(splitArray[i] + "<br>");
            }
        </script>
        </body>
        </html>
```

**EXPLANATION**

1   A new array object is created.

2   The string *"apples   pears,peaches:plums,oranges"* is assigned to the variable called *myString*. The delimiters are a tab, comma, and colon.

3   The regular expression /[\t:,]/ is assigned to the variable called *regex*.

**EXPLANATION** (CONTINUED)

4   The *String* object's *split()* method splits up the string using a tab, colon, or comma as the delimiter. The delimiting characters are enclosed in square brackets, which in regular expression parlance is called a character class. (See "Getting Control— The Metacharacters" on page 414.) In simple terms, any one of the characters listed within the brackets is a delimiter in the string. The *split()* method will search for any one of these characters and split the string accordingly, returning an array called *splitArray.*

5   Each of the array elements is displayed in the page. See Figure 13.8.

**Figure 13.8**   The string is split on tabs, colons, and commas.

# 13.3 Getting Control—The Metacharacters

Regular expression metacharacters are characters that do not represent themselves. They are endowed with special powers to allow you to control the search pattern in some way (e.g., find the pattern only at the beginning of line, or at the end of the line, or if it starts with an upper- or lowercase letter, etc.). Metacharacters will lose their special meaning if preceded with a backslash. For example, the dot metacharacter represents any single character, but when preceded with a backslash is just a dot or period.

If you see a backslash preceding a metacharacter, the backslash turns off the meaning of the metacharacter, but if you see a backslash preceding an alphanumeric character in a regular expression, then the backslash is used to create a metasymbol. A metasymbol provides a simpler form to represent some of regular expression metachacters. For example, *[0-9]* represents numbers in the range between 0 and 9, and *\d*, the metasymbol, represents the same thing. *[0-9]* uses the bracketed character class, whereas *\d* is a metasymbol (see Table 13.6).

## EXAMPLE 13.10

```
/^a...c/
```

## EXPLANATION

This regular expression contains metacharacters (see Table 13.6). The first one is a caret (^). The caret metacharacter matches for a string only if it is at the beginning of the line. The period (.) is used to match for any single character, including a whitespace. This expression contains three periods, representing any three characters. To find a literal period or any other character that does not represent itself, the character must be preceded by a backslash to prevent interpretation.

The expression reads: Search at the beginning of the line for an *a*, followed by any three single characters, followed by a *c*. It will match, for example, *abbbc, a123c, a   c, aAx3c*, and so on, but only if those patterns were found at the beginning of the line.

**Table 13.6**  Metacharacters and metasymbols.

| Metacharacter/Metasymbol | What It Matches |
|---|---|
| Character Class: Single Characters and Digits | |
| . | Matches any character except newline |
| [a–z0–9] | Matches any single character in set |
| [^a–z0–9] | Matches any single character not in set |
| \d | Matches one digit |
| \D | Matches a non-digit, same as [^0–9] |
| \w | Matches an alphanumeric (word) character |
| \W | Matches a non-alphanumeric (non-word) character |
| Character Class: Whitespace Characters | |
| \0 | Matches a null character |
| \b | Matches a backspace |
| \f | Matches a formfeed |
| \n | Matches a newline |
| \r | Matches a return |
| \s | Matches whitespace character, spaces, tabs, and newlines |
| \S | Matches non-whitespace character |
| \t | Matches a tab |

**Table 13.6**    Metacharacters and metasymbols. (continued)

| Metacharacter/Metasymbol | What It Matches |
|---|---|
| Character Class: Anchored Characters | |
| ^ | Matches to beginning of line |
| $ | Matches to end of line |
| \A | Matches the beginning of the string only |
| \b | Matches a word boundary (when not inside [ ]) |
| \B | Matches a non-word boundary |
| \G | Matches where previous *m//g* left off |
| \Z | Matches the end of the string or line |
| \z | Matches the end of string only |
| Character Class: Repeated Characters | |
| *x?* | Matches 0 or 1 of *x* |
| *x\** | Matches 0 or more of *x* |
| *x+* | Matches 1 or more of *x* |
| *(xyz)+* | Matches one or more patterns of *xyz* |
| *x{m,n}* | Matches at least *m* of *x* and no more than *n* of *x* |
| Character Class: Alternative Characters | |
| *was\|were\|will* | Matches one of *was*, *were*, or *will* |
| Character Class: Remembered Characters | |
| *(string)* | Used for backreferencing (see "Remembering or Capturing" on page 443) |
| \1 or $1 | Matches first set of parentheses |
| \2 or $2 | Matches second set of parentheses |
| \3 or $3 | Matches third set of parentheses |
| New with JavaScript 1.5 | |
| *(?:x)* | Matches *x* but does not remember the match. These are called non-capturing parentheses. The matched substring cannot be recalled from the resulting array's elements *[1], ..., [n]* or from the predefined *RegExp* object's properties $1, ..., $9. |

**Table 13.6**  Metacharacters and metasymbols. (continued)

| Metacharacter/Metasymbol | What It Matches |
|---|---|
| New with JavaScript 1.5 (continued) | |
| x(?=y) | Matches *x* only if *x* is followed by *y*. For example, /Jack(?=Sprat)/ matches *Jack* only if it is followed by *Sprat*. /Jack(?=Sprat|Frost)/ matches *Jack* only if it is followed by *Sprat* or *Frost*. However, neither *Sprat* nor *Frost* are part of the match results. |
| x(?!y) | Matches *x* only if *x* is not followed by *y*. For example, /\d+(?!\.)/ matches a number only if it is not followed by a decimal point. /\d+(?!\.)/.exec("3.141") matches *141* but not *3.141*. |

If you are searching for a particular character within a regular expression, you can use the <u>dot</u> metacharacter to represent a single character, or a <u>character class</u> that matches on one character from a set of characters. In addition to the dot and character class, JavaScript has added some backslashed symbols (called metasymbols) to represent single characters. See Table 13.7 for the single-character metacharacters, and Table 13.8 on page 423 for a list of metasymbols.

**Table 13.7**  Single-character and single-digit metacharacters.

| Metacharacter | What It Matches |
|---|---|
| . | Matches any character except newline |
| [a–z0–9_] | Matches any single character in set |
| [^a–z0–9_] | Matches any single character <u>not</u> in set |

## 13.3.1  The Dot Metacharacter

The dot metacharacter matches for any single character with exception of the newline character. For example, the regular expression /a.b/ is matched if the string contains an *a*, followed by any one single character (except the \n), followed by *b*, whereas the expression /.../ matches any string containing at least three characters.

## EXAMPLE 13.11

```
        <html><head><title>The dot Metacharacter</title>
        </head>
        <body>
        <script language="JavaScript">
1           var textString="Norma Jean";
2           var reg_expression = /N..ma/;

3           var result=reg_expression.test(textString);   // Returns true
                                                           // or false
            document.write("<font size='+1'><b>"+result+"<br>");
4           if ( reg_expression.test(textString)){         //  if (result)
                document.write("<b>The reg_ex /N..ma/ matched the
                string\""+ textString +"\".<br>");
            }
            else{
5               document.write("No Match!");
            }
        </script>
        </body>
        </html>
```

## EXPLANATION

1   The variable *textString* is assigned the string *"Norma Jean"*.

2   The regular expression */N..ma/* is assigned to the variable *reg_expression*. A match is found if the string being tested contains an uppercase *N* followed by any two single characters (each dot represents one character), and an *m* and an *a*. It would find *Norma*, *No man*, *Normandy*, etc.

3   The *test* method returns *true* if the string *textString* matches the regular expression and *false* if it doesn't. The variable *result* contains either *true* or *false*.

4   If the string *"Norma Jean"* contains regular expression pattern */N..ma/*, the return from the *test* method is true, and the output is sent to the screen as shown in Figure 13.9.

5   If the pattern is not found, *No Match!* is displayed on the page.

Address  C:\sambar50\docs\regex\dot.html

**true**
**The reg_ex /N..ma/ matched the string"Norma Jean".**

**Figure 13.9**   The user entered *Norma Jean,* an *N* followed by any 2 characters, and *ma.*

## 13.3.2 The Character Class

A character class represents <u>one</u> character from a set of characters. For example *[abc]* matches either an *a*, *b*, <u>or</u> *c*; and *[a-z]* matches one character from a set of characters in the range from *a* to *z*; and *[0-9]* matches one character in the range of digits between *0* to 9. If the character class contains a leading caret, ^, then the class represents any one character not in the set; thus, *[^a-zA-Z]* matches a single character <u>not</u> in the range from *a* to *z* or *A* to *Z*, and *[^0-9]* matches a single digit not in the range between 0 and 9.

JavaScript provides additional symbols, called metasymbols, to represent a character class. The symbols \d and \D represent a single digit and a single non-digit, respectively; the same as *[0-9]* and *[^0-9]*; whereas \w and \W represent a single word character and a single non-word character, respectively; same as *[A-Za-z_0-9]* and *[^A-Za-z_0-9]*.

### EXAMPLE 13.12

```
              <html><head><title>The Character Class</title>
              </head>
              <body>
              <script language="JavaScript">
1                 var reg_expression = /[A-Z][a-z]eve/;
2                 var textString=prompt("Type a string of text","");
3                 var result=reg_expression.test(textString);   // Returns true
                                                                 // or false
                  document.write("<font size='+1'><b>"+result+"<br>");
                  if ( result){
                      document.write("<b>The reg_ex /[A-Z][a-z]eve/ matched the
                      string\""+ textString +"\".<br>");
                  }
                  else{
                      alert("No Match!");
                  }
              </script>
              </body>
              </html>
```

### EXPLANATION

1   The variable is assigned a bracketed regular expression containing alphanumeric characters. This regular expression matches a string that contains at least one uppercase character ranging between A and Z, followed by one lowercase character ranging between a and z, followed by *eve*.

2   The variable *textString* is assigned user input, in this example *Steven lives in Cleveland* was entered.

3   The regular expression *test()* method will return *true* since *Steven* contains an uppercase character, followed by a lowercase character, and *eve*. *Cleveland* also matches the pattern. The variable *result* contains either *true* or *false*. See the output in Figures 13.10 and 13.11.

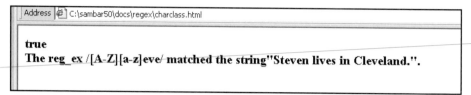

**Figure 13.10**   The user entered *Steven lives in Cleveland,* one uppercase letter *(A-Z)*, followed by one lowercase letter *(a-z)*, followed by *eve*. This matches both *Steven* and *Cleveland*.

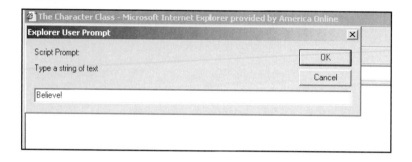

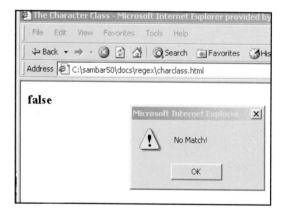

**Figure 13.11**   When the user entered *Believe!* (top), it didn't match (bottom). It would have matched if he had entered *BeLieve*. Why?

## EXAMPLE 13.13

```
    <html><head><title>The Character Class</title>
    </head>
    <body>
    <script language="JavaScript">
    // Character class
1       var reg_expression = /[A-Za-z0-9_]/;      // A single alphanumeric
                                                  // word character
2       var textString=prompt("Type a string of text","");
3       var result=reg_expression.test(textString);   // Returns true
                                                      // or false
        document.write("<font size='+1'><b>"+result+"<br>");
        if (result){
           document.write("<b>The reg_ex /[A-Za-z0-9_]/ matched the
           string\""+ textString +"\".<br>");
        }
        else{
           alert("No Match!");
        }
    </script>
    </body>
    </html>
```

## EXPLANATION

1 A regular expression object, an alphanumeric character in the bracketed character class *[A-Za-z0-9_]* is assigned to the variable called *reg_expression*. This regular expression matches a string that contains at least one character in the character class ranging between *A* and *Z*, *a* and *z*, *0* and *9*, and the underscore character, _.

2 User input is entered in the prompt dialog box and assigned to the variable *textString*. In this example the user entered *Take 5*.

3 The regular expression test method will return true since this string *Take 5* contains at least one alphanumeric character. See Figure 13.12.

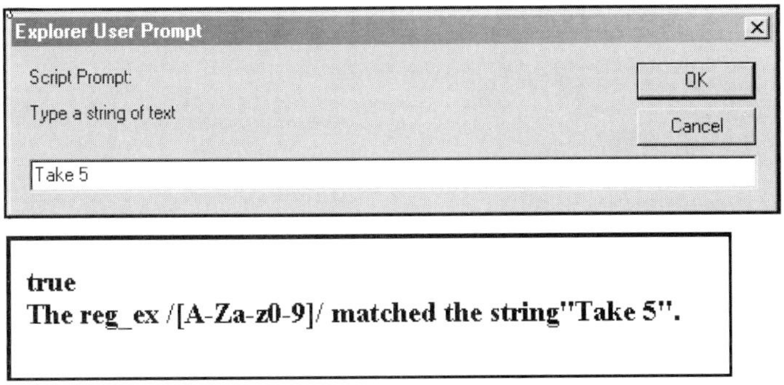


**Figure 13.12** User entered *Take 5* (top). The string contained at least one alphanumeric character (bottom).

**EXAMPLE** 13.14

```
<html><head><title>The Character Class and Negation</title>
</head>
<body>
<script language="JavaScript">
//  Negation within a Character Class
    var reg_expression = /[^0-9]/;
    var textString=prompt("Type a string of text","");
    var result=reg_expression.test(textString);  // Returns true
                                                  // or false
    document.write("<font size='+1'><b>"+result+"<br>");
    if (result){
        document.write("<b>The reg_ex /[^0-9]/ matched the
        string\""+ textString +"\".<br>");
    }
    else{
        alert("No Match!");
    }
</script>
</body>
</html>
```

Lines 1, 2, 3 marked in left margin beside the `var reg_expression`, `var textString`, and `var result` lines respectively.

**EXPLANATION**

1   The caret inside a character class, when it is the first character after the opening bracket, creates a negation, meaning any character not in this range. This regular expression matches a string that <u>does not</u> contain a number between 0 and 9.

2   User input is assigned to the variable *textString*. In this example, *abc* was entered.

3   The regular expression *test()* method will return true since the string *abc* does not contain a character ranging from 0 to 9.

---

> **true**
> **The reg_ex /[^0-9]/ matched the string"abc".**

**Figure 13.13**   The user entered *abc*. It contains a character that is <u>not</u> in the range between 0 and 9.

## 13.3.3  Metasymbols

Metasymbols offer an alternative way to represent a character class. For example, instead of representing a number as *[0-9]*, it can be represented as \d, and the alternative for representing a non-number *[^0-9]* is \D. Metasymbols are easier to use and to type than metacharacters.

**Table 13.8** Metasymbols.

| Symbol | What It Matches | Character Class |
|--------|----------------|-----------------|
| \d | One digit | [0-9] |
| \D | One non-digit | [^0-9] |
| \s | One whitespace character (tab, space, newline, carriage return, formfeed, vertical tab) | |
| \S | One non-space character | |
| \w | One word character | [A-Za-z0-9_] |
| \W | One non-word character | [^A-Za-z0-9] |

**EXAMPLE 13.15**

```
       <html><head><title>The Digit Meta Symbol</title>
       </head>
       <body>
       <script language="JavaScript">
1          var reg_expression = /6\d\d/;
2          var textString=prompt("Type a string of text","");
3          var result=reg_expression.test(textString);   // Returns true
                                                          // or false
       document.write("<font size='+1'><b>"+result+"<br>");
       if (result){
           document.write("<b>The regular expression /6\\d\\d/ matched
           the string\""+ textString +"\".<br>");
       }
       else{
           alert("No Match!");
       }
       </script>
       </body>
       </html>
```

**EXPLANATION**

1 The variable is assigned a regular expression containing the number 6, followed by two single digits. The metasymbol \d represents the character class [0-9].

2 The variable *textString* is assigned user input; in this example, *126553* was entered.

3 The regular expression *test()* method will return true since this string *abc* does not contains a 6 followed by any two digits. See Figure 13.14.

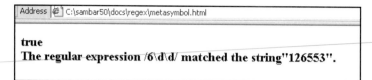

Address ⬚ C:\sambar50\docs\regex\metasymbol.html

**true**
**The regular expression /6\d\d/ matched the string"126553".**

**Figure 13.14**   The user entered *126553*. It contains a 6 followed by any two digits.

## EXAMPLE  13.16

```
         <html><head><title>The Digit Meta Symbol Negated</title>
         </head>
         <body>
         <script language="JavaScript">
1            var reg_expression = /[a-z]\D\D/;
2            var textString=prompt("Type a string of text","");
3            var result=reg_expression.test(textString);  // Returns true
                                                           // or false
             document.write("<font size='+1'><b>"+result+"<br>");
             if (result){
                 document.write("<b>The regular expression /[a-z]\\D\\D/
                 matched the string\"" + textString +"\".<br>");
             }
             else{
                 alert("No Match!");
             }
         </script>
         </body>
         </html>
```

## EXPLANATION

1   The variable is assigned a regular expression containing a letter, followed by two single non-digits. The metasymbol \D represents the character class *[^0-9]*.

2   The variable *textString* is assigned user input; in this example, *Hello!* was entered.

3   The regular expression *test()* method will return *true* since this string *Hello!!* matches a lowercase letter, followed by two non-digit characters. See Figure 13.15.

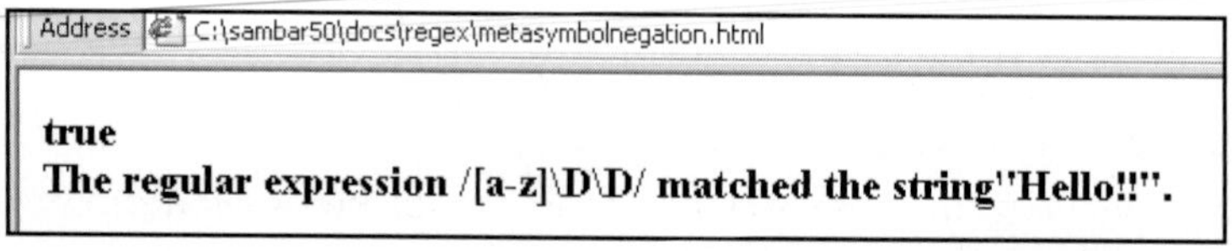

Address ⬚ C:\sambar50\docs\regex\metasymbolnegation.html

**true**
**The regular expression /[a-z]\D\D/ matched the string"Hello!!".**

**Figure 13.15**   The user entered a lowercase letter followed by two non-digits.

EXAMPLE 13.17

```
<html><head><title>Word and Space Metasymbols</title>
</head>
<body>
<script language="JavaScript">
1     var reg_expression = /\w\s\w\W/;
2     var textString=prompt("Type a string of text","");
3     var result=reg_expression.test(textString);  // Returns true
                                                    // or false
      document.write("<font size='+1'><b>"+result+"<br>");
      if (result){
          document.write("<b>The regular expression /\\w\\s\\w\\W/
          matched the string\""+ textString +"\".<br>");
      }
      else{
          alert("No Match!");
      }
</script>
</body>
</html>
```

EXPLANATION

1   The variable is assigned a regular expression containing an alphanumeric word character \w, followed by a space \s, followed by another alphanumeric word character, followed by a non-alphanumeric word character \W. The metasymbol \w represents the character class *[A-Za-z0-9_]*. The metasymbol \W represents the character class *[^A-Za-z0-9_]*, and the metasymbol \s represents a whitespace character (tab, space, newline, carriage return, formfeed).

2   The variable *textString* is assigned user input; in this example, *ABC D%* was entered first.

3   The regular expression *test()* method will return *true* since the string *ABC D%* matches an alphanumeric character (*C*), followed by a space, another alphanumeric character (*D*) and a non-alphanumeric character (*%*) (see Figure 13.16). An example of output where the pattern failed is shown in Figure 13.17.

---

**true**
**The regular expression /\w\s\w\W/ matched the string"ABC D%".**

---

**Figure 13.16**   The user entered *ABC D%*. It contained a word character, followed by a whitespace, another word character, followed by a non-whitespace.

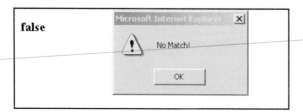

**false**

**Figure 13.17** The user entered *ABCD#*. To match, the string needs a space between the *C* and *D*.

## 13.3.4 Metacharacters to Repeat Pattern Matches

In the previous examples, the metacharacter matched on a single character. What if you want to match on more than one character? For example, let's say you are looking for all lines containing names and the first letter must be in uppercase, which can be represented as *[A-Z]*, but the following letters are lowercase and the number of letters varies in each name. *[a-z]* matches on a single lowercase letter. How can you match on one or more lowercase letters, or zero or more lowercase letters? To do this you can use what are called <u>quantifiers</u>. To match on one or more lowercase letters, the regular expression can be written */[a-z]+/* where the + sign means "one or more of the previous characters"; in this case, one or more lowercase letters. JavaScript provides a number of quantifiers as shown in the Table 13.9.

**Table 13.9** Quantifiers: The greedy metacharacters.

| Metacharacter | What It Matches |
| --- | --- |
| *x?* | Matches 0 or 1 of *x* |
| *(xyz)?* | Matches zero or one pattern of *xyz* |
| *x\** | Matches 0 or more of *x* |
| *(xyz)\** | Matches zero or more patterns of *xyz* |
| *x+* | Matches 1 or more of *x* |
| *(xyz)+* | Matches one or more patterns of *xyz* |
| *x{m,n}* | Matches at least *m* of *x* and no more than *n* of *x* |

**The Greed Factor.**   Normally quantifiers are "greedy"; that is, they match on the largest possible set of characters starting at the left-hand side of the string and searching to the right, looking for the last possible character that would satisfy the condition. For example, given the string:

```
var string="ab123456783445554437AB"
```

and the regular expression:

```
/ab[0-9]*/
```

If the *replace()* method were to substitute what is matched with an *"X"*:

```
string=string.relace(/ab[0-9]/, "X");
```

the resulting string would be:

```
"XAB"
```

The asterisk is a greedy metacharacter. It matches for zero or more of the preceding character. In other words, it attaches itself to the character preceding it; in the above example, the asterisk attaches itself to the character class *[0-9]*. The matching starts on the left, searching for *ab* followed by zero or more numbers in the range between 0 and 9. It is called greedy because the matching continues until the last number is found; in this example, the number 7. The pattern *ab* and all of the numbers in the range between 0 and 9 are replaced with a single *X*.

Greediness can be turned off so that instead of matching on the maximum number of characters, the match is made on the minimal number of characters found. This is done by appending a question mark after the greedy metacharacter. See Example 13.18.

## EXAMPLE 13.18

```
        <html><head><title></title>
        </head>
        <body>
        <script language="JavaScript">
1           var reg_expression = /\d\.?\d/;
2           var textString=prompt("Type a string of text","");
3           var result=reg_expression.test(textString);  // Returns true
                                                          // or false
            document.write("<font size='+1'><b>"+result+"<br>");
            if (result){
                document.write("<b>The regular expression /\\d\\.?\\d/
                matched the string\""+textString +"\".<br>");
            }
            else{
                alert("No Match!");
            }
        </script>
        </body>
        </html>
```

## EXPLANATION

1   The variable is assigned a regular expression containing a decimal character \d, and followed by either one or zero literal periods, \.?. The question mark (zero or one) controls the character preceding it, in this case a period. There is either one period or no period at all in the string being matched.

2   The variable *textString* is assigned user input; in this example, *3.7* was entered.

3   The regular expression test method will return *true* since the string *3.7* matches a decimal number, 3, followed by a period (or not one) and followed by another decimal number, 7. See the examples in Figure 13.18.

---

**true**
**The regular expression /\d\.?\d/ matched the string"3.7".**

---

**true**
**The regular expression /\d\.?\d/ matched the string"456".**

---

**Figure 13.18**   The user entered *3.7*, or number, period, number (top); the user entered *456*, or number, no period, number (middle); the user entered *5A6*, but there must be at least two consecutive digits for a match (bottom).

EXAMPLE 13.19

```
        <html><head><title></title>
        </head>
        <body>
        <script language="JavaScript">
        // Greediness
1       var reg_expression = /[A-Z][a-z]*\s/;
2       var textString=prompt("Type a string of text","");
3       var result=reg_expression.test(textString);  // Returns true
                                                      // or false
        document.write("<font size='+1'><b>"+result+"<br>");
        if (result){
            document.write("<b>The regular expression /[A-Z][a-z]*\\s/
            matched the string"+ textString +"\".<br>");
        }
        else{
            alert("No Match!");
        }
        </script>
        </body>
        </html>
```

**EXPLANATION**

1   The variable is assigned a regular expression containing an uppercase letter, *[A-Z]*, followed by zero or more lowercase letters, *[a-z]\**, and a space, *\s*. There are either zero or more lowercase letters.

2   The variable *textString* is assigned user input; in this example, *Danny boy* was entered.

3   The regular expression test method will return *true* since the string *Danny boy* matches an uppercase letter *D*, followed by zero or more lowercase letters *anny*, and a space. See Figure 13.19.

---

true
**The regular expression /[A-Z][a-z]\*\s/ matched the string"Danny boy".**

---

true
**The regular expression /[A-Z][a-z]\*\s/ matched the string"DANNY BOY".**

---

**Figure 13.19** The user entered *Danny boy,* or one uppercase letter, zero or more lowercase letters, and a space (top); the user entered *DANNY BOY,* or one uppercase letter, zero lowercase letters, and a space (bottom).

**EXAMPLE**   13.20

```
<html><head><title></title>
</head>
<body>
<script language="JavaScript">
1       var reg_expression = /[A-Z][a-z]+\s/;
2       var textString=prompt("Type a string of text","");
3       var result=reg_expression.test(textString);   // Returns true
                                                       // or false
        document.write("<font size='+1'><b>"+result+"<br>");
        if (result){
            document.write("<b>The regular expression /[A-Z][a-z]+\\s/
            matched the string\""+ textString +"\".<br>");
        }
        else{
            alert("No Match!");
        }
</script>
</body>
</html>
```

**EXPLANATION**

1   The regular expression reads: Search for an uppercase letter, followed by one or more lowercase letters, followed by a space.

2   The user is prompted for input.

3   The regular expression *test()* method checks that the string *textString* entered by the user, matches the regular expression and returns true or false. See Figure 13.20.

---

**true**
**The regular expression /[A-Z][a-z]+\s/ matched the string"Danny Boy".**

---

**false**

**Figure 13.20**   The user entered *Danny Boy* or one uppercase letter, one or more lowercase letters, and a space (top); the user entered *DannyBoy* and gets no match, since there was no space (bottom).

---

**EXAMPLE  13.21**

```
<html><head><title></title>
</head>
<body>
<script language="JavaScript">
1     var reg_expression = /abc\d{1,3}\.\d/;
2     var textString=prompt("Type a string of text","");
3     var result=reg_expression.test(textString);  // Returns true
                                                    // or false
      document.write("<font size='+1'><b>"+result+"<br>");
      if (result){
          document.write("<b>The regular expression
          /abc\\d{1,3}\\.\\d/ matched the string\""+
          textString +"\".<br>");
      }
      else{
          alert("No Match!");
      }
</script>
</body>
</html>
```

---

**EXPLANATION**

1  The variable is assigned a regular expression containing the pattern *abc\d{1,3}\.\d*, where *abc* is followed by at least one digit, repeated by up to three digits, followed by a literal period, and another another digit, \d.

2  The variable *textString* is assigned user input; here, *abc456.5xyz* was entered.

3  The regular expression contains the curly brace {} metacharacters, representing the number of times the preceding expression will be repeated. The expression reads: Find at least one occurrence of the pattern \d and as many as three in a row. See Figure 13.21.

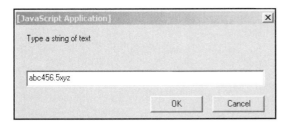

true
**The regular expression /abc\d{1,3}\.\d/ matched the string"abc456.5xyz".**

**Figure 13.21**  The user entered *abc* followed by between one and three numbers, followed by a literal period, and *xyz* (top); the entered string matched *true* (bottom).

**EXAMPLE  13.22**

```
          <html><head><title></title>
          </head>
          <body>
          <script language="JavaScript">
          //Repeating patterns
1         var reg_expression = /#\d{5}\.\d/;
2         var textString=prompt("Type a string of text","");
3         var result=reg_expression.test(textString);   // Returns true
                                                         // or false
          document.write("<font size='+1'><b>"+result+"<br>");
          if (result){
              document.write("<b>The regular expression /#\\d{5}\\.\\d/
              matched the string ""+ textString +"\".<br>");
          }
          else{
              alert("No Match!");
          }
          </script>
          </body>
          </html>
```

**EXPLANATION**

1   The variable is assigned a regular expression that reads: Find a # sign, followed by exactly five repeating digits \d{5}, a period, and another digit \d.

2   The user is prompted for input.

3   The *test()* method returns *true* if the regular expression pattern was found in the input string. See Figure 13.22.

---

**true**
**The regular expression /#\d{5}\.\d/ matched the string"#34234.6".**

---

**true**
**The regular expression /#\d{5}\.\d/ matched the string"abac#12345.56789".**

---

**false**

**Figure 13.22**
The user entered *#34234.6*, or a # sign, followed by five repeating digits, a period, and a number (top). This returns *true*. The user entered *abac#12345.56789* (middle). This returns *true*; but when the user entered *#234.555* (there are not five repeating digits after the # sign), no match was made (bottom).

**EXAMPLE   13.23**

```
        <html><head><title></title>
        </head>
        <body>
        <script language="JavaScript">
        //Repeating patterns
1           var reg_expression = /5{1,}\.\d/;
        var textString=prompt("Type a string of text","");
        var result=reg_expression.test(textString);  // Returns true
                                                      // or false
        document.write("<font size='+1'><b>"+result+"<br>");
        if (result){
            document.write("<b>The regular expression #\\5{1,}\\.\\d/
            matched the string\" "+ textString +"\".<br>");
        }
        else{
            alert("No Match!");
        }
        </script>
        </body>
        </html>
```

---

**true**
**The regular expression /5{1,}\.\d/ matched the string "abc5555555.2".**

---

**true**
**The regular expression /5{1,}\.\d/ matched the string "5.6".**

---

**Figure 13.23**   The user entered *abc5555555.2*, or the number 5 at least 1 time, followed by a literal period, and any digit, *\d* (top). This returns *true*; the user entered *5.6* (bottom). This also returns *true*.

**Metacharacters That Turn off Greediness.**  By placing a question mark after a greedy quantifier, the greed is turned off and the search ends after the first match, rather than the last one.

---

**EXAMPLE** 13.24

```
      <html><head><title>Greed</title>
      </head>
      <body bgcolor=lightblue>
      <script language="JavaScript">
1         var myString="abcdefghijklmnopqrstuvwxyz";
          document.write("<font size='+1'>Old string:<b>
             "+myString+"<br>");
2         myString=myString.replace(/[a-z]+/, "XXX");
          document.write("</b>New string:<b> "+   myString+"<br>");
      </script>
      </body>
      </html>
```

**EXPLANATION**

1   The variable, called *myString*, is assigned a string of lowercase letters.
2   The regular expression reads: Search for one or more lowercase letters, and replace them with *XXX*. The + metacharacter is greedy. It takes as many characters as match the expression; i.e., it starts on the left-hand side of the string grabbing as many lowercase letters as it can find until the end of the string.
3   The value of *myString* is printed after the substitution, as shown in Figure 13.24.

---

Old string: **abcdefghijklmnopqrstuvwxyz**
New string: **XXX**

**Figure 13.24**   The + sign is greedy. One or more lowercase letters are replaced with *XXX*; i.e., the whole string.

**EXAMPLE  13.25**

```
                <html><head><title></title>
                </head>
                <body>
                <script language="JavaScript">
1                   var myString="abcdefghijklmnopqrstuvwxyz";
                    document.write("<font size='+1'>Old string: <b>"
                                    +myString+"<br>");
2                   myString=myString.replace(/[a-z]+?/, "XXX");
                    document.write("</b>New string: <b>"+myString+"<br>");
                </script>
                </body>
                </html>
```

**EXPLANATION**

1   The variable called *myString* is assigned a string of lowercase letters, just exactly
    like the last example.

2   The regular expression reads: Search for one or more lowercase letters, but after
    the + sign, there is a question mark. The question mark turns off the greed factor.
    Now instead of taking as many lowercase letters as it can, this regular expression
    search stops after it finds the first lowercase character, and then replaces that char-
    acter with *XXX*.

```
Old string: abcdefghijklmnopqrstuvwxyz
New string: XXXbcdefghijklmnopqrstuvwxyz
```

**Figure 13.25**   This is not greedy. Output from Example 13.25.

### 13.3.5  Anchoring Metacharacters

Often it is necessary to anchor a metacharacter down, so that it matches only if the pattern is found at the beginning or end of a line, word, or string. These metacharacters are
based on a position just to the left or to the right of the character that is being matched.
Anchors are technically called <u>zero-width assertions</u> because they correspond to positions, not actual characters in a string; for example, /^abc/ will search for *abc* at the
beginning of the line, where the ^ represents a position, not an actual character. See
Table 13.10 for a list of anchoring metacharacters.

**Table 13.10**  Anchors (assertions).

| Metacharacter | What It Matches |
|---|---|
| ^ | Matches to beginning of line or beginning of string |
| $ | Matches to end of line or end of a string |
| \b | Matches a word boundary (When not inside [ ]) |
| \B | Matches a non-word boundary |

### EXAMPLE 13.26

```
       <html><head><title></title>
       </head>
       <body>
       <script language="JavaScript">
1          var reg_expression = /^Will/;   // Beginning of line anchor
2          var textString=prompt("Type a string of text","");
3          var result=reg_expression.test(textString);  // Returns true
                                                         // or false
           document.write("<font size='+1'><b>"+result+"<br>");
           if (result){
               document.write("<b>The regular expression /^Will/ matched
               the string\""+ textString +"\".<br>");
           }
           else{
               alert("No Match!");
           }
       </script>
       </body>
       </html>
```

### EXPLANATION

1   The variable is assigned a regular expression containing the beginning of line anchor metacharacter, the caret, followed by *Will*.

2   The variable *textString* is assigned user input; in this example, *Willie Wonker* was entered.

3   The regular expression *test()* method will return *true* since this string *Willie Wonker* begins with *Will*. See Figure 13.26.

> **true**
> **The regular expression /^Will/ matched the string"Willie Wonker".**

**false**

**Figure 13.26**  The user entered *Willie Wonker*. *Will* is at the beginning of the line, so this tests true (top); if the user enters *I know Willie*, and *Will* is not at the beginning of the line, the input would test *false* (bottom).

---

**EXAMPLE** 13.27

```
<html><head><title>Beginning of Line Anchor</title>
</head>
<body>
<script language="JavaScript">
1    var reg_expression = /^[JK]/;
2    var textString=prompt("Type a string of text","");
3    var result=reg_expression.test(textString);  // Returns true
                                                   // or false
     document.write("<font size='+1'><b>"+result+"<br>");
     if (result){
         document.write("<b>The regular expression /^[JK]/ matched
         the string\""+ textString +"\".<br>");
     }
     else{
         alert("No Match!");
     }
</script>
</body>
</html>
```

## EXPLANATION

1   A regular expression contains a beginning of line anchor, the caret. The regular expression reads: Find either an uppercase *J* or uppercase *K* at the beginning of the line or string.

2   The variable *textString* is assigned user input; in this example, *Jack and Jill*.

3   The regular expression *test()* method will return *true* since the string *Jack* matches an uppercase letter *J* and is found at the beginning of the string. See Figure 13.27.

---

**true**
**The regular expression /^[JK]/ matched the string"Jack and Jill".**

---

**true**
**The regular expression /^[JK]/ matched the string"Karen Evich".**

---

**Figure 13.27**   The string must begin with either a *J* or *K*. The user entered *Jack and Jill* (top) and this returns *true*; the user entered *Karen Evich* (bottom) and this also returns *true*.

## EXAMPLE 13.28

```
      <html><head><title>End of Line Anchor</title>
      </head>
      <body>
      <script language="JavaScript">
1         var reg_expression = /50$/;
2         var textString=prompt("Type a string of text","");
3         var result=reg_expression.test(textString);  // Returns true
                                                        // or false
      document.write("<font size='+1'><b>"+result+"<br>");
      if (result){
          document.write("<b>The regular expression /50$/ matched
          the string\""+ textString +"\".<br>");
      }
      else{
          alert("No Match!");
      }
      </script>
      </body>
      </html>
```

## EXPLANATION

1   The regular expression */50$/* is assigned to the variable. The pattern contains the dollar sign ($) metacharacter, representing the end of line anchor only when the $ is the last character in the pattern. The expression reads: Find a *5* and a *0* followed by a newline.

## EXAMPLE   13.29

```
<html><head><title>Anchors</title>
</head>
<body>
<script language="JavaScript">
1      var reg_expression = /^[A-Z][a-z]+\s\d$/;
           // At the beginning of the string, find one uppercase
           // letter, followed by one or more lowercase letters,
           // a space, and one digit.
2      var string=prompt("Enter a name and a number","");
3      if ( reg_expression.test(string)){
           alert("It Matched!!");
       }
       else{
           alert("No Match!");
       }
</script>
</body>
</html>
```

## EXPLANATION

1   The regular expression reads: Look at the beginning of the line, ^, find an uppercase letter, *[A-Z]*, followed by one or more lowercase letters, *[a-z]+*, a single whitespace, *\s*, and a digit at the end of the line, *\d$*.

2   The user is prompted for input.

3   The regular expression *test()* method tests to see if there was a match and returns *true* if so, and *false* if not. See Figures 13.28 and 13.29.

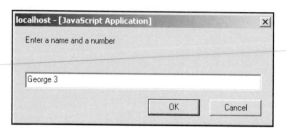

**Figure 13.28**  The string begins with a capital letter, followed by one or more lowercase letters, a space, and ends with one digit (left); the input sequence matched, so this message is displayed (right).

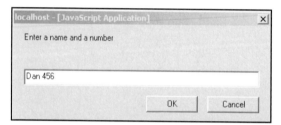

**Figure 13.29**  The regular expression does not match because the string ends in more than one digit (left); the input sequence did not match, so this message is displayed (right).

---

**EXAMPLE** 13.30

```
     <html><head><title>The Word Boundary</title>
     </head>
     <body>
     <script language="JavaScript">
     // Anchoring a word with \b
1        var reg_expression = /\blove\b/;
         var textString=prompt("Type a string of text","");
2        var result=reg_expression.test(textString);   // Returns true
                                                         // or false
         document.write("<font size='+1'><b>"+result+"<br>");
         if (result){
             document.write("<b>The regular expression /\blove\b/
             matched the string \""+ textString +"\".<br>");
         }
         else{
             alert("No Match!");
         }
     </script>
     </body>
     </html>
```

1    The regular expression contains the \b metacharacter, representing a word bound-
     ary, not a specific character. The expression reads: Find a word beginning and
     ending with *love*. This means that *gloves, lover, clover,* and so on, will not be found.

2    The regular expression *test()* method will return *true* since the string *love* is within
     word boundary anchors \b. See Figure 13.30.

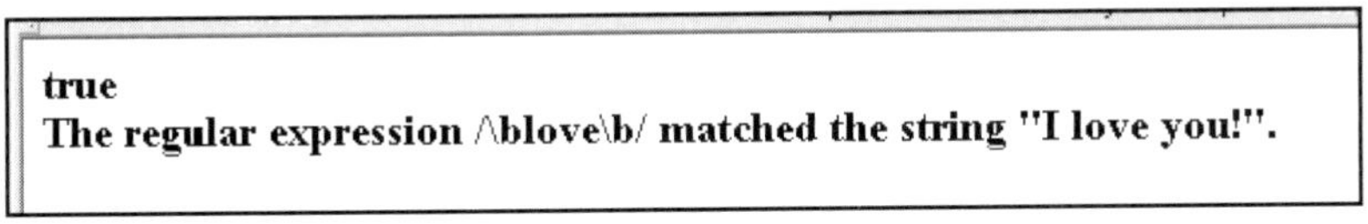

---

true
**The regular expression /\blove\b/ matched the string "I love you!".**

---

**Figure 13.30**  The user entered *I love you!*. The word *love* is between word boundaries ( \b).
The match was successfull.

### 13.3.6   Alternation

Alternation allows the regular expression to contain alternative patterns to be matched;
for example, the regular expression */John|Karen|Steve/* will match a line containing *John*
or *Karen* or *Steve*. If *Karen, John,* or *Steve* are all on different lines, all lines are matched.
Each of the alternative expressions is separated by a vertical bar (the pipe symbol, |) and
the expressions can consist of any number of characters, unlike the character class that
only matches for one character; thus, */a|b|c/* is the same as *[abc]*, whereas */ab|de/* cannot
be represented as *[abde]*. The pattern */ab|de/* is either *ab* or *de*, whereas the class *[abcd]*
represents only <u>one</u> character in the set *a, b, c,* or *d*.

**EXAMPLE  13.31**

```
       <html><head><title>Alternation</title>
       </head>
       <body>
       <script language="JavaScript">
       // Alternation: this or that or whatever...
1      var reg_expression = /Steve|Dan|Tom/;
       var textString=prompt("Type a string of text","");
2      var result=reg_expression.test(textString);  // Returns true
                                                     // or false
       document.write("<font size='+1'><b>"+result+"<br>");
       if (result){
           document.write("<b>The regular expression /Steve|Dan|Tom/
           matched the string\""+ textString +"\".<br>");
       }
       else{
           alert("No Match!");
       }
       </script></body></html>
```

## EXPLANATION

1   The pipe symbol, |, is used in the regular expression to match on a set of alternative patterns. If any of the patterns, *Steve*, *Dan*, or *Tom*, are found, the match is successful.

2   The *test()* method will return *true* if the user enters either *Steve*, *Dan*, or *Tom*. See Figure 13.31.

---

**true**
**The regular expression /Steve|Dan|Tom/ matched the string"Do you know Tommy?".**

---

**true**
**The regular expression /Steve|Dan|Tom/ matched the string"Dan is my son.".**

---

**true**
**The regular expression /Steve|Dan|Tom/ matched the string"Steve Dobbins is Christian's daddy.".**

**Figure 13.31**   The user entered *Do you know Tommy?*. Pattern *Tom* was matched in the string.

**Grouping or Clustering.**   If the regular expression pattern is enclosed in parentheses, a subpattern is created. Then, for example, instead of the greedy metacharacters matching on zero, one, or more of the previous single characters, they can match on the previous subpattern. Alternation can also be controlled if the patterns are enclosed in parentheses. This process of grouping characters together is also called <u>clustering</u>.

## EXAMPLE 13.32

```
<html><head><title>Grouping or Clustering</title>
</head>
<body>
<script language="JavaScript">
// Grouping with parentheses
1      var reg_expression = /^(Sam|Dan|Tom) Robbins/;
2      var textString=prompt("Type a string of text","");
3      var result=reg_expression.test(textString);  // Returns true
                                                     // or false
```

**EXAMPLE   13.32 (CONTINUED)**

```
        document.write("<font size='+1'><b>"+result+"<br>");
        if (result){
            document.write("<b>The regular expression /^(Sam|Dan|Tom)
            Robbins/ matched the string\""+ textString +"\".<br>");
        }
        else{
            alert("No Match!");
        }
    </script>
    </body>
    </html>
```

**EXPLANATION**

1   By enclosing *Sam, Dan,* and *Tom* in parentheses, the alternative now becomes ei-
    ther *Sam Robbins, Dan Robbins,* or *Tom Robbins.* Without the parentheses, the reg-
    ular expression matches *Sam,* or *Dan,* or *Tom Robbins.* The caret metacharacter ^
    anchors all of the patterns to the beginning of the line.

2   The user input is assigned to the variable called *textString.*

3   The *test()* method checks to see if the string contains one of the alternatives: *Sam
    Robbins* or *Dan Robbins* or *Tom Robbins.* If it does, *true* is returned; otherwise, *false*
    is returned. See Figure 13.32.

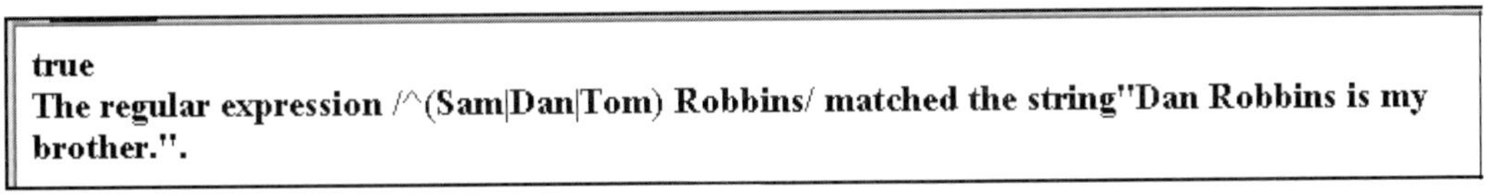

---

**true**
**The regular expression /^(Sam|Dan|Tom) Robbins/ matched the string"Dan Robbins is my**
**brother.".**

---

**Figure 13.32**   The user entered *Dan Robbins* as one of the alternatives. *Sam Robbins* or *Tom
Robbins* would also be okay.

**Remembering or Capturing.**   If the regular expression pattern is enclosed in
parentheses, a subpattern is created. The subpattern is saved in special numbered class
properties, starting with $1, then $2, and so on. which will be applied to the *RegExp*
object, not an instance of the object. These properties can be used later in the program
and will persist until another successful pattern match occurs, at which time they will
be cleared. Even if the intention was to control the greedy metacharacter or the behavior
of alternation as shown in the previous example, the subpatterns are saved as a side
effect.[2] For more information on this go to *http://developer.netscape.com/docs/manuals/
communicator/ jsguide/reobjud.hmt#1007373.*

---

2.  It is possible to prevent a subpattern from being saved.

## EXAMPLE 13.33

```
<html><head><title>Capturing</title>
</head>
<body>
<script language="JavaScript">
1      textString = "Everyone likes William Rogers and his friends."
2      var reg_expression = /(William)\s(Rogers)/;
3      myArray=textString.match(reg_expression);
4      document.write(myArray);   // Three element array
5      document.write(RegExp.$1 + " "+RegExp.$2);
       // alert(myArray[1] + " "+ myArray[2]);
       // match and exec create an array consisting of the string, and
       // the captured patterns. myArray[0] is "William Rogers"
       // myArray[1] is "William"  myArray[2] is "Rogers".
</script>
</body>
</html>
```

## EXPLANATION

1   The string called *textString* is created.

2   The regular expression contains two subpatterns, *William* and *Rogers*, both enclosed in parentheses.

3   When either the *String* object's *match()* method or the *RegExp* object's *exec()* method are applied to the regular expression containing subpatterns, an array is returned, where the first element of the array is the regular expression string, and the next elements are the values of the subpatterns.

4   The array elements are displayed, separated by commas.

5   The subpatterns are class properties of the *RegExp* object. *$1* represents the first captured subpattern, *William*, and *$2* represents the second captured subpattern, *Rogers*. See Figure 13.33.

William Rogers,William,RogersWilliam Rogers

**Figure 13.33**   Output from Example 13.33.

EXAMPLE 13.34

```
<html>
<head><title>Capture and Replace</title>
<font size="+1"><font face="helvetica">
<script language = "JavaScript">
1       var string="Tommy Savage:203-123-4444:12 Main St."
2       var newString=string.replace(/(Tommy) (Savage)/, "$2, $1");
3       document.write(newString +"<br>");
</script>
</head><body></body>
</html>
```

EXPLANATION

1   A string is assigned to the variable, called *string*.

2   The *replace()* method will search for the pattern *Tommy Savage*. Since the search side of the *replace()* method contains the pattern *Tommy* enclosed in parentheses and the pattern *Savage* enclosed in parentheses, each of these subpatterns will be stored in $1 and $2, respectively. A third pattern would be stored in $3 and a fourth pattern in $4, etc. On the replacement side of the *replace()* method, $2 and $1 are replaced in the string, so that *Savage* is first, then a comma, and then *Tommy*. The first and last names have been reversed.

3   The new string is displayed.

Savage, Tommy:203-123-4444:12 Main St.

**Figure 13.34**   Output from Example 13.34.

EXAMPLE 13.35

```
<html>
<head>
<title>Capture and Replace</title></head>
<body>
<font size="+1">
<font face="helvetica">
<script language = "JavaScript">
1       var string="Tommy Savage:203-123-4444:12 Main St."
2       var newString=string.replace(/(\w+)\s(\w+)/, "$2, $1");
3       document.write(newString +"<br>");
</script>
</body>
</html>
```

## EXPLANATION

1  A string is created to be used by the *replace()* method in step 2.

2  The *replace()* method searches for one or more alphanumeric word characters, followed by a single space, and another set of alphanumeric word characters. The word characters are enclosed in parentheses, and thus captured. *$1* will contain *Tommy*, and *$2* will contain *Savage*. On the replacement side, *$1* and *$2* are reversed. After the replacement is made, a new string is created.

3  The value of *newString* shows that the capturing and the substitution occurred successfully, leaving the remainder of the string as it was. See Figure 13.35.

Savage, Tommy:203-123-4444:12 Main St.

**Figure 13.35**   Subpatterns are used in string replacement.

# 13.4 Form Validation with Regular Expressions

When you fill out a form on the Web, you are typically asked for your name, phone, address (a pop-up menu of all the states is usually provided), and then all sorts of credit card stuff. Sometimes it takes four or five tries to get it right because you didn't complete the form exactly the way you were asked. A message will appear and you won't be allowed to submit the form until you get it right. Behind the scenes a JavaScript program is validating the form.

## 13.4.1 Checking for Empty Fields

There's a form waiting to be filled out. Some of the fields are optional, and some are mandatory. The question is, did the user fill in the mandatory fields? If he didn't, the form can't be processed properly. Checking for empty or null fields is one of the first things you may want to check.

## EXAMPLE 13.36

```
        <html>
        <head>
        <title>Checking for Empty Fields</title>
        <script language="JavaScript">
1       function validate_text(form1) {
2           if ( form1.user_name.value == "" || form1.user_name.value  ==
                  null){
                alert("You must enter your name.");
                return false;
            }
3      .    if ( form1.user_phone.value == "" || form1.user_phone.value ==
                  null){
                alert("You must enter your phone.");
                return false;
            }
            else {
4               return true;
            }
        }
        </script>
        </head>
        <hr>
        <body>
        <h2> Checking for Empty fields </h2>
5       <form name="formtest" action="/cgi-bin/form1.cgi" method="get"
           onSubmit="return validate_text(formtest)">
        Please enter your name: <br>
6       <input type="text" size=50 name="user_name">
        <p>
        Please enter your phone number: <BR>
7       <input type="text" size=30 name="user_phone">
        <p>
        <input type=submit value="Send">
        <input type=reset value="Clear">
        </form>
        </html>
```

## EXPLANATION

1   A user-defined function called *validate_text()* is defined. It takes one parameter, a reference to a form.

2   If the value in the first text field is an empty string (represents a string with no text) or null (represents no value), the user is sent an alert asking him to fill in his name. If a *false* value is returned, the form is not submitted.

3   If the value in the second text field is an empty string or null, the user is sent an alert asking him to fill in his phone. If a *false* value is returned, the form is not submitted.

4   If both text boxes were filled out, a *true* value is returned, and the form will be submitted to the server's CGI program whose URL is listed in the *action* attribute of the form.

5   The *onSubmit* event is triggered when the user presses the submit button. The handler function, *validate_text()*, will be called with a reference to this form.

6   The input type for this form is a text box that will get the name of the user.

7   Another text box is created to hold the phone number of the user. See Figure 13.36.

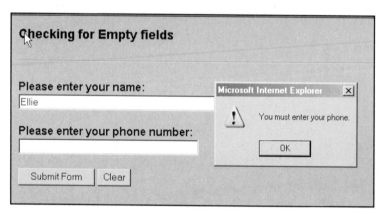

**Figure 13.36**   The user left the phone field empty, so the form was not submitted.

## 13.4.2   Checking for Numeric Zip Codes

If you ask the user for a five-digit zip code, it is easy to check using a regular expression by matching for exactly five digits:

```
/^\d{5}$/
```

Another way to say the same thing:

```
/^[0-9][0-9][0-9][0-9][0-9]$/
```

Some longer zip codes contain a dash followed by four numbers. This long zip code format could be represented as:

```
/^\d{5}-?\d{4}$/
```

The beginning and end of line anchors prevent the matched string from containing any extraneous characters at either end of the string. See Example 13.37.

```
        <html>
        <head><title>Testing for a Valid Zip Code</title>
        <script language="JavaScript">
1       function ok_Zip(zip){
2           var regex=/^\d{5}$/;   // Match for 5 numbers
3           if ( regex.test(zip.value) == false) {
                alert("Zip code must contain exactly five numbers!");
                zip.focus();
                return false;
            }
4           if ( zip.value == ""){
                alert("You must enter a zip code");
                zip.focus();
                return false;
            }
            return true;
        }
        </script></head>
        <body><font face="arial" size="+1">
        <form name="ZipTest" action="/error" >
        Enter your zip code:
        <input type="text"
            name="zipcode"
            size=5>
        <input type="button"
            value="Check zip"
5           onClick="if( ok_Zip(ZipTest.zipcode)) {alert('Zip is
            valid.')}">
        <br><input type="reset">
        </form>
        </body>
        </html>
```

1   The function, called *ok_Zip()*, is defined to validate the zip code entered by the user.

2   The regular expression reads: Look for exactly five digits. The beginning of line and end of line anchors ensure that there will not be any extraneous characters before or after the five digits.

3   The regular expression *test()* method checks that the value entered by the user is a valid zip code. If not, an alert dialog box will tell the user, focus will returned to the text box, and *false* will be returned.

4   If the user doesn't enter anything, an alert dialog box will appear, focus will be returned to the text box, and *false* will be returned.

5   The *onClick* event is triggered when the user clicks the "Check zip" button. A JavaScript statement to call the *ok_Zip()* function is assigned to the event. If the user entered a valid zip code, the alert dialog box will pop up and say so. See Figure 13.37.

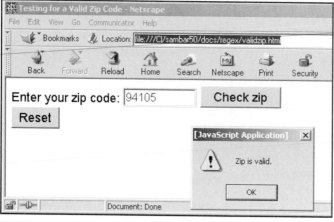

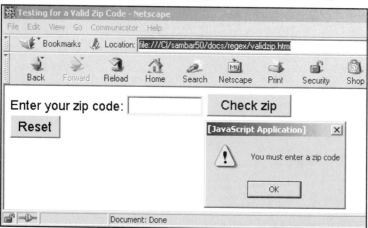

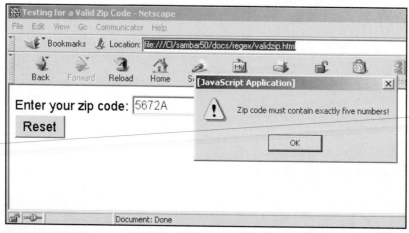

**Figure 13.37**   The user enters a five-digit zip code (top); the user enters nothing (middle); the user enters 4 digits and 1 letter (bottom).

### 13.4.3 Checking for Alphabetic Data

To test for entries that must consist strictly of alphabetic input, such as a name, state, or country field, the regular expression character set can be used; for example, /[a-zA-z]+/ is a regular expression that matches a string containing one or more uppercase or lowercase letters, and /^[a-zA-Z]+$/ matches a string containing only one or more uppercase or lowercase letters, because the character set is enclosed within the beginning and ending anchor metacharacters. To represent one or more alphanumeric word characters, [A-Za-z0-9_], you can use the \w metasymbol; for example, /\w+/ represents one or more alphanumeric word characters.

**EXAMPLE 13.38**

```
      <html>
      <head><title>Testing for Alphabetic Characters</title>
      <script language="JavaScript">
1     function okAlpha(form){
2        var regex=/^[a-zA-Z]+$/; //Match for upper- or lowercase letters
         if ( regex.test(form.fname.value) == false) {
            alert("First name must contain alphabetic characters!");
            form.fname.focus();
            return false;
         }
3        if ( form.fname.value == ""){
            alert("You must enter your first name.");
            form.fname.focus();
            return false;
         }
4        return true;
      }
      </script>
      </head>
      <body><font face="arial" size="+1">
5     <form name="alphaTest"
         method="post"
         action="/cgi-bin/testing.pl"
6        onSubmit="return okAlpha(this)" >
         Enter your first name:
         <input type="text"
7           name="fname"
            size=20>
         <p>
8        <input type="submit" value="Submit">
         <input type="reset">
      </form>
      </body>
      </html>
```

# EXPLANATION

1  A function called *okAlpha()* is defined. It takes one parameter, a reference to a form. Its purpose is to make sure the user entered only alphabetic characters in the form.

2  A regular expression is created. It reads: Starting at the beginning of the line, find one or more uppercase or lowercase letters in the character class *[A-Za-z]* followed by the end of line anchor (*$*). The regular expression is tested against the input that came in from a text box named *text*. If it doesn't match, the alert box will notify the user, and *false* is returned to the *onSubmit* handler on line 6. The form will not be submitted.

3  If the user didn't enter anything at all and the field is empty, another alert will be sent to the user, and *false* will be returned. The form will not be submitted.

4  If the user entered only alphabetic characters in his name, *true* will be returned, and the form will be submitted.

5  This is where the HTML form starts.

6  The *onSubmit* handler will be triggered when the user presses the submit button, and the *okAlpha()* function will be called, passing a reference to the form called *alphaTest*.

7  The user enters his name in the text field called *fname*.

8  After filling out the form, the user will press the submit button, thereby triggering the *onSubmit* handler on line 6. See Figure 13.38.

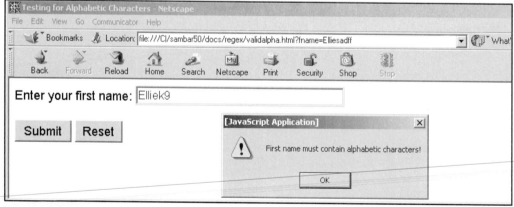

**Figure 13.38**  The user has a digit in his name. He can only enter alphabetic characters, or he will see the warning.

### 13.4.4 Removing Extraneous Characters

**Removing Spaces and Dashes.**   To remove any unwanted spaces or dashes from user input, the *String* object's *replace()* method can be used to find the characters and replace them with nothing, as shown in Example 13.39.

```
        <html>
        <head>
        <title>Removing Spaces and Dashes</title>
        </head>
        <body bgcolor="magenta">
        <font size="+1" font face="arial">
        <h2>Removing Spaces and Hyphens</h2>
        <script language = "JavaScript">
1           var string="444- 33 - 12 34"
2           var regex = /[ -]+/g;
3           var newString=string.replace(regex, "");
            document.write("The original string: "+string);
            document.write("<br>The new string: "+ newString +"<br>");
        </script>
        </body>
        </html>
```

**EXPLANATION**

1   The string contains numbers, spaces, and dashes.

2   The variable called *regex* is assigned a regular expression, which means: Search for one or more spaces or dashes, globally (multiple occurrences within the string).

3   The *replace()* method searches in the string for spaces and dashes, and if it finds any, replaces them with the empty string, *""*, returning the resulting string to *newString*. To change the original string, the return value of the *replace()* method can be returned back to the original string: *var string=string.replace(regex, "");*

---

## Removing Spaces and Dashes

The original string: 444- 33 - 12 34
The new string: 444331234

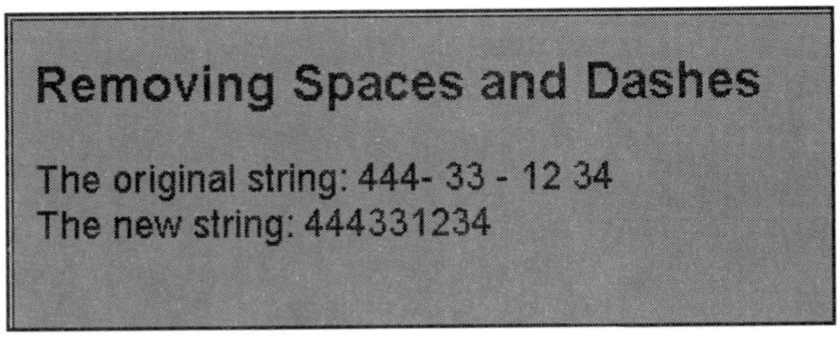

**Figure 13.39**   The *replace()* method is used to remove any spaces or dashes.

**Removing Unwanted Parentheses.**   You may also want to remove parentheses surrounding area codes or telephone numbers. This is a relatively simple regular expression used in the *replace()* method, as shown in next last example.

---

**EXAMPLE  13.40**

```
<html>
<head>
<title>Removing Parens</title>
</head>
<body bgcolor="magenta">
<font size="+1">
<font face="arial">
<h2>Removing Unwanted Parentheses, Spaces, and Dashes</h2>
<script language = "JavaScript">
1       var string="(408)-332-1234"
2       var regex = /[() -]+/g;
3       var newString=string.replace(regex, "");
        document.write("The original string: "+string);
        document.write("<br>The new string: "+ newString +"<br>");
</script>
</body>
</html>
```

**EXPLANATION**

1  The string contains numbers,  parentheses, spaces, and dashes.

2  The variable called *regex* is assigned a regular expression, which means: Search for one or more parens (open or closed), spaces or dashes, globally (multiple occurrences within the string).

3  The *replace()* method searches in the string for parens, spaces, and dashes, and if it finds any, replaces them with the empty string, *""*, returning the resulting string to *newString*. To change the original string, the return value of the *replace()* method can be returned back to the original string: *var string=string.replace(regex, "");*

---

**Removing Unwanted Parentheses, Spaces, and Dashes**

The original string: (408)-332-1234
The new string: 4083321234

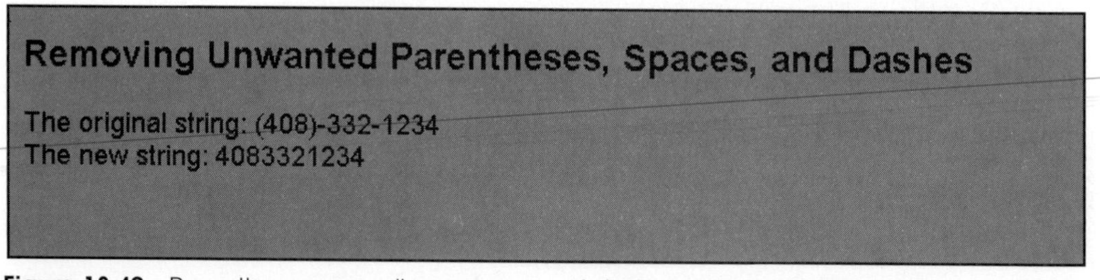

**Figure 13.40**   Parentheses, as well as spaces and dashes, are removed. Numbers or letters will remain.

**Removing any Non-Digits.**   A character that is not a digit can be represented as *[^0-9]* or as *\D* in a regular expression. You may want to remove any characters that are not digits in the user's input such as zip codes or phone numbers. This can also be done simply with a regular expression and the *replace()* method, as shown in the following example.

```
      <html>
      <head>
      <title>Removing all Non-digits</title>
      </head>
      <body bgcolor="magenta">
      <font size="+1" face="arial">
      <h3>If it's not a number, remove it!</h2>
      <script language = "JavaScript">
1         var string="phone is (408)-//[332]-1234@#!!!"
2         var newString=string.replace(/\D/g, "");
          document.write("The orginal string: "+string);
3         document.write("<br>The new string: "+ newString +"<br>");
      </script>
      </body>
      </html>
```

**EXPLANATION**

1    The string contains all kinds of characters, many which are not numbers.

2    The *replace()* method searches in the string for all non-digit characters, *\D/g*, and if it finds any, replaces them with the empty string, *""*, returning the resulting string to *newString*. To change the original string, the return value of the *replace()* method can be returned back to the original string: *var string=string.replace(regex, "")*;

3    The new string is diplayed after all the non-digit characters were replaced with nothing; i.e., they were removed.

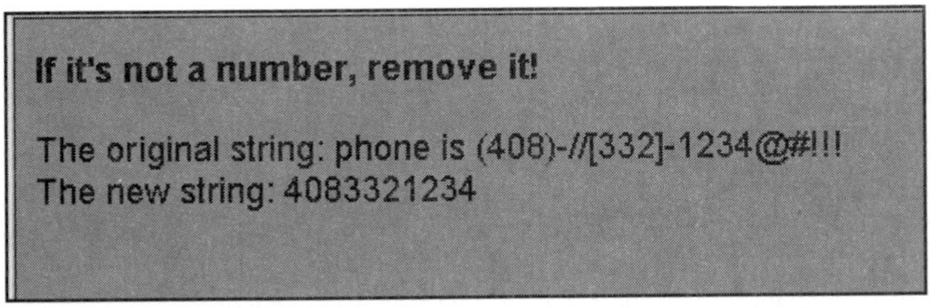

**If it's not a number, remove it!**

The original string: phone is (408)-//[332]-1234@#!!!
The new string: 4083321234

**Figure 13.41**   Only numbers will remain in the string. All other characters are removed.

**Removing any Non-Alphanumeric Characters.** A non-alphanumeric word character *[^0-9a-zA-Z_]*, any character that is not a letter, number, or the underscore, can be represented as \W. Again we can use the *replace()* method to remove those characters from a string.

## EXAMPLE 13.42

```
<html>
<head>
<title>Removing Non-Alphanumeric Characters</title>
</head>
<body bgcolor="magenta">
<font size="+1">
<font face="arial">
<h3>If it's not a number or a letter, remove it!</h2>
<script language = "JavaScript">
    var string="(408)-//[332]-1234@#!!!"
    var newString=string.replace(/\W/g, "");
    document.write("The original string: "+string);
    document.write("<br>The new string: "+ newString +"<br>");
</script>
</body>
</html>
```

Line numbers: 1, 2, 3

## EXPLANATION

1. The string contains all kinds of characters, many which are not letters or numbers.

2. The regular expression, \W/g, means: Search globally for any non-alphanumeric characters (\W). The *replace()* method searches for non-alphanumeric characters and replaces them with the empty string, *""*, returning the resulting string to *newString*. To change the original string, the return value of the *replace()* method can be returned back to the original string: *var string=string.replace(regex, "")*;

3. The new string is diplayed after all non-alphanumeric characters are removed.

---

**If it's not a number or a letter, remove it!**

The original string: (408)-//[332]-1234@#!!!
The new string: 4083321234

---

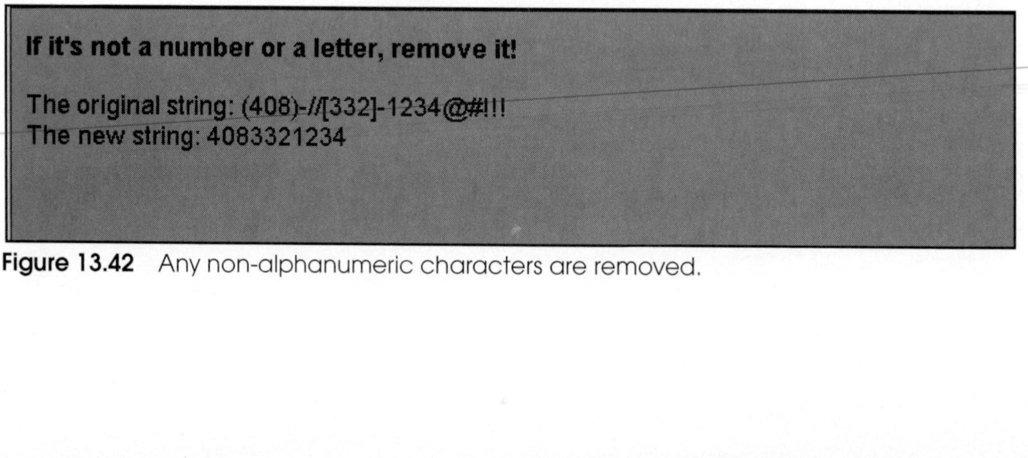

**Figure 13.42**   Any non-alphanumeric characters are removed.

## 13.4.5 Checking for Valid Social Security Numbers

A Social Security number contains exactly nine numbers. There may be dashes to separate the first three numbers and the last four numbers. The dashes should be optional. Example 13.43 demonstrates a regular expression that tests for three digits, followed by an optional dash, followed by two more digits, an optional dash, and finally four digits. The beginning and end of line anchors ensure that the user does not enter extraneous characters on either end of his Social Security number, such as *abd444-44-4444xyz*.

**EXAMPLE** 13.43

```
      <html>
      <head><title>Testing for a Social Security Number</title>
      <script language="JavaScript">
1     function okSocial(sform){
2         var regex=/^\d{3}-?\d\d-?\d{4}$/;
3         if ( regex.test(sform.ssn.value) == false) {
              alert("Social Security number invalid!");
              sform.ssn.focus();
              return false;
          }
4         if ( sform.ssn.value == "" ){
              alert("Please enter your Social Security number.");
              sform.ssn.focus();
              return false;
          }
          return true;
      }
      </script>
      </head>
      <body><font face="arial" size="+1">
      <center>
      <form name="snnTest"
          method=post
          action="/cgi-bin/testing"
5         onSubmit="return okSocial(this)" >
      Enter your Social Security number: xxx-xx-xxxx
      <p>
6     <input type="text"
          name="ssn"
          size=11>
      <p>
7     <input type="submit" value="Submit">
      <input type="reset">
      </form>
      </body>
      </html>
```

## EXPLANATION

1   The function *okSocial()* is defined. Its purpose is to validate a Social Security number.

2   The regular expression reads: Start at the beginning of the line, look for three digits, one dash (or not one), two more digits, another possible dash, and ending in four digits.

3   The regular expression *test()* method will return *true* if a valid Social Security number was entered and *false*, if not.

4   If nothing was entered in the text box, the user will be alerted, focus will go to the text field, and the form will not be submitted.

5   The *onSubmit* event handler will be triggered when the user presses the submit button, line 7.

6   The input type is a text field that will hold up to 11 characters.

7   When the user presses the submit button, the *onSubmit* event handler will be triggered. It will call the *okSocial()* function to validate the Social Security number. See Figure 13.43.

**Figure 13.43**   User enters a valid Social Security number.

## 13.4.6   Checking for Valid Phone Numbers

A valid U.S. phone number has ten digits: an area code of three digits, followed by the subscriber number of seven digits. There may be parentheses surrounding the area code, and dashes or spaces separating the numbers in the subscriber number. With regular expressions you can test for any or all of these conditions and then, if necessary, remove the extraneous characters, leaving just numbers. Example 13.44 demonstrates how to validate a simple U.S. phone number.

**EXAMPLE   13.44**

```
    <html><head><title>Validating Phone Numbers</title>
    <script language="JavaScript">
    function ok_Phone(phform){
1       var regex = /^\(?\d{3}\)?-?\s*\d{3}\s*-?\d{4}$/;
2       if(regex.test(phform.user_phone.value)){
            return true;
        }
        else{
            alert("Enter a valid phone number");
            return false;
        }
    }
    </script>
    </head><hr><body><h2>
    Checking for a Valid Phone Number </h2>
3   <form name="formtest"
        action="http://localhost/cgi-bin/environ.pl" method="post"
4       onSubmit="return ok_Phone(this);">
    <p>
        Please enter your phone: <BR>
5       <input type="text" size=40 name="user_phone">
    <p>
        <input type=submit value="Submit">
        <input type=reset value="Clear">
    </form></body></html>
```

**EXPLANATION**

1   The regular expression reads: Start at the beginning of the string, look for an optional literal opening parenthesis, followed by exactly three digits, and an optional closing parenthesis (the area code), followed by an optional dash, zero or more spaces, exactly three digits, zero or more spaces, an optional dash, and ending in exactly four digits, such as (222)-111-2345 or 222-111-2345 or 2221112345.

2   The regular expression is matched, *phform.user_phone.value*, the *test()* method will return *true*, and the form will be submitted; otherwise, the user will be alerted to enter a valid phone number.

3   The HTML form starts here and is named *formtest*.

4   The *onSubmit* event handler is assigned as an attribute of the *<form>* tag. It will be activated when user presses the submit button. The handler, *ok_Phone*, passes the form as an argument. The *this* keyword refers to the form named *formtest* and returns a *true* or *false* value. If *true*, the form will be submitted.

5   The user will enter his phone number in a text field. See Figure 13.44

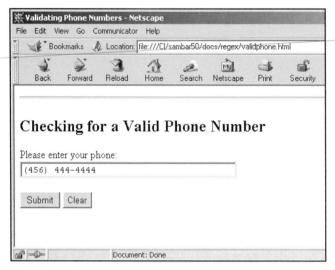

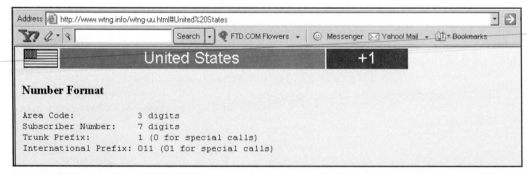

**Figure 13.44**   The user enters a valid phone number (top). Parentheses and the dash are optional; the user enters a number with too many digits, and an alert box appears (bottom).

Go to *http://www.wtng.info*, the World Wide Telephone Guide, to get a listing of phone formats for the world, country by country.

**Figure 13.45**   Go to *http://www.wtng.info/* to look up phone formats around the world.

For international phone numbers, the following formats are accepted:

```
+1 (123) 456 7888
+1123456 7888
+44 (123) 456 7888
+44(123) 456 7888 ext 123
+44 20 7893 2567
02345 444 5555 66
```

## 13.4.7 Checking for Valid E-Mail Addresses

When validating an e-mail address, you are looking for the typical format found in such addresses. There may be some domain names that are more than three characters, but it isn't typical. Also, just because the user types what looks like a valid e-mail address, that does not mean that it is; for example, the e-mail address *santa@northpole.org* uses a valid syntax, but that fact does not prove that *santa* is a real user.

E-mail addresses usually have the following format:

- An @ sign between the username and address (*lequig@aol.com*)
- At least one dot between the address and domain name ( *.com*, *.mil*, *.edu*, *.se*)
- At least six characters (*a@b.se*)[3]

Examples of valid e-mail addresses:

*username@mailserver.com*
*username@mailserver.info*
*username@mailserver.org.se*
*username.moretext@mailserver.mil*
*username@mailserver.co.uk*
*user-name.moretext.sometext@mailserver.se*

To break down the regular expression

```
/^((([\-\w]+)\.?)+@((([\-\w]+)\.?)+\.[a-zA-Z]{2,4}$/;
```

use the following steps:

**Step 1:** `^`      Go to the beginning of the line.

**Step 2:** `([\-\w]+)\.?`      The user name consists of one or more dashes or word characters grouped by parentheses, followed by one (or not one) literal period. Because the dot is outside the parentheses there will be either one or zero dots for the list of word characters, not two or three dots in a row.

---

3. As of this writing, domain names have at least two characters.

Step 3:      `((\[\-\w\]+)\.?)+`          The user name may consist of more than one set of word characters separated by a single dots, as in *Joe.Shmoe.somebody*.

Step 4:      `@`          A literal @ symbol is required in the e-mail address.

Step 5:      `(\[\-\w\]+)\.?)+`          The mail server's name is like the user's name, a group of word characters separated by a dot. Same as step 3.

Step 6:      `[a-zA-Z]{2,4}`          The domain name follows the mail server's name. A single dot separates the server from the domain. The domain name consists of between two and four alphabetic characters; e.g., *savageman@imefdm.usmc.mil* or *patricia.person@sweden.sun.com*.

Step 7:      `$`          The end of the line anchor assures that no extra characters can be added onto the end of the e-mail address.

Example 13.45 uses a regular expression to check for a valid e-mail address.

**EXAMPLE  13.45**

```
    <html><head><title>Validating E-Mail Addresses</title>
    <script language="JavaScript">
1   function ok_Email(eform){
2      var regex = /^((\[\-\w]+)\.?)+@((\[\-\w]+)\.?)+\.[a-zA-Z]{2,4}$/;
3      if(regex.test(eform.user_email.value)){
4         return true;
       }
       else{
5         alert("Enter a valid email address");
          return false;
       }
    }
    </script>
    </head>
    <hr>
    <body>
    <h2> Checking for Valid Email Address </h2>
6   <form name="formtest"
7      action="http://localhost/cgi-bin/environ.pl"
       method="post"
8      onSubmit="return ok_Email(this);">
    <p>
    Please enter your email address: <BR>
    <input type="text" size=40 name="user_email">
    <p>
    <input type=submit value="Send">
    </body></html>
```

## EXPLANATION

1   A function called *ok_Email* is defined. It takes one parameter, a reference to the form started on line 6.

2   The regular expression is assigned the variable *regex*. The regular expression reads: Start at the beginning of the string (^), look for one or more alphanumeric characters and/or a dash followed by a literal dot (or not one). The literal period is outside the parentheses, meaning that in each group of word characters, there will be only one (or not one) period; e.g., *abc.xyz*. The entire expression is in parentheses followed by a + sign. This means that the pattern can be repeated one or more times; e.g., *abc.xyz.yaddy.yady.yady*. Next comes a literal @ symbol, required in all e-mail addresses. The mail server name comes right after the @ sign. Like the user name, it is represented by one or more alphanumeric characters or a dash, followed by a literal dot (\.). Now we have *Joe.Blow@aol* or *Dan-Sav@stamford*, etc. This pattern, like the first pattern, can be repeated one or more times. The domain name part of the address comes next; a literal dot, and at least two but not more than four alphabetic characters, *[a-zA-Z]{2,4}*; e.g., *JoeBlow@Chico.com, danny@Stamford.edu, .se, .uk*, etc. There are other varieties that could also be considered, such as *john@localhost*, but for most e-mail addresses, the regular expression used in this example should suffice.

3   The regular expression *test()* method takes the value of the user input, *user_email.value*, and returns *true* if the pattern in the regular expression matched the user's input.

4   The e-mail address entered is tested to be valid. A *true* value is returned and the form will be submitted to the server. A valid e-mail address does not mean that if mail is sent to that address it will necessarily be delivered; e.g., *santa@north-pole.org* is syntactically valid, but there is no guarantee that *santa* is a real user (unless you still believe!).

5   If an invalid e-mail address was entered, the alert box will appear with this message. The *ok_Email()* function will return *false*, and the form will not be submitted.

6   The form named *formtest* starts here.

7   This is the URL of the CGI script that will be called on the server side when the form is submitted.

8   The *onSubmit* event handler is triggered when the user presses the submit button. The value assigned to the event is a function called *ok_Email* that will return *true* if the e-mail address is valid and *false*, if not. The form will be sent to the server only if the return value is *true*. See Figure 13.46.

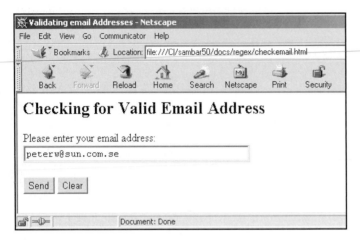

**Figure 13.46**   The user enters a valid e-mail address.

## 13.4.8   Credit Card Validation

When validating a credit card number, you can do some preliminary checking but real card validation is done on the server side through a software product designed specifically for that purpose.[4] Before issuing a card, there are certain rules that must be followed when creating card numbers, such as how many numbers there are, what prefix is used by a particular card type, whether the entire number fits a certain formula, and valid expiration dates. For preliminary checking, you can test, for example, to see if a person enters valid digits for a Visa card and that the expiration date is later than the current date, but you can't really tell if the user's card has gone over the limit, was cancelled or stolen, or that he even owns it. Checking whether the card is active and has a sufficent balance to cover a sale is performed by the banking system backing the card.

**The Expiration Date of the Card.**   A valid expiration date is a month and year that haven't gone by. The month and year are represented as two digits: 01 for January, 11 for November, and 03 for the year 2003. The following example defines a function to test for a valid expiration date based on a one to two-digit month and a two-digit or four-digit year.

---

4. For a guide to credit card validation software, go to *http://www.winsite.com/business/cc/*.

**EXAMPLE 13.46**

```
     <html>
     <head>
     <title>Testing Expiration Dates</title>
     <script language="javascript">
1    function validExpire(form) {
2        var now = new Date();
3        var thismonth = (now.getMonth() + 1);
4        var thisyear = now.getFullYear() ;
5        var expireYear = parseInt(form.expireYear.value);
         var yearLength = form.expireYear.value.length;
         var expireMonth = parseInt(form.expireMonth.value);
         if( yearLength == 2 ){
             expireYear += 2000;
         }
6        if ((expireMonth < thismonth  && expireYear == thisyear)
                 || expireMonth > 12){
             alert("Invalid month");
             return false;
         }
7        else if ( expireYear < thisyear) {
             alert("Invalid year");
             return false;
         }
         else {
             return true;
         }
     }
     </script>
     </head>
     <body>
8    <form name="myForm"
         action="http://127.0.0.1/cgi-bin/env.cgi"
9        onSubmit="return validExpire(this)">
     <p>
     Enter the month (02 or 2):
     <input name="expireMonth" type="text" size=5>
     <p>
     Enter the year (2003 or 03):
     <input name="expireYear" type="text" size=5>
     <input type="submit" value="submit">
     <input type="reset" value="clear">
     </form>
     </body>
     </html>
```

## EXPLANATION

1  A function called *validExpire()* is defined. It takes one parameter, a reference to a form. Its purpose is to validate the expiration date of a credit card.

2  A new *Date* object is created and assigned to the variable called *now*.

3  Using the *getMonth()* method, we get this month (months start at zero) and add 1.

4  Using the *getFullYear()* method, we get the current year, as *2003*.

5  The *parseInt()* function converts the expiration year, as typed in by the user, to an integer. Then we get the length of the year, and convert the month into an integer. If the number of characters in the year, *yearLength*, is 2, then 2000 is added to the *expireYear* value. If the user typed 02, then the new value is 2002.

6  If the value of *expireMonth* is less than the value of *thisMonth* and the value of *expireYear* is equal to the value of *thisyear,* or the value of *expireMonth* is greater than 12, the number entered is invalid. So a card in invalid if it has a month prior to this month and the card expires this year, or the month is over 12, because there are only 12 months in a year.

7  If the expiration year is prior to this year, it is also invalid.

8  The form starts here.

9  The *onSubmit* event handler is triggered after the user fills out the form and presses the submit button. When he does, the function called *validExpire()* is called. It will return *true* if the expiration date is valid, and the form will be sent to the URL assigned to the *action* attribute of the form. See Figure 13.47.

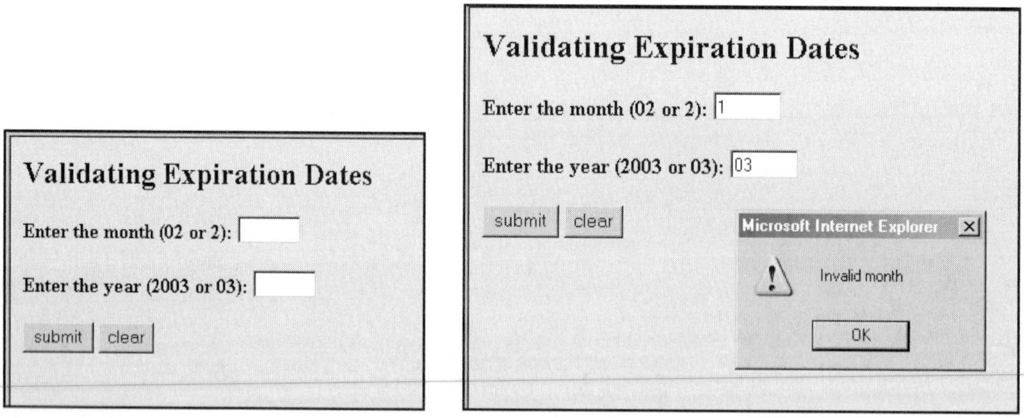

**Figure 13.47**  The form before the user enters anything (left); the user enters a month and year, but the month has already gone by (right).

**Checking for Valid Type, Prefix, and Length.**   In Figure 13.49 the major credit cards are listed along with the identifying characteristics of account numbers for each. All the characters must be numbers. Each type of card has a prefix value; e.g., MasterCard's prefix is a number between 51 and 56, and Visa's is the number 4. Validation routines to check for a prefix and the correct number of characters are shown in Example 13.47.

Steps for credit card validation:

1. Remove any spaces or dashes, then test that the result is a numeric value.
2. Check to see if the user has selected a valid credit card type such as MasterCard or Visa, the correct prefix for the card, and a valid length for the number of characters in the card.
3. Apply the Lunh formula for further validation.

**EXAMPLE   13.47**

```
        <html>
        <head>
        <title>Checking for Valid CC Type and Length</title>
        <script language="JavaScript">
1       function checkCC(myForm){
            var cc_type;
            var cc_length;
2           if (myForm.select1.selectedIndex==0){
                cc_type="Visa";
            }
            else if( myForm.select1.selectedIndex==1){
                cc_type="MasterCard";
            }
            else if( myForm.select1.selectedIndex==2){
                cc_type="Discover";
            }
            else {
                alert("You didn't select a card type.");
            }
3           cc_length=myForm.text.value.length;
4           switch(cc_type){
5           case "Visa" :
6               if ( cc_length == 13 || cc_length == 16){
                    return true;
                }
                else{
                    alert("Invalid length");
                    return false;
                }
                break;
```

EXAMPLE 13.47 (CONTINUED)

```
7       case "MasterCard":
           if ( cc_length == 16){
              return true;
           }
           else{
              alert("Invalid length");
              return false;
           }
           break;
8       case "Discover":
           if ( cc_length == 16){
              return true;
           }
           else{
              alert("Invalid length");
              return false;
           }
           break;
        default:
           alert("Invalid type");
           return false;
           break;
        }
    }
    </script>
    </head>
    <body bgcolor="lightblue">
    <font size="+1" face="arial">
9   <form name="form1" onSubmit="return checkCC(this);">
    Please select a credit card from the menu:
    <p>
10  <select name="select1" size="3">
        <option value="Visa">Visa</option>
        <option value="MC">MasterCard</option>
        <option value="Dis">Discover</option>
    </select>
    <p>
    Please enter your card number:
    <p>
11  <input type=textbox name="text" size=30>
    <p>
12  <input type=submit value="Check card">
    <input type=reset>
    </form>
    </body>
    </html>
```

## EXPLANATION

1   A function called *checkCC()* is defined. It takes one parameter, a reference to a form.

2   If the value of *selectedIndex is 0*, the first option in the *select* list was chosen, a Visa card. The rest of the statements in this *if* block check to see which card was selected if it wasn't this one.

3   The variable *cc_length* is assigned the number of characters that were typed into the text box; that is, the number of characters in the credit card number.

4   The *switch* statement will be used to check for valid card number lengths for whichever card the user selected from the select menu. The variable *cc_type* contains the card type: Visa, MasterCard, or Discover.

5   If the card is a Visa card, the *case* statements will be used to check for a valid length.

6   The valid length for the Visa credit card number is between 13 and 16 characters (as shown in Figure 13.49). If the card number length is between these numbers, *true* is returned.

7   MasterCard is checked here. Its number must consist of 16 characters.

8   Discover is checked here. Its number must consist of 16 characters.

9   The form starts here. The *onSubmit* handler will be triggered when the user presses the submit button. At that time the credit card will be checked for a valid number of characters in the number provided by the user. This is not a complete check. You can combine the other functions from this section to provide a more thorough check; we haven't checked here to see if the value entered is numeric, has strange characters, or empty fields.

10  The select menu starts here with three options, each a credit card type.

11  This is the text box where the user enters the card number.

12  When the user presses the submit button, the *onSubmit* handler is invoked, and if the credit card number passes the validity test, off goes the form!

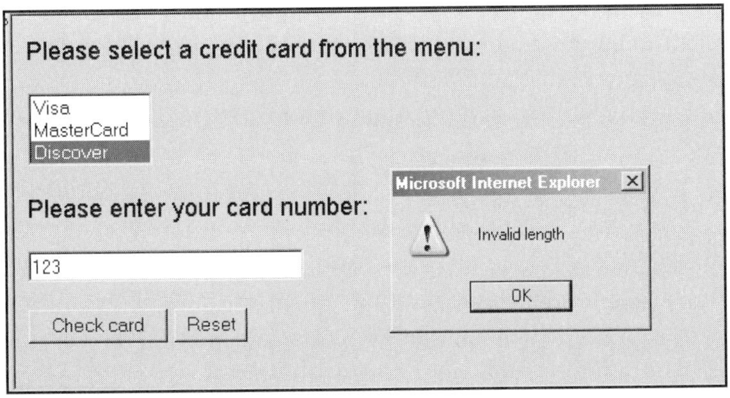

**Figure 13.48**
The number of characters in the credit card number should be 16 for Discover card.

| CARD TYPE | Prefix | Length | Check digit algorithm |
|---|---|---|---|
| MASTERCARD | 51-55 | 16 | mod 10 |
| VISA | 4 | 13, 16 | mod 10 |
| AMEX | 34 <br> 37 | 15 | mod 10 |
| Diners Club/ Carte Blanche | 300-305 <br> 36 <br> 38 | 14 | mod 10 |
| Discover | 6011 | 16 | mod 10 |
| enRoute | 2014 <br> 2149 | 15 | any |
| JCB | 3 | 16 | mod 10 |
| JCB | 2131 <br> 1800 | 15 | mod 10 |

**Figure 13.49**  Some valid credit cards, their prefix, length, and whether they pass the Lunh test based on modulus 10, shown below. Source: *http://www.beachnet.com/~hstiles/ cardtype.html*.

**The Lunh Formula.**    The credit card number can be subjected to an additional mathematical test, called the Lunh formula, which it must pass in order to be valid. The following steps are required to validate the primary account number:

Step 1:  Double the value of every other digit starting with the next-to-right-most digit.

Step 2:  If any of the resulting values has more than two digits, then its digits must be added together to produce a single digit.

Step 3:  Add the sum of all the digits <u>not</u> doubled in Step 1 to the sum of the digits transformed from Steps 1 and 2.

Step 4:  If the result is exactly divisible by 10 (that is, if the result ends in a zero, 30, 40, 50, etc.), then the number is valid—providing of course that it's of the correct length and bears a correct prefix for that type of card.

For example, to validate the primary account number *49927398716*:

Step 1:  Starting from the next to the right-most digit, multiply every other number by 2 (the number in bold text).

```
4   9   9   2   7   3   9   8   7   1   6
    9x2     2x2     3x2     8x2     1x2
    18      4       6       16      2
```

Step 2: If any numbers resulting from Step 1 have more than one digit, add those numbers together.

```
(1+8)   (1+6)
_____
   9       7
```

Step 3: Add up the top row of numbers that were not doubled (not in bold) to the bottom row of numbers after Step 2 was finished. Bottom numbers are in parentheses.

```
4 + (9) + 9 + (4) + 7 + (6) + 9 +( 7) + 7 + (2) + 6
```

Step 4: If the result of Step 3 is divisible exactly by 10 (i.e., leaves no remainder), the card is valid. The result of Step 3 is 70. The card number is valid if the card type is valid, as long as the length of numbers entered is valid, and it has the correct prefix for that type of card.

## 13.4.9 Putting It All Together

After writing the functions that validate each field of the form, they will be put together in a single script to check all form entries. The following example combines just two of the functions, to keep the example from being too large. One function, *ok_Form()*, calls the functions that check individual entries; for example, *ok_Email()* checks for valid e-mail and returns either *true* or *false*, and *ok_Phone()* checks for a valid phone number. After all of the entries have been checked, the *ok_Form()* function returns either *true* or *false* to the *onSubmit* event handler. If *ok_Form()* returns *true*, the form will be submitted to the server; if not, it is stopped. If we add in all the credit card validation functions, this program will get really large. Why don't you try it?

### EXAMPLE 13.48

```
        <html><head><title>Validating a Form</title>
        <script language="JavaScript">
1       function ok_Email(emform){
2           var regex=/^(([\-\w]+)\.?)+@(([\-\w]+)\.?)+\.[a-zA-Z]{2,4}$/;
3           if(regex.test(eform.user_email.value)){
                return true;
            }
            else{
                alert("Enter a valid email address");
                return false;
            }
```

**EXAMPLE  13.48 (CONTINUED)**

```
4   function ok_Phone(phform){
5       var regex = /^\(?\(?\d{3}\)\)?-?\s*\d{3}\s*-?\d{4}$/;
6       if(regex.test(phform.value)){
            return true;
        }
        else{
            return false;
        }
    }
7   function ok_Form(myform){
8       if (ok_Email(myform.user_email)== false){
9           alert( "Invalid email address");
10          myform.user_email.focus();
11          myform.user_email.select();
12          return false;
        }
13      if (ok_Phone(myform.user_phone) == false){
            alert( "Invalid phone number");
            myform.user_phone.focus();
            myform.user_phone.select();
            return false;
        }
14      return true;
    }
    </script>
    </head>
    <hr>
    <body bgcolor="lightgreen"> <font face="arial" size="+1">
    <h2> Checking Form Input</h2>
    <form name="myform"
        action="http://localhost/cgi-bin/environ.pl" method="post"
15      onSubmit="return ok_Form(this);">
    <p>
    Please enter your email address: <BR>
    <input type="text" size=40 name="user_email">
    <p>
    Please enter your phone number: <BR>
    <input type="text" size=12 name="user_phone">
    <p>
    <input type=submit value="Send">
    </form>
    </body>
    </html>
```

# EXPLANATION

1   The function to validate an e-mail address is defined. It is called by the *ok_Form()* function on line 8.

2   The local variable called *regex* is assigned a regular expression, explained in Example 13.45.

3   The e-mail address entered by the user, *eform.user_email.value*, is tested against the regular expression for validity. The regular expression *test()* method returns *true* or *false* to the *ok_Form* function, line 8.

4   The function to validate a phone number is defined. It is called by the *ok_Form()* function on line 13.

5   The local variable called *regex* is assigned regular expression .

6   The phone number entered by the user, *eform.user_phform.value*, is tested against the regular expression for validity. The regular expression *test()* method returns *true* or *false* to the *ok_Form* function, line 13.

7   This is the big function that returns the final verdict. Did the user provide a valid e-mail address and phone number? If so, the function returns *true*, line 14.

8   The *ok_Email()* function is called with the user's e-mail input. If the *ok_Email()* function returns *false*, the user entered an invalid address, and he will be alerted.

9   The alert dialog box sends this message if the e-mail address is not valid.

10  The *focus()* method puts the cursor in the text box, so that the user can start typing there.

11  The *select()* method highlights the text in a field.

12  If *false* is returned to the *onSubmit* handler on line 15, the form will not be submitted.

13  If an invalid phone number was entered, *false* will be returned to the *onSubmit* handler on line 15.

14  If both the e-mail address and the phone number are valid, the *ok_Form()* function returns *true* to the event handler on line 15, and the form will be submitted to the server's URL assigned to the form's *action* attribute.

15  The *onSubmit* event is triggered when the user presses the submit button. The handler is a function called *ok_Form()*. It is the main validation function for this form. If *true* is returned, the form will be submitted; otherwise, not. See Figures 13.50 and 13.51.

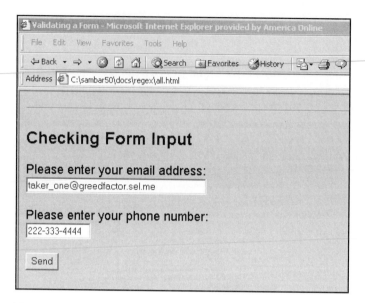

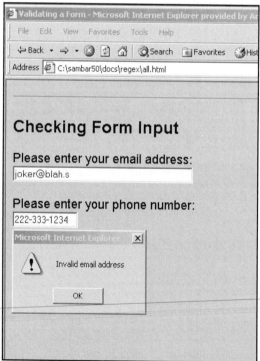

**Figure 13.50**    The user enters a valid e-mail address (top); the user entered an invalid e-mail address because there is only one letter in the domain name (bottom).

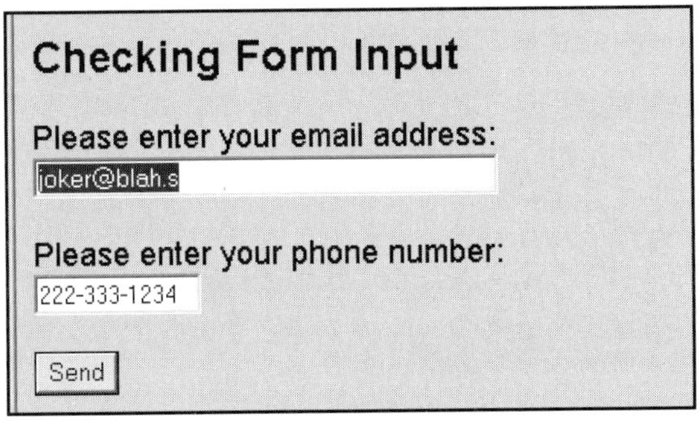

Checking Form Input

Please enter your email address:
joker@blah.s

Please enter your phone number:
222-333-1234

Send

**Figure 13.51** The *focus()* and *select()* methods focus on and highlight the invalid entry.

## EXERCISES

1. Write a regular expression that will:
   a. Return *true* if a string begins with letters between *a* and *f*, either upper- or lowercase.
   b. Return *true* if a string contains a number.
   c. In the string *My friend is Betsy Ann Savage*, capture the first and last name and display them in reverse, as *Savage, Betsy*.
   d. Replace *Betsy* with *Elizabeth* in the previous string.
   e. In the string *123abcdefg584*, replace all the letters with *XXX*.
   f. Prompt the user for a string of text, then print *true* if the string ends in three or more numbers.
   g. Prompt the user for a string of text, then display the first three characters in the string.
   h. Prompt the user for a string of text that includes letters and numbers, then print *true* if the string does <u>not</u> contain the number 4 or the letter *a*, or print *false* if not.
   i. Prompt the user for his first and last name. Display *true* if the name starts with an uppercase letter followed by lowercase letters. The last name would be similar to the following: *Jones, Smith, McFadden, O'Reilly*, and *Jones-Smith*.

2. Validate an international phone number that is represented as follows:

   *011 49 762 899 20*

3. Start with a one- or two-character code for a United Kingdom postal district, such as B for Birmingham or RH for Red Hill, followed by a one- or two-digit number to represent a sector within that district. For example, RH1 is Red Hill district, sector 1; CM23 is the Chelmsford district, sector 23; and B1 is Birmingham district, sector 1. Following the district and sector is a space, followed by a digit and two characters, such as 4GJ.

   For example: *CM23 2QP*          where:
                                     *CM* = Chelmsford district
                                     *23* = sector 23
                                     *2QP* = a particular road.

   Create a regular expression to validate a UK postal code as described above.

4. Validate a credit card number using the Lunh formula.

# chapter

# 14

# Cookies

## 14.1 What Are Cookies?

The Web protocol, HTTP, was designed to be stateless to keep transactions between a browser and server brief and cut down on the overhead of keeping connections open. Stateless means that after a transaction takes place between the browser and server, the connection is lost and neither the browser nor server have any recollection of what transpired between one session and the next. But as the Internet grew and people started filling up shopping carts with all kinds of goodies, ordering everything from groceries to music, books, prescription drugs, and even cars and homes, it became necessary for merchants to remember what their customers purchased, their preferences, registration numbers, IDs, and so on. Enter Netscape way back in 1994 with the cookie. A cookie is a local file used to store information, and it is persistent; that is, it is maintained between browser sessions and remains even when the user shuts down his computer. The cookie idea became very popular and is now supported by all major browsers.

The term "cookie" comes from an old programming trick for debugging and testing routines in a program. A text file, called a "magic cookie" was created. It contained text that was shared by two routines so that they could communicate with each other. The cookie feature started by Netscape[1] is also just a little piece of textual data that is stored in a file (often called the cookie jar) on the hard drive of the client (browser). It contains information about the viewer that can be retrieved and used at a later time to welcome him to your site, and based on past visits, show him a new book by his favorite author, display the latest stock quotes, or take him to CNN Europe when he wants to view the news. The HTTP server sends the cookie to the browser when the browser connects for the first time and from then on, the browser returns a copy of the cookie to the server each time it connects. The information is passed back and forth between the server and browser via HTTP headers.

---

1. See *www.netscape.com/newsref/std/cookie_spec.html* for cookie specification.

Cookies can make a Web page personal and friendly, and store important information about the user's language, reading, or music preferences, how many times he has visited your site, track items in a shopping cart, and more. But they can also be annoying, and some question the security of putting unknown data on their hard drive. Love 'em or hate 'em, they're an intrinsic part of the Web. But you do have a say about whether or not to use them. If you don't like cookies, you can turn them off, and remove all of them from your hard drive. For example, if using IE, you can delete cookies by going to the Tools menu and then to Internet options (see Figure 14.1); in Navigator, look at the Tools menu, go to Cookie Manager, and from there you can block all cookies for this site (see Figure 14.2).

Unlike Grandma's old-fashioned cookie jar that could be packed full of sugar cookies (and the calories kept out of sight), Web browser cookies occupy a limited amount of space. Browsers usually can't store more than 300 cookies and servers not more than 20. Storage is usually limited to only 4 kilobytes per cookie, so you can't store a lot of information. The actual filename that holds the cookie data varies on different platforms. Netscape Navigator (Windows) stores cookies in a file named *cookies.txt* in Navigator's system directory; IE stores them in the Window\Cookies directory, and on the Mac, they are found in a file called *MagicCookie*.

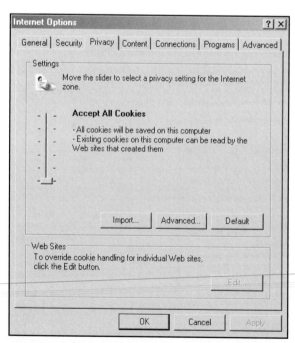

**Figure 14.1**   Internet Explorer—Enabling and disabling cookies.

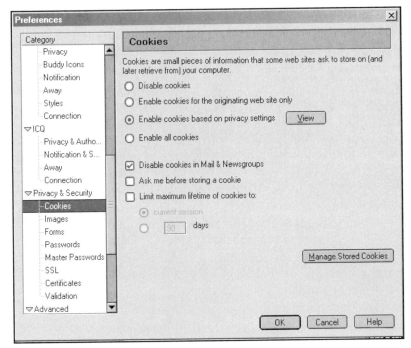

**Figure 14.2**  Netscape 7—Enabling and disabling cookies.

## 14.1.1  Cookie Ingredients

Cookies are often sent from a CGI program on the server side to the browser through HTTP request and response headers, but with JavaScript you can set cookies on the local browser, eliminating the need for the CGI program to handle them, and thereby cutting down on server activity. The cookie's default lifetime is the length of the current session. Then they are destroyed. See the expiration attribute below.

Cookies are composed of text in the form of key/value pairs, often nicknamed "crumbs," and up to 20 pairs can be stored in a single cookie string. The browser stores only one cookie per page.

When making cookies, the crumbs consist of *name=value* pairs, called attributes, that must be terminated with a semicolon. Within the string, semicolons, commas, or whitespace characters are not allowed. The HTTP *Set-Cookie* header has the following format:

**FORMAT**

```
Set-Cookie: name=value; [expires=date}; [path=path];
[domain=domainname]; [secure];
```

Example:

```
Set-Cookie: id="Bob";expires=Monday, 21-Oct-05 12:00:00
GMT;domain="bbb.com"; path="/"; secure;
```

## 14.1.2   The Attributes of a Cookie

When setting the cookie, it is important to understand the components of a cookie. It has a name and a value and another set of optional attributes to determine the expiration date, the domain, path, and whether the cookie must be sent over a secure communications channel (HTTPS). All of these attributes are assigned as strings.

**Name.**   The actual cookie text consists of the name of the cookie and the value stored there. It can be a session ID, a user name, or whatever you like.

**FORMAT**

```
nameofcookie=value;
```

Examples:

```
id=456;
email=joe@abc.com;
name=Bob;
```

Don't confuse the value with what the cookie is named. The name of the cookie is on the left-hand side of the = sign and the cookie text that gets stored there is on the right-hand side. The value assigned is a string. To add multiple values to the string, you must use unique characters to separate the values, such as *Bill*Sanders*345*. (With JavaScript you can also use the built-in *escape()* method, which returns URL encoding for a string, acceptable to the browser. See "Assigning Cookie Attributes" on page 482.)

**Expiration Date.**   The cookie normally expires when the current browser session ends, which gives it little value, but you can specify an expiration date that will let it persist, by using the following format:

**FORMAT**

```
;expires=Weekday, DD-MON-YY  HH:MM::SS GMT
```

Example:

```
;expires= Friday, 15-Mar-04 12:00:00 GMT
```

The day of the week is specified by *Weekday*, the day of the month by *DD*, the first three letters of the month by *MON*, and the last two numbers of the year by *YY* (e.g., *03* or *04*). The hour, minutes, and seconds are specified in *HH:MM:SS* and the GMT time zone is always used. Some cookies last for days, but it's possible for them to even last for years. It's up to the designer to decide how long a cookie should live. Setting the expiration date also limits the amount of possible damage that could be done if the cookie is intercepted by some hacker. Once the cookie has expired it is called stale and is automatically destroyed.

**Domain Name.**   The domain name, not commonly used, specifies a general domain name to which the cookie should apply. It allows the cookie to be shared among multiple servers instead of just the one you're on. If you don't use the full *http://domain* syntax, then a leading dot must precede the domain name.

**FORMAT**

```
; domain=.domain_name
; domain=http://somedomain.com
```

Example:

```
; domain=.kajinsky.com
; domain=http://kajinksy.com
```

**Path.**   The path is used to specify where the cookie is valid for a particular server. Setting a path for the cookie allows other pages from the same domain to share a cookie.

**FORMAT**

```
; path=pathname
```

Example:

```
; path=/home
```

**Secure.**   If a cookie is secure, it must be sent over a secure communication channel (HTTPS server).

## 14.2 Creating a Cookie with JavaScript

In the following examples, we will create a cookie, view the cookie, and then destroy it. It is important to note when you are setting cookies that they are stored in the browser's memory and not written to the hard drive until you exit the browser.

### 14.2.1   The Cookie Object

The cookie is stored by JavaScript as a document object for both reading and writing cookie data. Cookies are made by assigning attributes to the *cookie* property. When you start your browser, if there are cookies, they pertain to the current document. The *document.cookie* property contains a string of *name=value* pairs representing the names of all the cookies and their corresponding values, such as a session ID number or a user ID. All the other attributes set for the cookie, such as expiration date, path, and secure, are not visible. In a JavaScript program, if you execute the statement shown in Figure 14.3, you will see all the cookies set for this page.

**Figure 14.3**   Using *alert(document.cookie);*.

When you reload the page, the *document.cookie* property will contain all the cookie text saved for that page.

### 14.2.2   Assigning Cookie Attributes

To create a cookie, assign the *name=value* pairs to the *document.cookie* property. Be careful with quotes, making sure the variables you use are not quoted, but the text that the cookie needs, such as the word *"name"*, and *"="* are quoted. Also, this will be a big string where the different parts are concatenated together with the + operator. The following format sets a cookie using all possible attributes. Those attributes enclosed in square brackets are optional:

## FORMAT

```
name=value;[expires=date];[path=path];[domain=somewhere.com];[secure]
```

**Example:**

```
document.cookie="id=" + form1.cookie.value ";expires=" +
expiration_date+";path=/";
```

**The *escape()* and *unescape()* Built-In Functions.**   It is important to know that when assigning string *name=value* attributes to a cookie, you cannot use whitespace, semicolons, or commas. The *escape()* function will encode the string object by converting all non-alphanumeric characters to their hexadecimal equivalent, preceded by a percent sign; for example, *%20* represents a space and *%26* represents an ampersand. In order to send information back and forth between browser and server, the browser encodes the data in what is called URI encoding. You can see this encoding in the location bar of your browser; when you go to Google and search for something, you will see the search string in the location bar of the browser all encoded. Since the browser handles cookies, the cookie strings can be encoded with JavaScript's built-in *escape()* function to ensure that the cookie values are valid.

The *unescape()* function converts the URI-encoded string back into its original format and returns it. The *encodeURI()* and *decodeURI()* built-in functions are a more recent version of *escape()* and *unescape()* and do not encode as many characters.

## EXAMPLE 14.1

```
        <html><head><title>The escape() Method</title>
        </head><center><h2>URL Encoding </h2>
        <script language="JavaScript">
1       function seeEncoding(form){
            var myString = form.input.value;
2           alert(escape(myString));
        }
3       function seeDecoding(form){
            var myString = form.input.value;
4           alert(unescape(myString));
        }
        </script>
        <body background="cookebg.jpg" >
```

EXAMPLE 14.1 (CONTINUED)

```
<form name="form1">
    Type in a string of text:
    <p>
    <input type="text" name="input" size=40>
    <p>
    <input type="button"
        value="See encoding"
5       onClick="seeEncoding(this.form);">
    <p>
    <input type="button"
        value="See decoding"
6       onClick="seeDecoding(this.form);">
    <p>
</form>
</center>
</body>
</html>
```

**EXPLANATION**

1   A function called *seeEncoding()* is defined. It takes a reference to a form as its only parameter.

2   The built-in *escape()* function is used to URI encode the string that was entered as input by the user.

3   A function called *seeDecoding()* is defined. It takes a reference to a form as its only parameter.

4   The built-in *unescape()* function is used to convert the URI encoded string back into its original ASCII format.

5   When the user clicks this button, the *onClick* event is triggered and the encoded string will appear in an alert dialog box.

6   When the user clicks this button, the *onClick* event triggers a function that will decode the encoded string. See Figures 14.4 and 14.5.

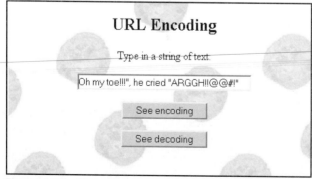

**Figure 14.4**  Using the *escape()* and *unescape()* functions.

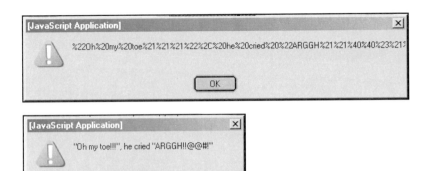

**Figure 14.5** The user pressed the "See encoding" button (top); the user pressed the "See decoding" button (bottom).

### 14.2.3 Let's Make a Cookie!

Now that we have all the ingredients, let's put them together and make a cookie, then pull it out of the oven (your program) and voila! a delicious cookie for your browser. The following example creates a cookie called *"name"*. The value assigned to it will be the user's name. You will see this *name=value* pair in the *document.cookie* property.

**EXAMPLE 14.2**

```
        <html><head><title>Making a Cookie</title>
        <script language="JavaScript">
1   function makeCookie(form){
2       var when = new Date();
        when.setTime(when.getTime() + 24 * 60 * 60 * 1000);
                                        // 24 hours from now
3       when.setFullYear(when.getFullYear() + 1);
                                        // One year from now
        yname=form.yourname.value;
4       document.cookie=escape("name")+"="+escape(yname)+
            ";expires="+when.toGMTString();
        alert(document.cookie);
    }
5   function welcome(myForm){
        you=myForm.yourname.value;
6       var position=document.cookie.indexOf("name=");
        if ( position != -1){
            var begin = position + 5;
            var end=document.cookie.indexOf(";", begin);
            if(end == -1){ end=document.cookie.length;}
7       you= unescape(document.cookie.substring(begin, end));
8       alert("Welcome " + you);
    }
```

**EXAMPLE** 14.2 (CONTINUED)

```
          else{ alert("No cookies today");}
     }
     </script>
     </head>
     <body background="cookiebg.jpg" onLoad="document.form1.reset()" >
     <center>
     <h2> Got milk?</h2>
     <form name="form1">
          What is your name?
          <br>
 9        <input type="text" name="yourname" >
          <p>
10        <input type="button" value="Make cookie"
               onClick="makeCookie(this.form);">
          <p>
11        <input type="button"
               value="Get Cookie" onClick="welcome(this.form);">
          <p>
     </form>
     </body>
     </html>
```

**EXPLANATION**

1   A function called *makeCookie()* is defined. It takes a reference to a form as its only parameter. This is the function that creates the cookie.

2   A new *Date* object is created and assigned to the variable called *when*.

3   The *Date* object creates a date a year from now. This will be the expiration date for the cookie.

4   The cookie is created. Its name is *"name"* and its value is the user's name, stored in *yname*. The attributes are escaped just in case the user added unwanted characters, such as spaces, commas, or semicolons. The expiration date is set to a year from now and is converted to GMT time, the required format for the *"expires"* attribute. Notice the quotes. If the text is literal for the attribute it must be quoted; if it is a variable value, then it is not quoted or JavaScript can't interpret it—very tricky getting these right.

5   A function called *welcome()* is created. It takes a reference to a form as its only parameter. Its purpose is to greet the user based on the cookie value.

6   The following statements are used to parse out the *value* attribute of the cookie. The beginning index position is set to where the *"name="* string starts in the cookie string. It will be at position 5 in this example. Starting at index position 0, position 5 takes us to the character directly after the = sign. The end position is either at the first semicolon or at the end of the string, whichever applies.

7   After getting the substring, the *value* part of the cookie, the *unescape()* function, will convert the URI-encoded string back into its original ASCII format.

8    The user is welcomed, all based on the value extracted from the cookie. The cookie lets Web sites know who you are so that you can get a personal greeting when you return to the site.

9    The user will enter his name in a text box field. See Figure 14.6.

10   When the user clicks this button, the *onClick* event is triggered, and the cookie will be made. See Figure 14.7.

11   When the user clicks this button, the *onClick* event is triggered, and the user will be welcomed by the name he entered in the text box. See Figure 14.8.

**Figure 14.6**
Making a cookie.

**Figure 14.7**
After making the cookie, the value of the *document.cookie* property is displayed.

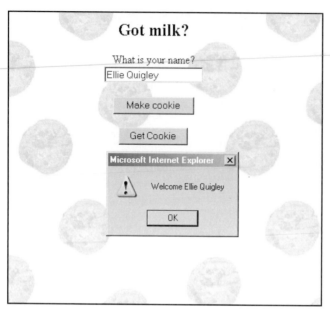

**Figure 14.8**    Retrieve the cookie and welcome the user!!

## 14.2.4  Retrieving Cookies from a Server

When retrieving cookies, you can only get those that were written for the server you are
on and written by you. You cannot read and write cookies that belong to someone else
or reside on a different server. In the last example, we got one cookie; in the following
example all the cookies for this page are displayed.

---

**EXAMPLE  14.3**

```
      <html><head><title>See my Cookies</title>
      </head>
1     <body background="cookebg.jpg" onLoad="document.form1.reset()" >
      <center>
      <h2> Got milk?</h2>
2     <form name="form1">
         Click to see document.cookie property
         <p>
3        <input type="button" value="See Cookie" onClick="seeCookie();">
         <p>
      </form>
      <script language="JavaScript">
4        function seeCookie(){
5           if(document.cookie == ""){
                document.write("No cookies");
            }
```

EXAMPLE   14.3 (CONTINUED)

```
          else{
6             var myCookie = document.cookie.split("; ");
7             for(var i=0;i<myCookie.length; i++){
                 document.write("<body bgcolor=darkblue>
                                 <font face=verdana color=white>");
              //   document.write("<b>Cookie: " +
                                 myCookie[i].split("=")[0] +"<br>");
8                document.write("<b>Cookie: " + myCookie[i] +
                                 "<br>");
              }
           }
        }
     </script>
     </center>
     </body>
     </html>
```

**EXPLANATION**

1   After the document is loaded, the *onLoad* event is triggered and the values in the
    form are cleared with the *reset()* method.

2   This is the start of an HTML form, called *form1*.

3   When the user clicks the button, the *onClick* event is triggered, and the *seeCook-
    ie()* function will be called to display all the cookies for this page.

4   A function called *seeCookie()* is defined.

5   First, we check to see if there are any cookies at all. If not, the alert box will say so.

6   The *split* function splits up the cookie string by semicolons and returns an array
    called *myCookie*.

7   The *for* loop iterates through each element of the *myCookie* array until the end of
    the array, *myCookie.length*, is reached.

8   The value of the cookie is displayed. See Figure 14.9.

Cookie: name=Ellie%20Quigley

**Figure 14.9**   IE cookies.

## 14.2.5   Deleting a Cookie

If you want to delete a cookie for the current page, set the expiration date of the cookie to a date earlier than the current date. This will cause the cookie to be deleted when the session ends.

**EXAMPLE** 14.4

```
         <html><head><title>Delete Cookie</title><head>
         <script name = "JavaScript">
          var i = 0;
1        function delCookie (cookieName){
2           document.cookie = cookieName + "=" +"; expires=Thu, 01-Jan-1970
               00:00:01 GMT";
            alert("Cookie was deleted!");
            seeCookie();
         }
3        function seeCookie(){
            if(document.cookie == ""){
               alert("No cookies");
               return false;
            }
            else{
4              var myCookie = document.cookie.split("; ");
               if ( i < myCookie.length ){
5              document.form1.cookietype.value =
                  myCookie[i].split("=")[0];
                  i++;   // Increase the index value to see the next cookie
               }
               else{alert("No more cookies");}
            }
         }
         </script>
         </head>
6        <body background="cookebg.jpg" onLoad="seeCookie()" >
         <center>
         <h2> Got milk?</h2>
7        <form name="form1">
8           Is this the cookie you want to delete?
            <br>
            <input type="text" name="cookietype" >
            <p>
9           <input type="radio"
               name="radio"
               value="choice"
9              onClick="delCookie(document.form1.cookietype.value);">Yes
```

**EXAMPLE   14.4 (CONTINUED)**

```
            <input type="radio"
                name="radio"
                value="choice"
10              onClick="seeCookie();">No
            <p>
        </form>
        </center>
        </body>
        </html>
```

**EXPLANATION**

1   The function called *delCookie()* will remove a requested cookie. The name of the cookie, *cookieName*, is passed as a parameter to the function.

2   The expiration date of the cookie is set to the beginning of UNIX time, also called epoch time—January 1, 1970. Certainly this date has passed and the cookie will be deleted. After the cookie has been deleted, the *seeCookie()* function will be called, and the user will be presented with another cookie. If he clicks on the Yes radio button, that cookie will be removed.

3   The function called *SeeCookie()* will check to see if there are any cookies remaining in the *document.cookie* property. If not, the program is over. To actually see if the cookies were deleted, close this session, and then reopen it.

4   By splitting up the *document.cookie* property by semicolons, an array is created consisting of a *name* and *value* attribute of the cookie.

5   The first element of the array, the name of the cookie, is assigned to the text box represented as *document.form1.cookietype.value*. It will appear in the text box for the user to see. Each time the function is called, the next cookie will be assigned to the text box, giving the user the option to delete that cookie.

6   When the document has finished loading, the *onLoad* event is triggered, and calls the *seeCookie()* function. The first cookie name will appear in the text box.

7   The HTML form starts here.

8   The text box input type will be used to hold the cookie name.

9   This radio button, when clicked, will called the *delCookie()* function. The user wants to remove this cookie. See Figure 14.10.

10   This radio button, when clicked, means the user doesn't want to delete this cookie but would like to see the next cookie. When the user clicks No, the *seeCookie()* function will be called. After all the cookies have been shown, the alert message will say "*No more cookies*".

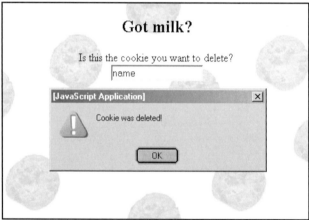

**Figure 14.10**   The cookie's name is *name*. If the user clicks Yes (top), the cookie will be removed (bottom).

**Using the Browser to Remove Cookies.**   Another way to delete cookies is to go in your browser to the Tools menu in Navigator, then to the Cookie Manager, and then to Manage Stored Cookies. In IE, go to the Tools menu and Internet Options. See Figure 14.11. Then you can remove all or some cookies from the hard drive.

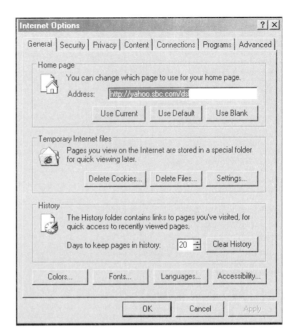

**Figure 14.11**   Netscape Navigator 7 Cookie Manager from the Tools menu (left); Internet Explorer from the Tools menu (right).

## 14.2.6   Cookie Help

Whether you like them, or hate them, you have complete control over whether to accept all cookies, some cookies, delete cookies, and so on. Check your particular browser for all of your options. For example, under the Help option in Navigator and IE, some of the cookie topics you might review are shown in Figure 14.12.

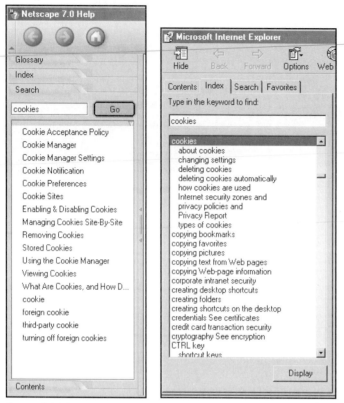

**Figure 14.12**   Cookie Help!

## EXERCISES

1. Create a form that contains a set of checkboxes with different types of coffees—
   espresso, cappucino, mocha, and so on. Ask the user for his name and room
   number and to select a type of coffee. Tell him you will be sending the coffee to
   his room number. Create a cookie to remember his preference. The next time
   he brings up the page, tell him there is a special rate for his (use the cookie
   value) favorite coffee.

2. Create a cookie that is assigned the user's favorite color. Change the background color of the document to that color.

# 15

# Dynamic HTML: Style Sheets, the DOM, and JavaScript

## 15.1 What Is Dynamic HTML?

Dynamic HTML, called DHTML, is really more than just a lively version of HTML. It consists of HTML4, the Document Object Model (DOM), JavaScript, and CSS (Cascading Style Sheets). CSS was introduced by the World Wide Web Consortium to help designers get more control over their Web pages by enhancing what HTML can do—it is used to stylize the content of a Web page. CSS is to a Web page what a hair stylist is to your hair. You can get a simple haircut for $9 or you can go to a fancy salon and hire a stylist to give you a really cool new look. Plain HTML gives you the $9 Web page, and DHTML takes your page to the styling salon to give it a dramatic new appearance. Whereas HTML is concerned with the structure and organization of a document, CSS is concerned with its layout and presentation. Since the initial style of the content is done with CSS, we'll start there. After that we'll use the DOM and JavaScript to dynamically change the style of the page after it has been loaded. For a complete discussion of Cascading Style Sheets (both CSS1 and CSS2) see *http://www.w3org/Style/CSS*.

## 15.2 What Is a Style Sheet?

*Webster's Dictionary* defines "style" as a manner of doing something very grandly; elegant, fashionable. Style sheets make HTML pages elegant by allowing the designer to create definitions to describe the layout and appearance of the page. This is done by creating a set of rules that define how an HTML element will look in the document. For example, if you want all *H1* elements to produce text with a green color, set in an Arial 14-point font face centered in the page, normally you would have to assign these attributes to each *H1* element as it occurs within the document, which could prove quite time consuming. With style sheets you can create the style once and have that definition apply to all *H1* elements in the document. If you don't have a lot of time to learn how to create style sheets, an excellent alternative is Macromedia's Dreamweaver MX. For more on authoring tools, see *http://www.w3.org/Style/CSS/#editors*.

### 15.2.1   What Does CSS Mean?

CSS is short for Cascading Style Sheets and is a standard defined by the World Wide Web Consortium (W3C), first made official in December of 1996. They are called cascading because the effects of a style can be inherited or cascaded down to other tags. This gets back to the parent/child relationship we talked about in Chapter 12, "Handling Events," and the DOM. If a style has been defined for a parent tag, any tags defined within that style may inherit that style. Suppose a style has been defined for a *<p>* tag. The text within these tags has been set to blue and the font is set to Arial. If within the *<p>* tag, another set of tags is embedded, such as *<b>* or *<em>*, then those tags will inherit the blue color and the Arial font. The style has cascaded down from the parent to the child. But this is a simplistic definition of cascading. The rules can be very complex and involve multiple style sheets coming from external sources as well as internal sources. And even though a browser may support style sheets, it may resolve the conflicting CSS information differently or it may not support the cascading part of it at all.

### 15.2.2   What Is a CSS-Enhanced Browser?

A CSS-enhanced browser supports CSS and will recognize the style tag *<style>* as a container for a style sheet, and based on the definition of the style, will produce the document accordingly. Most modern browsers, such as IE4+, Netscape 4+, Opera 3.5+, and Apple's Safari Web browser and Mozilla support CSS, and the majority of Web users are running a CSS-enhanced browser. However, just because a browser is CSS enhanced, doesn't mean that it is flawless or without limitiations. And just because a browser is not CSS enhanced, doesn't mean that it can't see the content of a page.[1]

Traditionally, browsers have silently ignored unknown tags, so if an old browser happens to encounter a *<style>* tag, its content will be treated simply as part of the document. It is also possible to hide the *<style>* tag within HTML comments if the browser is too old to recognize CSS, or it might just be a good time to upgrade to a newer model. (See "CSS Comments" on page 498 for more on this.)

### 15.2.3   How Does a Style Sheet Work?

A style sheet consists of the style rules that tell your browser how to present a document. The rules consist of two parts: a selector—the HTML element you are trying to stylize, and the declaration block—the properties and values that describe the style for the selector.

---

1. For an updated overview of available browsers, see the W3C overview page:
   *http://www.w3.org/Style/CSS/#browsers*.

## FORMAT

```
selector { property: value }
```

*declaration block*

Example:

```
H1 { color: red }
```

This rule sets the color of the *H2* element to blue:

```
H2 { color: blue }
```

A rule, then, consists of two main parts: the <u>selector</u> (e.g., *H2*) and the declaration block (e.g., *color: blue*). The following example demonstrates this simple rule.

## EXAMPLE  15.1

```
    <html><head><title>First Style Sheet</title>
1   <style type="text/css">
2       h1 { color: red }
        h2 { color: blue  }
    </style>
    </head>
    <body bgcolor=silver>
3       <h1>Welcome to my Stylin' Page</h1>
4       <h2>What do you think?</h2>
    </body>
    </html>
```

## EXPLANATION

1  The style sheet starts with the HTML *<style>* tag and specifies that the style sheet consists of text and CSS. The purpose of this style sheet is to customize HTML tags, thus giving them a new style.

2  A selector is one of any HTML elements, such as *h1, h2, body, li, p,* or *ul.* In this example, the *h1* and *h2* elements are selectors. The declaration has two parts: property (*color*) and value (*red*). Every time an *<h1>* tag is used in the document, it will be red, and every time an *<h2>* tag is used, it will be blue. (There are approximately 50 properties beyond the color property that are defined in the CSS specification!)

3  The *<h1>* tag will be displayed in red, based on the rule in the style sheet.

4  The *<h2>* tag will be displayed in blue, based on the rule in the style sheet.

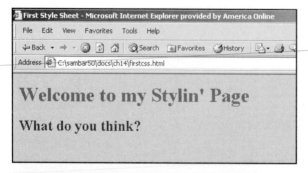

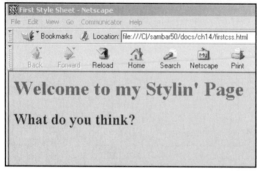

**Figure 15.1**   Style sheet with Internet Explorer (top) and with Nescape (bottom). If this book was in color, you would be able to see that the *h1* is in red, and the *h2* is in blue.

**CSS Comments.**   CSS comments, like C language comments, are enclosed in /* */. They are the textual comments that are ignored by the CSS parser when your style is being interpreted, and are used to clarify what you are trying to do. They cannot be nested.

```
H1 { color: blue }    /* heading level 1 is blue */
```

**Grouping.**   Grouping is used to reduce the size of style sheets. For example, you can group selectors in comma-separated lists, if you want the same rule to apply to all of the elements:

```
H1, H2, H3 { font-family: arial; color: blue }
```

Now all three heading levels will contain blue text in an Arial font face.

You can also group a set of declarations to create the style for a selector(s). The following rule combines a number of declarations describing the font properties for an *H1* element:

```
H1 {
    font-weight: bold;
    font-size: 12pt;
    line-height: 14pt;
    font-family: verdana;
}
```

And you can group the values for a particular property as follows:

```
h2 {font: bold 24pt arial}
```

## EXAMPLE 15.2

```
        <html>
        <head><title>Grouping Properties</title>
        <style type="text/css">
1       h1,h2,h3 { color: blue }    /* grouping selectors */
2       h1 {                        /* grouping declarations */
            font-weight: bold;
            font-size: 30pt;
            font-family: verdana;
        }
3       h2 {                    /* grouping a property's values */
            font: bold 24pt arial
        }
        </style>
        </head>
        <body bgcolor=silver>
4       <h1>Welcome to my Stylin' Page</h1>
5       <h2>What do you think?</h2>
6       <h3>Groovy!</h3>
        </body>
        </html>
```

## EXPLANATION

1   Three selectors, *h1*, *h2*, and *h3*, are grouped together. The declaration block enclosed in curly braces sets the color property to *blue*. Whenever any one of the *h1*, *h2*, or *h3* elements is used in the document, its text will be blue.

2   The declaration block for the *h1* selector consists of a group of properties and values to further define the font style for this heading.

3   The *font* property, in this example, groups the font values as a list, rather than creating individual property/value pairs as done on line 2.

4   Now the *h1* tag is tested to see if the style was applied, and it is!

5   The style for the *h2* tag is tested and it has been applied.

6   The only style set for the *h3* tag is a blue font, and that's all we get, as shown in Figure 15.2.

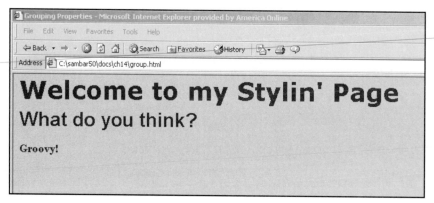

**Figure 15.2**  Grouping selectors and declarations for *h1, h2,* and *h3* HTML elements.

**Units of Measurement.**  You can express the size of a given property in different units of measurement; for example, a font size can be expressed in pixels or ems or points (the default is pixels). Colors can also be expressed in combinations of red, green, and blue, either by the name of the color, or its hexadecimal value.

Measurement is used in three categories: absolute units, relative units, and proportional units. For example, a point size measurement (e.g., *14pt*) would be the actual size (absolute) of a particular font; a value (e.g., *5em*) could be relative to the size of the current font; and a color (e.g., *50%80%100%*) could represent red, green, and blue as a percentage value of the original color. Table 15.1 introduces the types of measurements that are often used in style sheets.

**Table 15.1**  CSS units of measurement.

| Unit of Measurement | Description |
| --- | --- |
| % | Relative value as a percentage of parent element |
| cm | Centimeter |
| deg | Degree; angular measure used in aural styles |
| em | Relative length value proportional to current font size; width of the letter *M* for that font |
| ex | Vertical height of letter *x* relative to current font; height of a lowercase *x* for that font |
| float | Can be specified if a property value has no applicable unit of measurement, same as *integer* |
| hz | Hertz; for audio content |
| in | Inch, 2.54 cm |

**Table 15.1**  CSS units of measurement. (continued)

| Unit of Measurement | Description |
|---|---|
| *integer* | Can be specified if a property value has no applicable unit of measurement, same as *float* |
| *mm* | Millimeter |
| *ms* | Millisecond, $1/1000$ sec |
| *pc* | Pica, 12 points |
| *pt* | Point size, $1/72$ inch |
| *px* | Pixel (based on the resolution of the monitor) |
| *rgb(#,#,#)* | Red, green, blue; e.g., *rgb(203,55,266)* |
| *rgb(R%,G%,B%)* | Red, green, and blue percentage values of a color; e.g., *rgb(80%,20%,100%)* |
| *#rrggbb* or *#RRGGBB* | color values (red, green, blue) |
| *sec* | Second, 1000 ms |

Examples:

- `font-size: 10pt`
- `top: 20px`
- `margin: 1em`
- `margin-right: 20%`
- `color: blue`

## 15.2.4  Common Style Sheet Properties (Attributes)

In the previous examples, *font-family* and *color* are properties (also called attributes), and by assigning values to them, the style of the document is defined. Listed in Table 15.2 are some of the properties commonly used in style sheets. Many of these properties are used in the style sheets defined throughout this chapter and later as properties of the style object used with JavaScript. The Web Design Group provides a complete listing of this information at *http://www.htmlhelp.com/reference/css/properties.html*.

**Table 15.2**  Style sheet properties.

| Property | Value/Example | Tags Affected |
|----------|---------------|---------------|
| **Fonts** | | |
| *font* | 12pt/14pt sans-serif, 80% sans-serif, x-large/110% arial, normal small-caps | All |
| *font-family* | serif, sans-serif, cursive, fantasy, monospace; or any specific font typeface name may be used | All |
| *font-size* | 12pt, larger, 150%, 1.5em | All |
| *font-size-adjust* | xx-small, x-small, small, medium, large, x-large, xx-large, smaller, larger, 12pt, 25% | All |
| *font-stretch* | normal, wider, narrower, ultra-condensed, extra-condensed, condensed, semi-condensed, semi-expanded, expanded, extra-expanded, ultra-expanded | All |
| *font-style* | normal, italic, oblique | All |
| *font-variant* | normal, small-caps | All |
| *font-weight* | normal, bold, bolder, lighter,100, 200...900 | All |
| **Colors and Background** | | |
| *background-attachment* | scroll, fixed | All |
| *background-color* | red, blue, #F00, transparent | All |
| *background-image* | URL (bay.gif), none | All |
| *background-position* | right top, top center, center, bottom, 100% 100%, 0% 0%, 50% 50% | Block-level and replaced elements |
| *background-repeat* | repeat, repeat-x (horizontally), repeat-y (vertically), no-repeat | All |
| *color* | red, green, #F00, rgb(255,0,0) | All |
| **Text Alignment** | | |
| *letter-spacing* | normal, 0.1em | All |
| *line-height* | normal, 1.2, 1.2em, 120% | All |
| *text-decoration* | underline, overline, line-through, blink | All |
| *text-transform* | capitalize, uppercase, lowercase, none | All |
| *text-align* | left, right, center, justify | All |

**Table 15.2**   Style sheet properties. (continued)

| Property | Value/Example | Tags Affected |
|---|---|---|
| **Text Alignment (continued)** | | |
| *text-indent* | 3em, 15% | Block-level elements |
| *vertical-align* | baseline, sub, super, top, text-top, middle, bottom, text-bottom, 50% | Inline elements |
| *word-spacing* | normal, 2em | All |
| **Margins and Borders** | | |
| *border-bottom* | <border-bottom-width> or <border-style> or <color> | All |
| *border-bottom-width* | thin, medium, thick, 2em | All |
| *border-color* | red, green, #0C0 | All |
| *border-left* | <border-left-width> or <border-style> or <color> | All |
| *border-left-width* | thin, medium, thick, 3em | All |
| *border-right* | <border-right-width> or <border-style> or <color> | All |
| *border-right-width* | thin, medium, thick, 1cm | All |
| *border-style* | [none], dotted, dashed, solid, double, groove, ridge[inset,outset]{1,4} | All |
| *border-top* | <border-top-width> or <border-style> or <color> | All |
| *border-top-width* | thin, medium, thick, 3em | All |
| *border-width* | thin, medium, thick, .5cm | All |
| *clear* | none, left, right, both (allows or disallows floating elements on its sides) | All |
| *float* | left, right, or none (wraps text around an element, such as an image) | All |
| *height* | 12em, auto | Block-level and replaced element |
| *margin* | 5em, 3em, 2em,1em (top, right, bottom, left) | All |
| *margin-bottom* | 100px, 50% | All |
| *margin-left* | .5in, 40% | All |

**Table 15.2**   Style sheet properties. (continued)

| Property | Value/Example | Tags Affected |
|---|---|---|
| *Margins and Borders (continued)* | | |
| *margin-right* | 20em,45% | All |
| *margin-top* | 1cm, 20% | All |
| *padding* | 2em, 4em, 6em (right, bottom, left) | All |
| *padding-bottom* | 2em, 20% | All |
| *padding-left* | .25in, 20% | All |
| *padding-right* | .5cm, 35% | All |
| *padding-top* | 20px, 10% | All |
| *width* | 12em, 30%, auto (initial width value) | Block-level and replaced element[a] |

a.   A replaced element has set or calculated dimensions, such as *img, select, textarea.*

**Working with Colors.**   What is style without color? Table 15.3 lists the properties for managing color. You can use these properties to create color for the document's background and fonts, margins, borders, and more. The colors can be expressed with real names (e.g., *red, blue, yellow, magenta*) or their corresponding hexadecimal values (e.g., *#FF0000, #0000Ff, #ffff00, #ff00FF*) (see Tables B.1 and B.2 in Appendix B for a full list).

Sometimes colors don't look as crisp and bright as you would expect; pink might look like red, or some of the colors in a field of flowers might be dull. In Chapter 10, "The Browser Objects: Navigator, Windows, and Frames," we discussed the *screen* object. It has a property called *colorDepth* that will tell you how many colors in bits a computer can handle. For example, a color-bit depth of 4 will display 16 colors and a color-bit depth of 32 will provide 16.7 million colors. How many colors can your computer display?

There are a number of color charts available on the Web that provide Web-safe color palettes. See *www.lynda.com, www.paletteman.com,* or *www.visibone.com.*

**Table 15.3**   Color properties.

| Property | Value/Example | Elements Affected |
|---|---|---|
| *background-color* | red, blue, #F00 | All |
| *color* | red, green, #F00, rgb(255,0,0) | All |

**EXAMPLE  15.3**

```
        <html><head><title>Colors</title>
        <style type="text/css">
1           body { background-color: blue }
2           h1 {color: #FFFF33;}
3           p { color: white;  }
        </style>
        </head>
4       <body>
            <font size="+2">
5           <h1>Welcome to my Stylin' Page</h1>
6           <p>This paragraph is all white text on a blue background.<br>
            Do you like it?
            </p>
        </body>
        </html>
```

**EXPLANATION**

1   A style is defined for the background of the document. It will be blue.

2   The text for all *<h1>* tags will be yellow (*#FFFF33* is yellow).

3   Paragraphs will have white text.

4   The body of the page will be blue.

5   The heading level *<h1>* is displayed in its yellow style.

6   Any text enclosed in *<p> </p>* will be white against a blue body. See Figure 15.3 for output.

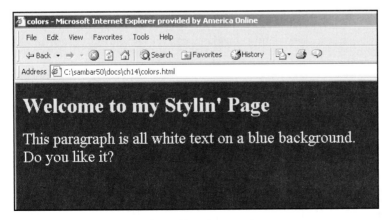

**Figure 15.3**  Colored text and background.

**Working with Fonts.**   The presentation of a document would be quite boring if you only had one font face and size available. CSS lets you specify a style for the fonts in a document in a variety of ways—by family, size, color, and others (see Table 15.4). There are a huge number of fonts to pick from, although it's a good idea to specify fonts that users are likely to have installed. Like the HTML *<font>* tag, CSS lets you specify several font families (see Table 15.5), and will go from left to right, selecting the one available on your computer.

**Table 15.4**   Font properties.

| Property | Value/Example | Elements Affected |
|---|---|---|
| *font* | 12pt/14pt sans-serif, 80% sans-serif, x-large/110% arial, normal small-caps | All |
| *font-family* | serif, sans-serif, cursive, fantasy, monospace; or any specific font family typeface name may be used | All |
| *font-size* | 12pt, larger, 150%, 1.5em | All |
| *font-style* | normal, italic, oblique | All |
| *font-variant* | normal, small-caps | All |
| *font-weight* | normal, bold, bolder, lighter, 100, 200...900 | All |

**Table 15.5**   Font families.

| Family Names | Specific Family Typeface Names |
|---|---|
| Serif | Times, Palatino, Bookman |
| Sans-serif | Arial, Helvetica, GillSans |
| Monospace | Courier, OCRB, WALLSTREET |
| Cursive | ZapfChancery, Mural Script, Virante |
| Fantasy | Celtic, Impact, Marriage |

**EXAMPLE 15.4**

```
        <head><title>Fonts</title>
        <style type="text/css">
            body { background-color: darkblue; }
1       h1 { color: yellow; font-size:x-large;
            font-family: lucida, verdana, helvetica; }
2       h2 { color:lightgreen; font-size:large;
            font-family:courier; }
```

**EXAMPLE** 15.4 (CONTINUED)

```
3          h3 { color:lightblue; font-size:medium;
               font-family:helvetica; }
4          p { color:white; font-size: 22pt;
               font-style: italic;
               font-family: arial;
               font-variant:small-caps; }
       </style>
       </head>
       <body>
          <font size="+2">
          <h1>My name is Papa Bear</h1>
5         <h2>My name is Mama Bear</h2>
          <h3>and I'm the Baby Bear</h3>
          <p>Once upon a time, yaddy yaddy yadda...</p>
       </body>
       </html>
```

**EXPLANATION**

1   The *h1* element will have yellow text, an extra-large font size from the Lucida family of fonts. If that font is not available in this browser, Verdana will be used, and if not Verdana, then Helvetica.

2   The *h2* element will have a light-green, large, Courier font.

3   The *h3* element will have a light-blue, medium, Helvetica font.

4   Paragraphs will have white text, with an italic, Arial font size of 22 points, all in small caps.

5   The *<h2>* tag is displayed in its big style. See Figure 15.4.

**Figure 15.4**  Changing fonts.

**Working with Text.**    If you want to make a business card, how do you put extra space between each of the letters of your company name? If you're writing a science term paper, how do you deal with exponents, equations, or subscripts? And how do you make it double-spaced? If you're writing a cool poem and want your text in the shape of an hourglass or a circle to give it visual appeal, or you just want to emphasize certain words to make your point for a presentation, then what to do?  The CSS controls listed in Table 15.6 may be your answer.

**Table 15.6**   Text alignment properties.

| *Property* | *Value/Example* | *Elements Affected* |
| --- | --- | --- |
| *letter-spacing* | normal, 0.1em | All |
| *line-height* | normal, 1.2, 1.2em, 120% | All |
| *text-align* | left, right, center, justify | All |
| *text-decoration* | underline, overline, line-through, blink | All |
| *text-indent* | 3em, 15% | Block-level elements |
| *text-transform* | capitalize, uppercase, lowercase, none | All |
| *vertical-align* | baseline, sub, super, top, text-top, middle, bottom, text-bottom, 50% | Inline elements |
| *word-spacing* | normal, 2em | All |

**EXAMPLE  15.5**

```
      <html><head><title>First Style Sheet</title>
      <style type="text/css">
1         #title{
2             word-spacing: 10px;
              letter-spacing: 4px;
              text-decoration: underline;
              text-align: center;
              font-size: 22pt ;
              font-family:arial;
              font-weight: bold;
          }
3         p { line-height: 2;
              text-indent: 6%;
              font-family:arial;
              font-size:18; }
          }
      </style>
      </head>
```

## EXAMPLE   15.5 (CONTINUED)

```
        <body bgcolor="coral">
4           <p id=title>The Color Palette
5           <p>The world is a colorful place. Web browsers display
        millions of those colors every day to make the pages seem
        real and interesting. Browser colors are displayed in
        combinations of red, green, and blue, called RGB. This is a
        system of indexing colors by assigning values of 0 to 255 in
        each of the three colors, ranging from no saturation (0) to
        full saturation (255). Black has a saturation of 0 and
        white has a saturation of 255. In HTML documents these
        colors are represented as six hexadecimal values, preceded
        by a # sign. White is #FFFFFF and black is #000000.
6           <p>
        Although there are millions of different combinations of color,
        it is best when working with Web pages to use what are
        called Web-safe colors.
        </body>
        </html>
```

## EXPLANATION

1   *#title* is called an ID selector, a way in the style sheet that we can allow any selector to use a style. In this example, the title of the page is going to be distinct from the text in the rest of the page. For example, if the *<p>* tag is used, it can identify itself with this ID selector in order to produce the text style described in the declaration block (see line #4). If the ID is not used, the rest of the paragraphs will display text as defined by the rule in line #3. More discussion on ID selectors is presented in "The ID Selector" on page 524.

2   Text controls are defined in the rule. The text will be centered, underlined, with a 22pt, bold Arial font. The spacing between each letter and each word is defined in pixels.

3   When the *<p>* tag is used, a line height of 2 will produce double-spaced lines. The first line of each paragraph will be indented by 2% from the left margin.

4   This paragraph is identifying itself with the *title* ID. This means that for this paragraph, the style will follow the rule defined after line 1.

5, 6   Both of these paragraphs take on the style provided by the rule in line 3.

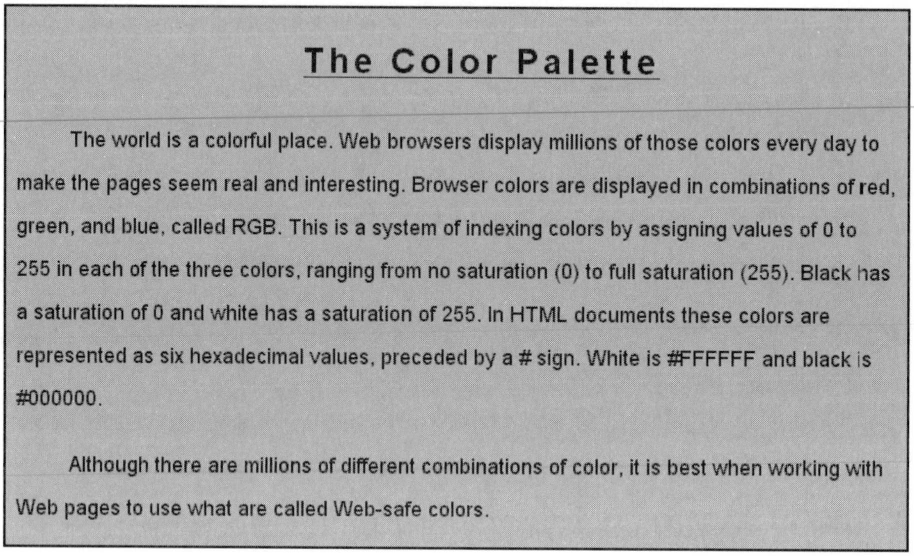

## The Color Palette

The world is a colorful place. Web browsers display millions of those colors every day to make the pages seem real and interesting. Browser colors are displayed in combinations of red, green, and blue, called RGB. This is a system of indexing colors by assigning values of 0 to 255 in each of the three colors, ranging from no saturation (0) to full saturation (255). Black has a saturation of 0 and white has a saturation of 255. In HTML documents these colors are represented as six hexadecimal values, preceded by a # sign. White is #FFFFFF and black is #000000.

Although there are millions of different combinations of color, it is best when working with Web pages to use what are called Web-safe colors.

**Figure 15.5**  A report with a centered title, double-spaced lines, and indented paragraphs.

**Working with Backgrounds and Images.**  The same way that wallpaper in a guest room can create a sense of warmth or calm, background images can add decoration and design to an otherwise blah page. CSS gives you a number of ways to control the appearance of background images. Refer to Table 15.7.

**Table 15.7**  Image and background properties.

| Property | Value/Example | Elements Affected |
|---|---|---|
| *background-attachment* | scroll, fixed | All |
| *background-image* | URL (bay.gif), none | All |
| *background-position* | right top, top center, center, bottom, 100% 100%, 0% 0%, 50% 50% | Block-level and replaced elements |
| *background-repeat* | repeat, repeat-x (horizontally), repeat-y (vertically), no-repeat | All |

EXAMPLE   15.6

```
        <html>
        <head><title>Backgrounds</title>
        <style type="text/css">
1           body {background-color:"pink" ;
2              background-image: url(greenballoon.gif);
3           repeat-x };
4          h1 {font-size: 42pt;text-indent: 25%;
                color:red; margin-top: 14%;
                font-family:fantasy; }
        </style>
        </head>
5       <body>
6          <h1>Happy Birthday!!</h1>
           <h1>Happy Birthday!!</h1>
        </body>
        </html>
```

**EXPLANATION**

1   The rule for the *body* element is to give it a pink background color.

2   The background image will come from a file called *greenballoon.gif*, in the current directory. The URL specifies the location of the image.

3   The image will repeat itself horizontally across the screen.

4   The rule for the *h1* element is a red 42-point fantasy font, indented 25% from the left of the block, where the margin is 14% from the top.

5   The body of the document reflects the style that was set for it in line #1.

6   The *<h1>* tag reflects the rule set for it in line 4.

**Figure 15.6**
Background color and a repeating image.

**Working with Margins and Borders.**     When you look at your document, it is composed of a number of containers. The *<body>* tag is a container and it may contain a heading, a paragraph, a table, or other elements. Each of these elements also can be thought of as a container. Each container has an outer margin, and the margin can have some padding (space between it and the next container). The padding is like the *CELL-PADDING* attribute of a table cell. On the inside of the padding is a border that separates the container from its contents. The border is normally invisible. You can change the margin, create colorful borders, or increase or decrease the padding, to give the page more style. See Figure 15.7 for a graphic representation, and Table 15.8 for a list of margin and border properties. Different browsers might handle the borders differently. Margins and borders will behave better if enclosed within *<div>* tags.

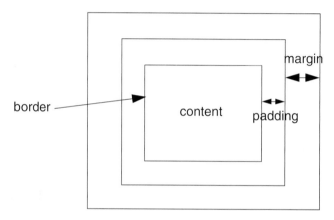

**Figure 15.7**   How an element is contained.

**Table 15.8**   Margin and border properties.

| Property | Value/Example | Elements Affected |
|----------|---------------|-------------------|
| *border-bottom* | <border-bottom-width> or <border-style> or <color> | All |
| *border-bottom-width* | thin, medium, thick, 2em | All |
| *border-color* | red, green, #0C0 | All |
| *border-left* | <border-left-width> or <border-style> or <color> | All |
| *border-left-width* | thin, medium, thick, 3em | All |
| *border-right* | <border-right-width> or <border-style> or <color> | All |
| *border-right-width* | thin, medium, thick, 1cm | All |
| *border-style* | [none], dotted, dashed, solid, double, groove, ridge [ inset,outset ]{1,4} | All |

**Table 15.8**   Margin and border properties. (continued)

| Property | Value/Example | Elements Affected |
|---|---|---|
| *border-top* | <border-top-width> or <border-style> or <color> | All |
| *border-top-width* | thin, medium, thick, 3em | All |
| *border-width* | thin, medium, thick, .5cm | All |
| *margin* | 5em, 3em, 2em, 1em (top, right, bottom, left) | All |
| *margin-bottom* | 100px, 50% | All |
| *margin-left* | .5in, 40% | All |
| *margin-right* | 20em, 45% | All |
| *margin-top* | 1cm, 20% | All |
| *padding* | 2em, 4em, 6em (right, bottom, left) | All |
| *padding-bottom* | 2em, 20% | All |
| *padding-left* | .25in, 20% | All |
| *padding-right* | .5cm, 35% | All |
| *padding-top* | 20px, 10% | All |

**EXAMPLE   15.7**

```
        <html>
        <head><title>Margins and Borders</title>
        <style type="text/css">
1           body { margin-top: 1cm; margin-left: 2cm ;
2               margin-bottom: 1cm; margin-right: 2cm;
3               border-width: thick;
                border-style:solid;
                border-color: red blue green yellow; padding:15px;
            }
            h1{ /* grouping properties */
                font-weight: bold;
                font-size: 30pt;
                font-family: verdana;
            }
            h2 { /* grouping a property's values */
4               border-style:dotted; border-color:purple;
                font: bold 24pt arial
            }
```

**EXAMPLE**   15.7 (CONTINUED)

```
    </style>
    </head>
    <body bgcolor=silver>
    <h1>Crossing the Border!</h1>
    <h2>Welcome!</h2>
    <h3>Nice country.</h3>
    </body>
    </html>
```

**EXPLANATION**

1    The margins and borders are defined for the body of this document.

2    The margin bottom is 1 centimeter up from the bottom of the document and 2 centimeters in from the left. There will be more whitespace around the headings, paragraphs, and other elements within the body because of the increased margin sizes.

3    A thick, rainbow-colored border is placed on the inside of the margin.

4    The border style for *h2* elements is purple dots. See Figure 15.8.

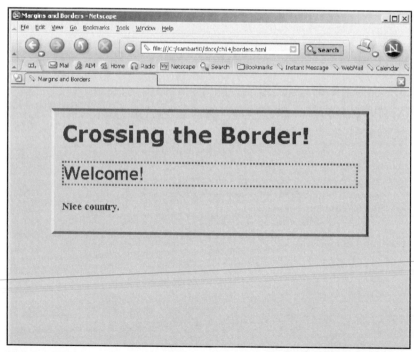

**Figure 15.8**   Playing with margins and borders. This is how the colorful border appears in NN7. (The border looks different in IE6. It surrounds the entire window.)

# 15.3 Types of Style Sheets

There are several ways to define style sheets within a document:

1. Embedded—the style is defined within the *<style>* tags for the HTML document.
2. Inline—the style is defined for a specific HTML element.
3. External—the style is defined in an external file.

## 15.3.1   The Embedded Style Sheet

A style sheet that is created with the HTML *<style></style>* tags right in the current document is called an embedded style sheet.

**The *<style>* Tag.**   The *<style></style>* tags were introduced into HTML to allow the style sheets to be inserted right into an HTML document. They are used to create a set of rules to define the style of an HTML element(s). The *<style></style>* tags are placed between the *<head></head>* tags in the document, as shown here:

```
<html><title>CSS Example</title>
<head>
    <style>
        h1 { color: blue ; }
    </style>
</head>
```

**The *type* Attribute.**   Because it is possible to have more than one style sheet language, you can tell the browser what type of style sheet you are using with the *type* attribute of the  HTML *<style>* tag. When the browser loads the page, it will ignore the style sheet if it doesn't recognize the language; otherwise it will read the style sheet.

The following example specifies that the type is *text/css*; that is, text and cascading style sheet.

**FORMAT**

```
<style type="style sheet language">
```

**Example:**

```
<style type="text/css">
```

**EXAMPLE 15.8**

```
    <html>
    <head><title>Cascading Style Sheets</title>
1   <style type="text/css">
    <!--
2       body { background-color: lightblue; }
3       p { background:yellow;
            text-indent:5%;
            margin-left: 20%;
            margin-right: 20%;
            border-width:10px;
            border-style:groove;
            padding: 15px;
            font-family: times,arial;
            font-size:150%;
            font-weight:900 }
4       h1, h2, h3 {
            text-align: center;
            background:blue;
            border-width:5px;
            border-style:solid;
            border-color:black;
            margin-left:20%;margin-right:20%;
            font-family:courier, arial;
            font-weight:900;
            color: white; }
5       h2,h3 { font-size:24; }
6       em { color: green;
            font-weight: bold }
    -->
7   </style>
    </head>
    <body>
8   <h1><center>Stylin' Web Page</center></h1>
9   <p>HTML by itself doesn't give you much other than structure in a
    page and there's no guarantee that every browser out there will
    render the tags in  the same way. So along came style sheets.
    Style sheets enhance HTML as a word processor enhances plain text.
    <p>But... no guarantees what a browser might do with a style
    sheet, any more than what a stylist might do to your hair, but we
    can hope for the best.
10  <h2><center>An H2 Element</center></h2>
    <h3><center>An H3 Element</center></h3>
11  <p>This is not a <em>designer's dream style</em>, but it
    illustrates the power.
    </body>
    </html>
```

## EXPLANATION

1    The HTML *<style>* tag belongs within the *<head></head>* tags. The is the start of an embedded CSS.

2    A rule is defined for the HTML *body* element. The background color of the document will be light blue.

3    A rule is defined for the HTML *p* (paragraph) element. The left and right margins are set at 20%, meaning that they will be moved inward 20% from their respective edges. They will be surrounded by a grooved border, with the text given a 15-pixel size padding. The font face is Times or Arial (whichever works on your browser), point size 150% bigger than its default, weight 900 is the boldest of the bold.

4    A rule is defined for a group of selectors (heading levels *h1*, *h2*, and *h3*). They will be centered on the page, the text will be white against a blue bordered background, in a Courier or Arial font face.

5    The rule for the *h2* and *h3* tags sets the font size to 24 points.

6    A rule is defined for an *em* element. Text will be italicized, green, and bold.

7    This marks the end of the HTML header that encloses the style sheet.

8    As shown in the output (see Figure 15.9), the heading level is displayed according to the style defined in the style sheet, line 4.

9    This paragraph is displayed according to the rule set in the style sheet, line 3. Notice how both the left and right margins have moved toward the center.

10    The heading level is displayed according to the rule set in the style sheet, lines 4 and 5, and the first paragraph is indented.

11    The *<em>* tag is embedded within the *<p>* tag. It inherits from the *<p>* tag everything but the font color and weight. These paragraph properties were overridden in the style sheet defined on line 6 for the *em* element.

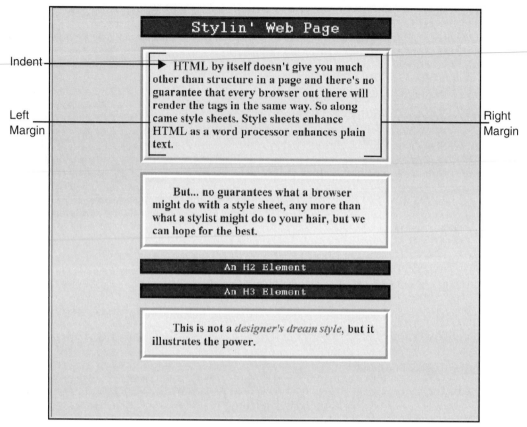

**Figure 15.9**   HTML and CSS—An embedded style sheet.

## 15.3.2   The Inline Type and the *<style>* Attribute

Inline style sheets are also embedded within an HTML document, but are assigned as an attribute of the *<style>* tag in the <u>body</u> of the document and are useful for overriding an already exisiting style for a particular element in a linked style sheet. On the negative side, they have to be redefined for any element that requires that style, element by element. For example, if the *h1* element has been defined to be blue and you want to temporarily change it to red, you can define the style as an attribute of the style tag for that element:

```
<h1 style= "color: red; "> This is red text</h1>
```

**EXAMPLE** 15.9

```
        <html><head><title>Inline Style Sheets</title>
1       <style type="text/css">
2           body { background-color: orange;
                   color:darkblue;  /* color of text */ }
        </style>
        </head>
        <body>
3       <h1 style="color:darkred;
            text-align:center;
            text-decoration:underline;">Inline Stylin'</h1>
4       <p style="color:black;
            background:white;
            font-family:sans-serif;font-size:large">
        This paragraph uses an inline style. As soon as another paragraph
        is started, the style will revert back to its default.
5       <p> This paragraph has reverted back to its default style, and so
        has the following heading.
        <h1>Default heading</h1>
        </body>
        </html>
```

1   A CSS starts here in the head of the document.

2   The background color is set to orange and the color of the font is set to dark blue.

3   This *h1* uses an inline style, an attibute of the *<h1>* tag and effective for this heading only. The color will be red, the text centered and underlined.

4   This is an inline style for the paragraph tag. It is an attribute of the *<p>* tag and is only good for this paragraph. The text of the paragraph will be black, the background color of the paragraph will be white, and the font family, sans-serif, large. The next time a *<p>* tag is used, the style will revert to its former style.

5   This paragraph has reverted to its former style. See Figure 15.10.

## Inline Stylin'

This paragraph uses an inline style. As soon as another paragraph is started, the style will revert back to its default.

This paragraph has reverted back to its default style, and so has the following heading

### Default heading

**Figure 15.10**   Inline styles are temporary.

## 15.3.3  The External Type with a Link

External style steets are the most powerful type if you want the style to affect more than one page; in fact, you can use the same style for hundreds, thousands, or millions of pages. As the name implies, external style sheets are stored in an external file, not the current HTML file. The filename for the external style sheet has a *.css* extension, just as the HTML file has an *.html* or *.htm* extension. To link the external file to the existing HTML file, a link is created as shown here:

```
<link rel=stylesheet href="style_file.css" type="text/css">
```

The following examples demonstrate the use of external style sheets. The first example is the HTML file containing a link to the external file and the second example is the *.css* file. It contains the style sheet.

---

**EXAMPLE 15.10**

```
      <html><head><title>External Style Sheets</title>
1         <link rel=stylesheet type="text/css"  href="extern.css">
          <!-- Name of external file is extern.css. See Example 15.11 -->
2     </head>
3     <body>
          <h1><u>External Stylin'</u></h1>
          <h2>Paragraph Style Below</h2>
          <p>The style defined for this paragraph is found in an external
          CSS document. The filename ends with <em>.css</em>.
          Now we can apply this style to as many pages as we want to.
          <h2>An H2 Element</h2>
          <h3>An H3 Element</h3>
          <p>This is not a <em>designer's dream style</em>, but it
          illustrates the power. Don't you think so?<p>
      </body>
      </html>
```

**EXPLANATION**

1   The *link* tag is opened within the *<head>* tags of your HTML document. The *link* tag has a *rel* attribute that is assigned *stylesheet*. This tells the browser that the link is going to a style sheet type document. The *href* attribute tells the browser the name of the CSS file containing the style sheet. This is a local file called *extern.css*. If necessary, use a complete path to the file. The *link* tag is closed with a >.

2   The *<head>* tag ends here.

3   In the body of the document, each of the HTML tags will be affected by the style defined in the external CSS file. The output for Examples 15.10 and 15.11 is shown in Figure 15.11.

## EXAMPLE 15.11

```
(The external extern.css file)
1   body { background-color: pink; }
2   p {
        margin-left:20%;
        margin-right:20%;
        font-family: sans-serif;
        font-size: 14
3   }
    h1, h2, h3 { text-align: center;
                 font-family: sans-serif;
                 color: darkblue
    }
4   em { color: green;
         font-weight: bold
    }
```

## EXPLANATION

1   This is the external CSS file that will be linked to the file in Example 15.10. Using an external CSS file keeps the main file size smaller and allows the style sheet to be shared by multiple files.

2   The paragraph *<p>* style is set to have a margin in 20% from the left and right, the text in size 14, and font family sans-serif.

3   The heading levels 1, 2, and 3 styles are set to be centered with a dark blue font, from the sans-serif family.

4   The *<em>* style will be a bold, green font.

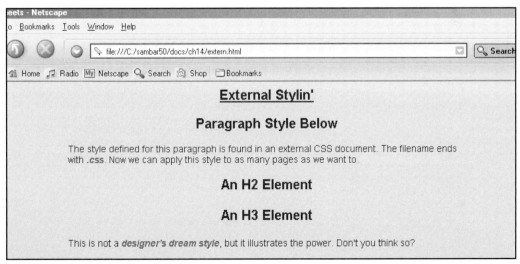

**Figure 15.11** External style sheets.

## 15.3.4  Creating a Style Class

Rather than globally defining a style for an element, you can customize the style by defining a class. The class style can be applied to individual tags when needed. The class name, called the class selector, is preceded by a period and followed by the declaration enclosed in curly braces.

**FORMAT**

```
.classname { style rules; }
```

Example:

```
.header { font-family: verdana, helvetica ; }
```

Once you have defined a class, it can be used on any of the HTML elements in the body of the document as long as that element understands the style you have applied to it. To apply the class, you use the *class* attribute. The class attribute is assigned the name of the class; for example, for the *<p>* tag, you would stipulate *<p class=name>* where *name* is the name of the class.

**EXAMPLE  15.12**

```
     <html><title>CSS Class Name</title>
1    <head>
2    <style>
3        p { margin-right: 30%;font-family: arial;
             font-size: 16pt;
             color:forestgreen; }
4        .bigfont { font-size: x-large; color:darkblue;
                    font-style:bold;}
5        .teenyfont {font-size:small; font-style: italic;color:black;}
     </style>
     </head>
     <body>
6    <p>The text in this paragraph is green and the point size is 16.
     The font family is <em>arial</em>.
7    <p class="bigfont"> This paragraph has a bigger font and is dark
     blue in color.
8    <p>The font style is specified as a class called
     <em>.bigfont</em>.
9    <h1 class="bigfont">Testing the Class on an H1 Element</h1>
10   <p class="teenyfont">Is this a small font?"
     <p>Let's start a new paragraph. This is green with a font size of
     16. What style is in effect here?
     </body></html>
```

1 The style is defined in the *<head>* of the document.

2 The CSS starts here.

3 A rule is defined for the paragraph (*p* selector). All paragraphs will have a right-hand margin, 30% in from both left and right. The Arial font will be 12 point and forest green.

4 A class selector called *.bigfont* is defined. Class names start with a period. When used on an HTML element, the font will be extra large, dark blue, and bold.

5 The class selector called *.teenyfont* is defined. All HTML elements that use this class will have a small, italic, black font.

6 The paragraph is styled according to the rule on line 3.

7 This paragraph is assigned the *bigfont* class. The text will be in the style defined for this class on line 4.

8 This paragraph reverts to the style rule on line 3.

9 The *<h1>* tag is using the *bigfont* class defined on line 4.

10 The *<p>* tag is using the *teenyfont* class defined on line 5. See Figure 15.12.

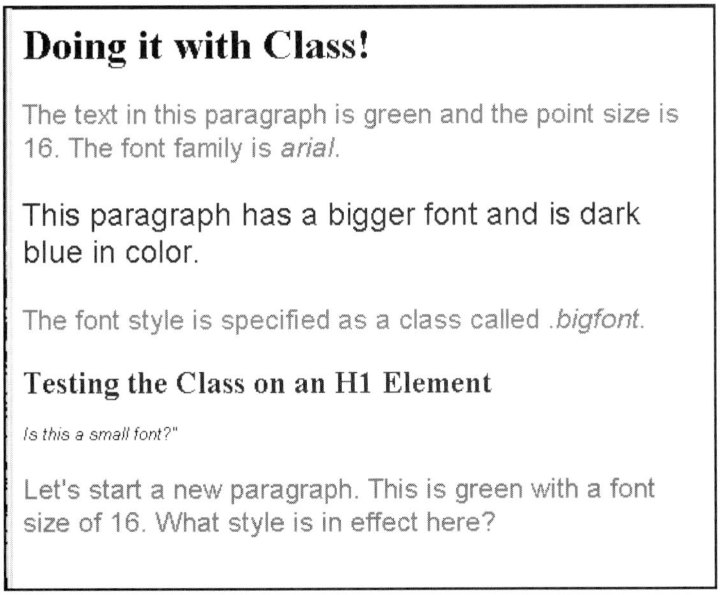

# Doing it with Class!

The text in this paragraph is green and the point size is 16. The font family is *arial*.

## This paragraph has a bigger font and is dark blue in color.

The font style is specified as a class called *.bigfont*.

### Testing the Class on an H1 Element

*Is this a small font?"*

Let's start a new paragraph. This is green with a font size of 16. What style is in effect here?

**Figure 15.12** Using a CSS class.

## 15.3.5   The ID Selector

The ID selector is another way to create a style that is independent of a specific HTML tag. By using the ID selector, you can choose the style for the element by assigning it a unique ID. The name of the ID selector is always preceded by a hash mark (also called a pound sign, #). The declaration block, consisting of properties and values, follows the ID selector and is enclosed in curly braces.

### FORMAT

```
#IDselector { declaration ; }
```

**Example:**

```
#menu1 { font-family: arial;
         font-size: big;
         color: blue; }
```

To apply an ID to an HTML tag, use the *id* attribute. The attribute will be assigned the same name given to the ID selector; so, to apply an ID selector to a *<p>* tag, you would stipulate *<p id=name>* where *name* is the name of the ID selector. (See Example 15.13.)

When JavaScript enters the picture, the *id* attribute is used to identify each element as a unique object so that it can be manipulated in a JavaScript program. The ID should be unique for an element and not used more than once on a page. If you need to use the style more than once for multiple elements, it would be better to use the class selector instead. The ID selector can be used with a class selector of the same name, as *#big, .big { }*.

### EXAMPLE   15.13

```
      <html><head><title>ID's</title>
1     <style type="text/css">
2        p{ font-family:arial,sans-serif,helvetica;
           font-style:bold;
           font-size:18
         }
3        #block { /* The ID selector */
                color: red;
                text-decoration:underline;
         }
      </style>
      </head>
      <body >
4     <p>When making my point, I will get quite red and underline what
      I say!!</p>
5     <p id="block">This text is red and underlined!!</P>
6     <p>and now I am somewhat appeased.
      </body>
      </html>
```

1    This is the start of a style sheet; it is placed between the *<head></head>* tags in the document.

2    The style of the paragraph element is defined. This style will take effect anywhere in the document where the *<p>* tag is used. Note that point sizes may be different on different browsers. Pixels will give you more accuracy.

3    The ID selector is called *block* and must be preceded by a hash mark. It can be used by any HTML element to produce red, underlined text. ID selectors should only be used once on a page to serve as a unique ID for the element.

4    A paragraph containing text will be displayed according to the style defined in the style sheet on line 2.

5    By adding the ID called *block*, the style for this paragraph will be changed to red, underlined text.

6    The *<p>* tag will revert to the style defined on line 2. See Figure 15.13.

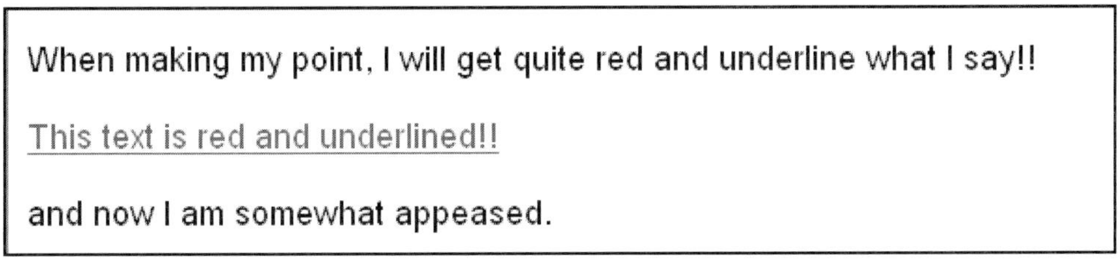

When making my point, I will get quite red and underline what I say!!

This text is red and underlined!!

and now I am somewhat appeased.

**Figure 15.13**    Using the ID selector in style sheets.

## 15.3.6    The *<span>* Tag

The *<span></span>* tags are used if you want to change only a selected portion of text. By doing so, you can create an inline style that will be embedded within another element and apply only to that portion of the content. In this way you can add or override a style to an element for which a style has already been defined. Carriage returns and breaks in the text will not occur with these tags.

In the following example, the paragraph style has been defined in a CSS. But later in the body of the document, the *<span>* tag is used to override the font size and to add margins to the text.

**EXAMPLE 15.14**

```
       <html><head><title>Margins</title></head>
       <style type="text/css">
1          body { margin:10%;
                  border-width: 10px; border-style:solid;
                  border-color: white; padding:5px;}
2          p { color=black;
               font-size: 22pt;
               margin-left:10;
               margin-right:10;
               padding:5px;
               border-style:groove;
               border-color:white;
               background-color:cyan;}
       </style>
       <body bgcolor=blue>
       <p>
3      <span style="margin-left:10%;font-size:26pt;">The Three Little
       Bears</span>
4      </p>
       Once upon a time there were three little bears,
       Mama bear, Papa bear, and Baby bear.
       They lived very happily in the deep woods.
       <p>And then there was Goldilocks!</p>
       </body>
       </html>
```

**EXPLANATION**

1   The style rule for the *body* element is defined. It will have a margin distance increased by 10% on all sides and a solid, white border with a padding of 5 pixels between the margin and the border. Margin borders will differ in appearance depending on your browser.

2   The style rule for the paragraph defines black text of a 22 point font, with both right and left margins of 10 pixels, contained within a grooved, white border, against a cyan background.

3   The *<span>* tag defines a left-hand margin increased by 10% relative to this paragraph, and changes the font size to 26 points. The only part of the document to be affected is the paragraph in which the *<span></span>* tags are enclosed. The text *The Three Little Bears* will be displayed according to this style.

4   The *<span>* tags have no effect on this paragraph. The style reverts to the rule in the style sheet. See Figure 15.14.

**Figure 15.14**   The *<span>* tag only affects a specific portion of the text.

### 15.3.7   Contextual Selectors

Contextual selectors have an inheritance basis. For example, if a *<b>* tag is nested with-ing a *<p>* tag, then the *<b>* tag takes on the characteristics assigned to its parent. If the *<p>* is green, than the bold text will also be green. If a bullet list *<ul>* has *<li>* tags nested within it, the bullets take on the characteristics of its parent. If the *ul* element is red, then all the bullets and the accompanying text will be red.

When you create a contextual selector, the last element in the selector list is the one that is affected by the style when it is used in context of the elements preceding it. For example, if you have a selector list: *table td em { color: blue ;}*, then the *em* element, the last in the list, will be affected by the style only when it is inside a table cell, *td*, at which point the table cell will be contain blue italic text.

**EXAMPLE  15.15**

```
      <head><title>Contextual Selector</title>
      <style type="text/css">
1         table td { color: blue; /* Table cells will take this style */
                    font-size: 18pt;
                    font-family: verdana; }
      </style>
      </head>
      <body bgcolor=silver><center>
         <h1><em>The Three Bears</em></h1>
         <table cellspacing="20" cellpadding="20%" border="3">
            <tr>
2              <td>Mama Bear</td>
            <tr>
3              <td>Papa Bear</td>
            <tr>
4              <td>Baby Bear</td>
            </tr>
         </table>
      </center>
      </body>
      </html>
```

**EXPLANATION**

1   A rule is defined for a table cell. The table's data will be blue, the font size 18 points, and the font family, Verdana. Whenever you create a table, each of the table cells, defined by the *<td>* tag, will have this style.

2–4   The table data in these cells will take on the style described in line 1.

**Figure 15.15**
A table with stylized cells.

**EXAMPLE   15.16**

```
        <html>
        <head><title>Contextual Selector</title>
        <style type="text/css">
1           table td em { color: blue; /* Table cells take this style */
                          font-size: 18pt;
                          font-family: verdana; }
        </style>
        </head>
        <body bgcolor=silver><center>
2           <h1><em>The Three Bears</em></h1>
            <table cellspacing="20" cellpadding="20%" border="3">
                <tr>
3                   <td><em>Mama Bear</em></td>
                <tr>
4                   <td>Papa Bear</td>
                <tr>
5                   <td>Baby Bear</td>
                </tr>
            </table>
        </center>
        </body>
        </html>
```

**EXPLANATION**

1  When a table is defined, the data cells will take on this style only if the *<em>* tag is used within the cell. See line 3.

2  The *<em>* tag used within this *<h1>* tag is not affected by the contextual selector because it is not within a table cell; that is, it is out of context.

3  The *<em>* tag is embedded within a *<td>* tag. The table's data will follow the style defined on line 1; it is in context.

4  This table cell is not using the *<em>* tag, so will not be affected by the style rule on line 1. It can only be affected if in context.

5  This table cell will not be affected by the style rule either because it doesn't use the *<em>* tag. See Figure 15.16.

**Figure 15.16**  A table cell is defined by the contextual selector.

## 15.3.8  Positioning Elements and Layers

One of the most important features of CSS is the ability to position objects on a page, to size them, and to make them either visible or invisible. This feature makes it possible to move objects to different sections of a page, move text and images, create animation, tool tips, scrolling text, and more. Normally when you place tags in an HTML document, the flow is from top to bottom. Now, with style sheets, you can set the position of an element, even layering one on top of the other.

A note about Netscape layers. Netscape 4 introduced layer (*<layer><ilayer>*) tags, a prototype of CSS positioning, to control the position and visibility of elements on a page, and then with Netscape 6 abandoned the whole thing. This book does not address the Netscape 4 layer technology since it is fast becoming a thing of the past. However, the term "layer" is still in use, and is used to refer to objects using the *id* attribute.

**Table 15.9**  Positioning styles.

| Property | What It Specifies |
|---|---|
| *bottom, right* | The placement of the bottom, right edges of an element |
| *clip* | A specified region of the element that will be seen |
| *display* | Whether an element is displayed |

**Table 15.9**  Positioning styles. (continued)

| Property | What It Specifies |
|---|---|
| *overflow* | What to do if there is an overflow; i.e., there isn't enough space for the element |
| *position* | How to position the element on the page |
| *top, left* | The placement of the top, left edges of an element |
| *visibility* | Whether an element can be seen |
| *width, height* | The size in width and height of an element's content, not additional padding, margins, borders, etc. |
| *z-index* | The third dimension in a stack of objects |

**Absolute Positioning.**    Absolute positioning places an element in a specific location on the page and can be used to achieve full animation; for instance, moving an image across a page. It is used to specify the absolute coordinates $(x,y)$ of the element in terms of the browser window itself. The *top* and *left* properties are used to determine the coordinates. (See Figure 15.17.) If not specified, the browser will assume the top left corner of the browser window, where $x$ is 0 and $y$ is 0. The top left corner of the window is position 0,0 and the bottom right corner depends on the resolution of the screen. If the screen resolution is set to 800 pixels in width and 600 pixels in height, the bottom right corner is positioned at coordinates 800, 600.

If an absolutely positioned element is nested within another absolutely positioned element, it will be positioned relative to that element.

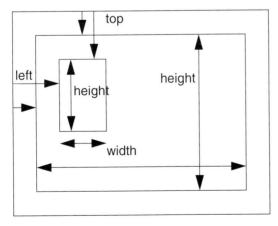

**Figure 15.17**  Absolute positioning.

**EXAMPLE** 15.17

```
      <html>
      <head>
      <title>layers</title>
      <style type="text/css">
      <!--
2         #first{
                background-color: red;
                border-style: solid;
                font-weight:bold;
                top: 20;
2               position: absolute;
                left: 20;
                height: 100;
                width: 100;
          }
3         #second{
                  background-color: blue;
                  border-style: solid;
                  font-weight:bold;
                  top: 30 ;
                  position: absolute;
                  left: 60;
                  height: 100;
                  width: 100;
          }
4         #third{
                background-color: orange;
                border-style: solid;
                font-weight:bold;
                top: 40 ;
                position: absolute;
                left: 100;
                height: 100;
                width: 100;
          }
      </style>
5     <body>
6         <p id="first">
              First position
          </p>
7         <p id="second">
              Second position
          </p>
8         <p id="third">
              Third position
          </p>
      </body>
      </html>
```

## EXPLANATION

1  An ID selector called *#first* sets the pixel positions for a red block that will be absolutely positioned 20 pixels from the top of the window, 20 pixels from the left-hand side, and have a size of 100 × 100 pixels (width × height).

2  The *position* attribute is specified as absolute. It is independent of all other elements in the body of this document.

3  An ID selector called *#second* sets the pixel positions for a blue block that will be absolutely positioned 30 pixels from the top of the window, 60 pixels from the left-hand side, and have a size of 100 × 100 pixels (width × height). The blue box will appear to be layered over the red one.

4  An ID selector called *#third* sets the pixel positions for an orange block that will be absolutely positioned 40 pixels from the top of the window, 100 pixels from the left-hand side, and have a size of 100 × 100 pixels (width × height). The orange box will appear to be layered over the blue one.

5  The *<body>* serves as the container for the four objects. The red, blue, and orange boxes will appear in the window at the absolute positions assigned to them in relationship to their container, the body of the document.

6  The paragraph element is positioned and styled according to the rule for the *first* ID selector.

7  The paragraph element is positioned and styled according to the rule for the *second* ID selector.

8  The paragraph element is positioned and styled according to the rule for the *third* ID selector. See Figure 15.18.

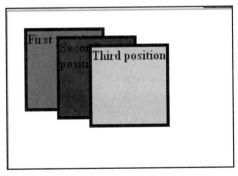

**Figure 15.18**  Three layers based on absolute positioning (IE5, NN7).

***Top, Left, Bottom, Right—Absolute Positions.***  As shown in the previous example, once the position has been set, the *left, top, right,* and *bottom* attributes can be used to specify exactly where on the page the element should be located. Although we used *left* and *top* to define the position of the element within the body of the document, *right* and *left bottom* can also position the element on the page. In the following example, four elements are placed in four corners of the document.

**EXAMPLE  15.18**

```
        <html>
        <head>
        <title>layers</title>
        <style type="text/css">
        <!--
1           #first{
                    background-color: red;
                    border-style: solid;
                    font-weight:bold;
                    position: absolute;
                    top: 100;
                    right: 200;
                    height: 100;
                    width: 100;
            }
2           #second{
                    background-color: blue;
                    border-style: solid;
                    font-weight:bold;
                    position: absolute;
                    bottom:200;
                    left:200;
                    height: 100;
                    width: 100;
            }
3           #third{
                    background-color: orange;
                    border-style: solid;
                    font-weight:bold;
                    position: absolute;
                    top: 100 ;
                    left: 200;
                    height: 100;
                    width: 100;
            }
4           #fourth{
                    background-color: yellow;
                    border-style: solid;
                    font-weight:bold;
                    position: absolute;
                    bottom: 200 ;
                    right: 200;
                    height: 100;
                    width: 100;
            }
```

**EXAMPLE  15.18 (CONTINUED)**

```
    </style>
5   <body>
6       <p id="first">
            First position
        </p>
7       <p id="second">
            Second position
        </p>
8       <p id="third">
            Third position
        </p>
9       <p id="fourth">
            Fourth position
        </p>
    </body>
    </html>
```

**EXPLANATION**

1   An ID selector called *#first* sets the pixel positions for a red block that will be ab-
    solutely positioned 100 pixels from the top of the window, 200 pixels from the
    right-hand side, and have a size of 100 × 100 pixels (width × height).

2   An ID selector called *#second* sets the pixel positions for a blue block that will be
    absolutely positioned 200 pixels from the bottom of the window, 200 pixels from
    the left-hand side, and have a size of 100 × 100 pixels (width × height).

3   An ID selector called *#third* sets the pixel positions for an orange block that will
    be absolutely positioned 100 pixels from the top of the window, 200 pixels from
    the left-hand side, and have a size of 100 × 100 pixels (width × height).

4   An ID selector called *#fourth* sets the pixel positions for a yellow block that will
    be absolutely positioned 200 pixels from the bottom of the window, 200 pixels
    from the right-hand side, and have a size of 100 × 100 pixels (width × height).

5   The body is called the container for the elements within it. The red, blue, orange,
    and yellow boxes will appear in the window at the absolute positions assigned to
    them in relationship to their container, the body of the document.

6   The paragraph element is positioned and styled according to the rule for the *first*
    ID selector, the top, right-hand corner.

7   The paragraph element is positioned and styled according to the rule for the *sec-
    ond* ID selector, the left-hand, bottom corner.

8   The paragraph element is positioned and styled according to the rule for the *third*
    ID selector, the top, left-hand corner.

9   The paragraph element is positioned and styled according to the rule for the *fourth*
    ID selector,  the bottom right-hand corner. See Figure 15.19.

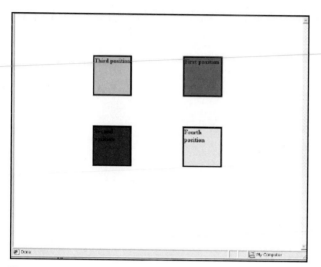

**Figure 15.19**   Absolute positions with four blocks.

**The *<div>* Tag.**   One of the most important containers is the *<div>* tag. It serves as a container where you can put other elements, give them color, borders, margins, etc. The *<div>* tag is also used for absolute positioning of a block of text that separates itself from other content in the document. It allows you to create a paragraph style independent of the *<p>* tag. Within the block, the *<span>* tags can be used to introduce other styles.

In the following example, the *<div>* tag is used to create a block. It is absolutely positioned in the window at position 0,0, which is the top, left-hand corner.

---

**EXAMPLE  15.19**

```
      <html><head><title>Positioning</title>
      </head>
1     <style>
2         .divStyle {background-color:blue;
3                    position: absolute;
                     width: 250px; height: 150px;
          }
      </style>
      </head>
      <body>
          <font size="+2">
4         <div class="divStyle">
5             <p>
                  This is a paragraph.
              </p>
          </div>
      </body>
      </html>
```

## EXPLANATION

1    The style sheet starts here with the *<style>* tag.

2    A class called *divStyle* is defined.

3    This style will produce a blue box, 250 pixels wide and 150 pixels high. It will be positioned at the top, left-hand corner of the window (0,0) because the *top* and *left* properties are undefined.

4    The *div* element will use the style defined by the *divStyle* class.

5    The paragraph element is embedded within the *<div>* tags. The div box is like a mini window. It will placed at the top, left-hand corner of the window, because its position has not been defined. See Figure 15.20.

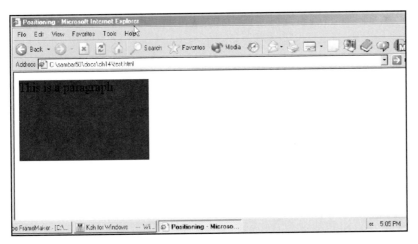

**Figure 15.20**    The *div* block is absolutely positioned in the window.

**Relative Positioning.**    Relative positioning places the element in a position relative to the element where it is defined in the document. In the following example the *.ParaStyle* class is positioned relative to where it should be placed within its container, a *div* block.

## EXAMPLE    15.20

```
      <html><head><title>Positioning</title>
      </head>
1     <style>
2        .divStyle { background-color:lightblue;
3                    position: absolute;
4                    width: 250px; height: 150px;
                     border-style: solid;
                     border-color: darkblue;
          }
```

**EXAMPLE    15.20 (CONTINUED)**

```
5       .paraStyle { color:darkblue;
6                   position: relative;
        }
    </style>
    </head>
    <body>
        <font size="+2">
7       <div style="left:50px; top:50px" class="divStyle">
8           <p style="left:15%; top:30%" class="paraStyle">
                This is a paragraph.
            </p>
        </div>
    </body>
    </html>
```

**EXPLANATION**

1   The style sheet starts here.

2   A style class called *divStyle* is defined for the *div* element.

3   The *div* box will be absolutely positioned in terms of the browser window.

4   The dimensions of width and height of the *div* box are set. The border around the *div* container is a solid, dark blue.

5   A style class called *paraStyle* is defined for the paragraph (*p*) element. The color of the text will be dark blue.

6   The position will be relative to the *div* box where the paragraph is contained. If *top* and *left* properties are not defined, the paragraph will be in the top, left-hand corner of the box, position 0,0 relative to the *div* container where it is placed.

7   An inline style is set for the *div* element, placing the box 50 pixels from both the top and the left-hand side of the browser window.

8   An inline style is set for the *p* element, placing the paragraph at a percentage of 15% from the left and 30% from the top based on the dimensions of the *div* box. See Figure 15.21.

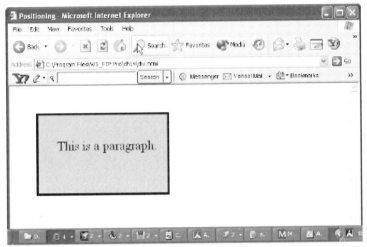

**Figure 15.21**   The paragraph is postioned relative to the *div* style.

**The *z-index* and Three Dimensions.**   The last type of position sets the precedence of a stack of overlapping elements. The absolute position properties include three coordinates: $x$, $y$, and $z$, where $x$ is the left side of an object, $y$ is the right side, and $z$ is the value of the stacking position. If you have three containers layered on top of each other, the $z$ position of the bottom layer is 0; the next layer, 1; and the top layer in the stack is layer 2. In the next section, JavaScript will allow us to move these objects around, rearranging the stacking order dynamically, by manipulating the $z$-position.

**EXAMPLE   15.21**

```
      <html><head><title>layers</title></head>
      <body bgcolor=lightgreen>
1     <span style="position: absolute; z-index:0;
          background-color: red; width: 200;height:250;
          top: 50px; left:160px;"></span>
2     <span style="position: absolute; z-index:1;
          background-color:yellow; width: 90;height:300;
          top: 20px; left:210px;"></span>
3     <span style="position: absolute; z-index:2;
          background-color: blue; width: 250;height:100;
          top: 125px; left:134px;"></span>
4     <span style="position: absolute; z-index:3;
          background-color: white; width: 50;height:50;
          top: 140px; left:230px;"></span>
      </body></html>
```

**EXPLANATION**

1   A *span style* is used to create a red rectangle, size 200 pixels × 250 pixels, in the top left-hand corner of the screen. A *z-index* of 0 means that this rectangle will be the bottom layer in a stack.

2   A *span style* is used to create a yellow rectangle, size 90 pixels × 300 pixels, positioned above the red rectangle, *z-index* of 1, or on top of it in the stacking order.

3   A *span style* is used to create a blue rectangle, size 250 pixels × 100 pixels, positioned above the yellow rectangle, *z-index* of 2, or on top of it in the stacking order.

4   A *span style* is used to create a white square, size 50 pixels × 50 pixels, positioned above the blue rectangle, *z-index* of 3, or on top of it in the stacking order.

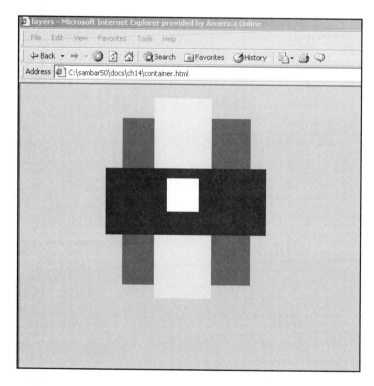

**Figure 15.22**
Three dimensions and the *z-index*.

## 15.4 Where Does JavaScript Fit In?

The W3C DOM (level 1) provides JavaScript applications a standard way to access all the elements of the document. In order for JavaScript to change the style of a document dynamically, the HTML tags must be represented as objects. We have already discussed the hierarchical tree-like structure of the document object model in Chapter 11, "The Document Objects: Forms, Images, and Links."

## 15.4.1 How the DOM Works with Nodes

Now we will take the DOM to a new level. Just as we used the DOM to access forms, images, and links as objects, now we can use the DOM to access every element in an HTML document. The standard DOM level 1 currently consists of two parts: the DOM core and the DOM HTML (see *http://www.w3.org/TR/REC-DOM-Level-1/introduction.html*). The DOM core specifies a standard way to manipulate document structures, elements, and attributes; the DOM HTML just extends that functionality to HTML. Recall that the DOM represented an HTML document as a tree: with the DOM, every HTML element can be defined as part of the tree, as shown in Figure 15.23.

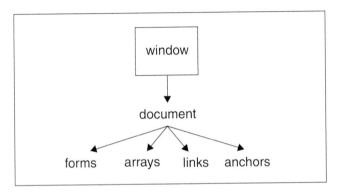

**Figure 15.23**   The tree-like hierarchy of the document object model.

   The purpose of the hierarchal tree is to provide a logical structure to represent a document and a way to navigate that structure, and to add, modify, or delete elements and content from it. Starting with the document at the top of the tree, you can traverse down the tree to every element until you reach the element, attribute, or text you are seeking. The core DOM identifies each element in the tree as a <u>node</u> object. There are parent and child nodes, sibling nodes, and more (see Table 15.10).

**Table 15.10**   Some DOM objects.

| Object | Definition |
| --- | --- |
| Node | The primary data type that represents an HTML element |
| Document | The root of the document tree |
| Element | An element within an HTML document |
| Attribute | Attributes of an HTML tag |
| Text | The text between markup tags, such as the text between <h1> and </h1> |

The DOM views every HTML element shown in Figure 15.24 as a node. In the tree, the top node is the *<html>* tag, called the root node of the document. Below it are the *<head>* and *<body>* tags, which are called child nodes of the HTML element. In the *<title>* is the text *My Title,* which is also a node, called a text node. Since it is the last node, the tree-like structure terminates at that node, also called a leaf node. The nodes are divided into three types of nodes: the element node, attribute node, and the text node. These types are numbered 1, 2, and 3, for element, attribute, and text node, respectively. In the example, the *<title>* and *</title>* tags are element nodes, and the text between the tags, *My Title,* is an example of a text node. An attribute node is represented as a property of the HTML element to which it is assigned. The *<a>* tag has an *href* attribute. In the example, *<a href="http://www.prenhall.com">, href* is an attribute node and the URL is called its *nodeValue.* (The text nodes are not supported on all browsers.)

Refer to Tables 15.11 and 15.12 for a list of node properties and node methods.

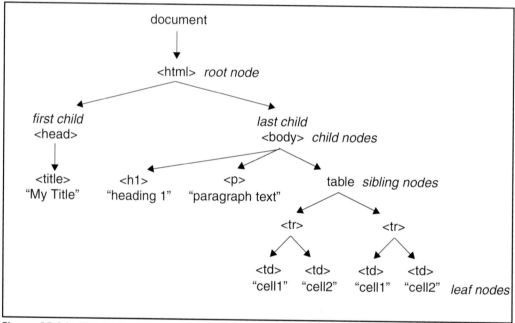

**Figure 15.24**   The node hierarchy.

**Table 15.11**   Node properties.

| Property | What It Does |
| --- | --- |
| *firstChild* | Returns the first child node of an element |
| *lastChild* | Returns the last child node of an element |
| *nextSibling* | Returns the next child node of an element at the same level as the current child node |

**Table 15.11**   Node properties. (continued)

| Property | What It Does |
|---|---|
| nodeName | Returns the name of the node |
| nodeType | Returns the type of the node as a number: 1 for element, 2 for attribute, 3 for text |
| nodeValue | Sets the value of the node in plain text |
| ownerDocument | Returns the root node of the document that contains the node |
| parentNode | Returns the element that contains the current node |
| previousSibling | Returns the previous child node of an element at the same level as the current child node |

**Table 15.12**   Node methods.

| Method | What It Does |
|---|---|
| appendChild(new node) | Appends a new node onto the end of the list of child nodes |
| cloneNode(child option) | Makes a clone of a node |
| hasChildNodes() | Returns *true* if the node has children |
| insertBefore(new node, current node) | Inserts a new node in the list of children |
| removeChild(child node) | Removes a child node from a list of children |
| replaceChild(new child, old child) | Replaces an old child node with a new one |

**Siblings.**   A sibling is a node on the same level as another node. In the example,

```
<p>
    <em>this is </em>some <b>text</b>
</p>
```

the parent node is *<p>* and has two children, the *<em>* node and the *<b>* node. Since the *<em>* and *<b>* are at the same level within the text, they are called siblings, like brother or sister nodes.

**Parents and Children.**   When looking at the structure of the tree hierarchy, some nodes are above others. A node above another node is a parent node, and the ones below the parent node are its children. See Figure 15.25. Any HTML tags that have both an opening and a closing tag are always parent nodes, for example, <p> and </p>.

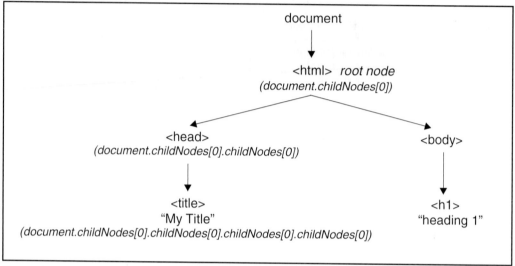

**Figure 15.25**   Tree hierarchy of nodes.

Attributes of an element are not child nodes, but are considered to be separate nodes in their own right. For example, the *href* attribute of the *<a>* tag is an attribute node, not a child of the *<a>* tag.

**The *nodeName* and *nodeType* Properties.**   When walking down DOM tree, you can find out the name of a node and the type of the node with the *nodeName* and *node-Type* properties. Table 15.13 gives the value for each of the properties.

**Table 15.13**   *nodeName* and *nodeType* properties.

| Node | nodeName Property | nodeType Property |
|------|-------------------|-------------------|
| Attribute | Name of the attribute (*id, href*) | 2 |
| Element | Name of the element (*h1, p*) | 1 |
| Text | *#text* | 3 |

EXAMPLE   15.22

```
      <html>
      <head><title>The Nodes</title></head>
      <body><font size="+2">
         <h1>Walking with Nodes</h1>
         <p>Who knows what node?</p>
1     <script name="javascript">
2        var Parent=document.childNodes[0];
3        var Child=Parent.childNodes[0];
         document.write("The parent node is: ");
4        document.write(Parent.nodeName+"<br>");
         document.write("The first child of the parent node is: ");
5        document.write(Child.nodeName+"<br>");
         document.write("The node below the child is: ");
6        document.write(Child.childNodes[0].nodeName+"<br>");
         document.write("The text node below title is: ");
7        document.write(Child.childNodes[0].childNodes[0].nodeName+"
            <br>");
         document.write("The first child of the parent is: ");
8        document.write(Parent.firstChild.nodeName+"<br>");
         document.write("The last child of the parent is: ");
9        document.write(Parent.lastChild.nodeName+"<br>");
         document.write("The node below the body is: ");
10       document.write(Parent.lastChild.childNodes[0].nodeName+
            "<br>");
         document.write("The next sibling of the h1 element is: ");
11       document.write(Parent.lastChild.childNodes[0].nextSibling.
            nodeName);
         document.write("<br>The last child's type is: ");
12       document.write(Parent.lastChild.nodeType);
      </script>
      </body>
      </html>
```

1   The JavaScript program will access the HTML elements through the DOM where each element is viewed as a node.

2   The first node, *childNodes[0]*, is the first node in the HTML hierarchy, the parent node. This node is assigned to a variable, *Parent*. The only reason to create the variable is to cut down on the amount of typing and propensity for errors when we go further down the document tree. Note: Watch your spelling when working with the DOM in JavaScript.

3   The parent node's first child is *document.childNodes[0].childNodes[0]*. This portion of the tree is assigned to the variable *Child*.

4   The name of a node is found in the *nodeName* property. The parent node is *HTML*, the highest element in the HTML hierarchy.

**EXPLANATION** (CONTINUED)

5   The *nodeName* of the first child of the parent node is *HEAD*.

6   The next node in the hierarchy is the child of the *HEAD* element. It is the *title* element:

```
<html>
   <head>
        <title>
```

7   Continuing the walk down the DOM tree, we come to the text node. It contains the text between the *<title> </title>* tags. The name of the text node is preceded by a # mark.

8   Using the *firstChild* property to simplify things, the first child of the parent again shows to be the *HEAD* element.

9   The last child of the HTML parent is the *BODY* element:

```
<html>
   <head>
   <body>
```

10  The node directly below the body is the *FONT* element:

```
<body><font size=+2</font>
```

11  The node below the body, *document.childNodes[0].lastChild.nodeName*, is the *H1* element.

12  The parent's last child node's type is 1. An element node type is type 1, an attribute type is type 2, and a text node is type 3. See Figure 15.26.

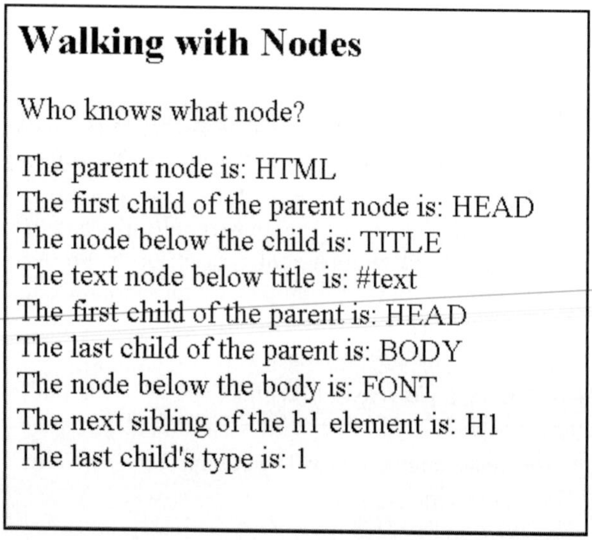

---

# Walking with Nodes

Who knows what node?

The parent node is: HTML
The first child of the parent node is: HEAD
The node below the child is: TITLE
The text node below title is: #text
The first child of the parent is: HEAD
The last child of the parent is: BODY
The node below the body is: FONT
The next sibling of the h1 element is: H1
The last child's type is: 1

**Figure 15.26**
Using the nodes to access
HTML elements.

**Working with the Elements.**   As you know, an HTML document is largely a set of elements, enclosed in < >, called tags. *H2* is an element, *<H2>* is a tag. The DOM is represented as a hierarchal tree of these elements, where each element is represented as a node. But walking with the nodes is just too much trouble most of the time, so the W3C DOM provides additional methods and properties to help make the walk easier.

**Table 15.14**   HTML element properties to represent HTML attributes.

| Property | Description | Example |
|---|---|---|
| *className* | Represents the class of a CSS element | `div2.className="blue";` *div2* refers to an HTML element. It is being assigned the CSS class called *blue* (see Example 15.29) |
| *dir* | Specifies the text direction for a document; e.g., read left to right (English), or right to left (Hebrew) | `element.dir="ltr";` |
| *id* | Value of the unique *id* of the current element | (see Section 15.4.2) |
| *lang* | Specifies the language in which the text of the document is written; e.g., *en* for English, *ja* for Japanese, and *sp* for Spanish | `if(document.lang=="ja")` |
| *style* | Value of the CSS inline style attribute (CSS2) | `div.style.color="green";` (see Section 15.4.4) |
| *title* | Returns the title of the document found between the *<title>* and *</title>* tags | `<title>My Book</title>` `strTitle = document.title` `strTitle contains "My Book"` |

## 15.4.2   All Those DOMs

You will often hear terms, like the Netscape DOM, the IE DOM, and the standard DOM. Before the W3C was able to create a standard, fourth-generation browsers introduced their own DOMs. Netscape 4, for example, implemented a *layer* DOM to control the positioning and visibility of elements, whereas Internet Explorer provided the *all* DOM to control positioning, visibility, and appearance of elements. They were not compatible and when you created a page, you had to perform cross-browser checking to determine which DOM should be used. This book addresses the W3C DOM, which has been embraced by most modern browsers, including NN6+ and IE5+.[2]

All browsers that comply with the W3C's DOM should implement the *ID* method for accessing the elements in a document. (See the next section for details.)

---

2. See *http://www.mozilla.org/docs/dom/domref/dom_el_ref.html* for a complete DOM elements interface.

Here is a little test code you can run to see if your browser is W3C DOM compliant:

```
isNetScape = (document.layers) ? true:false;
isInternetExplorer = (document.all) ? true: false;
if (document.getElementById){
    alert("DOM compliant!"); // Netscape 6+ and IE5+
```

Go to *http://developer.apple.com/internet/javascript/sniffer.html* to see examples of "browser sniffer" programs—programs that can tell what browser is being used.

### The *getElementById()* Method.

All that node stuff can be really tricky and vary on different browsers, but by combining the HTML *id* attribute with the *getElementById()* method of the *document* object, it is much easier to get a handle on any HTML object. The *getElementById()* method returns a reference to the HTML element that can then be manipulated by a JavaScript program. Suppose you have a *<body>* tag defined with an *id* attribute, as:

```
<body id="bdy1">
```

Now in JavaScript you can reference the body element with the *getElementById()* method as follows:

```
bdyreference = document.getElementById("bdy1")
```

Before the DOM was standardized, Internet Explorer (version 4+) provided another mechanism for accessing <u>all</u> HTML elements within the document, called the *all* property of the *document* object. The statement shown above written for IE could be written:

```
bdyreference = document.all["bdy1"];
```

And Netscape 4 provided yet another format:

```
bdyreference = document.layers["bdy1"]
```

Starting with IE5+ and NN6+, the W3C's *getElementID()* method is used rather than the *all* or the *layers* property. The newer browsers support the W3C standardized DOM although many Web pages were written using the older formats.

---

**EXAMPLE   15.23**

```
     <html>
     <head><title>The Dom and Id's</title></head>
1    <body id="body1">
2        <h1 id="head1">Heading Level 1</h1>
3        <p id="para1">
             This is a paragraph
         </p>
     </body>
     <script name="javascript">
4        var h1tag=document.getElementById("head1");
5        var bodytag=document.getElementById("body1");
6        var paratag = document.getElementById("para1");
7        h1tag.style.fontFamily="verdana";
         h1tag.style.fontSize="32";
         paratag.style.fontSize="28";
         paratag.style.color="blue";
         bodytag.style.backgroundColor="pink";
8        document.write(document.getElementById("body1")+"<br>");
         document.write(document.getElementById("head1")+"<br>");
         document.write(document.getElementById("para1")+"<br>");
     </script>
     </body>
     </html>
```

**EXPLANATION**

1   The *<body>* tag is given an *id* called *"body1"*.

2   The *<h1>* tag is given an *id* called *"head1"*.

3   The *<p>* tag is given an *id* called *"para1"*.

4   In the JavaScript program, the *getElementById()* method returns a reference to an *H1* element, and assigns that value to the variable called *h1tag*.

5   The *getElementById()* method returns a reference to a *BODY* element, and assigns that value to the variable called *bodytag*.

6   The *getElementById()* method returns a reference to a *P* element, and assigns that value to the variable called *paratag*.

7   Now, by using the *style* property (for a complete discussion, see "The style Object and CSS" on page 554), the elements are assigned new values for font size and color, causing them to change change dynamically.

8   The value returned by the *getElementById()* method is displayed for each of the elements by using their respective IDs. As shown in the output, each one of these HTML elements is an object. See Figure 15.27.

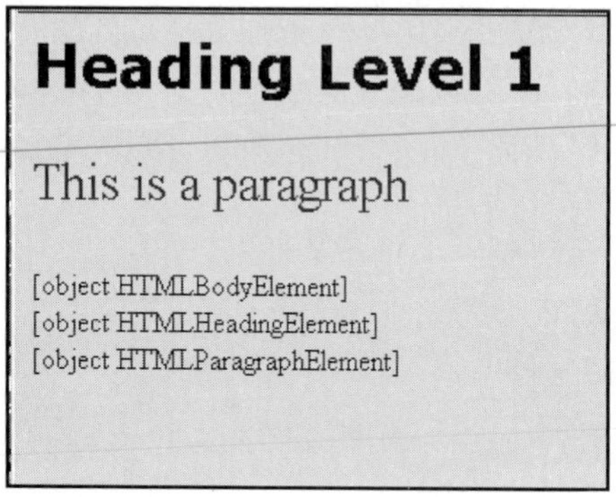

**Heading Level 1**

This is a paragraph

[object HTMLBodyElement]
[object HTMLHeadingElement]
[object HTMLParagraphElement]

**Figure 15.27**   HTML elements are objects.

**The *getElementsByTagName()* Method.**   To reference a collection of elements, such all the *<p>* tags, *<h1>* tags, or *<a>* tags in your document, you can use the *getElementsByTagName()* method. This method takes the name of the element as its argument and returns a list of all the nodes of that name in the document. If you need to collectively change the values of a particular element, such as all the links in an *<a>* tag, do this by manipulating the reference returned by the *getElementsByTagName()*.

**EXAMPLE** 15.24

```
    <html><head><title>Working with Tags</title>
    </head>
    <body bgcolor=lightblue>
1       <h1> First</h1>
        <h1> Second</h1>
        <h1> Third</h1>
    <font size="+2">
2   <script language="JavaScript">
        var heading1=document.getElementsByTagName("h1");
3       document.write(heading1 + "<br>");
        document.write("There are "+
4           heading1.length+ " H1 tags.<br>");
    </script>
    </body>
    </html>
```

**EXPLANATION**

1   Three *<h1>* tags are used in this document.

2   Because of the top-down processing by the HTML renderer, be sure to put the JavaScript program at the end of the document. This way, the tags will already have been identified before they are put into the HTML collection returned by the *getElementsByName()* method.

3   The HTML collection of H1 tags is stored as an array of nodes in the variable, *heading1*.

4   The length of the array is 3 in this example because there are three H1 elements in the document. See Figure 15.28.

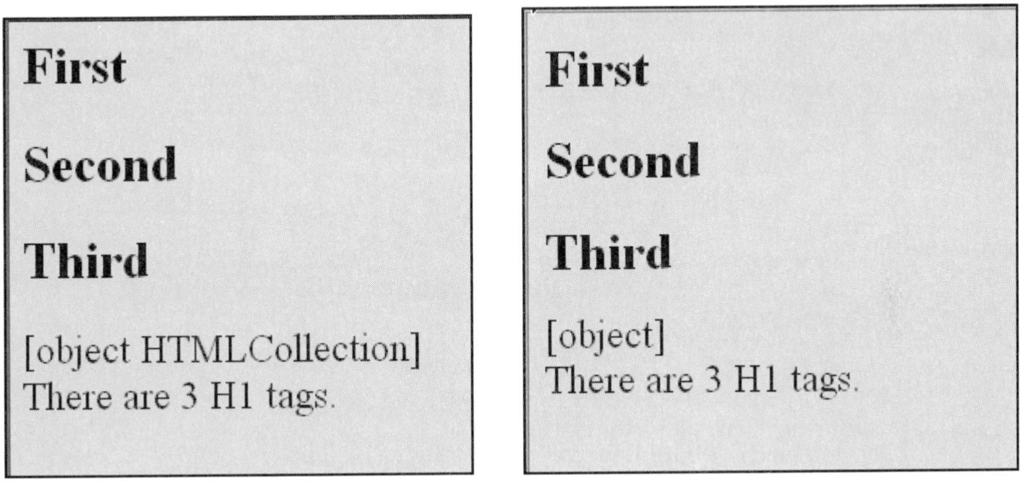

**First**

**Second**

**Third**

[object HTMLCollection]
There are 3 H1 tags.

**First**

**Second**

**Third**

[object]
There are 3 H1 tags.

**Figure 15.28**   Netscape 7 (left), IE 6 (right).

### 15.4.3   Scrolling with the Nodes

Although the title of this section may sound more like a title for a *Star Trek* drama, it is really about dynamic HTML. By using the *getElementById()* method and a little node knowledge, a scrolling marquee is created in Example 15.25. In Chapter 10 we saw scrolling in the window's status and title bar. Now we can scroll within the body of the document. In the following example, a message will continuously scroll across the screen. The original message is placed within a *<div>* container. By first identifying the HTML *div* element—*getElementById()*—JavaScript can then reference its child node, which is the text of the message (*firstChild*). This is depicted in Figure 15.29.

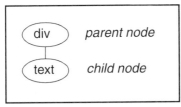

**Figure 15.29**   Referencing a child node requires first identifying the *div* element.

EXAMPLE 15.25

```
      <html><head><title>Scrolling Text</title>
      <style>
1         #div1 { background-color:darkgreen;
              color: white;
              font-family:courier;
              font-weight: bold;
              position:absolute;
              border-style:groove;
              border-color:white;
              padding-left:10px;
              top:20px;
              left:10px;
2             width: 595px; height: 6%;
3             overflow: hidden;
          }
4         img { position: absolute; top: 10px;left:60px;
                border-style:solid;border-color="darkgreen";}
      </style>
      <script language="JavaScript">
      <!--
5     /*Modification of text box marquee by Dave Methvin,
        Windows Magazine */
6         var scroll_speed = 200;    // 200 milliseconds
          var chars = 1;
7         function init(){
              divElement=document.getElementById("div1");
          }
8         function scroller() {
9             window.setTimeout('scroller()',scroll_speed);
10            var msg=divElement.firstChild.nodeValue;
11            divElement.firstChild.nodeValue = msg.substring(chars)
                            + msg.substring(0,chars);
          }
12        scroller();
      //-->
      </script>
      </head>
13    <body bgcolor="#669966" onLoad="init()";>
          <img src="BubyanIsland.JPG" width="450" length="500">
14        <div id="div1">
              The latest news from Baghdad is not good tonight. Sand and
              rain are hindering our troops. The number of refugees
              continues to increase in the north...
          </div>
      </body>
      </html>
```

## EXPLANATION

1   An ID selector is defined with a style for the *div* element on line 14.

2   The size of the *div* container is defined.

3   If the text within the *div* container will not fit within the dimensions of the box, the *overflow* property will adjust it to fit.

4   The image is fixed at this absolute position on the screen and has a dark green, solid border.

5   The *scroller()* routine (line 8) was found at the Java Planet Web site and submitted by Dave Methvin. (Thank you Dave, wherever you are!) I have greatly modified the original.

6   The initial values used for the *scroller()* function are assigned values. One is the speed for the timer, the other the value of an argument to the *substr()* method.

7   This function, called *init()*, is called after the document has been loaded. Its purpose is to get a reference to the *div* element. The *getElementById()* method returns a reference to the *div* element.

8   The function called *scroller()* is defined. Its function is to cause the text found in the *<div>* container to scroll continuously from the right-hand side of the container.

9   The window's *setTimeOut()* method is used to call the *scroller()* function every 200 milliseconds (.2 seconds). It's the timer that creates the action of actually scrolling.

10  The *div* element is a parent node. It has a child node. The value of its first child, *divElement.firstChild.nodeValue*, is the textual content of the message; that is, the text found between the *<div></div>* tags. The variable *msg* gets the value of the child node.

11  The value returned by *msg.substr(1)* is "*he latest news from Baghdad is not good tonight. Sand and rain are hindering our troops. The number of refugees continues to increase in the north...*" Notice that the first character in the message has been removed. The next substring method will return the first character—*substring(0,1)*—and append it to the first value resulting in "*he latest news from Baghdad is not good tonight. Sand and rain are hindering our troops. The number of refugees continues to increase in the north...T*". All of this is assigned back to the value of the child node. In 200 milliseconds, the *scroller()* function is called again, and the message becomes "*e latest news from Baghdad is not good tonight. Sand and rain are hindering our troops. The number of refugees continues to increase in the north...Th*", and so on.

12  The *scroller()* function is called for the first time here.

13  In the *<body>* tag, the *onLoad* event is triggered as soon as the document has loaded.

14  The *<div>* tags contain the text of the message that will be scrolled. Its ID, "*div1*", defines the CSS style that will be used, and is the unique identifier that will be used by JavaScript to get a reference to it. See the output in Figure 15.30.

**Figure 15.30**   A scrolling marquee continues to print news across the image. (The U.S. Marine is Major Tom Savage, my son, alongside a fellow officer.)

### 15.4.4   The *style* Object and CSS

The *style* object contains a set of properties corresponding to the CSS attributes supported by your browser. Each HTML object has a *style* property (starting with IE4 and NN6) used to access the CSS style attributes assigned to it; for example, an *H1* element may have been defined with a CSS *font-style*, *color*, and *padding*. The *style* object has properties to reflect each of the CSS atributes. See Table 15.15.

Many of the CSS style attributes, such as *background-color*, *font-size*, and *word-spacing*, contain hyphens in their names. Like all objects we have seen in JavaScript, there is a convention for spelling the name of the object. The name would not contain a hyphen, and multiple words after the first word are usually capitalized. Therefore, the CSS naming convention is different with the properties of the *style* object. The hyphen is removed and the first letter of each word after the hypen is capitalized. For example, the CSS attribute, *background-color*, when used as a style property, is spelled *backgroundColor*, *font-size* is *fontSize*, and *border-right-width* is *borderRightWidth*.

### FORMAT

```
elementname.style.property="value";
```

**Example:**

```
div2.style.fontFamily = "arial";
```

**Table 15.15**   *style* object properties.

| Property | Example CSS Value | HTML Tags Affected |
|----------|-------------------|--------------------|
| Fonts | | |
| *font* | 12pt/14pt sans-serif, 80% sans-serif, x-large/110% arial, normal small-caps | All |
| *fontFamily* | serif, sans-serif, cursive, fantasy, monospace | All |
| *fontSize* | 12pt, larger, 150%, 1.5em | All |
| *fontStyle* | normal, italic, oblique | All |
| *fontVariant* | normal, small-caps | All |
| *fontWeight* | normal, bold, bolder, lighter, 100, 200...900 | All |
| Colors | | |
| *backgroundColor* | red, blue, #F00 | All |
| *color* | red, green, #F00, rgb(255,0,0) | All |
| Images | | |
| *backgroundAttachment* | scroll, fixed | All |
| *backgroundImage* | URL (bay.gif), none | All |
| *backgroundPosition* | right top, top center, center, bottom, 100% 100%, 0% 0%, 50% 50% | Block-level and replaced elements |
| *backgroundRepeat* | repeat, repeat-x (horizontally), repeat-y (vertically), no-repeat | All |
| Text Alignment | | |
| *letterSpacing* | normal, 0.1em | All |
| *lineHeight* | normal, 1.2, 1.2em, 120% | All |

**Table 15.15** *style* object properties. (continued)

| Property | Example CSS Value | HTML Tags Affected |
|---|---|---|
| **Text Alignment (continued)** | | |
| *textAlign* | left, right, center, justify | All |
| *textDecoration* | underline, overline, line-through, blink | All |
| *textIndent* | 3em, 15% | Block-level elements |
| *textTransform* | capitalize, uppercase, lowercase, none | All |
| *verticalAlign* | baseline, sub, super, top, text-top, middle, bottom, text-bottom, 50% | Inline elements |
| *wordSpacing* | normal, 2em | All |
| **Margins and Borders** | | |
| *align* | | All |
| *borderStyle* | none, solid, 3D | All |
| *borderWidth* | thin, medium, thick, 2em | All |
| *margin* | 5em, 3em, 2em, 1em (top, right, bottom, left) | All |
| *marginBottom* | 100px, 50% | All |
| *marginLeft* | .5in, 40% | All |
| *marginRight* | 20em, 45% | All |
| *marginTop* | 1cm, 20% | All |
| *padding* | 2em, 4em, 6em (right, bottom, left) | All |
| *paddingBottom* | 2em, 20% | All |
| *paddingLeft* | .25in, 20% | All |
| *paddingRight* | .5cm, 35% | All |
| *paddingTop* | 20px, 10% | All |
| *length* | | Block-level elements |
| *width* | 12em, 30%, auto (initial width value) | Block-level element |

For a complete list of properties, see *http://www.w3.org/TR/REC-CSS2/propidx.html*.

**EXAMPLE   15.26**

```
    <html>
    <head><title>Changing Background Color Dynamically</title>
1   <script language="JavaScript">
2   function bodyColor(){
3       var i = document.form1.body.selectedIndex;
4       bodycolor = document.form1.body.options[i].value;
5       document.getElementById("bdy").style.backgroundColor =
            bodycolor;
    }
    </script>
    </head>
6   <body ID="bdy">
    <p>
        Pick a background color for this page.
    </p>
7   <form name="form1">
    <b> Color </b>
8   <select name="body" onChange="bodyColor();">
        <option value="pink">pink</option>
        <option value="lightblue">blue</option>
        <option value="yellow">yellow</option>
        <option value="lightgreen">green</option>
    </select>
    <br>
    </form>
    <p>
        This is a test.
    </p>
    </body>
    </html>
```

**EXPLANATION**

1   The JavaScript program starts here.

2   A JavaScript user-defined function called *bodyColor()* is defined.

3   The number, *selectedIndex*, of the option chosen from a select list is assigned to variable *i*.

4   The value of the selected option is one of the colors listed in the select list on line 8.

5   The *getElementById()* method returns a reference to the *body* tag, whose ID is *bdy*. With the *style* property, the background color of the document is changed with this statement.

6   The *body* tag is given an *id* attribute by which to identify it.

7   An HTML form called *form1* starts here.

8   A select menu is defined to give the user options to change the background color of the document on the fly. The *onChange* event is triggered when one of the options is selected, and is handled by invoking the function *bodyColor()*. The output is shown in Figure 15.31.

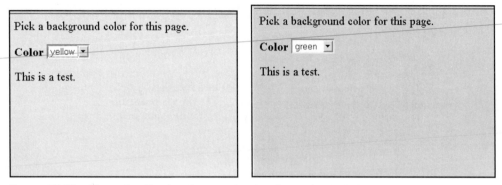

**Figure 15.31**   Changing the background color dynamically (left); now the color is green (right).

**Positioning Text with the *style* Property.**   By assigning a position to the *style* property it is possible to place an element in different sections of the page. In the following example, by assigning positions, the text is moved after the document has been loaded.

---

**EXAMPLE**   **15.27**

```
     <html><head><title>Positioning</title>
1    <script language="javascript">
        var div1,div2,div3;
2       function init(){
3           div1=document.getElementById("first");
            div2=document.getElementById("second");
            div3=document.getElementById("third");
        }
4       function movePosition(){
5           div1.style.left = 50;
            div1.style.top = 150;
6           div2.style.left = 100;
            div2.style.top = 100;
7           div3.style.left = 150;
            div3.style.top = 50;
        }
     </script>
     </head>
8    <body onLoad="init()">
     <font size="+2">
9    <div id="first" style="position:absolute; top:50px">one</div>
     <div id="second" style="position:absolute; top:100px">two</div>
     <div id="third" style="position:absolute; top:150px">three</div>
     <form>
     <input type="button" value="move text"
10      onClick="movePosition()">
     </form></body>
     </html>
```

## EXPLANATION

1   The JavaScript program starts here.

2   The first function defined is *init()*. It will be called after the document has been loaded.

3   The *getElementById()* method returns references to three *div* block objects.

4   A function called *movePosition()* is defined. It is responsible for moving the text to different positions on the screen.

5   The first block of text will be positioned at 50 pixels from the left-hand side of the screen and 150 pixels from the top.

6   The second block of text will be positioned at 100 pixels from the left-hand side of the screen and 100 pixels from the top.

7   And the third block of text will be positioned 150 pixels from the left-hand side of the screen and 50 pixels from the top.

8   The *onLoad* event is triggered just after the page has been loaded, and will invoke the *init()* function.

9   The *div* containers are assigned absolute positions on the page. Each *div* block will contain a string of text.

10  When the user clicks on the button labeled "move text", the *onClick* event will be triggered, causing the text to be moved to a different location on the page. See Figure 15.32.

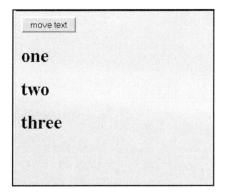
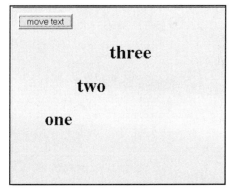

**Figure 15.32**   Before clicking the button (left); after clicking the button (right).

Now we will change the position values in the program, as shown in Example 15.28. The output is shown in Figure 15.33.

**EXAMPLE 15.28**

```
(See Example 15.27 for the complete program.)

    function movePosition(){
        div1.style.left = 50;
        div1.style.top = 50;

        div2.style.left = 100;
        div2.style.top = 100;

        div3.style.left = 150;
        div3.style.top = 150;
    }
```

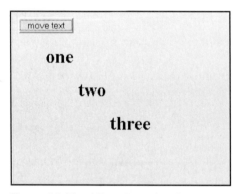

**Figure 15.33**  After changing the x,y positions in the program.

**Changing Color with the *className* Property.**  The *className* property is defined for all HTML elements. With the *className* property, you can change an element dynamically by assigning it the name of a class defined in a CSS. The following example contains a cascading style sheet with three classes.

**EXAMPLE 15.29**

```
    <html><head><title>Coloring Text</title>
    <style type="text/css">
        body { background-color: yellow;
                font-size: 22pt;
                font-weight: bold;
        }
```

**EXAMPLE   15.29** (CONTINUED)

```
1       .red { color:rgb(255,0,0);    /* Defining classes */
            font-style: verdana;
            font-size: 32;
        }
2       .blue { color:blue;
             font-style: verdana;
             font-size: 36;
        }
3       .green { color: green;
             font-style: verdana;
             font-size: 40;
        }
    </style>
    <script language="javascript">
4       function init(){
            div1=document.getElementById("first");
            div2=document.getElementById("second");
            div3=document.getElementById("third");
        }
5       function colorText(){
            div1.style.left = 50;
            div1.style.top = 50;
6           div1.className="red";
            div2.style.left = 100;
            div2.style.top = 100;
7           div2.className="blue";
            div3.style.left = 150;
            div3.style.top = 150;
8           div3.className="green";
        }
    </script>
    </head>
9   <body onLoad="init()">
        <div id="first"  style="position:absolute; top:50px">It's a
            one,</div>
        <div id="second"  style="position:absolute; top:100px">and a
            two,</div>
        <div id="third"  style="position:absolute; top:150px">and
            three!</div>
    <form>
        <input type="button" value="move and color text"
10          onClick="colorText()">
    </form>
    </body>
```

## EXPLANATION

1  A CSS class for a style is defined. Text will be a red, Verdana font, point size 32. The rgb (red, green, blue) color is used here for demonstration. It would be easier to just assign *red* to the *color* property.

2  A CSS class for another style is defined. The text will be a blue, Verdana font, point size 36.

3  A CSS class for a third style is defined. The text will be a green, Verdana font, point size 40. Notice that each class not only changes the color of the font, but increases its point size.

4  When the *onLoad* event is triggered, just after the document has been loaded, the user-defined *init()* function is called. The *getElementById()* method returns references to three *div* objects.

5  A function called *colorText()* is defined. It sets the position of the *div* containers and defines the color for the text in each container.

6  The *className* property is used to reference the CSS class named *red*, defined in the document.

7  The *className* property is used to reference the CSS class named *blue*, defined in the document.

8  The *className* property is used to reference the CSS class named *green*, defined in the document.

9  The *onLoad* event is triggered just after the document is loaded. It will invoke the *init()* function.

10  When the user clicks on this button, the *onClick* event is triggered. It invokes the *colorText()* function, which will move and change the text in each of the *div* containers.

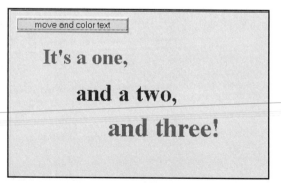

**Figure 15.34**  The initial appearance of the document (left); after clicking the button, the color, position, and size of the text is changed (right).

## 15.4.5   Event Handling and the DOM

We have been discussing events since Chapter 1. They are what allow the program to react to user-initiated events. After browsers got to their fourth version, the events became full-fledged objects. The *event* object has knowledge about the event: what caused it, what triggered it, where it occured on the screen, and even the parent of the tag that triggered it. The *event* object, like other objects, has a collection of properties and methods associated with it. Not all browsers support the same event model and not all browsers refer to the event in the same way or even use the same properties.

**Trickling and Bubbling.**   The way that the events are captured differs by the browser. In Netscape 4, for example, the event comes to life at the window level and is sent down the tree of nodes until it finally reaches the target object for which it was intended; whereas with IE the event springs to life for the target it was intended to affect, and then sends information about the event back up the chain of nodes. With Netscape 4, the event trickles down from the top to its target, and with the IE approach the event bubbles up from its target. Handling the way events propagate is another browser compatibility issue.

The W3C DOM level 2 provides an Events module that allows the DOM nodes to handle events with a combination of these methods, but defaults to the bubble up propagation model. This is supported by Netscape 6+, but not IE 6.

There are a number of event types defined by the DOM HTML Events module, as shown in Table 15.16.

**Table 15.16**   Event properties.

| Name | What It Describes |
|---|---|
| *bubbles* | Boolean to test whether an event can bubble up the document tree |
| *canceleable* | Boolean to test whether the event can be cancelled |
| *currentTarget* | The node currently being processed by a handler (NN) |
| *eventPhase* | A number specifying the phase of the event propagation |
| *fromElement* | Refers to the object where the mouse was pointing before the mouseover event was triggered (IE) |
| *srcElement* | Refers to the object of the tag that caused the event to fire |
| *target* | The node on which the event occurred, not necessarily the same as *currentTarget* |
| *timeStamp* | When the event occurred (a *Date* object) |
| *type* | The type of the event that occurred, such as *click* or *mouseOut* |

In the following example, *mouseOver* and *mouseOut* events will be used to change the style of a block of text to give it emphasis. When the mouse rolls over a specific block of text, the event handler invokes a function that can check to see what block of text the mouse is on and detect when it leaves the box. The node where the event occurred can be found in the *currentTarget* property (NN) or the *fromElement* property (IE).

**EXAMPLE   15.30**

```
         <html><head><title>Positioning</title>
1        <link rel=stylesheet type="text/css"
             href="externstyle.css">
         <script language="javascript">
             function init(){
                 div1=document.getElementById("first");
                 div2=document.getElementById("second");
                 div3=document.getElementById("third");
             }
2        function colorText(e){
3            if(e.currentTarget.id == "first") {
                         // Use e.fromElement.id (IE6)
4                div1.className="red";
             }
             else if(e.currentTarget.id == "second"){
                 div2.className="blue";
             }
             else{ div3.className="green";}
         }
3        function unColorText(e){
             if(e.currentTarget.id == "first"){
                         // use e.srcElement.id (IE6)
                 div1.className="black";
             }
             else if(e.currentTarget.id == "second"){
                 div2.className="black";
             }
             else{
                 div3.className="black";
             }
         }
         </script>
         </head>
```

**EXAMPLE**   15.30 (CONTINUED)

```
          <body onLoad="init()">
4            <div id="first"
                 style="position:absolute; top:50px"
5               onMouseover="unColorText(event);"
6               onMouseout="colorText(event);">Roll over me! </div>
             <div id="second"
                 style="position:absolute; top:100px"
                 onMouseover="unColorText(event);"
                 onMouseout="colorText(event);">and then me,</div>
             <div id="third"
                 style="position:absolute; top:150px"
                 onMouseover="unColorText(event);"
                 onMouseout="colorText(event);">and me too.</div>
          </body>
          </html>
```

**EXPLANATION**

1   The style for this document is coming from an external style sheet. It's the same style used in the previous example and can be found on the CD-ROM in the back of this book.

2   A function called *colorText()* is defined. It takes one argument, a reference to the event that caused it to be invoked.

3   The *current.Target.id* is a property that references the *id* of the tag where this event occurred: the *<div>* tag with the *id* of *"first"*. If this doesn't work for you, use the IE *fromElement* property for the *mouseOver* event. To get the *id* name for the *div* container, use *e.fromElement.id*. For the *mouseOut* event, use the *src.Element* property and *e.srcElement.id*.

4   The first *div* container is defined with an *id* name *"first"*.

5   When the mouse is moved onto the second *div* container, the *onMouseover* event is triggered and the *colorText()* function is called. It passes a reference to the *event* object to the function allowing the function to know more about the event that just occurred and what *div* container it applies to.

6   When the mouse is moved away from the *div* container, the *onMouseout* event is triggered, and the function *colorText* is called, passing a reference to the *event* object. The output is shown in Figure 15.35.

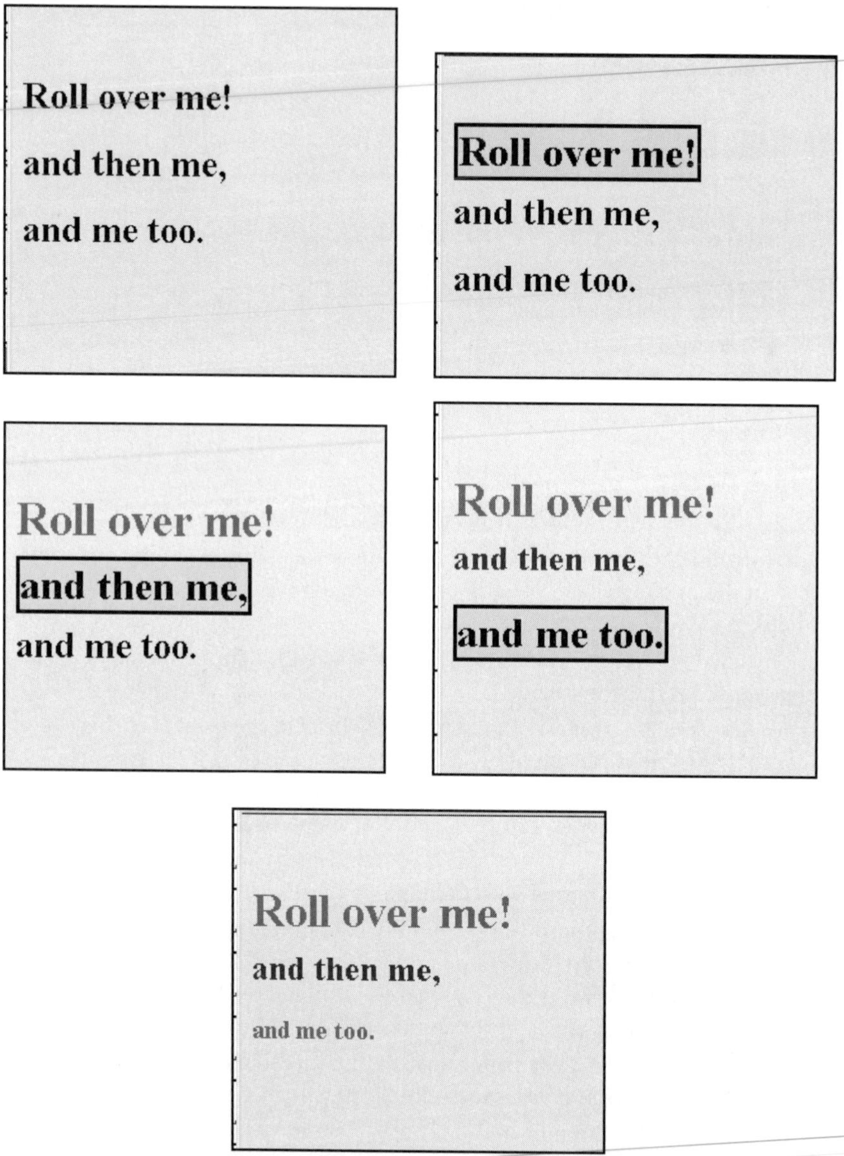

**Figure 15.35** Before the mouse rolls over the first *<div>* block (top left); when the mouse rolls over the first *<div>* block (top right); when the mouse leaves the first *div* container and rolls over the next one (midddle left); now the mouse has rolled over the last *<div>* container (middle right); after the mouse has left all three containers (bottom).

### 15.4.6 Back to the *z-index* and Dynamic Positioning

In the CSS section of this chapter, the *zIndex* property was described to create a three-dimensional effect with a stack of *<div>* containers. In the following example a JavaScript program manipulates the containers so that they can be moved into different positions.

**EXAMPLE 15.31**

```
      <html><head><title>layers</title>
      <script language="JavaScript">
1     function moveUp(id){
2         var box= document.getElementById(id);
3         if(box.style.zIndex == 100){    // Can't stack higher than 100
4             box.style.zIndex=2;
          }
5         else if(box.style.zIndex != 3){
              box.style.zIndex=100;
          }
          else{
6             box.style.zIndex=0;
          }
      }
      </script>
      </head>
      <body bgcolor=lightgreen>
7     <span id="red" style="position: absolute;z-index:0;
          background-color:red; width:200; height:250;
          top:50px; left:160px;"
8         onClick="moveUp(id);"></span>

9     <span id="yellow" style="position: absolute;z-index:1;
          background-color:yellow; width:90; height:300;
          top:20px; left:210px;"
          onClick="moveUp(id);"></span>

10    <span id="blue" style="position: absolute;z-index:2;
          background-color:blue; width:250; height:100;
          top:125px; left:134px;"
          onClick="moveUp(id);"></span>

11    <span id="white" style="position: absolute;z-index:3;
          background-color:white; width:50; height:50;
          top:140px; left:230px;"
          onClick="moveUp(id);"></span>
      </body>
      </html>
```

## EXPLANATION

1    The JavaScript user-defined function called *moveUp()* is defined. It has one parameter, the *id* of the tag from where it was called.

2    The *getElementById()* method returns a reference to the object that called this function and assigns it to the variable, called *box*.

3    If the *zIndex* of the object evaluates to 100, it must be at the top of the stack, because that is as high as the stack gets.

4    This sets the stack level of the *zIndex* to 2, causing it to move toward the bottom of the stack.

5    If the *zIndex* for the object is not 3, it is not at the top. Its *zIndex* will be set to 100, moving it to the top of the stack.

6    The object is moved to the bottom of the stack with a *zIndex* of 0.

7    The *<span>* tag is used to create a rectangular red box on the screen. With a *zIndex* of 0, it will be positioned at the bottom of the stack.

8    When the user clicks on the button, the *onClick* event is triggered, and the handler function, *moveUp(id)*, is called.

9    A yellow rectangular box is created with the *<span>* tag. With a *zIndex* of 1, it will be positioned above the last block in the stack.

10   A blue square box is created with the *<span>* tag. With a *zIndex* of 2, it will be positioned above the last block in the stack.

11   A small white rectangular box is created with the *<span>* tag. With a *zIndex* of 3, it will be positioned at the top of the stack. See Figure 15.36.

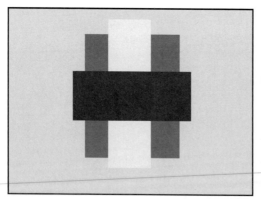 

**Figure 15.36**   The original configuration of the four rectangles (left); after manipulating the rectangles by reassigning the *z-index* (right).

## 15.4.7   Setting Visibility

The *visibility* property lets you hide an object and then bring it back into view. You can also use the *visibility* property to determine the state: it "visible" or "hidden"?[3] This property is useful when creating interfaces such as drop-down menus, slide shows, and pop-ups such as extra text to explain a link or image map.[4]

**Drop-Down Menus.**   Drop-down menus are commonly used in Web pages to create submenus that appear and then disappear when no longer needed. The following example demonstrates the use of the *visibility* property to create this type of menu. When the user clicks on one of the links in the main menu, a drop-down menu will appear. If he double-clicks anywhere within the drop-down menu, it will be hidden from view. Each of the drop-down menus is defined within a *<div>* container.

**EXAMPLE   15.32**

```
         <html><head><title>Drop-Down Menu</title>
         <style type="text/css">
1            a {  font-family: verdana, arial;
                  color: darkblue;
                  font-weight: bold;
                  margin-left: 4px; } /*link style for main menu*/
2            #menu, .menu { font-stye: verdana;
                        font-size:10pt;
                        color:black; }
                        /* link style for drop-down menu */
3            #menu { position:absolute;
                     top:40px;
                     border-style:solid;
                     border-width:1px;
                     padding: 5px;
                     background-color:yellow;
                     width:75px;
                     color: black;
                     font-size: 12pt;
4                    visibility:hidden; }
5            #menu2 { position:absolute;
                      top:40px;
                      left:3.2cm;
                      border-style:solid;
                      border-width:1px;
                      padding: 5px;
```

---

3. Netscape 4 specifies a value of *show* or *hide* with the *visibility* property of the *Layer* object.

4. The *visibility* property applies to an entire object. The *clip* property allows you to designate how much of an element will be visible.

**EXAMPLE** 15.32 (CONTINUED)

```
                background-color:orange;
                width:80px;
                color: black;
                font-size: 12pt;
                visibility:hidden; }

6       #menu3 { position:absolute;
                top:40px;
                left:6.2cm;
                border-style:solid;
                border-width:1px;
                padding: 5px;
                background-color:pink;
                width:80px;
                color: black;
                font-size: 12pt;
                visibility:hidden; }
7   </style>
    <script language="JavaScript">
8   function showMenu(id){
9       var ref = document.getElementById(id);
10      ref.style.visibility = "visible";   // Make the drop-down
                                            // menu visible
    }
11  function hideMenu(id){
12      var ref = document.getElementById(id);
13      ref.style.visibility = "hidden";    // Hide the drop-down menu
    }
    </script>
    <body bgColor="lightblue">
14  <table width="350" border="2" bgcolor="lightgreen" cellspacing="1"
        cellpadding="2">
    <tr>
        <td width="100">
15          <div id="menu" onDblClick="hideMenu('menu');">
16              <a class="menu" href="#">US</a><br>
                <a class="menu" href="#">World</a><br>
                <a class="menu" href="#">Local </a><br>
            </div>
17          <a href="#" onClick="showMenu('menu');">News</a>
        </td>
        <td width="100">
18          <div id="menu2" onDblClick="hideMenu('menu2');">
19              <a class="menu" href="#">Basketball</a><br>
                <a class="menu" href="#">Football</a><br>
                <a class="menu" href="#">Soccer</a><br>
            </div>
20          <a href="#" onClick="showMenu('menu2');">Sports</a>
        </td>
        <td width="100">
```

**EXAMPLE**   15.32 (CONTINUED)

```
21            <div id="menu3" onDblClick="hideMenu('menu3');">
                 <a class="menu" href="#">Movies</a><br>
                 <a class="menu" href="#">Plays</a><br>
                 <a class="menu" href="#>">DVD's</a><br>
              </div>
              <a href="#" onClick="showMenu('menu3');">Entertainment</a>
           </td>
22      </tr></table>
        </body>
        </html>
```

**EXPLANATION**

1   The *a* selector is followed by the style definition for the links that appear in the main menu.

2   An ID selector and a class are defined. This style will be used on links in the drop-down menus.

3   This ID selector defines the style of the first drop-down menu. When the user clicks the News link, this yellow drop-down menu will appear directly under the table cell containing the News link.

4   Initially, the first drop-down menu is *hidden* from view.

5   This ID selector defines the style of the second drop-down menu. It will be orange and drop down directly under the Sports link.

6   This ID selector defines the style of the third drop-down menu. It will be pink and drop down directly under the Entertainment link.

7   The CSS ends here, and the JavaScript program begins on the next line.

8   A function called *showMenu* is defined. Its only parameter is the *id* attribute of a *div* object, that is, the ID of one of the three drop-down menus.

9   The *getElementById()* method returns a reference to the *div* object which contains the drop-down menu.

10  The *visibility* property is set to *visible*. The drop-down object comes into view, right below the main menu item where the user clicked on the link.

11  A function called *hideMenu()* is defined. Its only parameter is the *id* attribute of a *div* object. When this function is invoked, the drop-down menu being referenced will be *hidden* from view.

12  The *getElementById()* method returns a reference to the *div* object that contains the drop-down menu.

13  The *visibility* property is set to *hidden*. The object being referenced disappears from view.

14  An HTML table is defined. It will be light green, 350 pixels wide, and contain one row and three data cells.

**EXPLANATION** (CONTINUED)

15  The first cell of the table contains a *<div>* container that is positioned and styled by the CSS *#menu* ID selector. If the user double-clicks from within this tag, it will be hidden from view.

16  The links within the *<div>* container are described by the CSS *.menu* class. The links are deactivated for this example.

17  When the user clicks on this link, the main link for the cell, called News, the *on-Click* event will be triggered. A function called *showMenu* will be invoked, causing the drop-down menu to appear.

18  The second drop-down menu is created and will be made visible when the user clicks on the Sports link.

19  The drop-down menu is defined here.

20  When the user clicks on the Sports link, the *onClick* event handler will cause a drop-down menu to be made visible.

21  Like the other two links, the Entertainment link also has a drop-down menu associated with it which will be made visible when the user clicks on it, and made invisible when the user double-clicks on the drop-down list.

22  The table row and table are closed. See Figure 15.37.

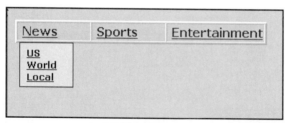

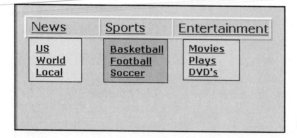

**Figure 15.37**
The first drop-down menu off the main menu—if the user double-clicks his mouse anywhere on the drop-down menu, it will be hidden from view (top); the second drop-down menu (middle); the third drop-down menu (bottom).

**Tool Tips.**   When a user's mouse rolls over a section of text or an image, a little tool tip might appear as a little rectangular box of text to give helpful hints or clues to clarify the presentation. And when he moves his mouse away from the area, the tool tip will disappear. You can use the HTML *title* attribute to create simple tool tips, or you can create your own by taking advantage of the CSS *visibility* property and JavaScript event handlers.

**EXAMPLE   15.33**

```
      <html><head><title>A tool tip</title>
      <style type="text/css">
1        #divclass { font-size:12pt;
                     font-family: arial;
                     font-weight: bold;
                     background-color:aqua;
                     border:thin solid;
                     width: 210px;
                     height:40px;
2                    visibility: hidden;    /* Can't see the container */
                     position:absolute;
                     top: 50px;
                     left: 175px;
3                    z-index: 1;   /* Put the div container on top */
         }
4        a {
             font-family: cursive;
             font-size: 18pt;
             font-weight: bold;
             color:white;
             position: absolute;
             left: 60px;
         }
5        img { position:absolute; top: 50px; z-index:0; }
      </style>
      <script language = "JavaScript">
         var div1;
6        function init(){
             div1=document.getElementById("divclass");
         }
7        function showHideTip(e) {
8            if(e.type == "mouseover")
                 div1.style.visibility="visible";
9            else if(e.type == "mouseout"){
                 div1.style.visibility="hidden";
             }
         }
      </script>
      </head>
```

## EXAMPLE  15.33 (CONTINUED)

```
10    <body bgcolor=black onLoad="init();">
11        <a href="http://www.servant.xxx"
12            onMouseover="showHideTip(event);"
13            onMouseout="showHideTip(event);"
              >At Your Service!
          </a>
          <br>
13        <img src="waiter.gif">
14        <div id="divclass">Always tip me at least 20%!</div>
      </body>
      </html>
```

## EXPLANATION

1   A CSS style is defined for the ID selector, *#divclass*.

2   The *visibility* property for this style is set to *hidden*; it will not be seen.

3   The *z-index* property is set to 1, putting above the image which is set to *z-index* 0. Remember, the higher the *z-index* number, the higher the element is placed on the stack.

4   The style for a link is defined.

5   A style for positioning an image is defined. Its *z-index* is 0, placing it below any other elements.

6   The *init()* function is defined to get the ID of a *div* element. In this example, this will be the ID for the tool tip.

7   The *showHideTip()* function is defined. It takes one parameter, a reference to an event object. It contains information about the event that caused this function to be called.

8   If the event was caused by the mouse going over the link, a *mouseOver* event, then the tool tip will be made visible.

9   If the event was caused by the mouse moving away from the link, a *mouseOut* event, then the tool tip will be hidden from view.

10  As soon as the document has finished loading, the *onLoad* event is triggered, and the *init()* function invoked.

11  This is the link that displays as "At Your Service!". Rolling the mouse over it will cause the tool tip to appear.

12  The *onMouseOver* event is triggered when the user puts his mouse on the link. The tool tip will be shown.

13  When the user moves his mouse away from the link, the tool tip disappears.

14  The image for the waiter is below the tool tip, because its *z-index* is 0, whereas the tool tip's *z-index* is 1.

15  The *<div>* container is used to hold the tool tip text and style defined by the CSS ID selector called *divclass*. The output is shown in Figure 15.38.

**Figure 15.38**  Before the mouse moves over the link (left), and after (right).

## 15.4.8  Simple Animation

Animation on a Web page can be either captivating and attractive or just plain annoying. It all depends on the design. Whether you are creating banners, slide shows, or animated logos, buttons, or icons, they are attention getters. With dynamic HTML you can create your own animations. There are a number of programs available for this, such as Macromedia Fireworks, Stone Design's GIFfun for Mac OS X, and Adobe Photoshop.

The following example takes four GIF images and with the help of a timer, rapidly displays an increasingly smaller image on different positions of the screen, giving the sensation of simple animation—a green balloon rising into the sky.

**EXAMPLE  15.34**

```
        <html><head><title>balloon</title>
        <script language="JavaScript">
           var position, up, upper, uppermost, upperupmost;
           function init(){
1              var position = 1;
2              var up = new Image();
               up.src = "greenballoon.gif";
3              var upper = new Image();
               upper.src= "greenballoon2.gif";
               var uppermost = new Image();
               uppermost.src = "greenballoon3.gif";
               var upperupmost=new Image();
               upperupmost.src = "greenballoon4.gif";
               ball = document.getElementById("balloon");
           }
```

## EXAMPLE 15.34 (CONTINUED)

```
4       function move() {
5           if ( position == 1){
                document.ballooimg.src=up.src;
                ball.balloon.style.left = 50;
                ball.balloon.style.top = 200;
6               position = 2;
            }
7           else if (position == 2){
                document.ballooimg.src=upper.src;
                ball.style.left = 100;
                ball.style.top = 150;
                position = 3;
            }
        }
            else if (position == 3){
                document.ballooimg.src=uppermost.src;
                ball.style.left = 150;
                ball.style.top = 100;
                position = 4;
            }
            else if (position == 4){
                document.ballooimg.src=upperupmost.src;
                ball.style.left = 200;
                ball.style.top = 10;
                position = 1;
            }
        }
    </script>
    </head>
7   <body bgColor="silver" onLoad="init();">
8   <span id="balloon" style="position:absolute; left:10; top:250">
        <img name="ballooimg" src="greenballoon.gif" >
    </span>
    <form>
        <input type="button" name="move" value=" Move "
9           onClick="startMove=setInterval('move()',900);">
        <input type="button" name="stop" value=" Stop "
            onClick="clearInterval(startMove);">
10  </form>
    </body>
    </html>
```

## EXPLANATION

1    The variable *position* will be assigned 1. This will be the image of the first balloon to be placed on the screen after the user calls the *move()* function below.

2    A reference to an image object is assigned to variable, *up*. The source for the image is a file named *greenballoon.gif*.

3    Another image object is created. Its source file is *greenballoon2.gif*. Each balloon image is scaled down in size.

4    The *move()* function is defined. Its purpose is to place, in rapid intervals, the balloon images in different sections of the screen to give the illusion of movement.

5    With position 1, the first image (*greenballoon.gif*) is positioned at the left bottom part of the screen. The value of the position is set to 2. When the timer calls the *move()* function, (approximately 1 second from now), the position value is 2 and control goes to line 5.

6    Position 2 puts the balloon *greenballoon2.gif* in the middle of the screen.

7    After the document has been loaded, the *onLoad* event is triggered and the *init()* function will be invoked to initialize variables and get a reference to the balloon object.

8    The *<span>* tag creates the position of the initial image 10 pixels from the left-hand side of the screen and 250 pixels from the top.

9    When the Move button is clicked, the *onClick* event is triggered and the *setInterval()* method will start calling the *move()* function every 900 milliseconds. The balloon appears to move from the left to the right, and upward on the screen, getting smaller as it goes to indicate distance.

10   When the Stop button is clicked, the *setInterval()* timer is turned off. The output is shown in Figure 15.39.

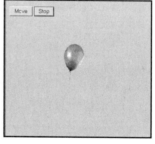

**Figure 15.39**   When the user clicks the Move button, the balloon image changes every second (top); Up, up, and away in my little green balloon... (bottom row).

## EXERCISES

1. Create a CSS style sheet that makes all *h1* elements italic and blue.

2. Define a class called *title* that can be used on an element to make the font face Arial, extra large, and bold.

3. Create a style for a paragraph with a unique ID that will define a style for a font family, font size, and font color.

4. Create a style that will affect all the cells in an HTML table.

5. Create a style that be used with a *<div>* tag to produce a light green box, positioned in the left-hand corner of the screen, with a solid, dark green border. The *<div>* container will contain a paragraph of italic text.

6. Write a JavaScript program that will tell you the name and version of your browser and whether it is DOM compliant.

7. Rewrite Example 15.34 to use an *Array* constructor in the *init()* function. Each image will be referenced as an array element when the *Image* constructor is called.

8. Create an animation of a stickman running. You will need to draw several stickmen of the same size in different running positions. Your program will give the illusion of the stickman running.

# JavaScript Web Resources

FreewareJava.com:
*http://freewarejava.com/javascript/index.shtml*
This site contains a collection of JavaScript tutorials and sample scripts.

The JavaScript Planet:
*http://www.geocities.com/SiliconValley/7116/*
This site contains a broad collection of free JavaScripts.

CodingForums.com:
*http://www.codingforums.com/*
This site contains a JavaScript forum where programmers help each other solve Java-
Script problems.

JavaScript Central on Netscape's devedge site:
*http://devedge.netscape.com/central/javascript/*
This site contains a top-notch collection of JavaScript tools and tutorials.

CGI resources:
*http://hoohoo.ncsa.uiuc.edu/cgi/intro.html*
*http://cgi.resourceindex.com/*
*http://www.scriptarchive.com/*
*http://www.icthus.net/CGI-City/*

# appendix

# B

# HTML Documents:
# A Basic Introduction

## by Joan Murray

## B.1  Intro to the Intro

The progress of HTML (HyperText Markup Language) in the age of the Internet and the World Wide Web has unfolded much in the way of classic Alpine skiing and X-treme skiing. Even people who don't ski know about the rules: bend the knees, hold onto the poles, stay on the trails, and follow a curved path down the slope. There is no mention of snowboarding, hot-dogging, playing catch on skis, or combining skiing with sky-diving. What used to be a winter pastime of country folk now requires special equipment, clothing, accessories, lodging, and transportation. Like skiing, HTML started out simply and can still be used simply, but if you follow the trail to the big time you'll find all the fancy and dangerous complications involved in fashionable pursuits, which is how HTML got mixed up with a scripting language like Perl in the first place.

## B.2  What Is HTML?

HTML is described in various ways:

1. A subset of SGML (Standard Generalized Markup Language), the standard for markup languages
2. A collection of platform-independent styles defining various components of a WWW (World Wide Web) document.
3. Put simply, HTML documents are plain-text (ASCII) files with markup (identifier) tags

### B.2.1  HTML: It Used to Be as Easy as Falling Off a Log

The basics still apply, but modern technology, new standards, and the Great Browser Wars have made inroads. This overview covers what endures, though that too may change. Our secret weapon is using commercially available Web tools to keep up with the changes. Each section of the overview will contain an update where changes have crept (and in some cases galloped) in.

The introduction of Web site building software like FrontPage and Dreamweaver might make you think that knowing HTML is no longer necessary. However, even the best product doesn't always produce desired results, so you need to be able to tweak where necessary. That brings us to the question:

*Why learn HTML code?*

1. To know what you're looking at and know how it's done, and, what's better, to be able to do the same yourself
2. To help judge WYSIWYG (what you see is what you get) software products used to create Web pages
3. To get by when you don't have the high-tech tools—even a basic knowledge of HTML will enable you to create a presentable Web site

*Why did "They" think this up in the first place?*

The Internet had existed for a decade or two as a way to send and receive messages and other documents when someone decided that since monitors had replaced teletype as standard output it might be nice to be able to read material in an orderly fashion on the monitor. One of the results was the invention of a system of embedded codes that would make this possible. The rules set up for HTML reflect the original interested parties, the military and universities, using the system and the state of personal computing devices at the time. They reveal themselves in the default colors, sizes, fonts, and text types and order.

## B.3    HTML Tags

The nice part about the basic HTML is that it is easy to do. It is time-consuming and complicated, but it is not difficult. Everything you need is contained in the tags, which are the code identifying an HTML document and the various parts of its contents to a browser.

The tags all follow a set form—start and stop:

- Left angle bracket (<), tag name, right angle bracket (>) for start tag
- Left angle bracket (<), slash (/), tag name, right angle bracket (>) for stop tag

These are usually paired in start/stop set (e.g.,<H1> and </H1>). These tags define various parts of the HTML document. Only a small set of tags is required; the others are advisable to make the document easier for the user to read.

### B.3.1   Required Elements

| | |
|---|---|
| *<HTML>, </HTML>* | Defines the HTML document |
| *<HEAD>, </HEAD>* | Defines the part of the document for the browsers use |
| *<TITLE>, </TITLE>* | Identifies the document to the Web |
| *<BODY>, </BODY>* | Defines the part of the document we see and use |

Believe it or not, this is all that is required in an HTML document. The head and title part are required for use by the browser. Unless they peek behind the scene, users see only what is presented between the two body tags.

### B.3.2   The Order of the Required Elements and Their Tags

*<HTML>*
*<HEAD>*
*<TITLE> </TITLE>*
*</HEAD>*
*<BODY>*
*</BODY>*
*</HTML>*

### B.3.3   The Elements: What They Are and How They Are Used

*<HTML>*

This tag tells the browser the file contains HTML-coded information. The file extension *.html* identifies an HTML document. With DOS-based files use *.htm*; Windows- and Mac-based files can use *.htm* or *.html*. Currently, UNIX files should use only *.html*.

*<HTML> UPDATE!*

There now are *.shtml*, *.stm*, *.asp*, and *.xml* Web pages, to name a few. UNIX servers undoubtedly recognize these also, but they are beyond the scope of this overview.

*<HEAD>*

This tag identifies first part of HTML-coded document. It contains the title. (This does not appear on the page itself.)

*<TITLE>*

This tag contains the document title. It is displayed on a browser window only and is not visible on the page itself. On the Web, it identifies a page subject to search engine criteria. It is used as a "hotlist," "favorites," or "bookmark" entry. It should be short, descriptive, and unique.

*<HEAD> UPDATE!*

Most Web page heads contain more than titles. The following are examples of what can be found there.

    Metatags: make site topics known to (some) search engines
    Style sheets/cascading style sheets (CSS): define aspects of the body
    Java scripts and JavaScript: add jazzy elements to the body of the document

*<BODY>*

This tag contains content of the document organized into various units:

    Headings (*<H1>* to *<H6>*)
    Paragraphs *<P>*
    Lists, which can be ordered *<OL>* or unordered *<UL>*
    Preformatted text *<PRE>*
    Addresses *<ADDRESS>*
    Space dividers *<BR>*, *<HR>*
    Graphic items

*<BODY> UPDATE!*

Preformatted text is rarely used unless you want something to look like a typed page. Tables replace preformatted text in most cases. The address portion is now often replaced by a reply form or e-mail address. Many of the interactive elements such as reply forms use CGI (Common Gateway Interface) scripts, usually written in Perl.

## B.4   The Minimal HTML Document

```
<HTML>
<HEAD>
<TITLE>Simple HTML Document. Only the browser sees this title </TITLE>
</HEAD>
<BODY>
<H1>Sample Heading -- You and I see this heading</H1>
<P>This is a sample text representing a paragraph. It will ignore
spaces and keep on being one paragraph <P>This is another paragraph
</BODY>
</HTML>
```

### B.4.1   Headings

Don't confuse these with *<HEAD>*, which is not visible to the end user. The heading is at the top of the Web document. Think "Headline." There are six heading tags ordered by size: *<H1>* is the largest and *<H6>* the smallest. According to the original rules it isn't fair to pick and choose headings by appearance. *<H1>* is a primary heading *<H2>* a secondary heading, etc. Those who have been doing this a long time claim it is virtually impossible to distinguish between *<H4>*, *<H5>*, and *<H6>*.

There are a million ways to solve the heading problem. In some fonts, *<H1>* is so huge you would only use it for something of great importance, such as "War is Declared." Because HTML now interacts with Web tools like Java and XML, the *<P>* tag now requires a matching *</P>* tag. Strictly speaking, this is not an HTML requirement because it is not HTML that is having trouble knowing that the paragraph has finished.

## B.4.2   Tags to Separate Text

NOTE: Formerly these did NOT require end tags.

*<P>*
This tag separates text into paragraphs—a hard return with space (line feed). Originally this tag came after the paragraph, but since we use monitors and not actual print devices we don't need to signal a hard return. So now *<P>* indicates to the browser that what follows is a paragraph.

*<BR>*
This breaks text into lines—a hard return with no space between lines.

*<HR>*
This is a horizontal rule—a graphic representation of a line to separate text areas.

## B.4.3   Lists

Lists are perennial favorites of organizations. When the Web began, they represented ways to break up text in a helpful fashion. They could (and still can) be used for definitions, tables of contents, or just plain lists. The numbered list is a favorite of the academic community; the bulleted list that of the military; otherwise, they are really self-explanatory.
There are two types of lists:

1. Ordered (numbered) list
   *<OL>*
   *<LI>* Item number one
   *<LI>* Item number two
   *</OL>*
2. Unordered (bulleted) list
   *<UL>*
   *<LI>* First item
   *<LI>* Next item
   *</UL>*

Lists are old fashioned. Use them with discretion. Avoid long lists; instead block topics as subpage(s). Use tables or links (or both) where possible.
The *<LI>* tag has suffered the same fate as the *<P>* tag. You must use an *</LI>* tag to be truly up to date. Originally there were several subcategories of lists, but they've pretty much done away with most of them.

## B.4.4   Tables for Fun and Profit

Tables are scary when you look behind the scene and see all those tags and indents. To make a table, use the same principle as the traveler on the 1,000-mile journey: one step at a time. This overview covers simple tables, the kind that replaced preformatted <PRE> text. Though complicated they are no more exasperating than counting all the spaces between words in preformatted text to make the results come out even.

**The Basic Table Tags:**

<TABLE> </TABLE>          Defines table
<TR> </TR>                Defines table row
<TD> </TD>                Defines table cell (data)

The principle is the same as with the HTML document as a whole: The table <TABLE> contains rows <TR>, which contain data cells <TD>.

**Tailoring Tables:**

<TABLE ALIGN="CENTER">
 <TABLE BORDER ALIGN="CENTER">
 <TABLE BGCOLOR="#FEFEFF">,  <TABLE BGCOLOR="AQUA">

You can use many of the same tag elements you use to tweak other page elements. The ALIGN= command puts items including tables to left, right, or center on page.

Some browsers allow you to add color to the background (Netscape, Internet Explorer). The same is true of background images, but Netscape and IE treat them differently.

Similar rules guide formatting of table rows and cells. You can adjust text position and background in these units.

**How Table Tags Are Used:**

This will yield a simple table with two rows and two cells.

<TABLE>
<TR><TD>data</TD><TD>more data</TD></TR>
<TR><TD>data</TD><TD>maybe a picture</TD></TR>
</TABLE>

By adding spacing, alignment, color, and other tags, you can manipulate tables. You can enlarge the table by increasing the number of rows or data cells. You can specify header rows, make data cells span more than one row and/or column, put background colors, borders, and more. It's all in the details.

# B.5   Character Formatting

There are two ways to indicate text formatting:

1. Logical—according to its meaning
2. Physical—according to its appearance

As you familiarize yourself with both of these, you can see the committee mentality at work. Either two groups already had different codes in place, or someone wanted to go home.

Many pages use physical tags even though logical tags are standard. The rule is, BE CONSISTENT.

WYSIWYGs like FrontPage and Dreamweaver, which don't require a lot of text entry, use the logical tags. (If you don't have to type *<STRONG></STRONG>* again and again, you don't really care that the software package chose to use it over *<B></B>*.)

Cascading style sheets (more on them later) will make font/text tags even more interesting than they are now.

## B.5.1   Logical Tags

| | |
|---|---|
| *<EM>* | For emphasis—usually *italics* |
| *<STRONG>* | For strong emphasis—usually **bold** |
| *<CODE><KBD>* | Various—`Fixed-width font` |

## B.5.2   Physical Tags

| | |
|---|---|
| *<B>* | **Bold text** |
| *<I>* | *Italic text* |
| *<TT>* | `Typewriter Text` |

# B.6   Linking

This is what makes hypertext hyper. It is also the reason to use HTML in the first place. If you like to read, get a book. If you need to connect to various references, hypertext is the way to go. HTML links text and/or images to other documents or other parts of the same document using anchors.

The hypertext tag is *<A>* for anchor; the reference part of tag is *HREF="File"*. The hypertext reference contains the pathname (relative or absolute) of the document (file) you are trying to access.

## B.6.1   Creating a Link

If you can get this next bit, you have mastered the magic of hypertext. Notice that the cue to the user does not have to be the pathname to the link. (When the Web was young, site builders did not understand this and often would spell out the path on the Web page, thus causing anxiety in the user.) In the example below, *newfile.html* is referred to in the text as *My Special Page*.

All hypertext link tags take this form:

*<A HREF="filename.html">Hot Link</A>*

Sample reference:

*<A HREF="newfile.html">My File</A>*

Put whatever you wish here leading to <u>My Special Page</u>. The same deal over here.

### B.6.2   Links to a URL (Uniform Resource Locator)

The hypertext link tag is the same form for a URL as for any other link:

*<A HREF="URLname.html">Hot Link</A>*

The *URLname* portion is written exactly as it appears in the browser's URL window:

*http://host.domain/path/filename*

## B.7   Adding Comments

Form for comments:

*<!-- Put Comment Here -->*

"Commenting out" questionable code is considered bad form in HTML. Use commenting only for real comments except as directed to hide Java, JavaScript, XML, CSS, and other scripts from the browser.

## B.8   Case Sensitivity

HTML per se is not case sensitive. The following tags are only three examples that are all the same to HTML:

  *<Body>*
  *<BODY>*
  *<body>*

UNIX ties are case sensitive:
  "Escape sequences" (*&gt*)
  Filenames (*HooXd.u*)
  *<A HREF="jones.html">Jones &amp Co.</A>*

XML, Java, JavaScript, and CSS all have to be just right.

Sometime during the great parade that the World Wide Web has become, someone noticed that HTML was the only unit that was not in step with the march of progress. So, beginning with HTML 4.0, all tags are to be in lowercase to conform with the other elements that make up part of modern Web sites. You can still build a simple Web site without worrying about case sensitivity, but once you start using the sophisticated tools of Web building, lowercase will be the rule. (In this review I will stick to UPPERCASE for tags so that they are more visible, but don't try this at home.)

# B.9   Graphics and Images

## B.9.1   Creating an Inline Image

To include an image inline (next to text) or otherwise, use the form:

  *<IMG SRC="ImageName">*

Graphic files are usually *.gif* or *.jpg*. *.jpg* appears as *.jpeg* in Windows environments. While the *.jpg* extension can be used on Windows, most UNIX environments currently do not support *.jpeg*.

## B.9.2   The Complex Tag

The coding used to create and place images introduces complexity to the tag. The opening anchor tag *<A>* for a hyperlink uses this complexity to identify the link (HREF). The image tag *<IMG>* adds SRC to identify the image. Since images on a page create complexity (increased load time, increased file size), complex, not to say complicated, tags become the norm. You use this complex tag form to define other elements of the Web page such as headings, paragraphs, and tables.

## B.9.3   Sizing and Placing the Image

The warring factions of the Web world are constantly debating what a Web site should be. Much of the debate centers on images and their effect on page loading time. While many points of the image debate are beyond the scope of this overview, one is not: the image size attributes. Everyone agrees that it is best to include the width and height of an image to speed page loading. The browser window can give you the information if you know what to do and where to look. We will use Netscape directions for our example.

Launch Netscape, click on **File** in the text menu bar, select **Open Page**, then **Choose File** in the pop-up window, and locate the image on your computer. **NOTE**: make sure the "Types of Files" bar is set to "All Files (*.*)."  Select the image whose dimensions you want to know and click the **OK** button. The blue bar at the very top of the browser window contains the measurements in pixels: width then height.

> *<IMG SRC=picture.gif WIDTH="40" HEIGHT="100" >*

You position the image on the page by adding *ALIGN="LEFT"* (or *"RIGHT"* or *"CENTER"*) inside the image tag.

## B.9.4   Creating a Text Alternative for an Image

Not all browsers support graphics; LYNX, one of the oldest, does not.

Some users turn image-loading off, and most graphics are impractical for sight-impaired users. Using a text label to identify graphic images is good manners and practical. The ALT tag inside the *<IMG>* tag identifies text alternatives for graphics.

> *<IMG SRC="UpArrow.gif" ALT="UP">*

The portion identifying the image does not have to be one word or a repeat of the image filename. Newer Browsers show ALT text when you "mouse over" the image, and inserting a user-friendly phrase such as *View of downtown Rochester, 1948* or *Back to Top* rather than *photo_main_47.jpg* and *arrow.gif* can provide additional information to Web spiders that the image would otherwise conceal.

## B.9.5   Where Do I Find Graphics?

The Web has many sites full of free graphics. You need to use discretion since some folks think that if butterflies are free, so are Bugs Bunny, Snoopy, Homer Simpson, and the Nike Swoosh, and there they all are on their "free graphics" Web site. The most useful graphics are part of the 4 B's: buttons, bars, ball, and backgrounds. They used to be very easy to find; every free Web graphics site had them, but with the new Web tools the trend is toward the "unique" (read baroque). One site that has the old reliables is the All Free Original Clipart page. Their URL is *http://www.free-graphics.com/*. The site is well organized so it is easy to review the small graphic objects you want. To get to the type of item you want, choose a category from the menu on the left side of the page. Each section has directions on how to download the image you want to use. When you work on the exercise to create a page of images you may want to use selections from this site.

### B.9.6  Background Graphics

All but the earliest versions of Netscape and Microsoft Internet Explorer support background graphics, colors, and textures. You can get images from a Web graphic site such as the one listed above. Since some early browsers (and they're still out there) don't support background images, you can include code in the tag for a background color as well. The browser will pick up the color. This is useful, too, for those users who turn graphics off.

### B.9.7  Creating Backgrounds

Since a background color or image can be included in as an attribute, the <BODY> tag can become quite complex. For a background image the form is the following:

<BODY BACKGROUND="filename.gif">

Background color is a bit tricky; it uses hexadecimals, but there are several sites on the Web that list these, and Web building tools include these codes. Basically, *000000* represents black and *FFFFFF* represents white. The form for background color follows:

<BODY BGCOLOR="#FF90CB">

To simplify things, there are some standard colors you can add using their name only. The current HTML standard names 16 of these colors; aqua, black, blue, fuchsia, gray, green, lime, maroon, navy, olive, purple, red, silver, teal, yellow, and white.

### B.9.8  Default Colors

When the standards for the Web were first created, color monitors were VGA at best, and modems were 300 to 1200 baud. So, the default colors are rather mundane. The default background, referred to as light gray, is more of a battleship gray. Regular text is black. For hotlinks, "Unvisited" hotlink text is blue, an "Active" hotlink text is red, and "Visited" hotlink text is violet. Additionally, All hotlinks are underlined.

Now in the time of streaming media, monitors capable of displaying thousands of colors, and 56K modems, backgrounds can be anything, and an Active link changes so quickly to Visited it hardly matters what color it is. For best contrast on background, try white (*FFFFFF*) or black (*000000*). Experiment with near misses; word on the street is that off-white or black is easier on the eyes.

Besides the 16 named colors there are 216 "Websafe" colors that work on most browsers without doing strange things. Most graphics tools have a Websafe palette option. See Tables B.1 and B.2.

Hotlinks should be obvious to the user. Purists say stick to the default blue and purple for unvisited and visited. Newer browsers can disable hotlink underline. Leave the underline intact when you build a site and let the user decide.

**Table B.1**   Named colors for HTML 4.01 and CSS2.

| Color Name | Hex 6 | Hex 3 | RGB | RGB% | Websafe | Reallysafe |
|---|---|---|---|---|---|---|
| black | #000000 | #000 | 0,0,0 | 0%,0%,0% | Yes | Yes |
| silver | #C0C0C0 | #CCC | 192,192,192 | 75%,75%,75% | No | No |
| gray | #808080 | #888 | 128,128,128 | 50%,50%,50% | No | No |
| white | #FFFFFF | #FFF | 255,255,255 | 100%,100%,100% | Yes | Yes |
| maroon | #800000 | #800 | 128,0,0 | 50%,0%,0% | No | No |
| red | #FF0000 | #F00 | 255,0,0 | 100%,0%,0% | Yes | Yes |
| purple | #800080 | #808 | 128,0,128 | 50%,0%,50% | No | No |
| fuchsia | #FF00FF | #F0F | 255,0,255 | 100%,0%,100% | Yes | Yes |
| green | #008000 | #080 | 0,128,0 | 0%,50%,0% | No | No |
| lime | #00FF00 | #0F0 | 0,255,0 | 0%,100%,0% | Yes | Yes |
| olive | #808000 | #880 | 128,128,0 | 50%,50%,0% | No | No |
| yellow | #FFFF00 | #FF0 | 255,255,0 | 100%,100%,0% | Yes | Yes |
| navy | #000080 | #008 | 0,0,128 | 0%,0%,50% | No | No |
| blue | #0000FF | #00F | 0,0,255 | 0%,0%,100% | Yes | Yes |
| teal | #008080 | #088 | 0,128,128 | 0%,50%,50% | No | No |
| aqua | #00FFFF | #0FF | 0,255,255 | 0%,100%,100% | Yes | Yes |

The HTML 4.01 and CSS2 color names with their corresponding numerical values. Members of the Websafe and Reallysafe palletes are marked. The information in this table is copyright 2003 Jupitermedia Corporation. All rights reserved. Used with permission from http://www.webreference.com.

**Table B.2** Proprietary color names for Internet Explorer.

| Color Name | Hex 6 | Hex 3 | RGB | RGB% | Websafe | Reallysafe |
|---|---|---|---|---|---|---|
| aliceblue | #F0F8FF | #FFF | 240,248,255 | 94%,97%,100% | No | No |
| antiquewhite | #FAEBD7 | #FED | 250,235,215 | 98%,92%,84% | No | No |
| aqua | #00FFFF | #0FF | 0,255,255 | 0%,100%,100% | Yes | Yes |
| aquamarine | #7FFFD4 | #7FD | 127,255,212 | 49%,100%,83% | No | No |
| azure | #F0FFFF | #FFF | 240,255,255 | 94%,100%,100% | No | No |
| beige | #F5F5DC | #FFD | 245,245,220 | 96%,96%,86% | No | No |
| bisque | #FFE4C4 | #FEC | 255,228,196 | 100%,89%,76% | No | No |
| black | #000000 | #000 | 0,0,0 | 0%,0%,0% | Yes | Yes |
| blanchedalmond | #FFEBCD | #FEC | 255,235,205 | 100%,92%,80% | No | No |
| blue | #0000FF | #00F | 0,0,255 | 0%,0%,100% | Yes | Yes |
| blueviolet | #8A2BE2 | #82E | 138,43,226 | 54%,16%,88% | No | No |
| brown | #A52A2A | #A22 | 165,42,42 | 64%,16%,16% | No | No |
| burlywood | #DEB887 | #DB8 | 222,184,135 | 87%,72%,52% | No | No |
| cadetblue | #5F9EA0 | #59A | 95,158,160 | 37%,61%,62% | No | No |
| chartreuse | #7FFF00 | #7F0 | 127,255,0 | 49%,100%,0% | No | No |
| chocolate | #D2691E | #D61 | 210,105,30 | 82%,41%,11% | No | No |
| coral | #FF7F50 | #F75 | 255,127,80 | 100%,49%,31% | No | No |
| cornflowerblue | #6495ED | #69E | 100,149,237 | 39%,58%,92% | No | No |
| cornsilk | #FFF8DC | #FFD | 255,248,220 | 100%,97%,86% | No | No |
| crimson | #DC143C | #D13 | 220,20,60 | 86%,7%,23% | No | No |
| cyan | #00FFFF | #0FF | 0,255,255 | 0%,100%,100% | Yes | Yes |
| darkblue | #00008B | #008 | 0,0,139 | 0%,0%,54% | No | No |
| darkcyan | #008B8B | #088 | 0,139,139 | 0%,54%,54% | No | No |
| darkgoldenrod | #B8860B | #B80 | 184,134,11 | 72%,52%,4% | No | No |
| darkgray | #A9A9A9 | #AAA | 169,169,169 | 66%,66%,66% | No | No |
| darkgreen | #006400 | #060 | 0,100,0 | 0%,39%,0% | No | No |
| darkkhaki | #BDB76B | #BB6 | 189,183,107 | 74%,71%,41% | No | No |

**Table B.2**  Proprietary color names for Internet Explorer. (continued)

| Color Name | Hex 6 | Hex 3 | RGB | RGB% | Websafe | Reallysafe |
|---|---|---|---|---|---|---|
| darkmagenta | #8B008B | #808 | 139,0,139 | 54%,0%,54% | No | No |
| darkolivegreen | #556B2F | #562 | 85,107,47 | 33%,41%,18% | No | No |
| darkorange | #FF8C00 | #F80 | 255,140,0 | 100%,54%,0% | No | No |
| darkorchid | #9932CC | #93C | 153,50,204 | 60%,19%,80% | No | No |
| darkred | #8B0000 | #800 | 139,0,0 | 54%,0%,0% | No | No |
| darksalmon | #E9967A | #E97 | 233,150,122 | 91%,58%,47% | No | No |
| darkseagreen | #8FBC8B | #8B8 | 143,188,139 | 56%,73%,54% | No | No |
| dodgerblue | #1E90FF | #19F | 30,144,255 | 11%,56%,100% | No | No |
| forestgreen | #228B22 | #282 | 34,139,34 | 13%,54%,13% | No | No |
| indianred | #CD5C5C | #C55 | 205,92,92 | 80%,36%,36% | No | No |
| lavender | #E6E6FA | #EEF | 230,230,250 | 90%,90%,98% | No | No |
| lemonchiffon | #FFFACD | #FFC | 255,250,205 | 100%,98%,80% | No | No |
| lightgrey | #D3D3D3 | #DDD | 211,211,211 | 82%,82%,82% | No | No |
| lightseagreen | #20B2AA | #2BA | 32,178,170 | 12%,69%,66% | No | No |
| mediumslateblue | #7B68EE | #76E | 123,104,238 | 48%,40%,93% | No | No |
| navy | #000080 | #008 | 0,0,128 | 0%,0%,50% | No | No |
| orange | #FFA500 | #FA0 | 255,165,0 | 100%,64%,0% | No | No |
| salmon | #FA8072 | #F87 | 250,128,114 | 98%,50%,44% | No | No |
| slateblue | #6A5ACD | #65C | 106,90,205 | 41%,35%,80% | No | No |
| yellowgreen | #9ACD32 | #9C3 | 154,205,50 | 60%,80%,19% | No | No |

Internet Explorer's proprietary color names with their corresponding numerical values. Members of the Websafe and Reallysafe palletes are marked. The information in this table is copyright 2003 Jupitermedia Corporation. All rights reserved. Used with permission from http://www.webreference.com.

### B.9.9 Bars, Bullets, and Icons

You can get these simple graphics from the *All Free Graphics* Web site to spruce up your page. The temptation is to use a lot of them because you can; don't yield to it. Be especially careful with animated GIFs. An envelope or mailbox constantly opening and closing at the bottom of a Web page can be mighty irritating.

Use bars in place of *<HR>* (hard rule) separators. Position them carefully.

*<P ALIGN="CENTER"><IMG SRC="somebar.gif"><P>*

Bullets are used to attract attention. (NEW!) is always popular. Small balls fall into the bullet category.

Icons, those small graphical representations, make great clickable images (links to other files). The image replaces the text that identifies the hotlink. This is the principle behind all those "Click here for…" banner graphics you see on every Web site.

*<A HREF="Some.html"><IMG SRC="icon.gif"></A>*

To eliminate the "hot" blue border around a linked icon, add *BORDER="0"* to the image tag.

*<A HREF="Some.html"><IMG SRC="icon.gif" BORDER ="0"></A>*

### B.9.10 Graphics Update

Flash 5—Need I say more? Types of graphics fall in and out of favor. The understated look is always good.

### B.9.11 External Sights 'n' Sounds

You can use anchor and reference to link to an image as a separate entity. This will open a page to a stand-alone image. Many sites use this device to keep slow loading, large graphics below the main page.

*<A HREF="Image.gif">link anchor</A>*

The syntax is the same for a sound (*.au*, *.wav*) or movie (*.mov*, *.mpg*)

NOTE: Sound and movies are slow loaders and not everyone can access these.

## B.10 Troubleshooting

Even pages put seamlessly together using WYSIWYG software can turn out not quite as expected. Usually the problem is something involving fancier HTML elements. (FrontPage is notorious for constantly trying to second-guess the author.) For those who are drawers of water and hewers of HTML, the problems are much more mundane.

The following covers the most common errors. Believe me when I say everybody who has written HTML has done all of these.

1. Watch out for overlapping tags:
   <B>Example of <I>overlapping</B> tags<I>
   <!-- here the author wants the last two words in italics, and everything but the last word to be bold. -->
   <B>It should be <I>this</I></B><I> instead</I>
   <!-- That's what keeps them buying FrontPage -->

2. Make sure all the tags are matched.
   <H1>Win a million dollars! </H1>
   Forgetting to stop an action can result in interesting effects such as *an entire page in italics* or headline sized type.

3. Be sure there are no missing parts to a tag ( /, <, >, or " ).

4. Embed only anchors and character tags inside defining tags.
   <H1><A HREF="file.html">Hot Stuff</A> </H1>

5. Watch out for misspellings such as HREP or Hl (letter el) for H1 (one).

## B.10.1   Ask Heloise!

The more popular browsers will correct most errors they detect. That doesn't mean that your page doesn't look hosed on someone else's browser. If that person is trying to get some useful information, the error may thwart his efforts.

Ideally, all pages should be validated. This process checks for missing parts, overlapping tags, unmatched tags, and other problems. The W3 consortium has a validator on its site at *www.w3.org*.

Check your code against more than one browser. Only standard-issue HTML works on both Netscape and IE, and the latest standard may not work on earlier browser versions. Metatags and style sheets, the norm by today's standards, have to be commented out because the earlier browsers will print them code and all, right on the user's screen.

To be safe put all tag content after the equal sign in double quotes.

<BODY BGCOLOR="aqua" BACKGROUND="grandma.jpg">
<P ALIGN="RIGHT">

Sometimes browsers get cranky and won't recognize a qualifier even when it's a clone of a tag you've used countless times with no trouble.

Even if you use a WYSIWYG editor double check all your ALT tags. The WYSIWYG will put in *ALT="00187.gif"* or *"fzzypic1.jpg"* because that's what the image source is called. If you can't figure out how to make them more user friendly using the WYSIWYG side, add them on the HTML side. Dreamweaver files can be opened in Notepad, and FrontPage has a nice HTML source code page incorporated in it.

### B.10.2  Some Sites that Help You with HTML

*www.w3c.org*

World Wide Web Consortium—This is the authority on all things involving the Web.

*hotwired.lycos.com/webmonkey*

WebMonkey—Full of hip tutorials on all sorts of Web-related topics.

*www.ncsa.uiuc.edu/General/Training*

National Center for Supercomputing—the home of Mosaic.

*www.ncsa.uiuc.edu/General/Training/HTMLIntro/HTML.Help.html*

The ultimate beginner's manual: read it online and print it out for future reference.

*www.htmlgoodies.com*

HTML Goodies—excellent tutorials by Joe Burns, Ph.D.; subscribe to his newsletters.

# B.11  Metatags, Cascading Style Sheets, and Java

These are some topics that you should know about.

- Metatags: more than you want anyone to know about your site but really need to tell them
- Cascading style sheets: giving a "pulled together" look to even the largest sites
- Java scripts and JavaScript: where the action is

### B.11.1  Metatags Example (Part 1)

Metatags are a study in themselves. Each part of the following example shows you the most common tags used. Some sites put the tags in Part 1 of the example first, followed by the *TITLE* tag and then the real metatag meat. They all follow the complex tag form seen below. The *META NAME* portion stays the same. You change the part in quotes after the *CONTENT=* to fit your situation. The first part is standard. You can copy it verbatim except for the *CONTENT* portion of the *META NAME="Author"* tag.

```
<HEAD>
<TITLE>Simon Says Put the Title First</TITLE>
<META NAME="Author" CONTENT="myownwebpage.com">
<META NAME="distribution" CONTENT="global">
<META NAME="resource-type" CONTENT="document">
<META NAME="language" CONTENT="en">
</HEAD>
```

## B.11.2   Metatags Example (Part 2)

This part illustrates the keywords that identify your site to some search engines. Notice the great variety of keywords used by this site. Most of them are common to many sites. It's not so much a case of trying to be different but of giving the people what they want. The trick is to pick words that match what your audience is looking for (note the word "free"), which explains why a Web search can lead to some very strange results indeed.

META NAME="Keywords" CONTENT="SHOPPING, JOB BANK, Sign Up!, Find-A-Job, Post-A-Job, CLASSIFIEDS, Search Ads, Place Ad, Change Ad, Delete Ad, Cool Notify, Hot List, DIRECTORIES, ActiveX, ASP, C/C++, CGI, Databases, Emerging Tech, HTML/DHTML, Intranets, Java, JavaScript, Middleware, Perl, Visual Basic, XML, What's Cool, What's New, Japanese Pages, REFERENCE, Online Reference Library, LEARNING CENTER, Course Catalog, Tutorials, Experts Q&A, JOURNAL, Tech Focus, Tech Workshop, Staff Picks, Users' Choice, Profiles, NEWS CENTRAL, Archive, DOWNLOADS, Free Graphics, Free Scripts, COMMUNITY, Discussions, J.D.A., Whos Who, CALENDAR, Online Events, Industry Events, Conferences, ABOUT US, Who We Are, What We Do, News About Us, Advertising Info, Vendor Info, Job Openings, Awards, FAQs, email, highlights, developers, Current issues">

## B.11.3   Metatags Example (Part 3)

This tag describes your site and your purpose. When users do a Web search the description is what the search engine retrieves and prints (together with the title) in the search results.

<META NAME="description" CONTENT="myownwebpage.com is the leading online service for novice Web page developers. It includes So Help Me Mama, the unofficial and utterly useless directory for Java, as well as news, information, tutorials, and directories for other Internet technologies including ActiveX, JavaScript, Perl, VRML, Java Beans, push technologies, and other Internet and intranet technologies. myownwebpage.com is also the home of Really Cheap Software, the Unprofessional Developer's Store, where naïve developers can purchase and download thousands of Web, authoring, and other development products at some of today's highest prices.">

## B.11.4   Style Sheet Example

Originally, Web pages were all about information and not about formatting; certainly not about style. Discreet additions of color and subtle graphics were one thing but spinning, screaming, flashing page parts quite another. Not only was this not dignified, but the variety of colors and styles meant more work for the developer maintaining the Web site. As things got more complicated, style sheets were introduced as a way to create a look without so much hand tweaking.

The site developer puts the requirements for color and text elements in one of three places, and these determine the look of the site. For special cases you can define the requirements inside a tag, such as the body tag. For a simple site with few pages to maintain you can define the requirements in the *<HEAD>* portion of each page. (See the example below.) For a large site or one that keeps changing its look you can define the requirements in a separate document. The cascading part of CSS (cascading style sheets) comes from the way style requirements are prioritized. Local (inside tag) requirements take precedence over document (inside the head portion) requirements, which take precedence over global (separate document) requirements. In this introductory overview we will use as an example the within-document form. NOTE: this is not as straightforward as old-fashioned HTML. It doesn't use the traditional start/stop tags except to identify the section as style.

Because older browsers can't deal with style sheets, everything defining the style must be placed between comment tags and contained in a section surrounded by *<STYLE>* tags. Various elements are defined using an identifier and its qualifiers. You must put these attributes inside curly braces. A qualifier (such as font size or font family) is followed by a colon and a specifier (such as 24 pt or sans serif). A semicolon separates sets of attributes for each element you choose to define. The example shown uses standard elements and suggested attributes.

```
<HEAD>
<TITLE>You call that a style sheet?</TITLE>
<STYLE="text/css">
<!--
BODY {background: #FFFFFF}
H1 {font-size: 24pt; font-family: arial}
H2 {font-size: 18pt; font-family: braggadocio}
H3 {font size: 14pt; font-family: sans-serif}
-->
</STYLE>
</HEAD>
```

## B.11.5   JavaScript Example

JavaScript adds action to a Web page. Its advantages are that it is not compiled and doesn't have to run on a server. Web developers use JavaScript to create small "events" such as pop-up windows (see the example below) and image rollovers. As with style sheets, older browsers can't handle JavaScript so it must be hidden inside comment tags. The example shown causes three pop-up windows to appear successively on a Web page when launched. Like other special effects on the Web, this sort of thing can be overdone.

```
<head> <title>First Exercise</title>
<script language="JavaScript">

<!-- hide me

alert("Here's a little script");
alert("Just to show");
alert("That I know JavaScript!");
```

```
// end hide -->

</script>
</head>
```

## B.12 Looking Behind the Scenes (or, What Did We Do Before the Right-Click?)

To borrow source code or download graphics use your right mouse button to open a menu of selections. If you wish to view source code, right-click on a clear area of the background. Good old IE launches a separate Notepad document you can save with a new filename to examine at your leisure. If you are interested in capturing an image, right-click on the image. Choose "save image/picture as." It's usually good to rename the file, especially if it's called something like *0018dr.jpg*.

To capture some text, highlight it with your mouse and copy it using <Ctrl>-c. Paste it into a document using <Ctrl>-v.

## B.13 What About Frames?

The way things are going, frames, like sex, politics, and religion, will be a topic that one may not discuss in polite company. People either love them or loath them. WebMonkey has several tutorials on frames. Go to *hotwired.lycos.com/webmonkey/authoring* and click on the frames topic.

## B.14 Some Final Thoughts

Consider how your page will be used. If people have to read a lot, they don't want attention-getting elements distracting them. Finally, here are a few general tips to keep in mind:

- The current standard for HTML tags is lowercase.
- Container is the jazzy new word for any HTML element (<P>, <TD>).
- With the advent of style sheets, <DIV> is the hip new tag. Its main use is as a container to identify style elements you've created and named yourself versus the standard type shown in the style example. It's one of those complex tags with parts. Check out online tutorials from HTML Goodies or WebMonkey to learn more about this.
- If you are going to create a table, draw it first. Write the necessary code in those fields that will need special tabs, and use the annotated sketch as a reference for coding.
- Visible e-mail addresses can attract spam (junk e-mail); CGI forms offer more control.

- Check Web sites devoted to HTML to learn of the latest developments (see "Some Sites that Help You with HTML" on page 599).
- Examine the source code on pages you like to help you develop your own pages.

## *About the Author of This Tutorial*

I work for the Navy in Monterey, California. In 1996 my employer, Fleet Numerical Meteorology and Oceanography Center, which supplies weather data for the Navy's ships and planes, was preparing to launch a Web site for its users. No adequate software package was available, but the job had to be done. As part of a "train the trainer" endeavor, I took a class on the Internet and the information superhighway at the nearby Naval Postgraduate School. One project, building a Web page using HTML, led me to create and teach a class in HTML basics that helped provide talented co-workers with the knowledge to launch our first Internet pages. Even though we now use more sophisticated Web-building tools, I've taught that basic class many times.

— *Joan Murray*

# C

# CGI and Perl:
# The Hyper Dynamic Duo

## C.1  What Is CGI?

Thoughout this book everything has happened in the browser because we have been talking about client-side JavaScript. When we discussed HTML forms, we learned how to create a form and validate it, but we stopped there. We mentioned that the form, if submitted, would be sent to a server program for further processing, normally by a CGI script. This server program was assigned to the ACTION attribute of the HTML <form> tag, but we never really covered what happened on the server side. Now we will discuss how the browser communicates with the server, how the information is sent between the browser and server, and what the happens to information when it gets to the server. The standard we will use on the server side is called CGI.

CGI stands for the Common Gateway Interface (CGI), a simple protocol that allows a Web or HTTP server to talk to a program or script. Through this gateway a program recieves information from the server and sends information back. The program can further validate forms, query databases, send email, communicate with electronic banking applications, etc. The programming language that is connected to the gateway is called a CGI program. In this Appendix we will use the Perl language because it is the most popular for writing CGI scripts, although any programming language that can be executed on the server is fine, including C++, C, Fortran, AppleScript, TCL, and Visual Basic.

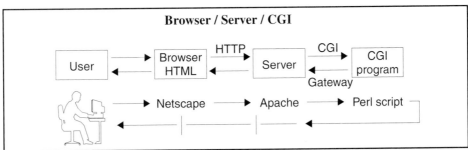

**Figure C.1**  The relationship between the browser, server, and CGI program.

## C.2 Internet Communication Between Client and Server

### C.2.1 The HTTP Server

On the Internet, communication is also handled by a TCP/IP connection. The Web is based on this model. The server side responds to client (browser) requests and provides feedback by sending back a document, by executing a CGI program, or by issuing an error message. The network protocol that is used by the Web so that the server and client know how to talk to each other is the Hypertext Transport Protocol, or HTTP. This does not preclude the TCP/IP protocol being implemented. HTTP objects are mapped onto the transport data units, a process that is beyond the scope of this discussion; it is a simple, straightforward process that is unnoticed by the typical Web user. (See *www.cis.ohio-state.edu/cgi-bin/rfc/rfc2068.html* for a technical description of HTTP.) The HTTP protocol was built for the Web to handle hypermedia information; it is object-oriented and stateless. In object-oriented terminology, the documents and files are called **objects** and the operations that are associated with the HTTP protocol are called **methods**. When a protocol is stateless, neither the client nor the server stores information about each other, but manages its own state information.

Once a TCP/IP connection is established between the Web server and client, the client will request some service from the server. Web servers are normally located at well-known TCP port 80. The client tells the server what type of data it can handle by sending *Accept* statements with its requests. For example, one client may accept only HTML text, whereas another client might accept sounds and images as well as text. The server will try to handle the request (requests and responses are in ASCII text) and send back whatever information it can to the client (browser).

---

**EXAMPLE** C.1

```
(Client's (Browser) Request)
GET /pub HTTP/1.0
Connection: Keep-Alive
User-Agent: Mozilla/4.0 Gold
Host: severname.com
Accept: image/gif, image/x-xbitmap, image/jpeg, image/pjpeg,*/*
```

**EXAMPLE** C.2

```
(Server's Response)
HTTP/1.1 200 OK
Server: Apache/1.2b8
Date: Mon, 22 Jan 2001  13:43:22 GMT
Last-modified: Mon, 01 Dec 2000 12:15:33
Content-length: 288
Accept-Ranges: bytes
Connection: close
Content-type: text/html

<HTML><HEAD><TITLE>Hello World!</TITLE>
          ---continue with body---
</HTML>
Connection closed by foreign host.
```

The response confirms what HTTP version was used, the status code describing the results of the server's attempt (did it succeed or fail?), a header, and data. The header part of the message indicates whether the request is okay, what type of data is being returned (for example, the content type may be *html/text*), and how many bytes are being sent. The data part contains the actual text being sent.

The user then sees a formatted page on the screen, which may contain highlighted hyperlinks to some other page. Regardless of whether the user clicks on a hyperlink, once the document is displayed, that transaction is completed and the TCP/IP connection will be closed. Once closed, a new connection will be started if there is another request. What happened in the last transaction is of no interest to either client or server; in other words, the protocol is stateless.

HTTP is also used to communicate between browsers, proxies, and gateways to other Internet systems supported by FTP, Gopher, WAIS, and NNTP protocols.

## C.2.2   HTTP Status Codes and the Log Files

When the server responds to the client, it sends information that includes the way it handled the request. Most Web browsers handle these codes silently if they fall in the range between 100 and 300. The codes within the 100 range are informational, indicating that the server's request is being processed. The most common status code is 200, indicating success, which means the information requested was accepted and fulfilled.

Check your server's access log to see what status codes were sent by your server after a transaction was completed.[1] The following example consists of excerpts taken from the Apache server's access log. This log reports information about a request handled by the server and the status code generated as a result of the request. The error log contains any standard error messages that the program would ordinarily send to the screen, such as syntax or compiler errors.

---

1. For more detailed information on status codes, see *www.w3.org/Protocols/HTTP/HTRESP.html*

**Table C.1**  HTTP status codes.

| Status | Code Message |
|--------|--------------|
| 100 | Continue |
| 200 | Success, OK |
| 204 | No Content |
| 301 | Document Moved |
| 400 | Bad Request |
| 401 | Unauthorized |
| 403 | Forbidden |
| 404 | Not Found |
| 500 | Internal Server Error |
| 501 | Not Implemented |
| 503 | Service Unavailable |

## EXAMPLE C.3

```
(From Apache's Access log)
1   susan - - [06/Jul/1997:14:32:23 -0700] "GET /cgi-bin/hello.cgi
    HTTP/1.0" 500 633
2   susan - - [16/Jun/1997:11:27:32 -0700] "GET /cgi-bin/hello.cgi
    HTTP/1.0" 200 1325
3   susan - - [07/Jul/1997:09:03:20 -0700] "GET /htdocs/index.html
    HTTP/1.0" 404 170
```

## EXPLANATION

1   The server hostname is *susan*, followed by two dashes indicating unknown values, such as user ID and password. The time the request was logged, the type of request is *GET* (see "The GET Method" on page 633), and the file accessed was *hello.cgi*. The protocol is HTTP/1.0. The status code sent by the server was 500, *Internal Server Error*, meaning that there was some internal error, such as a syntax error in the program, *hello.cgi*. The browser's request was not fulfilled. The number of bytes sent was 633.

2   Status code 200 indicates success! The request was fullfilled.

3   Status code 404, *Not Found*, means that the server found nothing matching the URL requested.

## C.2.3   The URL (Uniform Resource Locator)

URLs are what you  use to get around on the Web. You click on a hotlink and you are transported to some new page, or you type a URL in the browser's Location box and a file opens up or a script runs. It is a virtual address that specifies the location of pages, objects, scripts, etc. It refers to an existing protocol such as HTTP, Gopher, FTP, mailto, file, Telnet, or news (see Table C.2). A typical URL for the popular Web HTTP protocol looks like this:

```
http://www.comp.com/dir/text.html
```

**Table C.2**   Web protocols.

| Protocol | Function | Example |
|----------|----------|---------|
| *http:* | Hyper Text Transfer Protocol | *http://www.nnic.noaa.gov/cgi-bin/netcast.cgi* open Web page or start CGI script |
| *ftp:* | File Transfer Protocol | *ftp://jague.gsfc.nasa.gov/pub* |
| *mailto:* | Mail protocol by e-mail address | *mailto:debbiej@aol.com* |
| *file:* | Open a local file | *file://opt/apache/htdocs/file.html* |
| *telnet:* | Open a Telnet session | *telnet://nickym@netcom.com* |
| *news:* | Opens a news session by news server | *news:alt.fan.john-lennon Name or Address* |

The two basic pieces of information provided in the URL are the protocol *http* and the data needed by the protocol, *www.comp.com/dir/files/text.html*. The parts of the URL are further defined in Table C.3.

**Table C.3**   Parts of a URL.

| Part | Description |
|------|-------------|
| protocol | Service such as HTTP, Gopher, FTP, Telnet, news, etc. |
| host/IP number | DNS host name or its IP number |
| port | TCP port number used by server, normally port 80 |
| path | Path and filename reference for the object on a server |
| parameters | Specific parameters used by the object on a server |
| query | The query string for a CGI script |
| fragment | Reference to subset of the object |

The default HTTP network port is 80; if an HTTP server resides on a different network port, say *12345* on *www.comp.com*, then the URL becomes

```
http://www.comp.com.12345/dir/text.html
```

Not all parts of a URL are necessary. If you are searching for a document in the Locator box in the Netscape browser, the URL may not need the port number, parameters, query, or fragment parts. If the URL is part of a hotlink in the HTML document, it may contain a relative path to the next document, that is, relative to the root directory of the server. If the user has filled in a form, the URL line may contain information appended to a question mark in the URL line. The appearance of the URL really depends on what protocol you are using and what operation you are trying to accomplish.

---

**EXAMPLE  C.4**

```
1   http://www.cis.ohio-state.edu/htbin/rfc2068.html
2   http://127.0.0.1/Sample.html
3   ftp://oak.oakland.edu/pub/
4   file://opt/apache_1.2b8/htdocs/index.html
5   http://susan/cgi-bin/form.cgi?string=hello+there
```

**EXPLANATION**

1   The protocol is *http*.
    The hostname *www.cis.ohio-state.edu/htbin/rfc2068.html* consists of the following parts:[a]
        The hostname translated to an IP address by the Domain Name Service, DNS.
        The domain name is *ohio-state.edu*.
        The top-level domain name is *edu*.
        The directory where the HTML file is stored is *htbin*.
        The file to be retrieved is *rfc20868.html,* an HTML document.

2   The protocol is *http*.
    The IP address is used instead of the hostname; this is the IP address for a local host.
    The file is in the server's document root. The file consists of HTML text.

3   The protocol is *ftp*.
    The host *oak.oakland*.
    The top-level domain is *edu*.
    The directory is *pub*.

4   The protocol is file. A local file will be opened.
    The hostname is missing. It then refers to the local host.
    The full path to the file *index.html* is listed.

5 The information after the question mark is the query part of the URL, which may have resulted from submitting input into a form. The query string is URL encoded. In this example, a plus sign has replaced the space between *hello* and *there*. The server stores this query in an environment variable called *QUERY_STRING*. It will be passed on to a CGI program called from the HTML document. (See "The GET Method" on page 633.)

a.  Most Web severs run on hostnames starting with *www*, but this is only a convention.

**File URLs and the Server's Root Directory.**   If the protocol used in the URL is *file*, the server assumes that file is on the local machine. A full pathname followed by a filename is included in the URL. When the protocol is followed by a server name, all pathnames are relative to the document root of the server. The document root is the directory defined in the server's configuration file as the main directory for your Web server. The leading slash that precedes the path is not really part of the path as with the UNIX absolute path, which starts at the root directory. Rather, the leading slash is used to separate the path from the hostname. An example of a URL leading to documents in the server's root directory:

```
http://www.myserver/index.html
```

The full UNIX pathname for this might be

```
/usr/bin/myserver/htdocs/index.html
```

A shorthand method for linking to a document on the same server is called a partial or relative URL. For example, if a document at *http://www.myserver/stories/webjoke.html* contains a link to *images/webjoke.gif*, this is a relative URL. The browser will expand the relative URL to its absolute URL, *http://www.myserver/stories/images/webjoke.gif*, and make a request for that document if asked.

# C.3  Creating a Web Page with HTML

In order to write Web pages, you must learn at least some of what makes up the HTML language. There are volumes written on this subject. Here we will cover just enough to introduce you to HTML and give you the basics so that you can write some simple dynamic pages with forms and CGI scripts. See Appendix B for a succinct tutorial on HTML.

As previously stated, Web pages are written as ASCII text files in HTML. HTML consists of a set of instructions called **tags** that tell your Web browser how to display the text in the page.[2] When you type in the URL or click on a hyperlink in a page, the

---

2. If you have ever used the UNIX programs *nroff* and *troff* for formatting text, you'll immediately recognize the tags used for formatting with HTML.

browser (client) communicates to the server that it needs a file and the file is sent back to the browser. The file contains HTML content that may consist of plain text, images, audio, video, and hyperlinks. It's the browser's job to interpret the HTML tags and display the formatted page on your screen. (To look at the source file for a Web page, you can use the View Document menu under View in the Netscape browser, or using Internet Explorer select the View menu and then select Source to see the HTML tags used to produce the page.)

**Creating Tags.**    The HTML source file can be created with any text editor. Its name ends in *.html* or *.htm* to indicate it is an HTML file. The HTML tags that describe the way the document looks are enclosed in angle brackets < >. The tags are easy to read. If you want to create a title, for example, the tag instruction is enclosed in brackets and the actual text for the title is sandwiched between the marker that starts the instruction, *<TITLE>*, and the tag that ends the instruction, *</TITLE>*. The following line is called a **TITLE element**, consisting of the *<TITLE>* start tag, the enclosed text, and the *</TITLE>* end tag. A tag may also have attributes to further describe its function. For example, a text input area may allow a specified number of rows and columns, or an image may be aligned and centered at the top of the page. The elements and attributes are case-insensitive.

```
<TITLE>War and Peace</TITLE>
```

When the browser sees this instruction, the title will be printed in the bar at the top of the browser's window as a title for the page. To put comments in the HTML document, the commented text is inserted between <!-- and -->.

Because HTML is a structured language, there are rules about how to place the tags in a document. These rules are discussed below.

**A Simple HTML Document.**    The following HTML file is created in your favorite text editor and consists of a simple set of tagged elements.

**EXAMPLE** C.5

```
(The HTML Text File)
1    <HTML>
2    <HEAD>
3    <TITLE>Hyper Test</Title>
4    </HEAD>
5    <BODY>
6    <H1>Hello To You and Yours!</H1>
7    <H2 ALIGN="center">Welcome
8    </H2>
9    <P>Life is good. Today is <I>Friday.</I></P>
10   </BODY>
11   </HTML>
```

## EXPLANATION

1   All of the text for the HTML document is between the *<HTML>* start tag and the *</HTML>* end tag. Although HTML is the standard language for creating Web pages, there are other markup languages that look like HTML; The HTML element identifies this as an HTML document. You can omit these tags and your browser will not complain. It is just more official to use them.

2   Between the *<HEAD>* tag and *</HEAD>* tag information about the document is inserted, such as the title. This information is not displayed with the rest of the document text. The *<HEAD>* tag always comes right after the *<HTML>* tag.

3   The *<TITLE>* tag is used to create the title shown at the top of the browser window.

4   This is the closing tag for the *<HEAD>* tag.

5   The main part of the document appears in the browser's window, and is enclosed between the *<BODY>* start tag and *</BODY>* end tag.

6   A level 1 heading is enclosed between the *<H1>* and *</H1>* start and end tags.

7   This is a level 2 heading. The *ALIGN* attribute tells the browser to center the heading on the page.

8   This is the end tag for a level 2 heading.

9   The *<P>* starts a new paragraph. The string *Friday* will be printed in italicized text. *</P>* marks the end of the paragraph.

10  This tag marks the end of the body of the document.

11  This tag marks the end of the HTML document.

**Figure C.2**   The HTML document from Example C.5, as displayed in Internet Explorer.

**Table C.4**   Simple HTML tags and what they do.

| Tag Element | Function |
|---|---|
| *<!-- text -->* | Commented text; nothing is displayed. |
| *<BASE HREF="http://www.bus.com/my.html">* | Where this document is stored. |
| *<HTML>*document*</HTML>* | Found at the beginning and end of the document, indicating to a browser that this is an HTML document. |
| *<HEAD>*headinginfo*</HEAD>* | First element inside the document. Contains title, metatags, JavaScript, and CSS. Only the title is displayed directly. |
| *<TITLE>*title of the document*</TITLE>* | Title of the document; displayed outside the document text in a window frame or top of the screen. Can be placed in the bookmark list. |
| *<BODY>*document contents*</BODY>* | Contains all the text and other objects to be displayed. |
| *<H1>*heading type*</H1>* | Creates boldface heading elements for heading levels 1 through 6. The levels elements are: H1, H2, H3, H4, H5, and H6. The largest, topmost heading is H1. |
| *<P>*text*</P>* | Paragraph tag. Marks the beginning of a paragraph. Inserts a break after a block of text. Can go anywhere on the line. Ending paragraph tags are optional. Paragraphs end when a *</P>* or another *<P>* (marking a new paragraph) is encountered. |
| *<B>*text*</B>* | Bold text. |
| *<I>*text*</I>* | Italic text. |
| *<TT>*text*</TT>* | Typewriter text. |
| *<U>*text*</U>* | Underlined text. |
| *<BR>* | Line break. |
| *<HR>* | Horizontal shadow line. |
| *<UL>* | Start of an unordered (bulleted) list. |
| *<LI>* | An item in a list. |

**Table C.4**   Simple HTML tags and what they do.  (continued)

| Tag Element | Function |
| --- | --- |
| *<LI>* | Another item in a list. |
| *</UL>* | The end of the list. |
| *<OL>* | Start of an ordered list. |
| *<DL>* | Descriptive list. |
| *<DT>* | An item in a descriptive list |
| *<DT>* | Another item in a descriptive list. |
| *</DL>* | End of the descriptive list. |
| *<STRONG>* | Bold text. |
| *<EM>* | Italic text. |
| *<BLOCKQUOTE>*text*</BLOCKQUOTE>* | Italicized blocked text with spaces before and after quote. |
| *<A HREF SRC="URL">* | Creates a hotlink to a resource at address in URL on the Web. |
| *<IMG SRC="URL">* | Loads an image into a Web page. URL is the address of the image file. |

# C.4  How HTML and CGI Work Together

As previously discussed, HTML is the markup language used to determine the way a Web page will be displayed. CGI is a protocol that allows the server to extend its functionality. A CGI program is executed on behalf of the server mainly to process forms such as a registration form or a shopping list. If you have purchased a book or CD from Amazon.com, you know what a form looks like. When a browser (client) makes a request of the server, the server examines the URL. If the server sees *cgi-bin* as a directory in the path, it will go to that directory, open a pipe, and execute the CGI program. The CGI program gets its **input from the pipe** and sends its **standard output back though the pipe** to the server. **Standard error** is sent to the server's **error log**. If the CGI program is to talk to the server, it must speak the Web language, since this is the language that is ultimately used by the browser to display a page. The CGI program then will format its data with HTML tags and send it back to the HTTP server. The server will then return this document to the browser where the HTML tags will be rendered and displayed to the user.

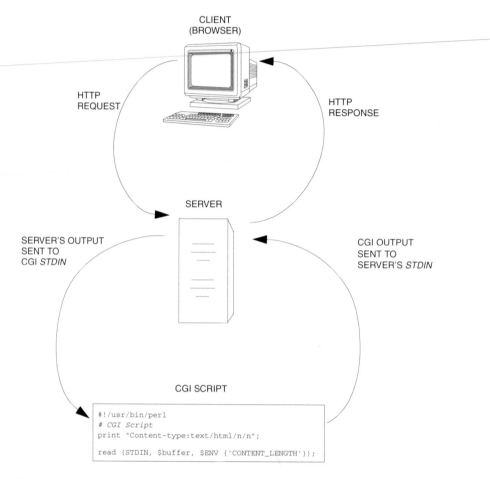

**Figure C.3**   The client/server/CGI program relationship.

## C.4.1   A Simple CGI Script

The following Perl script consists of a series of *print* statements, most of which send HTML output back to *STDOUT* (piped to the server). This program is executed directly from the CGI directory, *cgi-bin*. Some servers require that CGI script names end in *.cgi* or *.pl* so that they can be recognized as CGI scripts. After creating the script, the execute permission for the file must be turned on. For UNIX systems, at the shell prompt type

```
chmod 755 <scriptname>
```

   or

```
chmod +x <scriptname>
```

The URL entered in the browser Location window includes the protocol, the name of the host machine, the directory where the CGI scripts are stored, and the name of the CGI script. The URL will look like this:

```
http://servername/cgi-bin/perl_script.pl
```

**The HTTP Headers.**   The first line of output for most CGI programs is an HTTP header that tells the browser what type of output the program is sending to it. Right after the header line, there must be a blank line and two newlines. The two most common types of headers, also called **MIME** types (which stands for multipurpose Internet extension), are "Content-type: text/html\n\n" and "Content-type: text/plain\n\n." Another type of header is called the **Location** header, which is used to redirect the browser to a different Web page. And finally, **Cookie** headers are used to set cookies for maintaining state; that is, keeping track of information that would normally be lost once the transaction between the server and browser is closed.

**Table C.5**   HTTP headers.

| Header | Type | Value |
| --- | --- | --- |
| Content-type: | text/plain | Plain text |
| Content-type: | text/html | HTML tags and text |
| Content-type: | image/gif | GIF graphics |
| Location: | http://www.... | Redirection to another Web page |
| Set-cookie: NAME=VALUE... | Cookie | Set a cookie on a client browser |

Right after the header line, there must be a blank line. This is accomplished by ending the line with \n\n in Perl.

## EXAMPLE C.6

```
1   #!/bin/perl
2   print "Content-type: text/html\n\n";      # The HTTP header
3   print "<HTML><HEAD><TITLE> CGI/Perl First Try</TITLE></HEAD>\n";
4   print "<BODY BGCOLOR=Black TEXT=White>\n";
5   print "<H1><CENTER> Howdy, World! </CENTER></H1>\n";
6   print "<H2><CENTER> It's ";
7   print "<!--comments -->";   # This is how HTML comments are
                                              included
8   print `date`;   # Execute the UNIX date command
9   print "and all's well.\n";
10  print "</H2></BODY></HTML>\n";
```

## EXPLANATION

1  This first line is critical. Many Web servers will not run a CGI script if this line is missing. This tells the server where Perl is installed.

2  This line is called the **MIME header**. No matter what programming language you are using, the first output of your CGI program must be a MIME header followed by two newlines. This line indicates what type of data your application will be sending. In this case, the CGI script will be sending HTML text back to the server. The \n\n cause a blank line to be printed. The blank line is also crucial to success of your CGI program.

3  The next lines sent from Perl back to the server are straight HTML tags and text. This line creates the header information, in this case, a title for the document.

4  This defines the background color as black and the textual material as white.

5  <H1> is a level 1 heading. It is the largest of the headings and prints in bold text. *Howdy, World!* will be formatted as a level 1 heading and centered on the page.

6  All text from this point until line 10 will be formatted as a level 2, centered heading.

7  This is how comments are inserted into an HTML document. They are not displayed by the browser.

8  The UNIX *date* command is executed and its output is included as part of the centered, second-level heading. A better way to get the date so that your program is portable is to use *localtime*, a Perl built-in. Try changing line 9 to

   *$now = localtime;*
   *print "$now\n";)*

9  This line is printed as part of heading level 2.

10 These tags end the second level heading, the body of the document and the HTML document itself.

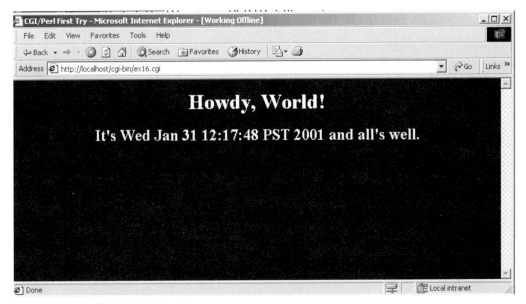

**Figure C.4** Output from the CGI program in Example C.6.

# C.5 Log Files

**Error Logs and *STDERR*.**   Normally, error messages are sent to the terminal screen (*STDERR*) when something goes wrong in a Perl script, but when launched by a server as a CGI script, the errors are not sent to the screen, but to the server's error log file. In the browser you may see "Empty Document" or "Internal Server Error," which tells you nothing about what went wrong in the program.

Always check your syntax at the shell command line with the -c switch before handing the script to the server. Otherwise, you will not see your error messages unless you check the log files. **Check the syntax of your Perl scripts with the -c switch.**

---

**EXAMPLE C.7**

```
(At the Command line)
1   perl -c perlscript
2   perlscript syntax OK
```

**EXAMPLE C.8**

```
(Perl syntax errors shown in the Apache server's error log)

[Mon Jul 20 10:44:04 1998] access to /opt/apache_1.2b8/
    cgi-bin/submit-form failed for susan, reason: Premature end
    of script headers
[Mon Sep 14 11:11:32 1998] httpd: caught SIGTERM, shutting down
[Fri Sep 25 16:13:11 1998] Server configured -- resuming normal
    operations
```
1   **Bare word found where operator expected at welcome.pl line 21,**
    **near "/font></TABLE"**
```
(Missing operator before TABLE?)
```
2   **syntax error at welcome.pl line 21, near "<TH><"**
```
syntax error at welcome.pl line 24, near "else"
[Fri Sep 25 16:16:18 1998] access to /opt/apache_1.2b8/
    cgi-bin/visit_count.pl failed for susan, reason:
    Premature end of script headers
```

**Access Logs and Status Codes.**   Check your server's access log to see what status codes were sent by your server after a transaction was complete.[3] The following example consists of excerpts taken from the Apache server's access log. This log reports information about a request handled by the server and the status code generated as a result of the request.

**Table C.6**   HTTP status codes.

| Status | Message Code |
|--------|--------------|
| 100 | Continue |
| 200 | Success, OK |
| 204 | No Content |
| 301 | Document Moved |
| 400 | Bad Request |
| 401 | Unauthorized |
| 403 | Forbidden |
| 404 | Not Found |
| 500 | Internal Server Error |
| 501 | Not Implemented |
| 503 | Service Unavailable |

---

3. For more detailed information on status codes, see *www.w3.org/Protocols/HTTP/HTRESP.html*

**EXAMPLE** C.9

```
(Status codes from the Apache server's access log)

1    susan - - [08/Oct./1999:10:45:36 -0700]
     "GET /cog-bin/visit_count.pl HTTP/1.0" 500 388
2    susan - - [08/Oct./1999:10:45:59 -0700]
     "GET /cgi-bin/visit_count.pl HTTP/1.0" 200 426
```

## C.6   Where to Find CGI Applications

There are a number of Web sites that provide online resources to help you get started in writing your own CGI scripts. Most house prebuilt scripts that you can freely download, examine, and modify. Browsing through some of following sites can also give you a good idea of how Web pages are designed.

**Table C.7**   Web sites for CGI beginners and developers (just a few of thousands!).

| The Web Site | What It Is |
| --- | --- |
| www.virtualville.com/library/cgi.html | An introduction to CGI |
| www.virtualville.com/library/scripts.html | Scripts to Go. A collection of CGI scripts |
| www.scriptarchive.com | Matt's Script Archive |
| www.extropia.com/opensource.html | Open-source Web software, formerly Selena Sol's Public Domain CGI Script Archive |
| www.perl.com/CPAN/ | The Comprehensive Perl Archive Network |
| cgi-lib/berkeley.edu | The cgi-lib.pl Home Page |
| dir.yahoo.com/Computers_and_Internet/Software/Internet/World_Wide_Web/Servers/Server_Side_Scripting/Common_Gateway_Interface__CGI_/ | Yahoo CGI Resources |

## C.7   Getting Information Into and Out of the CGI Script

The server and the CGI script communicate in four major ways. Once the browser has sent a request to the server, the server can then send it on to the CGI script. The CGI script gets its input from the server as:

1. Environment variables
2. Query strings
3. Standard input
4. Extra path information

After the CGI program gets the input from the server it parses and processes it, and then formats it so that the server can relay the information back to the browser. The CGI script sends output through the gateway by

1. Generating new documents on the fly
2. Sending existing static files to the standard output
3. Using URLs that redirect the browser to go somewhere else for a document

## C.7.1   CGI Environment Variables

The CGI program is passed a number of environment variables from the server. The environment variables are set when the server executes the gateway program, and are set for all requests. The environment variables contain information about the server, the CGI program, the ports and protocols, path information, etc. User input is normally assigned to the *QUERY_STRING* environment variable. In the following example, this variable has no value because the user never was asked for input; that is, the HTML document has no INPUT tags.

The environment variables are set for all requests and are sent by the server to the CGI program. In a Perl program, the environment variables are assigned to the *%ENV* hash as key/value pairs. They are shown in Table C.8.

**Table C.8**   CGI environment variables.

| Name | Value | Example |
|---|---|---|
| *AUTH_TYPE* | Validates user if server supports user authentication | |
| *CONTENT_TYPE* | The MIME type of the query data | *text/html* |
| *CONTENT_LENGTH* | The number of bytes passed from the server to CGI program | *Content-Length=55* |
| *DOCUMENT_ROOT* | The directory from which the server serves Web documents | /opt/apache/htdocs/index.html |
| *GATEWAY_INTERFACE* | The revision of the CGI used by the server | CGI/1.1 |
| *HTTP_ACCEPT* | The MIME types accepted by the client | image/gif, image/jpeg, etc |
| *HTTP_CONNECTION* | The preferred HTTP connection type | Keep-Alive |

**Table C.8**   CGI environment variables. (continued)

| Name | Value | Example |
|------|-------|---------|
| HTTP_HOST | The name of the host machine | susan |
| HTTP_USER_AGENT | The browser (client) sending the request | Mozilla/3.01(X11;I; Sun05.5.1 sun4m) |
| PATH_INFO | Extra path information passed to a CGI program | |
| PATH_TRANSLATED | The PATH_INFO translated to its absolute path | |
| QUERY_STRING | The string obtained from a GET request from the URL (information following the ? in the URL) | http://susan/cgi-bin/ form1.cgi?Name=Christian+ Dobbins |
| REMOTE_HOST | The remote hostname of the user making a request | eqrc.ai.mit.edu |
| REMOTE_ADDR | The IP address of the host making a request | 192.100.1.11 |
| REMOTE_PORT | The port number of the host making a request | 33015 |
| REQUEST_METHOD | The method used to get information to the CGI program | GET,  POST, etc |
| SCRIPT_FILENAME | The absolute pathname of the CGI program | /opt/apache/cgi-bin/hello.cgi |
| SCRIPT_NAME | The relative pathname of the CGI program; a partial URL | /cgi-bin/hello.cgi |
| SERVER_ADMIN | E-mail address of the system administrator | root@susan |
| SERVER_NAME | The server's hostname, DNS alias, or IP address | susan, 127.0.0.0 |
| SERVER_PROTOCOL | The name and version of the protocol | HTTP/1.0 |
| SERVER_SOFTWARE | Name and version of the server software | Apache/1.2b8 |

**An HTML File with a Link to a CGI Script.**    The following example is an HTML file that will allow the user to print out all the environment variables. When the browser displays this document, the user can click on the hotlink *here* and the CGI script, *env.cgi*, will then be executed by the server. In the HTML document the string *here* and the URL *http://susan/cgi-bin/env.cgi* are enclosed in the *<A></A>* anchor tags. If the hotlink is ignored by the user, the browser displays the rest of the document. The following example is the HTML source file that will be interpreted by the browser. The browser's output is shown in Figure C.5.

## EXAMPLE C.10

```
(The HTML file with a hotlink to a CGI script)
1   <HTML>
2   <HEAD>
3   <TITLE>TESTING ENV VARIABLES</TITLE>
    </HEAD>
    <BODY>
    <P>
    <H1> Major Test </H1>
4   <P> If you would like to see the environment variables<BR>
    being passed on by the server, click .
5   <A HREF="http://localhost/cgi-bin/env.cgi">here</A>
    <P>Text continues here...
    </BODY>
    </HTML>
```

## EXPLANATION

1    The *<HTML>* tag says this document is using the HTML protocol.

2    The *<HEAD>* tag contains the title and any information that will be displayed outside the actual document.

3    The *<TITLE>* tag is displayed in the top bar of the browser window.

4    The *<P>* tag is the start of a paragraph. The *<BR>* tag causes the line to break.

5    The *<A>* tag is assigned the path to the CGI script, *env.cgi*, on server *localhost*. The word *here* will be displayed by the browser in blue underlined letters. If the user clicks on this word, the CGI script will be executed by the server. The script will print out all of the environment variables passed to the script from the server. This is one of the ways information is given to a CGI script by a Web server. The actual CGI script is shown below, in Example C.11.

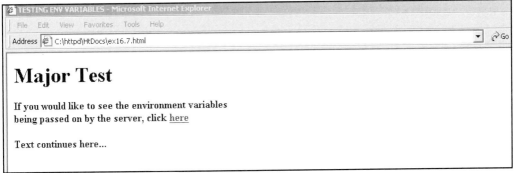

**Figure C.5** Output of the HTML file in Example C.10. It contains a hotlink to the CGI script.

---

**EXAMPLE C.11**

```
(The CGI Script)
1   #!/bin/perl
2   print "Content type: text/plain\n\n";
3   print "CGI/1.1 test script report:\n\n";
4   # Print out all the environment variables

5   while(($key, $value)=each(%ENV)){
6       print "$key = $value\n";
    }
```

**EXPLANATION**

1   The #! line is important to your server if your server is running on a UNIX platform. It is the path to the Perl interpreter. The line must be the correct pathname to your version of perl or you will receive the following error message from your server:
    *Internal Server Error ...*

2   The first line generated by the CGI script is a valid HTTP header, ending with a blank line. The header contains a content type (also called a MIME type) followed by *text/plain*, meaning that the document will consist of plain text. If the script were to include HTML tags, the content type would be *text/html*.

3   The version of the Common Gateway Interface used by this server is printed.

4   This is a Perl comment line.

5   The %ENV hash contains environment variables (keys and values) passed into the Perl script from the server. The *each* function will return both the key and the value and store them in scalars, $key and $value, respectively.

6   The $key/$value pairs are printed back to *STDOUT*, which has been connected to the server by a pipe mechanism.

CGI/1.1 test script report: QUERY_STRING =
CONTENT_TYPE =
HTTP_REFERER =
PROCESSOR_IDENTIFIER = x86 Family 6 Model 8 Stepping 6, GenuineIntel
HTTP_USER_AGENT = Mozilla/4.76 [en] (Windows NT 5.0; U)
HTTP_ACCEPT = image/gif, image/x-xbitmap, image/jpeg, image/pjpeg, image/png, */*
REMOTE_HOST =
GATEWAY_INTERFACE = CGI/1.1
REMOTE_IDENT =
TMP = C:\WINNT\TEMP
OS2LIBPATH = C:\WINNT\system32\os2\dll;
SCRIPT_NAME = /cgi-bin/env.cgi
TEMP = C:\WINNT\TEMP
SERVER_NAME = localhost
USERPROFILE = C:\Documents and Settings\Default User
OS = Windows_NT
TMPDIR = C:/WINNT/TEMP
HTTP_COOKIE = preference=blue
CONTENT_LENGTH = 0
PATH = C:\Perl\bin\;C:\mksnt;C:\WINNT\system32;C:\WINNT;C:\WINNT\System32\Wbem;;C:\ATF;;C:\httpd\php
SHELL = C:\mksnt/sh.exe
COMPUTERNAME = LEARNING-2LS8XZ
COMMONPROGRAMFILES = C:\Program Files\Common Files
PATHEXT = .COM;.EXE;.BAT;.CMD;.VBS;.VBE;.JS;.JSE;.WSF;.WSH
PROGRAMFILES = C:\Program Files
PROCESSOR_ARCHITECTURE = x86
SYSTEMROOT = C:\WINNT
PROCESSOR_REVISION = 0806
ALLUSERSPROFILE = C:\Documents and Settings\All Users
SERVER_PROTOCOL = HTTP/1.0
COMSPEC = C:\WINNT\system32\cmd.exe
SYSTEMDRIVE = C:
PATH_TRANSLATED = C:\httpd\CGI-BIN/env.cgi
WINDIR = C:\WINNT
SERVER_SOFTWARE = OmniHTTPd/2.07
PATH_INFO = /cgi-bin/env.cgi
REMOTE_USER =
REMOTE_ADDR = 127.0.0.1
PROCESSOR_LEVEL = 6
NUMBER_OF_PROCESSORS = 1
ROOTDIR = C:/
HOME = C:/
REQUEST_METHOD = GET
AUTH_TYPE =
SERVER_PORT = 80

**Figure C.6**   The environment variables displayed by the CGI script in Example C.11.

# C.8  Processing Forms with CGI

Processing user input is one of the most common reasons for using a CGI script. This is normally done with forms. The form offers you a number of methods, called **virtual input devices**, with which to accept input. These include radio buttons, checkboxes, pop-up menus, and text boxes. All forms are in HTML documents and begin with a *<FORM>* tag and end with a *</FORM>* tag. A method attribute may be assigned. The method attribute indicates how the form will be processed. The *GET* method is the default and the *POST* method is the most commonly used alternative. The *GET* method is preferable for operations that will not affect the state of the server; that is, simple document retrieval and database lookups, etc., whereas the *POST* method is preferred for handing operations that may change the state of the server, such as adding or deleting records from a database. These methods will be described in the next section. The *ACTION* attribute is assigned the URL of the CGI script that will be executed when the data is submitted by pressing the Submit button.

The browser gets input from the user by displaying fields that can be edited. The fields are created by the HTML *<INPUT TYPE=key/value>* tag. These fields might take the form of checkboxes, text boxes, radio buttons, etc. The data that is entered into the form is sent to the server in an encoded string format in a name/value pair scheme. The value represents the actual input data. The CGI programmer must understand how this input is encoded in order to parse it and use it effectively. First let's see how input gets into the browser by looking at a simple document and the HTML code used to produce it. The user will be able to click on a button or enter data in the text box. The input in this example won't be processed, thereby causing an error to be sent to the server's error log when the Submit button is selected. Nothing will be displayed by the browser. The default for obtaining input is the *GET* method.

A summary of the steps in producing a form is

1. START: Start the form with the HTML *<FORM>* tag.
2. ACTION: The *ACTION* attribute of the *<FORM>* tag is the URL of the CGI script that will process the data input from the form.
3. METHOD: Provide a method on how to process the data input. The default is the *GET* method.
4. CREATE: Create the form with buttons and boxes and whatever looks nice using HTML tags and fields.
5. SUBMIT: Create a Submit button so that the form can be processed. This will launch the CGI script listed in the *ACTION* attribute.
6. END: End the form and the HTML document.

## C.8.1  Input Types for Forms

**Table C.9**  Form input types.

| *Input Type* | *Attributes* | *Description* |
|---|---|---|
| *CHECKBOX* | *NAME, VALUE* | Displays a square box that can be checked. Creates name/value pairs from user input. Multiple boxes can be checked. |
| *FILE* | *NAME* | Specifies files to be uploaded to the server. MIME type must be multipart/form-data. |
| *HIDDEN* | *NAME, VALUE* | Provides name/value pair without displaying an object on the screen. |

**Table C.9**   Form input types. (continued)

| Input Type | Attributes | Description |
|---|---|---|
| *IMAGE* | *SRC, VALUE, ALIGN* | Same as the Submit button, but displays an image instead of text. The image is in a file found at SRC. |
| *PASSWORD* | *NAME, VALUE* | Like a text box but input is hidden. Asterisks appear in the box to replace characters typed. |
| *RADIO* | *NAME, VALUE* | Like checkboxes, except only one box (or circle) can be checked at a time. |
| *RESET* | *NAME, VALUE* | Resets the form to its original position; clears all input fields. |
| *SELECT* | *NAME, OPTION SIZE, MULTIPLE* | Provides pop-up menus and scrollable lists. Only one can be selected. Attribute *MULTIPLE* creates a visibly scrollable list. A *SIZE* of 1 creates a pop-up menu with only one visible box. |
| *SUBMIT* | *NAME, VALUE* | When pressed, executes the form; launches CGI. |
| *TEXT* | *NAME* <br> *SIZE, MAXLENGTH* | Creates a text box for user input. *SIZE* specifies the size of the text box. *MAXLENGTH* specifies the maximum number of characters allowed. |
| *TEXTAREA* | *NAME, SIZE* <br> *ROWS, COLS* | Creates a text area that can take input spanning multiple lines. *ROWS* and *COLUMNS* specify the size of the box. |

## C.8.2   Creating an HTML Form

**A Simple Form with Text Fields, Radio Buttons, Checkboxes, and Pop-up Menus.**   First let's see how input gets into the browser by looking at a simple document and the HTML code used to produce it. The user will be able to click on a button, or enter data in the text box. The input in this example won't be processed, thus causing an error to be sent to the server's error log when the Submit button is selected. Nothing will be displayed by the browser. The HTML file is normally stored under the server's root in a directory called *htdocs*. If the HTML file is created on the local machine, then the *file:///* protocol is used in the Location box with the full pathname of the HTML file, which would normally end with an *.html* or *.htm* extension.

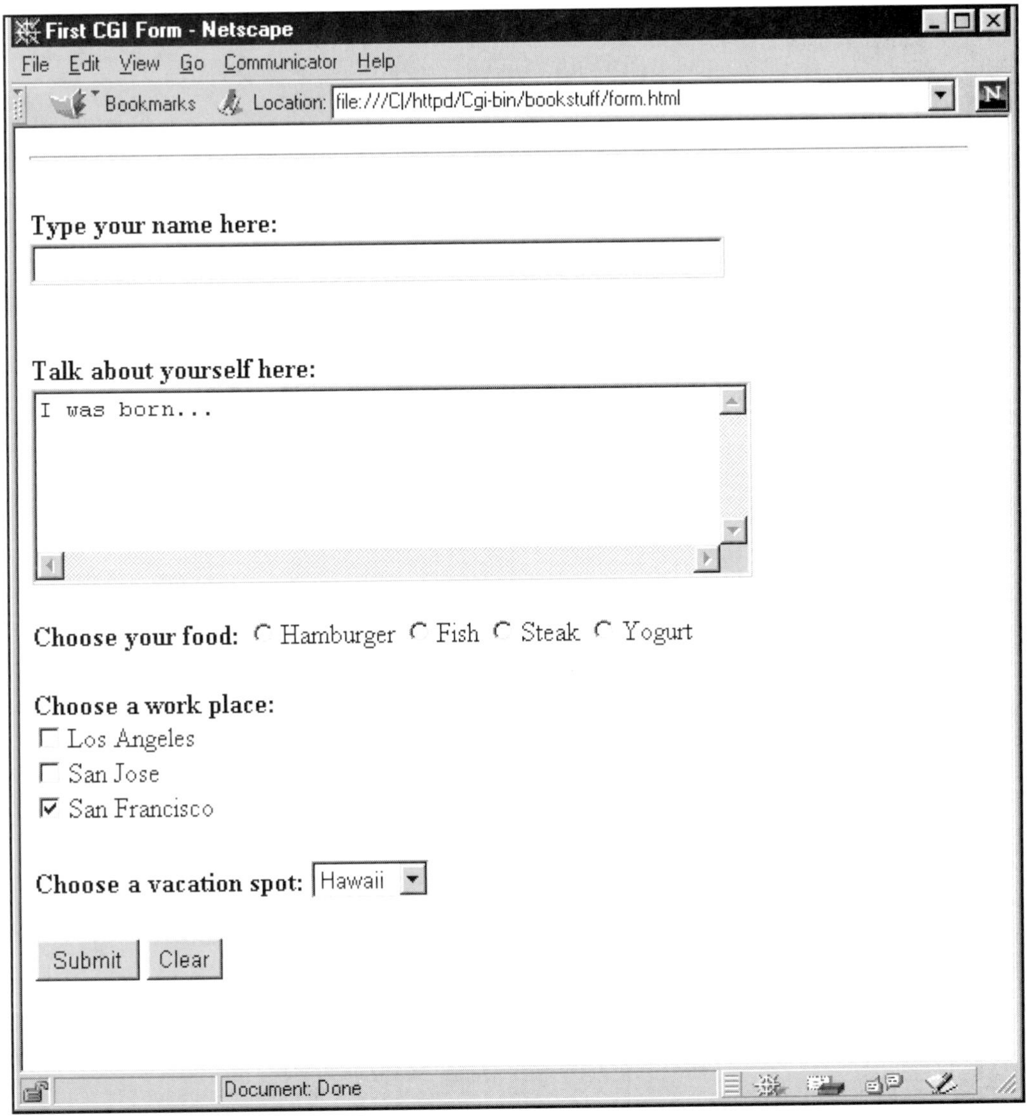

**Figure C.7** A form as it is initially displayed.

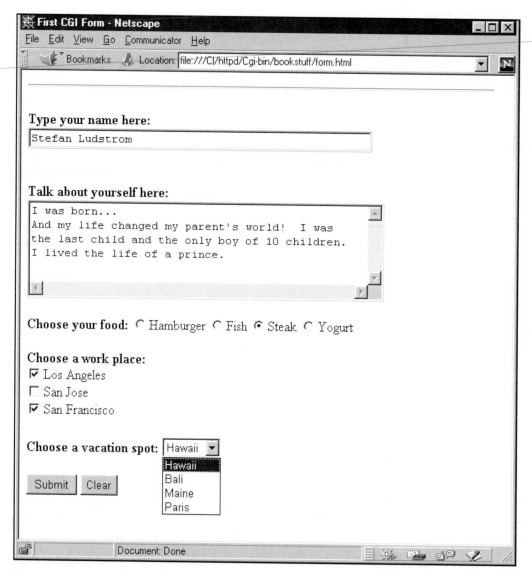

**Figure C.8** A form filled with user input.

EXAMPLE   C.12

```
(The HTML Form Source File)
1    <HTML><HEAD>
2    <TITLE>First CGI Form</TITLE></HEAD>
     <HR>
3    <FORM ACTION="/cgi-bin/bookstuff/form1.cgi" >
4    <P><B> Type your name here:
5    <INPUT TYPE="text" NAME="namestring" SIZE=50>
6    <P><BR> Talk about yourself here: <BR>
7    <TEXTAREA NAME="comments" ROWS=5 COLS=50>I was born... </TEXTAREA>
     </B>
8    <P> Choose your food:
9    <INPUT TYPE="radio" NAME="choice" VALUE="burger">Hamburger
     <INPUT TYPE="radio" NAME="choice" VALUE="fish">Fish
     <INPUT TYPE="radio" NAME="choice" VALUE="steak">Steak
     <INPUT TYPE="radio" NAME="choice" VALUE="yogurt">Yogurt
     <P> <B>Choose a work place:</B> <BR>
10   <INPUT TYPE="checkbox" NAME="place" VALUE="LA">Los Angeles
     <BR>
     <INPUT TYPE="checkbox" NAME="place" VALUE="SJ">San Jose
     <BR>
     <INPUT TYPE="checkbox" NAME="place" VALUE="SF" Checked>
        San Francisco
     <P>
11   <B>Choose a vacation spot:</B>
12   <SELECT NAME="location"> <OPTION SELECTED VALUE="hawaii"> Hawaii
     <OPTION VALUE="bali">Bali
     <OPTION VALUE="maine">Maine
     <OPTION VALUE="paris">Paris
     </SELECT> <P>
13   <INPUT TYPE="SUBMIT" VALUE="Submit">
14   <INPUT TYPE="RESET" VALUE="Clear">
     </FORM> </HTML>
```

**EXPLANATION**

1   This tag says that this is the start of an HTML document.
2   The *<TITLE>* tag; the title appears outside of the browser's main window.
3   The beginning of a *<FORM>* tag, which specifies where the browser will send the input data and the method that will be used to process it. The default method is the *GET* method. When the data is submitted, the CGI script will be executed by the server. The CGI script is located under the server's root directory in the *cgi-bin* directory, the directory where CGI scripts are normally stored. In this example, the CGI script is stored in a directory called *bookstuff*, below the *cgi-bin* directory.

**EXPLANATION** (CONTINUED)

4  The *<P>* tag starts a new paragraph. The *<B>* tag says the text that follows will be in bold type. The user is asked for input.

5  The input type is a text box that will hold up to 50 characters. When the user types text into the text box, that text will be stored in the user-defined *NAME* value, *namestring*. For example, if the user types *Stefan Lundstom*, the browser will assign *namestring=Stefan Lundstrom* to the query string. If assigned a *VALUE* attribute, the text field can take a default; i.e., text that appears in the text box when it is initially displayed by the browser.

6  The user is asked for input.

7  The text area is similar to the text field, but will allow input that scans multiple lines. The *<TEXTAREA>* tag will produce a rectangle (name comments) with dimensions in rows and columns (5 rows by 50 columns) and an optional default value (*I was born...*).

8  The user is asked to pick from a series of menu items.

9  The first input type is a list of radio buttons. Only one button can be selected. The input type has two attributes: a *TYPE* and a *NAME*. The value of the *NAME* attribute *choice*, for example, will be assigned *burger* if the user clicks on the *Hamburger* option. *choice=burger* is passed onto the CGI program. And if the user selects *Fish*, *choice=fish* will be assigned to the query string, and so on. These key/value pairs are used to build a query string to pass onto the CGI program after the Submit button is pressed.

10  The input type this time is in the form of checkboxes. More than one checkbox may be selected. The optional default box is already checked. When the user selects one of the checkboxes, the value of the *NAME* attribute will be assigned one of the values from the *VALUE* attribute such as *place=LA* if *Los Angeles* is checked.

11  The user is asked for input.

12  The*<SELECT>* tag is used to produce a pop-up menu (also called a drop-down list) or a scrollable list. The *NAME* option is required. It is used to define the name for the set of options. For a pop-up menu, the *SIZE* attribute is not necessary; it defaults to 1. The pop-up menu initially displays one option and expands to a menu when that option is clicked. Only one selection can be made from the menu. If a *SIZE* attribute is given, that many items will be displayed. If the *MULTIPLE* attribute is given (e.g., *SELECT MULTIPLE NAME=whatever*), the menu appears as a scrollable list, displaying all of the options.

13  If the user clicks the Submit button, the CGI script listed in the form's *ACTION* attribute will be launched. In this example, the script wasn't programmed to do anything. An error message is sent to the server's error log and to the browser.

14  If the *Clear* button is clicked, all of the input boxes are reset back to their defaults.

### C.8.3   The *GET* Method

The simplest and most widely supported type of form is created with what is called the *GET* method. It is used every time the browser requests a document. If a method is not supplied, the *GET* method is the default. It is the only method used for retrieving static HTML files and images.

Since HTML is an object-oriented language, you may recall that a method is a name for an object-oriented subroutine. The *GET* method passes data to the CGI program by appending the input to the program's URL, usually as a URL-encoded string. The *QUERY_STRING* environment variable is assigned the value of the encoded string.

Servers often have size limitations on the length of the URL. For example, the UNIX size is limited to 1240 bytes. If a lot of information is being passed to the server, the *POST* method should be used.

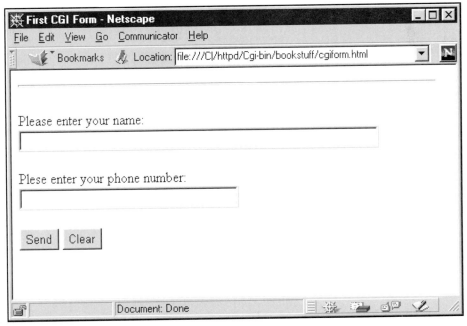

**Figure C.9**   The HTML form created in the following Example C.13.

## EXAMPLE C.13

**HTML Source File** with a Form Tag and ACTION Attribute

```
--------------------------------------------------------------------
      <HTML><HEAD><TITLE>First CGI Form</TITLE></HEAD>
      <HR>
1     <FORM ACTION="/cgi-bin/form1.cgi" METHOD=GET>
      <! When user presses "submit", cgi script is called to process
      input >
2     Please enter your name: <BR>
3     <INPUT TYPE="text" SIZE=50 NAME="Name">
      <P>
      Please enter your phone number: <BR>
4     <INPUT TYPE="text" SIZE=30 NAME="Phone">
      <P>
5     <INPUT TYPE=SUBMIT VALUE="Send">
      <INPUT TYPE=RESET VALUE="Clear">
6     </FORM>
      </HTML>
```

## EXPLANATION

1 The <FORM> tag specifies the URL and method that will be used to process a form. When a user submits the form, the browser will send all the data it has obtained from the browser to the Web server. The *ACTION* attribute tells the server to call a CGI script at the location designated in the URL and send the data on to that program to be processed. The *METHOD* attribute tells the browser how the input data is to be sent to the server. The *GET* method is the default, so it does not need to be assigned here. The CGI program can do whatever it wants to with the data and, when finished, will send it back to the server. The server will then relay the information back to the browser for display.

2 The user is asked for input.

3 The input type is a text box that will hold up to 50 characters. The *NAME* attribute is assigned the string *Name*. This will be the key part of the key/value pair. The user will type something in the text box. The value entered by the user will be assigned to the *NAME* key. This *NAME=VALUE* pair will be sent to the CGI script in that format; for example, *Name=Christian*.

4 The *NAME* attribute for the input type is *Phone*. Whatever the user types in the text box will be sent to the CGI program as *Phone=VALUE*; for example, *Phone=510-456-1234*

5 The *SUBMIT* attribute for the input type causes a Submit button to appear with the string *Send* written on the button. If this box is selected, the CGI program will be executed. The input is sent to the CGI program. The *RESET* attribute allows the user to clear all the input devices by clicking on the *Clear* button.

6 The </FORM> tag ends the form.

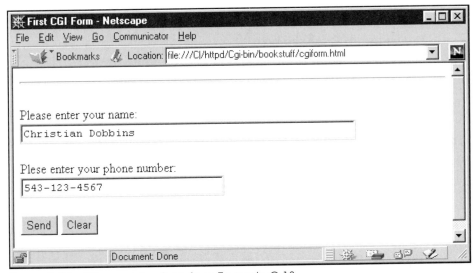

**Figure C.10**  Filling out the form from Example C.13.

---

**EXAMPLE  C.14**

```
(The CGI Script)
1   #!/bin/perl
    # The CGI script that will process the form information sent
    # from the server
2   print "Content-type: text/html\n\n";

    print "First CGI form :\n\n";
    # Print out only the QUERY_STRING environment variable

3   while(($key, $value)=each(%ENV)){
4       print "<H3>$key = <I>$value</I></H3><BR>"
                    if $key eq "QUERY_STRING";

    }
```

**EXPLANATION**

1   The #! line tells the server where to find the Perl interpreter.

2   Perl's output goes to the browser rather than the screen. The content type (also called the MIME type) is *text/html* text since there are HTML tags in the text.

3   Perl's input comes from the server. The *while* loop is used to loop through all of the environment variables in the *%ENV* hash. These variables were passed into the Perl script from the Web server.

4   This line will be printed only when the value of the *QUERY_STRING* environment variable is found. It wasn't really necessary to loop through the entire list. It would have been sufficient to just type  *print "$ENV{QUERY_STRING}<BR>";*.

## C.8.4   Processing the Form

**The Encoded Query String.**   When using the *GET* method, information is sent to the CGI program in the environment variable, *QUERY_STRING*.[4] The string is URL-encoded. In fact, all data contained in an HTML form is sent from the browser to the server in an encoded format. When the *GET* method is used, this encoded data can be seen on the URL line in your browser preceded by a question mark. The string following the *?* will be sent to the CGI program in the *QUERY_STRING* environment variable. Each key/value pair is separated by an ampersand (*&*) and spaces are replaced with plus signs (+). Any non-alphanumeric values are replaced with their hexadecimal equivalent, preceded by a percent sign (%). After pressing the Submit button in the previous example, you would see the input strings in your browser's Location box (Netscape), appended to the URL line and preceded by a question mark. The highlighted part in the following example is the part that will be assigned to the environment variable, *QUERY_STRING*. The *QUERY_STRING* environment variable will be passed to your Perl script in the *%ENV* hash. To access the key/value pair in your Perl script, add a *print* statement: *print  $ENV{QUERY_STRING};*

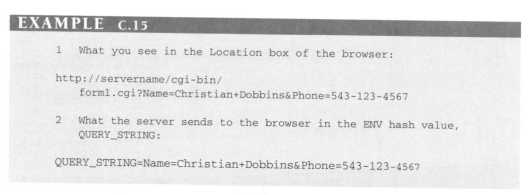

```
EXAMPLE  C.15

1    What you see in the Location box of the browser:

http://servername/cgi-bin/
    form1.cgi?Name=Christian+Dobbins&Phone=543-123-4567

2    What the server sends to the browser in the ENV hash value,
     QUERY_STRING:

QUERY_STRING=Name=Christian+Dobbins&Phone=543-123-4567
```

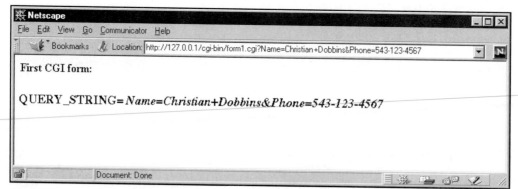

**Figure C.11**   Output of the CGI script from Example C.13.

---

4. When using the *POST* method, input is assigned to a variable from *STDIN* and encoded the same way.

**Decoding the Query String with Perl.** Decoding the query string is not a difficult task because Perl has such a large number of string manipulation functions, such as *tr*, *s*, *split*, *substr*, *pack*, etc. Once you get the query string from the server into your Perl program, you can parse it and do whatever you want with the data. For removing &, +, and = signs from a query string, use the substitution command, *s*, the *split* function, or the translate function, *tr*. To deal with the hexadecimal-to-character conversion of those characters preceded by a % sign, the *pack* function is normally used.

**Table C.10** Encoding symbols in a query string.

| Symbol | Function |
|--------|----------|
| & | Separates key/value pairs. |
| + | Replaces spaces. |
| %xy | Represents any ASCII character with a value of less than 21 hexadecimal (33 decimal), or greater than 7f (127 decimal) and special characters ?, &, %, +, and = . These characters must be escaped with a %, followed by the hexadecimal equivalence (xy) of that character, e.g., %2F represents a forward slash, and %2c represents a comma. |

**Table C.11** URL hex-encoded characters.

| Character | Value |
|-----------|-------|
| Tab | %09 |
| Space | %20 |
| ! | %21 |
| " | %22 |
| # | %23 |
| $ | %24 |
| % | %25 |
| & | %26 |
| ( | %28 |
| ) | %29 |
| , | %2C |

**Table C.11**  URL hex-encoded characters. (continued)

| Character | Value |
| --- | --- |
| . | %2E |
| / | %2F |
| : | %3A |
| ; | %3B |
| < | %3C |
| = | %3D |
| > | %3E |
| ? | %3F |
| @ | %40 |
| [ | %5B |
| \ | %5C |
| ] | %5D |
| ^ | %5E |
| ` | %60 |
| { | %7B |
| \| | %7C |
| } | %7D |
| ~ | %7E |

**Parsing the Form's Input with Perl.**  After the Perl CGI script gets the input from the form, it will be decoded. This is done by splitting up the key/value pairs and replacing special characters with regular text. Once parsed, the information can be used to create a guest book, a database, send e-mail to the user, and so on.

The routines for parsing the encoded string can be stored in subroutines and saved in your personal library, or you can take advantage of the *CGI.pm* library module, part of Perl's standard distribution, which eliminates all the bother.

**Decoding the Query String.**   Steps to decode are handled with Perl functions. The following shows a URL-encoded string assigned to *$ENV{QUERY_STRING}*.

```
Name=Christian+Dobbins&Phone=510-456-1234&Sign=Virgo
```

The key/pair values show that the URL has three pieces of information separated by the ampersand (&): *Name*, *Phone*, and *Sign*:

```
Name=Christian+Dobbins&Phone=510-456-1234&Sign=Virgo
```

The first thing to do would be to split up the line and create an array (see step 1 below). After splitting up the string by ampersands, remove the + with the *tr* or *s* functions and split the remaining string into key/value pairs with the split function using the = as the split delimiter (see step 2 below).

```
1.  @key_value = split(/&/, $ENV{QUERY_STRING});
    print "@key_value\n";
```

```
2.  Output:
        Name=Christian+Dobbins  Phone=510-456-1234   Sign=Virgo
```

The @key_value array created by splitting the query string:

| Name=Christian+Dobbins | Phone=510-456-1234 | Sign=Virgo |
|---|---|---|

```
3.  foreach $pair ( @key_value){
        $pair =~ tr/+/ /;
        ($key, $value) = split(/=/, $pair);
        print "\t$key: $value\n";
        }
```

```
4.  Output:
        Name: Christian Dobbins
        Phone: 510-456-1234
        Sign: Virgo
```

---

## EXAMPLE   C.16

```
(Another URL-Encoded String assigned to $ENV{QUERY_STRING})

1   $input="string=Joe+Smith%3A%2450%2c000%3A02%2F03%2F77";
2   $input=~s/%(..)/pack("c", hex($1))/ge;
3   print $input,"\n";

Output:
string=Joe+Smith:$50,000:02/03/77
```

## EXPLANATION

1   This string contains ASCII characters that are less than 33 decimal and greater than 127, the colon, the dollar sign, the comma, and the forward slash.

2   The *pack* function is used to convert hexadecimal-coded characters back into character format.

3   The search side of the substitution, /%(..)/, is a regular expression that contains a literal percent sign followed by any two characters (each dot represents one character) enclosed in parentheses. The parentheses are used so that Perl can store the two characters it finds in the special scalar, $1.

On the replacement side of the substitution, the *pack* function will first use the *hex* function to convert the two hexadecimal characters stored in $1 to their corresponding decimal values and then pack the resulting decimal values into an unsigned character. The result of this execution is assigned to the scalar, $input.

Now you will have to remove the + sign.

## C.8.5   Putting It All Together

**The GET Method.**   Now it is time to put together a form that will be processed by a Perl CGI program using the GET method. The CGI program will decode the query string and display the final results on the HTML page that is returned after the form was filled out and the Submit button pressed.

The following examples demonstrate

1.  The HTML fillout form

2.  The HTML source file that produced the form

3.  The form after it has been processed by the CGI script

4.  The Perl CGI script that processed the form

## EXAMPLE   C.17

```
(The HTML source file)

     <HTML><HEAD><TITLE>CGI Form</TITLE></HEAD><BODY>
     <HR>
1    <FORM ACTION="http://127.0.0.1/cgi-bin/getmethod.cgi" METHOD=GET>
     <!When user presses "submit", cgi script is called to process
     input >
2    Please enter your name: <BR>
3    <INPUT TYPE="text" SIZE=50 NAME=Name>
     <P>
     Plese enter your salary ($####.##): <BR>
     <INPUT TYPE="text" SIZE=30 NAME=Salary>
     <P>
     Plese enter your birth date (mm/dd/yy): <BR>
     <INPUT TYPE="text" SIZE=30 NAME=Birthdate>
     <P>
4    <INPUT TYPE=SUBMIT VALUE="Submit Query">
     <INPUT TYPE=RESET VALUE="Reset">
5    </FORM>
     </BODY></HTML>
```

## EXPLANATION

1   The form is started with the <FORM> tag. When the user presses the Submit button on the form, the *ACTION* attribute is triggers the HTTP server on this machine (local host is IP address 127.0.0.1) to start up the script called *getmethod.cgi* found under the server's root in the *cgi-bin* directory.

2   The user is asked for information.

3   The user will fill in the text boxes with his name, salary, etc.

4   When the user presses the Submit button, the CGI script assigned to the *ACTION* attribute will be activated.

5   This is the end of the form tag.

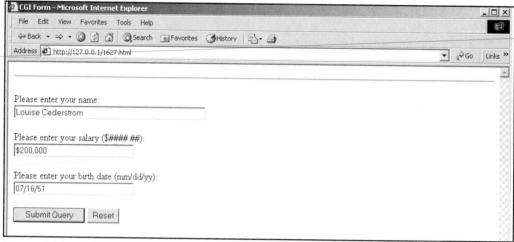

**Figure C.12**  The HTML form from Example C.17.

---

**EXAMPLE C.18**

```perl
#!/usr/bin/perl
# The CGI script that processes the form shown in Figure C.12.
1   print "Content-type: text/html\n\n";
    print "<H2><U>Decoding the query string</U></H2>";

    # Getting the input
2   $inputstring=$ENV{QUERY_STRING};
    print "<B>Before decoding:</B><BR>";
    print "<H3>$inputstring</H3>";

    # Translate + signs to space
3   $inputstring =~ tr/+/ /;

    # Decoding the hexadecimal characters
4   $inputstring=~s/%(..)/pack("C", hex($1))/ge;

    # After decoding %xy
    print "-" x 80, "<BR>";
    print "<B>After decoding <I>%xy</I>:</B>";
5   print "<H3>$inputstring</H3>";
    # Extracting & and creating key/value pairs
6   @key_value=split(/&/, $inputstring);
7   foreach $pair ( @key_value){
        ($key, $value) = split(/=/, $pair);
```

**EXAMPLE** C.18 (CONTINUED)

```
8    %input{$key} = $value;      # Creating a hash
        }
     # After decoding
     print "-" x 80, "<BR>";
     print "<B>After decoding + and &:</B>";
9    while(($key, $value)=each(%input)){
10      print "<H3>$key: <I>$value</I></H3>";
     }
     print "<B>Now what do we want to do with this information?"
```

**EXPLANATION**

1   This MIME header line describes the format of the data returned from this program to be HTML text. The two newlines (required!) end the header information.

2   The *%ENV* hash contains the key/value pairs sent to this Perl program by the Web server. The value of the *QUERY_STRING* environment variable is assigned to a scalar, *$inputstring*.

3   The *tr* function translates all + signs to spaces.

4   The *pack* function converts any hexadecimal numbers to their corresponding ASCII characters.

5   The value of the scalar *$inputstring* is sent from the Perl script to the server and then on to the browser.

6   The scalar *$inputstring* is now split by ampersands. The output returned is stored in the three-element array,*@key_value*, as:
    *Name=Louise Cederstrom&Salary=$200,000&Birthdate=7/16/51*

7   The *foreach* loop is used to iterate through the *@key_value* array. The resulting key/value pairs are created by splitting each array element by the = sign.

8   A new hash called *%input* is created with corresponding key/value pairs.

9   The *while* loop is used to iterate through the hash.

10  The new key/value pair is printed and sent back to the Web server. The browser displays the output. Now that the Perl script has parsed and stored the input that came from the form, it is up to the programmer to decide what to do with this data. He may send back an e-mail to the user, store the information in a database, create an address book, etc. The real work is done!

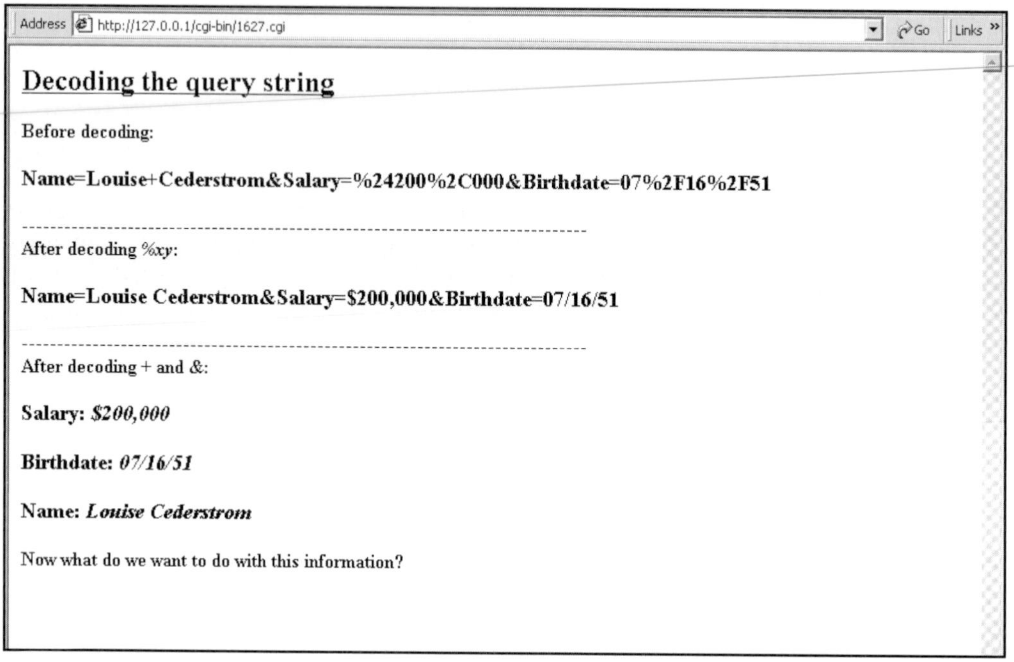

| Address | 🔖 http://127.0.0.1/cgi-bin/1627.cgi | ▾ | 🔗 Go | Links ≫ |

## Decoding the query string

Before decoding:

Name=Louise+Cederstrom&Salary=%24200%2C000&Birthdate=07%2F16%2F51

-------------------------------------------------------------

After decoding %xy:

Name=Louise Cederstrom&Salary=$200,000&Birthdate=07/16/51

-------------------------------------------------------------

After decoding + and &:

Salary: *$200,000*

Birthdate: *07/16/51*

Name: *Louise Cederstrom*

Now what do we want to do with this information?

**Figure C.13**  Output after CGI/Perl processing, Example C.18.

**The *POST* Method.**    The only real difference between the *GET* and *POST* methods is the way that input is passed from the server to the CGI program. When the *GET* method is used, the server sends input to the CGI program in the *QUERY_STRING* environment variable.

When the *POST* method is used, the CGI program gets input from standard input, *STDIN*. Either way, the input is encoded in exactly the same way. One reason for using the *POST* method is that some browsers restrict the amount of data that can be stored in the *QUERY_STRING* environment variable. The *POST* method doesn't store its data in the query string. Also, the *GET* method displays the input data in the URL line in the Location box of the browser, whereas the *POST* method hides the data. Since the *POST* method does not append input to the URL, it is often used in processing forms where there is a lot of data being filled into forms.

In an HTML document, the <FORM> tag starts the form. The *ACTION* attribute tells the browser **where** to send the data that is collected from the user, and the *METHOD* attribute tells the browser **how** to send it. If the *POST* is method used, the output from the browser is sent to the server and then to the CGI program's standard input, *STDIN*. The amount of data, that is, the number of bytes taken as input from the user, is stored in the *CONTENT_LENGTH* environment variable.

Rather than assigning the input to the *QUERY_STRING* environment variable, the browser sends the input to the server in a message body, similar to the way e-mail messages are sent. The server then encapsulates all the data and sends it on to the CGI program.

The CGI program reads input data from the *STDIN* stream via a pipe.

The Perl *read* function reads the *CONTENT_LENGTH* amount of bytes, saves the input data in a scalar, and then processes it the same way it processes input coming from the query string. It's not that the format for the input has changed; it's just **how** it got into the program. Note that after the *POST* method has been used, the browser's Location box does not contain the input in the URL as it did with the *GET* method.

**EXAMPLE C.19**

```
(The HTML source file)
<HTML>
<HEAD>
<TITLE>CGI Form</TITLE>
<HR>
1   <FORM ACTION="http://127.0.0.1/cgi-bin/postmethod.cgi"
    METHOD=POST>
    <!When user presses "submit", cgi script is called to process
    input >
2   Please enter your name: <BR>
3   <INPUT TYPE="text" SIZE=50 NAME=Name>
    <P>
    Please enter your salary ($####.##): <BR>
    <INPUT TYPE="text" SIZE=30 NAME=Salary>
    <P>
    Please enter your birth date (mm/dd/yy): <BR>
    <INPUT TYPE="text" SIZE=30 NAME=Birthdate>
    <P>
4   <INPUT TYPE=SUBMIT VALUE="Submit Query">
    <INPUT TYPE=RESET VALUE="Reset">
5   </FORM>
    </HTML>
```

**EXPLANATION**

1   The <FORM> tag starts the form. The *ACTION* attribute is assigned the URL of the CGI script, *postmethod.cgi*, that will be executed whent the Submit button is pressed by the user, and the *METHOD* attribute is assigned *POST* to indicate how the data coming from the form will be handled.

2   The user is asked for input.

3   Text Fields are created to hold the user's name, salary, and birth date.

4   The Submit button is created.

5   The form is ended.

## EXAMPLE C.20

```
(The CGI Script)
    #!/bin/perl
    # Scriptname: postmethod.cgi
1   print "Content-type: text/html\n\n";
    print "<H2><U>Decoding the query string</U></H2>";

    # Getting the input
2   if ( $ENV{REQUEST_METHOD} eq 'GET'){
3       $inputstring=$ENV{QUERY_STRING};
        }
    else{
4       read(STDIN, $inputstring, $ENV{'CONTENT_LENGTH'});
    }
5   print "<B>Before decoding:</B><BR>";
    print "<H3>$inputstring</H3>";

    # Replace + signs with spaces
6   $inputstring =~ tr/+/ /;

    # Decoding the hexadecimal characters
7   $inputstring=~s/%(..)/pack("C", hex($1))/ge;
    # After decoding %xy
    print "-" x 80, "<BR>";
8   print "<B>After decoding <I>%xy</I>:</B>";
    print "<H3>$inputstring</H3>";

    # Extracting the & and = to create key/value pairs

9   @key_value=split(/&/, $inputstring);
10  foreach $pair ( @key_value){
11     ($key, $value) = split(/=/, $pair);
12     %input{$key} = $value;    # Creating a hash to save the data
    }
    # After decoding
    print "-" x 80, "<BR>";
    print "<B>After decoding + and &:</B>";
13  while(($key, $value)=each(%input)){
        # Printing the contents of the hash
        print "<H3>$key: <I>$value</I></H3>";
    }
    print "<B>Now what do we want to do with this information?";
```

## EXPLANATION

1   The content being sent to the browser is text interspersed with HTML tags.
2   One of the environment variables sent by the server to the script is $ENV{REQUEST_METHOD}, which will have a value of either GET or POST.
3   If the value of the $ENV{REQUEST_METHOD} variable is GET, the scalar, $inputstring will be assigned the value of the query string, $ENV{QUERY_STRING}.
4   If the value of the $ENV{REQUEST_METHOD} variable is POST, the scalar, $inputstring will be assigned the input coming from the standard input stream via the read function. The amount of data read is found in the environment variable, $ENV{CONTENT-LENGTH}.
5   The value of $inputstring is printed with the URL encoding still in place; for example, a space is represented by a + sign, the key/value pairs are separated with an &, and the % sign is followed by the hexadecimal value of the character it represents.
6   All + signs are translated to single spaces.
7   This line replaces the hexadecimal characters with their corresponding ASCII values.
8   After decoding the % hex values, the value of $inputstring is printed.
9   The split function uses the & as a field separator.
10  The foreach loop iterates through array, assigning each element, in turn, to $pair.
11  Key/value pairs are created by splitting the string at = signs.
12  A hash, %input, is being created on the fly. It will consist of key/value pairs created by splitting up the input string.
13  The each function extracts the key/value pairs from the %input hash. Each time through the loop the next key/value pair is extracted and displayed in the browser.

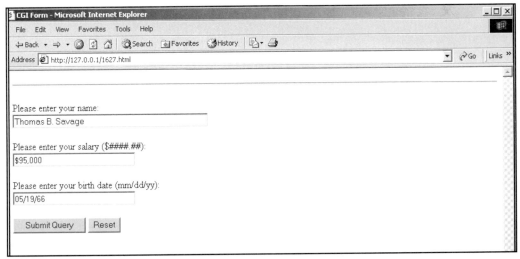

**Figure C.14**   The HTML input form from Example C.19.

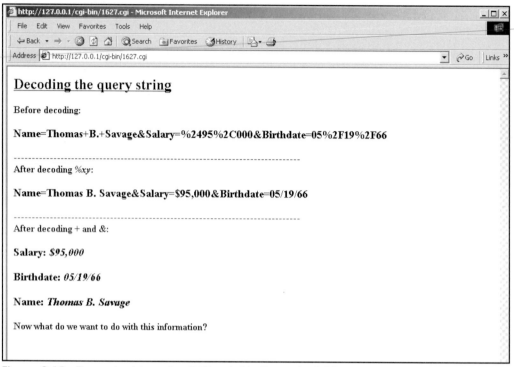

**Figure C.15**   The output from the CGI script in Example C.20.

## C.8.6   Handling E-Mail

**The SMTP Server.**   When processing a form, it is often necessary to send e-mail before exiting. You may be sending e-mail to the user and/or to yourself with the submitted form data. E-mail cannot be sent over the Internet without a valid SMTP (Simple Mail Transfer Protocol) server. [5]

The SMTP server is an instance of a mail daemon program that listens for incoming mail on Port 25. SMTP is a TCP-based client/server protocol where the client sends messages to the server. UNIX systems commonly use a mail program called *sendmail* to act as the SMTP server listening for incoming mail. Normally you would run *sendmail* at the command line with the recipient's name as an argument. To end the e-mail message, a period is placed on a line by itself. In a CGI script, the mail will not be sent interactively, so you will probably want to use the *sendmail* options to control these features. See Table C.12.

---

5.  The format for Internet mail messages is defined by RFC822.

**Table C.12**  *sendmail* options.

| Option | What It Does |
|---|---|
| *-o* | A *sendmail* option follows |
| *-t* | Reads headers *To, From, Cc,* and *Bcc* information from message body |
| *-f "email address"* | Message is from this e-mail address |
| *-F "name"* | Message is from *name* |
| *-i* | Periods will be ignored if on a line by themselves |
| *-odq* | Queues up multiple e-mail messages to be delivered asynchronously |

For Windows, two programs similar to *sendmail* are *Blat,* a public domain Win32 console utility that sends e-mail using the SMTP protocol (see *www.interlog.com/~tcharron/blat.html*), and *wSendmail,* a small utility that can send e-mail from programs, the command line, or directly from an HTML form (see *www.kode.net/wsendmail.html or www.softseek.com/Internet/E_Mail/E_Mail_Tools*). Go to CPAN and find the *MailFolder* package, which contains modules such as *Mail::Folder, Mail::Internet,* and *Net::SMTP,* to further simplify the sending and receiving e-mail. For a complete discussion on *sendmail,* see *www.networkcomputing.com/unixworld/tutorial008.*

**EXAMPLE C.21**

```
(From the HTML form where the e-mail information is collected)

<FORM METHOD="post" ACTION="http://127.0.0.1/cgi-bin/submit-form">
<INPUT TYPE="hidden" NAME="xemailx"
       VALUE="elizabeth@ellieq.com">
<INPUT TYPE="hidden" NAME="xsubjext"
       VALUE="Course Registration">
<INPUT TYPE="hidden"  NAME="xgoodbyex"
       VALUE="Thank you for registering.">
<P>
<A NAME="REGISTRATION">
<TABLE CELLSPACING=0 CELLPADDING=0>
<TR>
    <TD ALIGN=right><B>First Name:</B></TD>
    <TD ALIGN=left><INPUT TYPE=text NAME="first_name*" VALUE="">
    </TD>
</TR>
```

**EXAMPLE** C.21 (CONTINUED)

```
<TR> <TD ALIGN=right><B>Last Name:</B></TD>
   <TD ALIGN=left><INPUT TYPE=text NAME="last_name*"
      VALUE=""></TD>
</TR>
<TR>
   <TD ALIGN=right><B>Company:</B></TD>
   <TD ALIGN=left><INPUT TYPE=text SIZE=30 NAME="company*"
      VALUE=""></TD>
</TR>
<TR>
   <TD ALIGN=right><B>Address1:</B></TD>
   <TD ALIGN=left><INPUT TYPE=text SIZE=30
      NAME="address1*" VALUE=""></TD>
</TR>
<TR>
   <TD ALIGN=right><B>Address2:</B></TD>
   <TD ALIGN=left><INPUT TYPE=text SIZE=30 NAME="address2"
      VALUE=""></TD>
</TR>
<TR>
   <TD ALIGN=right><B>City/Town:</B></TD>
   <TD ALIGN=left><INPUT TYPE=text SIZE=30 NAME="city*"
      VALUE=""></TD>
</TR>
<TR>
   <TD ALIGN=right><B>State/Province:</B></TD>
   <TD ALIGN=left><INPUT TYPE=text SIZE=10 NAME="state"
      VALUE=""><FONT SIZE=-1> Abbreviation or code</TD></TR>
<TR>
   <TD ALIGN=right><B>Postal/Zip Code:</B></TD>
   <TD ALIGN=left><INPUT TYPE=text SIZE=10 NAME="zip"
       VALUE=""></TD>
   </TR>


------------------------------------------------------------


<continues here>
```

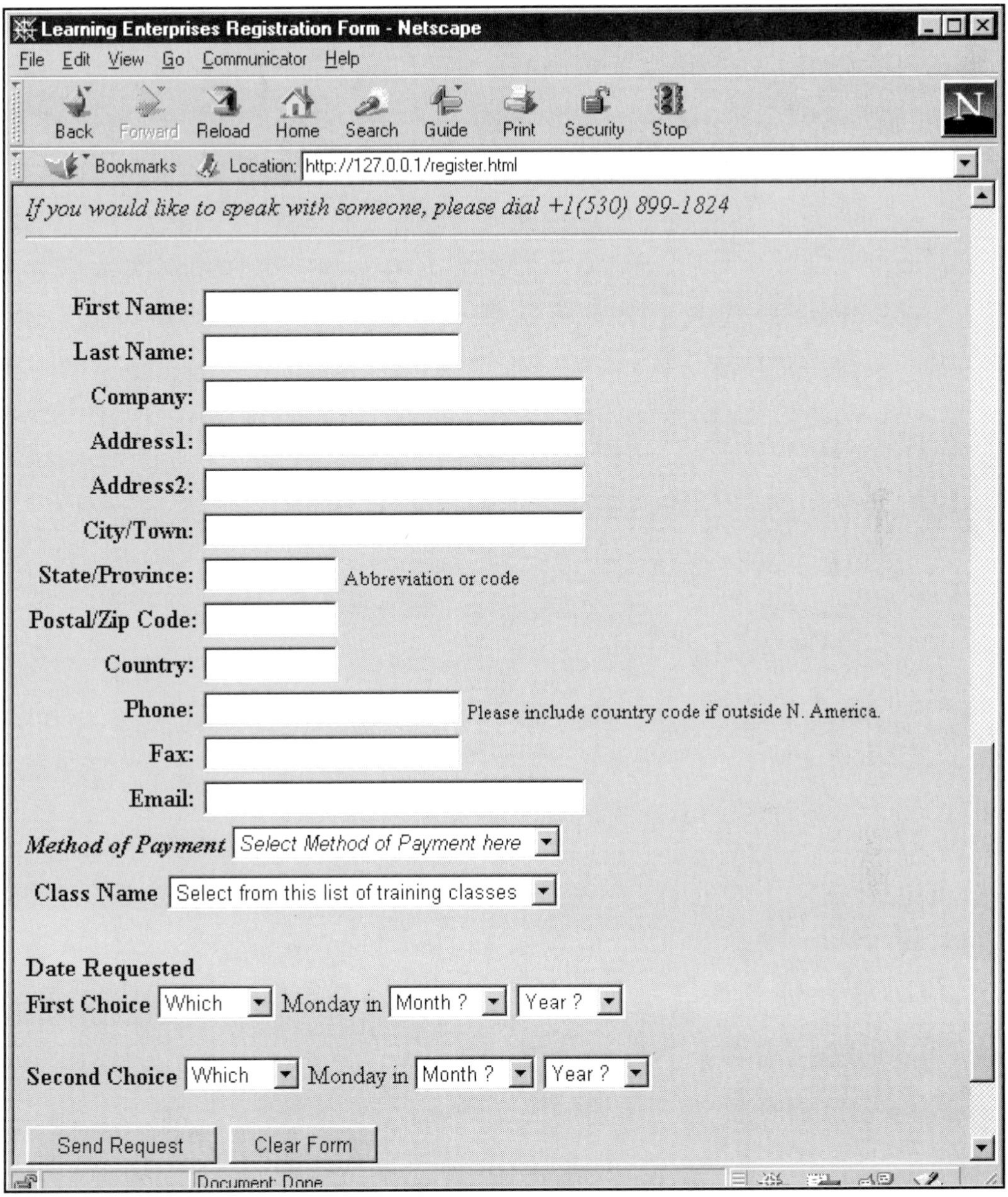

**Figure C.16**   Portion of the HTML registration form from Example C.21.

## EXAMPLE C.22

```
(From a CGI script)
# An HTML Form was first created and processed to get the name of the
# user who will receive the e-mail, the person it's from, and the
# subject line.
1   $mailprogram="/usr/lib/sendmail";   # Your mail program goes here
2   $sendto="$input{xemailx}";          # Mailing address goes here
3   $from="$input{xmailx}";
4   $subject="$input{xsubjext}";


5   open(MAIL, "|$mailprogram -t  -oi") || die "Can't open mail
        program: $!\n";
    # -t option takes the headers from the lines following the mail
    # command -oi options prevent a period at the beginning of  a
    # line from meaning end of input
6   print MAIL "To: $sendto\n";
    print MAIL "From: $from\n";
    print MAIL "Subject: $subject\n\n";


7   print MAIL <<EOF;    # Start a "here document"

    Registration Information for $input{$first_name}
        $input{$last_name}:
    Date of Registration: $today
    -----------------------------------------------
    First Name:             $input{$first_name}
    Last Name:              $input{$last_name}
    Street Address:         $input{$address}
    City:                   $input{$city}
    State/Province:         $input{$state}

    <Rest of message goes here>


8   EOF
9   close MAIL;  # Close the filter
```

## EXPLANATION

1  The name of the mail program being used here is *sendmail*, located in the UNIX subdirectory, */usr/lib*.

2  This line will be assigned to the *To:* header in the e-mail document.

3  This line will be assigned to the *From:* header in the e-mail document.

4  And this line is the *Subject:* header in the e-mail document.

## EXPLANATION (CONTINUED)

5   Perl is going to open a filter called *MAIL* that will pipe the user's e-mail message to the *sendmail* program. The *-t* option tells *sendmail* to scan the e-mail document for the *To:*, *From:*, and *Subject:* lines (instead of from the command line) and the *-i* option tells the mail program to ignore any period that may be found on a line by itself.

6   These are the header lines indicating to whom the mail is going, where it's going, and the subject of the mail. These values were pulled from the form.

7   A *here document* is started. The text between EOF and EOF is sent to the sendmail program via the *MAIL* filter.

8   EOF marks the end of the *here document*.

9   The *MAIL* filter is closed.

**The *Mail::Mailer* Perl Module.**   *Mail::Mailer* provides a simple interface for sending Internet mail with *sendmail* and *mail* or *mailx*.

## EXAMPLE C.23

```
(From a CGI script)
1   use Mail::Mailer;
2   my $mailobj = new Mail::Mailer("smtp", Server=>"www.ellieq.com");
3   $mailer -> open( {
            To => $emailaddress,
            From => $sender,
            Subject => "Testing email..."
    } );
    # The mail message is created in a here document
4   print $mailobj << EOF;
    This is a test to see if the Mail::Mailer module is working for
    us. Thankyou for participating in this little experiment!
    EOF

5   close $mailobj;
```

## EXPLANATION

1 After downloading *Mail::Mailer* from CPAN, it is to be used in the CGI script.
2 The constructor *new* is called with the name of the SMTP server passed as the first argument. Mail will use the *Net::SMTP* Perl module to send the mail. The server will relay the message on to the e-mail address listed in the *To:* header. A pointer to the mail object is returned.
3 The *Mail::Mailer*'s *open* method is called with an anonymous hash as an argument, consisting of three attributes: the *To:* field with the recipient's address, the *From:* field with the sender's address, and the *Subject:* field. The *open* method creates a Perl output filter. Output from the script will go as input to mail program.
4 A *here document* is created to send the e-mail message.
5 The object is closed; that is, the mail filter is closed.

**E-mail and the *mailto:* Protocol.** HTML anchors can be used to create links to files and to e-mail adresses. When a user selects the e-mail hyperlink, their e-mail program starts an e-mail message to the address specified in the *HREF* attribute. The *mailto:* protocol is followed by the valid e-mail address.

## EXAMPLE C.24

```
(Portion of the HTML form showing the e-mail hyperlink)
</MENU>
<P>
Students unable to send appropriate payment information will be
    dropped from the class unceremoniously.
<P>
<I>
If you would like to speak to one of our staff, please dial
    +1(530)899-1824.
<BR>
If you have a question , <A HREF="mailto:elizabeth@ellieq.com">click
    here.</A>
<BR>
<I><FONT SIZE=2>Provide as much detail in your request as possible, so
    that we may reply quickly and as informative as possible.</I>
</TD>
</TR>
<BR>
<BR>If you would like to speak with someone, please dial +1(530) 899-
    1824
<HR>


-----------------------------------
```

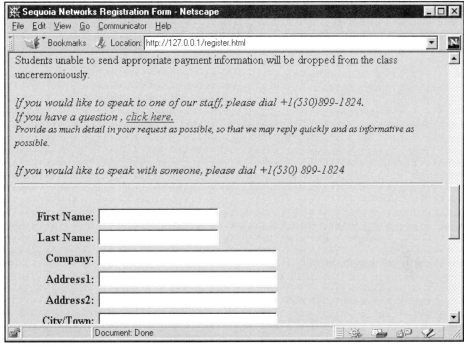

**Figure C.17**   The HTML form and hyperlink to an e-mail address, from Example C.24.

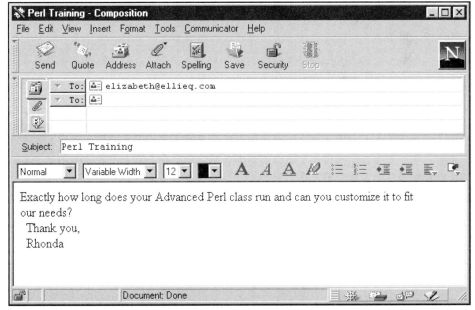

**Figure C.18**   E-mail window that appears after clicking on the hyperlink, from Example C.24.

## C.8.7   Extra Path Information

Information can also be provided to the CGI script by appending some extra path information to the URL of the HTML document. The path information starts with a forward slash (/) so that the server can identify where the CGI script ends and the new information begins. The information can then be processed in the CGI script by parsing the value of the *PATH_INFO* environment variable where this extra information is stored.

If the information appended is a path to another file, the *PATH_TRANSLATED* environment variable is also set, mapping the *PATH_INFO* value to the document root directory. The document root directory is found in the *DOCUMENT_ROOT* environment variable. The pathname is treated as relative to the root directory of the server.

---

**EXAMPLE** C.25

```
(The HTML Document)

1    <HTML>
2    <HEAD>
     <Title>Testing Env Variables</title>
     </HEAD>
     <BODY>
     <P>
     <H1> Major Test </h1>
     <P> If You Would Like To See The Environment Variables<Br>
     Being Passed On By The Server, Click .

3    <A Href="Http://susan/cgi-bin/pathinfo.cgi/color=red/
        size=small">here</a>
     <P>
     Text Continues Here...
     </BODY>
     </HTML>
```

## EXAMPLE C.26

```
(The CGI Script)

    #!/bin/perl

1   print "Content type: text/html\n\n";

    print "CGI/1.0 test script report:\n\n";

    print "The argument count is ", $#ARGV + 1, ".\n";
    print "The arguments are @ARGV.\n";
    # Print out all the environment variables

2   while(($key, $value)=each(%ENV)){
3       print "$key = $value\n";
    }

    print "=" x 30, "\n";
4   print "$ENV{PATH_INFO}\n";
5   $line=$ENV{PATH_INFO};
6   $line=~tr/\// /;
7   @info = split(" ", $line);
8   print "$info[0]\n";
9   eval "\$$info[0]\n";
10  print $color;
```

## EXPLANATION

1   The content type is *text/html*.
2   The loop iterates through each of the *ENV* variables, assigning the key to $key and the corresponding value to $value.
3   Each key and value is printed.
4   The value for the $ENV{PATH_INFO} environment variable is printed.
5   The value of $ENV{PATH_INFO} variable is assigned to the scalar $line.
6   All forward slashes are replaced with spaces. */color=red/size=small* will become *color=red size=small* and assigned to $line.
7   The *split* function splits the scalar $line into an array, using spaces as the separator.
8   The first element of the array, *color=red*, is printed.
9   The *eval* function evaluates the expression and assigns *red* to $color.
10  When the scalar $color is printed, the value is *red*.

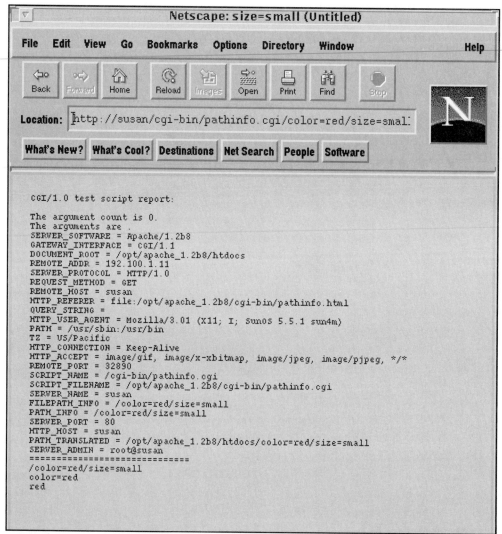

Figure C.19   CGI output with extra path information, from Example C.26.

## C.8.8   Server Side Includes

It is not always necessary to produce a full-blown CGI script just to get a small amount of data on the fly from a static HTML document. If you just wanted to know the name of a remote server, the current file, or the date and time, etc., it would seem silly to have to write a CGI script. Now most servers support a shortcut feature that allows the HTML document to output these small amounts of information without requiring an HTTP header. The feature is called *SSI*, short for Server Side Includes, which are really just HTML directives that are inserted into the HTML document; this type of file normally ends with *.shtml*.

## FORMAT

```
<!--command option=value -->
```

## EXAMPLE C.27

```
<!--#exec cgi="/cgi-bin/joker/motto"-->
```

## EXPLANATION

Executes the CGI program enclosed in quotes as though it was called from an anchor link.

**Table C.13** Some common SSI commands.

| Command | Example | Meaning |
|---------|---------|---------|
| config | `<!-- #config sizefmt="bytes" -->` | Sets the format for display size of the file in bytes |
| echo | `<!-- #echo var="DATE_GMT" -->` | Prints the date in Greenwich Mean Time (same as UTC); other values are shown in Example C.28 |
| exec | `<!-- #exec cmd="finger" -->` | Executes shell command *finger* |
| flastmod | `<!-- $flastmod file="test.html" -->` | Inserts a file in the current directory or in a subdirectory |
| fsize | `<!-- #fsize file="test.html" -->` | Prints the size of the file |
| include | `<!-- #include file="myfile.html" -->` | Inserts a file in the current directory or in a subdirectory |

The following example is the HTML source test file from an *OmniHTTPd* Web server.

## EXAMPLE C.28

```
     <HTML>
     <HEAD>
     <Meta Http-equiv="Pragma" Content="No-cache">
     <Title>CGI And SSI Test</title>
     </head>
     <Body Bgcolor="#ffffff">
     <H1>CGI And SSI Test</h1>

     <Hr>
     <H2>standard CGI Test</h2>
     You Are Visitor # <Img Src="/cgi-bin/visitor.exe"><P>
     <Hr>

  1  <H2>Server Side Includes</h2>
     If Server Side Includes Are Enabled, You Will See Data Values
     Below:
     <P>
  2  The Date Is: <!--#echo Var="Date_local"--><Br>
  3  The Current Version Of The Server Is:
         <!--#echo Var="Server_software"--><Br>
  4  The CGI Gateway Version Is:
         <!--#echo Var="Gateway_interface"--><Br>
  5  The Server Name Is:  <!--#echo Var="Server_name"--><Br>
  6  This File Is Called: <!--#echo  Var="Document_name"--><Br>
  7  This File's Uri Is: <!--#echo Var= "Document_uri"--><Br>
  8  The Query String Is:
         <!--# Echo Var="Query_string_unescaped"--><Br>
  9  This File Was Last Modified:
         <!--#echo Var="Last_modified"--><Br>
 10  The Size Of The Unprocessed File Is
         !--#fsize Virtual="/test.shtml"--><Br>
 11  You Are Using <!--#echo Var="Http_user_agent"--><Br>
 12  You Came From <!--#echo Var="Http_referer"--><P>
     <Br>
     <Input Type="Submit" Value="Go!">
     </FORM>
     <HR>
     </BODY>
     </HTML>
```

**EXPLANATION**

1 Server side includes is enclosed in heading tags to print. If server side includes are enabled, you will see data values below:

2 The date is: *Jul 22 1999*
3 The current version of the server is: *OmniHTTPd/2.0a2(Win32;i386)*
4 The CGI gateway version is: *CGI/1.1*
5 The server name is: *ellie.Learn1.com*
6 This file is called: *C:\HTTPD\HTDOCS\test.shtml*
7 This file's URI is: */test/shtml*
8 The query string is:
9 This file was last modified: *Jun24 1997*
10 The size of the unprocessed file is *1989*
11 You are using Mozilla/2.01KIT *(Win95; U)*
12 You came from *http://127.0.0.1/default.htm*

**An Object-Oriented Perl/CGI Program.** If you would like to study a complete CGI program, written by a professional Web developer, go to Appendix B.

# C.9 The *CGI.pm* Module

## C.9.1 Introduction

The most popular Perl 5 library for writing dynamic CGI programs such as guestbooks, page counters, feedback forms, etc., is the *CGI.pm* module written by Lincoln Stein; it is included in the standard Perl library starting with version 5.004. The most recent version of *CGI.pm* can be found at *www.perl.com/CPAN*. *CGI.pm* not only takes advantage of the object-oriented features that were introduced in Perl 5, it also provides methods (*GET* and *POST*) to interpret query strings, handle forms, and hide the details of HTML syntax.

Lincoln Stein has also written *Official Guide to Programming with CGI.pm*[6] (*www.wiley.com/compbooks/stein*), an excellent, easy-to-read guide from which much of the following information was gleaned.

---

6. Stein, L., *Official Guide to Programming with CGI.pm, The Standard for Building Web Scripts*, Wiley Computer Publishing, 1998.

## C.9.2   Advantages

1. *CGI.pm* allows you to keep a fillout form (HTML) and the script that parses it, all in one file under the *cgi-bin* directory. In this way your HTML file (that holds the form) and your CGI script (that reads, parses, and handles the form data) are not so far apart.[7]

2. After the user has filled out a form, the results appear on the same page; in other words, the user doesn't have to backpage to see what was on the form and the fillout form does not lose data, it maintains its state. Data that doesn't disappear is called "sticky." To override stickiness, see "The override Argument" on page 692.

3. All the reading and parsing of form data is handled by the module.

4. Methods are used to replace HTML tags for creating text boxes, radio buttons, menus, etc. to create the form, as well as for assigning standard tags such as headers, titles, paragraph breaks, horizontal rule lines, breaks, etc.

5. To see what HTML tags are produced by the *CGI.pm* module, from the View menu, select Source (in Internet Explorer) after the form has been displayed.

6. Accepting uploaded files and managing cookies is easier with the *CGI.pm* module.

## C.9.3   Two Styles of Programming with *CGI.pm*

**The Object-Oriented Style.**   Using the object-oriented style, you create one or more CGI objects and then use object **methods** to create the various elements of the page. Each CGI object starts out with the list of named parameters that were passed to your CGI script by the server. You can modify the objects and send them to a file or database. Each object is independent; it has its own parameter list. If a form has been filled out, its contents can be saved from one run of the script to the next; that is, it maintains its **state**. (Normally the HTML documents are **stateless**, in other words, everything is lost when the page exits.)

---

**EXAMPLE**  C.29

```
1    use CGI;
2    $obj=new CGI;   # Create the CGI object
3    print $obj->header,      # Use functions to create the HTML page
4    $obj->start_html("Object oriented syntax"),
5    $obj->h1("This is a test..."),
     $obj->h2("This is a test..."),
     $obj->h3("This is a test..."),
6    $obj->end_html;
```

---

7. Ibid.

The following output can be seen by viewing the source from the browser. It demonstrates the HTML output produced by the *CGI.pm* module.

```
<!DOCTYPE html
PUBLIC "-//W3C//DTD XHTML 1.0 Transitional//EN"
"DTD/xhtml1-transitional.dtd">
<html xmlns="http://www.w3.org/1999/xhtml" lang="en-US">
<head><title>Object oriented syntax</title></head><body>
<h1>This is a test...</h1>
<h2>This is a test...</h2>
<h3>This is a test...</h3>
</body
</html>
```

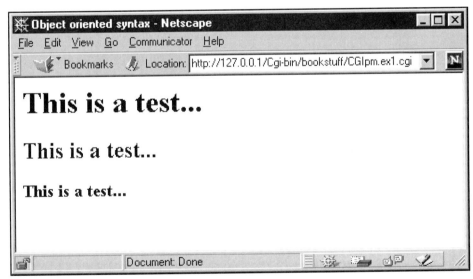

**Figure C.20**   Output from the object-oriented CGI script in Example C.29.

**Function-Oriented Style.**   The function-oriented style is easier to use than the objectoriented style, because you don't create or manipulate the CGI object directly. The module creates a default CGI object for you. You use the same built-in functions to manipulate the object, pass parameters to the functions to create the HTML tags, and retrieve the information passed into the form.

Although the function-oriented style provides a cleaner programming interface, it limits you to using one CGI object at a time.

The following example uses the function-oriented interface. The main differences are that the *:standard* functions must be imported into the program's namespace, and you don't create a CGI object. It is created for you.[8]

**EXAMPLE  C.30**

```
     #!/usr/bin/perl
1    use CGI qw(:standard);      # Function-oriented style uses a set of
                                 # standard functions
2    print header,
3    start_html("Function oriented syntax"),
4    h1("This is a test..."),
     h2("This is a test..."),
     h3("This is a test..."),
5    end_html;
```

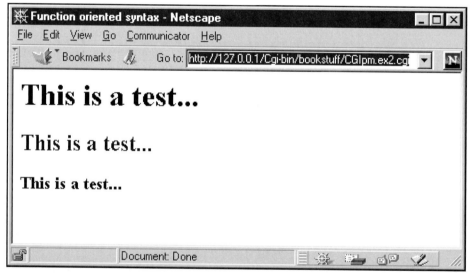

**Figure C.21**　Output from the function-oriented CGI script in Example C.30.

## C.9.4　How Input from Forms Is Processed

A CGI script consists of two parts: the part that creates the form that will be displayed in the browser, and the part that retrieves the input from the form, parses it, and handles the information by sending it back to the browser, to a database, to e-mail, etc.

---

8. A default object called *$CGI::Q* is created, which can be accessed directly if needed.

**Creating the HTML Form.**   Methods are provided to simplify the task of creating the HTML form. For example, there are methods to start and end the HTML form, methods for creating headers, checkboxes, pop-up menus, radio buttons, Submit and Reset buttons, etc. Table C.14 lists the most used of the HTML methods provided by *CGI.pm*.

When passing arguments to the *CGI.pm* methods, two styles can be used:

- **Named arguments**—passed as key/value pairs. Argument names are preceded by a leading dash and are case insensitive.

---

**EXAMPLE** C.31

```
(Named Arguments)
1   print popup_menu(-name=>'place',
                     -values=>['Hawaii','Europe','Mexico', 'Japan' ],
                     -default=>'Hawaii',
                    );
2   print popup_menu(-name=>'place',
                     -values=> \@countries,
                     -default=>'Hawaii',
                    );
```

**EXPLANATION**

1   The arguments being passed to the *popup_menu* method are called **named parameters** or **argument lists**. The argument names in this examples are *-name*, *-values*, and *-default*. These arguments are always preceded by a leading dash and are case insensitive. If the argument name might conflict with some built-in Perl function or reserved word, quote the argument. Note that the arguments are passed to the method as a set of key/value pairs. The *-values* key has a corresponding value consisting of an anonymous array of countries.

2   This is exactly like the previous example, except that the value for the *-values* key is a reference to an array of countries. Somewhere else in the program, the array *@countries* was created and given values.

---

- **Positional arguments**—passed as strings, they represent a value. They are used with simple HTML tags. For example, *CGI.pm* provides the *h1()* method to produce the HTML tags, *<H1>* and *</H1>*. The argument for *h1()* is the string of text that is normally inserted between the tags. The method is called as follows:

```
print  h1("This is a positional argument");
```

which translates to

```
<H1>This is a positional argument</H1>
```

If using HTML attributes,[9] and the first argument is a reference to an anonymous hash, the attribute and its values are added after the leading tag into the list. For example:

```
print h1({-align=>CENTER}, "This heading is centered");
```

translates to

```
<H1 ALIGN="CENTER">This heading is centered</H1>
```

If the arguments are a reference to an anonymous list, each item in the list will be properly distributed within the tag. For example:

```
print li( ['apples', 'pears', 'peaches'] );
```

translates to three bulleted list items:

```
<LI>apples</LI> <LI>pears</LI> <LI>peaches</LI>
```

whereas

```
print li( 'apples', 'pears', 'peaches' );
```

translates to one bulleted list item:

```
<LI>apples pears peaches</LI>
```

---

**EXAMPLE** C.32

```
(The CGI script)
    # Shortcut calling styles with HTML methods
    use CGI qw(:standard);  # Function-oriented style print header
1   start_html("Testing arguments"),
    b(),
2   p(),
3   p("red", "green", "yellow"),
4   p("This is a string"),
5   p({-align=>center}, "red", "green", "yellow"),
6   p({-align=>left}, ["red","green","yellow"]),
    end_html;
```

---

9.  Attributes do not require a leading dash.

**EXAMPLE**  C.32 (CONTINUED)

(**Output produced by** *CGI.pm* **methods**)
```
1    Content-Type: text/html; charset=ISO-8859-1<!DOCTYPE html
     PUBLIC "-//W3C//DTD XHTML 1.0 Transitional//EN"
     "DTD/xhtml1-transitional.dtd">
     <html xmlns="http://www.w3.org/1999/xhtml" lang="en-US">
     <head><title>Testing arguments</title></head>
     <body>
     <b />
2    <p />
3    <p>red green yellow</p>
4    <p>This is a string</p>
5    <p align="center">red green yellow</p>
6    <p align="left">red</p> <p align="left">green</p>
     <p align="left">yellow</p>
     </body>
     </html>
```

**EXPLANATION**

1   The function-oriented style of the *CGI.pm* module is used. The *START_HTML* method generates the header information and starts the body of the HTML document.

2   The *p()* (paragraph method) generates a paragraph tag that takes no arguments. It is a start tag only.

3   The quoted list of comma-separated arguments produces a single string argument. The paragraph's text is displayed as one line on the brower: *red green yellow.* It consists of a start tag, the arguments as a single string, and an end tag.

4   The string is also displayed as a single string. It consists of a start tag, the string, and and end tag.

5   The string is a centered paragraph. This paragraph tag consists of a start tag, attributes, arguments, and an end tag.

6   This paragraph tag displays each word, left-justified, on a line by itself. It consists of a start tag, with the attributes for left alignment distributed across each of the listed arguments. The arguments are listed as a reference to an anonymous array.

To avoid conflicts and warnings (-*w* switch), enclose all arguments in quotes.

**Table C.14** HTML methods.

| Method | What it Does | Attributes |
|---|---|---|
| a() | Anchor tag <br> *<A>* | *-href, -name, -onClick, -onMouseOver, -target* |
| applet() (:html3 group) | Embedding applets <br> *<APPLET>* | *-align, -alt, -code, -codebase, -height, -hspace, -name, -vspace, -width* |
| b() | Bold text <br> *<B>* | |
| basefont() (:html3) | Set size of base font <br> *<FONT>* | *-size* (sizes 1–7) |
| big (:netscape group) | Increase text size <br> *<BIG>* | |
| blink (:netscape group) | Creates blinking text <br> *<BLINK>* | |
| br() | Creates a line break <br> *<BR>* | |
| button() | Creates a push button to start a JavaScript event handler when pressed | *-name, -onClick, -value, -label* |
| caption (:html3) | Inserts a caption above a table <br> *<CAPTION>* | *-align, -valign* |
| center() (:netscape group) | Center text <br> *<CENTER>* | Doesn't seem to work <br> Use the *<CENTER>* tag. |
| cite() | Creates text in a proportional italic font <br> *<CITE>* | |
| checkbox() | Creates a single named checkbox and label | *-checked, -selected, -on, -label, -name, -onClick, -override, -force, -value* |
| checkbox_group() | Creates a set of checkboxes linked by one name | *-columns, -cols, -colheaders, -default, -defaults, -labels, -linebreak, -name, -nolabels, -onClick, -override, -force, -rows, -rowheaders, -value, -values* |
| code() | Creates text in a monospace font <br> *<CODE>* | |
| dd() | Definition item of definition list *<DD>* | |

**Table C.14**   HTML methods. (continued)

| Method | What it Does | Attributes |
|--------|--------------|------------|
| *defaults()* | Creates a fillout button for submitting a form as though for the first time; clears the old parameter list | |
| *dl()* | Creates a definition list <DL>; see *dd()* | *-compact* |
| *dt()* | Term part of definition list <DT> | |
| *em()* | Emphatic (italic) text | |
| *end_form()*, *endform()* | Terminate a form </FORM> | |
| *end_html()* | Ends an HTML document </BODY></HTML> | |
| *font()* (:netscape group) | Changes font | *-color, -face, -size* |
| *frame()* (:netscape group) | Defines a frame | *-marginheight, -marginwidth, -name, -noresize, -scrolling, -src* |
| *frameset()* (:netscape group) | Creates a frameset <FRAMESET> | *-cols, -rows* |
| *h1()...h6()* | Creates heading levels 1–6 <H1>, <H2> ... <H6> | |
| *hidden()* | Creates a hidden, invisible text field, uneditable by the user | |
| *hr()* | Creates a horizontal rule <HR> | *-align, -noshade, -size, -width* |
| *i()* | Creates italic text <I> | |
| *img()* | Creates an inline image <IMG> | *-align, -alt, -border, -height, -width, -hspace, -ismap, -src, -lowsrc, -vrspace, -usemap* |
| *image_button()* | Produces an inline image that doubles as a form submission button | *-align, -alt.-height, -name, -src, -width* |
| *kbd()* | Creates text with keyboard style | |

**Table C.14** HTML methods. (continued)

| Method | What it Does | Attributes |
|---|---|---|
| li() | Creates list item for an ordered or unordered list | -type, -value |
| ol() | Start an ordered list | -compact, -start, -type |
| p() | Creates a paragraph <P> | -align, -class |
| password_field() | Creates a password field; text entered will be stars | |
| popup_menu() | Creates a pop-up menu <SELECT><OPTION> | -default, -labels, -name, -onBlur, -onChange, -onFocus, -override, -force, -value, -values |
| pre() | Creates preformatted typewriter text for maintaining line breaks, etc. <PRE> | |
| radio_group() | Creates a set of radio buttons all linked by one name | -columns, -cols, -colheaders, -default, -labels, -linebreak, -name, -nolabels, -onClick, -override, -force, -rows, -rowheaders, -value, -values |
| reset() | Creates form's Reset button | |
| scrolling_list() | Controls a scrolling list box form element | -default, -defaults, -labels, -multiple, -name, -onBlur, -onChange, -onFocus, -override, -force, -size, -value, -values |
| Select() | Creates a select tag; Note the uppercase "S" to avoid conflict with Perl's built-in select function. <SELECT> | |
| small() (:netscape group) | Reduce size of text | |
| start_form(),startform() | Starts an HTML form <FORM> | |
| start_multipart_form(), | Just like start_form, but used when uploading files | |
| strong() | Bold text | |
| submit() | Creates a Submit button for a form | -name, -onClick, -value, -label |

**Table C.14**   HTML methods. (continued)

| Method | What it Does | Attributes |
|---|---|---|
| sup() (:netscape group) | Superscripted text | |
| table() (:html3 group) | Creates a table | -align,bgcolor, -border, -bordercolor, -bordercolor-dark, -bordercolorlight, -cellpadding, -hspace, -vspace, -width |
| td() (:html3 group) | Creates a table data cell <TD> | -align, -bgcolor, -bordercolor, -bordercolorlight,-bordercolordark, -colspan, -nowrap, -rowspan, -valign, -width |
| textarea() | Creates a multiline text box | -cols, -columns, -name, -onChange, -onFocus,OnBlur, -onSelect, -override, -force, -value, -default, -wrap |
| textfield() | Produces a one-line text entry field | -maxLength, -name, -onChange, -onFocus, -onBlur, -onSelect, -override, -force, -size, -value, -default |
| th() (:html3 group) | Creates a table header <TH> | |
| Tr() (:html3 group) | Defines a table row; Note the uppercase "T" to avoid conflict with Perl's tr function. <TR> | -align,bgcolor, -bordercolor, -bordercolordark, -bordercolorlight, -valign |
| tt() | Typewriter font | |
| ul() | Start unordered list | |

**Processing the Form's Data with *param()*.**   After the user has filled in a form, *CGI.pm* will take the input from the form and store it in name/value pairs. The names and values can be retrieved with the *param()* function. When *param()* is called, if null is returned, then the form has not yet been filled out. If the *param()* function returns true (non-null), then the form must have been filled out, and the *param()* function can be used to retrieve the form information. If you want an individual value, the *param()* can retrieve it by its name. The following example illustrates the two parts to the CGI program: the HTML form, and how to get the information with the *param()* function. For a list of other methods used to process parameters, see Table C.16.

## EXAMPLE C.33

```perl
#!/usr/bin/perl
1   use CGI qw(:standard);
2   print header;
3   print start_html(-title=>'Using the Function-Oriented Syntax',
                      -BGCOLOR=>'yellow');
4   print img({-src=>'/Images/GreenBalloon.gif', -align=LEFT}),
5       h1("Let's Hear From You!"),
        h2("I'm interested."),

6       start_form,
7       "What's your name? ", textfield('name'),
8       p,
        "What's your occupation? ", textfield('job'),
        p,
9       "Select a vacation spot. ", popup_menu(
            -name=>'place',
            -values=>['Hawaii','Europe','Mexico', 'Japan' ],
                                    ),
        p,
10          submit,
11      end_form;

    print hr;

12  if ( param() ){  # If the form has been filled out,
                     # there are parameters
13      print "Your name is ", em(param('name')),
        p,
            "Your occupation is ", em(param('job')),
        p,
            "Your vacation spot is", em(param('place')),
        hr;
    }
```

## EXPLANATION

1 The *use* directive says that the *CGI.pm* module is being loaded and will import the *:standard* set of function calls, which use a syntax new in library versions 1.21 and higher. This syntax allows you to call methods without explicitly creating an object with the *new* constructor method; that is, the object is created for you. The *Official Guide to Programming with CGI.pm* by Lincoln Stein contains a complete list of shortcuts.

2 The header method *header* returns the *Content-type: header.* You can provide your own MIME type if you choose, otherwise it defaults to *text/html.*

3 This will return a canned HTML header and the opening <BODY> tag. Parameters are optional and are in the form *-title*, *-author*, and *-base*. Any additional parameters, such as the Netscape unofficial *BGCOLOR* attribute, are added to the <BODY> tag; for example, *BGCOLOR=>yellow.*

4 The *img* method allows you to load an image. This GIF image is stored under the document's root in a directory called *Images*. It is aligned to the left of the text. Note: The *print* function here does not terminate until line 11. All of the CGI functions are passed as a comma-separated list to the *print* function.

5 This will produce a level 1 heading tag. It's a shortcut and will produce the *<H1>* HTML tag.

6 This method starts a form. The defaults for the form are the *ACTION* attribute, assigned the URL of this script, and the *METHOD* attribute, assigned the *POST* method.

7 The *textfield* method creates a text field box. The first parameter is the *NAME* for the field, the second parameter representing the *VALUE* is optional. *NAME* is assigned *name* and *VALUE* is assigned "".

8 The *p* is a shortcut for a paragraph *<P>*.

9 The *popup_menu* method creates a menu. The required first argument is the menu's name (*-name*). The second argument, *-values*, is an array of menu items. It can be either anonymous or named.

10 The *submit* method creates the Submit button.

11 This line ends the form.

12 If the *param* method returns non-null, each of the values associated with the parameters will be printed.

13 The *param* method returns the value associated with *name*; in other words, what the user typed as input for that parameter.

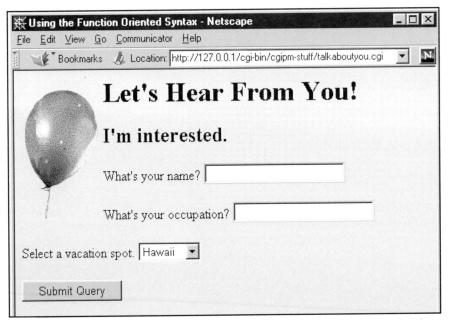

**Figure C.22** Output from lines 1–11 in Example C.33 before filling out the form.

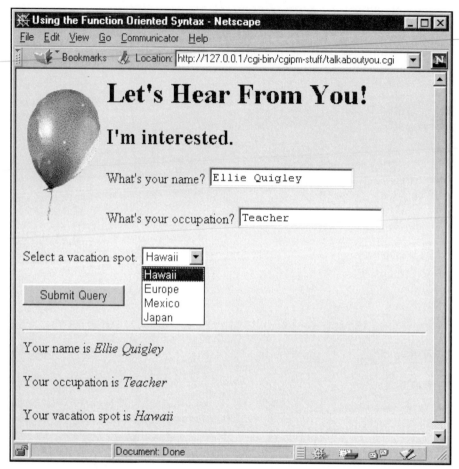

**Figure C.23**   The completed form and result of *CGI.pm* processing.

**Checking the Form at the Command Line.**   If you want to see the HTML tags generated by the *CGI.pm* form, you can run your script at the command line, but you will probably see the following error message:

```
(Offline mode: enter name=value pairs on standard input)
```

You can handle this by typing in key/value pairs and then pressing *<Ctrl>-d* (UNIX) or *<Ctrl>-z* (Windows) or by passing an empty parameter list. When the parameter list is empty, the output will let you see the HTML tags that were produced without any values assigned. See Example C.34.

**EXAMPLE  C.34**

```
(At the Command Line)
1  $ perl talkaboutyou.pl
   (Offline mode: enter name=value pairs on standard input)
   name=Dan
   job=Father
   place=Hawaii
   <Now press Ctrl-d or Ctrl-z>

(Output)
   Content-Type: text/html

   <!DOCTYPE HTML PUBLIC "-//IETF//DTD HTML//EN">
   <HTML><HEAD><TITLE>Using the Function Oriented Syntax</TITLE>
   </HEAD><BODY BGCOLOR="yellow">
   <H1>Let's Hear From You!</H1>
   <H2>I'm internested.</H2>
   <FORM METHOD="POST"  ENCTYPE="application/x-www-form-urlencoded">
       What's your name? <INPUT TYPE="text" NAME="name"
       VALUE="Dan"><P>What's your occupation? <INPUT TYPE="text"
       NAME="job" VALUE="Father"><P>Select a vacation spot.
       <SELECT NAME="place">
   <OPTION SELECTED VALUE="Hawaii">Hawaii
   <OPTION  VALUE="Europe">Europe
   <OPTION  VALUE="Mexico">Mexico
   <OPTION  VALUE="Japan">Japan
   </SELECT>
   <P><INPUT TYPE="submit" NAME=".submit"></FORM>
       <HR>Your name is <EM>Dan</EM><P>Your occupation is <EM>Father
       </EM><P>Your vacation spot is <EM>Hawaii</EM><HR>

(At the Command Line)
2  $ perl talkaboutyou.pl < /dev/null   or perl talkaboutyou.pl ' '
   Content-Type: text/html

(Output)
   <!DOCTYPE HTML PUBLIC "-//IETF//DTD HTML//EN">
   <HTML><HEAD><TITLE>Using the Function Oriented Syntax</TITLE>
   </HEAD><BODY BGCOLOR="yellow">
   <H1>Let's Hear From You!</H1>
   <H2>I'm interested.</H2><FORM METHOD="POST"
       ENCTYPE="application/x-wwwform-urlencoded">
       What's your name? <INPUT TYPE="text" NAME="name"
       VALUE=""><P>What's your occupation? <INPUT TYPE="text"
       NAME="job" VALUE=""><P>Select a vacation spot.
       <SELECT NAME="place">
   <OPTION  VALUE="Hawaii">Hawaii
   <OPTION  VALUE="Europe">Europe
   <OPTION  VALUE="Mexico">Mexico
   <OPTION  VALUE="Japan">Japan
   </SELECT>
   <P><INPUT TYPE="submit" NAME=".submit"></FORM><HR>Your name is
       <EM><P>Your occupation is <EM><P>Your vacation spot is <EM><HR>
```

## EXPLANATION

1   When running in offline mode, you can enter the key/value pairs as standard input. You need to check the form so that you get the right keys and then supply the values yourself. In this example, *name=Dan, job=Father, place=Hawaii* were supplied by the user. After pressing *<Ctrl>-d* (UNIX) or *<Ctrl>-z* (Windows), the input will be processed by *CGI.pm*.

2   By passing an empty parameter list, you can see the HTML output as it appears without the values assigned. If using UNIX, */dev/null* is the UNIX bit bucket (black hole), and reading from that directory is the same as reading from an empty file. By supplying a set of empty quotes as an argument, the effect is the same.

## C.9.5  *CGI.pm* Form Elements

**Table C.15**   CGI methods.

| Method | Example | What It Does |
|---|---|---|
| append | $query–>append(-name=>'value'); | Appends values to parameter |
| checkbox | $query–>checkbox(-name=>'checkbox_name', -checked=>'checked', -value=>'on', -label=>'clickme'); | Creates a standalone checkbox |
| checkbox_group | $query–>checkbox_group(-name=> 'group_name', -values=>[ list ], -default=>[ sublist ], -linebreak=>'true', -labels=>\%hash); | Creates a group of checkboxes |
| cookie | $query–>cookie(-name=>'sessionID', -value=>'whatever', -expires=>'+3h', -path=>'/', -domain=>'ucsc.edu', -secure=>1); | Creates a Netscape cookie |
| defaults | $query–>defaults; | Creates a button that resets the form to its defaults |
| delete | $query–>delete('param'); | Deletes a parameter |
| delete_all | $query–>delete; | Deletes all parameters; clears $query, the object |
| endform | $query–>endform; | Ends the <FORM> tag |
| header | $query–>header(-cookie=>'cookiename'); | Puts a cookie in the HTTP header |
| hidden | $query–>hidden(-name=>'hidden', -default=>[ list ] ); | Creates a hidden-from-view text field |
| image_button | $query–>image_button(-name=>'button', -src=>'/source/URL', -align=>'MIDDLE'); | Creates a clickable image button |
| import_names | $query–>import_names('namespace'); | Imports variables into namespace |

**Table C.15**   CGI methods. *(continued)*

| Method | Example | What It Does |
|---|---|---|
| *keywords* | @keywords = $query–>keywords; | Obtains parsed keywords from the *Isindex* input string and returns an array |
| *new* | $query = new CGI; | Parses input and puts it in object *$query* for both the *GET* and *POST* methods |
|  | $query = new CGI(INPUTFILE); | Reads contents of form from previously opened filehandle |
| *param* | @params = $query–>param(-name=>'name', -value=>'value'); | Returns an array of parameter names passed into the script |
|  | $value = $query–>('arg'); | Returns a value (or list of values) for the @values = $query–>('arg') parameter passed |
| *password_field* | $query–>password_field(-name=>'secret' -value=>'start', -size=>60, -maxlength=>80); | Creates a password field |
| *popup_menu* | $query–:                        me=>'menu' -values=>@items, -defaults=>'name', -labels=>\%hash); | Creates a pop-up menu |
| *radio_group* | $query–>radio_group(-name=>'group_name', -values=>[ list ], -default=>'name', -linebreak=>'true',  -labels=>\%hash); | Creates a group of radio buttons |
| *reset* | $query–>reset; | Creates the Reset button to clear a form boxes to former values |
| *save* | $query–>save(FILEHANDLE); | Saves the state of a form to a file |
| *scrolling_list* | $query–>scrolling_list(-name=>'listname', -values=>[ list ], -default=> [ sublist ], -multiple=>'true', -labels=>\%hash); | Creates a scrolling list |
| *startform* | $query–>startform(-method=> -action=>, -encoding); | Returns a <FORM> tag with optional method, action, and encoding |
| *submit* | $query–>submit(-name=>'button', -value=>'value'); | Creates the *Submit* button for forms |
| *textarea* |  | Same as text field, but includes multiline text entry box |
| *textfield* | $query–>textfield(-name=>'field', -default=>'start', -size=>50, -maxlength=>90); | Creates a text field box |

**Table C.16**   CGI parameter methods.

| Method | What It Does | Example |
|---|---|---|
| *delete(), Delete()* | Deletes a named parameter from parameter list. Delete must be used if you are using the function-oriented style of *CGI.pm*. | *$obj–>delete('Joe');*<br>*$obj–>delete(-name=>'Joe');*<br>*Delete('Joe');*<br>*Delete(-name=>'Joe');* |
| *delete_all(), Delete_all()* | Deletes all CGI parameters. | *$obj–>delete_all();*<br>*Delete_all();* |
| *import_names()* | Imports all CGI parameters into a specified namespace. | |
| *param()* | Retrieves parameters from a fillout form in key/value pairs. Can return a list or a scalar. | *print $obj–>param();*<br>*@list=$obj–>param();*<br>*print param('Joe');*<br>*$name=$obj–>param(-name=>'Joe');* |

**Methods For Generating Form Input Fields.**   The following examples use the object-oriented style, and can easily be replaced with the function-oriented style by removing all object references. The *print_form* subroutine will cause the form to be displayed in the browser window and the *do_work* subroutine will produce output when the *param* method returns a true value, meaning that the form was filled out and processed.

### The texfield() Method

The *textfield* method creates a text field. The text field allows the user to type in a single line of text into a rectangular box. The box dimensions can be specified with the *-size* argument, where the size is the width in characters, and *-maxlength* (a positive integer) sets an upper limit on how many characters the user can enter. If *-maxlength* is not specified, the default is to enter as many characters as you like. With the *-value* argument, the field can be given a default value, text that will appear in the box when it is first displayed.

### FORMAT

```
print $obj->textfield('name_of_textfield');
print $obj->textfield(
    -name=>'name_of_textfield',
    -value=>'default starting text',
    -size=>'60',         # Width in characters
    -maxlength=>'90');   # Upper width limit
```

## EXAMPLE C.35

```perl
#!/usr/bin/perl
1   use CGI;
2   $query = new CGI;
    # Create a CGI object
3   print $query->header;
4   print $query->start_html("Forms and Text Fields");
5   print  $query->h2("Example: The textfield method");

6   &print_form($query);
7   &do_work($query) if ($query->param);
    print $query->end_html;

8   sub print_form{
9       my($query) = @_;
10      print $query->startform;
        print "What is your name? ";
11      print $query->textfield('name');   # A simple text field
        print  $query->br();

12      print "What is your occupation? ";
13      print $query->textfield(-name=>'occupation',   # Giving values
                                -default=>'Retired',   # to the
                                -size=>60,             # text field
                                -maxlength=>120,
                               );
        print $query->br();
14      print $query->submit('action', 'Enter ');
15      print $query->reset();
16      print $query->endform;
        print $query->hr();
    }
17  sub do_work{
        my ($query) = @_;
        my (@values, $key);
        print $query->("<H2>Here are the settings</H2>");
18      foreach $key ($query->param){
            print "$key: \n";
19          @values=$query->param($key);
            print join(", ",@values), "<BR>";
        }
    }
```

## EXPLANATION

1   The *CGI.pm* module is loaded. It is an object-oriented module.
2   The CGI constructor method, called *new*, is called and a reference to a CGI object is returned.
3   The HTML header information is printed; for example, *Content-type: text/html*.
4   The *start_html* method produces the HTML tags to start HTML, the title *Forms and Textfields*, and the body tag.
5   The *h2* method produces an *<H2>*, heading level 2, tag.
6   This user-defined *print_form* function is called, with a reference to the CGI object is passed as an argument.
7   The *do_work* function is called with a reference to the CGI object passed as an argument. This is a user-defined function that will only be called if the *param* function returns true, and *param* returns true only if the form has been filled out.
8   The *print_form* function is defined.
9   The first argument is a reference to the CGI object.
10  The *startform* method produces the HTML <FORM> tag.
11  The *textfield* method produces a text box with one parameter, *name*. Whatever is assigned to the text box will be assigned to *name*.
12  The user is asked to provide input into the text box.
13  This *textfield* method is sent arguments as key/value hash pairs to further define the text field. The default will show in the box. See the output of this example in Figure C.24.
14  The *submit* method creates a Submit button with the text *Enter* in the button.
15  The *reset* method creates a Reset button with the default text *Reset* in the the the button.
16  The *endform* method creates the HTML </FORM> tag.
17  This is the user's *do_work* function that is called after the user fills out the form and presses the Submit (*Enter*) button. It processes the information supplied in the form with the *param* function.
18  The *param* function returns a key and a list of values associated with that key. The key is the name of the parameter for the input form and the values are what were assigned to it either by the user or in the form. For example, the key named *occupation* was filled in by the user as *jack of all trades*, whereas the *action* key in the Submit button was assigned *Enter* within the form before it was processed.

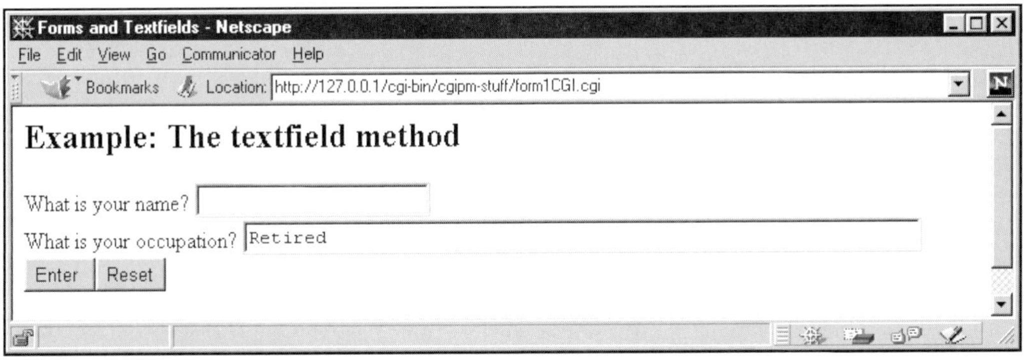

**Figure C.24** Output for text field form, Example C.35.

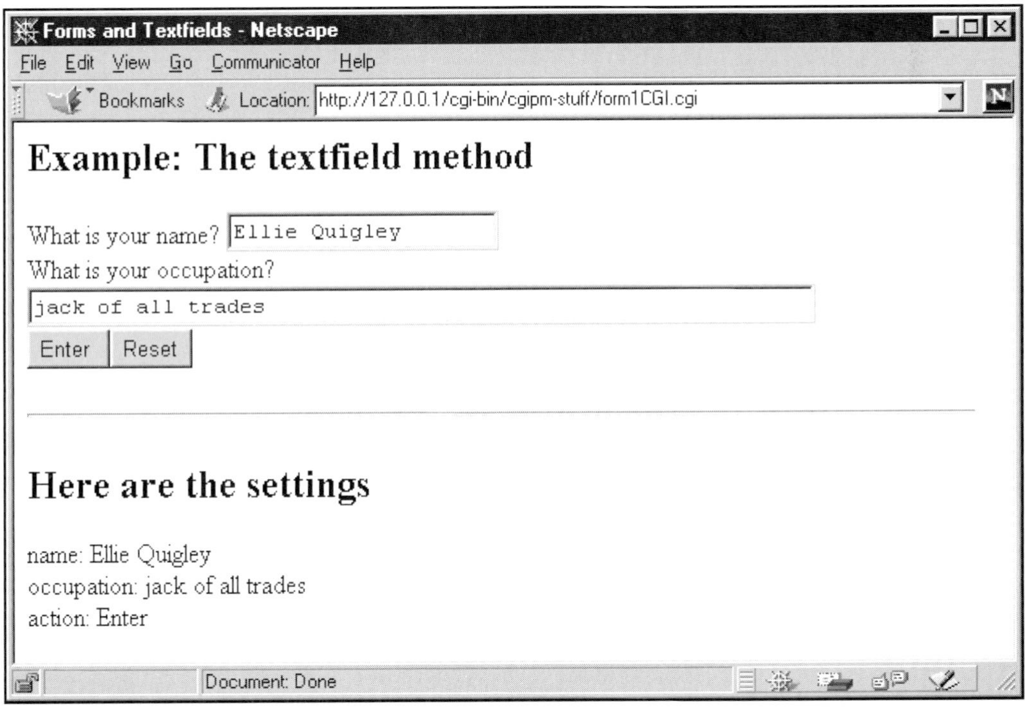

**Figure C.25** Output after the form was filled out and processed, Example C.35.

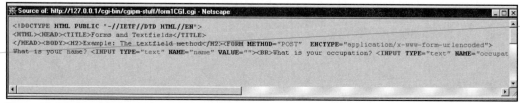

**Figure C.26**   The HTML source that was produced by *CGI.pm.*

### The checkbox() Method

The *checkbox()* method is used to create a simple checkbox for a *yes* or *no* (Boolean) response. The checkbox has *NAME* and *VALUE* attributes, where *-name* gives the CGI parameter a name and *-value* contains one item or a reference to a list of items that can be selected. If the *-checked* is assigned *1*, the box will start as checked. If *-label* assigned a value, it will be printed next to the checkbox; if not, the *-name* value of the checkbox will be printed. If not selected, the checkbox will contain an empty parameter.

The *checkbox_group()* method creates a set of checkboxes all linked by a single name. The options are not mutually exclusive; that is, the user can check one or more items. If *-linebreak* is assigned a non-zero number, the options will be vertically aligned. Ordinarily, the options would be displayed in a horizontal row. (See Example C.36.)

## FORMAT

```
print $obj->checkbox(-name=>'name_of_checkbox',
                     -checked=>1,
                     -value=>'ON'
                     -label=>'Click on me'
                    );


%labels = ('choice1'=>'red',
           'choice2'=>'blue',
           'choice3'=>'yellow',
          );
print $obj->checkbox_group(-name=>'name_of_checkbox',
                           -values=>[ 'choice1', 'choice2',
                                      'choice3', 'green',...],
                           -default=>[ 'choice1', 'green' ],
                           -linebreak => 1,
                           -labels=>\%labels
                          );
```

**EXAMPLE**  C.36

```perl
                 #!/usr/bin/perl
                 use CGI;
                 $query = new CGI;
                 print $query->header;
                 print $query->start_html("The Object Oriented CGI and Forms");
                 print "<H2>Example using Forms with Checkboxes</H2>\n";

                 &print_formstuff($query);
                 &do_work($query) if ($query->param);

                 print $query->end_html;
                 sub print_formstuff{
                     my($query) = @_;
    1                print $query->startform;

                     print "What is your name? ";
                     print $query->textfield('name');    # A simple text field
                     print "<BR>";

                     print "Are you married? <BR>";
    2                print $query->checkbox(-name=>'Married',
                                            -label=>'If not, click me' );
                                            # Simple checkbox
                     print "<BR><BR>";
                     print "What age group(s) do you hang out with? <BR>";
    3                  print $query->checkbox_group(-name=>'age_group',
                                            -values=>[ '12-18', '19-38',
                                                       '39-58','59-100' ],
                                            -default=>[ '19-38' ],
                                            -linebreak=>'true',
                                            );
    4                print $query->submit('action', 'Select');
    5                print $query->reset('Clear');
                     print $query->endform;
                     print "<HR>\n";
                 }

    6            sub do_work{
                     my ($query) = @_;
                     my (@values, $key);
                     print "<H2>Here are the settings</H2>";
    7                foreach $key ($query->param){
                         print "$key: \n";
    8                    @values=$query->param($key);
                         print join(", ",@values), "<BR>";
                     }
                 }
```

## EXPLANATION

1 The *startform* method produces the HTML *<FORM>* tag.

2 The is the simplest kind of checkbox. If the user is not married, he should click the box. The name of the checkbox is *Single*, the label, *If not, click me* is displayed next to the checkbox. If *-checked* is assigned *1*, the box will be checked when it is first displayed.

3 This an example of a checkbox group where a set of related checkboxes are linked by a common name, *age_group*. The *-values* argument is assigned a reference to a list of options that will appear to the right of each of the checkboxes. If *-labels* were used it would contain a hash consisting of key/value pairs that would be used as the labels on each of the checkboxes. The *-default* argument determines which boxes will be checked when the checkboxes are first displayed. The *-line-break* argument is set to a non-zero value, true, which will cause the options to be displayed as a vertical list.

4 When the user presses the Submit button, labeled *Select*, the form will be processed.

5 The Reset button clears the screen only if the user has not yet submitted the form. To override "stickiness," that is, to set the checkboxes back to original default values, set the *-override* argument to a non-zero value.

6 The *do_work* function is called when the form is submitted. This is where all the reading and parsing of the form input is handled.

7 Each of the parameters that came in from the form (key/value pairs) are printed.

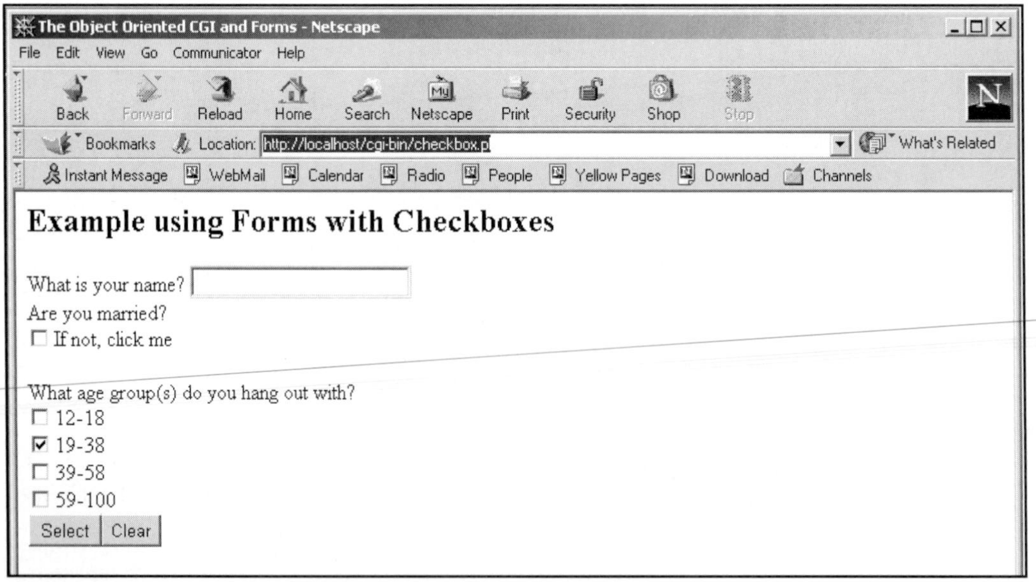

**Figure C.27**   Output for checkbox form in Example C.36.

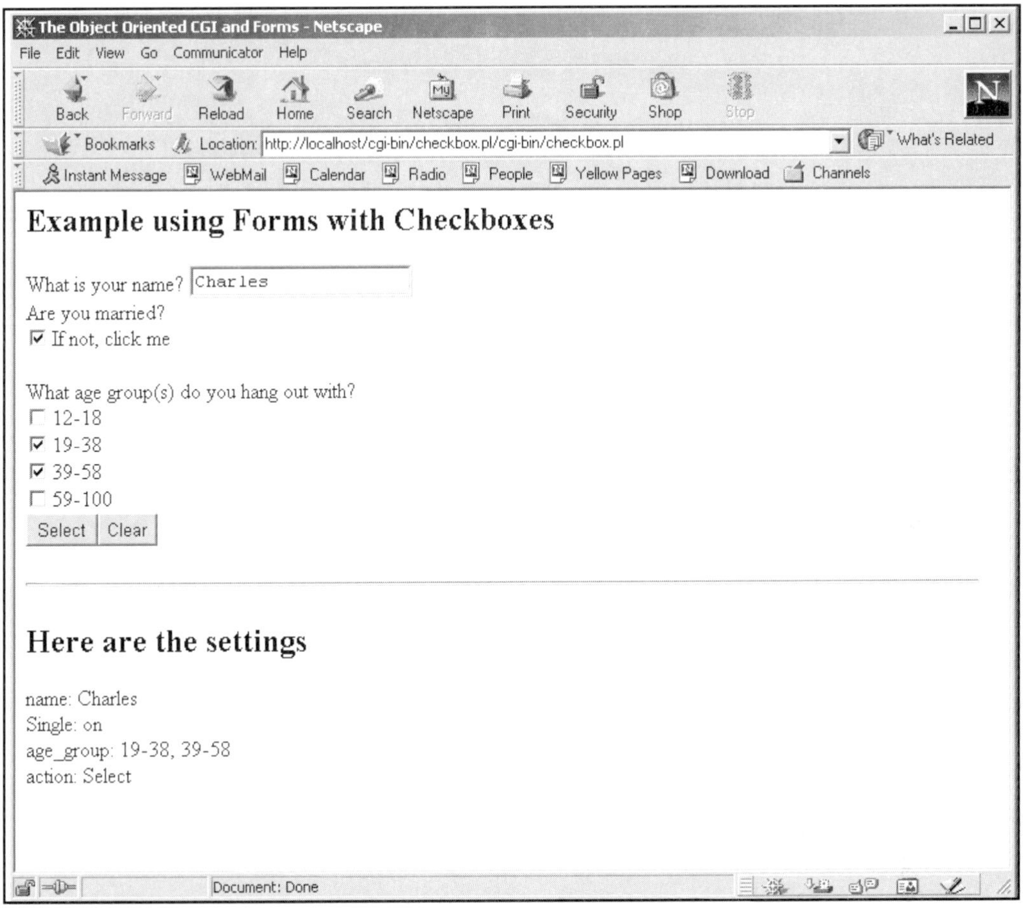

**Figure C.28**   Output after the form was filled out and processed, Example C.36.

### *The radio_group() and popup_menu() Methods*

To select among a set of mutually exclusive choices, you can use radio buttons or pop-up menus. Radio button groups allow a small number of choices to be grouped together to fit in the form; for a large number of choices, the pop-up menu is better. They both have arguments consisting of name/value pairs. Since the value argument consists of more than one selection, it takes a reference to an array. The *-default* argument is the value that is displayed when the menu first appears. The optional argument *-labels* is provided if you want to use different values for the user-visible label inside the radio group or pop-up menu and the value returned to your script. It's a pointer to an associative array relating menu values to corresponding user-visible labels. If a default isn't given, the first item is selected in the pop-up menu.

## FORMAT

```
%labels = ('choice1'=>'red',
           'choice2'=>'blue',
           'choice3'=>'yellow',
          );
print $obj->radio_group(-name=>'name_of_radio_group',
                        -values=>['choice1','choice2',
                                  'choice3', 'green', ...],
                        -default=>[ 'choice1', 'green' ],
                        -linebreak => 1,
                        -labels=>\%labels
                       );

%labels = ('choice1'=>'red',
           'choice2'=>'blue',
           'choice3'=>'yellow',
          );
print $obj->popup_menu(-name=>'name_of_popup_menu',
                       -values=>['choice1','choice2','choice3',
                                 'green',...],
                       -default=>[ 'choice1', 'green' ],
                       -linebreak => 1,
                       -labels=>\%labels
                      );
```

## EXAMPLE C.37

```
   #!/bin/perl
1  use CGI;
   $query = new CGI;
   print $query->header;
   print $query->start_html("The Object-Oriented CGI and Forms");
   print "<H2>Example using Forms with Radio Buttons</H2>\n";
   &print_formstuff($query);
   &do_work($query) if ($query->param);
   print $query->end_html;

   sub print_formstuff{
   my($query) = @_;
   print $query->startform;
   print "What is your name? ";
   print $query->textfield('name');  # A simple text field
   print "<BR>";
   print "Select your favorite color? <BR>";
```

---

**EXAMPLE** C.37 (CONTINUED)

```
2    print $query->radio_group(-name=>'color',
                               -values=>[ 'red', 'green',
                                          'blue','yellow' ],
                               -default=>'green',
                               -linebreak=>'true',
                              );
     print $query->submit('action', 'submit');
     print $query->reset('Clear');
     print $query->endform;
     print "<HR>\n";
     }
     sub do_work{
         my ($query) = @_;
         my (@values, $key);
         print "<H2>Here are the settings</H2>";
3        foreach $key ($query->param){
             print "$key: \n";
4            @values=$query->param($key);
             print join(", ",@values), "<BR>";
         }
     }
```

---

**EXPLANATION**

1  The *CGI.pm* module is loaded.

2  A radio group is created in the form by calling the CGI *radio_group* method with its arguments. The values of the individual radio buttons will be seen to the right of each button. The default button that will be checked when the form is first displayed is *green*. The *-linebreak* argument places the buttons in a vertical position rather than in a horizontal line across the screen. The user can select only **one** button.

3  After the user has filled out the form and pressed the Submit button, the *param* method will return the keys and values that were sent to the CGI script.

4  The key/value pairs are displayed.

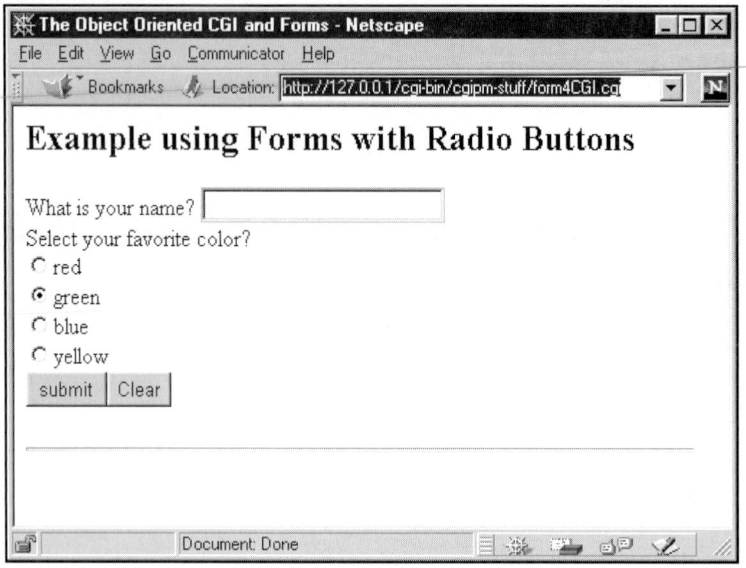

**Figure C.29**    Output for radio button form, Example C.37.

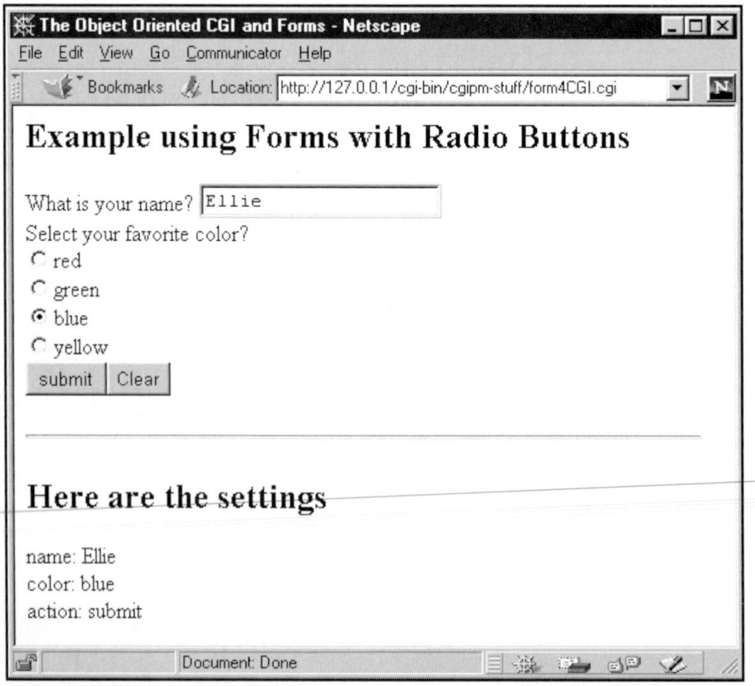

**Figure C.30**    Output after form was filled out and processed, Example C.37.

*Labels*

Labels allow the buttons to have user-friendly names that are associated with different corresponding values within the program. In the following example, the labels *stop*, *go*, and *warn* will appear beside radio buttons in the browser window. The values returned by the *param* method will be *red*, *green*, and *yellow*, respectively.

**EXAMPLE   C.38**

```
( The -labels Parameter -- Segment from CGI script)
    print $query->startform;
    print "What is your name? ";
    print $query->textfield('name');      # A simple text field
    print "<BR>";
    print "We're at a cross section. Pick your light.<BR>";
1   print $query->radio_group(-name=>'color',
2                              -values=>[ 'red', 'green', 'yellow' ],
                               -linebreak=>'true',
3                              -labels=>{red=>'stop',
                                         green=>'go',
                                         yellow=>'warn',
                                         },
4                              -default=>'green',
                              );
    print $query->submit('action', 'submit');
    print $query->reset('Clear');
    print $query->endform;
    }
```

**EXPLANATION**

1   The *radio_group* method is called with its arguments. Only one value can be selected.
2   The values that the *params* function returns will be either *red*, *green*, or *yellow*.
3   The labels are what actually appear next to each radio button. The user will see *stop*, *go*, and *warn* in the browser, but the CGI parameters associated with those labels are *red*, *green*, and *yellow*, respectively. If, for example, the user clicks on the *stop* button, the key/value pair passed to the script will be *color=>red*.
4   The default button is to have the button labeled *go* checked.

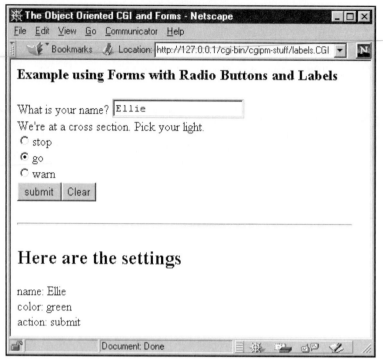

**Figure C.31**   Output for labels form after being filled out and processed, Example C.38.

### The popup_menu() Method

The **pop-up menu** is also referred to as a **drop-down list**. It is a list of selections that will be displayed when the user clicks on the scrollbar icon to the right of the text. Only one selection can be made.

---

**EXAMPLE C.39**

```perl
#!/usr/bin/perl
use CGI;
$query = new CGI;
print $query->header;
print $query->start_html("The Object-Oriented CGI and Forms");
print "<H2>Example using Forms with Pop-up Menus</H2>\n";
&print_formstuff($query);
&do_work($query) if ($query->param);
print $query->end_html;
```

**EXAMPLE   C.39** (CONTINUED)

```
sub print_formstuff{
my($query) = @_;
print $query->startform;
print "What is your name? ";
print $query->textfield('name');   # A simple text field
print "<BR>";
print "Select your favorite color? <BR>";
print $query->popup_menu(-name=>'color',
                         -values=>[ 'red', 'green', 'blue',
                                    'yellow' ],
                         -default=>'green',
                         -labels=>'\%labels',
                        );
print $query->submit('action', 'submit');
print $query->reset('Clear');
print $query->endform;
print "<HR>\n";
}

sub do_work{
    my ($query) = @_;
    my (@values, $key);
        print "<H2>Here are the settings</H2>";
        foreach $key ($query->param){
            print "$key: \n";
            @values=$query->param($key);
            print join(", ",@values), "<BR>";
    }
}
```

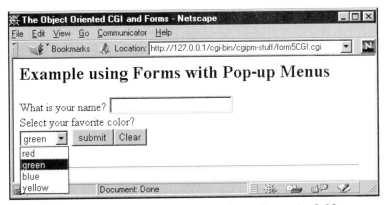

**Figure C.32**   Output for pop-up menu form, Example C.39.

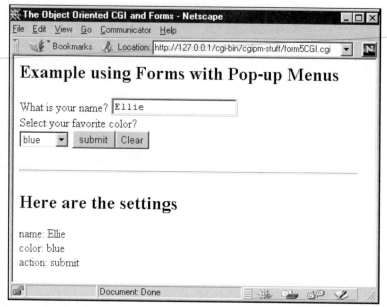

**Figure C.33**   Output for pop-up menu form after being filled out and processed, Example C.39.

### The submit() and reset() Methods

The *submit()* method creates a button that, when pressed, sends form input to the CGI script. If given an argument, you can label the button, often for the purpose of distinguishing it from other buttons if several Submit buttons are used.

The *reset()* method is used to clear all the entries in a form. It restores the form to the state it was in when last loaded, not to its default state. (See "The defaults Method," below.)

## Clearing Fields

### The override Argument

Note that if you press the Reset button or restart the same form, the previous information is sticky; in other words, the input box is not cleared. You can force the entry to be cleared by using the *-override* or *-force* argument with a non-zero value; for example:

```
textfield(-name=>'name', -override=>1);
```

### The defaults Method

The *defaults()* method clears all entries in the form to the state of the form when it was first displayed in the browser window; that is, the parameter list is cleared. To create a user-readable button, call the defaults method; for example:

```
print defaults(-name=>'Clear All Entries');
```

### Error Handling

When your *CGI.pm* script contains errors, the error messages are normally sent by the server to error log files configured under the server's root. If the program aborts, the browser will display "Document contains no data" or "Server Error." These messages are not very helpful.

#### *The carpout and fatalsToBrowser Methods*

*CGI.pm* provides methods, not only to store errors in your own log file, but also to see fatal error messages in the browser's window. The *carpout* function is provided for this purpose. Since is not exported by default, you must import it explicitly by writing:

```
use CGI::Carp qw(carpout);
```

The *carpout* function requires one argument, a reference to a user-defined filehandle where errors will be sent. It should be called in a *BEGIN* block at the top of the CGI application so that compiler errors will be caught. To cause fatal errors from *die*, *croak*, and *confess* to also appear in the browser window, the *fatalsToBrowser* function must also be imported.

---

### EXAMPLE   C.40

```
       #!/usr/bin/perl
1      use CGI;
2      BEGIN{ use CGI::Carp qw(fatalsToBrowser carpout);
3          open(LOG,">>errors.log") ||die "Couldn't open log file\n";
4          carpout(LOG);
       }
       $query = new CGI;
       <Program continues here>
```

### EXPLANATION

1   The *CGI.pm* module is loaded.
2   The *CGI::Carp* module is also loaded. This *Carp* module takes two arguments: *fatalsToBrowser* and *carpout*. The first argument, *fatalstobrowswer*, sends Perl errors to the browser and *carpout* makes it all possible by redirecting the standard error from the screen to the browser and error log.
3   A file called *errors.log* is opened for creation/appending. This log file will contain the error messages that will also be seen in the browser.
4   The *carpout* function will send errors to the *errors.log* file. Here is a line from that file:

*[Thu Feb  8 18:59:04 2001] C:\httpd\CGI-BIN\carpout.pl: Testing error messages from CGI script.*

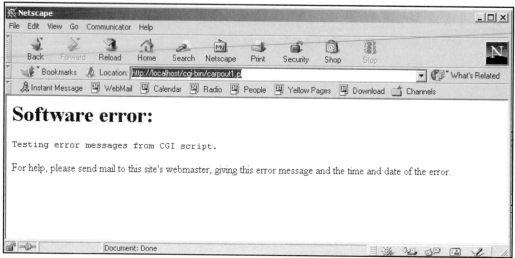

**Figure C.34**   Redirecting errors with *carpout* and *fatalsToBrowser*.

**Changing the Default Message.**   By default, the software error message is followed by a note to contact the Webmaster by e-mail with the time and date of the error. If you want to change the default message, you can use the *set_message* method, which must be imported into the programs namespace.

## FORMAT

```
use CGI::Carp qw(fatalsToBrowser set_message);
set_message("Error message!");
set_message(\reference_to_subroutine);
```

## EXAMPLE C.41

```
1    use CGI;
2    BEGIN{ use CGI::Carp qw(fatalsToBrowser carpout);
3        open(LOG,">>errors.log") ||die "Couldn't open log file\n";
4        carpout(LOG);
5        sub handle_errors {
6            my $msg = shift;
7            print "<h1>Software Error Alert!!</h1>";
             print "<h2>Your program sent this error:<br><I>
                 $msg</h2></I>";
         }
     }
8    set_message(\&handle_errors);
9    die("Testing error messages from CGI script.\n");
```

## EXPLANATION

1    The *CGI.pm* module is loaded.

2    The *CGI::Carp* module is also loaded. The *Carp.pm* module takes two arguments: *fatalsToBrowser* and *carpout*. The first argument, *fatalsToBrowser* sends Perl errors to the browser and *carpout* makes it all possible by redirecting the standard error from the screen to the browser and error log.

3    A file called *errors.log* is opened for creation/appending. This log file will contain the error messages that will also be seen in the browser.

4    The *carpout* function will send errors to the *errors.log* file.

5    A user-defined subroutine called *handle_errors* is defined. It will produce a customized error message in the user's browser window.

6    The first argument to *handle_errors* subroutine is the error message coming from a *die* or *croak*. In this example, the *die* message on line 9 will be be assigned to *$msg*, unless the *die* on line 3 happens first. This message will also be sent to the log file, *errors.log*.

7    This error message will be sent to the browser.

8    The *set_message* method is called with a reference to the user-defined subroutine *handle_errors*, passed as an argument. *handle_errors* contains the customized error message.

9    The *die* function will cause the program to exit, sending its error message to the *handle_errors* subroutine via *set_message*.

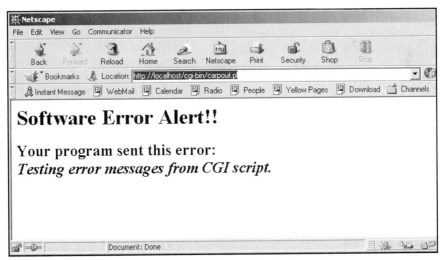

**Figure C.35** Output of error message from Example C.41.

## EXAMPLE C.42

```
(Contents of the errors.log file created by carpout)
carpout.pl syntax OK
[Thu Feb  8 18:27:48 2001] C:\httpd\CGI-BIN\carpout.pl: Testing err
rom CGI script.
[Thu Feb  8 18:30:01 2001] C:\httpd\CGI-BIN\carpout.pl: <h1>Testing
es from CGI script.
[Thu Feb  8 18:55:53 2001] C:\httpd\CGI-BIN\carpout.pl: Undefined s
in::set_message called at C:\httpd\CGI-BIN\carpout.pl line 11.
[Thu Feb  8 18:55:53 2001] C:\httpd\CGI-BIN\carpout.pl: BEGIN faile
n aborted at C:\httpd\CGI-BIN\carpout.pl line 12.
[Thu Feb  8 18:56:49 2001] carpout.pl: Undefined subroutine &main::
alled at carpout.pl line 11.
[Thu Feb  8 18:56:49 2001] carpout.pl: BEGIN failed--compilation ab
out.pl line 12.
```

**Cookies.**   The HTTP protocol, by design, is stateless in order to keep the connections brief. After a transaction is completed, the connection is lost and the browser and server have no recollection of what transpired from one session to the next. But now that the Internet is used as a huge shopping center, it is often necessary to keep track of users and what they have purchased, their preferences, registration information, etc. Netscape introduced **cookies** in order to establish a persistent state; that is, keep information around that would normally be lost at the end of a transaction. Cookies offer a way to keep track of visitors and their preferences after they have visited a site.

The cookie is a piece of data that is sent by the server from your CGI script to the visitor's browser where it is stored in a file (often called *cookie.txt* or just *cookie*) for as long as you specify. It is a string assigned to an HTTP header that gets entered into the memory of the browser (client) and then stored in a file on the hard drive. The browser maintains a list of cookies on disk that belong to a particular Web server and returns them back to the Web server via the HTTP header during subsequent interactions. When the server gets the cookie it assigns the cookie values (name/value pairs) to the *HTTP_COOKIE* environment variable. The cookie, then, is passed back and forth between the browser and the server. The CGI program can set the cookie in a cookie response header (*Set-Cookie*) and retrieve values from the cookie from the environment variable, *HTTP_COOKIE*.

By default, the cookie is short-term and expires when the current browser session terminates, but it can be made persistent by setting an expiration date to some later time, after which it will be discarded. The path decides where the cookie is valid for a particular server. If not set, it defaults to the location of the script that set the cookie. The path it refers to is the server's path, where the server's root is /. The domain name is the domain where the cookie is valid; that is, the current domain as in *127.0.0.1* or *www.ellieq.com*.

Cookies are set in the HTTP cookie header as follows:

```
Set-Cookie:  Name=Value; expires=Date; path=Path; domain=Domainname; secure
```

## EXAMPLE   C.43

```
#!/bin/perl
# A simple CGI script to demonstrate setting and retrieving a cookie.
# Run the program twice:  the first time to set the cookie on the
# client side, and second to retrieve the cookie from the browser
# and get its value from the environment variable,
# $ENV{HTTP_COOKIE, coming from the server.

1   my $name = "Ellie";
2   my $expiration_date = "Friday, 17-Feb-01 00:00:00: GMT";
3   my $path = "/cgi-bin";

4   print "Set-Cookie: shopper=$name, expires=$expiration_date,
        path=$path\n";
    print "Content-type: text/html\n\n";

5   print <<EOF;
    <html><head><Title>Cookie Test</Title></Head>
    <body>
    <h1>Chocolate chip cookie!!</h1>
    <h2>Got milk?</h2>
    <hr>
    <p>
    What's in the HTTP_COOKIE environment variable?
    <br>
6   $ENV{HTTP_COOKIE}
    <p>
    <hr>
    </body></html>
    EOF
```

## EXPLANATION

1   The variable is set for the shopper's name.
2   The expiration date is set for when the cookie will be deleted.
3   This is the path on the server where the cookie is valid.
4   This is the HTTP header that is assigned the information that will be stored in the cookie file in the browser.
5   This is the start of the *here document* that will contain the HTML tags to be rendered by the browser.
6   The value of the *HTTP_COOKIE* environment variable displays the cookie information that was retrieved and sent back to the server from the browser in an HTTP header.

**Figure C.36**    The *HTTP_Cookie* environment variable.

**Table C.17**    Cookie values.

| | |
|---|---|
| Name | Name of the cookie. The term *Name* is the actual name of the cookie; for example, it could be *preference=blue* where *preference* is the name of the cookie and *blue* is the data assigned to the cookie. |
| Value | Data assigned to the cookie; spaces, semicolons, commas, not allowed. |
| Date | When the cookie will expire: *s* = seconds; *m* = minutes; *h* = hours; *d* = days; *now, M* = months; *y* = years; *Fri,15-Mar-00 12:35:33 GMT*; e.g., *+30m* is 30 minutes from now; *-1d* is yesterday;  *+2M* is two months from now; and *now* is now. |
| Path | Path where cookie is valid. |
| Domain | Domain name refers to the domain where the script is running and the cookie is valid. |
| Secure | Makes the cookie invalid unless a secure connection is established. |

The values of the cookie are stored in the *HTTP_COOKIE* environment variable. Netscape limits the number of cookies to *300*. *CGI.pm* makes it easy to use cookies. See the following Example C.44.

## EXAMPLE C.44

```perl
    #!/usr/bin/perl
1   use CGI;
2   $query = new CGI;
3   if ( $query->param && $query->param('color') ne ""){
4       $color=$query->param('color') ;    # Did the user pick a color
    }
5   elsif ( $query->cookie('preference')){      # Is there a cookie
                                                # already?
6       $color=$query->cookie('preference');   # Then go get it!
    }
    else{
7   $color='yellow';}  # Set a default background color if
                       # a cookie doesn't exist, and the user didn't
                       # select a preference
8   $cookie=$query->cookie(-name=>'preference',
                           -value=>"$color",   # Set the cookie values
                           -expires=>'+30d',
                          );
9   print $query->header(-cookie=>$cookie);
                        # Setting the HTTP cookie header

10  print $query->start_html(-title=>"Using Cookies",
                             -bgcolor=>"$color",
                            );
    print $query->h2("Example: Making Cookies");

    &print_prompt($query);
    &do_work($query) if ($query->param);

    print $query->end_html;

11  sub print_prompt{
        my($query) = @_;
        print $query->startform;
        print "What is your name? ";
        print $query->textfield(-name=>'name',
                                -size=>30);  # A simple text field
        print "<BR>";
        print "What is your occupation? ";
        print $query->textfield(-name=>'occupation',  # Giving values
                                -default=>'Retired',  # to text field
                                -size=>30,
                                -maxlength=>120
                               );
```

## EXAMPLE C.44 (CONTINUED)

```
            print "<BR>";
            print "What is your favorite color? ";
            print $query->textfield(-name=>'color');    # Giving values
            print $query->br();
            print $query->submit('action', 'Enter');
            print $query->reset();
            print $query->endform;
            print $query->hr();
         }
12   sub do_work{
            my ($query) = @_;
            my (@values, $key);
            print "<H2>Here are the settings</H2>";
13          foreach $key ($query->param){
            print "$key: \n";
            @values=$query->param($key);
            print join(", ",@values), "<BR>";
            }
         }
```

## EXPLANATION

1  The module is loaded into this script.

2  The CGI module's constructor, *new*, is called and a reference to a CGI object is returned and assigned to *$query*. We will be using the object-oriented form of *CGI.pm* in this example.

3  If the form was filled out and if the user selected a color, the *param* function will return true; in other words, if *param* is not a null string, the value of the selected color will be assigned to the scalar, *$color*.

4  If the form has been filled out, and a cookie was sent back to the server, the value of the cookie will be retrieved and store it in the scalar, *$color*.

5  If the user didn't select a color, and there was no cookie, then the default background will be set to *yellow*.

6  If a cookie was set, retrieve the value of the preference from the cookie. The *cookie* method will extract the value of the *HTTP_COOKIE* environment variable.

7  If this is the first time this script has been run, a default value of *yellow* will be set for the background color.

8  Key/value pairs for the cookie are set. The cookie is set to expire after 30 days. If no expiration date is set, the cookie is only good for the current session of the browser.

9  The *header* method creates the HTTP cookie.

10  The background color for the HTML page is set by the *start_html* method.

11  The method that displays the HTML form is defined.

12  The method that parses the form after it has been filled out is defined.

13  Each of the key/value pairs produced by the *param* method are displayed.

EXAMPLE   C.45

(What the Cookie HTTP header looks like)

Set-Cookie: preference=yellow; path=/form1CGI.cgi; expires=Sun,
17-Sep-2000 09:46:26 GMT

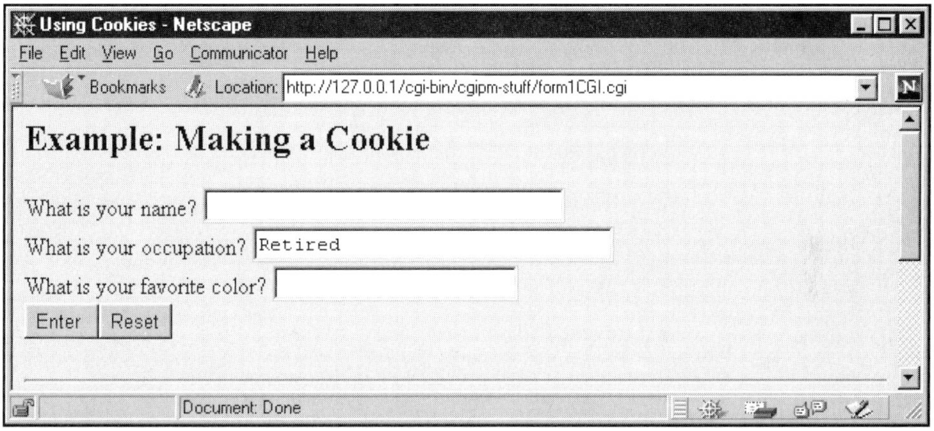

**Figure C.37**   The default background color was set to *yellow.*

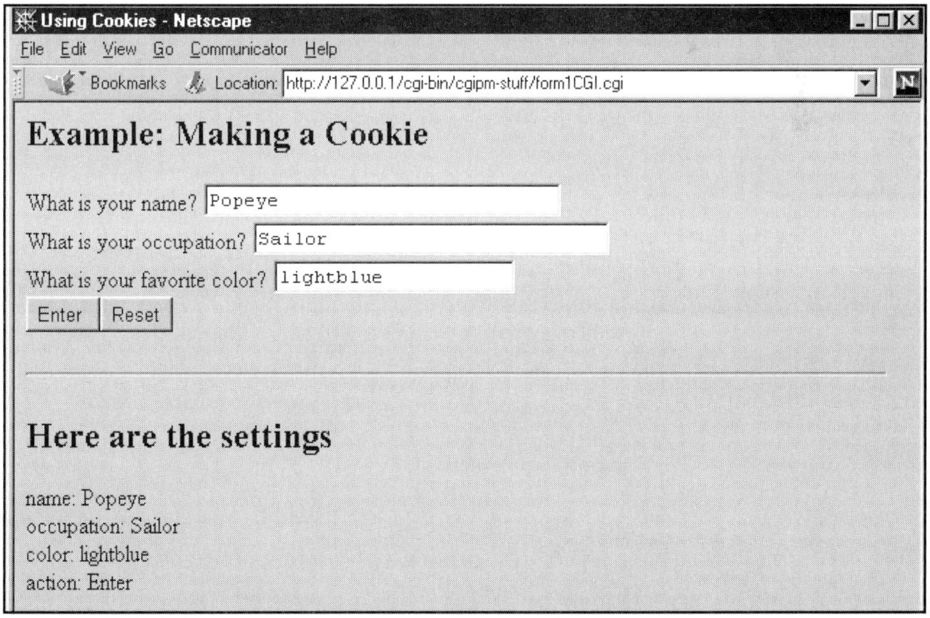

**Figure C.38**   The user's preference, *lightblue,* is stored in a cookie.

## C.9.6   HTTP Header Methods

A cookie is assigned to an HTTP header as shown in the previous example. Table C.18 lists other methods that can be used to create and retrieve information from HTTP headers.

**Table C.18**   HTTP header methods.

| HTTP Header Method | What It Does |
| --- | --- |
| *accept()* | Lists MIME types or type |
| *auth_type()* | Returns authorization type for the current session |
| *cookie()* | Creates and retreives cookies |
| *header()* | Returns a valid HTTP header and MIME type |
| *https()* | Returns information about SSL for a session |
| *path_info()* | Sets and retrieves addtional path information |
| *path_translated()* | Returns additional path information |
| *query_string()* | Returns the URL encoded query string |
| *raw_cookie()* | Returns a list of unprocessed cookies sent from the browser |
| *redirect()* | Generates an HTTP header with a redirection request to the browser to load a page at that location |
| *referer()* | Returns the URL of the page the browser displayed before starting your script |
| *remote_addr()* | Returns the IP address of the remote host, possibly a proxy server |
| *remote_ident()* | Returns remote user's login name if the identity daemon is activiated |
| *remote_host()* | Returns the DNS name of the remote host |
| *remote_user()* | Returns the account name used to authenticate a password |
| *request_method()* | Returns the HTTP method, *GET*, *POST*, or *HEAD* |
| *script_name()* | Returns the URL of this script relative to the server's root |
| *self_url()* | Returns the URL of the CGI script: protocol, host, port, path, additional path info, and parameter list; can be used to reinvoke the current script |
| *server_name()* | Returns the name of the Web server |
| *server_software()* | Returns the name and version of the Web server |
| *server_port()* | Returns the port number for the current session (usually 80) |
| *url()* | Returns URL of the current script without additional path information and query string |
| *user_agent()* | Returns browser information |
| *user_name()* | Returns remote user's name if it can |
| *virtual_host()* | Returns the name of the virtual host being accessed by the browser |

**EXAMPLE** C.46

```
     #!/usr/bin/perl
     use CGI qw(:standard);
1    print header;
2    print start_html(-title=>'Using header Methods'),
     h1("Let's find out about this session!"),
     p,
3    h4 "Your server is called ", server_name(),
     p,
4    "Your server port number is ", server_port(),
     p,
5    "This script name is: ", script_name(),
     p,
6    "Your browser is ", user_agent(), "and it's out of date!",
     p,
7    "The query string looks like this: ", query_string(),
     p,
8    "Where am I? Your URL is: \n", url(),
     p,
9    "Cookies set: ", raw_cookie();

10   print end_html;
```

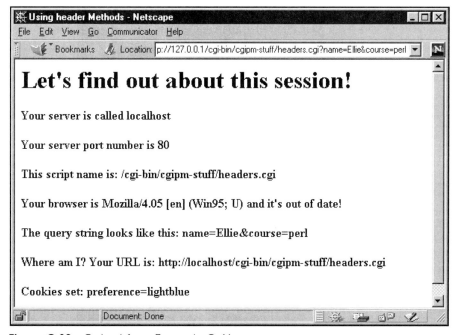

**Figure C.39**   Output from Example C.46.

## EXERCISE C.1

1. **The Environment Variables and CGI**

   Create a CGI script that will print to the browser:

   *The name of the server is:  <Put the values here.>*
   *The gateway protocol is:*
   *The client machine's IP address:*
   *The client machine's name:*
   *The document root is:*
   *The CGI script name is:*

   (Hint: Use the *%ENV* hash.)

2. **Creating A CGI Program**

   a.  Write a CGI script called *town_crier* that will contain HTML text and Perl statements.

   b.  The script will contain two subroutines: &*welcome* and &*countem*.

   c.  The *welcome* subroutine will print *Welcome Sir Richard!!*. Use a blue font that blinks the welcome. (Note: Internet Explorer ignores *blink*.) The subroutine will also print today's date. (Use the *ctime* library function.)

   d.  The subroutine called *countem* will be written in a file called *countem.pl*. The *town_crier* script will call *countem* passing its name (*town_crier*) as an argument to the subroutine. Remember, the name of the script is stored in the *$0* variable, e.g., &*countem ($0);*. The subroutine will return the number of times the page has been visited.

   e.  See Figure 10.40 for an idea of how this script will display its output in the browser's window.

   f.  The *countem* function should be designed to

   - Take an argument—the name of the file that called it. Unless there is a file called *town_crier.log* already in the directory, the file will be created. Either way, the file will be opened for reading and writing. (If the *countem* function were called from another Perl script, then the log file created would have the name of that script, followed by the *.log* extension.)

   - If the log file is empty, *countem* will write the value *1* into the file; otherwise a line will be read from the file. The line will contain a number. The number will be read in and stored in a variable. Its value will be incremented by *1*. Each time *town_crier* is executed, this function is called.

   - The new number will be sent back to the file, overwriting the number that was there.

   - The log file will be closed.

   - The *countem* subroutine will return the value of the number to the calling program. (In the example, I put the number in a cell of an HTML table and sent the whole string back to the *town_ crier*. Don't bother to try to create the table if you don't have time. Just send back the number.)

- If running on a UNIX system, use the *flock* function to put an exclusive lock on the log file while you are using it and will remove the lock when you are finished.

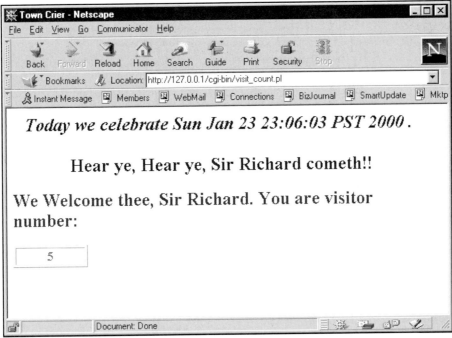

**Figure C.40**    Output of the CGI program in Exercise C.1.

## EXERCISE C.2

1. Creating Forms—HTML
   a. Create a Web page called Stirbucks that contains a form to order coffee, similar to the order form in Figure C.41.
   b. In the *action* attribute of the initial *<FORM>* tag, specify a URL that directs the server to a CGI script using the default *GET* method.
   c. Test your file in a browser.
   d. The CGI script will print the value of the *QUERY_STRING* environment variable.

2. Processing Forms—CGI

   a. Write a CGI script that will send back to the user an HTML page that thanks him for his order and tells him the coffee he selected will be delivered to his shipping address. Use the *GET* method. After getting the information from the form, write your own fuction to parse the input.

   b. Redesign the form to include the *POST* method. The program will test which method was used and call the parse function.

   c. Create a DBM file that keeps a list of the e-mail addresses submitted. When a user submits an order, his e-mail address will be listed in the DBM file. Make sure there are no duplicates. Design a function to do this.

   d. The CGI script will handle e-mail. Send e-mail to yourself confirming the information that was submitted. Design another function to handle e-mail.

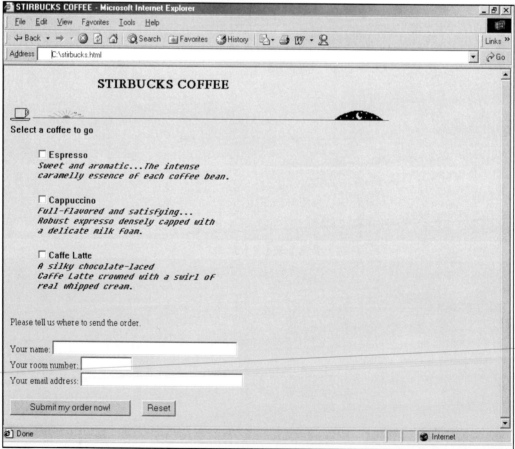

**Figure C.41**   The Stirbucks Web page order form.

3. Rewrite the *Stirbucks* program so that the HTML form and the CGI script are in one CGI program created with the *CGI.pm* module. Use the function-oriented style.

4. Add to the *Stirbucks* program a cookie that will save the user's preferences so that each time he orders coffee, he will get a free sweet. If he doesn't state a preference, he will get a bagel with his coffee. The bagel or the alternate choice for a free sweet is saved in a Netscape cookie. The cookie should not expire for 1 week. (See Figure C.42.)

5. Write a CGI script (with the *CGI.pm* module) that will replace the *ATM* script you wrote in Chapter 11. The new CGI script will provide a form in the browser that will produce a menu of items; that is, deposit, withdraw, balance, etc. Use the object-oriented CGI methods to create the HTML form. In the same script, the *param* function will check which selection was checked, and, based on the selection, the appropriate method will be called from *Checking.pm*. After the form has been filled out and submitted, the results of processing will appear on the same page.

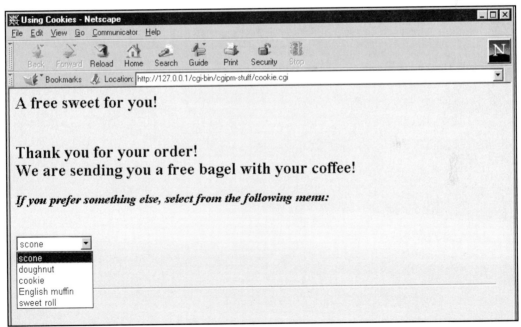

**Figure C.42**  Cookie output.

# INDEX

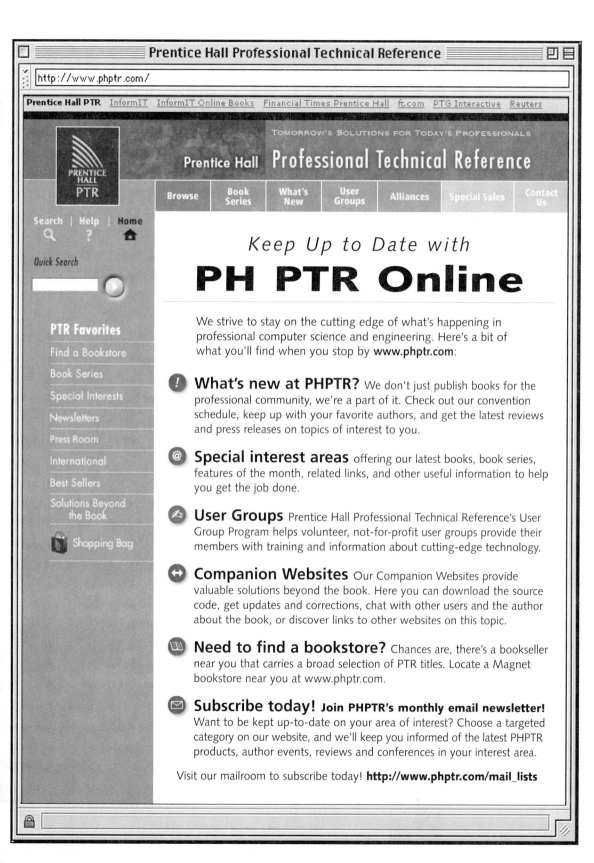

# LICENSE AGREEMENT AND LIMITED WARRANTY

READ THE FOLLOWING TERMS AND CONDITIONS CAREFULLY BEFORE OPENING THIS SOFTWARE PACKAGE. THIS LEGAL DOCUMENT IS AN AGREEMENT BETWEEN YOU AND PRENTICE-HALL, INC. (THE "COMPANY"). BY OPENING THIS SEALED SOFTWARE PACKAGE, YOU ARE AGREEING TO BE BOUND BY THESE TERMS AND CONDITIONS. IF YOU DO NOT AGREE WITH THESE TERMS AND CONDITIONS, DO NOT OPEN THE SOFTWARE PACKAGE. PROMPTLY RETURN THE UNOPENED SOFTWARE PACKAGE AND ALL ACCOMPANYING ITEMS TO THE PLACE YOU OBTAINED THEM FOR A FULL REFUND OF ANY SUMS YOU HAVE PAID.

1.    **GRANT OF LICENSE:** In consideration of your payment of the license fee, which is part of the price you paid for this product, and your agreement to abide by the terms and conditions of this Agreement, the Company grants to you a nonexclusive right to use and display the copy of the enclosed software program (hereinafter the "software") on a single computer (i.e., with a single CPU) at a single location so long as you comply with the terms of this Agreement. The Company reserves all rights not expressly granted to you under this Agreement.

2.    **OWNERSHIP OF SOFTWARE:** You own only the magnetic or physical media (the enclosed software) on which the software is recorded or fixed, but the Company retains all the rights, title, and ownership to the software recorded on the original software copy(ies) and all subsequent copies of the software, regardless of the form or media on which the original or other copies may exist. This license is not a sale of the original software or any copy to you.

3.    **COPY RESTRICTIONS:** This software and the accompanying printed materials and user manual (the "Documentation") are the subject of copyright. You may not copy the Documentation or the software, except that you may make a single copy of the software for backup or archival purposes only. You may be held legally responsible for any copying or copyright infringement which is caused or encouraged by your failure to abide by the terms of this restriction.

4.    **USE RESTRICTIONS:** You may not network the software or otherwise use it on more than one computer or computer terminal at the same time. You may physically transfer the software from one computer to another provided that the software is used on only one computer at a time. You may not distribute copies of the software or Documentation to others. You may not reverse engineer, disassemble, decompile, modify, adapt, translate, or create derivative works based on the software or the Documentation without the prior written consent of the Company.

5.    **TRANSFER RESTRICTIONS:** The enclosed software is licensed only to you and may not be transferred to any one else without the prior written consent of the Company. Any unauthorized transfer of the software shall result in the immediate termination of this Agreement.

6.    **TERMINATION:** This license is effective until terminated. This license will terminate automatically without notice from the Company and become null and void if you fail to comply with any provisions or limitations of this license. Upon termination, you shall destroy the Documentation and all copies of the software. All provisions of this Agreement as to warranties, limitation of liability, remedies or damages, and our ownership rights shall survive termination.

7.    **MISCELLANEOUS:** This Agreement shall be construed in accordance with the laws of the United States of America and the State of New York and shall benefit the Company, its affiliates, and assignees.

8.    **LIMITED WARRANTY AND DISCLAIMER OF WARRANTY:** The Company warrants that the software, when properly used in accordance with the Documentation, will operate in substantial conformity with the description of the software set forth in the Documentation. The Company does not warrant that the software will meet your requirements or that the operation of the software will be uninterrupted or error-free. The Company warrants that the media on which the software is delivered shall be free from defects in materials and workmanship under normal use

for a period of thirty (30) days from the date of your purchase. Your only remedy and the Company's only obligation under these limited warranties is, at the Company's option, return of the warranted item for a refund of any amounts paid by you or replacement of the item. Any replacement of software or media under the warranties shall not extend the original warranty period. The limited warranty set forth above shall not apply to any software which the Company determines in good faith has been subject to misuse, neglect, improper installation, repair, alteration, or damage by you. EXCEPT FOR THE EXPRESSED WARRANTIES SET FORTH ABOVE, THE COMPANY DISCLAIMS ALL WARRANTIES, EXPRESS OR IMPLIED, INCLUDING WITHOUT LIMITATION, THE IMPLIED WARRANTIES OF MERCHANTABILITY AND FITNESS FOR A PARTICULAR PURPOSE. EXCEPT FOR THE EXPRESS WARRANTY SET FORTH ABOVE, THE COMPANY DOES NOT WARRANT, GUARANTEE, OR MAKE ANY REPRESENTATION REGARDING THE USE OR THE RESULTS OF THE USE OF THE SOFTWARE IN TERMS OF ITS CORRECTNESS, ACCURACY, RELIABILITY, CURRENTNESS, OR OTHERWISE.

IN NO EVENT, SHALL THE COMPANY OR ITS EMPLOYEES, AGENTS, SUPPLIERS, OR CONTRACTORS BE LIABLE FOR ANY INCIDENTAL, INDIRECT, SPECIAL, OR CONSEQUENTIAL DAMAGES ARISING OUT OF OR IN CONNECTION WITH THE LICENSE GRANTED UNDER THIS AGREEMENT, OR FOR LOSS OF USE, LOSS OF DATA, LOSS OF INCOME OR PROFIT, OR OTHER LOSSES, SUSTAINED AS A RESULT OF INJURY TO ANY PERSON, OR LOSS OF OR DAMAGE TO PROPERTY, OR CLAIMS OF THIRD PARTIES, EVEN IF THE COMPANY OR AN AUTHORIZED REPRESENTATIVE OF THE COMPANY HAS BEEN ADVISED OF THE POSSIBILITY OF SUCH DAMAGES. IN NO EVENT SHALL LIABILITY OF THE COMPANY FOR DAMAGES WITH RESPECT TO THE SOFTWARE EXCEED THE AMOUNTS ACTUALLY PAID BY YOU, IF ANY, FOR THE SOFTWARE.

SOME JURISDICTIONS DO NOT ALLOW THE LIMITATION OF IMPLIED WARRANTIES OR LIABILITY FOR INCIDENTAL, INDIRECT, SPECIAL, OR CONSEQUENTIAL DAMAGES, SO THE ABOVE LIMITATIONS MAY NOT ALWAYS APPLY. THE WARRANTIES IN THIS AGREEMENT GIVE YOU SPECIFIC LEGAL RIGHTS AND YOU MAY ALSO HAVE OTHER RIGHTS WHICH VARY IN ACCORDANCE WITH LOCAL LAW.

### ACKNOWLEDGMENT

YOU ACKNOWLEDGE THAT YOU HAVE READ THIS AGREEMENT, UNDERSTAND IT, AND AGREE TO BE BOUND BY ITS TERMS AND CONDITIONS. YOU ALSO AGREE THAT THIS AGREEMENT IS THE COMPLETE AND EXCLUSIVE STATEMENT OF THE AGREEMENT BETWEEN YOU AND THE COMPANY AND SUPERSEDES ALL PROPOSALS OR PRIOR AGREEMENTS, ORAL, OR WRITTEN, AND ANY OTHER COMMUNICATIONS BETWEEN YOU AND THE COMPANY OR ANY REPRESENTATIVE OF THE COMPANY RELATING TO THE SUBJECT MATTER OF THIS AGREEMENT.

Should you have any questions concerning this Agreement or if you wish to contact the Company for any reason, please contact in writing at the address below.

Robin Short
Prentice Hall PTR
One Lake Street
Upper Saddle River, New Jersey 07458

# About the CD-ROM

Welcome to *JavaScript by Example*. This CD-ROM contains the JavaScript code examples that correspond with the examples shown in the book. It also contains Netscape's Core JavaScript Guide version 1.5, and Netscape's Core JavaScript Reference version 1.5.

## Using the CD-ROM Contents

To use the contents of the CD-ROM, start your Web browser, and open the file *index.html* located in the top-level directory of the CD-ROM. From there, you will see links to all of the code examples used in the book. You will also see links to the two Netscape manuals.

## System Requirements

You must have installed Internet Explorer version 5 or higher, Netscape Navigator version 7 or higher, or Mozilla version 1.0 or higher; and any operating system supporting one of these browsers.

## License Agreement

Use of the software accompanying *JavaScript by Example* is subject to the terms of the License Agreement and Limited Warranty, found on the previous two pages.

## Technical Support

Prentice Hall does not offer technical support for any of the programs on the CD-ROM. However, if the CD-ROM is damaged, you may obtain a replacement copy by sending an e-mail that describes the problem to: *disc_exchange@prenhall.com*.